The Municipal Bond Handbook

II

The Municipal Bond Handbook

Edited by **Sylvan G. Feldstein
Frank J. Fabozzi
Irving M. Pollack**

II

DOW JONES-IRWIN
Homewood, Illinois 60430

ISBN 0-87094-421-5

Library of Congress Catalog Card No. 83–70058

Printed in the United States of America

1 2 3 4 5 6 7 8 9 0 BC 0 9 8 7 6 5 4 3

Dedicated to
A. E. Buck and Luther Gulick

The Original Think Tank of
Municipal Bond Research

Preface

Of all the municipal bonds that were rated by a commercial rating company in 1929 and plunged into default by 1932, 78 percent had been rated Aa or better, and 48 percent had been rated Aaa. Since then the ability of rating agencies to assess the credit worthiness of municipal obligations has evolved to a level of general industry acceptance and respectability. In the large majority of instances, they adequately describe the financial condition of the issuers and identify the credit risk factors. However, a small but significant number of instances have caused market participants to re-examine their reliance on the opinions of the rating agencies. This book is intended to provide investors with a framework for analyzing municipal bonds and notes themselves. The need for such a book has been apparent for sometime.

The troubled bonds of the Washington Public Power Supply System (WPPSS) should first be mentioned. Both commercial rating companies gave their highest ratings to these bonds in the early 1980s. One commercial rating company, Moody's, had given the WPPSS Projects 1, 2, and 3 bonds its very highest credit rating of Aaa and the Projects 4 and 5 bonds its rating of A-1. This latter investment-grade rating is defined as having the strongest investment attributes within the upper medium grade of credit worthiness. Another major commercial rating company, Standard & Poor's, also had given the WPPSS Projects 1, 2, and 3 bonds its highest rating of AAA and the Projects 4 and 5 bonds its rating of A+—which is comparable to Moody's A-1 rating. While these high-quality ratings were in effect, WPPSS sold over $8 billion in long-term bonds. By June of 1983 Moody's did not rate at all the Projects 1, 2, and 3 bonds or the Projects 4 and 5 bonds. Standard & Poor's also had no assigned rating for the Projects 1, 2, and 3 bonds and rated the Projects 4 and 5 bonds CC—which is highly speculative.

In fact, since 1975 all of the major municipal debt defaults initially had been given investment-grade ratings. As some examples, the notes of the Urban Development Corporation that defaulted in 1975 had been rated MIG-2 by Moody's. Moody's also had given New York City's notes that defaulted its MIG-1 and MIG-2 ratings. The defaulted bonds of both Midlands Community Hospital in Sarpy County, Nebraska, and the Hilton Head Hospital of Beaufort County, South Carolina, originally had been given investment-grade ratings by both Standard & Poor's and Moody's. The construction loan notes of the Oklahoma Housing Finance Agency, at the time of their default on June 1, 1982, were still rated MIG-1 and AAA by Moody's and Standard & Poor's, respectively. This last default highlights the concern of the investment community that the rating companies may not closely monitor their ratings once they are assigned.

Near defaults should also be mentioned. The general obligation bonds of New York City and the bonds of the Urban Development Corporation, among others, had been given investment-grade ratings. The bonds and notes of the Chicago Board of Education, which were on the brink of default in 1980, at issuance had been given investment grade ratings by Moody's. Also, the distressed state of Ohio's Recycle Energy Revenue Bonds for Akron had been given investment-grade ratings by both commercial rating companies. While the investor may not have lost a single coupon payment, if the investor bought the securities when they had high investment-grade ratings and had to sell them prior to maturity and after their ratings had been suspended or lowered, he would have had a substantial loss.

We wish to reiterate our belief that in the majority of instances, ratings of the commercial rating companies adequately reflect the condition of the credit. In fact, their ratings on small, new issue general obligation bonds tend to be sound. However, unlike 20 years ago when the commercial rating companies would not rate many kinds of revenue bond issues, today they seem to view themselves as assisting in the capital formation process.[1] This is of particular concern since the commercial rating companies now receive fees for their ratings that sometimes are very substantial. The major companies are part of large, growth-oriented conglomerates. Moody's is an operating unit

---

[1]See, Victor F. Zonana and Daniel Hertzberg, "Moody's Dominance in Municipals Market Is Slowly Being Eroded," *The Wall Street Journal*, November 1, 1981, pp. 1, 23.

of the Dun & Bradstreet Corporation, and Standard & Poor's is part
of the McGraw-Hill Corporation. As of early 1983, Moody's charged
fees as high as $67,500 per bond sale, and Standard & Poor's charged
up to $25,000.

Also, it should be noted that the timely review of ratings outstanding is believed to be one of the largest difficulties facing investors and
the rating agencies. A commercial rating company may have as many
as 20,000 ratings outstanding. Periods up to 10 years and even longer
may elapse between published reviews of ratings. For the seller, for
the buyer, and for the trader of municipal bonds, the possibility that
ratings may be outdated, and therefore of questionable reliability, is
distressful.

As the result of the above, there has developed on Wall Street as
well as among larger, more sophisticated investors—such as bond
funds, insurance companies, and bank trust departments—the recognition that municipal bonds and notes should be independently reviewed for their credit worthiness. Many of them now do their own
research.

What we have done in this book is draw upon this new talent as
much as possible. Our contributors present the "state-of-the-art" in
credit analysis. Needless to say, we have been activist editors during
the two and a half years that it has taken us to compile this book.
We have required each contributor to meet our standards, and we
thank them for cheerfully tolerating and accepting our suggestions.

In Section I the background for state and local government bond
analysis is presented. In Section II are described the legal frame-
works for general obligation and revenue bonds. The analytical
framework for analyzing specific types of municipal bond structures
is set forth in the 13 chapters in Section III, while Section IV provides
the analytical framework for analyzing hybrid and special bond securities. Credit analysis of municipal notes is covered in Section V,
and the principles of municipal accounting are described in Section VI.

We also have 28 case studies in the book. The first 14 discuss recent
municipal bond and note defaults and near misses. The other 14 case
studies describe security structures unique to specific state and local
jurisdictions. In the appendix is a discussion of the 1978 federal bankruptcy law and how it applies to municipals. At the end of the book
is a glossary of terms, which we hope the reader will find useful.

We note that the views expressed here are those of the editors and
not necessarily those of the organizations they are employed by.

Finally, we have dedicated our book to Arthur Buck and Luther
Gulick. Their 1926 book, entitled *Municipal Finance,* was the original research book in this area. We hope our book follows in their

footsteps. Additionally, we hope our book will be of value to investors and that it will make a positive contribution to the literature on securities analysis.

Sylvan G. Feldstein
Frank J. Fabozzi
Irving M. Pollack

Contributors

Jeffrey J. Alexopulos   Vice President, T. Rowe Price Associates, Inc.

Eileen Titmuss Austen   Corporate Vice President, Director of Municipal Research, Drexel Burnham Lambert Inc.

Arnold J. Bornfriend   Professor of Management and Public Administration, Worcester State College

William C. Brashares   Partner, Cladouhos & Brashares

Charles Buschman   Attorney, Debevoise & Plimpton

Walter D. Carroll   Vice President, Merrill Lynch, Pierce, Fenner & Smith, Inc.

John W. Coleman, Jr.   Municipal Credit Analyst, The Citizens and Southern National Bank, Atlanta, Georgia

Joseph F. Coleman   Municipal Bond Department, Goldman, Sachs & Co.

John De Jong   Vice President, National Securities and Research Corporation

Theodore Diamond   Judge, New York City Civil Court

Jere Dodd, Jr.   Vice President, Robinson Humphrey/American Express Inc.

Robin Wiessmann Dougherty   Deputy Managing Director, City of Philadelphia

Frank J. Fabozzi   Professor of Economics, Fordham University

Sylvan G. Feldstein   Senior Municipal Specialist, Merrill Lynch, Pierce, Fenner & Smith, Inc.

John C. Fitzgerald Managing Director, Merrill Lynch White Weld Capital Markets Group

Alan W. Frankle Associate Professor of Finance, The University of Tulsa

Mark Fury Staff Writer, *The Bond Buyer*

Richard M. Gerwitz Associate, Merill Lynch White Weld Capital Markets Group

Robert J. Gibbons Attorney, Debevoise & Plimpton

Howard Gleckman Staff Reporter, *The Bond Buyer*

Alan J. Goldfarb Investment Officer, The First National Bank and Trust Company of Oklahoma City

James J. Goodwin II Director, Division of Bond Finance, State of Florida

Michael A. Gort Vice President and Manager, Health and Education Finance Group, Lehman Brothers Kuhn Loeb, Inc.

Arthur R. Guastella Executive Vice President, Blyth Eastman Paine Webber Health Care Funding, Inc.

Donald Haider Professor of Public Management, J. L. Kellogg Graduate School of Management, Northwestern University

David Herships Vice President, Public Finance Division, Marine Midland Bank, N.A.

Cadmus M. Hicks Research Analyst, John Nuveen & Co., Incorporated

John W. Illyes, Jr. Analyst, John Nuveen & Co., Incorporated

James C. Joseph Manager, Municipal Bond Division, State of Oregon

Andrea L. Kahn Partner, Kraft & Hughes

Michael Kluger Associate, Merrill Lynch White Weld Capital Markets Group

Edward M. Lehr Originator—Public Finance, Boland, Saffin, Gordon & Sautter

James A. Moyer LeBoeuf, Lamb, Leiby & Macrae

Charles T. Noona Senior Vice President, L. F. Rothschild, Unterberg, Towbin

Kenneth D. Ough Associate, Merrill Lynch White Weld Capital Markets Group

Kent Pierce Staff Reporter, *The Bond Buyer*

George B. Pugh, Jr. Senior Vice President and Managing Director, Craigie Incorporated

J. Michael Rediker Partner, Ritchie and Rediker

R. Scott Richter Vice President, Ehrlich-Bober Advisors, Inc.

Rhonda S. Rosenberg Assistant Vice President, Drexel Burnham Lambert Inc.

Allan A. Ryan III Senior Vice President, Smith Barney, Harris Upham & Co., Inc.

Steven E. Scheinberg Financial Consultant

Tifton Simmons, Jr. Senior Vice President, Smith Barney, Harris Upham & Co., Inc.

Abraham J. Simon Professor of Accounting and Information Systems, Queens College, City University of New York

James E. Spiotto Managing Partner, Chapman and Cutler

Dell H. Stevens Consultant, L. F. Rothschild, Unterberg, Towbin

Diana L. Taylor Associate, Lehman Brothers Kuhn Loeb, Inc.

Judy Wesalo-Temel Municipal Bond Department, Goldman, Sachs & Co.

George Yacik Staff Writer, *The Bond Buyer*

Contents

    ***Alan W. Frankle*   54**

    Introduction: *The Financial Function.* Tax and Revenue Management:
    Revenue Sources. Treasury Management: *Cash Mobilization and Bank
    Services. Investment of Idle Funds.* Debt Management: *Methods of Fi-
    nancing. Capital Improvement Projects. Debt Financing Alternatives.*

5. **State and Local Government Revenues, Taxpayer Revolts,
    and Crises, *Robin L. Weissmann Dougherty*   69**

    Historical Perspective. Linkage between Tax Revolts and Financial
    Crises. Major Factors Influencing Financial Position: *External and In-
    ternal Danger Signals. Internal Factors.* Response and Effects.

**SECTION TWO
THE LEGAL SECURITY**

6. **The Legal Framework for General Obligation Bonds,
    Andrea L. Kahn   87**

    The Pledge of Security. Enforceability of Pledge, and Creditors' Rem-
    edies: *Sovereign Immunity. Attachment of Municipal or Private Assets.
    Mandamus. Inviolability of Contract. Bankruptcy.*

7. **The Legal Framework for Revenue Bonds, *Charles Buschman
    and Robert J. Gibbons*   98**

    Basic Legal Background: *Who May Issue Revenue Bonds—Tax Consid-
    erations. Who May Issue Revenue Bonds and under What Circum-
    stances—State Law Considerations. Statutory Security Devices. Unilat-
    eral Contractual Changes after Issuance. Blocking Enforcement of
    Contractual Provisions.* Provisions of a Typical Revenue Bond Inden-
    ture or Resolution: *Pledge of Revenues and Other Assets—Flow of
    Funds. Dilution by Issuance of Parity Bonds. Covenants—Outside Se-
    curity. Redemption and Other Terms. Defeasance. The Trustee and De-
    fault Provisions.*

**SECTION THREE
CREDIT ANALYSIS OF MUNICIPAL BONDS**

8. **General Obligation Bonds, *Sylvan G. Feldstein*   121**

    Introduction. Basic Information Required when Analyzing a General
    Obligation Bond: *On the Issuer's Debt Structure. On the Issuer's Bud-
    getary Operations. On the Issuer's Revenue Structure. On the Economy.*
    The Negative Indicators. The More Important Debt Ratios.

ments. Sources and Uses Financial Statements. Proprietary Funds and Other Nonexpendable Funds. General Purpose Financial Statements: *Combined Balance Sheet. Hypothetical Combined Financial Statements on Real and Financial Activities over the Course of a Fiscal Period. Comparison of Actual and Budget on a Basis Other than GAAP.* The Comprehensive Annual Financial Report. Diagramatic Overview of Financial Reporting per *NCGA Statement 1. Appendix A: An Illustrative Title Page for a Comprehensive Annual Financial Report. Appendix B: An Illustrative Table of Contents for a Comprehensive Annual Financial Report. Appendix C: An Illustrative Letter of Transmittal from the Chief Executive Officer for a Comprehensive Annual Financial Report. Appendix D: An Illustrative Finance Director's Letter of Transmittal that Functions as an Introductory Section for a Comprehensive Annual Financial Report. Appendix E: An Illustrative Certificate of Conformance in Financial Reporting for a Comprehensive Annual Financial Report. Appendix F: An Illustrative Independent Auditor's Audit Report for a Comprehensive Annual Financial Report. Appendix G: An Illustrative Set of General Purpose Financial Statements that Is a Part of a Comprehensive Annual Financial Report. Appendix H: An Illustrative Set of Notes to Financial Statements where Such Notes Are Considered an Integral Part of the General Purpose Financial Statements of the Comprehensive Annual Financial Report.*

CASE STUDIES
DEFAULTS AND RELATED PROBLEMS

CASE STUDIES
LOCAL BOND SECURITIES

Background

Section ONE

Introduction

CHAPTER **1**

Sylvan G. Feldstein, Ph.D.
Senior Municipal Specialist
Merrill Lynch, Pierce, Fenner & Smith, Inc.

THE REASONS FOR INCREASED INTEREST IN CREDIT RISK ANALYSIS

Historically, while investing in municipal bonds has been considered second in safety only to that of U.S. debt, beginning in the decade of the 1970s and continuing into the 1980s there developed among many investors ongoing concerns about the credit risks of municipal bonds. This was true regardless of whether or not the bonds had been given high investment-grade credit ratings by the rating companies.

Defaults and the Federal Bankruptcy Law

The first reason for this concern results primarily from the New York City billion dollar financial crisis in 1975. The financial crisis sent a loud and clear warning to municipal bond investors in general. That warning was that regardless of the supposedly ironclad legal protections for the bondholder, when issuers such as large cities have severe budget-balancing difficulties, the political hues, cries, and fi-

3

nancial stakes of public employee unions, vendors, and community groups may be dominant forces in the budgetary process.

This reality was further reinforced by the new federal bankruptcy law, which took effect on October 1, 1979, and which makes it easier for municipal bond issuers to seek protection from bondholders by filing for bankruptcy. Of course, the investor should always avoid bonds of issuers that may go into bankruptcy. The judicial process usually involves years of numerous court hearings and litigation which no bond investor should want to be a party to regardless of whether or not he may eventually "win."

New Financing Techniques and Legally Untested Security Structures

The second reason for increased interest in credit risk analysis results from the proliferation in the municipal bond market of innovative financing techniques to secure new bond issues. In addition to the more traditional general obligation bonds and toll road, bridge, and tunnel revenue bonds, there are now more nonvoter-approved, innovative, and legally untested security mechanisms. These innovative financing mechanisms include "moral obligation" housing bonds, "take or pay" electric utility bonds with "step-up" provisions requiring the participants to increase payments to make up for those that may default, "lease rental" bonds, medicare- and medicaid-dependent hospital bonds, commercial bank-backed letter of credit bonds, "put" bonds, and tax-exempt commercial paper. What distinguishes these newer bonds from the more traditional general obligation and revenue bonds is that there is no history of court decisions and other case law which firmly establishes the rights of the bondholders and the obligations of the issuers. For the newer financing mechanisms, it is not possible to determine the probable legal outcome if the bond securities were challenged in court. Therefore, credit analysis has become important in order to identify those bonds which—because of strong finances and other characteristics—are not likely to result in serious litigation.

Cutbacks in Federal Grant-In-Aid Programs

The third reason, and one that began with the electoral victory of President Reagan in 1980, is the impact that the scaling down of federal grants and aid programs will have on the credit worthiness of both general obligation and revenue bonds. As an example of the change in federal funding policies, the president in December 1981 signed into law an extension of the Clean Water Act of 1970. Among other changes, the new amendments reduce the total federal contribution to local waste treatment programs from $90 billion projected under the old law to $36 billion. Additionally, after October 1, 1984, the federal matching contribution to local sewerage construction projects will decline from 75 percent to 55 percent of the costs. Over the previous 20 years, many state and local governments had grown dependent on this and other federal grant programs as direct subsidies to their own capital construction and operating budgets. These federal grants had provided indirect subsidies to their local economies as well.

The new, fiscally conservative federalism can be expected to continue through the 1980s. The Reagan victory—as well as the Republican party victories in the U.S. Senate at the same time—where for the first time in 25 years the Republicans are in the majority—has been seen as an electoral message from the American people that they want a major change in federal-state financial relationships. With the continued support from a broad-based, fiscally conservative national political constituency, we can expect the scaling-down process of federal aid to state and local governments to continue even if there is a change in national leadership. The increased population growth in the more conservative Sun Belt regions of the country would indicate a further strengthening of this electoral base for fiscal conservatism. What this means for credit analysis is that many general obligation and revenue bond issuers may undergo serious financial stresses as the federal grant and aid reductions are implemented over the coming years.

Decline of the Durable Goods Sector

The fourth reason for investor concern is that the American economy is undergoing a fundamental change, which is resulting in a decline of the durable goods sector of the economy. This decline has widespread implications for whole regions of the country. Many general obligation and revenue bond issuers can be expected to undergo significant economic deterioration which could negatively impact their tax collections and wealth indicators such as personal income, bank deposits, retail sales, and real property valuations.

The Strong Market Appetite for Municipal Bonds in the 1970s and 1980s

The fifth reason for the increased interest in municipal bond credit risk analysis is derived from the changing nature of the municipal bond market. For most of the 1970s the municipal bond market was characterized by strong buying patterns among both private investors and institutions. This was caused in part by high federal, state, and local income tax rates. Additionally, inflation, or "bracket creep," pushed many investors into higher and higher income tax brackets. Tax-exempt bonds increasingly became an important and convenient way for sheltering income. One corollary of the strong buyer's demand for tax exemption was an erosion of the traditional security provisions and bondholder safeguards that had grown out of the default experiences of the 1930s. General obligation bond issuers with high tax and debt burdens, declining local economies, and chronic budget-balancing problems had little difficulty finding willing buyers. Also, revenue bonds increasingly were brought to market with legally untested security provisions, modest rate covenants, reduced debt reserves, and weak additional bonds tests.

In regard to the rate covenant, while it is desirable that the rates charged should provide cover to the extent necessary to pay for debt service, operations, and prudent reserves, more and more rate covenants were structured to provide cover only to the extent necessary to pay debt service, operations, and *required* improvements. Excess monies were credited against the succeeding year's revenue requirements. Such an arrangement is known as "Chinese coverage." This form of coverage has become more of a norm in the industry instead of an exception, which it had been in the past. Because of the widespread weakening of security provisions, it has become more important than ever before that the prudent investor carefully evaluate the credit worthiness of a municipal bond before making a purchase.

"Buy and Hold" versus "Buy and Trade" Investment Strategies

The last reason for the increased interest in credit risk analysis results from a fundamental philosophical change which is developing among large institutional investors, such as fire and casualty insurance companies, commercial banks, and tax-exempt bond funds. More and more municipal bond buyers no longer "buy and hold" their municipal bonds to maturity—which had been the traditional investment approach. Instead, they try to "buy and trade." This new trading interest has grown out of two developments. First, because of the market decline since 1978 many "buy and hold" investors have seen the paper value of their assets decline by as much as 30 percent. Second, because of the great volatility in the market that now exists (where swings of up to 200 basis points have occurred in a single day), some investors see the opportunity for substantial capital gains through active trading. This could occur if they buy in a sector of the municipal bond market which has become underpriced or "cheap," and sell when the sector becomes overpriced or "rich." Of course, knowing which bonds are likely credit rating downgrades or upgrades can be very valuable to such an investor.

DEFINING THE CREDIT RISK FOR A MUNICIPAL BOND

While the purpose of a common stock analysis is for the analyst to predict the future earnings and profitability of individual corporations and product sectors, the role of municipal bond credit analysis, while less dramatic, is still nevertheless very important. It should be noted, furthermore, that there are several different approaches to municipal bond credit analysis. There are no universally accepted theories of municipal credit analysis, as there are in the fields of common stock and corporate bond analysis.

As an example of the diversity of municipal bond analysis, one can look at the relationship of intergovernmental aid programs to general obligation bond security. There is one viewpoint held in the investment community that the bonds of any local government such as a city, town, county, or school district which is heavily dependent upon outside revenue sources are less attractive as an investment than bonds for a community that has a strong local taxable economic base. However, the financial and budgetary operations of the bond issuer may be significantly strengthened by the outside support. For instance, the school district of Hoboken, New Jersey, issues its own general obligation bonds and maintains its own budgetary accounts. Since the late 1970s the school district has received approximately 75 percent of its revenues from the state, and an annually declining amount from local property taxpayers. In this instance it is a New Jersey state constitutional provision and a resulting statute which provide that if a community's property tax base declines, the state correspondingly makes up the difference with increased payments of state aid to education. Does this feature make the general obligation school bonds of Hoboken stronger or weaker credit risks?

While the field of municipal bond credit analysis is not characterized by standardized and universally accepted analytical techniques, there is general acceptance of the three basic purposes of a bond analysis. Additionally, it should be noted that while the municipal bond investor will not make a "killing" on the basis of a competent credit worthiness analysis, he or she should be aware of risk factors in three respects, discussed below. By knowing the degree of credit worthiness, he can better protect and utilize his investment funds.

Default Potential

First, the municipal bond credit risk analysis should determine whether the bond issuer is likely, under a reasonable economic and financial scenario, to ever default either permanently or temporarily in making bond and interest payments when due. That is, the first purpose of a municipal bond credit analysis is to determine if the bond is going to have serious problems in which the investor could lose his capital. Furthermore, it should be noted that over the past 25 years there have been some municipal bonds and notes which have indeed defaulted.[1] There even have been a few that have had to go to the federal bankruptcy courts. The Advisory Commission on Intergovernmental Relations reported in a 1976 study that, between 1960 and 1969 alone, there were recorded defaults by a total of 294 issuers. Of the 294 issuers that defaulted, 140 were municipalities, 60 school districts, 24 counties, and the other 70 special jurisdictions. Clearly, such bonds and notes were ones that the prudent investor should have avoided.

Degrees of Safety

Second, besides identifying the likely default candidates, a related purpose of the risk analysis is to identify among the nondefault candidates those that are financially and legally stronger than others as well as those that are the most strongly secured bonds. Terms such as *gilt-edged* are usually reserved for describing municipal bonds with very little credit risks and very remote default possibilities, whereas bonds identified as either not being for "widows and orphans" or as being "businessmen's risks" would be at the lower end of the investment risk spectrum.

It should be noted, furthermore, that while the rating companies give ratings which show degrees of safety, a shortcoming of relying on their ratings exclusively is that they tend to review a credit only when it comes to the new issue market. With credit deterioration possible over a very short period of time, the analyst or investor must look beyond the assigned credit rating.[2]

Short-Term versus Long-Term Opportunities

The third and final purpose of the credit risk analysis is to provide the investor with an indication of what direction the credit worthiness of a particular municipal bond is headed. Is the bond becoming stronger, deteriorating in quality, or remaining the same? Knowing the direction in which the bond is headed can provide tremendous short-term trading opportunities for the sophisticated investor who buys or sells on the basis of potential credit upgrades or downgrades. Additionally, the credit risk analysis of a bond may uncover certain attractive features of the bond security which are not generally recognized in the marketplace, are not adequately reflected in the credit

---

[1]These are discussed in the case studies sections of this book.
[2]Also see the Preface for additional information about the shortcomings of the rating companies.

ratings, but eventually may be.[3] Such bonds provide short-term investment opportunities as well.

As an example, certain bonds issued by the New York City Housing Authority were originally secured only by authority revenues and the guarantee of the city of New York.[4] In the late 1970s they were converted to a federal program whereby the debt service began to be paid directly by the federal government to the paying agent for the bonds. For some years, however, the bonds continued to be rated only "B" by Moody's. Some investors, aware of this new security feature, bought the bonds when they were priced as B-rated credits. After the Authority applied for the credit upgrade, Moody's assigned "Aaa" ratings to the bonds. Once this became known in the marketplace, the value of the bonds increased by 200–250 basis points.

A final point in determining the credit direction of a bond is for the investor to be aware that because demographic, economic, and financial changes can take place very rapidly, the time horizon of this credit risk analysis should not be expected to cover a longer period than a few years.

In this book is presented and explained the basic analytical tools for the analyst or investor to use in determining the credit worthiness of a municipal bond or note. We have also included case studies of defaulted bond issues in the "Defaults and Related Problems" section, which demonstrate that not all municipal bonds are second only to U.S. debt obligations in terms of safety. While the analysis of municipal bonds—and particularly, general obligation bonds—is more an art than a science, we have tried to set forth in this book the basic analytical questions and answers that should always be addressed.

---

[3]See Chapter 9, "Seaport Revenue Bonds." This is an example of an analytical approach which focuses on these objectives.

[4]See Case Study 22.

The Powers and Structure of State and Local Governments in the Federal System

CHAPTER **2**

Arnold J. Bornfriend, Ph.D.
Professor of Management and Public Administration
Worcester State College

THE FEDERAL BALANCE

Certainly America's most distinctive contribution to the art and practice of government is the federal system. Unlike unitary governments such as Great Britain, France, or Italy, federalism does not concentrate all powers in a central government; in practice they are shared among the nation and the states. When the nation was created, the Constitution reserved important powers to the states and guaranteed the separate identities of both levels.

Down through the years the federal share has grown—largely through Supreme Court decisions, constitutional amendments, and grants-in-aid—enabling the national government to intervene in matters that once were reserved for the states. The early development of the implied-powers doctrine, in conjunction with the broad interpretation of the interstate commerce clause, gave meaning to the constitutional power of Congress to tax and spend for the general welfare. This has led to the regulation of almost every kind of economic activity—including transportation, wages and hours, communications, banking, gas and electric utilities, food and drugs, and

10

corporate securities—through agencies such as the ICC, NLRB, FPC, FTC, FDA, and SEC. While one might question the wisdom of any given ruling, the authority of the federal government to deal with these matters has not been seriously challenged since the New Deal.

From the early 1970s on, resentment against Washington has mounted due to the convergence of three major federal initiatives. First, the "new wave" of alphabetic agencies such as the EPA, CPSC, and OSHA (that were created to protect the public from pollution, unsafe workplaces, and unsafe products) are not considered a legitimate exercise of federal power by vocal critics in the business community. These newer regulatory activities cut across industry lines and impose high costs on many smaller companies, which were not touched by the traditional bodies that focus on large industries. Secondly, federal court rulings, from civil rights to the newer social issues including busing, bilingual education, access for the handicapped, abortion, and pornography, have caused much regional public indignation and additional financial burdens for state and local governments. And finally, the sheer size, complexity, and dislike of the purposes of many federal grant-in-aid programs have culminated in President Reagan's proposal to consolidate 88 narrow categories into five block grants and name yet another advisory commission on federal-state relations.

To a large extent, the current furor over federal intervention obscures the reality that the center of gravity remains in the states. Unlike regional governments in most other nations, our states are not merely the instruments for implementation of national policies. Most of the laws, be they criminal or civil, are state laws. All elected national office holders—senators, members of the House of Representatives, and even the president—are not exclusively national officials but have direct ties to the states. National party organizations in effect are federations of 50 state parties. When congressmen consider allocation formulas for grant-in-aid programs, such as food stamps, school lunch programs, or basic educational opportunity grants, their aim is to broaden eligibility formulas to accommodate as many of their constituents as possible. Even when federal money or standards shape a national program, it is state or local administrators who locate and build the highways, determine teacher credentials and curriculum, and set payment levels and eligibility requirements for many forms of public assistance. Thus, expansion of federal programs has not been at the expense of state and local governments, since all levels have greatly increased their scope and operations. Since the early 1960s and until the recent financial crunch, both state and local spending and the number of public employees climbed at a faster rate than in the national government.

ADAPTING TO CHANGE

In contrast to the states, the identity of local government is not guaranteed by the constitution; nor are they even mentioned in that document, since in legal terms they are creatures of the state. The balance of this chapter presents an overview of the powers and kinds of governments to be found in the United States, followed by an appraisal of striking changes in state government operations over the past 20 years. A recurrent theme is the resiliency of these institutions and their capacity to respond to fundamental changes.

THE UNITS OF LOCAL GOVERNMENT

In the census taken in 1977 there were close to 80,000 units of local government in the United States, distributed among five categories—municipalities, counties, towns and townships, school districts, and special districts. Municipalities include cities, villages, boroughs, and towns that are incorporated places with significant population concentrations and that have received a charter from the state spelling out their duties and responsibilities. Nearly 90 percent of the population live in the nation's 3,042 counties, which are geographic subdivisions of the states. The traditional functions of counties are law enforcement, judicial administration, and construction and maintenance of roads. But counties today, particularly in urban areas, also have taken on duties once performed by the overburdened municipalities.

Towns or townships, found in about half of the states—from New England to the Midwest—are geographical subdivisions of the states and perform, on a grassroots level, many of the same functions as counties. In the Midwest, township government has dwindled due to rural population decline. But the New England town, the classic example of direct democracy, has remained a vital force in rural areas. In the larger urban areas, however, direct democracy has been replaced by representatives, called town meeting members, who are elected prior to the town meeting. The fastest growing and most numerous unit of local government is the special district. Excluding school districts, which are a type of special district, the number of units has jumped from 8,300 to nearly 26,000 at present. Most special districts perform one specific function such as sewage disposal or fire control, and they can either be located entirely within one community or serve several adjacent areas. They generally are not bound by tax and debt limits that states often set for other kinds of local government. School districts number 15,200 compared to 50,500 in 1957. Their decline in number is primarily the result of school district consolidation and reorganization.

Multiple governments are the norm for most Americans. Because of overlapping jurisdictions and functions, a given individual may support with taxes and receive services from more than one unit in each of the five categories—municipalities, counties, towns and townships, school districts, and special districts. Most of the population is concentrated in the 285 Standard Metropolitan Statistical Areas (SMSAs), which are composed of cities of at least 50,000 residents, the surrounding county, and adjacent counties having commuting ties with the central city. These 285 SMSAs contain nearly three quarters of the nation's population and have a mean average of approximately 95 governments that ranges from a high of 1,214 in Chicago to a low of 4 in Honolulu. Although larger SMSAs tend to have more local government, the number of these units decreases as population density increases. Between 1970 and 1979 the trend towards metropolitanization began to slow down, as rural communities and small towns on the fringes outpaced metropolitan areas in the rate of population growth. Nonetheless, about 73 percent of the population is concentrated in the SMSAs.

When describing this landscape of governments, typical phrases used by political scientists include, "a zoo of governments," "the metropolitan morass," "a maze of jurisdictions," and a "crazy-quilt pattern." But attempts to alter political boundaries to achieve some type of consolidation or integration (as will be shown later) have not been very successful.

DILLON'S RULE AND ITS CONSEQUENCES

One of the severest restrictions on the exercise of local government powers today is Dillon's Rule, named after an Iowa state judge who issued the ruling more than 70 years ago. If a function is not expressly granted or specified in the charter, a municipality is forbidden to do it; and any doubt whether powers exist will be resolved against the city. Dillon's Rule upends the presumption of constitutionality that is followed when either state or federal legislation is challenged in the courts. Unlike the states, municipalities do not have implied powers. One of the consequences is the exceptional length of some city charters, spelling out every conceivable area of legislation and ordinances. The resulting complexity tends to result in further intervention by the state courts since it is a hopeless task to anticipate every possible future contingency.

In an effort to reverse Dillon's Rule, more than half the states have included in their constitutions provisions for issuing home rule charters. While the theory behind home rule is to enable the city to do anything not specifically forbidden, this has not worked out in practice. Home rule has indeed permitted cities to draft their own charter as to the form and structure of government, instead of requesting a charter from the state legislature as was done in the past. But home rule has not given cities autonomy over substantive matters. For example, New York State grants its larger cities authority in dealing with their "property, affairs, or government." But if the matter is deemed to be a statewide concern by the courts, that declaration supersedes a municipal ordinance even when a locality previously operated unimpeded. Thus, in recent decades, attempted city regulation of the following matters were declared invalid because they were judged to be matters of statewide as opposed to municipal affairs: wages, hours, and pensions of city police and firemen; opening and closing hours of barbershops; taxation within a city's borders; regulation of plumbers; and regulations requiring that the date be stamped on milk containers.

Knowing that state courts may be on their side encourages individual taxpayers and interest groups who have lost a policy conflict to enter lawsuits claiming the action was illegal. To forestall these challenges, a city is forced to go to the state legislature for a special act signed by the governor to be sure that it can legally enact a program of its own. And once again Dillon's Rule takes its toll. Not only may states deny cities the right to increase or diversify taxes but they have placed local communities in a double bind by imposing mandates requiring them to undertake costly functions without providing additional state funds. A bitter source of conflict between state and local officials is the growing use of mandates to implement statewide goals such as affirmative action programs, environmental impact statements, and access for the handicapped. When the federal government imposes new requirements upon the states, a grant is often used to assure compliance; but state mandates usually only contain the stick, and not the carrot.

FORMS OF LOCAL GOVERNMENT

Mayors and Machines

All of the biggest cities in the United States with a population of over one million use the mayor-council form, which follows the traditional separation of powers between executive and legislative functions. Alarmed by the rampant growth of corruption in the latter part of the 19th century, mayors were stripped of control over many city services, their term of office frozen to two years, and their appointment and removal powers prescribed. This approach came to be known as the *"weak mayor"* version. (Case Study 14 provides an illustration of what can happen with a weak mayor.) Conditions worsened as the independent boards and commissions became splintered into enclaves captured by special interests. Moreover, the weak-mayor system encouraged the rise of the old-style political machine and the city boss, who usually was not a mayor himself but wielded power behind the scenes.

Through its ability to dominate nominations and elections as well as its virtual monopoly over governmental positions, the political machine provided a centralizing force that was lacking in the formal government structure.[1] In exchange for patronage in the form of jobs, favor, or cash, the machine maintained discipline over party workers, who in turn delivered sizable voting blocs. These operations were underwritten by business interests who provided payoffs and rebates in exchange for municipal franchises and contracts. While some machines might field a few excellent candidates, and the extent of corruption varied from city to city, the political machine's primary mission was control of the mechanics and prizes of politics and not issues or programs.

In the early part of the 20th century, the strong-executive movement was launched to counteract the twin evils of the weak mayor and machine politics. Reformers urged that powers be concentrated in the hands of the mayor, since he was the most visible and accountable figure in government. Some cities responded by lengthening his term to four years, broadening his appointment and removal power, transferring functions from boards to line agencies, and granting him the veto and budget control. National developments led to the decline of old-style politics. As large-scale immigration dropped, fewer people needed the services the machine furnished. From the New Deal to the Great Society, federal action provided alternatives to the jobs and favors, through welfare programs, the civil service, and Economic Opportunity programs. The rise of the middle-class, independent voter led parties to focus more on issues, undercutting the role of patronage. Nonoffice-holding party leaders lost their ability to dominate elections, and mayors began to dominate their respective party organizations.

Mayors as Leaders. No matter how strong a mayor's formal powers, they are not sufficient to enable him to govern effectively. Other resources such as party control, personality, desire for power, ability to build alliances, and the particular cultural and political environment are all factors that help determine and shape his leadership style. Essentially, leadership style is the way a mayor uses available resources to achieve his objectives. In the recent past, most big-

---

[1] Arnold J. Bornfriend, "Political Parties and Pressure Groups," in *Governing The City*, ed. Robert H. Connery and Demetrios Caraley (New York: Praeger Publishers, 1969), pp. 55–57.

city mayors have tended to be "opportunistic policy broker" or "policy innovator and champion" types.[2]

Richard Daley, mayor of Chicago from 1955 to 1976, is the classic example of an opportunistic policy broker. Operating under a weak-mayor government he became chairman of the Cook County Democratic Committee which enabled him to deal effectively with many independent commissions, a 50-person city council and the overlapping jurisdictions of the city and county. Daley seldom was the initiator of any public policy but functioned as an arbitrator between competing interests. Inasmuch as a policy broker's major goal is to increase his own personal power, policies are chosen not on the basis of their merit but on the lineup of forces for and against. Apparently Daley chose wisely, for Chicago gained the reputation of the best-run big city in the nation during his regime. In the same vein, Robert F. Wagner, who served three terms as mayor of New York, transformed procrastination into a formidable strategy. By delaying a decision he would wait until the opposition was neutralized to slip his proposal through.

During the 1960s a new breed of younger, policy-oriented champions emerged on the urban landscape. These mayors included Kevin White of Boston, Richard Lee of New Haven, Jerome Cavanaugh of Detroit, Carl Stokes of Cleveland, and Henry Maier of Milwaukee. In many ways John Lindsay of New York was a symbol of these policy champions. Mayor Lindsay was noted for a deep moral concern for the poor and the underprivileged, a strong commitment to take the heat to get programs enacted, and an unwillingness to compromise on basic principles. Yet by the end of his second and final term, his concern for the poor was widely perceived as caring only about blacks and Hispanics, and his moral commitments were considered to be sermonizing. Also, his failure to compromise made him many enemies. While Lindsay had significant accomplishments, such as enacting one of the nation's strongest antipollution laws and increasing police protection, as champion of the city he created very high expectations that were never fulfilled, alienating the electorate. The other policy-oriented mayors faced similar frustrations. Several chose not to run for reelection, and a mood of pessimism arose that cities are ungovernable.

Yet, Mayor Kevin White of Boston, one of the advocates of the 1960s, had managed to survive; he was sworn in for an unprecedented fourth term in January 1980. He has survived largely because he has shifted from a policy-innovator to a broker style with a machine politics emphasis that Mayor Daley would have envied.[3] For example, in

---

[2]For a more detailed analysis, see Demetrios Caraley, *City Governments and Urban Problems* (Englewood Cliffs, N. J.: Prentice-Hall, 1977), pp. 208–225.

[3]Martha W. Weinberg, "Boston's Kevin White: A Mayor Who Survives," *Political Science Quarterly*, Spring 1981, pp. 87–108.

the 1979 campaign Kevin White created a tight organization manned by city workers who knew that pay increases, and in fact their very jobs, would depend on getting out the vote in the precincts. White's critics point out that he has discarded his earlier commitment to solving racial and other urban problems in preference to seeking personal power for its own sake. Those who are more sympathetic to his dilemma indicate that stability in governance is still possible in American cities, but at the cost of abandoning substantive programs.

On the other hand, Edward Koch of New York City, one of the most popular mayors, artfully combines championing with brokerage aspects to achieve a distinctive and highly successful leadership style. In contrast to the Lindsay years when public expectations were high, Koch came into office just after a succession of budgetary cutbacks and near-bankruptcy, when the popular mood was at an all-time low. He too is a moralist, but his governing maxim—"don't spend what you don't have"—is in keeping with the mood for a balanced budget.[4] He is considered to be a champion of the vast middle class, rather than a friend of the poor and underprivileged.

This image of being evenhanded has led to strong criticism that black and Hispanic needs are being ignored. On the brokerage side, Koch has been effective in dealing with unions and other centers of power. His friendship with President Reagan may produce close to $2 billion to complete the long-stalled Westway Construction Project, a covered highway that will link midtown and downtown Manhattan. Similarly, Jane Byrne, mayor of Chicago, emerged for a period of time as an effective broker and policy champion. Byrne inherited the city's patronage system but not Richard Daley's control of the machine through his seat on the Cook County Democratic Committee. This absence of a power base had forced her to be more ruthless than Daley. But Byrne is said to have appointed one of the best boards of education in the history of Chicago and has undertaken redevelopment of the central business district. To overcome her low popularity rating, she moved into a predominantly black housing project in a decaying area. While the tactic gained a lot of favorable publicity for Byrne, it also focused public attention on the daily problems faced by the poor.

The Commission Form

The commission form of city government gives both legislative and executive powers to a small body, usually consisting of five members. The commission form originated as an alternative designed to end the divided responsibility between mayor and council. It gained wide-

---

[4]*Time*, June 15, 1981, p. 25.

spread acclaim when a tidal wave ravaged Galveston, Texas, in 1901 causing both physical and financial collapse. A few leading business-man literally were commissioned to deal with the crisis, fusing legis-lative and executive duties in the same hands. It worked in Galves-ton, and by 1915, about 500 communities had adopted the commission form in rapid sequence. Customarily, one of the commission members is the nominal mayor but has no more formal powers than his col-leagues. In practice, one commission member will become responsible for the operations of a given department, such as public works, fi-nance, or public safety. Poor, small, blue-collar communities find the small council and combining jobs attractive for reducing payroll costs. But when commissioners bicker among themselves for higher appro-priations, or if acrimony arises, the absence of coordination can lead to near-paralysis. Jersey City, home of the notorious Boss Hague, is the largest city that adopted this form. Since 1930 there have been virtually no new adoptions, and barely 5 percent of cities use this form today.

Council-Manager

Having origin similar to the commission plan, the council-manager form arose as yet another alternative to the weak-mayor system. It too gained the spotlight in the wake of a disaster when Dayton, Ohio, hired a city manager in 1914 to help recover from bankruptcy. After World War II, council-manager adoptions increased sharply, mainly due to the widespread abandonment of the commission plan and de-fections from mayor-council ranks by rapidly growing suburban com-munities. At present about 3,500 municipalities have a council-man-ager government, making it the most prevalent type for medium-sized cities of from 25,000 to 250,000 in population. A few large cities with over one-half million—notably Dallas, Phoenix, and San Diego—have city managers, but they adopted it prior to reaching their present size.

Essentially the council-manager form is inspired by the model of the business corporation. In formal terms the city manager serves as chief administrative officer at the pleasure of the council. As is his counterpart in the private sector, he is given wide managerial powers such as the authority to hire and fire, a professional staff, and bud-getary controls. The largely part-time council, analogous to a board of directors, may set policy guidelines but affords the manager free rein in day-to-day operations. Traditional party politics is down-played or excluded. More than 80 percent of council-manager govern-ments use nonpartisan ballots and at-large elections, as opposed to voting by wards or precincts. But as there is often a discrepancy be-tween the ideal of the corporation and the realities of corporate life, so there also is between the doctrine and practices found in council-manager governments. It is not unusual for skillful city managers to seize the initiative in public policy making, develop a loyal following, and enjoy tenure that outlasts the elected council. Similarly while the creed of the city manager profession encourages widespread citizen participation, many city managers view opposing viewpoints as chief executive officers would regard dissenting stockholders. Banishing party labels does not mean the elimination of politics or policy differences either. When differences of opinion arise, issues are likely to be settled among the "board" rather than discussed openly. There is also a wide gap between the manager's perceptions of his role and the council's expectations. More than a majority of city managers see themselves functioning as political leaders, contrasted with 12 percent of council members. This suggests effective managers are impelled to develop a subtle, perhaps manipulative leadership style.

Typical council-manager governments flourish best when conditions are homogeneous. This plan is associated with growing middle-class, white-collar communities having a low proportion of industrial workers, ethnic groups, and other minorities. The spending rate among council-manager cities is also less than for comparable cities with elected mayors. The insulation of the manager from the electorate and the absence of clearly identifiable political parties tends to dampen the formation of labor unions and organizations representing racial minorities and the poor. Opportunities for expressing dissenting viewpoints are limited. During the racial conflicts of the 1960s, manager cities were less equipped to handle the disturbances than mayor-council communities. If rancorous conflict develops over budget deficits and cutbacks, the impact may be quite harsh.

COUNTIES

Originating in colonial times as administrative subdivisions of the states, counties were one of the first attempts to decentralize services. Through constructing and maintaining roads and highways, administering justice, recording deeds, and handling other legal matters, counties enabled easier access to vital services, particularly for those citizens living in unincorporated areas. Soon the county courthouse became not only the center for the judicial system but also a key building block in the statewide political apparatus.

From the birth of the nation until the mid-20th century, counties were dubbed the "dark continent of American government" due to their archaic structure, obscure electoral arrangements, and poor performance. County commissioners were selected by complex forms of representation involving other local units and by gubernatorial appointment. Bedsheet ballots for numerous offices including auditors, treasurers, coroners, clerks, and sheriffs resulted in low voter turnout and excessive patronage. Powers of the county were restricted largely to state-mandated functions. As incorporated communities grew, counties became the depository of functions that other local governments did not want to undertake, such as operating prisons or asylums.

In the mid-1960s, however, county fortunes were on the upturn. The federal government's emphasis on a regional approach to housing, planning and zoning, and environmental control provided the impetus for county modernization. A revitalized National Association of Counties, in collaboration with other government interest groups, successfully lobbied to have counties administer these grants, on the grounds of their wide territorial jurisdiction.

In politics, as well as aesthetics, form follows function. Faced with these added responsibilities, counties reorganized, abetted by states granting them home rule powers and authority to take on optional functions. The first wave of reorganizations adapted the concepts of the city manager plan and established a county administrator. A newer trend which is becoming prevalent in densely populated metropolitan areas is the elected chief executive, inspired by the strong-mayor model. All told, close to 500 counties are governed by a county administrator or elected county executive. While this is a small number compared to the 3,000 counties in the United States, more than half of the population lives in a modernized county.

As a consequence of these changes, counties have taken on new regulatory functions in health, environmental and pollution control, planning, and zoning. There are a few urban counties that provide a range of services for the entire area, approximating a sophisticated big-city government, notably Dade County, Los Angeles County, and Milwaukee County.

DILEMMAS OF METROPOLITAN REFORM

During the 1950s and lasting through the late 1960s, the prevailing theme of many scholars and activists was to insist that the proliferation of governmental units—cities, towns, counties, special districts, and the like—was the principal cause of urban problems. The absence of a central authority with jurisdiction over both cities and suburbs meant that there was no adequate way to deal with concerns that crossed boundary lines, such as interurban transportation, water supply, waste and sewage disposal, public health regulations, pollution control, zoning, and even police and fire protection. Proponents claimed that metropolitan government with appropriate taxing and spending powers was essential to eliminate fiscal disparities between the richer and poorer communities. Autonomous suburban enclaves enabled the middle class to escape the ravages of crime, poor housing, and urban blight, and the loss of tax revenues worsened conditions in the core cities left behind. Through economies of scale, the construction and operation of mass transit, water supply, and sewage disposal facilities could be undertaken more efficiently. And finally, greater coordination could be achieved by overcoming the fragmentation of local governments.

In 1953 the municipality of Metropolitan Toronto was created, encompassing within its boundaries the city of Toronto and 12 suburban municipalities. This new level took on responsibility for a range of metropolitan functions area-wide, while local operations remained with the municipalities. This federal structure captured the imagination of reformers in the United States, and much debate centered on the appropriate divisions of functions. Looking back, the principal lesson of the Toronto experience was not grasped by reformers. Federation was *imposed* by an act of the provincial legislature and not *voted in* by the residents of the communities involved. In the United States popular referendums were invariably required. The closest version to the Toronto model was created in 1957 when Dade County was consolidated. Even though a new level of government was not created, the battle was fierce; only a slim majority carried the measure. Despite well-financed compaigns to achieve "Metro," attempts failed in such cities as Cleveland, St. Louis, and Seattle. When an occasional victory was won, as in Davidson County (Louisville), the circumstances were unique and reallocation of responsibilities was modest.

Let us consider the reasons for the failure of the metropolitan reform movement, and indicate the more viable approaches that are currently used as a consequence of those experiences. What is most striking is the wide discrepancy between the issues as defined by the media and the "real" issues perceived by the voters but not that openly discussed. Unlike the reformers, the vast majority of middle-class voters did not view fragmentation as an evil. Proliferation of governments provided enclaves which enabled suburbanites to maintain a distinctive lifestyle. While the campaigns emphasized improved physical facilities, voters were more concerned about unspoken social and cultural fears having to do with race, deteriorating property values, and crime. Similarly, it was felt elimination of fiscal disparities would mean higher taxes for those who recently escaped the core city.

Efforts to change political boundaries never developed a popular following, either in the central cities or suburbs. Reform was primarily a civic concern of business and communication interest with economic stakes in the urban core. It is ironic that the movement peaked about the time the black outbursts of the 1960s began, since a number of cities that launched campaigns for metropolitan government were also the first places where the violence erupted. In essence the metropolitan dilemma finally came to be seen not as a structural regional problem but one of national scope that could only be addressed by coordinated federal action and massive resources.

A new generation of scholars also began to challenge the premise that larger units of government are more effective and efficient.[5] A number of studies demonstrate that consolidation leads to higher overhead cost in the form of bureaucratic salaries, while less of the budget is used to provide direct services. Similarly, in many instances small local governments can be more efficient since they can shop around in the marketplace for goods and services. Competition among vendors also brings the price down. In addition, there are positive values attached to fragmentation of government. More choices are available to citizens, and communities will compete with one another to keep the tax rate down.

Metropolitan Special Districts

Metropolitan special districts are units of government that may serve all or a few localities in the region. Examples of large-scale districts include the Port of New York and New Jersey Authority, which operates piers, tunnels, airports, bridges, and the World Trade Center; BART (San Francisco) and METRO (Washington, D.C.) created to construct and operate modern rapid transit systems; The Metropolitan Sanitary District of Greater Chicago; and the Cleveland Metropolitan Park District. Metropolitan districts have several characteristics that make them highly suitable for operating services that cross existing boundaries. First, their flexible jurisdiction can extend over entire counties or even neighboring states. Secondly, where clientele usage is high (such as transit, water supply, or sewage disposal), they can take advantage of economies of scale and new technologies. Thirdly, financed in part by user charges, tolls, and revenue bonds, they permit a more equitable distribution between costs and benefits. If public subsidies are required, these come from the localities and not direct taxpayer payments. Their bonds are also not subject to the same borrowing limits of the communities served.

Charges leveled against metropolitan districts include insulation from popular control since directors are not elected but usually appointed by the governments involved, failure to use their surplus revenue to support other needed services, and contributing to the fragmentation of governments in metropolitan areas. Nonetheless metropolitan districts do not threaten existing political or community

---

[5]Vincent Ostrom, *The Intellectual Crisis in American Public Administration* (University: University of Alabama Press, 1973), pp. 69–73.

lifestyles, as the more comprehensive approaches to change would. Given the widespread public antipathy to federation, consolidation, or annexation, metropolitan districts are one of the few viable mechanisms for securing incremental improvement.

Interjurisdictional Agreements

Local governments contract with other units, the county government, or even with firms in the private sector to buy services or share the costs of operations. Typically, most are agreements between two communities over a single service. The prototypical contracting county is Los Angeles County, using a system known as the Lakewood Plan. Los Angeles will sell a package of services tailored to the needs of communities within its boundaries which enables them to gain political autonomy through incorporating and yet avoid an expensive bureaucracy. A number of counties provide services (such as health regulation, engineering, emergency ambulance, law enforcement, and fire protection) that require advanced technology or high start-up costs. Similarly many communities contract with private firms for refuse collection, legal services, and street lighting. Other agreements among municipalities take the form of mutual assistance pacts that operate on a standby basis. All in all, these agreements permit communities to retain their identity and to maintain, on a flexible basis, levels of service that they may not otherwise be able to afford.

Councils of Government

Councils of government are voluntary regional associations of local governments. Since 1967 they have grown to more than 130, due to the stimulus of federal funds for metropolitanwide planning agencies. More recently their clout has grown due to federal requirements that cities in metropolitan areas obtain the review of an areawide agency to qualify for grants and loans for housing, mass transit, and public works. Councils of government are most useful where a broad consensus exists and coordination can be achieved through the recognition of common interests. But when divisive issues erupt, the absence of legal authority diminishes their impact.

RESURGENCE OF THE STATES

When Jimmy Carter stepped from the state house in Georgia to the White House in 1976, he became the first governor to be elected president since Franklin Delano Roosevelt in 1932. Yet in the 20th century prior to World War II, five of the eight presidents were former governors and in 1980 the stature of the office of governor was confirmed as two former governors vied for the prize of national politics.

The revival of gubernatorial office as a career path to the presidency dramatizes the resurgence both of chief executives and of their states. Since the 1972 Watergate election, the tide of favorable public opinion has shifted from the federal government toward the states. While the senate remains the forum for foreign policy issues, the focus of popular concern is how to cope with domestic problems such as high taxes, unemployment, inflation, and governmental regulations. And many people feel that federal power is the cause of many problems that state and local governments are grappling with. In a 1976 Harris survey, those polled felt by a three-to-one margin that states rather than the federal government care more what happens to people and that the central government is more corrupt than the states.[6] Yet back in the 1960s, most of the public was confident that the national government could and would solve most of the nation's problems. The perception that states are now considered more trustworthy than the federal government is reinforced by attitudes about taxes. In an annual poll of the Advisory Commission on Intergovernmental Affairs, the federal income tax for the first time had an edge over the local property tax as the most onerous tax.

This more favorable popular mood towards the states is not due simply to declining federal fortune but also reflects the increased capabilities of state officials and institutions to govern. Let us first consider the formal powers accorded the chief executive. At one end of the spectrum there is the weak governor. He is limited to a two-year term and cannot be reelected. His appointment and removal powers are restricted by the state legislature or by independent boards and commissions. Heads of administrative agencies may also be elected. He lacks authority to reorganize, and is burdened by the cumbersome bureaucracy. In dealing with the state legislature, his veto is frequently overridden, and he can neither prepare nor control the size of the budget. At the other end of the spectrum, the strong governor enjoys powers that many presidents would envy. He can serve a four-year term and there are no limits to relection. His authority to appoint and dismiss subordinate officials is unencumbered by outside agencies. And if his managerial duties prove too burdensome, he can streamline the administrative apparatus. When he disagrees with legislative decisions, he can strike out the offensive titles through the item veto, and his decision is sustained.

Over the past two decades, the strong-governor model has become the norm in the vast majority of states; only a scant handful adhere

---

[6]Parris N. Glendening, "The Public's Perception of State Government and Governors," *State Government,* Summer 1980, pp. 115–19.

to the weak-governor variant. A four-year term is nearly universal. Only Arkansas, New Hampshire, Rhode Island, and Virginia continue to elect governors for a two-year term. Similarly, only five states would deny him an opportunity to run for a consecutive term— Kansas, Mississippi, New Mexico, South Carolina, and Virginia. Since 1965, 22 states have undergone major reorganizations broadening the governor's appointment and removal power, while most other states have reorganized one or more departments. Only North Carolina fails to grant its chief executive the veto power, and in 44 states he may use the item veto. In 34 states, the governor has complete responsibility for preparing and overseeing the budget. Another reform contributing to the greater visibility and prominence both of the governor and of state issues is the separation of gubernatorial and presidential selections. Only 13 governors are now elected in presidential years, compared to 27 in 1960. This enables gubernatorial hopefuls to formulate views different from the party platform and not rely on the national standard bearer.

While it is clear that the governor's formal powers have markedly increased, the relationship between the governor and his political party (a traditional resource of informal power) has also been transformed. In this case, however, the results are mixed. In several instances the changes benefit the governor; but others may weaken his standing. There are now only seven one-party states in the nation, all Democratic. There are 10 states which "lean" Democratic, but are in the process of converting to a more competitive status.[7] The remaining 33, which includes several formerly Republican states in the Farm Belt and New England, are competitive: either party has a good chance of capturing the governorship. It is a political axiom that competition leads to party unity—virtually assuring the renomination of the incumbent with a high probability of winning the general election. Incumbent governors have a better than 70 percent chance to succeed themselves. On the other hand, the growing numbers of voters labeling themselves as "independent" resulted in a great amount of ticket splitting during the 1970s which significantly increased divided control between the executive and one or both houses. This has led to policy stalemates and the inability of governors to secure cooperation during their administration.

Also a series of interviews with 15 former governors who have left office since 1976 reveals that modern chief executives tend to reject their traditional role as party leaders.[8] Basically these governors viewed party principles and platforms as irrelevant when it came to

[7]Sarah M. Morehouse, "The Politics of Gubernatorial Nominations," *State Government,* Summer 1980, pp. 125–28.

[8]Lynn Muchmore and Thad L. Beyle, "The Governor as Party Leader," *State Government,* Summer 1980, pp. 121–24.

the complex issues they confronted. In the same vein, most of them excluded patronage in making appointments that required expertise or managerial competence. While the governor is free to exercise more discretion, this can handicap his ability to secure cooperation from the legislative branch, which is organized along customary partisan lines. At the root of the matter, the party organization no longer can offer much in the way of money or other support for obtaining the nomination or securing reelection. The replacement by the direct primary of the now virtually extinct statewide nominating convention forces the gubernatorial aspirant to fend for himself. As a consequence, television, opinion polling, and campaign consultants are becoming key factors making for success or failure in the states as they have been for national office.

The Legislative Process

State legislatures also have undergone significant changes over the past two decades. In the 1960s a series of Supreme Court decisions which mandated the "one man–one vote" doctrine resulted in the almost universal reapportionment of state legislatures. More youthful and better-educated legislators, drawn from wider occupational backgrounds, were attracted to the state capitals. In addition, members of groups that formerly had been vastly underrepresented—such as women, ethnic minorities, and blacks—increased their numbers substantially.

Fueled by energies of these newcomers, state legislatures are now better organized to be more work oriented and responsive to their constituents than in the past. Virtually every state legislature now meets yearly; two decades ago the norm was biannually. Constitutional restrictions on the length of legislative sessions have also been relaxed, reducing the need for special legislative sessions which often produced erratic outcomes. In the mid-1950s, all legislatures combined processed 25,000 bills a year. By 1980 this number climbed to 175,000. (The proportion of bills enacted into laws also increased comparably.) Salaries have also grown from an average of $4,000 in the early 1960s to well over $20,000 by 1980. While turnover has been considerably reduced—about a third are new to their jobs each year—this is still more than twice the rate for the U.S. Congress.

To cope with the increased workload, there is greater emphasis on procedures for managing time. A number of states have reduced the number and size of standing committees and imposed deadlines to expedite legislation. Forty-four states now allow bills to be prefiled prior to the opening of the session, and a number place caps on the proliferation of bills.

State legislatures are in vigorous competition with the governor and executive branch to put their own stamp on governmental programs. There is a greater tendency for program innovations to arise in the legislative branch itself rather than being introduced, as was formerly the case, as part of the governor's package. For example, sunset laws providing automatic termination of government agencies unless renewed by the legislature are now in effect in 35 states.[9] Legislative oversight has also been strengthened by the use of the audit function to review the impact of federal assistance funds. There are now 40 states where the audit function is part of the legislative branch; and auditors also cover the evaluation of government programs.

Voter concerns and demands are reflected in rapid succession in the legislative output from state to state. Following Proposition 13 in California, 38 states provided property tax relief, while some form of income tax relief was enacted in 22 states. More than 20 states have legislation dealing with hazardous substances and wastes, modeled on anticipated federal regulations that have not yet taken effect. In accord with concern about public education, minimal competency testing of public school students is now required in 36 states. Several hastily enacted measures affect controversial and emotionally charged issues. In the past few years: some 20 states have passed new death penalty laws; adult motorcyclists were freed of helmet requirements; laetrile may be legally prescribed for cancer patients in about half the states; and several have placed restrictions on abortion funding and practices.

But it is just such emotionally charged issues as capital punishment, gun control, welfare reform, and abortion that present the greatest danger for legislators. The interests that are involved tend to be "single issue" constituencies. All expect complete agreement on every vote involving their issues, a good, solid overall record is not enough. Representatives are forced into polar positions, making compromise extremely difficult. The increase of these controversial matters has severely limited the discretion of representatives to study the matter carefully, then vote their own minds or consciences.

Governments as Shopping Malls

Related problems stem from the consequences of modernization of the institutions of state government. While it is clear that states operate more effectively than in the past, it is not so obvious why the more progressive states such as California, New York, and Massachusetts are those which have recently experienced the most popular discontent. One explanation suggests a paradox: it is modernization—

[9]Elaine S. Knapp, "Trends in State Legislation: 1978–79" in *Book of the States, 1980–1981* (Lexington, Ky.: Council of State Government, 1981), pp. 22–26.

marked by the increased professionalization of governors' offices, state legislatures, and executive departments—which is a central cause of the ailment.[10] Many of the staff who were attracted to the human service areas such as education, mental health, and public assistance are client-centered professionals, as distinct from the more traditional subject-matter specialists. These advocates are not simply interested in trying to solve existing problems, but in the process are constantly identifying new problems. Working in concert with their special interest group counterpart, they have generated a proliferation of expensive narrow programs that lack a coherent purpose. Thus in education there are programs for the disadvantaged, the handicapped, the bicultural, the gifted, women, blacks, native Americans, and more.

In effect, state government may be depicted as a modern shopping mall with small specialty shops, each catering to a small segment of the population. When business is good, all are crowded and can expand without worrying about those who are setting up new shops. The management of the mall is not particularly concerned with what each shop is selling when the overall cost of operations is being met. But when times are bad, shopkeepers compete for business and fight the addition of new stores in order to survive. Management is forced to think about whom to evict for not paying the rent, and how to attract and develop shops that would serve the needs of large numbers of customers. Perhaps only when budgets are tight can the purpose and priorities of state and local governments be addressed with vigor and clarity.

---

[10]Jerome T. Murphy, "The Paradox of State Government Reform," *The Public Interest,* Summer 1981, pp. 124–39.

The Financial Impact on Local Governments of Intergovernmental Aid Programs

CHAPTER 3

Donald Haider, Ph.D.
Professor of Public Management
J. L. Kellogg Graduate School of Management
Northwestern University

Any projections concerning the condition of state and local government finance in the 1980s is not a task for the fainthearted. Those who undertook this task in the 1960s and in the 1970s for the decade beyond widely missed the mark. Even with past hindsight, economic models and determinant studies of government expenditures are unlikely to provide any clear road map to the state and local government terrain in the 1980s. There are simply too many uncertainties.

Nowhere is this more the case than in the sphere of intergovernmental relations, which has experienced rather dramatic changes over the two preceding decades. In spite of some obvious continuities between the past and the present, the contrasts between intergovernmental relations in the 1960s and in the 1980s are enormous. As the Advisory Commission on Intergovernmental Relations (ACIR) observed of these changes: "Over the past 20 years the federal role has become bigger, broader, and deeper—bigger within the federal system both in the size of intergovernmental outlays and in the number

29

of grant programs, broader in its program and policy concerns, and deeper in its regulatory thrust and preemption proclivities."[1]

Beyond a changing federal role in the intergovernmental context, public finance in the 1980s faces a whole new range of problems that stem from inflation, such as erratic capital markets as well as tax and expenditure limitations. Public officials also will have to come to grips with rising pension obligations, problems associated with deferred capital maintenance, and new accounting, disclosure, and reporting standards. These events and trends are occurring at a time of slower governmental growth and intergovernmental retrenchment. Just as the federal government is attempting to redefine its relationship with states and localities, so are state governments with their local units. Not only will these changes require better financial planning and management by government but they also will bring into being new forms of financing, service delivery, and public-private relationships in conducting the public's business.

FORECASTING THE FISCAL OUTLOOK

In its 1966 study, *Fiscal Outlook for State and Local Government to 1975*, the Tax Foundation foresaw an overall improvement in the state-local fiscal condition for the decade ahead. Existing revenue structures coupled to federal aid growth provided sufficient margin necessary for the support of state and local governments. These increases were forecasted to average 7 percent annually through 1975, well above the projected rate for expenditures.[2]

Rather than moderating as anticipated, state-local revenues and expenditures surged ahead in the late 1960s at nearly twice the growth rate of the overall economy. Inflation rates tripled from the early to the late 1960s while welfare growth escalated. Not only did public sector employment expand, but average public employment compensation levels ran ahead of the private sector.

Noting these unanticipated changes, the Tax Foundation revised and updated its projections in 1972 for the decade, still viewing the state-local fiscal outlook optimistically, albeit more cautiously. The Tax Foundation's favorable outlook and conclusions found support from the President's Council of Economic Advisers, the American Enterprise Institute, the Brookings Institution, and many public finance experts. However, the deep 1973–75 recession coupled with double-digit inflation shattered these projections as well. New York City's

---

[1]Advisory Commission on Intergovernmental Relations, *An Agenda for American Federalism* (Washington, D.C., 1981), p. 1.

[2]Tax Foundation, *Fiscal Outlook for State and Local Government to 1980* (New York: Tax Foundation, 1972), p. 20.

default on its debt obligations and New York State's entanglement in this crisis marked a low point in the 1973–75 recession that severely damaged the ability of older large cities to finance public services. Once again, the assumptions on which these forecasts had been based had not anticipated the economic turbulence of the 1970s—uneven growth, high inflation, and a deep recession. They also neglected fundamental changes that had occurred in the state-local sector.

Among other shortcomings, these projections underestimated not only inflation but also the differential impacts it had on the revenue and expenditure side of governmental balance sheets. By using more representative inflation indices to measure impacts upon the state-local sector, it became clear that expenditures proved much more responsive to inflation than did own-source revenues. The purchasing power of state-local governments (townships, counties, school districts, etc.) also fell considerably from 1972 to 1976.[3]

Prior projections assumed too close of a relation (especially in education) between declining or static service demand and the number of, as well as compensation for, public employees. Between 1955 and 1973, employment by state and local governments rose from 7.5 percent to 12 percent of all workers, while average earnings of public employees increased from 92.5 percent to 103.5 percent of workers in all industries.[4] The surge in numbers and in compensation levels slowed during the mid-1970s, but not uniformly, as fringe benefits (employee pensions and social security coverage) continued to grow. Even where work-force reduction occurred, aggregate wages still increased rapidly due to previous labor agreements, age of work force, and wage supplements. From 1974 to 1977, private sector wages rose faster than public employees, but the inflationary wage push affected both simultaneously.

Uneven growth and unforeseen inflation impacted state and local governments in a highly volatile manner. The recession produced a drop-off in income and sales tax revenues, requiring combinations of retrenchment and tax increases. Renewed growth and inflation then produced high surpluses under more favorable economic conditions, only to be followed in 1978 by a record number of state tax reductions. In the midst of the recession, Congress responded to lost state-local revenues and cutbacks by pumping increased federal aid to these governments through countercyclical assistance. Instead of relying on tax cuts to stimulate the national economy, Washington

---

[3]Roy Bahl et al., "The Outlook for City Fiscal Performance in Declining Regions," in *The Fiscal Outlook for Cities,* ed. Roy Bahl (Syracuse, N.Y.: Syracuse University Press, 1978), p. 14.

[4]R. Bahl, J. Burkhead, and B. Junip, *Public Employment and State and Local Government Finance* (Cambridge, Mass.: Ballinger Publishing, 1980), pp. 11–14.

chose to use the state-local sector as instruments of macroeconomic policy. These programs continued through 1978, well after the recession had ended, and increased the flow of federal aid to states and localities.

In reviewing this history, it becomes clear that in our system of fiscal federalism there is a state sector, a local sector, and a state-local sector in which the state portion does not always move in the same direction as the local portion; for that matter, the state-local sector moves either entirely cyclically or countercyclically to the national economic business cycle. So, too, economic cyclical fluctuations impact governments in different ways depending upon their economic base, tax structures, and financial response.[5]

Generally, the steady improvement both in the elasticity and progressivity of state revenue systems dramatically increased the revenue yields of the state-local sector, while excessive tax cutting and mandated expenditure limits reduced many a governments' flexibility to respond to rapidly changing economic conditions. Inflation proved critical to both swings.

During the 1970s an enormous outpouring of academic and congressional studies focused on the financial condition of state and local governments, from measures of fiscal health to determinants of fiscal strain. The problem of forecasting, let alone developing an accurate measurement of a sector's fiscal health, is compounded by the way the financial position of subnational governments is measured in the National Income and Product Accounts. These accounts fail to distinguish between state and local governmental balances, while state accounts typically show wide variation between the high-growth, energy-surplus states and the low-growth, high-unemployment states. Moreover the disparities among regions, states, and localities, in terms of tax efforts and personal income growth, provide a more accurate dimension of their so-called fiscal blood pressure than does a single snapshot of the aggregate sector at a particular time. The state-local accounts often mix separate and restricted funds that result in an uneven picture of real surpluses. How government estimates or calculates this sector's condition not only affects decisions on macroeconomic federal policies, but also produces heated debates between governors and mayors and the Congress over federal aid distribution.

Once again, economic projections for the decade ahead paint a favorable picture for state and local government finance. This optimism is grounded in the strengthened state-local revenue systems and the

[5]See Robert Rafuse, "The State-Local Sector and the Economy," in *Essays in Public Finance and Financial Management,* eds. J. Peterson and C. Spain (Chatham, N.J.: Chatham House, 1978), pp. 127–40; and Advisory Commission on Intergovernmental Relations, *Countercyclical Aid and Economic Stabilization* (Washington, D.C., 1978).

slowing growth rate in the state and local sector.[6] Demographics also continue to work in these governments' favor. The decline in student enrollment at all levels, for example, is stabilizing if not reducing the percentage of state-local expenditures for education. Between 1974 and 1978, outlays for schools have declined from 5.3 percent of personal income to 4.6 percent. However, the principal determinant of the state-local condition turns on the condition of the overall economy. As Table 1 indicates, the Reagan administration's economic forecast through 1985 projects net revenues of $551 billion and $547 billion in expenditures for the state-local sector. A $4 billion surplus amounts only to a 1 percent safety margin and assumes both high growth/lower inflation and no increase in state-local tax rates.

Beyond the gradual but nonetheless pervasive impacts of demographic and economic changes, two key areas of intergovernmental finance in the 1980s involve: *(a)* changing federal priorities and the related intergovernmental assistance system and *(b)* the fiscal relations between states and their local governments.

Table 1
1985 Forecasts for State and Local Expenditures and Receipts in the National Income Accounts ($ billions of current dollars)

	1980	*1985*
Expenditures (constant real per capita):		
Total	$355.0	$547.2
Purchases	335.8	518.7
Net transfers	19.1	28.5
Revenues:		
Total	384.0	596.8
Tax forecast	230.0	395.9
Revised grants (Reagan fiscal year 1982 budget)	88.0	84.3
All other revenues	66.1	116.6
Less: NIA gross surplus	−29.1	−45.4
Net revenue available	$354.9	$551.4

Source: U.S. Treasury Department, 1981. Assumes population of 240.3 million in 1985 and NIA deflators for purchases equal 2.692.

SHIFTING FEDERAL PRIORITIES

The shift in federal resource allocation away from the state-local sector began well before the election of President Ronald Reagan in 1980. From fiscal year 1978 to fiscal year 1981, the annual rate of increase in federal aid to state and local governments slowed to 7.8

---

[6]Emil M. Sunley, Jr., "State and Local Governments," in *Setting National Priorities: The Next Ten Years*, eds. Henry Owen and Charles Schultz (Washington, D.C.: Brookings Institution, 1976), chap. 9; and G. Break, "Fiscal Federalism in the 1980s," *Intergovernmental Perspective* 6 (Summer 1980), pp. 10–14.

percent, nearly half the annual figure for the preceding 20 years. Indeed, federal aid peaked in 1978, according to Table 2, as measured by grants as a percentage of total federal outlays, total domestic outlays, or state-local expenditures. Following 1978, federal aid declined in constant dollar terms as inflation far exceeded increments in federal aid. By deleting grants to individuals (transfer payments) from the grant total, federal aid began to decline in current dollars as well. If it had not been for the 1973–75 recession and the federal countercyclical aid response (jobs, public works, and revenue aid), it is highly likely that federal aid would have begun its no-growth or downward slope far sooner than in 1978.

Between 1960 and 1980, federal grants to state and local government became one of the principal vehicles of government growth, leveraging state and local resources, employment, and service demands. The differences in the two periods may be best illustrated by the following contrasts and comparisons:

> Then, 130-odd intergovernmental fiscal transfer programs amounted to $7 billion or less than 2 percent of GNP, and 15 percent of state-local expenditures; 20 years later, the 500-plus programs amounted to $88 billion, or 3.4 percent GNP and 23.2 percent of state-local outlays.
>
> Then, almost all federal aid went to or through state governments; 20 years later, 25 percent passed directly to local governments with at least 80 percent of the 80,000 subnational governments receiving some federal aid.
>
> Then, there were few programs, with limited conditions attached to each; two decades later, with several hundred grant programs, several dozen conditions cut across all programs, deepening federal regulatory requirements and, indirectly, using grant conditions as a means of furthering national social, environmental, egalitarian, and other goals.
>
> In 1960, income maintenance and social welfare programs accounted for 50 percent of the total intergovernmental aid amount, and state-local

Table 2
Trends: Federal Grant-In-Aid Outlays (fiscal years; $ in millions)

	Composition of Grants			Grants as a Percent of Federal Outlays		
Year	Total Grants	Grants to Individuals	Other	Total	Domestic	State-Local Expenditures
1960	7,020	2,474	4,541	7.6%	15.9%	14.7%
1970	24,014	9,023	14,991	12.2	21.1	19.4
1976	59,093	21,023	38,070	16.1	21.7	24.4
1978	77,889	25,981	51,908	17.3	22.9	26.4
1979	82,858	28,765	54,093	16.8	22.4	25.6
1980 (est.)	88,945	34,202	54,744	15.8	21.0	25.3

Source: *Budget of the U.S. Government—Fiscal Year 1981, Special Analyses,* p. 254.

contribution constituted less than $2 billion; in 1980, they represent 63 percent of total aid, and state-local contribution is nearly $20 billion.[7]

The takeoff stage in federal grants to states and localities occurred during the "Great Society" years (1964–66), a period when an entire backlog of ideas, programs, and social reforms swept through the prolific 89th Congress. Federal resources were provided to subnational governments and to a host of new actors to enable the federal government to achieve national objectives rather than the reverse. These programs vastly changed intergovernmental relations.

During succeeding years, the full thrust of these programs and shift in public resource allocation actually occurred. Defense spending as a proportion of federal outlays declined from 43 percent to 24 percent of the federal budget during the Nixon and Ford administrations (1969–76), while benefit payments and grants to states and localities rose from 31 percent to 58 percent of outlays. From 1969 to 1976, federal aid to state and localities alone increased from 10 percent to 16 percent of federal outlays, and from 17 percent to a peak of nearly 26 percent of state-local expenditures.

Beginning in the 1960s, and increasing by a 2 percent rate annually, more of the federal budget became relatively uncontrollable due to expenditures mandated by existing statutes, prior-year contracts, or obligations. Social security and related income security programs increased at a rate nearly double that of the overall budget growth and 2.5 times faster than GNP. Between 1970 and 1975 alone, these entitlement and income security payments jumped from 33.6 percent of the total federal budget to 48 percent.[8] Once these entitlements provided for built-in inflation adjustments, they rose precipitously with surging inflation, further exacerbated by high unemployment, early retirement, and related benefits programs.

Consequently, a distinct reversal of relative financial positions occurred between the national and state-local governments from 1960 to 1980, from a federal position of relative ease to one of considerable fiscal strain. Former New York Governor Nelson Rockefeller exemplified an earlier view of these positions when he argued that "The federal government had the revenues, but states and local governments had all the problems." During the 1970s the federal government's fiscal position shifted dramatically due to uneven growth, inflation, and high unemployment. The momentum driving federal budgetary growth was simply incompatible with the limits imposed by economic growth. Inflation-driven expenditures and periodic

---

[7]ACIR, *An Agenda For American Federalism*, pp. 3–5.

[8]Executive Office of the President, *America's New Beginning: A Program for Economic Recovery* (February 18, 1981), p. 15.

congressionally induced tax cuts propelled expenditure growth rates that consistently outpaced current-year revenues.

Set against rising defense obligations, social security, and entitlement payments, the controllable portion of the federal budget—the grant sector—became the casualty of altered priorities. Dramatic evidence of this squeeze occurred when Congress rejected outright President Carter's 1978–80 proposals for new targeted fiscal assistance programs to aid fiscally stressed local governments and for authorization for a standby countercyclical revenue program. Indeed, the 96th Congress also eliminated the $2.3 billion annual state share from the three-year renewal of general revenue sharing. If the general revenue sharing renewal battle served as a fiscal bellweather for Congress's judgment of the condition of American federalism, then that body had resolved that the states had the revenue capacity to carry on without this additional federal assistance.

Thus, for the foreseeable future, the question is no longer whether federal aid to states and localities will slow, but rather by how much, in what form, with what attendant conditions, and with what impacts. As Table 3 indicates, the proposed Reagan administration shift in federal budget priorities will place heavy emphasis upon defense, maintenance of safety net programs, and a reduced grant portion of the federal budget through at least mid-1985. Given the prospects of using federal deficits for 1981–1983, aid to states and localities will remain under constant pressure for additional cuts. Nearly two thirds of the 1982 budget cuts fell on grant programs.

Slower growth rate in federal grants opens up their distribution to rather stiff competition between regions; states and local governments; governors, mayors, and local officials; executive and legislative bodies; program administrators and elected public officials; governmental units and nongovernmental organizations; and grant recipients and program beneficiaries.

Federal grants constitute one of several devices for sharing federal

Table 3
Reagan Administration Proposed Shift in Federal Budget Priorities ($ billions; percentages of total budget)

Year	1962		1981		1984	
Dept. of Defense–military	$ 46.8	43.8%	$157.9	24.1%	$249.8	32.4%
Safety net programs*	26.2	24.5	239.3	36.6	313.0	40.6
Net interest	6.9	6.4	64.3	9.8	66.8	8.6
All other	26.9	25.2	193.2	29.5	$142.0	18.4
Total	$106.8	100.0	$654.7	100.0	$771.6	100.0

*Defined as social insurance benefits for the elderly; basic unemployment benefits; cash benefits for dependent families, elderly, and disabled; and social obligation to veterans.

Source: Executive Office of the President, *America's New Beginning: A Program for Economic Recovery,* February 18, 1981, p. 11.

resources and authority with nonfederal actors: loans, loan guarantees, tax incentives, regulations, credit insurance, contracting, procurement, and the like. From its meager beginning in the 19th century, the grant-in-aid device expanded into a massive system of intergovernmental action which relies not simply on state and local governments to carry out federal purposes, but also special districts, nonprofit corporations, financial institutions, hospitals, schools, neighborhood organizations, and others. In many cases, federal grants helped create, support, and perpetuate these instrumentalities for conducting the publics' business. This entire modern grant economy may be overloaded, dysfunctional, inefficient, as many of its critics argue. Nonetheless, it is the political, social, and economic lifeline for thousands of claimants. Change will not come easily.

Federal grants are the most pervasive aspect of federal instrumentalities, involving a $100 billion distribution system. As a federal fiscal tool, grants involve the payment of funds by one level of government to be expended by another level for a specific purpose, usually on a matching basis and in accordance with prescribed standards or requirements. Grants have assumed three basic forms—categorical, block, and revenue sharing—that may be distinguished by amounts, program scope, recipient discretion, and funding criteria.

Categorical grants, the oldest and most numerous form, can be distributed either by legislative formula or by competition under agency guidelines (project grants). Categoricals number in the hundreds, are narrow in scope, and are specific in problem focus and in intended results. They are conditional in character, which means limited or restricted as to use, and entail other recipient conditions such as matching, advance planning, reporting, accounting, and the like. Project grants rapidly surpassed formula grants in use during the 1960s, investing considerable discretion in the grant administering agencies as to distributional criteria. Overall, categoricals constituted 98 percent of the federal aid system in 1966. This enormous growth was accompanied by problems of overlap, duplication, excessive categorization, varying matching and administrative requirements, and arbitrariness.

Congress enacted the first of several block grants during the mid-1960s. A block grant may be defined as a program which seeks to further some broad national purpose and in which funds are provided chiefly to general-purpose governmental units in accordance with a statutory formula for use in a broad functional area largely at the recipient's discretion. Block grants differ from categoricals due to their broader scope, recipient discretion, less administrative requirements, and statutory distribution. Between 1966 and 1980, only 5 of the 20 major block grants proposed by presidents have been enacted. Among other factors, this casualty rate suggests the great problem

Congress has in reaching agreement on funding, distribution, and use, as well as the balance between goals of state-local discretion and federal oversight.

Finally, general revenue sharing (GRS) has distributed more than $50 billion to 50 states and 39,000 units of local governments since its adoption in 1972. As the least restrictive form of federal aid distribution, it is the most popular federal assistance program from the vantage of state-local officials, and most disliked by Congress due to its unrestrictive nature. One third of the GRS allocations goes to state governments, and the remaining two thirds to all general purpose units of local government on a quarterly basis. Distribution occurs by formula which includes population, tax effort, and per capita income among other factors.

First enacted as a $30.2 billion, five-year entitlement program, GRS was extended in 1976 for four additional years at a $25.6 billion funding level. In 1980 Congress voted to eliminate the states' $2.3 billion share for fiscal year 1981, leaving open future disposition of the states' role, and funded local governments on an appropriation basis at $4.5 billion annually through fiscal year 1983. Thus, what was once the foundation of President Nixon's "New Federalism" and the principal wedge in broadening the federal aid system is in obvious decline. The program has grown only marginally since 1972 in current dollars, and relative to the inflation rate, its purchasing power has been reduced by more than half.

Still, efforts to balance federal aid distribution away from categoricals through use of GRS and block grants have progressed significantly since 1972. As Table 4 indicates, the latter two forms of aid constituted 27 percent of total federal assistance in 1978, and have slipped since. The Reagan administration seeks to further broaden flexible aid distribution by proposing six additional block grants. Four of these result from the consolidation of nearly 100 categorical programs within the Department of Health and Human Services to be channeled through the states for redistribution without requirements for matching funds, application, or maintenance of effort. The aggregate total of these block grants are to be 25 percent less than

Table 4
Outlays for General Purpose, Block, and Categorical Grants by Percent of Total Federal Aid: 1972–1981

Grant Type	*1972*	*1976*	*1978*	*1981 (est.)*
General purpose	1.5%	12.1%	12.3%	7.2%
Broad-based	8.3	10.6	14.8	10.8
Other	90.2	77.3	72.9	82.0
Total	100.0%	100.0%	100.0%	100.0%

Source: *Budget of the U.S. Government—Fiscal Year 1982, Special Analyses*, p. 255.

the sum of their current authorized levels. Another Reagan administration proposal combines programs for disadvantaged and handicapped students into one block grant and research, institutional, and curricula related grants into another. More substantial changes notwithstanding, block grant initiatives will be at the forefront of the Reagan agenda.

The record of block grants as compiled by the ACIR suggests that "they neither lived up to high expectations of their most enthusiastic supporters nor to the devastating predictions of doom from their most ardent critics."[9] The evidence shows that block grants can lead to improved economy and efficiency, greater decentralization and generalist control, and increased coordination. On the other hand, they are not well suited to achieve targeting of resources, innovation, or program growth, and may increase costs for recipients. These strengths and weaknesses have all been amply documented. Successful passage of block grants generally has required the availability of additional funding to "buy consolidation" and to overcome opposition.

Structural changes in federal assistance programs such as grant consolidation and block grants represent one response to the problems of a congested and overloaded intergovernmental system. Another involves administrative and procedural changes aimed at standardizing, unifying, and simplifying crosscutting grant regulations and conditions. In a broad sense, the issues of grant modernization and reform embrace all forms of federal assistance—the rules, regulations, processes, and procedures used by federal agencies to accomplish objectives set by Congress. This includes not only grants but other forms of assistance: contracts, cooperative agreements, subsidies, loans, insurance, and procurement. Rarely do Congress and federal agencies make systematic choices over what tools and strategies to employ in achieving stated objectives or, once a selection is made, provide guidance as to how much federal involvement is warranted in achieving particular policy objectives.

For more than a decade, pressures have built up for reform of grants management: centralizing guidance, reducing regulatory burdens, resolving disputes, strengthening accountability, and the like. Despite what has been a mixed record of results, procedural reforms will continue to be the most frequently used tool for intergovernmental management improvement. Compared to structural changes such as block grants and shifts in intergovernmental functional responsibility, the prospects for procedural changes are extremely promising for the 1980s.[10]

---

[9]Carol Weissert, "Block Grants: The Promise and Reality," *Intergovernmental Perspective* 7 (Spring 1981), pp. 16–17.

[10]See Office of Management and Budget, *Managing Federal Assistance in the 1980s* (Washington, D.C.: Office of Management and Budget, 1980).

The most ambitious and far-reaching changes in federal assistance involve a fundamental sorting out of functions among governmental levels. The ACIR, among others, has called for a reexamination of federal, state, and local roles in and contributions to the principal areas of public policy, including assessments of the desirability of fully nationalizing some functions while reducing, eliminating, or forestalling federal involvement in others. The commission recommended federal assumption of full financial responsibility for welfare, medicaid, employment security, housing assistance, and basic nutrition programs. Federalization of the human need functions would include uniform levels of benefit assistance, adjusted for cost-of-living variations, and consistent nationwide administration. The nation's governors and mayors are generally united in support of this position.

Closely linked to this sorting out process, the ACIR recommended termination, phaseout, and consolidation of federal programs that duplicate and overlap one another, or where federal involvement is small. This entire process of disentangling who does what, who pays for what, and who is responsible for what involves substantial trade-offs among government levels. National responsibility would be asserted for certain programs and functions, combined with devolution of responsibilities for others to state and local levels or the private sector. Table 5 indicates federal aid share of state and local expenditures for 11 major functions, while Table 6 represents a rough calculation of the aggregate national financial implications of certain potential trade-offs. This proposal represents one of several that have been offered by state-local officials, academics, and public finance experts to build greater accountability, responsibility, and rationality into the morass of intergovernmental relations.

Thus far, neither the Reagan administration nor the 52-member Presidential Advisory Committee on Federalism, which is to recommend ways to shift federal power from Washington to state and local government, has expressed much interest in a trade-off that would federalize human need programs, especially welfare. More than four decades of controversy and conflict have characterized federal-state relations over public assistance programs which, according to the ACIR, expanded into "a massive, chaotic, seemingly unalterable non-system despised by everyone—especially its beneficiaries."[11] Dating from its origin in 1935 (medicaid in 1966), the federal role has been secondary and financial. States and localities administer these programs, determine eligibility, and establish payment levels, while the Congress fixes reimbursement formulas for states' welfare spending.

---

[11]Advisory Commission on Intergovernmental Relations, *Public Assistance: The Growth of a Federal Function* (Washington, D.C.: ACIR, 1980), p. 106.

Table 5
Federal Aid Share of State and Local Expenditures for 11 Major Functions

Large (More than 50 Percent)*		Moderate (15–50 Percent)†		Small (Less than 15 Percent)‡	
Social insurance	87.2%	Airports	44.0%	Health and hospitals	11.0%
Housing and urban	80.0	Natural resources	38.5	Education	10.5
renewal		Highways	25.0	Libraries	7.6
Public welfare	53.2			Police and corrections	3.4
(includes medicaid, food stamps, social services, etc.)				Fire protection	0.1

*Potential federal assumption.
†Potential shared or mixed programs.
‡Potential state-local assumption.
Source: Advisory Commission on Intergovernmental Relations, *An Agenda for American Federalism*, (Washington, D.C., 1981), p. 122.

Table 6
Funding of Federal Aid Programs Involved in Rough Trade-Off Proposals ($ millions)

Federal Assumption of State-Local Costs		State-Local Assumption of Present Federal Aid Funding	
Public welfare (medicaid, social services, food stamps, etc.)	$17,628	Education	$11,602
		Libraries	103
		Fire protection	4
Social insurance (including unemployment insurance and workmen's compensation)	226*	Police and corrections (criminal justice)	551
		Health and hospitals	2,464
		Natural resources	551
Housing	730	Airports	719
Total	$18,584 −15,994	Total	$15,994
Net federal extra cost	$ 2,590		

*These are general fund expenditures. They exclude trust fund expenditures supported by payroll taxes.
Source: Advisory Commission on Intergovernmental Relations, *An Agenda For American Federalism*, (Washington, D.C., 1981), p. 124.

President Richard Nixon first proposed a comprehensive reform of public assistance known as the Family Assistance Plan—a limited guaranteed income program and a step toward federal assumption of costs. Three years later, President Carter sought a similar reform by cashing out many job and welfare-related programs into a single program. In both cases, these reforms failed either to sustain congressional interest or to meet budgetary goals. A related reason for failure stems from the condition that seven states currently bear two thirds of the total state share for public assistance, Aid for Families of

Dependent Children (AFDC) and nearly 60 percent of the state-local medicaid share (Table 7). With the exception of California, these large urban states are concentrated in the nation's Frost Belt region and have experienced slower growth in jobs, income, and population than the nation as a whole. This reform, then, is the source of considerable regional tension.

Compelling arguments can be made for a structural-functional overhaul of the intergovernmental aid system. However, such radical departures are not likely to occur, if for no other reason than the U.S. Senate—in which 43 states are not likely to come to the rescue of those 7 (and their cities) which bear a disproportionately large share of the welfare burden. On the other hand, welfare benefits are increasing outside the Northeast-Midwest area faster than in those regions, so that trade-offs of functions over time may overcome the current hostility between winners and losers.

Instead of functional trade-offs, the Reagan administration seems far more interested in "turnback policies," namely turning back over to states and localities shared functional responsibilities as well as the financial resources necessary to support them. The returning of resources to subnational governments can be accomplished through a variety of methods ranging from revenue or tax sharing to relinquishment of a federal tax. More important than resources are the questions of what functions or programs (e.g., welfare, education, medicaid) to return and the distributional effects of returned resources.

Table 7
Fiscal Year 1981 Funding of AFDC and Medicaid Benefits ($ millions)

	AFDC		*Medicaid*	
	Federal Share	*State-Local Share*	*Federal Share*	*State-Local Share*
California	$1,047	$1,047	$ 1,661	$ 1,661
Illinois	387	387	653	653
Massachusetts	283	263	580	541
Michigan	454	454	615	615
New York	975	975	2,041	2,041
Ohio	279	228	452	268
Pennsylvania	467	380	795	647
	$3,872	$3,734	$ 6,797	$ 6,526
Total national costs	$6,562	$5,649	$13,709	$11,135
Seven-state percentage of total state-local costs		66.1%	58.6%	
Seven-state percentage of total federal costs		59.0%	49.6%	

Source: U.S. Department of Health, Education, and Welfare, 1979 HEW estimates based on 1978 state outlays and fiscal year 1981 federal budget.

The resources, for example, may flow with the returned responsibilities, or the return may simply leave the tax resource at its place of origin. Finally, resources can be used to equalize resources relative to need. This "reverse functional realignment" undoubtedly will embroil the administration in bitter congressional battles, mobilize governors and mayors into the fray, and raise innumerable problems involving winners and losers from any turnback proposals.

In short, the Reagan administration's long-range intergovernmental policies are likely to go beyond cutting back grants, consolidating them, and liberalizing their uses. Although previous administrations have unsuccessfully attempted to disentangle, roll back, and turn back resources and functions in the past, the political climate appears to be more propitious for a comprehensive decentralization package. If successful over the long haul, the states could confront burgeoning pressures from above and below for structural-functional changes.

THE STATES: AN ALTERNATIVE VIEW

In contrast to procedural, structural, and functional changes at the federal level that would have varying degrees of impact upon state and local government finance in the 1980s, states have a comparable range of alternatives for dealing with their local units. Many of these changes can fundamentally alter functional, administrative, and financial responsibilities between state and local governments. The outcome of this evolutionary process may be even more critical to the condition of American federalism than what happens in Washington.

In reviewing the state-local sector over the past 30 years, the most striking feature is how dramatically high growth turned to slow growth, and even no growth. After growing nearly twice as fast as the economy since 1949, aggregate state-local spending began falling behind nominal GNP growth in 1975. Indeed state-local spending on a real per capita basis reached zero growth rates between 1978 and 1979 (-0.8 percent in 1979 and -1.1 percent in 1980). As Table 8 indicates, this formerly dynamic growth (especially during the 1960s) began its downward slope by the mid-1970s.

The peak real per capita growth period of the 1960s was not simply a function of rising federal aid, but rather a gradual transformation of state and local government revenue systems. During the 1950s, for example, the number of states employing an income tax remained the same, while five states added broad-based sales taxes. During the 1960s, 12 states adopted general sales taxes, and another 6 added personal income taxes. By 1970, then, 33 states made use of both taxes, whose revenue yields proved to be increasingly sensitive to economic growth and inflation. Between 1963 and 1973, for example, the average annual increase in receipts from these taxes soared: 18.2 per-

Table 8
State and Local Expenditures* For
Selected Years 1949–1980

Calendar Year	Percent of GNP	Per Capita (constant dollars)
1949	7.8%	$189
1959	9.6	302
1969	12.5	528
1975	15.1	670
1976	14.6	682
1978	14.3	710
1979	13.9	688
1980 (est.)	13.7	656

Source: Advisory Commission on Intergovernmental Relations, *Intergovernmental Perspective* 2 (Spring 1980), p. 29.
    *Expenditures include federal aid.

Table 9
State Share of Total State-Local Revenue

Frequency Distribution of States	1959	1967	1977
Less than 50 percent	20	14	5
50 to 60 percent	14	17	17
60 percent and up	16	19	28
Total	50	50	50

Source: Advisory Commission on Intergovernmental Relations, 1979.

cent for individual income taxes and 13.7 percent in general sales and gross receipts, compared to an 8.7 percent growth rate for property tax receipts.[12]

What also changed over this two-decade period was the relative revenue-raising ability of states compared to their localities. In 1959, 28 states raised more than half of combined state-local revenues. By the late 1970s, as indicated by Table 9, 45 states raised more than half of their own-source, state-local revenues. States had become senior fiscal partners to their local units.

STATE–LOCAL SLOWDOWN: TAX CUTS AND PUBLIC DEMANDS

As the states' largest functional expenditure area declined, namely education, the slowdown in state-local expenditures could be antici-

___

[12]Advisory Commission on Intergovernmental Relations, *Significant Features of Fiscal Federalism 1978–1979* (Washington, D.C.: 1979), p. 42.

pated. Perhaps equally predictable, however, should have been the eventual public demand for tax relief following the considerable rise in state-local taxes during the 1960s. The surge in inflation and the 1973–75 recession, among other factors, helped trigger the vast public opinion shift in the late 1970s from support for, or at least tolerance of, state-local growth to rising pressures for slower growth.

The relative position of the states within our federal system grew significantly during the 1960s. The most striking feature of this change, according to the ACIR and others, may be attributed to the personal income tax—the then fastest growing revenue source in the intergovernmental revenue system.[13] As the federal government repeatedly cut taxes to spur the economy or to offset inflation-induced tax increases, most states refrained from comparable actions, especially as they endured revenue shortfalls stemming from the 1973–75 deep recession. Following economic recovery in 1976 and renewed growth in inflation, income tax yields rose precipitously, especially for those 20 or so states whose income tax structures reflect moderate to high progressivity.

Consequently, a record number of 15 states in 1978 opted for major reductions in personal income taxes (rates, exemptions, or deductions), while another 14 reduced their general sales taxes. This trend continued in 1979 as tax reductions exceeded increases. Compounding the tax cut mood, inflation-driven property values, (especially residential property) rose at a faster rate than the income of many property owners. The demands for local property tax relief, controls, or limits culminated in 1978 when California voters approved Proposition 13—an amendment to the California constitution that not only rolled back property taxes and assessment levels, but also limited future local and state taxes to approval by extraordinary majorities.

California's high state-local tax burden, rising property taxes, and $5.5 billion state budget surplus provided ample grist for the so-called California tax revolt.[14] A wave of Proposition 13-type limits spread across state and local governments, leading to the adoption of numerous fiscal limitations upon government: indexed taxes, property tax relief, tax and expenditure restrictions, and other controls. Cries of fiscal disaster notwithstanding, the tax revolt subsided in 1979–80 as more states rejected limitations than accepted them. The public had exercised their demand for tax relief and slowdown, often through referenda, and this type of voter initiative augurs ill for renewed state-local spending in the 1980s. In the meantime the state-local tax

---

[13]Ibid, p. 3. See also, Advisory Commission on Intergovernmental Relations, *The Inflation Tax: The Case for Indexing Federal and State Income Taxes* (Washington, D.C., 1980).

[14]See Frank Levy, "On Understanding Proposition 13," *The Public Interest* 56 (Summer 1979), pp. 66–89.

revolt moved on to Washington as pressures mounted for a constitutionally prescribed, balanced federal budget.

USER CHARGES: THE THIRD SECTOR

The dramatic slowdown in state spending in the mid-1970s was accompanied by a slowdown in federal aid—a forecasted 20 percent real purchasing decline between fiscal years 1980 and 1982. By 1979, the amount of local government property tax receipts also had slowed to zero growth. For local governments, property taxes provided nearly 80 percent of local own-source revenues, down from the 90 percent range 20 years earlier. Thus, localities faced a fiscal pincer: caught between federal-state slowdown in aid and the further constraint of rising public disfavor with their dominant revenue source, the property tax.

Thus, local governments have begun to diversify their revenue sources. More than 30 states now permit their local jurisdictions to levy either sales or income taxes. This change over time will significantly reduce local government reliance on property tax levies. Equally significant, however, has been the enormous increase by local governments of user fees: licenses, fines, and charges. By the late 1970s, municipal revenue had become rather evenly divided among three sources: intergovernmental assistance, local taxation, and nontax revenues. Between 1957 and 1977, nontax revenues of municipal governments had moved from an amount equal to two thirds of municipal revenues to well above 80 percent.[15]

Several pressures have combined to compel local governments into greater use of these fees. The most obvious is intergovernmental retrenchment and the necessity to broaden their revenue bases. Another stems from municipal markets and public sector accounting systems that have moved local governments into establishing separate enterprise funds whereby the costs of providing goods and services— such as water, sewers, electric, gas, airport, and transit—are financed separately through charges upon users. Not only do such funds relieve general operating budgets, but they also provide a separate revenue stream to sustain operating, maintenance, and capital needs of major municipal functions. With a slowdown in federal capital aid and erratic market conditions, a revenue-financed system operated like a public utility offers significant advantages for localities for maintaining market access and fiscal balance for the short term.

In a very real sense, post-Proposition 13 local governments have entered the marketplace for pricing goods and services according to

---

[15]Lennox L. Moak, "The Revenue Source with Vitality—A New Look at Some Ancient Concepts—Nontax Revenues," in *Cities Under Stress,* eds. R. W. Burchell and David Lestokin (Rutgers, N.J.: Center for Urban Policy Research, 1981), pp. 475–92.

demand levels, actual costs, and identifiable consumers of public services. Such pricing mechanisms also have spread to intergovernmental agreements and contracts among adjacent communities. By the late 1970s, separate funds supported by user fees increased at a rate in excess of 13 percent annually, well above the growth rate for local government, own-source revenues. This "third sector" for local revenue diversification and growth will continue to cushion much of the loss incurred by slower federal-state intergovernmental assistance.

REGIONAL COMPETITION

The tensions and competition brought into play by differing rates of regional economic growth and needs will continue to be a major factor in intergovernmental relations of the 1980s. How much of a factor this will be depends on the rate of current demographic and economic trends as well as the general condition of the overall economy.

During the 1960s, regional issues turned largely on civil rights, public works, and defense contracts. On a regional basis, the South and West historically received more federal expenditures than they paid in federal revenues, although this advantage diminished as real incomes and tax revenues in these regions rose. The fact that poorer states were growing faster than wealthier states, and that, to a degree, federal aid encouraged greater equality among states and regions, seemed to be desirable national policy.

Accelerated growth in the South and West—as measured by population, employment, and income—reflected basic structural changes occurring within the nation's economy. On a demographic basis, the country experienced two trends simultaneously: the movement of households from older, high-density urban areas of the northeast and north central states to other regions; and exurban movement away from central cities to suburbia, smaller towns, and formerly rural areas. As these trends increased, propelled by the 1969–71 and 1973–75 recessions, regional battles intensified over federal aid, tax and economic policies, government procurement, and defense expenditures. By the mid-1970s, the new terminology—Frost Belt and Sun Belt—had come to epitomize these regional clashes. Regional caucuses within Congress and among governors became more active in their claims.

The rates at which these demographic and economic shifts continue are critical not only for federal policy, but also for financing the state-local sector in the 1980s. The ACIR's extensive studies suggest two conclusions—convergence and decentralization. Per capita income and ratios of federal government revenues and expenditures by state are converging, over the long pull, and seem to be slowing. So, too, decentralization of economic activity continues away from the earlier industrial states toward the newer, less developed sections of the country.[16]

Based on an index of fiscal and economic disparities among 50 state-local systems, it is obvious that certain states within the Frost Belt have and will continue to incur periodic fiscal stress (tax and welfare burdens/income growth, and employment). Two federal options for moderating these disparities, welfare takeover and regional growth policies, received considerable attention and support in the 1970s. Interest in the former has subsided, and the latter is being left largely to the states. Following the earlier example of southern states, nearly all Frost Belt states have made economic development a major objective for the 1980s. Given the increased competition among states for jobs and growth, state leaders will resist tax increases that may disadvantage their states in interstate competition, or otherwise detract from a positive business climate. Considerable disagreement exists as to the pulling power of state-local financial incentives as well as tax effects upon business location and relocation. Still, sensitivity to these factors will have a restraining influence upon state-local taxing decisions during the 1980s, especially in low-growth states.

Regional disputes transcend the Frost Belt–Sun Belt dichotomy to include energy surplus and energy deficient states. Soaring energy costs and oil-gas deregulation have provided a major revenue source for energy-rich states from severance taxes, royalty payments, income, sales, and property taxes. The energy production differences among states are enormous, ranging from high self-sufficiency in Louisiana, Wyoming, and Alaska to zero energy production in Delaware and Hawaii. Although these cleavages include the Northwest and exceptions such as Florida and the Carolinas, the "haves" include most growth states and the "have-nots" much of the Northeast and Midwest.

Estimates are that energy-related severance taxes—largely exportable as to tax burden—will yield nearly $10 billion in revenues by 1983, or about 3 percent of an estimated $328 billion in state-local tax revenues.[17] Under high tax rates and rising fuel costs, the energy-surplus states will accumulate significant tax advantages over other states. The interstate differences over severance taxes could escalate to include agriculture and mineral resource states which are com-

---

[16]Janet Pack, "Frostbelt and Sunbelt: Convergence over Time," *Intergovernmental Perspective* 4 (Fall 1978), 18. See also Advisory Commission on Intergovernmental Relations, *Regional Growth: Interstate Tax Competition* (Washington, D.C., 1981)

[17]Statement of Robert Rafuse, U.S. Treasury Department, before U.S. Senate Committee on Governmental Affairs, Subcommittee on Intergovernmental Relations, May 13, 1981. See also R. Corrigan and R. Stanfield, "Rising Energy Prices—What's Good for Some States Is Bad for Others," *National Journal* 12 (March 22, 1980), pp. 468–74.

pelled to impose similar taxes. For federal grant programs like revenue sharing, severance and energy-related taxes are included in calculations of state tax effort and burden, while user fees are not. These issues also divide governors and members of congress insofar as Frost Belt states lose federal funds and still bear higher taxes upon their individuals and businesses.

Hence, regional tensions and issues will likely increase, not decrease, during the 1980s even though variations among states within the same region are frequently greater than interregional differences. In general, Frost Belt demands will persist for social services, jobs, direct aid to cities, capital infrastructure replacement, and welfare reform. In the Sun Belt, interest runs high for government help in water resources, military outlays, dams, public works, roads, parks, and recreation facilities, and against high-cost, human service programs. These differences are not easily reconcilable in a no-aid growth climate and one in which congressional reapportionment will benefit the South and West.

LOCAL GOVERNMENTS AND CITIES

As previously indicated, states have become more senior partners in their relation to local governments. Still, there is a substantial range among states—from Hawaii which raises more than 80 percent of state-local revenues, to the most junior partner, New Hampshire, which finances less than 50 percent. Regional variations are equally striking from northeast and midcentral states—traditionally strong home rule and high local property tax effort states—to the South and West with greater state involvement in financing local functions.

Set against the prospects of no real growth in direct federal aid during the early 1980s and rather modest tax-induced revenue losses due to reductions in federal personal and corporate income tax rates, many states will operate under rising local government pressure for additional state assistance. High-growth states are experiencing demands from a growing population in schools and local services, while those experiencing population loss and declining school enrollment face pressures from older, fiscally strained cities.

In many respects, however, the states have emerged in a far better position than the federal government for sharing service burdens, assuming the costs of certain functions, and overcoming local fiscal disparities. During the early 1970s, states put nearly 80 percent of their additional resources into four functional areas—education, health and hospitals, transportation, and human resources. They also made significant strides in developing fiscal and functional strategies for meeting the needs of distressed urban and rural communities. A 1980 ACIR survey of state responses found, among other achievements, that: 23 states had a revenue sharing policy that equalizes the gap between poorer and wealthier communities; 27 states have assumed 90 percent or more of local public welfare responsibilities; 12 states reimburse localities for state-mandated responsibilities; and 16 states provide significant local access or assistance to the capital markets.[18]

These trends underscore the fact that only state government can reform local fiscal systems or grant broader local authority. In contrast, the federal government is limited by resources and authority in tailoring its programs to meet specific local problems. The forces besetting distressed communities, whether rural or urban, may defy state and even regional boundaries. Still, states possess the most immediate financial, legal, and administrative powers over these units and their adjacent communities. New York City's fiscal crisis further established the fiscal and economic interdependency between a state government and its largest city. It also reaffirmed the workings of the tax-exempt capital markets by which a state's own credit worthiness and market access can be affected by the fiscal condition of its localities. Brought to an end was the growing post-World War II era belief that municipal securities are a riskless investment.

URBAN DISTRESS

Cities are highly complex economic, political, and social systems. They exist legally and economically in an environment of regional, national, and international forces. From the first awakening to the "urban crisis" in the mid-1960s up through successive efforts by Democratic and Republican administrations to shape national urban policies, we have been sobered by the prospect that older large cities will continue to depopulate, to unload, and to undergo transformation.

Why cities grow and decline has been variously explained in terms of categories of factors: social, economic base, migration, regional cost variation, income growth and jobs, transportation, federal policy, and financial management. The most important difference among big cities tends to be regional. Less troubled cities with brighter prospects are newer cities, with a growing middle-income population and potential for annexation. In contrast, northeast-midwest cities with boundaries encompassing a small proportion of their metropolitan areas are characterized by problems of aging structures and a concentration of a high-cost, low-income population. These latter cities have proven to

[18]See, Advisory Commission on Intergovernmental Relations, *The States and Distressed Communities* (Washington, D.C., 1981); Advisory Commission on Intergovernmental Relations, *Central City–Suburban Fiscal Disparity and City Stress* (Washington, D.C., 1980); and National Academy of Public Administration, *The States and Urban Strategies: A Comparative Analysis* (Washington, D.C.: U.S. Department of Housing and Urban Development, 1980).

be increasingly vulnerable to economic recessions due to job and tax-base loss as well as high service demands and costs.

Central cities have had declining fiscal postures for more than a decade. What is relatively new is the demographic changes that have overtaken our largest metropolitan areas. They also began to experience a net out migration. Declining areas, at least temporarily, experience higher absolute outlays set against slower per capita income growth than smaller metropolitan areas, while increased taxes or vastly reduced services only compound the decline problem. Some older cities have been able to incur large population losses and eventually stabilize. Others like Detroit, Cleveland, and New York have teetered on bankruptcy only to be rescued by complex financial packages involving taxes, service cuts, municipal union wage freezes, and state and federal aid.

Since New York City's fiscal crisis, much effort has gone into measuring local government fiscal stress: need indices, hardship rankings among cities, and distress factors. These measurements may provide an early warning system of local fiscal collapse. They also have been incorporated into federal aid criteria for distributing federal assistance to those communities with the greatest need. Urban distress classifications generally produce similar results and correspond to municipal credit ratings.[19] Thus, policymakers have a much better feel for municipal finance than a decade ago. Municipal reporting systems still may lack uniformity and consistency, but fuller disclosure has opened up local finances to the public.

In light of these intergovernmental trends, many cities will be severely pinched between state and federal governments. To the extent that cities depend upon federal assistance to provide basic services and to finance capital projects, reduced federal assistance leaves three options: raising additional revenues, more efficiently providing services, or cutting services. So, too, as cities broaden their revenue systems to include income-elastic revenue sources, they also will become more vulnerable to economic fluctuations and to fiscal stress during recessions. The choices are difficult ones.

Fiscal retrenchment plus erratic tax-exempt market conditions in 1980–81 already have resulted in impaired market access and the decline in credit worthiness of many municipal bonds. Local capital spending increased in 1978 and 1979, but slowed significantly in 1980–81 due to soaring interest rates and reduced federal aid. A growing number of large cities reported operating deficits in 1978 and 1979. This trend toward operating deficits, if it continues, could erode many a city's fiscal assets and result in cash flow problems. Inflation

---

[19]See Burchell and Lestokin, *Cities under Stress,* Section II.

continues to drive expenditures faster than revenues. Reduced federal aid simply exacerbates this situation.[20]

Reduced federal aid will require cities to better define their priorities and to improve management practices. Local officials have the benefit of hindsight that stemmed from the 1970s—inflation, recession, and "feast and famine" in federal aid. The slowing rate of government expenditures and pervasive retrenchment suggest difficult times ahead even in the context of generally favorable forecasts for the total state-local sector.

CONCLUSIONS

The forecasts for the state-local government through the mid-1980s are cautiously optimistic. Beginning with decreased operating surpluses due to short-term economic weaknesses and reduced federal aid, higher growth and lower inflation will greatly benefit these governments during the 1983–85 period, as gauged by the income elasticities of the sector as a whole. In a worst-case scenario, however, this sector could incur severe financial difficulties under recessionary conditions.

The most fundamental departure in intergovernmental relations from the preceding decade involves the slowing growth rate of the state-local sector coupled to the prospects for no growth in federal aid. The former began in 1975, the latter in 1978, and together they suggest rather prolonged intergovernmental retrenchment in the early 1980s. The Reagan administration is committed to increased expenditures for defense and social security, and to maintain the 1981 tax cuts. The longer-range domestic policy points toward consolidation and decentralization of federal programs, and returning to states major functional responsibilities. To the extent the administration is successful in these efforts, intergovernmental relations would experience a substantial change in direction from its evolutionary development over the past 20 years.

The states will play an increasingly more important role in these fiscal and programmatic changes between Washington and local governments. They have established more diversified and balanced revenue structures, and become more deeply involved in new areas and functions. State competition will intensify, especially the regional component. States also will become more involved in dealing with the financial problems of their local governments and coping with fiscal disparities among their local units.

---

[20]Joint Economic Committee of the U.S. Congress, *Trends in the Fiscal Condition of Cities: 1979–1981* (May 18, 1981); and Joint Economic Committee of the U.S. Congress, *The Regional and Urban Impacts of the Administration's Budget and Tax Proposals* (August 1981).

Municipalities will have to adapt to this changing fiscal and intergovernmental environment. They too will seek to diversify their revenue bases, move away from traditional dependency on the property tax, and seek to get their states to share a greater proportion of their service burdens. Older large cities will experience chronic fiscal stress and more difficult times in retaining market access.

In light of the changes underway, one can conclude that intergovernmental relations will be quite different from the halcyon days of the 1960s and the traumatic adjustments of the 1970s. It is clear that resource constraints will continue to shape the state-local sector for the future.

The Financial Management of State and Local Governments

CHAPTER **4**

Alan W. Frankle, Ph.D.
Associate Professor of Finance
The University of Tulsa

INTRODUCTION

The objective of this chapter is to discuss the elements of good financial management. They involve reviewing tax and revenue management, treasury management, and debt management while critically describing the goals, objectives, and caveats in each function.[1]

The Financial Function

The pyramidal organizational structure of the private sector is well suited to be carried over to financial organizations of state and local government. Organizational structure in municipal government is often fragmented; however, the goal is to optimize output both by integration of similar activities and by reduction of friction among participating departments and employees. We initiate our study of finance functions by reviewing the general principles outlined by an analyst who was on the scene several years ago. He cited the follow-

---

[1]Organizational form is discussed in Chapter 2.

ing elements as being fundamental for an acceptable finance organization:

1. One who receives money or things of value may not also keep or have access to the control of the records of such receipt, nor have custody of such items for longer than needed to deliver them to the official custodian.
2. One who keeps control records shall not have access to the things of value recorded.
3. A custodian may maintain records of what is delivered into or released from custody. However, a custodian may not authorize either deposits or withdrawals, nor keep or have access to the general control records.
4. The person that controls post-audits may not be concerned with any of the activities or records to be audited.[2]

These basic rules provide a system of checks and balances to protect the flow of funds during the receipt, custodial, and disbursement stages. The postaudit function insures both a final check on all financial activities and reporting by an independent entity.

The previously discussed principles can be applied to all state and local finance activities. These activities can be grouped into three categories: tax and revenue management, treasury management, and debt management.

Prior to examining each of these functions we can propose some general questions to obtain an overview of the general performance of the financial function. First, can any past policy defects be observed and traced back to the finance function?[3] An example of such a defect, the lack of a capital improvements plan, will be expanded upon in the discussion on debt management. Another policy defect is the absence of an effective cash management operation within the treasury function. Policy oversights in areas such as these should alert the observer to review the governmental unit in close detail.

Another caution flag can be raised by the financial reporting system. Since the 1975 New York City note defaults, state and local governments have voluntarily moved in the direction of generally accepted principles of governmental accounting. The independent auditor's report will qualify their opinion, if the financial reporting is substandard, and reveal the problems incurred. Further inquiry can ascertain whether future changes will correct the noted irregularities.

A final, quick check of the financial soundness of a governmental unit can be accomplished by comparing the assessed and true real estate valuation figures for the municipality in question to other,

---

[2]Wade S. Smith, *The Appraisal of Municipal Credit Risk* (New York: Donnelley Printing Co.; The Lakeside Press, 1979), p. 82.
[3]Ibid., p. 85.

comparable communities. These figures provide insights into whether the wealth of the community is accurately stated and the current tax burden is reasonable.

Once general questions concerning governmental structure, policies, and reporting are answered, the analyst can proceed to evaluate each of the three major financial functions previously listed.

TAX AND REVENUE MANAGEMENT

State and local governments are expected to provide services so their residents can maintain a certain quality of life. These services include police and fire protection, government needs, water and sewer systems, education, parks, community hospitals, urban renewal projects, and many others. To maintain and expand these services, the responsible governmental unit must collect revenues and allocate them. However, they are constrained by state constitution and statutes. Especially important are the latest changes in state law which refer to current sources of revenue and their expansion or curtailment. State law will continue to describe the kind and amounts of taxes that may be imposed on state residents (see Chapter 2). State laws also include tax formulas, enforcement procedures, and possibly limitations on the use of tax proceeds. The tax structure and limitations affect a community's competitive position in terms of economic growth and well-being. Unfair or burdensome taxes force both individuals and corporate entities to seek alternative locations. Taxes that are too low to provide an acceptable quality of life restrict communities from attracting new residents and corporate employers. Governmental units must walk a fine line, providing services that attract and hold productive residents and yet keep taxes and fees below a level that would stimulate revolt. In this respect, fairness and effectiveness of revenue-producing should be closely scrutinized. An important rule for the analyst is to determine how well communities tax or charge their residents in proportion to the services they actually provide.

Revenue Sources

Local governments have historically obtained funds by the following means:

1. Property taxes (ad valorum).
2. Sales tax.
3. Income taxes.
4. Franchise taxes.
5. Service charges.

6. Licences and fees.
7. Fiscal aid.
8. Revenue sharing.[4]

A May 1981 study prepared for the Joint Economic Committee, Congress of the United States, reports the results of a survey from 275 respondents to the questionaire which was mailed to 594 cities with populations of 10,000 or more.[5] Table 1 gives results of that study pertaining to sources of funds for municipal governments. The trends from 1979 to 1981 show a lessened dependence on federal aid and a higher reliance on property and other local taxes. This trend should continue as we move toward President Reagan's "New Federalism." Trends in revenue sources should be studied, emphasizing both levels and rates of change for each revenue source, as well as the collectibility of forecasted amounts.

Municipalities also face an increasing problem due to the movement of the population to suburban communities. Many cities are searching for new ways to raise revenues from suburban commuters. Sources of revenue from individuals who reside outside of the city limits include city car tags, occupation taxes, and payroll taxes.[6]

City car tags provide revenue from all residents that drive and park within the city limits. It is a use charge and provides monies from residents and nonresident commuters alike. City car tags are difficult to administer and, if a flat fee is incurred, it is a regressive tax. A value-imposed fee creates a less regressive tax but increases administrative costs.

Another method of revenue production is the initiation of an occupation tax or a sales tax on services. Professional service growth is high in urban areas; thus an occupation tax would increase revenues over time. Relying on sales tax increases on merchandise creates a risk of driving merchants outside the city limits and actually reducing sales tax–generated revenue. The occupation tax, however, is also regressive and costly to administer.

Payroll taxes are an income tax levied on the incomes of persons employed within the city limits. Payroll taxes can be a large source of revenue for urban communities. Administrative costs of implementation are small, and regressivity can be reduced by creating a careful tax structure. Most important politically, payroll taxes shift a portion of the burden for city services to the nonresident, nonvoting commuters.

[4]Moak and Hillhouse, *Concepts and Practices*, pp. 55–61.

[5]U.S. Congress, Joint Economic Committee, Subcommittee on Fiscal and Intergovernmental Policy, *Trends in Fiscal Conditions of Cities: 1979–1981* (Washington, D.C.: Government Printing Office, 1981), p. 20.

[6]University of Tulsa, College of Business Administration, Office of Business Research, "Alternative Funding Sources: Meeting the Capital Expenditure Needs of the City of Tulsa", March 1982.

Table 1
Percent Composition of Current Revenues by City Size

Current Revenue Source	Percentage of Total		
	1979	1980	1981a*
Small cities (sample = 109):			
Property tax	33.9%	33.5%	35.1%
Other local taxes	19.9	20.4	19.2
User charges	6.8	6.9	6.8
Fees and miscellaneous	13.6	14.6	13.0
State aid	16.3	15.7	16.4
Federal aid	5.9	4.9	5.3
Transfers from enterprise funds	3.7	4.1	4.3
Medium cities (sample = 51):			
Property tax	37.0%	37.4%	39.2%
Other local taxes	16.5	17.6	18.1
User charges	5.2	5.1	6.0
Fees and miscellaneous	13.3	14.1	12.3
State aid	15.9	15.2	15.5
Federal aid	9.8	8.6	6.6
Transfers from enterprise funds	2.3	2.1	2.3
Large cities (sample = 47):			
Property tax	32.7%	33.1%	34.3%
Other local taxes	19.9	20.2	21.2
User charges	4.4	4.3	4.7
Fees and miscellaneous	13.2	14.6	12.8
State aid	15.1	14.4	14.5
Federal aid	12.4	11.1	10.2
Transfers from enterprise funds	2.3	2.4	2.3
Largest cities (sample = 29):			
Property tax	22.3%	22.2%	22.8%
Other local taxes	24.6	25.7	25.3
User charges	5.3	5.1	5.2
Fees and miscellaneous	11.4	13.4	13.1
State aid	18.7	17.6	18.0
Federal aid	16.1	14.5	14.3
Transfers from enterprise funds	1.5	1.6	1.3

*1981a = Budgeted or anticipated amounts for fiscal year 1981.
Source: U.S. Congress, Joint Economic Committee, Subcommittee on Fiscal and Intergovernmental Policy, *Trends in Fiscal Conditions of Cities: 1979–1981* (Washington, D.C.: Government Printing Office, 1981), p. 20.

Whatever the methods of raising revenue, ideally it must be perceived as fair and equitable for all persons and businesses that share the community-provided services. Inequities cause, at best, uncertainty and may cause serious problems of litigation and restrictive provisions. At worst, it causes corporate flight out of the city.

Reviewing revenue systems of state or local government can be initiated by conducting an inventory of both currently and legally available sources of revenue. Generally, a diversified revenue base is superior to one that obtains a large proportion of funds from one source and leaves other, legally available options untapped. Once the inventory is completed, taxes and fees can be compared to taxes and fees of other governmental units of equal size and circumstance. This cross-section analysis is useful in evaluating the unit's revenue system in respect to other similar systems.

In addition to a comparative analysis, the revenue sources should be checked for legal constraints and limits that could affect future revenue flows. Dependency on grant revenues should be given considerable attention, especially possible cutbacks appearing on the horizon. State and local governments that have previously relied heavily on federal aid could be facing financial problems if forced to find substitute sources of revenue.

Historical review of revenue sources reveals which sources fluctuate most widely over time, as well as the correlation between revenue sources. A sensitivity analysis is helpful in determining the effects of revenue variability on the governmental unit. Past fluctuations and current information provide input for estimating the range of flows considered by the forecast (e.g., a 20 percent reduction in fiscal aid for the coming year).

Finally, the analysis should compare revenues to expenditures over time and ascertain if past levels and percent changes in revenues and expenditures have been equivalent. Before comparisons are attempted, historical data should include adjustments for both price level and population changes as well as full adjustments for reserves and deficiencies. Municipal revenue flow in regard to debt issuance is also subsidized by direct assistance from state governments. Three kinds of programs can be observed. They include:

1. State backup of debt issues, where states promise to supplement local resources if they are not adequate to meet debt service requirements.
2. Financial intermediation on the part of the state, where the debt is issued by the state or designated state authority, and then proceeds are loaned from the state to its municipalities.
3. Direct subsidy grants for certain local projects or needs covering a portion of debt service requirements. The direct state subsidies are the preferred program as they provide a real dollar flow of funds to the municipality.[7]

These programs should be reviewed and evaluated with caution, as future state legislatures may have the power to withdraw these supports at any time. Although political ramifications reduce the proba-

[7]Ronald W. Forbes and John E. Peterson, *Building a Broader Market* (New York: McGraw-Hill, 1976).

bilities of this occurrence, the financial manager must be a political pragmatist when forecasting state support over a 5- to 10-year period. One critical question facing municipal governments is whether state debt-related assistance will keep pace with the cost of new-found responsibilities of local governments during the years to come.

TREASURY MANAGEMENT

The treasury function is an important part of state and local financial management primarily because of the large dollar amounts which flow through the governmental unit. One particularly sensitive aspect of the treasury function is pension fund management. The question of funding level is paramount because of the trend in recent years to compensate municipal employees with pension benefits rather than salary increases. If these pension benefits are not adequately funded or paid for in the same period they are incurred, large deficits can be generated. To avoid this possibility, many states have passed the responsibility for pension fund management from the local level to state-managed pension funds. The centralization of this function at the state level increases the chance that professional managers will oversee the benefit packages, their funding, and the investment of the gathered monies.

Other treasury functions are also extremely important in attaining efficient financial management. Having cash available for transactions, for good banking relationships at a reasonable cost, and for borrowing and investing short-term funds is a necessity for sound financial management.

Treasury management in state and local government is very similar to the function in private enterprise. The primary objective is to have funds available when they are needed. A major difficulty that is readily noticeable is a periodic need to issue short-term debt, as observed in New York State's spring ritual.[8] This practice reveals a chronic cash flow problem and should be avoided whenever possible.

Cash Mobilization and Bank Services

Many mechanical procedures can also be reviewed. Billing and collection procedures should expedite cash into the government coffers by early billing and, when economical, lockbox operations. The time, from actual service provided to deposit of payment for these services, should reflect an acceptable level of "float." This mobilization of cash includes the use of automated billing systems, lockbox systems, concentration and zero-balance accounts, and wire transfers. Unlike the

---

[8]Ronald W. Forbes, Louise Flynn, and Todd Whitestone, "Annual Rites of Spring: Short-Term Borrowing by New York State," *The Bond Buyer*, October 1977.

private sector, state and local governments are sometimes restricted in the use of modern cash management techniques. State statutes that prohibit investment of restricted funds are frequent constraints. Other state and local governments are hindered in efficient cash management because of outdated practices and lack of expertise.

Commercial banks can provide governmental units with many valuable services. Although some states continue by law to require inefficient banking relationships, the trend is toward an increasing use of competitive bidding for banking services. Since these services can be paid for on a fee basis or by compensating balances, some states have allowed the use of restricted funds in zero-interest accounts for compensating balances.

Investment of Idle Funds

Investment of idle funds is also included in the treasury function. Because of the high interest rates over the last decade, quality investment programs have generated considerable funds for state and local governments. There is little excuse for funds to sit idle in demand deposits and forego interest, unless they serve as compensating balances for bank services.

Investment of idle funds is governed by state law as well as sound judgment. Short-term investments must be high-quality–low-risk instruments and readily liquid. Maturities of the chosen instrument should match projected cash needs. Undue risk can be added to a portfolio by financial managers that attempt to predict movements of interest rates and ignore cash need patterns. Strategies such as "riding the yield curve" can increase portfolio yield, but can also cause large losses if liquidity is suddenly required. Also, such sophisticated techniques as hedging with financial futures can be helpful, but can also create extreme losses if speculation replaces hedging as the primary objective.

Four investments most used by state and local governments as investment vehicles for idle funds are (1) certificates of deposit, (2) time deposits, (3) repurchase agreements, and (4) U.S. treasury securities.[9] Most of these investments have relatively low risk and the treasury manager's objective is to maximize yield under the constraints of future cash needs. As shown in Chapter 25, however, repurchase agreements (repos) do present certain risks. Yield maximization objectives are sometimes debated by supporters of "keep the money at home." By increasing the amount of funds available for local residents and

---

[9]C. Wayne Stallings, *A Guidebook to Improved Financial Management for Small Cities and Other Governmental Units* (Chicago: Municipal Finance Officers Association, 1978), p. 105.

businesses, the local tax base is expanded and local government prospers. Empirical evidence to support the argument is, however, difficult to obtain and measure.

Investment strategy is influenced significantly by cash availability. Similar to revenue forecasting in general, cash forecasting is a more precise technique as specific timing is an essential ingredient to a successful investment program. Governmental units receive two distinct kinds of cash receipts: those that are deterministic—forecasted with certainty—and those that are stochastic—uncertain in timing and amount. The treasury manager's task is to establish past patterns of expenditures and receipts and to develop accurate estimates of future activities. Once the flows are determined, and combined when possible, an investment strategy for the coming year can be developed using many of the services provided by local banking institutions.

Coordination of activities in the treasury function is essential. Responsibility and authority for treasury functions should be centralized so that one official can oversee all activities including cash forecasting, banking relationships, and short-term financing and investing. These activities must be integrated for effective treasury management to prevail.

DEBT MANAGEMENT

The methods of funding long-term capital improvement projects by municipalities receives abundant debate. The reason for the interest and concern is because a readily visible product can be observed, and in many instances taxpayers have the final verdict on the need for the improvement. Whatever the purpose of the capital improvement, replacement of an old facility or expansion of existing facilities to accomodate growth, only three means are available to finance these projects. State and local governments can: (1) pay directly from current income (pay as you go), (2) pay directly from past years' income (accumulation), or (3) borrow funds from the capital markets.

Financing large capital projects is a complex issue from the standpoint of financing mechanics and also in terms of political and economic considerations. Extreme cases of liberal and conservative financing are not difficult to identify. The decade of the 1970s enlightened many to the fact that some states and municipalities have abused the concept of debt financing. Massachusetts and New York, for example, have been penalized for poor financial judgment in the nation's credit markets. Legal debt units have in many cases been circumvented, resulting in exorbitant taxes for residents and industry. These productive resources have been forced to seek alternative locations with more hospitable economic climates. On the other end of the continuum, the extreme no-borrowing philosophy has limited the potential of other states and municipalities. One of the prerequisites for maintaining quality of life for state and local residents is long-range planning of public services. These services should be provided when the demand occurs, and therefore must be planned and initiated prior to the actual need. State and local governments that lack this foresight play a continual game of catch-up resulting in less than optimal services for their residents and businesses.

Methods of Financing

Accumulation of funds to finance capital projects saves interest costs, but taxpayers lose the use of the project during the accumulation process as well as losing the opportunities to invest those tax funds at their own discretion. Additionally, in recent years, inflation has increased project costs dramatically, and now may more than outweigh the costs of interest on tax-exempt debt.

The borrowing alternative entails encumbering future income to pay interest on debt, but allows residents the immediate enjoyment of capital improvements. Borrowing avoids problems created by rampant inflation. In fact, inflation works to the debtor's advantage, allowing the municipality to repay with cheaper dollars. Another advantage of debt financing is socioeconomic. It spreads the cost of large capital projects over future generations of users, while accumulation puts the cost of capital improvements on residents that may never benefit from the completed project.

As previously mentioned, debt financing is not a cure-all for municipal needs. Well-managed municipalities will likely combine a pay-as-you-go strategy with borrowing. This combined strategy usually insures that the improvement will be well planned, and reduces the carrying cost of the project for future users. Often state bond laws require that all capital projects be financed with a certain percent of funds raised directly from current income. States and municipalities that employ a combination of borrowing and pay-as-you-go increase the number of paid-for public improvements and increase the credit quality of their debt issues. Such actions decrease the cost of future borrowing for the governmental unit. Borrowing limits are determined also by tax and debt limits set by law. In addition to these legislative constraints, economic constraints based on manageable debt service defined in terms of annual revenue are a limiting factor. The method of financing will also be influenced by the forecasted need for capital improvement projects.

Capital Improvement Projects

Primary to analyzing funding sources for state and local government is the development of a capital program. Generally, four- to six-year capital forecasts are developed that are referred to as capital programs or budgets. Such documents should follow the well-accepted guidelines for capital programs outlined by Moak and Killian in their manual on capital programming and capital budgeting. The authors list the essential functions of a capital program, including:

1. Design of capital-project request forms.
2. Review of project requests and requirements.
3. Preparation of financial analysis and projection of financing sources.
4. Preparation of a tentative capital improvements program and budget.
5. Overall supervision of budget.
6. Financial performance and reporting.[10]

A capital-project request form and review process are designed to compare and rank unlike projects by predetermined criteria. The task is not an easy one, as even the definition of capital project varies between departments and over time. The classification of items as capital projects is dependent upon cost and frequency. Expenditures that occur annually should not be considered capital projects, and generally a minimum cost must be exceeded before an item is given a capital-project classification. Some communities include a specification of the item's life expectancy as a requirement for capital-project status. Other municipalities look to the output side of the item and require that the project add to the physical worth of the city. Municipal accounting and auditing has defined capital outlay as "expenditures which result in the acquisition of or additions to fixed assets." They go on to define fixed assets as "assets of a long-term character, which are intended to continue to be held or used, such as land, buildings, machinery, furniture, and other equipment."[11]

While some cities still classify capital expenditures based on the accounting definition, most have revised their classifications subject to the economic interpretation previously mentioned. Once the definition of capital project is agreed upon, the community can create a framework for project selection. The selection process encompasses at least two major tasks. The first entails a comprehensive list of proj-

---

[10]Lennox L. Moak and Kathryn W. Killian, *A Manual of Suggested Practice for the Preparation and Adoption of Capital Programs and Capital Budgets by Local Governments* (Chicago: Municipal Finance Officers Association, 1964), p. 12.

[11]National Committee on Governmental Accounting, *Governmental Accounting, Auditing, and Financial Reporting* (Chicago: Municipal Finance Officers Association, 1968), p. 233.

ects by each department and agency. Before the departments can submit a viable needs list, they must know the current status of their present assets. An inventory list is required that includes each of the department's facilities, the age of the facility, condition of the facility, and estimate of usage, and a target year for replacement or expansion. The purpose of this list is to provide information for the assessment of future (perhaps undefined) capital outlays required for the upkeep of existing fixed assets. Secondly, a review committee must rank the projects from an overall list which consists of the comprehensive lists from each department. The review committee is responsible for selecting projects in accordance with a master plan that embellishes the current and future needs of the governmental unit.

Each department or agency should also provide information on the status of previously approved projects. This status report includes: (1) all completed projects during the last fiscal year; (2) projects to be continued in future years, with an estimate of funds needed on an annual basis; (3) projects to be deleted from the capital program, and the amount of released funds that can be reallocated to other projects. It is difficult to estimate future revenue needs without a capital program schedule that includes:

1. Status of projects in progress.
2. Condition of existing fixed assets.
3. Schedule of future capital projects, including timing and sources or project's dollar needs.

Once capital needs are properly identified, the financial manager can begin to identify funding sources for the various projects on a priority basis.

Debt Financing Alternatives

Paralleling the demand for debt financing by tax-exempt issuers has been a change in emphasis from general obligation debt (backed by tax revenues) to short-term, limited liability, and special assessment debt. By 1978, tax-supported new issues had declined to less than 40 percent of all new bonds sold. Governmental units have switched from general obligation issues to revenue-type bonds. However, in doing so, the governmental unit has given up some of its internal financing flexibility, as these specific payments are separated and unavailable for general-fund purposes.

Many factors contributed to the decline in use of general obligation bonds. These include: (1) a widening of the definition of public purpose to include "enterprise-type" projects; (2) constraints imposed by statutory or constitutional limits on tax-supported debt; (3) the demand that costs of public projects be borne by the beneficiaries of the projects through user charges; and (4) the grass roots tax revolt evidenced by the reluctance by voters to approve new general obligation debt issues.

Because of the factors listed above, public service enterprise debt has been increasingly used to finance municipal capital projects where services can be operated as a business and are partially or fully self-supporting. Public services such as water, sewer, electric, and gas systems have been financed using enterprise debt in the form of revenue bonds. Other semiprivate or quasi-public debts are also issued to support assessable improvements such as streets, sidewalks, lights, and parks. These improvements usually benefit a limited segment of the residents at the expense of the entire population. Many different tax-exempt debt issues have been created to fulfill the financing needs of state and local governments.

General obligation bonds are the most well-known tax-exempt debt offering. To be considered a general obligation bond, debt issuers must possess the unlimited power of general taxation. The issuance of general obligation bonds generally requires voter approval. Tax limitations usually do not affect general obligation bonds. Pledging of specific sources of funds (i.e., water and sewer) to aid in repayment does not affect the general obligation classification. These securities are considered "double-barrel" general obligation issues, as they are secured by a pledge of specific revenue as well as the general, unlimited taxing powers of the issuer. (See Chapter 8 for a discussion of general obligation bonds.)

Governmental units can issue another debt obligation, namely limited-tax bonds which rely on certain restricted taxing powers of the municipality but not the general, unlimited powers. The repayment pledge is restricted to revenues available from the collection of specifically defined taxes. One example of these obligations is the special assessment, limited liability bond. For instance, street paving, lighting, sewer collection lines, and other neighborhood improvements are provided by the municipality but paid for, by special assessments, by the residents who benefit. These improvements involve substantial costs, and a lum-sum outlay for their financing could create a severe burden on many residents. However, because these improvements carry such useful benefits over future periods, the municipality issues bonds to finance construction and pledges special assessment as a source of funds for repayment. Another example of limited tax bonds are issues secured by first liens on monies held in specific funds. Special taxes such as sales taxes, occupation taxes, payroll taxes, or car taxes could be designated for specific purposes.

Recently, many states have authorized the use of another tax-exempt financing alternative, namely tax-increment financing. This instrument is a very specialized form of tax-supported debt that has become increasingly popular. The bonds are generally issued by re-development agencies of a municipal government and are part of a financing program designed to revitalize urban core areas. Tax-increment financing works as follows:

> The city declares a section of its jurisdiction as a redevelopment district. Under statutory powers available, the city can then acquire and condemn, and proceed to redevelop and rehabilitate the area. As part of this process, the assessed valuation of properties will be fixed at some base value prior to redevelopment.
>
> The agency then attempts to draw private investment capital into the district to build hotels, office buildings, industrial parks, housing, etc., as a result of the infrastructure of services provided through the redevelopment program. In essence, the agency serves as a "land developer," providing public improvements.
>
> To carry out the public improvements, the agency will issue bonds payable solely from the incremental tax revenues generated from the incremental assessed value that results from the private investment. The agency has no authority to levy taxes. Instead, the taxing process works as follows:
>
> 1. The units of government with taxing power (city, county, school district) levy taxes, as established in the budgets of each unit, on all assessed properties in the redevelopment district.
> 2. But, the levying units collect only that portion of the levy produced by the base-year valuations.
> 3. The taxes received over and above the levy on base-year valuations are deposited in a *Special Fund* dedicated to the repayment of the tax-increment bonds.[12]

These bonds may face severe market pressure due to the tax-revolt legislation passed in many states. Restrictions, such as California's Proposition 13, placed on ad valorem taxes have hurt the credit quality and market acceptance of these issues. The success of these issues also depends upon the ability of the agency to attract sufficient private capital so that the growth of future taxable property will generate sufficient incremental tax revenues.

SUMMARY AND CONCLUSIONS

The soundness of state and local governments in the 1980s is dependent upon good planning and pragmatic management, especially in the financial function. The financial function should be led by professional managers that are cognizant of the "state of the art"

---

[12]This section is taken from an article by Ronald Forbes, Alan Frankle, and Philip Fisher, "The Effects of Proposition 13 on Tax-Supported Municipal Bonds in California: A Case Study of Bond Market Efficiency," in *The Property Tax Revolt: The Case of Proposition 13,* ed. George G. Kaufman and Kenneth T. Rosen, Cambridge, Mass.: (Ballinger Publishing, 1981), p. 120.

techniques in financial systems design, cash management, and capital market operations. An analyst can improve the selection of tax-exempt investments not only by gathering information in the traditional areas of economics and sociodemography but also by analyzing the financial management expertise. Being in the right geographical location will not, by itself, assure excellent fiscal health in the coming decade for state and local governments.

State and Local Government Revenues, Taxpayer Revolts, and Crises

CHAPTER 5

Robin Wiessmann Dougherty, J.D.

Deputy Managing Director
City of Philadelphia

HISTORICAL PERSPECTIVE

Fiscal crises and tax revolts are not new phenomena. Mismanagement of public business, and low productivity, shortfalls in revenue, boom and bust business cycles, and inequitable tax burdens have existed as long as governments.

One of the earliest reports we have of a fiscal distress comes from ancient Athens, circa 500 B.C. Immediately following his election as "finance director," Aristedes the Just realized that several of his friends and electors had been systematically mismanaging the city treasury. Aristedes exposed the fraud and for his trouble was vilified, ostracized, and banished.

The generally prosperous experience of young America was also marred by financial problems. The American depression of 1837–43 produced widespread unemployment and poverty and the first wave of municipal bond defaults. Because of relief efforts and revenue failures, state governments fell on hard times. During that time, many states had to resort to extensive borrowing to meet current obligations. As Samuel Rezneck noted:

> Like the federal government, few states escaped without a deficit in their ordinary budgets. Pennsylvania had a shortage of $1 million in

69

1839, and resorted to rather questionable methods in raising a loan to cover arrears. New York, with better credit, was able to borrow $3 million in 1841. Massachusetts pledged itself to meet future expenses by means of "taxation and retrenchment." Maryland adopted new taxes in 1841; Kentucky, Indiana, and Illinois increased their land taxes by as much as 50 percent. Many of the states were further embarrassed by the heavy burden of their debts, which in 1840 amounted to nearly $200 million. . . .

Especially serious, however, was the fact that after a time, some of the states could not meet the interest requirements at all; between 1841 and 1842, eight states went into default, and two or three even repudiated part of their debts. For several years, default and repudiation supplied the occasion for international recrimination and embittered public opinion on both sides. As early as 1840, the Senate lectured the states on their extravagance and rejected the proposal to transfer the state debts to the federal government.[1]

Localities faced multiple pressures on their fiscal stability as the general economy continued to worsen. Carl Chatters chronicled the state of municipal finance during the Great Depression as follows:

Deflation accompanies an economic depression. Public and private treasuries are deflated. Public morale is at a low state but still unbroken. Public services are curtailed but not entirely crippled. Tax levies have been reduced, and bond principal and bond interest must be paid in full. Deflationary forces have attacked municipal finance on all sides—by reducing income while increasing demands for unemployment relief and public works. Inflation is increasing the cost of performing services while municipal income continues its downward trend. Thus, caught between the upper and nether millstones, municipalities are being transformed by the sheer force of economic necessity.

The depression however, may serve to improve the financial administration of American cities. It brings to light the fallacy of extensive short-term borrowing, the burden caused by unwise and unwieldy bonded debts, and the necessity for financial planning by qualified personnel. If the public generally, and public administrators in particular, will seize the present opportunity to put into practice sound and conservative financial practices, the depression will have been a blessing in disguise.[2]

While it is true that those who ignore the lessons of history are condemned to repeat the mistakes of the past, nothing had prepared

[1]Samuel Reznock, "Business Depressions and Financial Panics," in *Essays in American Business and Economic History,* ed. Samuel Reznock (Westport, Conn.: Greenwood Publishing, 1971), p. 93.

[2]Carl H. Chatters, "Municipal Finance," in *What the Depression Has Done to Cities,* ed. Clarence E. Ridley and Orin F. Notling (Chicago: The International City Managers' Association, 1935), p. 1.

administrators, taxpayers, scholars, and the general public for the fiscal crisis that struck New York in 1975. Despite admonitions of fiscal and economic doom by critics, the temper of the times was limitless optimism. Nevertheless, the impossible happened, as described in the following passage:

> September 21, 1938, was a special day for one resident of Long Island. A war was about to explode in Europe; but on this morning he was more concerned with a long-awaited package that arrived in the mail. Excitedly he unwrapped his shiny new barometer, noticing that the needle pointed below 29, where the dial warned of "Hurricanes and Tornadoes." Ridiculous. It was a sunny day. As recounted by William Manchester in *The Glory and the Dream:* "He shook it and banged it against a wall; the needle wouldn't budge. Indignant, he repacked it, drove to the post office, and mailed it back. While he was gone, his house blew away."
>
> Something like that happened to New York 37 years later. For years, few believed the menacing storm clouds. Since 1898, New York had become America's largest and most important metropolis. Then, in the 1960s, New York stopped growing. Each year, the budget would come up short; each year, officials would devise a temporary solution by taxing a little here, borrowing a little there, fudging everywhere they could. Then, during the year and outside the normal budget review process, they would add a program here or there and fudge some more. By 1975, city expenditures totaled $12.8 billion, while revenues totaled only $10.9 billion. New York was borrowing to close an annual operating deficit of almost $2 billion. While city and state officials tinkered and wrestled with symptoms, New York was being blown away.[3]

New York has not been alone. Boston, Cleveland, Chicago, Buffalo, Philadelphia, Detroit, and others have experienced similar problems. At the same time as major urban areas were beset by extreme fiscal difficulties, various limits on taxation or spending were enacted in a number of jurisdictions. As of 1977, 41 states had partial limitations on property tax rates or receipts, or some limited restriction on spending.[4]

The overriding concern of taxpayers to exert more effective control over the size and activities of government, however, was dramatically demonstrated in 1978 when eight states adopted constitutional amendments and three states adopted legislation limiting taxation or spending.[5] By November 1980, 17 states had adopted measures pro-

---

[3]Ken Auletta, *The Streets Were Paved with Gold* (New York: Random House, 1979), Chap. 2, p. 29.

[4]Advisory Commission on Intergovernmental Relations, *State Limitations on Local Taxes and Expenditures,* (Washington, D.C.: 1977).

[5]Constitutional amendments in California, Tennessee, Arizona, Hawaii, Michigan, South Dakota, Texas; statutes in Colorado, New Jersey, North Dakota; and Robert C. Pitcher, *State Revenue and Spending Limits Since Proposition 13* (Washington, D.C.: Federation of Tax Administrators, Research Report No. 86, March 1980), p. 36.

viding overall limits on state spending or taxes or, in the case of California, both spending and taxes.[6] By March 1980, 17 states had adopted measures limiting the taxing or spending authority of local governments.[7] Thus, both by referenda and legislation, a critical attitude towards government spending and practical limitations on governments' ability to spend became legacy.

The purpose of this chapter is fourfold. First, it will describe the linkage between tax revolts and fiscal crises. Second, it will examine the major factors influencing a jurisdiction's financial position. Third, it will discuss responses to fiscal crises and tax revolts. Finally, it will review the effects of these phenomena.

LINKAGE BETWEEN TAX REVOLTS AND FINANCIAL CRISES

The phenomena of tax revolts and financial crises are inextricably intertwined. This relationship can be either explicit, in that it results from direct actions taken with forethought, or implicit, in that failure to act based on apprehension in a timely manner leads to a crisis. In each case, political judgments stand at the core of the problem. If a jurisdiction explicitly refuses to increase taxes or it imposes a tax or expenditure cap, budgets must be curtailed or other revenue sources tapped. In either case, these explicit decisions can provoke a fiscal crisis. The explicit actions which most often precipitate financial crises are tax caps or reductions in tax bases.

Proposition 2½ in Massachusetts has been a primary example of this linkage. In Massachusetts, efforts to reduce the levels of taxation have been underway for several years. Since November 1975, there were several tax reductions at the state level and relatively few tax increases (except conversion to a floating rate for the gasoline tax). Property taxes, virtually the state's sole source of revenue, continued to grow due to ever increasing assessments. With this growth came demands for relief from the tax. In 1977–78, Massachusetts was first in the nation in per capita property tax revenues, with approximately 6.59 percent of 1978 personal income going towards property taxes. Consequently, in November 1980 the voters adopted Proposition 2½.

In general, Proposition 2½ limits the property taxes which may be assessed in a city or town to 2½ percent of the full cash value of the real and personal property of the city or town. The statute provides for phasing down to the 2½ percent level by annual reduction of up to 15 percent in property tax levies, beginning in fiscal 1982. Motor vehicle excise taxes are also reduced by Proposition 2½, and rent pay-

---

[6]"A Dual Tax and Spending Cap for Philadelphia," Appendix B (Philadelphia: Pensylvania Economy League, Eastern Division, November 1980).

[7]Pitcher, *State Revenue and Spending Limits, p. 6.*

ers qualify for a deduction of half their rents against the state income tax.

The estimates of the effect of Proposition 2½ are constantly changing and subject to wide variation. Although earlier estimates had been higher, in March 1981 the Commissioner of Revenue estimated that Proposition 2½ would result in a reduction in fiscal year 1982 of local revenues of approximately $478 million and a reduction of $52 million at the state level. The anticipated revenue loss for fiscal 1982 was approximately 7 percent of all state and local tax revenues.

According to the March 25, 1981, Official Statement of the Commonwealth of Massachusetts, "to stay within the limits set by Proposition 2½ will require substantial cuts or economies in many instances unless other revenues are found. Because fixed costs such as debt service and pensions cannot be cut, discretionary costs (principally police, fire, and schools) may have to be cut more than 15 percent in many communities."[8] Furthermore, "the effects of the legislation will be felt unevenly, since it is typically the larger cities which have property tax levels significantly higher than 2½ of property values."[9]

The implicit effects of a perceived tax revolt often cause more insidious but equally devastating consequences. Officials, fearing either massive public controversy or voter backlash, continuously postpone needed increases in tax rates or expansion of revenue bases. The result usually is the failure of revenues to keep pace with increased expenditures. Often budgets are made to appear balanced by overestimating revenues and underestimating expenses.

An implicit expression of a tax revolt occurred in Philadelphia. During the period of 1971 to 1980, the assessed value of property in the city grew at an annual rate of 1.82 percent while the market value of property, measured by actual sales, increased by 7.01 percent. The explanation for this disparity was a judgment by individual assessors and the Board of Revision of Taxes itself that taxes were too high and taxpayers would be driven out of the city if assessments were increased. This lack of growth in assessment was extremely vexing to political leaders and, in 1976, contributed to an overestimation of revenues that resulted in a budget deficit of more than $87.8 million or 12.3 percent of total revenues. This provoked a financial crisis from which the city has not as yet fully recovered in terms of its reputation among municipal bond analysts and institutional investors.

Whether or not actions on the revenue side of the ledger precipitate a financial crisis depends largely on what happens to expendi-

---

[8]$125,000,000 Commonwealth of Massachusetts General Obligation Bonds Official Statement (March 25, 1981), p. 2.
[9]Ibid.

tures. If a spending cap exists simultaneously with diminution of revenues, a crisis can be explicitly provoked, requiring the immediate reduction of work-force and nonwage expenditures. The surest way to reduce the size of government (or keep it from growing), is to directly limit expenditures. Government cannot avoid the control, because it cannot resort to nonproperty tax revenue to make up the loss of property tax dollars. Expenditure limits, however, still face the issue of whether spending for certain purposes will be exempted. This has been the method utilized by many jurisdictions to avoid precipitous crises.[10] If exemptions are not allowed, however, control can be more restrictive than intended. Relatively uncontrollable fixed costs such as pensions and medical insurance may consume an ever increasing percentage of expenditures with little money left for other uses.

The state of New Jersey, for example, adopted legislation limiting state and local expenditures by reference to a base year, defined as the year's preceding budget expenditures with various adjustments. Most municipal and county budget increases are limited to 5 percent per year, but may be increased to a total cap of 8 percent if approved by a two-thirds majority of the governing body.[11]

Although there are various adjustments to and exclusions from New Jersey's cap,[12] the limitation has resulted in postponement of capital projects, increased borrowing for exempt purposes, layoffs, service cuts, sale of assets, and special district financing.[13] It is unquestionable that the cap is having an effect on provision of municipal services.[14] And, without exemptions, New Jersey would be facing much more devastating consequences.[15]

Massachusetts, and specifically Boston, is another example of this phenomenon. A 1979 state statute limits local government budgets and appropriation growth to 4 percent per annum,[16] and as discussed earlier, a 1980 statute limits taxation.

---

[10]Arizona has had a 10 percent limitation on increases in city and county spending since 1921. The state responded to problems, particularly in rapidly growing areas, by exempting certain parts of the budget. For example in Mohave County, the fastest growing in the state, more than 70 percent of the budget is in exempt categories. The limitation has not proved effective, however, since there is a high property tax rate. Steven D. Gold, *Property Tax Relief* (Lexington, Mass.: Lexington Books, 1979), p. 166.

[11]Sidney Glaser, "New Jersey's Limits on State and Local Spending—A Model for the Nation," *New Jersey Municipalities,* November 1978, p. 11.

[12]Ibid., p. 11. Excluded from New Jersey's cap on municipal expenditures are "debt service, cash deficits, reserves for uncollected taxes, programs funded wholly or in part by state or federal programs, programs mandated by state or federal law after the effective date of the law, revenues raised by the sale of municipal assets, new or revised fees, and revenues from increased valuations as a result of new construction."

[13]"Municipal Caps"—Date Report submitted to the Committee to Study the Impact of the Cap Staff Report—County and Municipal Government Study Commission, State of New Jersey, 1980, p. 1.

[14]Ibid.

[15]Gold, *Property Tax Relief,* p. 166.

[16]Pitcher, *State Revenue and Spending Limits,* p. 18.

Although exact fiscal impacts and further repercussions are uncertain, Boston anticipated an $87 million revenue loss in fiscal year 1982 due to Proposition 2½. Consequently, major cutbacks were implemented. As of November 1, 1981, 2,726 or 21 percent of city employees and 1,000 school district employees had been laid off. Budgets of operating departments had also been reduced by $735 million—for example, the police department ($18.1 million), the fire department ($16.7 million), and the public works department ($10.9 million).[17] Nevertheless, without further spending cuts or additional revenues, the city expected to incur a $30 million appropriation deficit in fiscal year 1982.

California, the paradigm, which has the most comprehensive state and local tax and spending limitations, is presently facing a fiscal crisis.[18] Initially, the effect of property tax reductions under Proposition 13 was mitigated by a large state surplus. In order to realign government services, California removed many state strings on school finance, giving local school districts discretion over use of funds.[19] California also assumed over 80 percent of the cost of public education and assumed responsibility for health and welfare assistance. Nevertheless, the combined effect of Proposition 13 and the recessionary slowdown in revenues is resulting in the enforced reduction of state government programs. In addition to the potential loss of nearly $550 million in federal aid previously received, the $5.3 billion allocated to local governments in 1981–82 was significantly reduced, there is no funding for new expenditures, and there were 2 percent across-the-board program cuts in order to balance the budget.[20]

The most common cause of a fiscal crisis is the failure of a revenue system to keep pace with inflation and the failure of management to come to grips with expenditure reduction. This often results in the double jeopardy of underestimating expenditures and overestimating revenue. A classic case of this occurred in Detroit. Since 1978, Detroit has experienced consecutive operating and fund balance deficits. Fiscal year 1980 ended with an $80.9 million deficit, and fiscal year 1981

[17]Boston Municipal Research Bureau, "Boston Faces $30 Million Appropriation Deficit" Staff Report—Boston Municipal Research Bureau, October 12, 1981.

[18]In the June 1978 primary, approval of Proposition 13 amended the state constitution by rolling back property taxes and restricting the levy of taxes to replace the lost revenue. Ad valorem taxes are limited to 1 percent of the full cash value of property as of the 1975 assessment. On November 6, 1979, the state constitution was amended by Proposition 4 to limit appropriations of state and local governments to the appropriation level of the preceding year, adjusted for changes in the cost of living and population. Revenues collected in excess of the appropriate amount must be refunded.

[19]Winnifred M. Austerman and Dan Pilcher, "The Tax Revolt Transformed," *National Conference of State Legislatures,* July–August 1980.

[20]Financial Research Department, State of California Department of Finance Sacramento, Calif.

a $119.6 million cumulative deficit. Caused by a variety of factors, this occurred despite the requirement that any year's deficit be funded in the succeeding year's budget. Revenues did not grow sufficiently because unemployment resulted in an actual decline of income tax receipts for fiscal years 1980 and 1981, and the city's assessed valuation, on which property taxes are collected, grew very slightly. Even though certain operating economies were instituted, such as hiring freezes, layoffs, and spending reductions (approximately $10 million in fiscal year 1979 and $20.9 million in fiscal year 1980), many other anticipated revenues such as countercyclical revenue sharing and distributable aid from the state were not realized in fiscal years 1979, 1980, and 1981.[21]

Concomitant with inadequate revenue growth was an increase in expenditures. Detroit experienced the same inflationary pressures as the rest of the country on items such as employee benefits, operating supplies, and purchase of services and equipment; arbitration awards for uniformed employees resulted in unexpected salary increases; and some unanticipated transit and hospital expenses were incurred.[22] Thus, even with the city divesting itself of various services and making substantial reductions in its employee level, operations were not balanced. Such a clear case of imbalance is attributable to unrealized revenues and unanticipated expenditures.

At the time of this writing, Detroit is implementing a three-part plan to bring its finances into balance. The three-pronged financial plan includes:

1. A legislative-and voter-approved 1 percent increase on both resident and commuter income taxes. Such increase raises the resident rate from 2 to 3 percent and the nonresident from ½ to 1½ percent. The increase in collections expected is, therefore, substantial; 1982 revenues are expected to be $230.5 million as compared with $127.4 million for 1982, an 81 percent increase.

2. Renegotiation of contracts with 22 of 57 bargaining units to provide for wage freezes at current levels through June 30, 1983. When added to nonunion employees, this represents over 63 percent of the city's work force of approximately 21,200.

3. Sale of $113 million of general obligation fiscal stabilization bonds dated September 1, 1981, due April 1, 1983, through April 1, 1986. This kind of response, stemming from an inability to alleviate a prospective financial squeeze, is typical of many jurisdictions. The cost of postponing tax increases or expenditure reductions may be calculated in two ways. First, there is the reduction of credit worthiness,

---

[21]$113,000,000 City of Detroit, Michigan, General Obligation Fiscal Stabilization Bonds Official Statement, August 13, 1981, pp. 27–29.

[22]The city had budgeted a "normal" wage increase for 1979, but an arbitration award resulted in $12.4 million more than was budgeted for.

which increases the cost of future borrowings significantly; second, the interest on deficit funding bonds (in Detroit's case a total of $42,759,166) is added to the taxpayer's burden.

In summary, links between financial crises and tax revolts make analysis of the two phenomena critical to the analyst's prognosis for one provoking the other. In order to project or predict how the two phenomena interact in any particular jurisdiction, it is necessary to analyze the underlying factors which influence financial position. These are presented in the next section.

MAJOR FACTORS INFLUENCING FINANCIAL POSITION

Even with a strong economy, a governmental entity can be severely restricted in its ability to repay indebtedness by a legal structure that does not confer the broad home rule powers necessary to control its own revenue destiny. An example of this can be seen in the financial problems of the Philadelphia school district. Although Philadelphia's economy has been relatively stable between 1977 and 1983, the fortunes of its school district suffer badly from inherent structural weaknesses.

First, the district is a creation of the state, which has the responsibility for education in Pennsylvania and is therefore subject to its jurisdiction. Second, the school district of Philadelphia is a governmental entity separate from the city but, because its board is appointed rather than elected, it has no taxing powers independent of the taxes levied on its behalf by the Commonwealth of Pennsylvania and the city of Philadelphia. Third, the board of education and the superintendent of schools are not directly accountable to the mayor and council for their fiscal decisions, or for the operation of the school system in general. Fourth, the district must adopt its own balanced budget before it has any assurance from either the state legislature or city council that sufficient revenues will be available. Therefore, the two components of the budget equation—revenues and expenditures—are controlled by different entities.

This structural straitjacket gives rise to the frustrating tautology that those who tax cannot control spending, and those who spend cannot control taxation. Failure to come to grips with either revenues or expenditures had, until recently, led to continuing crises.

The two most important tests of willingness to repay indebtedness stem directly from ability. Here the question that must be asked is, Given the economic means and legal ability, has a jurisdiction demonstrated consistently that it has the willingness to raise revenue and/or control expenditures to continuously provide moderate fund-balance surpluses? History and experience are the only way these factors can be consistently analyzed. A pattern of conservative revenue projections coupled with the demonstrated willingness to reduce service and expenditure levels when necessary indicate a willingness on management's part to live within its ability.

The most volatile factor, however, is always the growing reluctance of elected officials to authorize increases in revenue. This reluctance is itself an implicit offshoot of the tax revolt. In legislative bodies and on the part of executives, the emphasis is not on halting expenditure growth but on holding the line on taxes. While in the short run this can encourage good management of scarce resources, it is often carried to extreme and unrealistic budget cuts or mandated labor settlements which prove impossible to implement.

The willingness of a legislative body or an executive to act in a responsible fashion is the most difficult factor for an analyst to ascertain. Direct contact with the political leaders involved can help to clarify the situation. Also, communication of concerns by analysts can serve to more fully acquaint elected officials with the interrelationships and potential seriousness of their actions.

External and Internal Danger Signals

While understanding the overall capacity of a government to avoid crisis, and its willingness to make tough decisions is essential, it is necessary to go further in presenting an analysis of the jurisdiction and examining the danger signals that can assist an analyst in forming an overall opinion.

There are essentially two types of danger signals that forecast potential tax revolt and predict the vulnerability of the jurisdiction to a financial crisis. These danger signals are external and internal factors.

The first type is a series of external factors which are not directly under the immediate control of the officials of the jurisdiction. These include the economic health of the area, the equity of the tax structure, the political climate, the legal underpinnings of the government, demographic changes, intergovernmental revenue or expenditure changes, and inherent limitations on revenue growth. It is important to analyze each of these external factors to develop a framework for determining if the seeds of a financial crisis are present. Each is discussed in Chapter 8.

Internal Factors

Tax Inequity. Spurring Proposition 13 in California and Proposition 2½ in Massachusetts was the belief that the property tax was inequitable and out of control. As inflation pushed assessments ever higher, the ability of individuals to pay the tax eroded. This was particularly true for those on fixed incomes.

Examination of the equity of taxes in a jurisdiction, should include study of the overall mix of taxes, the perceived proportionate burden on various classes of taxpayers, and the real level of taxes as compared with other jurisdictions. A signficant portion of the analysis is the perception of taxpayers. While an analyst cannot measure this directly, constant sensitivity to this factor must be maintained. In the Philadelphia example cited earlier, assessors had been systematically overassessing certain areas while underassessing others. This phenomenon led to an inordinately high coefficient of dispersion among classes of property as well as between classes.[23] Public perception of the inequity was reflected in the myriad lawsuits filed by a broad cross section of taxpayers. The analyst should be sensitive to litigation of this type and should attempt to determine its potential effect either on ability to pay or on possible legislative curtailment of taxing authority.

When Philadelphia attempted to change this inequitable assessment pattern, vehement opposition came from those who felt that their tax burden was already too high and that services, particularly public education, were either irrelevant or inadequate. It became necessary to build a coalition to explain the nature of the inequity and to strike a compromise on the means of redressing the inequities to avoid a serious tax revolt. Philadelphia was greatly aided by the fact that its tax was among the very lowest in its region and also by the fact that only 18 percent of the city's total revenues came from the property tax.[24] This enabled city fiscal managers to allow a longer period of time for raising assessments than would have been possible if reliance were heavier.

Thus, in Philadelphia, despite a perceived inequity falling on a group whose assessments were being raised, no long-term adverse consequences occurred, because of a diverse revenue structure and a relatively low overall rate of property tax.

Political Climate. The most difficult factor to measure directly, but perhaps the most crucial in anticipating a tax revolt or a fiscal crisis, is the political climate. A history of long-term leadership in a jurisdiction and the demonstrated willingness of management to make the difficult decisions should give the analyst comfort. On the other hand, continual change of leadership, continuing contentiousness over the need for tax increases, and a decentralized decision-making structure can all lead to the worst kind of crisis, the crisis of inaction.

---

[23]*The Problems With Philadelphia Real Property Assessment Practices and Solutions,* (Philadelphia, Pennsylvania Economy League, Eastern Division, Report No. 417, August 1980), p. 7.
[24]Ibid.

Yonkers, New York, demonstrated the effects of constantly changing leadership and decentralized decision making in the mid-70s. The political structure of Yonkers featured a classic weak-mayor, strong-council, city-manager system. The council was continuously divided into factions and the city had four city managers in five years. The inability to agree on tax increases coupled with the inability to control expenditures, particularly in the board of education, precipitated a financial crisis. Like many crises, excessive short-term borrowing which came due without the ability to be paid down or rolled over triggered an acute financial problem. The primary response by the state legislature was to take management of the city financial affairs out of the hands of the city council and place it in an emergency financial control board. Could this crisis have been anticipated? Probably, by a careful monitoring of the political climate.

Legal Underpinnings of Government. The power of a government to control the major elements of its revenues and expenditures stems primarily from the legal structure under which the government operates. In general, broad home rule powers to raise revenues, freedom from excessive-expenditure mandates, and a simple process of budget approval are all positive signs to an analyst that a government has proper legal underpinnings. The earlier discussion of the Philadelphia school district is a good example of weak legal underpinnings.

RESPONSE AND EFFECTS

Faced with the reality of a crisis or a revolt, each jurisdiction finds its own particular solution, but certain patterns recur. The first item usually tackled is the governmental payroll. This tends to be the largest single item of expenditure and the easiest to bring under control. Administrators and taxpayers alike realize "that by far the largest government expenditure is for people, . . . that most states and municipalities spend between 50 and 80 percent of their budgets for public employees' salaries, pension programs, and other related benefits."[25] Simple analysis suggests that the original impetus for such tax and spending controls was public perception of rampant waste and inefficiency in government.[26]

The growth in overall local government wage bills during the last 20 years, in actual dollars as well as in average wages relative to the wages of the private sector, make this a productive and popular area for trimming. In 1960, city governments spent $6.8 billion for personal services. By 1980, personal service costs had reached $34.7 bil-

---

[25]Lois Friedland, "Public Employees Under Siege," *National Conference of State Legislatures,* July–August 1980.
[26]Gold, *Property Tax Relief,* p. 172.

lion, a staggering increase of 410 percent from 1960 to 1980[27] In addition to the overall increase in the payroll, individual salary growth of state-local general government employees outpaced private sector salary increases from 1955 to 1974. Most of the growth occurred between 1960 and 1970, with a tapering off of growth from 1970 until 1974. With Proposition 13 psychology, Reaganomics, and the presence of cost-of-living adjustments in the private sector in the late 70s/early 80s, private sector percentage increases have averaged roughly 10.5 percent over this period while public sector increases have been in the area of 7 percent.[28] Indicative of the new attitude toward public sector employee levels is the following: "This year the budget won't be in balance unless things are cut back. The only way we can reduce it is by cutting down on employees."[29]

The two typical ways of reducing payroll are by reducing force size (either by attrition or layoff) and freezing wages. The growing unionization of municipal workers makes either route difficult, but force reduction is usually less susceptible to union pressure. In the future, however, it is likely that unions will demand ever increasing job security, perhaps even accepting lower relative wage and fringe benefit increases in return.

A second response at each level of government has been to shift the responsibility for a particular service to the next lowest level of government. During the Great Society program of the 1960s, the federal government began assuming the responsibility for housing, education, health services, law enforcement, and other traditionally local responsibilities. States were often the conduits for the funding of these programs and, as such, were seen as taking on the functions as part of their responsibility. As the expense of these programs became evident to the federal government and funding was reduced, the response of many state governments was not to assume continued funding responsibilities but to notify local governments of the lack of funding and allow the municipality or the county to decide whether or not a service should be continued. While this certainly gives local decision makers greater control over program selection, it also shifts the burden of continuing programs from the broad-based progressive revenue structure of the federal government to the local level. The effects of these fiscal shifts cannot yet be seen. They are certain to result in the desired contraction of programs that the federal government sees as unnecessarily wasteful and expensive. The pressure on local governments to maintain existing service levels without in-

[27]U.S. Department of Commerce, Bureau of the Census, "City Government Finances in 1960," p. 6, "City Government Finances in 1969–70," p. 5, "City Government Finances in 1979–80," p. 7.

[28]U.S. Department of Labor, Bureau of Labor Statistics.

[29]Michigan State Senator Jack Faxon in Friedland, "Public Employees Under Siege," p. 36.

creased levels of local taxation should cause concern for the analyst. And, when cuts come in the middle of a local fiscal year, they are considerably more difficult to deal with than if they can be anticipated during the budgeting process.

Productivity improvement is often heralded as the proper response to diminished expectation for revenue. To be sure, every organization can benefit from the application of planning, control, and technology which can improve effectiveness. Yet two factors inhibit the widespread application of productivity improvements by state and local governments. The first, and by far the most important, is the nature of the services provided by local governments. Fire and police units are located to provide a particular amount of coverage within a defined response time. Unless coverage is decreased or response time increases, little can be done to improve productivity. Routing and scheduling can have an impact on the reading of meters, the collection of trash, and other route-oriented services. However, even here the easy-to-implement efficiencies are usually already present. Health, library, and recreation services require that posts be manned a certain number of hours each day so that the public can have access to the service. Productivity can be improved only by cutting the number of posts or the number of hours. In either case, a service reduction is required. While there is nothing wrong with service reduction, it is better to label it as such rather than to mislead people by claims of increased productivity.

The second limiting factor regarding productivity is the quality of resources available to local government and the motivation to employ them. The automobile industry is currently retooling. Its motivation to achieve higher profits in future years leads the managers of these firms to the conclusion that major changes are necessary. The manager of local government often does not have the luxury of planning within the context of applying the latest technologies. The annual budget is often a shortsighted document. Investment in tools with a longer payback can be extremely hard to justify if it requires an increase in the tax rate. Further, the manager typically is not compensated for improving productivity. This tends to encourage a more conservative management strategy of making do with what is on hand rather than pushing productivity to the limits.

Another key element of response is what official Washington calls "revenue enhancement." Utilizing service charges to support services that were previously within the general tax rate, creating authorities to provide services previously performed by a local government, raising tax rates, expanding bases, and finding new tax sources have all been elements used by governments responding to a revolt or seeking to avoid a crisis.

Probably the most important effect of revolts and crises is the possible change in management attitudes of both professional managers and politicians. Despite the problems mentioned above, more and more managers may be responding to the pressure for increased efficiency by adopting modern management techniques. The most fundamental change, however, could be in the attitudes of the political leaders. Tax and spending limitations promote an attitude of fiscal restraint, accountability, and effectiveness in governments. The fundamental question has shifted in many areas from, "How can we provide more and better service?" to "How much government can and should we support?" If the latter question is asked and answered in a responsible manner it will go a long way toward insuring against financial crises and preventing tax revolts.

The Legal Security

Section TWO

The Legal Framework for General Obligation Bonds

CHAPTER 6

Andrea L. Kahn, J.D.

Partner
Kraft & Hughes

General obligation bonds of municipalities, counties, school districts, and states are backed by a pledge of the full faith and credit of the issuing entity. This pledge generally is supported by a commitment of the issuer to levy and to collect taxes, without limitation as to rate or amount, for the payment of principal and interest on its bonds. The pledge of the taxing power is sometimes understood to create a lien upon all the property that is owned by the issuer or that is owned by the inhabitants in the district and is taxable by the issuer.

Traditionally, general obligation bonds of such issuers have been considered to be among the most secure investments. This belief, together with the exemption of interest on these investments from taxation, has resulted in low interest costs for the public projects financed through the issuance of such obligations. The shakeup of the municipal bond industry following the note default during the New York fiscal crisis in 1975 has resulted in an ebb in public confidence in the municipal bond industry and in a reconsideration of the time-honored concepts behind the municipal bond as an investment security. A positive effect of this has been greater public disclosure and

consideration of the economic and financial condition of municipal issuers in analyzing the value and the security of municipal obligations. An analysis of the legal security and the enforceability of municipal obligations will assist in understanding and in determining
the credit worthiness of these obligations.

THE PLEDGE OF SECURITY

A pledge of the full faith and credit of a municipal issuer means
that the issuer conclusively acknowledges the debt and obligates itself to do all things in its power to make timely payment on the obligation. The pledge of the taxing power without limitations as to rate
or amount is intended to commit the issuer to use the full extent of
its unlimited taxing power to raise the money necessary to make
timely payment on these debts. In order to understand these pledges,
it is necessary to consider the power or ability of the issuer to pay,
within the framework of other competing demands that challenge its
resources, and the concept of its unlimited ability to raise taxes.

In addition to being a debtor, a municipal issuer is a public body
created to exercise sovereign powers, to provide necessary public services, and to fulfill other governmental purposes. It is extremely important for a municipal issuer to make timely payment on its debts
in order to insure the availability of credit markets at reasonable
rates, which is essential to enable it to serve its governmental purposes. It is also essential for municipal governments to provide many
services, including law enforcement, administration of justice, fire
fighting, water and sewerage systems, road maintenance, traffic control, snow removal, solid waste removal and treatment, education,
transportation, recreation, and other social services. A municipal
bondholder has a claim to the revenues and the resources of the municipal issuer, but so do employees and other creditors and claimants.
A creditor might attach assets of a private debtor even if that results
in closing it down or driving it out of business. A municipal government cannot go out of business. A bondholder cannot expect to be paid
before the municipal issuer pays its employees and provides for basic
services. When entering into the contractual relationship with the
municipal issuer that results from the purchase of the municipal
bond, a bondholder implicitly accepts this principle inherent in the
concept of sovereignty.

As part of the contract, the municipal issuer has promised to raise
taxes sufficient to pay its obligations. Presumably this means that it
must raise taxes sufficient to enable it to meets its governmental responsibilities as well as to make timely payment on its debts. Legally
it may have the power to raise taxes without limitation as to rate or
amount. Practically, however, the concept of unlimited taxing power

must be questioned when exorbitant tax rates result in driving the tax base out of the taxing district. Municipal governments cannot tax in excess of the value of the services they provide without risking the loss of their tax base. There are limits to the amounts that citizens are willing and able to pay, as demonstrated in the "tax cut fever" that has manifested itself around the country, in the form of Proposition 13 in California and Proposition 2½ in Massachusetts, and in other ways elsewhere.

ENFORCEABILITY OF PLEDGE, AND CREDITORS' REMEDIES

The significance of the pledge of the full faith and credit of the municipal issuer and the pledge of its unlimited taxing power for payment of its debts depends upon the enforceability of these pledges within the framework of sovereignty and the realities of the ability of the issuer to pay. The enforceability of these pledges depends upon many factors including their legal basis, the duties and the prerogatives of sovereignty, the willingness of the courts to maintain and to police these rights, and the economic and financial condition of the issuer. Each of these factors must be considered within the jurisdiction of the issuer of a municipal bond in order to obtain an accurate analysis of the municipal bond as an investment.

Before an obligation of a municipal issuer will be upheld, a number of requirements must be met. The issuer must have the constitutional and statutory authority to undertake the obligation. The issuer must have the constitutional and statutory authority to raise the taxes it pledges in support of its obligation. The borrowing must be for a proper public purpose. There must be compliance with all procedural requirements for the authorization and the issuance of the debt. There must be compliance with all conditions precedent to the borrowing, including debt limitations, voter approval, and approvals of enforcement agencies in accordance with the constitutional or statutory scheme. For this reason, the investment community has always required that municipal obligations must be accompanied by the approving legal opinion of a nationally recognized bond counsel firm as to the validity of the obligation and the availability of the taxing power as the source of payment for the obligation.

Assuming a validly authorized municipal obligation and the legal authority of the issuer to levy and to raise taxes for payment of the obligation, the security of a general obligation bond must be evaluated in light of the remedies available to the holder or the owner of the municipal obligation in default. Under these circumstances the bondholder has an absolute right to payment. Nevertheless, there is generally no express statutory scheme of remedies available. The

availability of remedies must be derived from the contractual relationships that exist between the municipal issuer and its creditors as
limited by the principles of sovereignty inherent in that scheme.

A private creditor upon an event of default can reduce its claim to
a judgment and can obtain a writ of execution to authorize a sheriff
or other enforcement officer to attach an asset of the debtor. In attempting to follow this approach, a municipal creditor would run into
numerous obstacles.

Sovereign Immunity

In the past a bondholder seeking to recover on a municipal bond
faced a significant legal question as to whether the issuer has available to it as a defense the *doctrine of sovereign immunity*. Under the
doctrine of sovereign immunity, a state cannot be sued for the payment of money in its governmental capacity unless it has consented
to such an action. While the courts are not in full agreement, this
principle is applied often to municipalities as well. Many states have
laws expressly waiving sovereign immunity as a defense in a legal
action. Moreover, courts in many jurisdictions have held that the
state and its subdivisions impliedly waive sovereign immunity wher-
ever they lawfully enter into a contract. Today it seems unlikely that
the defense would be available in an action involving a default on a
municipal bond. Nevertheless, this is a question that must be considered in light of the statutory law and the case law of the jurisdiction
of the municipal issuer.

Attachment of Municipal or Private Assets

Once a judgment is rendered in favor of a bondholder, the bondholder has no clear procedure for compelling payment. In some jurisdictions, the legislature has expressly immunized municipal property
from execution by statute. Even where there is no express limitation
on such actions, a court would be reluctant to permit the attachment
of municipal assets. Municipal corporations exist and own property
for the purpose of performing governmental functions. To deprive
them of their property is to deprive them of their ability to serve their
public purposes. Accordingly, the attachment of municipal assets was
not recognized under common law, and courts have found such actions to be against public policy. Certainly such actions would be
enormously disruptive of the governmental process. Moreover, a court
might feel that a judicial writ of attachment on municipal assets violates the principle of separation of powers. In providing this type of
remedy the court would be interfering with the governmental process,
and it is not clear that a court has the power to do that. Without

express statutory authority, it is unlikely that a court would evolve a remedy that would give to an individual the right to interfere with the operation of government.

A possible exception to this rule might exist to permit the attachment of municipal assets not affecting the ability of the municipal corporation to carry out its governmental purposes. The characterization of certain activities as being governmental and certain activities as being proprietary has been used by courts to distinguish between the exercise of traditional sovereign powers by governments for the performance of essential services, and the involvement of governments in enterprises deemed to be of an enterpreneurial nature and not essential to the provision of important public services. Under such a theory, the attachment of municipal assets owned in a proprietary capacity could be permitted but not those owned in a governmental capacity. However, municipal corporations are created for governmental purposes, and all of their actions must be justified as serving governmental objectives. The legislative branch of government normally determines what functions the government will perform and what means it will use to accomplish its purposes. Under this theory, a court would have to substitute its wisdom for legislative wisdom in determining certain property to be owned in an essential governmental capacity and not subject to attachment, and other property to be owned in a proprietary or nonessential, nongovernmental capacity and subject to attachment. This theory would give the court the ability to interfere with certain functions or activities of government on the ground that they are not sufficiently "governmental." This creates a problem concerning the principle of separation of powers. Normally courts will be reluctant to interfere with legislative judgments as to the proper functions of government.

Without express statutory authorization, it is unlikely that a bondholder would be able to attach private property within the district of the issuer. While a few jurisdictions have interpreted the pledge of the full faith and credit as being secured by the privately owned real property within the district, most have held that this pledge does not create such rights. The rationale is that the bondholders have not bargained for that security.

In New Jersey the legislature has expressly provided by statute that the obligations of certain school districts are a lien upon the real estate situated in the district, the personal estates of the inhabitants of the district, and the property of the district, and that such property shall be liable for the payment of such debt. In this case the bondholders have a right to expect the enforceability of this lien. Nevertheless, there is still no clear statutory procedure for enforcement. If asked to attach school district assets, a court would be faced with difficult questions such as whether the lien was perfected properly, whether such liens can be enforced in light of competing constitutional requirements to provide a thorough and efficient education, and whether the judicial action required to enforce the lien violates the principal of separation of powers and deprives the school district of sovereign rights. If asked to attach private assets, a court would face questions as to whether the lien was perfected properly, whether the estates of one or more property owners could be attached for the full amount of the judgment, or whether they would be liable only for a pro rata share with the remedy being to bring actions against all property owners in the district, and other difficult questions.

The likelihood of attachment of municipal or private assets as an available remedy in the event of default on a municipal bond may depend upon the statutory scheme and the case law in a particular jurisdiction. It may also be a function of judicial activism. Therefore an examination of the law of a particular jurisdiction, as well as judicial attitudes within the jurisdiction towards the function of courts and their role in relation to other branches of government, is relevant in analyzing the security of a particular general obligation bond.

Mandamus

In the absence of such extraordinary remedies, a bondholder normally expects to receive payment from the general revenues of the municipal issuer. The pledge of the full faith and credit of a municipal issuer is generally coupled with a pledge to raise taxes sufficient to meet the required payments. Where the pledge of the taxing power is not expressly stated, it might be considered to be implicit in the pledge of full faith and credit. Alternatively, the pledge of full faith and credit alone might be considered to be merely a promise to make a good faith effort to use the resources, the credit, and the powers of the issuer to make payment on its debt. Where the pledge of full faith and credit is coupled with a pledge of the taxing power, the bondholder has a right to demand that the issuer levy and collect taxes sufficient to make the required payment.

The power to levy taxes belongs to the legislature and the power to collect taxes belongs to the executive branch. Ordinarily, a court will not exercise either power. Courts cannot seize the power to tax as an asset to be distributed, and they cannot exercise that power on behalf of creditors. In order to enforce this right to revenues to be raised through the taxing power, a bondholder would have to seek a writ of mandamus to compel the raising of the necessary revenues. A *mandamus* is a command from a court of competent jurisdiction, requiring a municipal corporation or any of its officers to perform a duty required by law in order to restore a claimant to rights or privileges from which he has been deprived illegally. The duty must be required by statute and must be nondiscretionary. Failure to comply with a mandamus could result in contempt proceedings and jail terms. Accordingly, a bondholder might seek a mandamus to compel the legislative body of a municipal issuer to levy taxes that it has the power and the duty to raise under existing law and to compel officials of the municipal issuer to collect such taxes.

Even when the bondholder has a clear right to such a remedy, the likelihood of this judicial action must be considered in light of existing political, social, and economic realities. If the municipal corporation has reached the point of insolvency and truly is unable to pay, the remedy is useless. In this context, the concept of municipal insolvency suggests that there are limits to the theoretically inexhaustible taxing power. As discussed previously, taxes cannot be so high as to drive out the tax base or make it impossible for taxpayers to pay. Taxation must not cause the abandonment or the loss of taxable properties through tax liens to municipal corporations, with their resulting loss as a source of revenues. In this context municipal insolvency must be defined as the point at which a court is unwilling to order taxation in an amount necessary to enable a municipal corporation to meet its debts. Moreover, at this point there is a good chance that the municipal issuer is making an attempt to restore its financial condition. In doing so, it may attempt to make agreements with creditors or to postpone payment of its debts. To what extent can or will a court interfere with the priorities of a municipal corporation that require the expenditure of funds? To what extent can or will a court interfere with the solutions that a municipal corporation attempts to pursue? An examination of the past actions of courts reacting to municipal defaults gives insight into the ability and the willingness of courts to act in light of the fundamental principle of the inviolability of contract and the concept of municipal bankruptcy.

Inviolability of Contract

Under the federal Constitution and under most state constitutions, states are prohibited from impairing the obligations of contracts. As interpreted, however, this prohibition is not absolute. It is limited by competing constitutional principles protecting the inherent police powers reserved to the states to provide for emergency situations and important public purposes. This philosophy developed in response to the unique financial emergencies created during the Great Depression. Nevertheless, these principles must be considered today in analyzing the security of a general obligation bond.

Debts are contracts and must be considered in light of the laws governing contracts. In consideration for the loan of a sum of money, the municipal issuer pledges its full faith and credit and promises to use its taxing power to make timely payments of principal and interest on its debt. These pledges are not absolute, however. In *Faitoute Iron & Steel Co.* v. *City of Asbury Park,* 316 U.S. 502 (1942), the U.S. Supreme Court approved a plan by which the city of Asbury Park, New Jersey, was permitted to adjust its general obligation debt under state law in order to preserve its taxing power. Under this plan, the existing debt was discharged, and new debt payable over a longer period of time was substituted for it. It was reasoned that the preservation of the taxing power was essential for the repayment of the debt at all. This action was justified on the ground that the inherent police powers reserved to the state to maintain public order, health, and safety could outweigh the principle of the inviolability of contract rights in the event of a true public disaster such as the financial crisis of the Great Depression.

Faitoute followed the rationale of *Home Building & Loan Association* v. *Blaisdell,* 290 U.S. 398 (1934), and *East New York Savings Bank* v. *Hahn,* 326 U.S. 230 (1945), which held that the police power may be invoked to modify the terms of a contract in a period of financial emergency where the state is acting to protect the vital interests of its people. These cases reasoned that the state's police power never can be contracted away and is an implied condition in every contract. Accordingly, the reasonable exercise of the police power, to suspend the enforcement of mortgagee's rights, could be justified to serve a legitimate end in avoiding wholesale foreclosures when the suspension was temporary and did not impair the substantial rights secured by the contract. The difference between *Faitoute* and the earlier cases is that the rationale was extended to permit the state to exercise its reserved police powers to abrogate contracts to which it was a party, not only contracts among private parties.

It is likely, however, that the rule in *Faitoute* will be limited to the unique circumstances of the Great Depression. In recent years, courts seem to be retracting from the positions taken in these cases. In *Flushing National Bank* v. *Municipal Assistance Corporation,* 40 N.Y. 2d 731, 358 N.E. 2d 848, 390 N.Y.S. 2d 22 (1976), the New York Court of Appeals struck down the Emergency Moratorium Act of 1975 as a violation of the New York State constitution's "Faith and Credit Clause." The act was passed in an emergency session of the legislature to prevent, for three years, the holders of short-term notes who refused to exchange them for Municipal Assistance Corporation (MAC) bonds from bringing an action to enforce their payment. (See Case 7.) The court held that the police power could not be used to override the intentional constitutional protection guaranteed by the Faith and Credit Clause of the New York constitution. Since this case relied on a provision unique to the New York constitution, it may have limited applicability. However, it adds a new dimension to the concept of the full faith and credit pledge. It adopted the position that the pledge of full faith and credit is a continuing commitment to make payment until the debt is discharged, not merely a commitment of the municipality to use good-faith efforts to use its taxing power to repay its debt. Also, it suggests that the pledge commits all the revenues of the municipality for repayment of the debt, not only tax revenues.

Another recent case, decided under the Contract Clause of the federal Constitution, significantly limits the theories followed in *Faitoute*. In *U.S. Trust Company of New York* v. *New Jersey,* 431 U.S. 1 (1977) rehearing denied, 431 U.S. 975(1977), the court prohibited the Port Authority of New York and New Jersey from abrogating its contract with bondholders. In response to the energy crisis, the Port Authority of New York and New Jersey wanted to expand its commuter operation. However, the legislatures of New York and New Jersey previously had enacted statutory covenants among each other and the holders of certain Port Authority bonds prohibiting the Port Authority from engaging in deficit rail operations. In 1974 the legislatures of both states repealed these covenants retroactively and the bondholders brought suit. The Supreme Court found that the Port Authority had entered into the contract under its spending and borrowing powers, which can be bargained away unlike the police power and some other powers. The court reasoned that an impairment of contract can be constitutional only if it is reasonable and necessary to serve an important public purpose. Essentially, the court found that the impairment was not reasonable under the particular circumstances since the alleged emergency was foreseeable when the covenant was enacted.

The situations involved in these two cases are different from the situations in the older cases. The New York financial crisis resulted from the mismanagement of city finances over a period of years, while the Great Depression was an economic disaster of major national proportions caused by numerous factors unrelated to the actions of any municipality. Moreover, the municipal actions could not be justified as reasonable in either *Flushing* or *U.S. Trust* in light of the availability of other remedies. These two cases suggest that today the courts will sparingly apply the principles carved out in *Faitoute*. It is doubtful that these principles will be applied to permit municipal corporations to avoid their contractual commitments except in the most extreme emergency.

Bankruptcy

Another factor distinguishing *Faitoute* is that it was decided at a time when there was no federal bankruptcy law. The availability of bankruptcy or insolvency proceedings is essentially a constitutionally permissible and federally authorized way of relieving municipal issuers of their contractual commitments under certain circumstances. One of the circumstances is the insolvency of the municipal corporation. Insolvency is a difficult concept to define, as suggested in previous discussions. However, in the event of insolvency when the municipal corporation is not deemed to have the ability to raise revenues sufficient to pay its debts as they come due, it is better to have an orderly procedure determined by federal statute than to leave the remedies in the hands of the judiciary without any guidance. With the availability of these remedies under federal law, the courts may not be faced with the kinds of pressures that the court in *Faitoute* had to face in resolving the difficult problems of an insolvent municipal corporation and its injured creditors. Therefore, the availability of the bankruptcy code can be a positive factor in analyzing the security of general obligation bonds.

On the negative side, however, the availability of bankruptcy proceedings threatens the security of municipal bonds in several ways. Creditors can be deprived of their right to bring an action for mandamus or to pursue other remedies. Municipal issuers can be authorized to issue additional debt with priority over existing debt. The bankruptcy proceedings can be forced upon creditors, but creditors cannot force a municipal issuer into bankruptcy. A trustee cannot be appointed to take over the operation except in limited capacities. Finally it is not clear whether general obligation bondholders will be found to be secured creditors or creditors of a special class with any priority over other unsecured general creditors.

Even with these negative aspects, it is better to have a defined procedure to deal with problems of insolvency. Without such a procedure courts could be forced to evolve remedies that might prove as harmful or more harmful to creditors. Since federal bankruptcy relief is available only in jurisdictions where expressly authorized by state law, an analysis of the security of a bond should consider whether federal bankruptcy proceedings are available to the issuer.

CONCLUSION

In analyzing the security of a general obligation bond and its value as an investment in light of that security, it is important to focus on a number of factors within the jurisdiction of the issuer. First of all, as explained in Chapter 8, the financial and economic condition of the municipal corporation must be examined to determine the likelihood of default. This review will focus on the sufficiency of the local economy to withstand hard times and to be able to produce tax revenues sufficient to support government services and to pay debts. It will also focus on the ability and the willingness of local officials to meet the demands of government and to respect the rights of its creditors. Next, the statutory framework of the municipal issuer should be examined to analyze what rights and what remedies a creditor has available to him. The history of the issuer should be considered to determine the attitude of the local officials and of the courts in the respect they afford to creditors' rights and concerns and in the policies they pursue in recognizing creditors' remedies. An analysis should be made of the case law in the jurisdiction interpreting the statutory framework for the authorization of debt, the rights of the municipality as sovereign, and the remedies available to a creditor in a judicial action in that jurisdiction. Finally, an inquiry should be made into the availability of federal bankruptcy proceedings. Creditors' rights can vary greatly from one statutory scheme to another and from one judicial jurisdiction to another, and consideration should be given to these factors in determining the relative value of general obligation bonds.

The Legal Framework for Revenue Bonds

CHAPTER **7**

Charles Buschman, J.D.
Attorney
Debevoise & Plimpton

Robert J. Gibbons, J.D.
Attorney
Debevoise & Plimpton

Under traditions dating back to the Magna Carta, the power of the purse in our governmental system has belonged to the people, to be exercised by them through legislators whose continuance in office depends on the popular will expressed through periodic elections. In today's terms, this means that moneys cannot be paid out from the federal treasury without an appropriation by Congress, or from a state treasury without an appropriation by the state legislature. In order to preserve the sovereignty of the electoral process in this regard, neither Congress nor the state legislatures can, as a general rule, appropriate moneys to be paid out after the current terms of their members expire, except for the remainder of a fiscal year begun before such expiration.

The most important exception to the above principle is the power of a legislative body to incur public debt—debt which, by law, must be paid regardless of what the legislative or popular mood may be when payment is due. Since this power is an exception to the traditional principle, it is generally cast in the form of a specific constitutional authorization. In the case of federal debt, this authorization is con-

98

tained in Article I, Section 8, clause 2 of the U.S. Constitution. Such clause is only 10 words long and contains no dollar ceiling or other restrictions.

In the case of state debt, the authorization usually occupies an entire, separate article of the constitution of the state involved and, in contrast to federal authorization, is loaded with restrictions. Such restrictions include the purposes for which debt of the state may be incurred and, in many cases, specific dollar ceilings on the amount which may be incurred for each such purpose. In addition, there are often referendum requirements in the case of various categories or amounts of debt. The "full faith and credit" of the state is said to stand behind debt incurred under the article, except to the extent, if any, which the same article also deals with revenue debt as described below. In many instances, the article will go on to provide further, specific measures to assure that such full-faith-and-credit debt will be paid. An example would be the pledging of certain taxes or other receipts, accompanied by a prohibition of any legislation that would lessen such taxes or other receipts. The existence of any such pledge does not imply a limitation of the sources of payment of the debt—all other resources of the state must be utilized for such payment if such taxes or other receipts are insufficient.

Besides bearing the label *full faith and credit,* debt like that described above is often called general obligation debt. Besides general obligation debt, most if not all the state constitutions authorize, either explicitly or implicitly, the issuance of what is called revenue debt. The essence of revenue debt is that a particular stream of revenues—from a project or enterprise, from a loan program, or sometimes from a special tax—is designated as the sole source for payment of the debt; the state is under no obligation to pay the debt from its general funds if such source proves inadequate or default is otherwise threatened. The issuance of revenue debt is usually subject to fewer and less severe restrictions than in the case of general obligation debt. This is because the purpose of such restrictions is to minimize the loss of popular control over the public purse—i.e., to protect future taxpayers against heavy tax burdens they must bear without their consent. Since future taxpayers need not come up with the money needed to pay revenue debt, the same degree of restriction is not necessary.[1]

States do not usually issue revenue debt in their own names. A commission, authority, corporation, or other entity will normally be

[1]The distinction between revenue debt and general obligation debt becomes blurred when the receipts from a special tax are pledged to pay an issue of revenue debt. Although there is no recourse to the state's general taxing power, there may exist a special covenant or an implied moral obligation to set the special tax at a high-enough level to ensure payment of the debt.

established for such purpose. Such entity may or may not be a legally separate "person" from the state itself. Counties and municipalities are also often empowered to issue revenue debt for various purposes, either under their own names or that of a commission, authority, corporation, or other entity which they are permitted to establish. Often an issuer will have outstanding two or more separate issues of revenue debt which depend for payment on separate streams of revenues. Generally, in such a case, if one issue should get into financial trouble, revenues pledged to another issue cannot be tapped to help pay it, and the entity need not, from a legal standpoint, help out with any other, unpledged funds in its possession.

This chapter will describe generally the legal framework of public revenue debt. The first part will describe, in more detail than above, the constitutional and statutory provisions behind the issuance of revenue debt, including the role of any constitutional and statutory pledges and other mechanisms set up to ensure payment. The second part will discuss the legal operation of the various key provisions within a typical revenue bond indenture or resolution. Consideration will be given to the soundness, from a legal standpoint, of the statutory pledges and other mechanisms of the sort discussed in the first part of this chapter and of any duplicative or additional security devices contained within a bond indenture or resolution—i.e., how well any such devices would stand up if the state, county, or municipality which issued the debt or which created the issuer got into serious financial difficulty and sought to tap the supposedly pledged revenues in order to maintain the operation of unrelated functions such as police, schools, or mass transportation.

Revenue debt is usually issued in the form of medium- or long-term bonds. Notes are frequently issued during the construction phase of a project or otherwise to provide temporary financing, to be paid at maturity from a portion of the proceeds of the bonds issued to provide permanent financing. This chapter will refer throughout to revenue "bonds," but the intended reference will in each case (unless otherwise specified) also be to notes or any other form an issuance of revenue debt may take.

BASIC LEGAL BACKGROUND

Who May Issue Revenue Bonds—Tax Considerations

Of great advantage to state and local governments is, of course, their power to issue bonds the interest on which, for federal tax purposes, is not included within the income of the person who receives it. The governing statutory language is that of section 103(a) of the Internal Revenue Code. Such section explicitly grants such tax exemption only to "obligations of a state, territory or a possession of the United States, or any political subdivision of any of the foregoing." This phrase clearly brings states, counties, and municipalities within the exemption, but is ambiguous as to entities such as special fire or sewer districts, housing or other authorities, or corporations established by states, counties, or municipalities.

Such ambiguity is addressed in regulations adopted by the Treasury under section 103(a), but has by no means been cured. Under the regulations, the term *political subdivision* is defined as "any division of any state or local governmental unit which is a municipal corporation or which has been delegated the right to exercise part of the sovereign power of the unit." The regulations go on to say that, under such definition, a political subdivision "may or may not . . . include special assessment districts such as road, water, sewer, gas, light, reclamation, drainage, irrigation, levee, school, harbor, port improvement, and similar districts." The regulations themselves provide no further elucidation as to what may or may not be a political subdivision. The inclusion in the above definition, however, of an entity "which has been delegated the right to exercise part of the sovereign power of the unit" means that the definition includes any entity which exercises police powers or has the power to levy taxes or to take private property by means of eminent domain. If a special district has any such power (most have the power of eminent domain or the power to levy taxes), it generally would qualify as a political subdivision.

As to authorities and corporations which do not possess any such power (e.g., state housing finance agencies) and which hence fail to qualify as political subdivisions, the door is opened to them in the regulations by a provision that obligations "of" a state or local governmental unit include obligations issued "on behalf of [the governmental] unit by constituted authorities empowered to issue such obligations." The regulations do not go on to say what constitutes a "constituted authority" or when obligations issued by such an authority are "on behalf" of a state or local government. Rulings of the Internal Revenue Service, however, indicate that authorities, corporations, or other entities established by statute and administered by public officials are included together with, under certain circumstances, nonprofit corporations founded by individuals to perform certain governmental or quasi-governmental functions. In 1976 the Treasury released proposed regulations containing a detailed set of rules as to "constituted authorities." The proposed regulations met with considerable adverse comment from state and municipal officials who considered them unduly restrictive, and they have never become effective.

Who May Issue Revenue Bonds and under What Circumstances—State Law Considerations

State law, beginning with the constitution of the state involved, determines under what circumstances the issuance of revenue bonds is legally authorized on the part of the state, its subdivisions, or other public entities in the state. State law also determines the extent to which each such entity is empowered to enter into related security arrangements, and under what circumstances a given entity may participate in a project financed by revenue debt issued by another public entity, whether as part of a security arrangement or in any other manner of participation.

As a general principle, a public entity's legal power to issue revenue bonds, or to enter into a proposed contractual arrangement as a third party in connection with revenue bonds to be issued by another public entity, is determined by a chain of laws, orders, or other acts of legal significance. Such chain also determines the procedural requirements for such issuance or for consummation of the related contractual arrangements. Regardless of the type of entity involved, the chain begins with the state constitution. From there down, the chain is different depending on the nature of the entity.

The State and Its Agencies and Authorities. As indicated earlier, state constitutions contain provisions authorizing and restricting the state's issuance of general obligation debt. Many also contain provisions respecting revenue debt which may be issued by the state itself or by its internal departments or agencies. An example is the Ohio constitution, which in Article VIII, Section 2i, authorizes the issuance of revenue bonds for designated purposes by the state itself or by internal state "boards, commissions," etc. Typically, the next link down in the chain of legal authorization, following the state constitution, is the state statute or statutes specifically authorizing the debt. This is sometimes followed by, in the case of departments or agencies, internal rules or procedures of the department or agency.

The New York constitution, on the other hand, has no provision that allows the issuance of revenue bonds by the state itself or any of its internal departments or agencies. The authorization in New York for revenue bonds is contained in Article 10, under which the state is empowered to create "public corporations," an example of which is the Power Authority of the state of New York. Such corporations may be authorized by the legislature to "contract indebtedness," which would include the issuance of revenue bonds. Most other states also permit the creation by the state of authorities, corporations, and similar entities empowered to issue revenue bonds.

In the case of revenue bonds issued by any such entities separate from the state, the next link down from the state constitutional provisions respecting the legislature's power to establish such entities is the state statute creating or authorizing the creation of the particular entity that is to issue the bonds. Such statute will usually delineate the entity's powers. In New York, for example, there is a lengthy statute creating the Power Authority and delineating its powers, including its power to issue revenue bonds. Similar statutes exist for many other state authorities established for various purposes.

The next link down in the chain of authorization is the entity's bylaws or other internal governing documents, rules, or procedures. Although various links within the chain determine to a certain extent the terms of the bonds or the security arrangements behind the bonds, the details of such are set forth in the bond indenture or resolution which the issuer enters into (in the case of an indenture) or adopts (in the case of a resolution) usually a short time before the bonds are issued or, in the case of bonds issued in series under a single indenture or resolution, a short time before the first series is issued.

In considering a proposed issue of revenue bonds, one must scrutinize carefully the statute and other documents governing each entity proposed to be involved, not only to see if debt of the type, in the amount, and for the purposes envisioned is authorized, but also to ensure that the entity has the power to pledge the revenues it intends to pledge, or to bind itself to any other security devices contemplated. Such scrutiny may become fairly tricky in the case of any entity involved in the project or program as a third party, as mentioned above. This is because, in addition to questions as to such third party's authority to involve itself in the desired manner, there may well arise the question of whether or not the financial commitments associated with its involvement amount to its incurring debt of its own. If this is the case, the amount involved may exceed the third party's debt ceiling, or the debt may otherwise be in violation of the third party's statute.

A good illustration of the problems which may arise in third-party arrangements is provided by lawsuits which have questioned the constitutionality of an arrangement commonly employed in connection with the issuance of bonds to provide money for state office buildings or other facilities needed by a state government. What the state has tried to do in such instances has been to characterize the bonds as revenue bonds, while in actuality there was not to be any flow of money to pay the bonds from any source other than the state government itself. First, the state creates a separate entity to issue the bonds and construct the office buildings or other facilities. Following construction, the entity leases the facilities to the state (the third party in the arrangement) for a period (or successive periods under renewal options) equal to the life of the bonds, the scheduled rental payments being in an amount sufficient to ensure that principal and interest on the bonds will be paid when due. As a general rule, the courts hearing such lawsuits have held that an obligation to make rental payments in future years does not constitute any present indebtedness of the state, at least where such obligation is expressly or implicitly made subject to future legislative appropriations and does not purport to bind the legislature to make such appropriations. This holding has been the basis for sustaining the arrangements at issue in many of the lawsuits.

In other such lawsuits, however, courts have gone on to recharacterize the "lease" within the arrangement as actually being a purchase of the facility or facilities in question.[2] Under such a recharacterization, the "rental" payments the state is to make are characterized as installment payments of the purchase price. If the court has so recharacterized the arrangement, the consequence has been that the installments have been viewed as a present indebtedness of the state contracted without compliance with the constitutionally mandated procedures for the state's incurring debt, the result being that the whole arrangement is unconstitutional.

Counties, Municipalities, and Other Local Governments and Their Agencies and Authorities. A state constitution will normally contain, in a separate article or as part of the article on state debt, provisions delineating the debt-incurring powers of counties, municipalities, and other local governments including special districts such as school districts, fire districts, and the like. Such provisions may well apply only to the incurrence of general obligation debt by such entities. In many instances, the authorization for revenue debt will not be explicit, but will instead have to be inferred from general "home rule" or other powers granted to local governments or from the general constitutional power of the state legislature to enact laws in the absence of a constitutional prohibition.

The next link in the chain is the state statute or statutes implementing the above constitutional provisions or based on such general powers. Then comes the local government's charter, bylaws, or other internal governing documents. As in the case of bonds issued by states and state-created agencies or authorities, the details of a bond issuance are set forth in an indenture or resolution entered into or adopted by the local government. In some cases, either the state constitution itself or the statute or statutes implementing the constitutional provisions regarding local governments will empower the local governments to establish authorities, corporations, or similar entities which may issue revenue debt.

---

[2]Whether or not the courts have made such a recharacterization has depended on a variety of factors, e.g., the extent to which the lease—or a succession of renewal leases—may be terminated at the option of the state.

Statutory Security Devices

Pledges, covenants, and other security devices are usually written into the indenture, resolution, or other documentation underlying an issuance of revenue bonds. Sometimes, however, they are contained in the statutory framework which establishes and governs the issuer and are not duplicated in such documentation.

Setting forth such security devices in the statutory framework, without setting them forth additionally in the indenture, resolution, or other documentation, raises the question whether or not the state can alter or even destroy such devices by amending or repealing the applicable statute or any other statutes necessary in order for the applicable statute to have the result intended. In the case of a pledge of receipts from a designated tax, this question would include whether or not the state can reduce or abolish the tax. The question addressed in this section overlaps that addressed in the next section of this chapter, which concerns to what extent a state legislature can in general interfere with its contractual commitments, including ones set forth in an indenture or resolution securing an issue of revenue bonds. As shall be shown there, any such interference risks running afoul of the clause within the U.S. Constitution which prohibits states from enacting laws that "impair the Obligation of Contracts." Here the question is whether or not a given statutory provision has the status of a contractual commitment. For if it does, its alteration or repeal may give rise to such a federal constitutional challenge; but if it does not, no such challenge would be available to any injured bond-holder.

A background statutory provision has contractual status when (in the words of the U.S. Supreme Court in a case to be termed herein the "Port Authority" case) "the language and circumstances evidence a legislative intent to create private rights of a contractual nature enforceable against the state."[3] The clearest instance would be where the statute explicitly provides that the state "covenants" or "agrees" with the issuer's bondholders that something will or will not be done, or where the statute expressly pledges certain assets or revenues for their benefit. Doubt may exist when the statutory language is less categorical, and in any such case the most prudent investor or analyst may want to see "locked in" the statutory provision or provisions in question, either by seeing them duplicated in the indenture or resolution underlying the bonds or by seeing a covenant to the effect that the bonds will be entitled to the benefits of such provision or provisions without regard to changes enacted after the time of issuance.

---

[3]*U.S. Trust Company of New York* v. *State of New Jersey,* 431 U.S. 1, 17 (1977).

Unilateral Contractual Changes after Issuance

The Port Authority case concerned the application of bridge, tunnel, and other revenues of the Port Authority of New York and New Jersey. Such revenues were pledged to the payment of certain of the Authority's bonds, but not so as to preclude various other uses for such revenues. The Port Authority was originally founded by a compact between New York and New Jersey. In 1962 the two states decided to apply a portion of such revenues to the operation of certain commuter railroad projects. In order not to shake investor confidence in the Authority's bonds secured by such revenues, including bonds to be issued in the future, the two states passed parallel statutes placing concrete restrictions on such application. Under the statutes, the states "covenant[ed] and agree[d] with each other and with the holders" of the affected bonds, that so long as any such bonds remained outstanding the Authority would apply such revenues only in connection with certain enumerated railroad lines and any other lines which would be "self-supporting" or the operation of which would not result in any deficits in excess of what were called "permitted deficits," defined by means of a formula.

The formula related such "permitted deficits" to the amount of Port Authority bonds outstanding at any given moment. No relation was established between such "permitted deficits" and any surplus of Authority bridge and tunnel revenues over what was necessary to pay debt service on the bonds, maintain required reserves, and provide for the Authority's bridge and tunnel operations. The result was that a big surplus could build up without any part of it being available for commuter railroad operations if losses from such operations should exceed a figure unrelated to, and far below, the amount of the surplus. By 1974, such a big surplus had indeed built up, so that a diversion of revenues to commuter railroad operations substantially in excess of "permitted deficits" might be accomplished without endangering the security of the bonds so long as revenues remained at their high levels. The statutory covenant, however, prohibited such a diversion. New York and New Jersey then sought to repeal the covenant, and to this end enacted statutes amending their respective 1962 statutes.[4] The trustee for the holders of certain of the affected bonds launched constitutional attacks on the two repeals in the courts of New York and New Jersey. The New Jersey case traveled up to the U.S. Supreme Court, the decision there being indirectly dispositive of the New York case as well.

The basis of the attack was Article I, Section 10, clause 1 of the

---

[4]In signing the New York statute into law, Governor Wilson offered bondholders a kind of apology in expressing his "great reluctance [in approving] a bill that overturns a solemn pledge of the state." 431 U.S. at 14.

U.S. Constitution, which reads, "No State shall . . . pass any . . . Law impairing the Obligation of Contracts . . . ." The Court agreed with the trustee and invalidated the repeal. In doing so, however, it spoke in terms strongly suggesting that in other circumstances holders of revenue bonds might not fare so well—that pledged revenues could in some circumstances be diverted or other security devices destroyed by state legislation enacted after the bonds were issued. Indeed, it should be noted that the Court's vote in the Port Authority case was 4 to 3, with the 3 dissenters stating that states should, from a constitutional perspective, be free to do in essence whatever they choose in respect of their obligations toward bondholders.[5]

The majority opinion focused on several aspects of the Port Authority case as reasons why repeal of the covenant was not allowed. In doing so, it established a number of somewhat vague tests as to the constitutionality of legislative contractual alterations of the kind at issue. Chief among such tests was whether or not the alteration was necessary.[6] The court in this regard contrasted the factual situation in the Port Authority case with that in a previous case in which the Court had upheld a legislative alteration, saying that the alteration then at issue "was regarded by this Court as 'quite clearly necessary' to achieve the state's vital interest in the orderly administration" of a certain program.[7] This "necessity" test was broken down into two subtests. The first was whether the desired result (operation of commuter railroads in the Port Authority case) could be accomplished without any change in the state's contractual obligations. As to this, the Court pointed out that New York and New Jersey had other sources of money which they could apply if they wanted to go ahead with the desired commuter railroad projects. The second subtest was whether such result could be accomplished by a less severe change. As to this, the Court hinted as to two or three less severe statutory changes that would have tied the amount of revenues allowed to be diverted to commuter railroads to the size of the Port

---

[5]"I would not want to be read as suggesting that the states should blithely proceed down the path of repudiating their obligations, financial or otherwise. Their credibility in the credit market obviously is highly dependent on exercising their vast lawmaking powers with self-restraint and discipline, and I, for one, have little doubt that few, if any, jurisdictions would choose to use their authority so foolish[ly] as to kill a goose that lays golden eggs for them. (*Erie R. Co.* v. *Public Util. Comm'rs,* 254 US, at 410, 65 L Ed 322, 41 S Ct 169.) But in the final analysis, there is no reason to doubt that appellant's financial welfare is being adequately policed by the political processes and the bond marketplace itself. The role to be played by the Constitution is at most a limited one. For this Court should have learned long ago that the Constitution—be it through the Contract or Due Process Clause—can actively intrude into such economic and policy matters only if my brethren are prepared to bear enormous institutional and social costs. Because I consider the potential dangers of such judicial interference to be intolerable, I dissent." Mr. Justice Brennan, 431 U.S. at 61–62.

[6]431 U.S. at 29.

[7]431 U.S. at 31.

Authority's surplus, thus leaving the bondholders with some protection if revenues fell off.

The Supreme Court's discussion of the necessity test sheds little light on just how necessary a legislative contractual change must be in order for it to pass constitutional muster. The examples used by the Court, however, together with the general tone of the Court's discussion, carry a strong implication that contractual obligations of a state or municipality will not be permitted to stand in the way when an alteration of them cannot, from a practical standpoint, be avoided in order to protect a truly "vital interest" of the state or municipality (using the words of the above quotation). If, for example, a state or municipality got into desperate financial straits and was unable to raise taxes any further without destroying its tax base, it might constitutionally be able to tap tax receipts or other revenues supposedly pledged to an issue of its own revenue bonds, or the revenues of a separate authority, corporation, or other entity (e.g., the Port Authority), in order to keep essential services running. The state or municipality would presumably be required to provide reimbursement when it became financially able, but the bondholders might have to wait for payment during the course of a declared moratorium or some other interval.

Another factor focused on by the Court was that the burden New York and New Jersey now wanted removed was exactly the burden they intended to bear when they enacted the restriction. This was clearly not a case where a contractual provision made a substantial time ago had come to have unintended side effects due to changed circumstances. In this regard, the Court pointed to a previous case where it had upheld a state's repeal of a 19th century statutory covenant which had come to have "effects that were unforeseen and unintended by the legislature when originally adopted," and as a result of which "speculators were placed in a position to obtain windfall benefits."[8] This statement by the Court, combined with certain other statements, distinctly suggests that the Obligation of Contracts clause cannot be made to do any more than prevent outright injury to bondholders or to other beneficiaries of contracts. Contractual provisions which are not needed otherwise than to preserve such a windfall benefit thus may well be subject to nullification at the will of the state legislature. If this is a correct view of the Court's position, such a position could have a wide application.

It should be noted that a contractual alteration that can pass muster under the Obligation of Contracts clause of the U.S. Constitution may nonetheless be prohibited by one or more state constitutional provisions. This was brought out in the litigation challenging the three-year moratorium on payment of New York City notes, enacted

---

[8]431 U.S. at 31.

into law by the New York State legislature in 1975. Various note-holders brought suit in the New York State courts, and the lower courts upheld the moratorium. The lower courts' opinions chiefly discussed the federal constitutional issue. They did not mention the Port Authority case, but voiced in essence the same necessity test outlined there. The Port Authority justices had come forth with this test on the basis of several prior U.S. Supreme Court cases which had upheld various state alterations of contractual obligations, and the lower New York courts, citing the dire needs of the city, relied on these older precedents. The lower courts' discussion of the *state* constitutional issues was very brief and seems to have incorporated this federal necessity test.

The New York Court of Appeals did not dispute the lower courts' position on the *federal* issues. It instead struck down the moratorium strictly on *state* constitutional grounds.[9] According to the court, the key state constitutional clause was not subject to any necessity test or similar qualification to which the Obligation of Contracts clause within the U.S. Constitution was subject. In the context of this chapter, it should be noted that this key clause pointed to by the Court of Appeals was the pledge, within the state constitution, of the city's "full faith and credit" to payment of the notes—not applicable to revenue bonds. In some states other than New York, however, revenue bonds may be protected by favorable language within the state constitution, which a state court might seize upon.

At this juncture, it should perhaps be mentioned that contractual obligations of a state or municipality have long been held to be subject to future application of the "police power"—i.e., the power of the state or municipality to pass laws for purposes of public health, safety, and morals. The long-voiced rationale is that no part of the police power can validly be granted away by the making of any covenant, by the pledging of any revenues or other assets, or by any other act. This principle became an issue in the New Jersey Supreme Court decision upholding the constitutionality of the New Jersey Sports and Exhibition Authority and its issuance of revenue bonds.[10] The judges' opinions there raised, but did not answer, the question whether this retention of the police power meant that the pledge to bondholders of pari-mutuel wagering net revenues at the New Jersey racetrack financed by the bonds might be subject to a future curtailment, or even elimination, of pari-mutuel wagering if the legislature thought that public health, safety, or morals would be furthered by such a curtailment or elimination.

It is clear, however, that any invocation of the police power in an attempt to alter a pledge of revenues or some other contractual pro-

---

[9]*Flushing National Bank* v. *Municipal Assistance Corporation for the City of New York*, 40 N.Y. 2d 731 (1976).

[10]*New Jersey Sports & Exposition Authority* v. *McCrane*, 61 N.J. 1 (1972).

vision would have to be based on an important public need. This qualification is illustrated by the New York Court of Appeals' decision in a suit brought on behalf of bondholders of the Jones Beach State Parkway Authority.[11] The suit challenged a state statute placing certain procedural restrictions on the Authority's power to raise parkway tolls. The bonds were protected by a covenant on the part of the Authority to raise tolls to whatever level was necessary to pay principal and interest after maintenance and other expenses were taken care of. The state argued that increased toll dodging resulting from a toll increase planned by the Authority, in the form of cars exiting from the parkway just before a toll booth and reentering just after, would constitute a public hazard which the statute sought to remedy. The statute was therefore, according to the state, a valid application of the state's police power. The Court of Appeals rejected such argument, saying that "the asserted traffic emergency [was not] a sufficiently important public purpose to warrant interference with contractual rights."

Blocking Enforcement of Contractual Provisions

If a state or municipality, or even the federal government, got into serious financial difficulty with respect to its outstanding debt, or in maintaining essential public functions while continuing to pay debt service or continuing to set aside revenues as security for its revenue bonds, one possible tactic could be to divert revenues, to postpone the maturity of the bonds, or to do any other contractually prohibited act, and then to close the courthouse doors to any suit attempting to challenge such a prohibited act. Reliance would be placed on the doctrine of sovereign immunity, according to which a government can supposedly be sued only with its consent.

Such an invoking of sovereign immunity was unsuccessfully attempted by the New York State legislature in connection with the New York City moratorium statute mentioned above. The actual form the moratorium took was not an outright postponement of the maturity of the city notes involved but rather a suspension of the right of any noteholder to bring any judicial action to enforce payment. The New York Court of Appeals, in reaching its conclusion (discussed above) that the moratorium violated the pledge within the state constitution of the city's full faith and credit, saw through this roundabout approach, in effect holding that the doctrine of sovereign immunity cannot be used to shield nonpayment of debt: "Moreover, in denying access to the courts, there is in effect a denial of all remedy. It is elementary that denial of a remedy is a denial of the right [for which the remedy is sought]."[12]

---

[11]*Patterson* v. *Carey,* 41 N.Y.2d 714, 723 (1977).
[12]40 N.Y.2d at 736.

Such a conclusion may be "elementary" in New York, but it may not be elementary or even correct in all jurisdictions, and a careful review of relevant judicial precedent in the jurisdiction concerned may be in order if one is making an exhaustive inquiry into the security behind a particular debt issuance. One intriguing example is the U.S. government, as its powers have been viewed by the federal courts. Two Supreme Court cases indicate a fundamentally different stance from that voiced by the New York Court of Appeals.

The first case concerned an act of Congress which repealed a federal insurance program. Congress had sought to make such repeal retroactive to the extent of denying payment on existing valid claims under policies issued pursuant to the program. The Court said that this amounted to an unconstitutional deprivation of property and was therefore void. In passing, however, it said that Congress could have achieved the result it wanted if it had employed the tactic of denying the courts jurisdiction to hear any suit for enforcement of an affected claim: "Although consent to sue was thus given when the [insurance] policy [was] issued, Congress retained the power to withdraw the consent at any time. For consent to sue the United States is a privilege accorded [and] may be withdrawn. . . . [I]mmunity from suit is an attribute of sovereignty which may not be bartered away . . . when the United States creates rights in individuals against itself, it is under no obligation to provide a remedy through the courts."[13]

The second instance was the famous "Gold Clause Case."[14] The Court's decision in this case resulted in holders of certain U.S. bonds receiving billions of dollars less than what was due to them under the terms of the bonds. The bonds at issue stated quite specifically that they were to be paid in dollars equal to the gold value of the dollar at the time of issuance, and were thus to be safe against any subsequent devaluation of the dollar in terms of gold. In 1933, however, the dollar had been devalued to 60 percent of its former value in gold, and Congress had passed a statute to the effect that such antidevaluation clauses in U.S. bonds were void. The Court held that the statute was unconstitutional as a repudiation of a federal obligation, but denied any remedy in the way of damages or otherwise. Such denial was based on other statutes, held valid by the Court, which prohibited gold ownership by private individuals (except in certain instances) and which, the Court held, had the side effect of reducing to zero the amount of damages that otherwise would have been available. The above *Lynch* case was cited in connection with a general discussion of the ability of the government to alter or destroy the possibility of enforcing a right in instances where it could not constitutionally destroy the right itself.

---

[13]*Lynch* v. *United States*, 292 U.S. 571, 581–82 (1934).
[14]*Perry* v. *United States*, 294 U.S. 330 (1935).

PROVISIONS OF A TYPICAL REVENUE BOND INDENTURE OR RESOLUTION

Pledge of Revenues and Other Assets—Flow of Funds

As stated earlier, payment of a revenue bond issue is dependent upon a particular source of funds, not upon any general governmental commitment to provide the amount needed for payment. It is therefore essential that the funds flowing from such source be firmly allocated exclusively for such payment, for building up required reserves, and for operating the project or program which generates the funds, except for any amount which because of its surplus nature is permitted to be applied to other uses. Such exclusive allocation is achieved by means of (1) formally pledging all funds flowing from the source as security for the bonds; (2) specifying the manner of their application, including restrictions on the alternative application of any surplus; and (3) covenanting not to apply any of such funds except as so specified.

The source of funds standing behind an issuance of revenue bonds usually comprises the receipts received in respect of some facility or enterprise (e.g., an electric power plant or system built with bond proceeds) or program (e.g., a veteran's mortgage subsidy program). As such revenues are received, they immediately become subject to the pledge established by the indenture or resolution securing the bonds. Indeed, it is typically provided in the indenture or resolution that such revenues are received by the issuer to be held in trust for the benefit of the bondholders, to be applied solely as specified in the indenture or resolution. In accordance with this quasifiduciary relationship, it is provided that, upon receipt of the revenues, they are to be deposited in a "trust fund" which is usually given some name such as the "Revenue Fund."

The indenture or resolution usually provides that moneys may be withdrawn from such fund (which would include any withdrawal from any bank account containing fund moneys) only for certain purposes and, in certain instances, only upon presentation of a requisition or certificate setting forth the purpose and the amount of the withdrawal. Such a requisition would be presented to some public official responsible for overseeing the fund, or to a bank or trust company appointed trustee under the indenture or resolution.

A typical allowed purpose for withdrawals is the payment of salaries to personnel of the issuer, together with other operating expenses of the project or program. Often, instead of having every such payout involve the procedures associated with a withdrawal from the fund, estimated operating expenses for the ensuing month or quarter will be withdrawn from the fund in a lump sum at the beginning of such month or quarter, the excess of such estimate over the amount actually expended during the mouth or quarter to be returned to the fund or credited to the amount to be withdrawn for the next month or quarter.

Other "trust funds" established by the indenture or resolution can include a special fund to accumulate the moneys necessary for the next upcoming debt service payment, and a fund into which is deposited the portion of original bond proceeds, if any, that is supposed to represent capitalized interest payments.

In addition to the funds described above, the indenture or resolution will often provide for one or more reserve funds, moneys from which can be withdrawn only to pay principal of or interest on the bonds if other sources are insufficient, or to redeem them in accordance with the terms of the indenture or resolution, including a redemption at the option of the issuer. It is sometimes provided that certain reserve fund moneys may be applied to operating expenses if other sources of money are insufficient.

Dilution by Issuance of Parity Bonds

A "closed" indenture or resolution is one under which no further bonds may be issued after the first issuance. This assures that the flow of revenues and other security standing behind the bonds will not have to be shared with other bonds. An "open" indenture allows for future issuances, but usually only upon conditions intended to ensure against a harmful dilution of the security for the bonds already outstanding. It is often the case that such an open indenture or resolution constitutes a better security for the original bonds, for the same reason that two or more farmers carrying eggs together to market might be wisest to distribute them in one another's baskets.

In the case of an open indenture, the conditions to be met for each additional issuance are cast usually in the form of certificates which must be rendered by this or that official. Some of these certificates relate to financial matters such as protection against dilution (referred to in the preceding paragraph). Most, however, are of a legal nature and are intended to ensure that the bonds to be issued are within the issuer's legal power, that all the proper steps have been taken to issue them, and that all security arrangements that are supposed to stand behind the bonds are themselves within the issuer's legal power and have been validly entered into. A further certificate is usually required to ensure that the bonds qualify for federal tax exemption. In addition to such certificates, the issuer will usually be required to secure legal opinions from independent counsel as to the legality of the issuance and of the underlying security arrangements, and as to such matters as federal tax exemption.

Covenants—Outside Security

The basic promise of an issuer of revenue debt is, of course, to pay principal and interest as they become due. Such promise is set forth explicitly in, and is embodied by, the bonds. Normally, however, this promise will not be enough to make an issue of revenue bonds attractive to investors. Other promises will be inserted into the indenture or resolution securing the bonds, their purpose being to ensure that steps will be taken prior to the due dates for principal and interest so that the issuer will remain in good financial health, or to ensure that it does not engage in activities which would endanger such good financial health. For example, in an issue the proceeds of which are to be spent building a facility the revenues from which are to pay principal and interest on the issue, the issuer might covenant that the facility be insured against fire and other casualties (including reference to the specific type and extent of coverage).

Many issues of revenue bonds are for the purpose of lending the proceeds to a third party which is then to spend them to build a facility which it will own. Such bonds are secured by the principal and interest payments to be made by the third party on such loan, which normally will be set to match, in timing and amount, the principal and interest payments to be made on the bonds. The most obvious example of the foregoing is, of course, an issue of industrial revenue bonds, in which the third party is a private company. Sometimes, however, the third party is another public entity.

Instead of a relending of bond proceeds, an industrial revenue bond issue will sometimes be structured so that the facility to be built with the proceeds is owned by the public entity which issued the bonds and is leased by such entity to the private company involved. In such an arrangement, the lease payments will, as in the case of a relending of bond proceeds, be set to match in timing and amount the payments of principal and interest due on the bonds. Alternatively, the facility may be sold to the company on an installment basis, the scheduled installments likewise set to match payments due on the bonds. Such arrangements can also exist between the issuer and another public entity. In many states, various constitutional limitations preclude the state from borrowing all the money it needs for state office facilities. A typical solution is for a separate public entity to issue revenue bonds the proceeds from which are used to build the facilities in an arrangement of the type alluded to in an example earlier in this chapter (but structured so as to avoid the constitutional problems described in the example). The facilities are then leased to the state, which thus serves as the third party, with the rental payments made by the state being used to pay principal and interest on the bonds.

No matter which of the above arrangements is chosen for a particular issue, there is usually no direct relationship between the company (or the public entity serving as the third party) and the bondholders, except sometimes in the form of a guaranty of the bonds. This means that any covenants made by the company (or such third-party public entity) constitute promises only to the issuer. As a result, the issuer could theoretically sign a further agreement with the company (or such third-party public entity) altering or even abolishing such covenants. Normally, however, the indenture or resolution securing the bonds will prevent the issuer from agreeing to any such alteration or abolition, at least with respect to certain of the covenants, without the consent of a specified percentage of the bondholders.

With increasing frequency these days, an issue of revenue bonds will be backed up by either a letter of credit from a bank or an insurance policy. When this is done, the bondholders receive a payment directly from the bank or insurance company if the issuer lacks funds to pay principal or interest. The indenture or resolution securing such bonds will usually contain covenants by the issuer to pay any fees or premiums owed to the bank or insurance company (unless they are prepaid "up front" for the life of the issue) and otherwise to do nothing that would result in the loss of the letter or policy. Any such covenants, however, are of very limited value to the bondholders, since by the time the letter or policy would come into play (when the bonds are in default), the issuer could easily be in violation of such covenants. Accordingly, the letter of credit or insurance policy must, in order to provide true protection, be issued under such circumstances that nothing the issuer might do or omit doing, including nonpayment of fees or premiums, can result in a diminution of the bank's or insurance company's obligations under the letter or policy.

Another kind of covenant often contained in an indenture or resolution—a covenant unrelated to the financial health of the issuer—is that the issuer will comply with all provisions of the Internal Revenue Code and regulations of the Treasury promulgated thereunder to maintain the tax-exempt status of the bonds. Particular attention in this regard is often focused on the arbitrage regulations.

Redemption and Other Terms

It is not uncommon for an issue of revenue bonds to have five or six different sets of redemption provisions, each set related to an occurrence or a list of occurrences (including, in the case of sinking fund provisions, the mere passage of time). Upon the happening of each such occurrence, the indenture or resolution will specify whether the bonds (or a certain percentage thereof) may be redeemed at the option of the issuer or, as the case may be, at the option of the holder or at the option of either the issuer or the holder. In the case of sinking fund redemptions and many other instances, the indenture or resolution will specify that a specified portion of the bonds must be redeemed no matter who may desire it. A common provision in an issue of bonds to be paid from revenues from a project constructed from proceeds of the bonds is that redemption of the whole issue becomes mandatory if the project is called off prior to completion, is abandoned following completion, or is destroyed before or after completion (unless it is to be rebuilt with insurance proceeds). In addition, a partial redemption may be mandatory if surplus construction moneys representing bond proceeds remain after construction has been completed.

There is usually a provision which allows the issuer to redeem the bonds simply if the issuer desires to. Usually, however, a time delay is provided before this can be done, and the redemption price for this kind of redemption usually is set, for the first year in which such redemption becomes permissible, at a figure greater than 100 percent of the principal amount of each bond to be redeemed, such price to decline year by year until 100 percent is reached. It should be noted that when a bond dealer or someone else says that a given bond is "callable beginning in 1990 at 105 percent," he is usually referring only to the optional redemption provision just described, and the bond may well under certain conditions be redeemable well before 1990 and at a price of only 100 percent.

Defeasance

Sometimes the pledges, covenants, and other provisions of an indenture or resolution come to impose burdens beyond those envisioned at the time when the bonds were issued. At other times, as in the Port Authority case, they interfere with new ideas or proposed initiatives on the part of the issuer or of the state or local government which is parent to the issuer.

In all but a few special instances, such pledges and covenants will terminate if the issuer redeems all the outstanding bonds of the affected issue or issues or pays them at maturity. Moreover, an indenture or resolution will usually provide that such pledges and covenants will terminate prior to maturity, without the bonds being redeemed, if the issuer deposits with the trustee appointed under the indenture or resolution a sum of money which is large enough to pay the principal of all the bonds when they do mature, or the redemption price (par or otherwise) earlier if the bonds will by then be redeemable and the issuer instructs the trustee to redeem them. Such amount must also be sufficient to pay all interest which will become payable during the period from the date of the deposit until the date of maturity or, if the bonds are to be redeemed, the date of the redemption.

The foregoing would be of limited utility were it not for a further provision in most indentures and resolutions. Such provision is that, in lieu of depositing a sum of money, the issuer may deposit a quantity of U.S. government securities the scheduled principal and interest payments on which are enough to assure absolutely that the trustee will have enough money on hand to pay the bonds at maturity or on the date of redemption and to make all interest payments in the interim. Such depositing of cash or securities, and the resulting termination of the pledges and covenants in an indenture or resolution, is called a "defeasance" of the bonds. The provisions governing defeasance are usually set forth in a separate article of the indenture or resolution.

The Trustee and Default Provisions

An indenture or resolution will normally appoint some bank or trust company as trustee. The duties of the trustee are generally fourfold: (1) as guardian and administrator of the pledged trust funds; (2) as registrar for the bonds in connection with transfers and lost or stolen bonds; (3) as the person who ascertains the fulfillment of the conditions precedent to future issuances in the case of an open indenture and similar technical matters; and (4) as the person who represents the collective interests of the bondholders in exercising available remedies in the event of default by the issuer, or in monitoring compliance with covenants or otherwise representing such collective interest prior to default. Sometimes, however, the state constitution or applicable state statutes give some or all of such functions to a designated state official instead of allowing them to be performed by a trustee.

Default by the issuer is normally given a technical definition in the indenture or resolution, so as to embrace not only nonpayment (sometimes after an allowed grace period) of principal or interest when due but also (sometimes after a grace period commencing with a notice from the trustee concerning the event in question) nonobservance of covenants or of financial tests on the part of the issuer or a third party (the company in industrial revenue issues), loss or destruction of pledged or certain nonpledged assets (often the facility financed), bankruptcy of the issuer or the third party, and so forth. Upon any such "event of default," a set of remedies becomes available to the trustee, though certain kinds of remedies may be restricted to certain kinds of defaults. One remedy often included is the power to accelerate the bonds—i.e., to declare all unpaid principal to be due

immediately, without regard to maturity date. A major purpose behind such an acceleration is to prevent assets of the issuer which
might be available to help pay the bonds from going to pay other
creditors of the issuer whose claims would come due before the bonds
were it not for such acceleration.

CONCLUSION

The foregoing discussion demonstrates the need for the participation of experienced bond counsel in any tax-exempt revenue bond offering. Proper legal representation is important to assure the investor
and the analyst that the revenue bond issue conforms to federal and
state requirements, that it will be accorded tax-exempt status, and
that the indenture will contain adequate protective covenants and
other provisions.

Credit Analysis of
Municipal Bonds

Section THREE

General Obligation Bonds*

CHAPTER 8

Sylvan G. Feldstein, Ph.D.
Senior Municipal Specialist
Merrill Lynch, Pierce, Fenner & Smith, Inc.

INTRODUCTION

General obligation bonds are secured by the pledge of the issuer's taxing powers (limited or unlimited). More commonly the general obligation bonds of local governments are paid from ad valorem property taxes and other general revenues.

It should be noted that there is no universally accepted theory of general obligation bond credit analysis. To a considerable extent it remains more an art than a science. It requires individual judgment and personal interpretation of a range of important factors. The following material provides some simple, clear guidelines for the investor or bond analyst to consider when reviewing a general obligation (GO) bond.

Information relating to the analysis of GO bonds may be grouped

---

*Derived in part from a chapter co-authored by Sylvan G. Feldstein in *Municipal Bonds* by R. Lamb and S. Rappaport, copyright © 1980 by McGraw-Hill, Inc. The author would also like to thank Walter Carroll of the Merrill Lynch municipal research department for his helpful suggestions.

into four categories: (1) debt, (2) budget, (3) revenues, and (4) the economics of the community.

These four categories, with slight modifications, may be applied to the GO bonds issued by states, counties, school districts, towns, or cities.

BASIC INFORMATION REQUIRED WHEN ANALYZING A GENERAL OBLIGATION BOND

On the Issuer's Debt Structure

The first question to ask is: What is the total amount of GO debt outstanding? This figure should include all bonds and notes secured by the general taxing powers, limited and unlimited, of the issuer.

Several issuers have limited-tax GO bonds outstanding. These bonds are secured by the limited power of the issuer to raise taxes. For example, while King County, Washington, issues unlimited-tax GO bonds, it also issues limited-tax bonds. The limited-tax bonds, although they are general obligations, are secured only by the revenues generated by a property tax that cannot exceed $1.80 per $1,000 of assessed value in the county. Nonetheless, when calculating the issuer's true total GO debt, the limited-tax bonds and the unlimited ones, which are secured by the full taxing powers of the issuer, are initially combined.

Information is also required on the GO debt trend for the previous five years. These figures show whether or not the issuer has been using debt to an increasing degree, possibly during periods of local economic adversity and decline when capital improvements are not required. An increase in debt is not automatically negative, however, if one takes into consideration the impact of inflation and the genuine needs of the community. On the one hand, many growing suburban communities have shown rapid increases in debt as they financed the construction of water and sewer systems, new roads, and schools. On the other hand, some declining areas (such as New York City) have turned in the past to GO debt as a way of financing budget deficits and priming the local economy. While determining the GO debt trend for five years, the issued GO notes must also be consistently reported. If the record of debt outstanding at the end of the issuer's fiscal year is used, the notes that were issued and redeemed during the course of the year could be overlooked. The analyst must determine the bonds outstanding at the year-end and must also indicate the notes sold during the course of the year.

Security for General Obligation Debt.   The security behind the GO bonds sold by states, counties, school districts, and municipalities usually includes a pledge that the issuer will use its full taxing powers to see that the bondholder receives bond principal and interest when due. Under various state and local government constitutions and charters, providing such security usually involves the levy of unlimited taxes on property, a first claim by the bondholder to monies in the issuer's general fund, and the legal duty or pledge of the governing body to pass any legislation needed to increase revenues.

Double-Barreled Bonds. While most GO bonds are secured by only the general taxing powers of the issuer, and by whatever monies are available in the issuer's general fund, some bonds are also secured by earmarked revenues which flow outside the general fund. For example, the state of Illinois issues GO Transportation, Series A bonds. These bonds are general obligations of the state and are secured by the gasoline taxes in the state's road fund. Because, as a matter of actual practice, debt service is paid from monies in the road fund, the bonds are considered to have a "double-barreled" security. If all other factors are equal, bonds having a double-barreled security should be considered a stronger credit than the issuer's straight GO bonds.

Net General Obligation Debt. In order to determine the debt ratios, it is necessary to determine the amount of the issuer's GO bonds that is not double-barreled, or supported by earmarked revenues, by reviewing the accounting reports of the issuer. While certain funds outside the issuer's general fund may be used to pay debt service, the source of monies in the specific fund will determine whether the bonds are operationally double-barreled or just straight GOs. For example, New York State has issued GO bonds for housing that are secured by monies in the state's housing fund. Although the annual debt service on these bonds is indeed paid out of the housing fund, the bonds are not genuinely self-supporting (or double-barreled). This peculiarity arises because most of the monies in the fund are appropriated by the state for grants to local governments; these monies are credited to the fund by the state comptroller for payments owed the fund by the local governments.

The net GO figure should include all those bonds that require monies from the general fund to pay debt service. The purpose of the figure is to show the amount of GO debt that the general unrestricted taxing powers of the issuer supports. Some analysts would deduct from this figure the amount of monies at year-end in any sinking funds or debt reserves. Since it is not always certain what these reserves are invested in, we would tend not to deduct these amounts from the debt figures.

Overlapping and Underlying Debt. Still another debt figure necessary for the analyst to determine is the total amount of GO debt for which the issuer's taxpayers are responsible. If the issuer is a municipality, the overlapping debt would include the GO debt of its county, school district(s), and special districts such as water and sewage authorities which have issued GO bonds secured by unlimited property taxes. In determining how much of a county's outstanding GO debt must be included in the municipality's overlapping debt, the analyst must determine the percentage of the full real estate property values of the municipality vis-à-vis that of the county. That percentage represents the county's overlapping debt that pertains to the municipality's real property taxpayers. Similar approaches are used to determine the overlapping debt of school districts and special districts applicable to the municipality's taxpayers.

When the issuer is a county government, the same procedure is used to determine the applicable GO debt of other jurisdictions. Here, however, the debt is underlying debt and not overlapping debt, though the concept is the same.

An analyst must be careful in determining what overlapping or underlying debt the taxpayer is indeed responsible for paying. For example, while Baltimore County, Maryland, physically surrounds the city of Baltimore, its jurisdiction stops at the city's borders. And the city is not legally considered to be within the county's jurisdiction. Therefore, taxpayers in the city of Baltimore are not responsible for the county's GO bonds, and the county taxpayers are not legally responsible for the city's GO bonds.

State Debt. Normally, when determining the overlapping or underlying debt of school districts, counties, or municipalities, the GO debt of their state is not considered. This is because states, unlike local governments, have broader revenue sources and potential powers under their constitutions to pay debt service on their GO bonds without reverting to property taxes, which are the major revenue sources of most local governments. Delaware is the one state which may be an exception. Because of the state's small size and because the state provides many of the services (such as highway and school construction) which in other states are provided by local governments, it may be prudent to use the Delaware state debt in determining the overlapping debt figure for the local units of government.

Special Debt. Besides the net GO debt and the overlapping or underlying GO debt, there are also three other debt obligations that many states, counties, and municipalities incur and which should be considered part of the issuer's debt load. They are outstanding leases, "moral obligation" commitments, and unfunded pension liabilities.

Lease Debt.[1] Many states and local governments have entered into leases or lease/purchase agreements for the construction of new buildings, highway repairs, and rentals for office space and data pro-

---

[1]For a more detailed discussion of lease bonds, see Cases 2 and 17.

cessing computers. The rental payments come from various sources, including general-fund revenues, earmarked tax revenues, student tuition, patient fees, and amusement park fees. In some instances, such as lease/rentals of computer equipment, the leases are also secured by the equipment itself. This area of borrowing has become increasingly important in the last 20 years. As examples of the magnitude of this debt, in 1982 alone New York City's lease payments totaled $112 million, and the total lease/rental debt of New York City was over $870 million. While the New Yorkers are leaders in the issuance of such debt, most GO debt issuers have lease/rental debt outstanding. Since this debt usually has a legal claim to the general revenues of the issuer, analysts should include it in their overall debt figures as well.

Moral Obligation Debt.[2] During the last 20 years many states have been issuing moral obligation municipal bonds. These bonds, structured as revenue bonds with one-year debt reserves, carry a potential state liability for making up deficiencies, should any occur, in their debt reserves. Under most state laws, if a drawdown of the reserve occurs, the bond trustee must report to the governor and state budget director the amount used. The state legislature in turn may appropriate the requested amount, though there is no legally enforceable obligation to do so. Bonds with this makeup provision are the so-called moral obligation bonds.

Unfunded Pension Liabilities. Still another special debt figure that the analyst must develop is the current unfunded pension liability of the issuer: What is the difference between the expected assets of the public employee pension system at current annual contribution rates and the future benefits to be paid out to the issuer's employees? In assessing this figure the analyst must determine when the pension system was last audited, who performed the audit, and what the auditor's assumptions were concerning (among other factors) the average age of public employee entry and retirement. The credit analyst should also determine whether the issuer has a plan in operation to reduce the unfunded liability and, if so, how long it will take (10, 20, or 50 years, for example) to eliminate the liability. Still another question to raise concerning pensions is their legal basis: Can pension benefits unilaterally be reduced by the local governments? Such reduction is allowed in some jurisdictions but not in others. An example of the latter would be New York State, where the state constitution prevents the reduction of pension benefits once they are granted to the public employees. Therefore, the unfunded pension liabilities of local governments in New York must be taken much more seriously than in states where such guarantees do not exist.

---

[2]For further discussion, see Chapter 30.

For purposes of determining the special debt figure—which represents the potential liability in a worst-case environment—the lease obligations, the moral obligations, and the unfunded pension liabilities are combined, and one figure is used.

Revenue Debt. Besides the general obligation, special lease, moral obligation, and pension liability, many governing bodies have also issued revenue bonds which are secured solely by the monies generated by the revenue-producing enterprises. Municipalities have issued water and sewer revenue bonds, and many states have issued toll road revenue bonds, most of which do not have a legal claim to the general taxing powers of the respective municipality or state. Nonetheless, the credit analyst should tabulate the issuer's outstanding revenue debt. Though this debt is not factored into the debt ratios, it is important to know the total borrowing activities of the issuer.

Future Bond Sales. While some GO issuers have small amounts of debt outstanding, they may be required to borrow significant amounts of money in the future. In order to factor this possibility into the credit assessment, the analyst must learn what the future financing plans are. As an example, a municipality that will have to issue large amounts of GO bonds to finance the construction of mandatory federal improvements for pollution control is of weaker quality than one that has already met the standards.

However, not all large-scale programs of capital construction are in themselves undesirable. Issuers that are borrowing heavily today to construct their physical infrastructures (such as new roads, schools, and water systems) may be better long-term investments than those issuers who have postponed making improvements and, as a result, have much less GO debt outstanding. The latter may very well face the prospect of extensive capital expenditures somewhere down the road in order to remain attractive for continued economic development and to meet the service demands of the taxpayers.

As an example, in the early 1960s the GO bonds of Newark, New Jersey, and Parsippany-Troy Hills, New Jersey, were rated by Moody's as A and Baa, respectively; Standard & Poor's gave the rating BBB for both. Newark was seen as a mature, developed community with little need for additional borrowing. In contrast, Parsippany-Troy Hills, a growing, youthful suburban community, had relatively higher borrowing needs in order to finance new streets and schools. Thus at the time, Moody's considered Parsippany-Troy Hills to be a weaker credit than Newark, but Standard & Poor's considered both communities comparable. Yet today, Moody's and Standard & Poor's credit ratings for Newark are Baa and BBB, respectively, and their credit ratings for Parsippany-Troy Hills are A-1 and A+, respectively. The credit analyst must make a qualitative judgment on the future of the issuer 10 to 15 years later—no matter how difficult or speculative it is to do so, and regardless of how sizable the financing plans for current or future bonds appear to be.

Debt Limits. For many years, some credit analysts viewed debt limits as major safeguards for the bondholder. Those GO debt limits which are restricted by the need for electoral approvals before bonds can be sold are still meaningful checks on excessive borrowing. However, debt limits which are tied to percentages of the issuer's real estate wealth have become less significant as a result of New York City's experience in 1974–75. In spite of state constitutional debt limits, the city had sold, over many years, amounts of GO bonds which were beyond its financial means and yet several billion dollars below its debt limits. The city's resulting fiscal crisis revealed the weakness of debt limits as a real safeguard for the bondholder.

On the Issuer's Budgetary Operations

The second general category of information required by the analyst is related to the budget. Here, we are concerned about questions of executive powers, budgetary control, public services, accounting history, and the potential impacts of taxpayer revolts.

Powers of the Chief Executives. Learning the form of government of the GO bond issuer is very important to the analyst. Governments that have strong executive systems (i.e., strong governors, strong county executives, or strong mayors) are, in general, preferred to those that do not, because strong, centralized executive systems have the potential to deal quickly and efficiently with unforeseen budgetary and economic problems. Perhaps the importance of this is best seen in the city of Cleveland. In 1978, Cleveland had a weak chief executive with very little power beyond his access to the press.[3] His limitations included: the need for electoral approval for increasing property and personal income taxes that were above the state-allowed levels; no control over many of the city's essential services; limited appointment and removal powers; and a term of office which at the time was only two years, so that he had to consistently focus on reelection strategies rather than policy directives. As a result of these limitations and the city's overall economic and political problems, the city defaulted in 1978 on its GO notes.

In the 1970s, the cities of Detroit, Baltimore, Newark, and Boston all had similar economic problems—in the cases of Newark and Detroit, economic problems far more serious than those of Cleveland—but they all managed to avoid defaults. One possible reason why these cities have been able to manage their problems is that they

---

[3]For a further discussion, see Case 14.

have strong executive forms of government, whereas Cleveland did not.

There are three basic components of a strong executive, regardless of whether the chief executive is a governor, county executive, or mayor. First, the chief executive must have at least a four-year term of office with the right to seek reelection without limit. Second, the chief executive must control three aspects of the annual budgetary process: (1) the preparation of the budget, which is presented to the legislative body for approval; (2) line-item veto powers over the approved budget; and (3) control over the implementation of the budget, including the power to determine allotment periods, to fill personnel lines, and to award contracts. The third component is the ability to control the bureaucracy through extensive personnel appointment and removal authority.

Services Directly Provided. In order to project future budgetary demands, it is necessary to determine the services which are provided by the issuer. In general, issuers that provide a full range of services have a weaker credit quality than those which provide only basic minimum services. For a municipality, basic services include utilties (such as water and sewage treatment), garbage pickups, street maintenance, police and fire protection, and recreational programs. Large municipalities that provide additional services—including extensive welfare programs, hospital care, housing, mass transportation, and higher education—usually have bureaus and departments that are captives of pressure groups which demand these services without regard to budgetary consequences.

General Budget Appropriations by Function. While many issuers provide the same services, quantitative distinctions should be made in order to determine what the budgetary priorities of the issuer really are. This is best done by determining the general budget appropriations in the current fiscal year by function, amount, and percentage of the total budget appropriation.

Accounting Procedures and Funds. The most desirable accounting system is known as a "modified accrual system." Generally, in this system revenues are only considered received when they are physically in the issuer's general fund. At the same time, expenditures are deemed to have occurred when contracts and other legal liabilities are entered into by the issuer, even though warrants for payment of these obligations may not have been made yet. The modified accrual system is the most honest and fiscally conservative accounting system. Many issuers, however, prefer other accounting systems which allow their governing bodies to have greater flexibility in the budgetary process. For example, for issuers who define revenues to include monies that are due but not necessarily received, a budget can quickly be balanced: The governing body levies a new tax or increases projected revenues from existing taxes and then adds the new amount to the revenue side of the budget. On the expenditure side, those issuers that use "cash expenditure accounting" can easily close their fiscal year with a budget surplus by just delaying actual payments until after the new fiscal year has begun.

Audit Procedures. Auditing is yet another important area of concern for the investor and bond analyst. The best auditing procedure is for the issuer to be audited annually by an outside certified public accountant (CPA) who applies generally accepted accounting principles, using the modified accrual system of accounting. For sound cost-related reasons, however, many issuers (states, in particular) do not have such audits performed.

If no audit by an outside CPA is commissioned, the next best safeguard for the bondholder is to have the issuer's accounts annually audited by a public official who is politically independent of the chief executive. Many states and municipalities have treasurers and comptrollers who are also elected public officials or appointees of the legislative branch. The institutional rivalry and competition between these elected public officials can provide checks and balances in the accounting areas.

Budget Trends. In order to determine the overall budgetary soundness of the issuer, it is necessary for the analyst to determine the revenues and expenditures of the issuer's general fund and all operating funds for at least a three-year period. This examination will show whether the issuer has balanced budgets, budget surpluses, or budget deficits. Clearly, those communities that have yearly budget deficits are serious investment risks, regardless of how positive the other analytical variables may appear to be.

Still another related question to ask is: What was the cash fund balance in the issuer's general fund at the end of the most recent fiscal year? While some issuers may show budget deficits during the previous three-year period, the deficits may be planned in order to reduce a fund balance surplus. Surpluses should accumulate in state governments which have elastic revenue structures made up of income and sales taxes. During expansions in the local economies or during inflationary periods, these revenues will greatly increase. Prudent states should build substantial, though not particularly excessive budget surpluses during such periods. They can then draw upon these surpluses either to meet revenue shortfalls caused by recessions or to meet increased wage and salary demands caused by inflation. Unfortunately, because of tax revolts, many states in the early 1980s—California, Oregon, and Washington, among others—have returned their state surpluses to their taxpayers. During recessionary periods these states have experienced severe budgetary stresses.

Short-Term Debt as a Percentage of the General Fund Receipts of the Prior Year. In order to determine how well the issuer matches revenue flows to expenditure flows, it is necessary to determine the percentage of short-term debt in relation to the issuer's general fund revenues of the prior year. The short-term debt does not include the issuer's bond anticipation notes (BANs), but does include both tax anticipation notes (TANs) and revenue anticipation notes (RANs). When committed to policies that require them to borrow large amounts of money to meet expenditure schedules, such issuers are clearly less attractive than issuers that have coordinated expenditure flow with revenue flow so as to minimize the need for issuing annual short-term debt. Of course, it should be noted that some issuers borrow short-term in order to generate additional General Fund revenues through arbitrage. That is, the interest rate on the note proceeds which are invested in U.S. bills is greater than the interest rate that must be paid to the GO noteholders.

Budgets and Taxpayer Revolts. In looking at budget trends, the analyst must also assess the potential impacts of newly enacted or anticipated budget and tax limitation measures. Examples of these include (1) the 5 percent "cap" laws in New Jersey, which since 1976 have limited the annual budget increases of the local governments to not more than 5 percent and (2) Proposition 13 in California, which significantly restricted local property tax revenue growth, the issuance of new GO bonds, and other functions. While each measure must be carefully reviewed, it can be said in general that taxpayer attempts to reduce taxes and government expenditures on the local levels in the long run have positive benefits for GO bonds. At the same time, these measures may have negative consequences for the overlapping GO bonds of the state governments. On the local level, such restrictions on budget expenditures and tax collections can result in reductions in some municipal services; these restrictions can also provide governing bodies and budget directors with the legal weapons and supportive political climates for resisting constituent demands for increased services and for bargaining with their organized local public employees—i.e., with the unions representing fire fighters, police, schoolteachers, etc. In the last 15 years, the militancy of these unions has been very costly. Since approximately two thirds of the annual expenditures by local governments are for salaries, pensions, and related purposes, curbs in these areas can be very beneficial in slowing down the escalating costs of local governments.

While the political activities and effectiveness of public employee unions and other pressure groups have lessened at the local government level, they may be correspondingly increased at the state government level. This pressure results from their attempts to have the states provide increased state aid to local governments or to have the state governments begin to finance and operate public programs that were originally the responsibility of the local governments. An example of this development is in California. Since the enactment of Proposition 13 in 1978 and as a result of increased political pressures, the funds that the state raised were used to replace the funds that localities were no longer permitted to raise. One result was that the percentage of certain local government budgets financed by local revenues decreased at the expense of the state's own budget surplus. From a long-term point of view the state's GO bonds should weaken in security as a result of this development, since its budgetary reserves have already declined dramatically.

When looking at both the GO bonds of the local governments and those of the states, credit analysts must determine both the direct and the indirect implications of specific tax and budget restrictions. This is important in order to determine in a budgetary sense who benefits from the specific restrictions, who is not affected, and who is hurt. Obviously, to answer these questions analysts must determine the relationships and interdependencies between pressure groups, such as public employee unions, and political parties and leaders. Credit analysts invite criticism by speculating on the political implications of proposed tax restrictions, particularly if they later are proved to be incorrect. They must nonetheless offer investors their opinions of the direct and indirect political effects of the proposals.

On the Issuer's Revenue Structure

The third general category of information covers data relating to the nature of the issuer's specific types and the amounts of revenue.

Primary Revenues. The initial question is: What are the issuer's primary revenues? In general, states have the most diversified revenue sources, which can include personal income taxes, a variety of corporation and business taxes, real and personal property taxes, death and gift taxes, sales taxes, motor vehicle taxes, severance taxes, user fees, and federal grants-in-aid. The attractiveness of state bonds over those of counties, municipalities, and school districts is largely a result of the diversity of a state's revenue sources and a state's ability, under its own laws, to make its revenue base even broader.

The local governments, in contrast, rely primarily on property taxes for their revenues. Some counties and municipalities have broadened their revenue bases through sales and income taxes. Such diversification is usually very difficult for a local government unit to initiate, since state legislative approvals are normally required. Nev-

ertheless, many cities in recent years have convinced their respective
state legislatures to grant them taxing powers beyond the property
tax.

General-Fund Revenue Trends. Besides learning what the
overall primary revenue sources are, the analyst should determine
what the specific revenues have been in the issuer's general fund over
a three-year period. This is the governmental fund account in which
all unrestricted revenues which can be used for debt service are
placed. The reason for going back three years is to identify trends
that may be developing in the issuer's revenue flows.

In the case of issuers who pay debt service on their GO bonds from
a debt service fund (which, for example, may receive property taxes
that do not pass through the general fund), this fund should also be
included. The reason for separating general-fund revenues from the
restricted ones is that many revenues received by issuers, such as
certain federal grants, are restricted as to purpose and cannot be used
for debt service on GO bonds. Since many local governments, such as
school districts and municipalities, include restricted monies in their
general-fund reporting, the analyst will have to separate the unrestricted portion from the restricted portion.

For urban counties, school districts, and municipalities, real property taxes, state grants, and federal aid monies are the major sources
of revenue. In many cities, state and federal monies have displaced
the property tax as the major revenue source. In most suburban and
rural areas, the property tax is the dominant source of revenue.

On the Economy

The fourth major category of information required by the analyst
concerns the overall economic health of the issuer. Indicators of economic activity and well-being include the trends of real estate valuation, population, unemployment, and total personal income.

While separately these economic indicators provide incomplete assessments of the economic vitality of the issuer, taken as a whole they
provide clues as to the strengths and weaknesses of each community.
Obtaining the data for the informational categories is easy, since data
is available from either the local governments themselves or publications of the U.S. Department of Labor, or from business sources.

Real Estate Valuation Trend. A major index of the growth of a
community is the yearly change in its real estate value. Here, analysts are not as interested in the assessed real values, which are used
for tax purposes, as they are in the full, or market, values of the real
estate. This would only include the taxable real property. Tracking
these values over a five-year period provides a good measure of the
health of the community and can indicate a declining or stagnant

community. It is also important to keep in mind that in an inflationary environment, growth in real estate values is not enough to indicate that a community is becoming wealthier; the annual growth must be higher than the annual inflation rate.

Ten Largest Taxable Properties. In looking at counties, municipalities, and school districts, it is useful to identify the 10 largest taxable properties in terms of their full real values and business purposes. In so doing, the analyst can determine how much of the real estate base may be dependent on railroads, utilities, and private corporations. In the Northeast some of the largest real estate holdings belonged to the Penn Central Transportation Company, which for many years paid no real estate taxes on its properties. Additionally, certain communities may be dependent on one major shopping center or a durable goods manufacturing plant for most of their property taxes. The viability of that single property will determine the community's overall economic viability.

Properties: Taxable or Tax-Exempt? When reviewing counties, municipalities, and school districts, it is necessary to learn what percentages of the total real estate wealth are exempt from local property taxes. Although a municipality can add new office buildings, hospitals, and governmental structures to its inner core, their contributions to the general real estate wealth of the community will be limited if they are tax-abated or tax-exempted. A corollary is to determine the distribution of the community's taxable property by purpose: What percentage is residential, commercial, industrial, held by a utility or railroad? From these figures the analyst can determine accurately which segments of the community's real estate are carrying the burden of the property taxes.

Building Permit Trend. In looking at counties, municipalities, and school districts, another component of economic vitality is the building permit trend. Here the analyst is looking for at least a five-year record of the annual total dollar value of all permits granted by the local governmental bodies for building and construction improvement. These figures are checked to make sure that building permits for tax-exempt properties are not included. One major value of this indicator is its ability to show the degree of business confidence in the future of the local economy.

Five Largest Employers. It is important to learn who the five largest employers are in each county, municipality, or school district to be analyzed. The analyst should determine the number of workers as well as the nature of the business. In this way the analyst can determine how stable the community is and how dependent the local economy may be on one industry, such as the automobile industry in Michigan, coal mining in West Virginia, and textiles in South Carolina.

Population Trend. Another useful index for investigating states and local governments is the population trend. An increasing population usually means a growing economy, while a declining or stagnant population usually indicates economic weakness. Besides having the raw population figures, it is worthwhile to break down the population by age group and by income level. A community that has a high percentage of senior citizens may have greater political demands for municipal services and reduced property taxes than one that does not. Also, communities with large numbers of unemployed or low-income residents usually require costly social services, and these services increase the budgets of the local schools, courts, welfare systems, and police departments.

Job Trend. Employment data are very necessary to the credit analyst. A 10-year comparison of the absolute number of employed people and their percentage of the population provides another clue as to the economic direction of the area. It is also helpful to determine the distribution of the nonfarm employment for at least the most recent year. The employment categories include manufacturing; retail/ wholesale trade; services; contract construction; and federal, state, and local government employment. This breakdown of employment according to type of job helps indicate, among other things, whether or not the economy is being supported by increased governmental jobs or by a vibrant private sector.

Unemployment Trend. It is helpful to compare local unemployment trends covering at least three years. It is useful to examine both the annual unemployment rate and the average number of workers unemployed during the year. For counties, municipalities, and school districts, the comparisons should focus on the unemployment rates within the boundaries of the local area, the state, and the nation. If the unit of local government is within a metropolitan area, it is also useful to include the unemployment rates of the metropolitan area.

Economic Activity Indicators for States. When reviewing the economies of states, there are five categories of information which are particularly useful:

1. Statewide personal income trend for the past three years.
2. Statewide retail sales trend for the past three years.
3. Statewide motor vehicle registration trend for the past three years.
4. Total number of people within a state who have received welfare for the past three years.
5. Per capita personal income today, compared with the figure five years ago and with the national per capita income figures.

The information gathered for these categories will quickly show, in absolute terms and when compared with other regions of the country, whether a state is becoming wealthier.

Economic Activity Indicators for Counties. When reviewing counties, municipalities, and school districts, the analyst will find that the following seven categories of information are useful:

1. Percentage of the population in the lower-income bracket.
2. Number of residents receiving welfare.
3. Per capita income, compared with the national average.
4. Median family income.
5. Median home value.
6. Percentage of owner-occupied housing.
7. Age distribution of the population.

THE NEGATIVE INDICATORS

Perhaps the most critical short-term function of the credit analysis of GO bonds is to identify the negative trends suggesting potential problems in the fiscal stability of states and municipalities. There are four categories of negative trends:

1. Revenue-based indicators:
   a. Decreasing value of taxable property.
   b. Increasing delinquent taxes.
   c. Increasing tax rate.
   d. Decreasing number and value of building permits issued.
   e. Increasing incidence of actual revenues below budgeted amounts.
2. Expenditure-based indicators:
   a. Increasing excesses of expenditures over local revenues.
   b. Increasing expenditures in excess of total revenues.
   c. Increasing expenditures in excess of the inflation rate.
   d. Increasing incidence of actual expenditures in excess of the approved budget.
   e. Continuing increases in the amount of the unfunded portions of the pension programs.
3. Cash management indicators:
   a. Reducing aggregate short-term investments.
   b. Increasing amounts of unpaid current obligations.
4. Debt indicators:
   a. Increasing amounts of bonded indebtedness while the property values remain stagnant.
   b. Increasing need to borrow in order to meet debt service requirements.
   c. Use of long-term debt to fund operation expenditures.
   d. Year-to-year increases in the amount of short-term borrowing remaining unpaid at the end of the fiscal year.

These are general signals which indicate the potential decline in the ability of a municipality to perform its functions within fiscally sound parameters.

THE MORE IMPORTANT DEBT RATIOS

In addition to looking for possible early warning signals, the analyst should develop debt-related ratios. The value of the ratios is two-fold: (1) the ratios are among the analytical tools for evaluating the credit worthiness of the issuer's GO bonds and (2) the per capita data allow the analyst to compare bonds of different communities.

Net GO Debt per Capita. This figure represents the nonself-supporting GO bonds divided by the population. In theory, it represents the amount of debt per person that is supported by the general taxing powers of the issuer in the issuer's general fund. In general, the lower the number, the more attractive the issuer.

Net GO, and Overlapping or Underlying Debt per Capita. This ratio applies not to states but to the local units of government. It is a per capita debt figure which includes the issuer's own net GO debt as well as the GO debt of overlapping or underlying jurisdictions.

Net GO Debt as a Percentage of Full Real Estate Valuation. This percentage indicates the debt as compared with the real estate wealth as represented in the most recent real estate evaluation. This statistic is perhaps one of the most important figures for the credit analyst, since it indicates the issuer's ability to pay.

Net GO and Overlapping or Underlying Debt as a Percentage of Full Real Estate Valuation. This figure is also used for counties, municipalities, and school districts. It represents the relationship of the issuer's full real estate value to the sum of the issuer's own GO and overlapping GO debt.

Net GO Debt as a Percentage of Personal Income. For a state this figure is another major indicator of the ability of the taxpayer to support its debt. While this figure is desirable when reviewing all GO bond issuers, such data are often only available concerning states.

GO Debt Payout in 10 Years. This figure shows whether the issuer has a relatively rapid and level debt retirement schedule, which is desirable, or debt service stretched out to, say, 30 or 40 years. In some cases, payment of debt service on bonds may continue beyond the useful life of the capital projects financed by the original bond proceeds. While the debt payout schedule is not a debt ratio, it is necessary for evaluating the actual ratio figures. For example, high debt ratios may be less significant if most of the issuer's debt will be retired within 10 years. But above-average debt ratios combined with a slow debt retirement schedule certainly weakens a security substantially.

CONCLUSION

After having determined whether the GO bonds are double-barreled or not (and if so, what the quality of the specific revenue stream is); after having gathered the information about the issuer's debt structure, budget, revenue operations, and economic forces; after having checked for the negative indicators; the analyst can make a generalization about the investment quality of the bond under review. While all these elements together are important indicators of bond quality, each provides, if taken separately, only a single isolated element not in itself sufficient for full-scale analysis. Therefore, the analyst must carefully review all these indicators so as to arrive at a judicious credit conclusion concerning the degree of risk involved in purchasing an issuer's GO bonds. As noted earlier in this chapter, this evaluation process is more an art than a science. Nonetheless, we have attempted here to identify the basic background information that is required for making an overall credit assessment.

Seaport Revenue Bonds

CHAPTER **9**

Jeffrey J. Alexopulos
Vice President
T. Rowe Price Associates, Inc.

Since the initial colonies were established in the new world, both air and seaports have played a major role in the development of what are now the 50 states. Over 130 domestic seaports currently provide facilities for the import and export of cargoes to all corners of the world. Cities such as Boston, New York, San Francisco, Philadelphia, and Baltimore grew rapidly in population and wealth as overseas trade flourished in the 18th and 19th centuries. Most major urban population centers today can be identified with either a seaport or airport facility. In addition to those just mentioned, cities such as Los Angeles, Chicago, Jacksonville, Atlanta, Dallas, Houston, and Seattle have evolved in part because of the ease of transporting people and cargo from a sea- or airport. Today, most seaports and airports are operated by independent public authorities.

Ports and port authorities are integral to the growth and vitality of more than just the cities in which they are located. They are vital to the region in which they compete for the business of providing facilities necessary in the loading and unloading of cargoes for transportation by land, air, and sea. For example, coal shipped from the

Port of Baltimore benefits the coal-producing areas of West Virginia, western Maryland, Virginia, and Pennsylvania. Should the costs of dredging the Baltimore ship channel to enhance the transporting of bulk cargoes such as coal be borne entirely by the state of Maryland? What is the probability that the region's states, which will also benefit from a deeper ship channel, will provide financial support in some manner? These are several of the types of questions which may be asked in an analysis of municipal bonds issued for port purposes.

The operations of port authorities range from seaport and airport facilities to properties management, ground and mass transportation services, and the ownership of toll bridge facilities. Security for bonds issued for port development include general obligations of the city or county owner, gross revenue and net revenue pledges of the operating authority, and specific lease agreements with the benefiting company. This broad base of security and product lines necessitates review of each port authority and its operating divisions from the ground up. Thorough research can result in the purchase of a security which is generally better than the assigned ratings of the major commercial rating companies would indicate and which could outperform similar-rated securities in other sectors of the municipal bond market.

WHY THE MUNICIPAL BOND MARKET?

Section 103B(4)(d) of the Internal Revenue Code provides for the tax exemption of interest on debt issued by a municipal issuer for port-related purposes. Public port authorities have taken advantage of this provision by issuing over $5 billion of revenue and industrial development bonds. Two of the largest issuers, the Trans-Alaska Pipeline System and the Louisiana Offshore Terminal Authority, have issued bonds secured by agreements with oil companies such as Exxon, Texaco, and Atlantic Richfield. Security of these issues is tied directly to the corporations' representation in the projects. However, the majority of port-related financings are revenue bonds payable from operations of the port authority.

The interest cost savings to the steamship company or airline using a port facility becomes evident when comparing the cost of capital. For example, the Dallas–Fort Worth Regional Airport issued $100 million of joint revenue bonds dated March 1, 1982, at a cost of 13.5 percent. A portion of the proceeds will be used for new terminal facilities and related improvements to accommodate an expansion by American Airlines, Inc. A long-term taxable bond issue by American Airlines, Inc, marketed during the same time period, would probably have cost the company 17 percent or more. Thus, the 350 basis point savings to the airline can be directly attributed to rates in the tax-exempt bond market and the security provided by the Dallas–Fort

Worth airport as an operating entity whose security is not tied directly to American Airlines or any other single company. The attraction of tax-exempt bonds is quite obvious in this example. Similar savings can be realized by steamship companies who need container facilities or grain elevators, but have little exposure in or access to the capital markets. Thus, port bonds have become the source of financing for various projects. This diversification of use is also a major underpinning of the strength of port revenue bonds.

MAJOR PORT AUTHORITIES

Of the approximately 130 identifiable, publicly operated port authorities, only a few are significant issuers of tax-exempt debt. The largest port authority in terms of debt issued, tonnage, and revenues is the Port Authority of New York and New Jersey. Operations of the Port Authority include seven marine terminals, four airports, two heliports, two tunnels, four bridges, two bus terminals, the twin-tower World Trade Center in lower Manhattan, and the PATH transportation system. This diversified system ended calendar year 1980 with gross operating revenues of $648 million, net income of $104 million, total assets of $3,650 million and bonded debt of $1,931 million. The Port Authority of New York and New Jersey is an example of revenue bonds being used for projects which are secured by net revenues of the consolidated system.

Other port authorities which have been active in the municipal bond market and their areas of operations include:

The Massachusetts Port Authority (Boston-Logan International Airport, Tobin Memorial Bridge, port properties, Boston Fish Pier).

Jacksonville Port Authority (Jacksonville International Airport, Craig Airport, Port of Jacksonville).

Port of New Orleans (port properties).

Los Angeles Harbor Department (port properties).

Port of Long Beach (port properties).

Port of Oakland (Metropolitan Oakland International Airport, port properties, commercial properties).

Port of San Francisco (port properties).

Port of Portland (Portland International Airport, two general-aviation airports, port properties, commercial and industrial properties).

Port of Seattle (Sea-Tac International Airport, port properties, commercial and industrial properties).

Port of Tacoma (port properties, commercial and industrial properties).

Numerous other port facilities are financed through the use of general obligation bonds or via an umbrella financing program such as the Maryland Department of Transportation (DOT). Maryland DOT issues debt which is secured by a consolidated transportation trust fund to finance improvements to the Port of Baltimore as well as for mass transportation, roads, bridges, and airports. Little significant competitive market advantage can be derived from analyzing port bonds which are financed either from general obligation bonds of the locality owning the port or under an umbrella system. Therefore, the analyst should concentrate on independently operated and financed port authorities such as those mentioned previously.

Industrial–development bond financing has been used quite extensively for port-related purposes. These are bonds issued by public bodies for projects which are leased to private enterprise. Security is provided by the strength of the company involved in the lease agreement. The bondholder has no recourse to the public body which issued the debt if there is a default on the lease. The Trans-Alaska Pipeline System Marine Terminal in Valdez, Alaska, was financed with over $1 billion of industrial development bonds. The bonds are secured solely by lease agreements with Atlantic Richfield Co., Exxon Corporation, Mobile Oil Corporation, Phillips Petroleum Co., Standard Oil Company of Ohio, British Petroleum Company Ltd., and Union Alaska Pipeline Company. The Louisiana Offshore Terminal Authority has issued $675 million in industrial development bonds (IDB) to provide funds for the acquisition and construction of a deepwater port and related facilities located in Louisiana and the Gulf of Mexico. These bonds are payable solely from revenues derived pursuant to a financing agreement with LOOP, Inc. LOOP, Inc. will obtain revenues pursuant to a throughput and deficiency agreement with Ashland Oil, Inc.; Marathon Oil Company; Murphy Oil Corporation; Shell Oil Company; and Texaco, Inc.

IDB financing is expected to be widely used during the 1980s for the development of coal-exporting facilities. Several billion dollars of identifiable coal projects have some probability of being financed. However, every proposed facility will not be feasible. If IDB financing is used, the financial health of the company or companies involved will be key determinants of the viability of the project and ultimately of the security of the bonds. Facilities which are built using revenue bonds on speculation, without firm commitments from coal shippers, should be avoided as overcapacity or variations in worldwide coal consumption could seriously impair the payment of principal and interest on debt issued to finance such a facility.

STRUCTURE OF PORT REVENUE BOND ISSUE

Port revenue bonds have been structured depending upon the pledged security, applicable state or local laws, and market conditions. However, there are a number of elements common to most issues that are secured by revenues of the port or port system and not specific projects leased to a private enterprise. Some of these elements are described below.

Authority for Issuance. This deals with the specific authorization for the issuance of the bonds by a municipal issuer. State, city, or local legal provisions may be cited. If the issuing body has other debt outstanding, new bonds may be distinguished by a series number or letter, such as the Series B bonds or the Series 1980 A bonds.

Maturity Schedule. The maturity breakdown of the issue may be divided into serial and term bonds. During periods of market turbulance, investors' preference for short maturities can be addressed through the use of rapid paydown of principal on a term maturity via a mandatory sinking fund. For example, the city of Long Beach, California, 1980 Harbor Revenue bonds included a 10 percent term bond due May 15, 2003. The average life of this maturity will actually be 18 years versus the 23-year stated maturity because of an active sinking fund which will begin in 1992. Interest-costs savings thus can be realized by reducing the average life of an issue, due to the positively sloped yield curve which generally prevails in the municipal bond market.

Purpose of the Issue. The use of bond proceeds should be explained both descriptively and numerically. The description will include the construction period, potential users of the facilities, leases (if any are signed), etc. A numerical breakdown for the uses of a hypothetical $100 million bond issue might be as follows:

Construction	$ 82,700,000
Debt service reserve fund	14,300,000
Costs of issuance	3,000,000
	$ 100,000,000

Security. Pledged revenues, rate covenants, reserve funds, and mortgage interest may all be included as security provisions of the indenture. Pledged revenues may consist of gross or net revenues, but for purposes of analysis, net revenue is a more conservative approach. The rate covenant is involved in the maintenance of rates and charges sufficient to produce adequate cash flow to provide for debt service payment in a timely manner. It may be set so low as to provide cash flow only equal to debt service, or as high as two times or more. A rate covenant requiring net revenues of 1.5 to 1.75 times debt service is an acceptable level. The inclusion of a mortgage on the proposed project does little to enhance the security if the facility is specialized in nature and is of limited value to anyone other than the proposed tenant. The presence of, or ability to, levy property or other taxes is a significant credit enhancement.

Debt Service Reserve Fund. A debt service reserve fund typically is funded from bond proceeds at a level equal to maximum debt service required in any future year. The fund may be partially financed from bond proceeds, with the remaining requirement accumulated from operating income over a 60-month period. Monies in this fund may be used during periods of cash flow difficulties to pay principal and interest payments if other funds are not available. Any withdrawals from this fund should be required to be restored within a 60-month period from operating income. Investment earnings on monies held in the fund should be used initially to restore the fund to its required level. Any remaining investment earnings may be transferred to the unrestricted funds of the authority.

Issuance of Additional Parity Bond. Additional parity debt should not be allowed to be issued unless rate covenants have been met. A prospective-rate test should also be included. This test would be based upon estimated income and expenses after completion of the proposed project, and generally requires the same percentage coverage as the historic rate covenant.

Reports and Accounts. The authority should provide an audited financial statement within 90 days of the close of the fiscal year. The audit should be done by an independent certified public accountant and in accordance with generally accepted accounting principles.

FINANCIAL ANALYSIS OF A PORT SYSTEM

Fundamental to any analysis of port bonds is a financial analysis of the authority. Past operations provide an excellent indication as to the capability of management, flow of funds, quality of income, and importance of various product lines to overall system vitality. The ability to generate funds for plant additions from operations is essential if a port is to maintain or increase its market share in the competitive environment which now exists. Access to the capital markets can be assured only if investors have a reasonable probability of recouping their investment. Analysis of past operations is invaluable in determining the potential for future coverage of debt service which will be acceptable to bondholders. The port which has shown operating losses in recent years will have a difficult task convincing potential bondholders that the future will be any different or that a rating downgrade is not justified.

There are several financial ratios which are useful in the analysis of port revenue bond. Debt service coverage is a widely used determinate of credit strength, but it remains only the result of many other factors such as competitive position, pricing, and mix of operations.

Several financial ratios and their uses, which are helpful in port analysis, follow.

Return on Equity. The pricing-policy trends of the port can be shown using this ratio, which is net income per the income statement divided by total equity at the beginning of the fiscal year. An increasing trend is viewed positively, especially if a major capital program is expected. Wide fluctuations in the return on equity can be an indication of cyclical operations, erratic management, and legal constraints which should be explored further. Declining trends are evidence of potential credit impairment, which must be viewed negatively, as ports should be run as business and not philanthropic organizations (see Illustration 1).

Illustration 1

Net income	= $ 10,000,000
Beginning equity	= $120,000,000
Return on equity	= $ 10,000,000 ÷ 120,000,000 = 8.33%

Equity Capitalization. This ratio indicates the extent to which the port depends upon external financing for additions to plant property and equipment. A declining trend of the percentage of equity may result from a large capital improvement program financed externally over a brief number of years. A very positive situation would be a large construction program underway coupled with a relatively stable equity capitalization ratio (see Illustration 2).

Illustration 2

Liabilities (other than current)	= $450,000,000
Equity	= $120,000,000
Total capitalization	= $570,000,000
Equity capitalization	= $120,000,000 ÷ $570,000,000 = 21.05%

Cash Flow to Additions to Plant, Property, and Equipment. Operating-cash flow after debt service requirements have been met can generally be used for any purpose including capital additions. This ratio is effective in measuring the ability of the port to finance its capital requirements without resorting to outside capital. Ratios above 50 percent are excellent. Although this ratio reflects the ability to expand without outside capital, the port does not have to use cash flow for capital purposes and actually may prefer bonding as a method of matching the asset and liability for pricing purposes (see Illustration 3).

Illustration 3

Operating cash flow	= $15,000,000
Additions to plant, property, and equipment	= $25,000,000
Cash flow to plant, property, and equipment	= $15,000,000 ÷ $25,000,000 = 60.00%

Margin of Safety. Operating-cash flow after debt service has been paid divided by total operating revenues provides the analyst with a measure of the ability of the port to remain viable under a worst-case scenario. The margin of safety indicates the extent to which operating revenues could have declined or operating expenses increased in order for cash flow to be zero (see Illustration 4).

Illustration 4

Operating cash flow	= $15,000,000
Total operating revenues	= $45,000,000
Margin of safety	= $15,000,000 ÷ 45,000,000 = 33.33%

Contribution of Product Line to Net Income before Interest Expenses. Many port authorities are engaged in several different product lines. The authority may operate an airport, marine terminal, and manage properties. The contribution of each operating component to net income, before interest expense is allocated, can provide an indication of the marginal or money-losing operations as well as the foundation upon which all operations depend. Investment income is included because of the potential for dramatic swings due to interest rate movements. Typically, marine-related operations contribute the heaviest percentage to net income.

Approximate Cost of Debt. Recent years have been characterized by ever increasing and volatile interest rates. A low, embedded cost of funds could aid a port in periods characterized by high interest rates. Also, the effect of a single, high-cost bond issue can be measured if the cost of the other debt is already known (see Illustration 5).

Illustration 5

Interest expense	= $10,000,000
Average debt for the year	= $80,000,000
Approximate cost of debt	= $10,000,000 ÷ $80,000,000 = 12.5%

Financial analysis should also include trend analysis of the port activity. Tonnage, airport passengers, and property activity are all important variables in the analysis. Negative activity trends should be carefully analyzed even if financial factors appear sound. Too aggressive pricing could result in short-run financial windfalls at the expense of long-run competitive realities. Stability of activity growth is preferred to erratic growth. Long-term construction programs should not be based upon one or two years of above-average activity.

The Port of Oakland, California, provides an excellent example for the financial analysis of a port authority revenue bond. Oakland operates an airport, marine terminal facilities, and commercial properties. Table 1 is a summary of the Port's operations over a seven-year period. Trends can be discerned quickly when financial operations are placed in a columnar format such as this.

SUBJECTIVE ASPECTS TO PORT ANALYSIS

Subjective areas of analysis can include management, competitive position, future outlook, effect of actions at the state or federal level, worldwide demand for certain types of cargoes, or mode of transportation. These factors are as important as the financial factors, but much more difficult to quantify. However, no thorough analysis is complete without a review of the environment in which a port exists, from the legislation which created it to the shippers whose continued use ultimately provides for the payment of debt service on the revenue bonds issued for construction purposes.

Questions of a general nature which can be asked include:

1. What is the background of senior management?
2. How involved is the city or county government which owns the port?
3. Is the city or county drawing cash out of the authority for use in its general fund?
4. Does the authority operate or lease terminal facilities?
5. Are adequate rail and road outlets available to support increased port activity?
6. What are competitor ports doing?
7. What are the effects of proposed actions, at the state or federal levels, which relate to port operations?
8. Are capital expenditures incurred on speculation or have leases been signed with proposed tenants?
9. What other non-marine-related activities may the port become engaged in, and what would be the effect of this upon financial health?
10. What markets will provide area of growth in the future?
11. Have there been problems with labor unions in the past, and are any contracts expiring in the near future?

Table 1

PORT OF OAKLAND, CALIFORNIA
Summary of Operations
year ended June 30
($000)

	1975	1976	1977	1978	1979	1980	1981
Operating revenues:							
Airport	$ 7,074	$ 7,750	$ 8,799	$ 10,781	$ 13,517	$ 14,480	$ 16,508
Marine terminals	9,364	8,860	10,554	15,355	17,328	21,305	24,660
Properties	3,837	4,155	4,187	4,706	5,233	5,168	4,657
Total operating revenue	20,274	20,766	23,540	30,842	36,088	40,953	45,825
Operating expenses	9,970	10,152	11,471	13,880	15,926	17,775	20,198
Net operating income	10,304	10,614	12,069	16,962	20,162	23,178	25,627
Other income and expenses	2,663	3,584	2,768	2,854	4,410	6,590	7,105
Revenue available for debt service (RADS)	12,967	14,198	14,837	19,816	24,572	29,768	32,732
Principal	2,105	2,108	3,510	2,493	2,930	3,339	3,581
Interest	5,576	6,792	6,939	7,558	8,117	9,613	10,682
Total debt service	7,672	8,900	10,449	10,051	11,047	12,952	14,262
Balance for corporate purposes	5,295	5,298	4,388	9,765	13,525	16,816	18,470
Depreciation	3,166	3,529	3,928	4,608	4,839	5,329	5,725
Long-term debt	93,623	108,027	123,032	122,526	141,079	173,858	144,878
Equity capitalization	48.34%	45.95%	44.00%	46.22%	45.45%	42.59%	49.74%
Margin of safety	26.12%	25.51%	18.64%	31.67%	37.48%	41.06%	40.31%
(RADS—depreciation/debt)	13.34%	11.77%	10.25%	12.12%	13.68%	14.06%	18.64%
Approximate cost of debt	7.27%	8.25%	7.04%	7.08%	6.02%	6.10%	6.70%
Coverage of debt service	1.69×	1.60×	1.42×	1.97×	2.22×	2.30×	2.30×
Return on equity	4.84%	4.15%	3.94%	8.46%	11.83%	15.00%	12.82%
Cash flow to additions to plant, property, and equipment	51.10%	26.88%	24.44%	65.26%	69.16%	49.94%	60.82%
Contribution to net income before interest expense:							
Airport	0.11%	3.72%	3.57%	(2.29%)	7.36%	9.14%	9.48%
Marine terminal	58.06%	42.72%	54.47%	58.25%	53.58%	57.08%	60.37%
Properties	16.89%	19.21%	19.06%	16.01%	13.51%	11.64%	8.45%
Other (primarily investment income)	24.96%	34.35%	22.90%	28.03%	25.55%	22.14%	21.70%
Airport traffic	2,215	2,256	2,500	2,788	2,772	2,530	2,451
Containerized cargo tonnage	5,648	6,705	7,309	8,062	8,900	9,200	9,036

12. What type of pricing mechanism does management apply?
13. What types of capital projects are planned, and how will they be financed?

Each analyst must decide the extent of subjective factors which will be used in the analystical process. Once these nonfinancial factors are gathered, their importance will depend upon the analyst.

Integrating subjective, technical, and financial factors is the final step in the rating process. Each analyst must decide the balance between the various factors. Good financial performance may offset weak technical provisions of the bond indenture. The proximity to a dynamic service area can overcome poor management decisions. Perceptive management may reduce the effects of negative actions by the state or federal governments. Fine tuning the degree of credit worthiness is more of a thought process than numerical ordering.

The essence of an above-average port bond would include:

a. Professional management.
b. Tight technical provisions of the bond indenture (1.5 × rate covenant, debt service reserve fund, and no provision for senior debt).
b. Location which requires little dredging.
d. Diversified mix of shippers and products (not a one-industry port).
e. Construction is initiated only after users have been identified and secured, such as via a lease agreement on the proposed facility, or because historic growth trends clearly indicate a need for the new facility.
f. The port has been operated on a financially sound basis.
g. All funds generated are maintained in the port's operating funds and not remitted to the city or county general fund for use on nonport-related activities.

THE MARKETPLACE

Many of the larger, independent port authorities would compare favorably when measured by the above criteria. The ports of New York and New Jersey, Long Beach, and Oakland and the Massachusetts Port Authority are healthy operating entities. The strength of the revenue bonds issued by these agencies can be evidenced from their performance in the marketplace. The bonds have traded well because of their insulation from property tax reforms and other problems facing state and local governments, as well as limited market involvement and excellent financial performance. These port authorities also are in states with high income tax rates, which has enhanced market performances. Performance for bonds issued by these four port authorities for 1981 are shown in Table 2.

Thus, port revenue bonds can be interesting to analyze as well as very good portfolio instruments. The relatively limited number of

Table 2
Changes in Municipal Bond Interest Rates

	Yields		Basis Point Change 12/31/80 to 12/31/81	Change in Prices 12/31/80 to 12/31/81	Total Return 12/31/80 to 12/31/81
	12/31/80	12/31/81			
Prime municipal notes—6 months	7.50%	6.90%	− 60 bp	0.0%	+ 7.4%
Prime municipal notes—1 year	7.25	7.25	0	0.0	+ 7.3
Bond buyer's 20 bond index:	9.76	13.30	+354	−24.3	−14.6
Port of Oakland	10.66	11.83	+117	− 9.0	+ 1.5
Port of Long Beach	10.40	11.94	+154	−11.8	− 1.5
Massachusetts Port Authority	11.70	12.95	+125	− 9.7	+ 1.8
Port Authority of New York & New Jersey	10.04	12.82	+278	−21.9	−12.1
Long-term revenue bonds:					
30 year hospital	11.65	15.00	+335	−22.0	−10.3
35-year housing authority	11.10	14.50	+340	−23.2	−12.1
40-year electric utility	10.55	14.50	+395	−27.1	−16.6
30 year pollution control	10.10	13.875	+378	−26.7	−16.6
30-year prime general obligation	9.40	12.75	+335	−25.5	−16.1

large port authorities issuing tax-exempt revenue bonds creates an aura of scarcity value for this type of bond. Financial performance has proven to be better than what is generally perceived, even during periods of weakness in the national economy. Port authority revenue bonds have provided the investor with a safe harbor investment during the interest rate turmoil and credit-quality declines which have characterized the municipal bond market since 1978.

"Waste-to-Energy," or Resource Recovery Revenue Bonds

CHAPTER 10

Sylvan G. Feldstein, Ph.D.
Senior Municipal Specialist
Merrill Lynch, Pierce, Fenner & Smith, Inc.

WHAT ARE "WASTE–TO–ENERGY," OR RESOURCE RECOVERY REVENUE BONDS?

"Waste-to-energy," or resource recovery revenue bonds are issued to finance the construction of industrial plants to process garbage, refuse, and other solid waste. Unlike the older, conventional municipal incinerators, these plants also convert the solid waste into commercially saleable energy such as electricity or steam, recoverable products such as steel scrap, and a residue to be landfilled.

Why Are They Issued?

A driving force in the creation of waste-to-energy plants is the rising costs of energy, particularly for oil and natural gas. One ton of garbage has the same energy equivalent as approximately 1.4 barrels of oil. Additionally, the increasing scarcity of landfills and the pollution control problems of many of the older municipal incinerators have forced local governments to consider garbage disposal alternatives. For a local government a successful waste-to-energy plant, if

151

properly designed and maintained, can be economically and environ-
mentally very attractive. For these reasons, municipal bonds have
been issued to finance the construction of resource recovery plants.

How Are They Secured?

Resource recovery revenue bonds have been issued which are secured in one of two ways, or a combination thereof.

The very earliest bonds were issued in the mid-1970s, and they
were structured as project enterprise, or pure, revenue bonds. That is,
the potential underlying economics of the specific resource recovery
plants represented the bondholders' securities. The bondholders were
to be paid principally by three revenue sources:

1. "Tipping fees" per ton, paid monthly by the haulers (both municipal and private) that deliver the garbage and other solid waste
   to the plants for disposal.
2. Revenues from the steam, electricity, or refuse-derived fuel which
   is sold to electric power companies or other energy users.
3. Revenues from the sale of recoverable materials found in the garbage such as aluminum and steel scrap.

Of course, in these project-enterprise security structures, the resource recovery plants had to be operational for the bondholders to be
paid.

Some of the earlier resource recovery plants have had operational
difficulties and have had trouble paying their bondholders. In fact,
one bond, the state of Ohio's Recycle Energy Revenue Bonds Series
1976 (City of Akron, Ohio Project) has been in technical default.[1]
Most resource recovery revenue bonds issued since then have a second barrel of security. These bonds, besides being structured as pure
revenue bonds, also have "put-or-pay" types of agreements with the
user communities involved.

Under the put-or-pay type of agreement, the communities are contractually obligated to haul or to have hauled a certain amount of
garbage to the plants each year for as long as the bonds are outstanding. They must pay tipping fees, or garbage disposal charges, which
are sufficient to operate the plants as well as provide for maintenance
and all capital costs related to the facility. These tipping fees must
also include amounts sufficient to pay the bondholders regardless of
whether or not the resource recovery plants have become fully operational. This financing mechanism is also known as a "base fee structure." Since the disposal of garbage is a vital function of local government, under a put-or-pay type of security structure, it is usually paid

---

[1]*The Bond Buyer,* October 12, 1982, p. 3.

out of a local government's operating budget and general fund. Therefore, the put-or-pay agreements usually should provide the bondholders with a level of security right below the general obligation bonds of the underlying local governments.

QUESTIONS FOR THE ANALYST OR INVESTOR TO ASK BEFORE BUYING A RESOURCE RECOVERY REVENUE BOND

In this section, 13 basic analytical questions are discussed which the analyst or investor should ask in determining the credit worthiness of a resource recovery bond. They are:

1. What Plant Technology is Used?

The first question to ask is what is the specific technology that the plant will use in converting the garbage to energy? The simplest and most proven is "mass burning." The next most proven is refuse-derived fuel, or shredding. The "gold-in-garbage" and more eclectic technologies require the most-detailed engineering evaluations by qualified specialists. Below are brief descriptions of these three types of waste-to-energy technologies which are used in plants that have been financed with municipal bonds.

Mass Burning. Mass burning is a generic name for the direct incineration process used to release the heat energy in garbage. This resource recovery system uses a "water-wall" type of heat exchange to produce electricity or steam. Based on decades of experience in Europe, three major U.S. firms have negotiated licensing agreements to use this proven technology in the American market:

1. In 1972, Von Roll, Switzerland, signed a licensing arrangement with the Wheelabrator-Frye Corporation; four years later the first modern resource recovery plant was built in Saugus, Massachusetts. Today this plant continues to process more than 1,200 tons per day of solid waste in its two refuse-combustion and steam-generating furnaces. This plant was financed in 1975 by the Saugus, Massachusetts, Solid Waste Disposal Revenue Bonds. Additionally, the issue of the Northeast Maryland Waste Disposal Authority, Resource Recovery Revenue Bonds, Series 1983 utilizes this technology.

2. The Deutsche Babcock Anlaten of Germany negotiated a licensing agreement with Grumman Corporation in 1974. Several years of intensive marketing produced no projects and in 1979 the marketing of this system was sold to Browning Ferris Industries of Houston.

3. UOP, a wholly owned subsidiary of the Signal Corporation represents the Joseph Martin Company of Munich, Germany. Martin plants in Chicago, Illinois, and Harrisburg, Pennsylvania, have been

running as incinerators since the late 1950s. UOP has completed construction of a new facility in Pinellas County, Florida. This plant was financed by the Pinellas County, Florida, Solid Waste and Electric Revenue Bonds, Series 1980 (Resource Recovery System)[2]. The mass-burning systems of Wheelabrator-Frye, Browning Ferris, and UOP use basically the same proven technology which has been in operation in Europe for many years. Mass burning is the simplest technology; the garbage is burned with very little processing.

Refuse-Derived Fuel. Although this process is not used in Europe, several American companies have developed plant technologies which preprocess garbage to produce a fuel by-product. The preprocessing of the garbage usually involves placing the garbage on a series of conveyer belts, where it is hammered or shredded into a more even consistency. This processed garbage, commonly referred to as refuse-derived fuel (RDF), generally has a higher heating value of 6,000 BTUs per pound. In its raw state, it resembles a papier-mache type of material. Although not commercially proven at the same level that the mass-burning plants have been, these plants generally take the RDF and co-fire it in an existing boiler, generally one that presently uses either powdered or stoker-fired coal. While there have not been any commercially successful applications of this technology to date, it does offer some unique economic advantages in certain circumstances, and when fired in a dedicated boiler, it can produce a more efficient steam load for the production of electrical energy or processed steam. In addition, the RDF can, as in many other multi-fuel-boiler applications, be mixed and matched as fuel availability affects the operation of the plant.

Gold-in-Garbage. Gold-in-garbage and other more eclectic approaches require the most-detailed engineering evaluations by qualified specialists, as well as strong bond security structures. Resource recovery plants with elaborate processing procedures and unproven technologies are sometimes known as the gold-in-garbage plants.

An example of such a resource recovery bond is the Connecticut Resources Recovery Authority's Greater Bridgeport System Revenue Bonds of 1976. The plant technology was to convert the garbage into fuel-like pellets, which were then to be mixed with oil and sold to the United Illuminating Company in Bridgeport. However, the technology was unproven, and the developer of the technology, Combustion Equipment Associates of New York, filed for bankruptcy.[3]

---

[2]In early 1983 the Signal Corporation purchased the Wheelabrator-Frye Corporation.

[3]*The Bond Buyer*, December 3, 1982, pp. 1, 32.

2. Is the Plant a Scaled-Up Model?

A primary risk in the construction and operation of a waste-to-energy plant is the possible "scale-up" problem. Many plants in the United States are of sizes that greatly exceed those in use in Europe. While the basic technologies may be sound, the scaled-up plants may present problems such as increased metallurgy in the furnace grates and excessive air pollution. Of course, the correction of these problems requires careful testing and adjustment of new devices, which takes time and is costly. While the investor should not altogether avoid waste-to-energy bonds that rely on a scaled-up plant model, he should determine if the bond issuer has established appropriate financial reserves and has carefully reviewed the potential scaling-up problems from an engineering perspective.

3. How Much Redundancy is Built into the Plant Design?

Another important consideration in plant design which could negatively impact the bondholder is the degree of "redundancy," or low utilization assumptions, built into the plant's operations. If the plant technology is very innovative, it is important for there to be sufficient redundancy to absorb any unforeseen problems once the plant comes on line. Most major mass-burning, water-wall incinerators are built around "process trains," or feeding lines that have capacities of about 750 tons of solid waste per day. These systems usually have an independent redundancy built into them which would allow one line, or boiler, to operate while the other boiler is under repair or down for periodic maintenance. Far more redundancy is required for the RDF-type plant where specific equipment trains should be replicated on several feeding lines. The resource recovery plant should have more than one feeding line and should have as much dual processing capability as possible.

4. Are the Bondholders Protected during the Construction Period?

Resource recovery plants can be divided into two periods—the construction, shakedown, and scale-up period and the commercial operation period. The risks to the bondholders are unique and specific during each period. During the construction, shakedown, and scale-up period, there should be unlimited performance guarantees, with liquidated damage provisions provided by the builder of the plant. In essence this is "turnkey" construction.

Another desirable safeguard is the "buy down" procedure. During the shakedown period, the plant might meet 90 percent of its design qualifications, but not 100 percent. It is desirable that the security arrangements are such that the performance standards can be reduced to the achievable level. This allows the economics to be locked in and the bondholder can expect to rely on the profitable revenue stream at the new reduced level. Of course, there have to be limits on the buy-down procedure so that the economics of the plant remain whole. If these provisions do not exist, then the bondholder is taking a risk which he should not be asked to do. A careful reading of the trust indenture or its summary in the official statement should indicate how well the bondholder is protected during the construction period.

5. How Experienced are the Construction Contractor and Plant Operator?

A key element in determining the credit worthiness of a resource recovery revenue bond is the level of experience and competency of the construction contractor and plant operator. Two primary problem areas can be either failures in the solid waste processing system or retrofitting existing and new boilers to burn the refuse-derived fuel. Contractors and plant operators with years of proven experience in these areas are clearly the most desirable.

Additional comfort should be provided to the bondholders to insulate them from equipment performance risks once the plant is constructed and operating. This basic technological protection should include performance and operating guarantees and warranties from the equipment vendors as well as commercial insurance.

6. Are There Adequate Financial Incentives for the Plant Operator?

In addition to knowing the degree of experience of the plant builder and operator, the investor should also determine what financial incentives exist for the plant operator to maintain the plant throughout its life, which usually is for 20 years. While the financial incentives are generally good in comparison to other types of projects in which these resource recovery plant builders and operators have traditionally engaged, the investor must remember that resource recovery plants have not yet gained large public acceptance in the United States. Generally, plant operators should have a rate of return of at least 30 percent on their investment. Moreover, since the increase in energy revenues can be higher than originally estimated, the plant operator as well as the community should benefit. For the former it would be increased profits, and for the latter it would be a reduction in the tipping fee. The plant operator should also be assured that the plant will have a virtual monopoly for providing garbage disposal services within the area for the life of the bonds. Other important upfront financial incentives for the plant operator are the tax advantages associated with resource recovery plants. Plant builders and operators can virtually recover their capital contribution within the first three to four years of construction, using the investment tax credit, energy tax credit, and accelerated depreciation allowances available under existing Internal Revenue Service regulations. Besides providing a means of developing additional cash reserves in case the plant develops technical difficulties, these tax advantages as well as the other financial incentives mentioned above should, if properly structured, provide adequate incentives both to compensate the plant operator for long-term risks and to provide the bondholder with comfort that the plant operator will stay with the plant even if technical problems should occur.

7. What Financial Risks is the Plant Operator Required to Take?

A key indication of the commitment of the plant operator to the resource recovery facility is the amount of financial risk the operator is willing to assume in the project. If a private corporation owns the plant, it should receive certain tax benefits associated with the facility. While the plant operator's financial commitment to the facility should at least include the total tax benefits accrued to the plant operator, a greater financial commitment is also sometimes desirable.

An example of the complexity of determining the dollar value of the tax benefits can be found in the Westchester County Industrial Development Agency's resource recovery bonds sold in 1982 on behalf of the Westchester Resco Company, a wholly owned subsidiary of Wheelabrator-Frye. In this project, after commercial start-up Wheelabrator-Frye's additional contributions are limited to the value of the tax benefits derived from the project. These benefits cannot easily be quantified in advance. In this instance, therefore, the analyst must rely more on the technology involved and the experience and business reliability of the plant operator in determining credit risk.

8. Are Annual Plant Reviews by Qualified Outside Engineers Required?

An additional safeguard for the bondholder is for the indenture for the bond issue to require annual plant reviews by qualified outside engineers. The reviews should not only evaluate the current operations of the plant but also identify maintenance work that should be

undertaken to keep the plant in operating order for the life of the
bond issue. Ideally, the repair recommendations by the outside engineers should be mandatory for the plant operator.

9. Is the Plant Adequately Insured?

The plant should at all times be fully insured during the construction stage. If the plant is not completed, the amount of the surety
insurance along with other assets should be adequate to retire all the
outstanding bonds.

10. Are Strikes by Garbage and Plant Workers a Problem?

Another risk to all major construction projects, and certainly to
those projects where public health services such as garbage disposal
is involved, are employee strikes by either those who collect the garbage or by those who operate the garbage disposal facilities. Generally, while strikes by garbage collectors do occur, are acrimonious,
and receive widespread coverage in the mass media, they tend to be
of short durations. Nonetheless, if the economics of a resource recovery revenue bond are dependent upon a relatively continuous stream
of garbage flow, the prudent investor should learn the history of public sector labor relations in that particular jurisdiction. If the local
and state political actors have histories of permissiveness toward
strikes in the public sector, the investor may want to avoid such resource recovery revenue bonds altogether.

In addition to strikes by garbage collectors, there also could be
strikes by the workers at the resource recovery plants themselves.
Although most, if not all, resource recovery plants are operated in
conjunction with the public sector, in most instances they are privately owned. Additionally, since most of these plants are still under
construction it remains to be seen as to what types of relationships
will develop between the new resource recovery plants and the existing workers in the solid waste industry. Nonetheless, there are certain features of resource recovery plants that the investor should be
aware of. First, there is a major difference in the educational and
skill levels required for workers who operate these plants and those
who currently operate waste collection vehicles and landfill disposal
sites. Second, if properly designed, operated, and maintained, resource recovery plants can offer a workplace environment that has all
the adequate protections necessary for the workers. Third, there are
real workplace health risks associated with the plants. How well and
how professionally the plant builders and operators look for and correct these problems during the shakedown and scale-up stages may
determine future labor-management relations in the plants.

11. What is the Responsibility of the Underlying Government or Governments?

A crucial element in assessing risk is the degree of involvement of state and local governments, such as counties and cities, in the resource recovery project. If the sponsoring governmental unit is legally responsible for paying bondholders, then the risk analysis begins initially with this governmental unit's budgetary and financial strengths and weaknesses. Of course, the most direct form of involvement is for the governmental jurisdiction to finance the construction of the facility with the sale of its own general obligation bonds. (For the analysis of general obligation bonds, see Chapter 8.) Here, we focus upon types of governmental liability other than the general obligation pledge.

Governmental involvement usually focuses around three issues. They are the tipping fee, the delivery of the garbage, and the vulnerability to change in federal law.

The Tipping Fee. The tipping, or garbage disposal, fee is intended to be one of the major sources of revenue for the resource recovery project. This is the amount of money paid per ton by the community that delivers the garbage to the facility for disposal. The strongest type of security arrangement is called a "put-or-pay" contract in which a community is obligated to put a specified amount of garbage into the plant each year, or pay a dollar amount equivalent to what a tipping fee would be for that annual amount of garbage. Additionally, the tipping fee should be sufficient along with other revenues to cover all operating, maintenance, and capital costs of the plant, including debt service.

A "put-and-pay" arrangement is one in which the tipping fees are dependent on the actual delivery of garbage and its acceptance by the plant for disposal.

It should also be noted that the tipping fee formula is usually delineated in the service contract between the community and the resource recovery facility.

The Delivery of the Garbage. Ideally, a state or local law requiring that all garbage in the area be delivered to the facility, and no place else does provide comfort to the investor. This is particularly so if the facility is also part of a landfill which can be used for garbage disposal when the plant is not operating. However, it should also be noted that, as discussed in Case Study 11, there could be legal risks for communities trying to control the waste supply, particularly in regard to anti-trust considerations.

The Power of Changes in Federal Law. Still another concern for the investor or analyst is the degree of risk involved if federal environmental standards are changed requiring extensive plant improvements. From the bondholder's point of view, it is desirable for the issuer to assume this responsibility at the time of the bond sale, though most communities are very reluctant to do so in advance.

12. How is the Produced Energy Priced and Sold?

Perhaps the most important factor in determining the economic viability of a waste-to-energy bond concerns the amount of revenues from the steam, electricity, or refuse-derived fuel that the plant produces. Generally, tipping fees and recovered metal revenues are insufficient by themselves since they usually only account for 25 percent to 40 percent of plant revenues. Without a strong market for the produced energy, the economic feasibility is impossible.

The market for the energy is best assured to the bondholder through a "take-and-pay contract." Such a contract should require that, to the extent energy is produced by the facility, the energy consumer (such as a utility) must purchase a specified amount or pay for it anyway. Additionally, a pricing formula that ties the price of the energy to future oil or gas prices is desirable since these fuels are expected to escalate over the next 10 years. Industrial energy consumers or utilities that currently utilize oil or gas are likely participants for take-and-pay contracts. Additionally, for start-up plants the analyst must look very closely at the feasibility study to determine how conservative its assumptions are, and whether it has assessed the economics of the project in a worst-case scenario; i.e. at times flat to lower energy prices and reductions in garbage processed.

13. Are There Adequate Financial Reserves?

Still another concern for the investor or analyst is how prudent the issuer has been in establishing financial reserves for protecting the bondholders should problems develop in the plant. A well-structured bond should have special reserves for debt service and required plant operation improvements. Below are three of the more important reserves that should be included in a resource recovery bond issue.

Debt Reserve. There should be held by the trustee a debt service reserve fund which ideally should be maintained in an amount at least equal to the maximum annual debt service on all outstanding bonds. This reserve should be fully funded from the original bond proceeds so that the bond trustee has available, at the very beginning, one year's debt service. Should a situation occur where the plant's revenues are not substantial and cannot pay the full debt service requirements, the trustee could draw down the debt service reserve to pay the bondholders while attempts are made to recover the monies from increased revenues of the plant. While the debt service reserve fund does not provide long-term security to the bondholders, it does provide a short-term security for possibly as long as 12 months.

Maintenance Reserve. A well-structured bond should also include a maintenance or contingency fund which can be used for making routine or minor plant repairs such as repairing grates in a mass-burning plant or hammers in a refuse-derived fuel plant. Of course, it should also be noted that in certain circumstances such a maintenance reserve may not be necessary or may be only funded at a very modest level—for example, if the plant builder and operator guarantee plant performance and are substantial companies that are capable and have histories of providing capital as required. For plants that utilize new waste-to-energy technologies or innovative plant designs with relatively inexperienced plant builders and operators, the maintenance or contingency fund is a necessary security structure for the bondholders. Usually this fund is established from the original bond proceeds and/or is to be maintained by revenues generated by the plant's operations.

Special Capital Improvement Reserve. In addition to the debt service reserve and maintenance funds, plants that present special engineering problems and have limited financial support from the plant builders and operators should also have special capital improvement reserves. Plants that utilize highly innovative technologies or have scale-up features should have monies available for making substantial plant modifications if necessary. A special capital improvement reserve fund for such plants should be maintained in an amount at least equal to 25 percent of the maximum annual debt service on the bonds. Usually this fund is established with the proceeds of the original bond issue and/or is to be maintained by revenues generated by the plant's operations.

CONCLUSIONS

Because of the newness of the financing techniques involved, the reliability of the legal opinions are of prime importance to the investor both in terms of state and local laws, arbitrage guidelines of the Internal Revenue Service, and vendor obligations. Legal opinions should be written by nationally recognized and experienced law firms. Additional comfort is provided if the bond issue is supported by direct case law. As an example, prior to the sale of the Pinellas County, Florida Solid Waste and Electric Revenue Bonds, Series 1980 (Resource Recovery System), the issuer sought a judicial review (known in Florida as a "validation" proceeding) and had confirmed in the state court system the legality of certain major security provisions in the bond resolution.

The analysis of resource recovery revenue bonds is particularly complicated. Credit worthiness or the degree of insulation from adversity for the bondholders is usually directly related to the economic feasibility of the project. The economic feasibility of the project, in turn, is dependent upon the long-term availability of a market for the plant's produced energy, the on-line operating performance of the plant, and the reliability of the garbage supply to fuel the plant.

While resource recovery revenue bonds usually have the above general features, the details of the provisions in a specific bond structure determine the credit worthiness. Credit worthiness in the past unfortunately has included some poorly secured resource recovery revenue bonds such as the state of Ohio's Recycle Energy Revenue Bonds Series 1976 (City of Akron, Ohio, Project)—which by the end of the 1970s had gone into technical default. It is hoped that this chapter will help investors avoid similarly structured resource recovery bonds in the future.

Hospital Revenue Bonds

CHAPTER 11

Arthur R. Guastella
Executive Vice President
Blyth Eastman Paine Webber Health Care Funding, Inc.

The volume of tax-exempt hospital revenue bonds issued in recent years has increased dramatically moving from $3.5 billion in 1980, representing 8 percent of all new long-term tax-exempts marketed in that year, to $9.2 billion in 1982 which accounted for 12 percent of that year's all-time record volume of $74.8 billion. Yet, most municipal bond analysts probably would concede that hospital revenue bonds are among the most complex to evaluate. After wrestling with regulatory, third-party reimbursement and other considerations unique to hospital revenue bonds, one longs for the relative simplicity of a sewer or power revenue bond. This complexity, coupled with market liquidity considerations resulting from relatively small average size, is reflected in the fact that hospital revenue bonds require higher yields to attract investors than most other classes of revenue bonds. The objective of this chapter is to chart a path through the complexity, identifying along the way the major signposts to credit worthiness.

The decline of charitable support, increasing technology of modern health care, and a growing awareness that health care is a public

163

responsibility have prompted most states to enact legislation authorizing the creation of public entities which can borrow on a tax-exempt basis for the benefit of not-for-profit hospitals. Many states have created statewide authorities, while others utilize local authorities; some, Illinois and Michigan for example, offer a choice. In any case the result is the same: to provide a tax-exempt capital-financing vehicle for private, not-for-profit hospitals and other health care facilities.

OFFICIAL STATEMENT

The preliminary official statement is the bond analyst's most important tool in assessing the credit worthiness of a proposed tax-exempt hospital revenue bond issue. A properly prepared official statement should contain at a minimum:

1. Description of the legal structure of the financing.
2. Details of bondholders' security.
3. History and description of the hospital.
   a. Five-year history of utilization data.
   b. Five-year summary of income statements and balance sheets.
   c. Description of the project.
   d. Audited financial statements.
4. Report on independent financial feasibility study.

LEGAL STRUCTURE

There are four basic legal structures which are employed in implementing tax-exempt revenue bond financings for hospitals: sale and leaseback; lease/sublease; loan agreement; and the so-called 63–20 not-for-profit corporation vehicle.

The last of these, based on an IRS ruling, is little used today because it requires that title to the financed facilities revert to the sponsoring governmental entity upon repayment of the debt. Obviously, a private, not-for-profit hospital with a history of serving the community for a generation or more is not eager to abdicate its responsibility to a governmental unit. Similarly, a municipality or a county has no wish to add to its problems by taking over and operating a highly specialized organization like a hospital. Which of the three remaining legal structures is utilized is largely dictated by the various state laws.

In the sale and leaseback arrangement, the hospital "sells" its facilities to the issuing entity for the "price" of the bond proceeds, and title to the hospital facilities is conveyed to the issuer of the debt. Simultaneously, the hospital leases back the facilities at rentals equal to the required interest and principal payments and regains title upon repayment of the debt. The lease/sublease arrangement is virtually identical to the sale and leaseback mechanism except that title to the hospital facility is not conveyed to the bond-issuing entity but "leased" to it for a single lease rental payment equal to the bond proceeds and subleased back at rentals sufficient to cover debt service payments on the bonds. The loan agreement is the simplest of the three legal structures in that the issuing entity lends the bond proceeds to the hospital, which agrees to unconditionally repay the loan in accordance with the debt service requirements on the bonds.

Regardless of the legal structure, the package of legal documents for a tax-exempt hospital revenue bond financing will include an agreement between the issuing entity and the hospital (lease, sublease, or loan agreement) and an agreement between a bond trustee, as representative of all bondholders, and the issuing entity (trust indenture or resolution). In situations involving leases or subleases, because of legal concerns about the status of a leasehold interest in bankruptcy, there will also be a guaranty agreement between the bond trustee and the hospital, in which the hospital unconditionally guarantees the full and prompt payment of principal and interest on the bonds.

Security Interest in Revenues

Whatever the package of legal instruments may contain, it is built around the major axiom of tax-exempt hospital revenue bond analysis: *The essence of security for a tax-exempt hospital bond is the ability of the institution to generate sufficient cash to meet its operating and debt service requirements; it is not the value represented by the physical plant and equipment.* The legal structure should provide for all of the major elements of such a revenue-based security. The most important of these is a security interest in revenues of the hospital. It should be noted that such security interest or pledge is important only if an institution develops financial problems. In the early years of tax-exempt hospital financing, a hospital was required to physically deliver its gross revenue daily to the bond trustee (acting in the capacity of depository agent) until such deposits equaled the amounted required monthly for debt service.

While it is evident that a hospital cannot function if it cannot pay operating expenses as well as debt service, it was believed that primary payment of debt service would force management to concentrate on keeping the facility operating. Today the more common arrangement is to leave day-to-day financial control to hospital management unless a debt service payment is missed—which would trigger a flow of hospital revenues to the trustee.

In addition to the security interest in revenues, there may be a mortgage of the hospital facilities, although it is generally believed that a mortgage on such a specialized facility as a hospital does not significantly improve credit quality. If there is no mortgage, there should be a so-called negative pledge covenant which provides that the revenue-generating facilities will not be otherwise pledged or mortgaged.

Other major security elements which are incorporated into the legal agreements and should be examined are: a debt service reserve, rate covenant, provision for additional parity indebtedness, and a depreciation reserve fund.

Debt Service Reserve Fund

The debt service reserve fund, while it is perceived as a burdensome requirement by many hospitals, provides an important element of additional security to the hospital as well as the bondholder. If properly structured, it should provide an earning asset under normal circumstances and a means of paying debt service for a year if a hospital finds itself in financial trouble.

Rate Covenant

The typical rate covenant requires the hospital, subject to legal or regulatory restrictions, to generate sufficient net revenue—before depreciation, interest, and amortization of financing expenses—to cover its annual debt service requirement on all long-term indebtedness by some fixed percent ranging generally from 110 to 125 percent. The primary purpose of the rate covenant in hospital revenue bond financing is not to require a hospital to set its rates at some arbitrary level, but to provide an early warning of financial problems. Generally, the rate covenant requires the institution to retain an independent management consultant if it fails to meet the required coverage level. This permits an outside expert to review hospital operations and make professional judgments and recommendations before a problem situation degenerates into financial default.

Additional Indebtedness

A hospital, like any public or private enterprise, must continue to keep up the vitality and adequacy of its revenue-generating facilities. Over the 30-year maturity of a typical tax-exempt revenue bond issue, this will require additional long-term capital financing. Accordingly, practically all such financing includes provisions for additional long-term debt financing on either a parity or nonparity basis. However, such borrowing is permitted only if the institution can meet both historical and future earnings tests. The historical test is basically a certification that the hospital has been meeting its rate covenant, while the future test requires an independent management consultant to determine that, in the first two years following completion of the facility being financed forecast net income before interest, depreciation, and amortization will exceed some fixed coverage factor. This factor is generally 1.25 times or higher depending on the institution involved. Certain financially strong institutions are permitted to issue a limited amount of such debt on the basis of just a historical test.

It should be pointed out that the earnings tests currently incorporated in most financings are quite liberal. In fact, tax-exempt revenue bonds of a hospital which could only barely meet a historical test of 1.10 times and a future test of 1.25 times could not be marketed without some additional financial backing.

As noted previously, the ability of an institution to generate sufficient cash flow is the major indicator of a given hospital's credit worthiness. Accordingly, the amount of indebtedness a hospital can incur depends primarily on its ability to generate future cash flow. *As used here, cash flow is defined as the hospital's excess of revenues over expenses before interest, depreciation and amortization.* The major factor affecting the ability of a hospital to generate sufficient excess of revenues is the method by which it is reimbursed for patient care by third-party payors such as medicare, medicaid, and Blue Cross.

Third-Party Payors. Medicare and medicaid represent hospital reimbursement programs created by certain provisions of the federal Social Security Act. Medicare is an exclusively federal program, and medicaid is a combined federal and state program. Both provide for payments to hospitals under formulas based on the lower of defined costs or charges for reimbursable services furnished to eligible patients. At present, reimbursable costs under medicare and medicaid regulations generally consist of operating expenses including interest and depreciation expense. Blue Cross hospital insurance programs vary widely from state to state, ranging from cost-based reimbursement to full charges.

The importance of these three programs to a hospital's financial well-being cannot be overstated, since collectively they may represent from 70 percent to as much as 90 percent of an individual hospital's sources of revenue.

The federal Tax Equity and Fiscal Responsibility Act of 1982 (TEFRA) and interim final rules promulgated by the Health Care Financing Administration under TEFRA have introduced certain Medicare reimbursement limitations that make the analyst's examination of a particular hospital's Medicare involvement more critical than ever. Apart from the fact that the new limitations are designed to limit reimbursement for services provided to Medicare beneficiaries, the effect of the changes will vary from hospital to hospital.

The dominance of third-party payors who make payments directly to hospitals on behalf of patients has been a mixed blessing. On the positive side they have reduced the proportion of patients for whom the hospital can expect to receive no payment. On the other hand, most third-party payors reimburse hospitals on the basis of current cash costs (including interest) of patient care plus the noncash expense of historical depreciation. A hospital's full charges for service rendered usually exceed the cost of providing those services and are a form of cost-plus payment. Commercial insurance companies and self-pay patients usually pay the hospital's full charges for services. The greater the volume of services rendered on a cost-plus basis, the greater the potential for revenues in excess of expenses. Thus, a hospital's ability to generate an excess of revenues over expenditures is principally based on the volume of services paid for on the basis of charges as supplemented by the hospital's nonoperating revenues.

Depreciation Reserve

There is one other major factor which affects the level of available cash flow and therefore the ability of a particular hospital to repay debt: the relationship of depreciation to the amortization of principal.

Most tax-exempt hospital revenue issues are marketed with level debt amortization schedules—equal annual payments which combine both principal and interest, much like the traditional home mortage. During the early years of such a loan, the major portion of the annual payment is applied to interest and the remainder to principal. In later years the interest portion becomes less as the outstanding principal decreases, so that a greater portion of the level annual payment is applied to the repayment of principal.

As mentioned previously, both interest and depreciation are currently reimbursed under cost formulas by third-party payors. Interest is reimbursed in accordance with the interest expense incurred each year during the term of the loan. Therefore, reimbursed interest is at its highest in the early years of the loan and is reduced as the loan is repaid. Depreciation, on the other hand, is reimbursed on a straight-line basis and is received as a relatively level amount each year during the life of the asset. Depreciation is used to repay the principal payment. In the early years of the loan, the reimbursement of depreciation exceeds the annual principal payment required, and in the later years the reimbursement of this item is generally less than the required payment. Therefore, the legal documents should provide a mechanism for assuring that the institution will have sufficient funds to meet principal payments in those years when annual depreciation is less than principal requirements.

FEASIBILITY STUDY

The feasibility study is particularly important to any analysis of hospital revenue bonds and should be prepared by an independent and experienced hospital consulting firm. As Standard and Poor's points out:

> A well-prepared study presents an extensive amount of pertinent material in a concise, logical format; it states the explicit assumptions upon which the utilization and financial forecasts are based, and it is an indication of management's willingness to expose the hospital and the capital project to objective, independent scrutiny. The study should include two major components: a market and demand analysis which defines the service area, examines demographic and utilization trends, and discusses competing institutions; and a financial analysis which examines staffing parameters, reimbursement, operating costs, and pricing of services.[1]

Since the analyst's task is to assess the relative ability of a hospital to make timely debt service payments, particular attention should be directed to the feasibility study's discussion of market position and share.

After examining those factors which are outside the control of an individual hospital, such as reimbursement patterns and demographic factors, the analyst should concentrate on those elements which are within an individual institution's control—management, medical staff and utilization, and financial factors. While it may be argued that good utilization and financials will logically result from good management, a negative demographic environment could result in comparatively poor financials however strong or efficient management may be.

Management

The board of trustees represents the institution's direct link to the community it serves, and as such it should be representative of that community. It should be active, meet regularly, and have a committee structure that provides a mechanism for continuous monitoring of hospital operations, particularly utilization and financial trends. Day-to-day operations, on the other hand, should be the province of trained professionals.

Medical Staff

The medical staff should be regarded as the engine that drives hospital admissions. As such, the characteristics of a desirable medical

---

[1]*Municipal and International Bond Ratings–An Overview,* Standard & Poor's Corporation, January 1, 1979.

staff are obvious: relatively young average age, no undue concentration of admissions by a relatively small number of physicians, broad range of specialties, many group practices with offices close to the hospital, and active ongoing recruitment.

Utilization and Financial Factors

Every analyst has a favored combination of financial and operating yardsticks. There are literally dozens of such indicators, many unique to hospitals, from which an analyst can form a general opinion as to the credit worthiness of a particular hospital. Indeed, a number of investment banking firms maintain a data base of financial and operating statistics of individual hospitals which have utilized tax-exempt revenue financings. Table 1 shows averages of a select group of such indicators for approximately 74 hospitals of "A" rated credit worthiness in 1981 and 1982.

Generally speaking, lenders favor issues of large hospitals having greater revenue bases which are perceived as being better able to withstand and adjust to changes in the economy and regulatory environment than small community hospitals. There is a direct relationship between credit quality and size expressed in terms of the number of beds, gross revenues, and occupancy. As is seen in Table 1, the average A-rated hospital had over 300 beds, occupancy of just over 80 percent, and gross patient revenues of $23.9 million. However, size alone is no assurance of credit worthiness.

FINANCIAL RATIOS

The art of analyzing hospital financial ratios has become quite sophisticated. The Hospital Financial Management Association (HMFA) provides hospital clients a ratio analysis service called Financial Analysis Service, developed for health care financial managers. While investment bankers' data-base ratios are designed to identify correlations between such ratios and credit ratings and to utilize both historical and forecasted data, the Hospital Financial Management Association's service is designed to permit a hospital to compare itself financially with comparably sized institutions on both a national and regional basis, and it utilizes only audited data.

The Financial Analysis Service utilizes 29 financial ratios classified into five major categories: liquidity, capital structure, activity, profitability, and other. Six of the 29 financial ratios—two each from liquidity, capital structure, and profitability—are explained below.[2]

---

[2]The author is indebted to the HFMA's *Financial Analysis Service User's Guide* for the lucid explanation of the ratios discussed in this chapter.

The particular ratios discussed are selected because they coincide with ratios commonly used in revenue bond analysis. Also included for each of the six ratios is a trend analysis covering the five years 1977, through 1981.[3]

Current Ratio

Definition

$$\text{Current ratio} = \frac{\text{Current assets}}{\text{Current liabilities}}$$

Desired position

Trend: Increasing values are favorable
Median: Values above medians are favorable

Discussion. The current ratio is one of the most widely used measures of liquidity. The value of the current ratio measures the number of dollars held in current assets per dollar of current liabilities. From an evaluation perspective, high values for the current ratio imply a good ability to pay short-term obligations and, thus, a low probability of technical insolvency.

It is not always safe to assume that a high value for the current ratio is good and a low value is bad. A hospital with a high current ratio may still have short-term payment problems if its current assets are not expected to be in liquid form (cash or short-term investments) in time to meet the expected payment dates of the current liabilities. Conversely, a hospital with a low current ratio may not have immediate payment problems if current liabilities include items that will not be paid from existing current assets, such as a construction account payable. Finally, large values for the current ratio may also imply either overinvestment in current assets such as cash, accounts receivable, and inventory, or underutilization of low-cost, short-term financing such as accounts payable.

Trend Analysis. There has been a steady pattern of decline in current ratios since 1978. The 1981 national median value of 1.873 was down significantly from the corresponding 1978 value of 2.064. This pattern warrants close attention because it may signal a general decline in the liquidity position of U.S. hospitals. Northeast hospitals have current ratios that are lower than other regions. Only the Southern region has had median current ratios in 1980 and 1981 which exceed the conventional wisdom standard of 2.0.

---

[3]The trend analysis is excerpted from the *Hospital Industry Analysis Report, 1981* prepared for the HFMA by William O. Cleverly, Ohio State University, Columbus.

Days in Patient Accounts Receivable

Definition

Days in patient   = Net patient accounts receivable

accounts receivable $$\dfrac{\text{Net patient service revenue}}{365}$$

Desired position

Trend: Decreased values are favorable

Median: Values below median are favorable

Discussion. The days in patient accounts receivable ratio is a liquidity ratio that may provide some rationale for changes in liquidity position. The value for this ratio provides a measure of the average time that receivables are outstanding, or the average collection period. High values for this ratio imply longer collection periods and thus a need for the hospital to finance this investment in accounts receivable. Changes in the values in patient accounts receivable are crucial in effective cash management. A hospital that expects an increase in its collection period should decide how to finance this increase. In most situations, the short-term solution would be to borrow on a short-term basis or to liquidate a portion of the investment portfolio. Ultimately, a permanent increase in the collection period will require an increase in the operating margin to provide the required amount of permanent equity financing. Low values for days in patient accounts receivable are not always favorable, just as high values may not always be unfavorable. These values are affected by seasonal factors. A hospital whose fiscal year ends when utilization is low will probably show a lower than normal value for days in patient accounts receivable. In summary, good management requires that any level of days in patient accounts receivable be analyzed to determine if there is anything that can be done to reduce the collection period. Possible strategies range from improving business office management to improving third-party payer relationships.

Trend Analysis. A slight decline in the average collection period in the hospital industry occurred during 1981. The 1981 national median value of 59.15 days was below the comparable 1980 value of 60.25 days. While this reduction is modest, it does reflect favorable hospital management. The economic recession did not appear to have had an adverse effect on days in patient accounts receivable during 1981. Days in patients accounts receivable declined during 1980 and 1981. This may, however, reflect different write-off policies.

Long-Term Debt to Equity Ratio

Definition

$$\text{Long-term debt to equity ratio} = \frac{\text{Long-term liabilities}}{\text{Unrestricted fund balance}}$$

Desired position

Trend: Decreasing values are favorable
Median: Values below median are favorable

Discussion. The long-term debt to equity ratio measures the relative importance of long-term debt in the hospital's permanent capital structure. Fund balance and long-term liabilities are often referred to as permanent capital, since they will not be repaid within one year. Hospitals with high long-term debt to equity ratios have relied extensively on debt as opposed to equity to finance their assets and are said to be leveraged. This means risk in the minds of many creditors and may be viewed unfavorably.

A high long-term debt to equity ratio may not prohibit future debt financing, nor does a low long-term debt to equity ratio guarantee a favorable credit review. It is not the amount of debt, but rather the ability to repay that debt, that is the central issue for both the creditor and borrower. Ability to pay is more directly tied to present and future cash flow and profitability positions. Also, the absence of long-term debt is usually not ideal. Credit experience is a factor in credit evaluations. A mixture of debt and equity may also minimize the overall cost of capital.

Trend Analysis. During the 1977–1981 period, the national median for this ratio has increasesd from .563 to .592. This modest increase is probably the result of continual replacement of fixed assets at ever inflating prices. Larger hospitals appear to have higher long-term debt to equity ratios than smaller hospitals. This may imply greater access to credit markets. Lenders may perceive less risk associated with loans to large hospitals than with loans to small hospitals.

Debt Service Coverage

Definition

$$\text{Debt service coverage} = \frac{\text{Cash flow} + \text{Interest expense}}{\text{Principal payment} + \text{Interest expense}}$$

Desired position

Trend: Increasing values are favorable
Median: Values above median are favorable

Discussion. The debt service coverage ratio measures total debt service coverage (interest plus principal) from the hospital's cash flow. Since cash flow is defined as the excess of revenues over expenses plus depreciation, debt service coverage is affected by both profitability and depreciation patterns. As is true of the times-interest-earned ratio, higher values for debt service coverage are viewed positively by creditors. One test of future debt service coverage employed by some credit analysts is the peak debt–historical coverage ratio. This ratio is derived by substituting the hospital's present cash flow and its maximum or peak debt service (interest plus principal) that is associated with a planned financing.

High values of debt service coverage can sometimes be misleading. Quite often in the early years of a capital expansion or renovation program, there is no principal or little principal retirement, but the depreciation expense on the newly acquired assets may have begun. This produces a very high debt service coverage ratio, but may be a distortion of future debt repayment ability. In this situation, the times-interest-earned ratio, the cash flow to total debt ratio, and the fixed-asset financing ratio may be better indicators of debt repayment ability. A very useful analytical tool in this respect is a graph of future depreciation and debt principal payment patterns. Provision for funding during periods when depreciation exceeds debt principal is highly desirable, if not mandated, in the bond indenture.

Trend Analysis. Debt service coverage ratios have been increasing in the hospital industry. The 1981 national median value of 3.25 was above the 1977 median value of 2.82.

Operating Margin

Definition

$$\text{Operating margin} = \frac{\text{Total operating revenue} - \text{Operating expenses}}{\text{Total operating revenue}}$$

Desired position

        Trend: Increasing values are favorable
        Median: Values above median are favorable

Discussion. The operating margin ratio defines the proportion of operating revenue (net of deductions) retained as revenue. This ratio focuses on the results of operations and does not consider nonoperating sources of income. It is used by many as the primary test of profitability in the hospital industry. Alternative measures of overall profitability are return on total assets or return on equity.

A favorable operating margin does not always indicate a favorable profitability position. Three major uses of operating income are working capital increases, debt retirement, and fixed-asset investment. Hospitals which have above-normal demands in any of the three areas need greater operating margins. In addition, the availability of nonoperating sources of income, such as contributions and investment, may moderate the need for operating income and permit the hospital to subsidize operations if this is board policy.

Trend Analysis. Operating margins have remained stable in the hospital industry during the five-year period 1977–1981. The 1981 national median value of 2.3 percent was slightly above the comparable 1977 value of 2.0 percent. There is an extremely important regional effect on operating margins. Northeast hospitals have operating margins significantly below other regions. The 1981 median Northeast value of .006 was only 25 percent of the next lowest regional value of .024. The Western regions (Near West and Far West) appear to be the most profitable. This regional impact on profitability most likely results from reimbursement and rate setting climates within these regions.

Deductible Ratio

Definition

$$\text{Deductible} = \frac{\text{Deductions}}{\text{Gross patient service revenue}}$$

Desired position

Trend: Decreasing values are favorable
Median: Values below median are favorable

Discussion. The deductible ratio measures the proportion of gross patient service revenue that is not expected to be realized in cash. The major categories of deductions are contractual allowances, bad debts, charity care, and courtesy discounts. Ideally, it would be useful to break down the deductible ratio by major-payer category. From a profitability perspective, increasing values of the deductible ratio are likely to result in declining profitability simply because a larger percentage of the total revenue is not being collected. In addition, a large deductible ratio usually results in cross-subsidization between payer categories.

A high deductible ratio does not necessarily imply poor profitability. A hospital may react to high deductibles by raising its rate or by increasing its nonoperating sources of funding. In addition, a hospital should examine the specific causes for the current deductible experience. For example, it may be possible to improve the collection of self-pay accounts by making billing process changes, instituting a bank financing policy, or changing the hospital's policy on charity care.

Contractual allowances may be reduced by improving reimbursement management. Whatever the final solution(s), it is important to monitor the deductible ratio closely. Small changes in this ratio can have a very profound impact on overall hospital profitability.

Trend Analysis. Values for this ratio have been increasing steadily over the five-year period. In 1981, the national median value was .140, which is above the comparable 1977 value of .116. The value for 1981 was above 1980; however, the increase was not unusually large. This result is interesting in light of the speculation that deductibles might increase because of the deepening recession.

Table 1
**Key Operating and Financial Ratios for
74 Hospitals Rated "A"**

Statistical:	
Number of beds	330
Occupancy	81.3%
Patient days	100,480
Average length of stay	7.32
Market share	37.24
Number of physicians	215
Percent board certified	67.5%
Patient revenues ($000s or percent)	
Gross revenues	$33,137
Net operating revenues	29,341
Expenses	25,482
Net income	1,313
Net income/gross patient revenues	4.2%
Medicare/medicaid	45.8%
Blue Cross	23.5%
Other	30.7%
Balance sheet ($000s)	
Current assets	$ 7,042
Net property, plant and equipment	15,112
Total assets	25,846
Working capital	3,098
Total liabilities	12,546
Unrestricted fund balances	13,300
Liquidity:	
Current ratio	2.21
Cash and investments/current assets	14.85%
Days in receivables	66.0
Debt:	
Long-term debt per bed	$83,438
Long-term debt to unrestricted fund balance	.65
Maximum debt service per patient day	$ 44.74
Debt service coverage	2.26 ×

Source: Blyth Eastman Paine Webber Health Care Funding, Inc.,
Hospital Data Base.

Student Loan Revenue Bonds

CHAPTER **12**

George B. Pugh, Jr.
Senior Vice President and Managing Director
Craigie Incorporated

INTRODUCTION

Since the enactment of the Education Amendments of 1976, the issuance of student loan revenue bonds has greatly increased, due to both increased demand for student loans in states which had central loan agencies prior to 1976 and to the creation or activation of central loan agencies in states which did not have such agencies prior to 1976. The structure of bond issues by these student loan agencies has varied tremendously.

Student loan revenue bonds are generally not well-perceived in the investment community. Many portfolio managers will not buy student loan revenue bonds because of the adverse publicity surrounding very high default rates on student loans and the abuse of the program by persons not really needing student loans. Because of this hysteria, student loan revenue bonds generally offer higher yields than comparably rated municipal revenue bond issues.

The market seems to have ignored the fact that these issues are secured by assets which have an indirect federal guarantee, and a significant portion of the revenues generated by the assets comes directly from the federal government. The relative cheapness of student loan revenue bond issues presents opportunities for investors who are able to identify well-secured, soundly structured financings. The purpose of this chapter is to provide a better understanding of the underlying assets and an analytical framework for evaluating student loan revenue bond issues.

BRIEF HISTORY OF THE GUARANTEED STUDENT LOAN PROGRAM

The guaranteed student loan program (GSLP) has been in existence since the mid-1960s. In its initial form, student loans were available through private lenders at a fixed rate of 6 percent. The federal government paid the interest for needy students (as determined by family income) while the student was in school. Such loans were either guaranteed directly by the federal government or by a state guarantee agency which could obtain 80 percent reinsurance of its guarantee liabilities from the federal government.

When market interest rates rose in the late 1960s and early 1970s, the fixed 6 percent rate on student loans caused private lenders' participation in the program to decline. To offset the obvious disincentive in the 6 percent rate, Congress initially raised the rate to 7 percent in the late 1960s, and in 1972 enacted a change which permitted the federal government to pay lenders a special allowance above the 7 percent fixed rate to make student loans more competitive with money market investments. The special allowances were determined quarterly by the secretary of the treasury and paid by the secretary of health, education, and welfare. Although the availability of special allowances helped somewhat to relieve the problem of loan accessibility, the program continued to be plagued by lenders dropping out or restricting their student loan volume. Most observers felt there was demand for student loans that was not being satisfied.

In 1976, to eliminate the uncertainty inherent in the determination of special allowance rates and to encourage states to establish loan guarantee agencies (it generally being felt that state guarantee programs produced lower default rates), Congress enacted the Education Amendments of 1976. Among other things, the new law provided that, quarterly, special allowances would be calculated as the bond equivalent average, less 3.5 percent, of 91-day Treasury bills auctioned during the quarter. The new law also extended federal reinsurance of state guarantee agencies from its original level of 80 percent up to as much as 100 percent, depending on default experience. In addition, the 1976 legislation increased the family income eligibility requirements for federal interest subsidies from an unadjusted annual level of $15,000 to $25,000. In 1978, as an alternative to the so-called Tuition Tax Credit, Congress further liberalized the federal student loan program by making all GSLP borrowers eligible for federal interest subsidies without regard to family income. As a result of the 1976 amendments and the removal of need as an eligibility factor, the annual volume of GSLP loans has almost doubled since 1978.

STUDENT LOANS—WHAT ARE THEY?

Types of Loans. There are basically three types of student loans: (1) loans made and administered directly by colleges with federal funds (NDSL loans), (2) federally insured student loans (FISL loans) made by private or public agency lenders, and (3) loans made by public agencies or private lenders that are guaranteed by a state guarantee agency and reinsured by the federal government (state-guaranteed loans). NDSL loans are very low rate loans to extremely needy students. The NDSL program, partly as a result of many colleges' inability to service the loans adequately, has been the source of most of the adverse publicity regarding high default rates. FISL and state-guaranteed loans are the only loans that are financed with student loans revenue bonds. Except for the different type of guarantee, FISL and state-guaranteed loans are identical. Moreover, FISL loans are available only in states that do not have a loan guarantee agency. Because the Education Amendments of 1976 encourage the creation of state loan guarantee agencies, most states either have established or are establishing student loan guarantee agencies. The state-guaranteed loan program therefore appears to be the program under which most student loans will be made in the foreseeable future.

Eligibility. To be eligible for a GSLP loan, a student must be enrolled in an institution of higher education on at least a half-time basis. Loans are available regardless of need, and in most cases individual credit standing is not a determining factor in the loan decision (although lenders may apply credit judgments if they do so uniformly). Institutional eligibility is determined by the federal government. Dependent undergraduate students may borrow up to $2,500 per year under the program, not to exceed a total GSLP indebtedness of $12,500. Independent undergraduate students may borrow $3,000 per year up to a maximum of $15,000. Graduate students may borrow $5,000 per year up to a limit of $25,000 (including graduate and undergraduate loans).

Terms. While a student is enrolled in school and for a grace period of nine months after leaving school (new federal legislation has reduced the grace period to six months for loans to first-time borrowers on or after October 1, 1980), interest only is payable at a fixed rate of 7 percent. The federal government pays the interest directly to the lender during this period. Nine months after leaving school, the borrower is required to consolidate student loan indebtedness and begin to amortize principal and pay interest on a monthly basis (based on level monthly payments of principal and interest). The borrower may elect to repay his or her indebtedness over a period not exceeding 10 years and may prepay this indebtedness at any time without penalty. Deferments in the repayment of principal are available to students for up to three years while serving in the armed forces, Peace Corps, or VISTA; for one year while seeking employment; and for graduate school.

Special Allowances. In addition to the 7 percent interest rate, lenders in GSLP programs are entitled to receive from the federal government an amount, payable quarterly, equal to the average bond equivalent yield of Treasury bills auctioned during the calendar quarter, less 3.5 percent, rounded up to the nearest ⅛ percent, calculated as a percentage of the average principal amount of student loans held by the lender and divided by four. This formula results in a quarterly loan-portfolio yield equal to the average 91-day Treasury bill yield plus 3.5 percent (7 percent + T bill − 3.5 percent). The federal government pays the special allowances for the entire term of the loans. The student borrower is responsible for paying only the base 7 percent beginning nine months after leaving school.

The Guarantee. FISL loans are directly insured by the federal government as to principal and interest. State-guaranteed loans are indirectly insured in the same manner, except that the guarantor generally is a state agency that administers a guarantee fund from which default claims are paid. (In some states, foundations or non-profit corporations serve as guarantors.) In order to collect a default claim, a loan must be 120 days delinquent and the lender must have exercised reasonable care and diligence in attempting to collect. Most loan servicers have prescribed collection procedures to follow in order to meet the "reasonable care" test.

Federal Reinsurance. State guarantee agencies generally pay 100 percent of principal and accrued interest on defaulted loans. Payments under their guarantee are reinsured, however, by the federal government. The federal government will reimburse a state guarantee agency for 100 percent of its payments on defaulted loans up to 5 percent of the amount of "loans in repayment" that are guaranteed by the agency at the beginning year. Reinsurance payments are 90 percent of claims submitted in excess of 5 percent of loans in repayment but less than 9 percent, and are 80 percent for claims exceeding 9 percent. Loans in repayment are defined to mean all loans guaranteed by the agency less (1) guarantee payments of principal made by the agency, (2) the principal amounts of loans that have been fully repaid, and (3) the principal amount of loans on which the first principal installment has not become due.

There are several relevant points here for the credit analyst. First, the amount received by the lender is not affected by the sliding percentage of reinsurance so long as the guarantee agency has funds sufficient to pay claims. Most guarantee agencies charge borrowers guarantee fees that are deducted from the loan prior to disbursement to the student. For example, the Virginia guarantee agency charges the maximum guarantee fee allowable under the federal law—$\frac{1}{12}$ of 1 percent of the principal amount of the loan times the number of months until one year after the student's expected graduation. For a freshman this formula would produce a guarantee of 5 percent, a sophomore 4 percent, and so on. In addition, some guarantee agencies have received appropriations from their state governments for their guarantee funds. The federal government also makes advances available to guarantee agencies to help establish their guarantee funds. While these advances are callable by the federal government, in practice the advances have become parts of the guarantee agencies' permanent capital.

Without question, however, the credit analyst must address the question of the ability of the guarantee agency to meet its guarantee obligations. Sources of income, operating expenses, and default rates are all relevant. The appendix to this chapter contains a calculation of the default rate at which guarantee fee income for the Virginia agency would not cover default payments.

Another pertinent point is that the reinsurance percentages are not default rates because the guarantee agency is also reimbursing lenders for accrued interest. For a 120-day delinquency, the amount paid by a guarantee agency on a 7 percent loan will equal 102$\frac{1}{3}$ percent of the principal amount of the loan. A 100 percent reimbursement rate up to 5 percent of loans in repayment will support a default rate of only 4.886 percent, and so on.

Sallie Mae. The Student Loan Marketing Association (Sallie Mae) was created in 1972 to maintain a secondary market in GSLP loans. Sallie Mae is authorized to buy such loans from eligible lenders and to enter into forward commitments to buy loans. Sallie Mae is authorized to issue federally guaranteed obligations directly to the Federal Financing Bank (FFB) through June 30, 1984, and pays the FFB a rate equal to $\frac{1}{8}$ of 1 percent above the rates for U.S. Treasury securities of comparable maturity. Until recently Sallie Mae was an aggressive purchaser of student loans at very favorable prices (generally at or near par). Sallie Mae in the early 1980s completed an evaluation of its inflation assumptions relative to servicing student loans acquired and, as a result, has become less aggressive in its purchases. Sallie Mae generally is not willing to pay par for loan portfolios having an average account size of less than $4,000, except in cases where the seller remains obligated to service the loan for a specified fee.

STRUCTURE OF STUDENT LOAN REVENUE BONDS

Student loan revenue bonds have been structured many ways, depending on different factors such as bond market conditions and the characteristics of the loan agency. The major difference in structure has been between long-term (15–18 years) issues with principal payments matched to expected loan payments and short-term issues (2–4 years) secured by Sallie Mae or bank forward commitments to purchase the loan portfolio prior to the maturity of the issue. Another significant difference has been between issues secured by a pledge of all loan net revenues (net revenue bonds)—including special allowances, after payment of loan servicing, and operating expenses—and those issues that have pledged to the payment of the bonds only the fixed 7 percent rate on the loans plus principal repayments, leaving the special allowances to the agency for servicing its loan portfolio and other operating expenses (split revenue bonds). In addition, some issues have been closed-ended, requiring excess revenues to be used to call bonds and not permitting parity bonds to be issued. Other issues have been structured on an open-ended basis, allowing for revenues to escape the lien of the bonds (after establishing certain reserves) and permitting the issuance of parity bonds.

An interesting aspect of most student loan revenue bond issues is that a debt service reserve fund does not serve the traditional purpose that most analysts perceive. The principal repayment period on a student loan is not determined until after the student leaves school, and certain deferment periods, such as service in the armed services or graduate school, are permitted. The revenues from an agency's loan portfolio are therefore very difficult to predict, although the agency is virtually assured of receiving interest and principal eventually (either from the borrower or from the guarantee agency). Therefore, the purpose of a debt service reserve generally is to make up, not for the insufficiency of revenues, but for the inevitable differences between actual loan repayment rates and those projected at the time the bonds are issued. It would not be at all unusual or unexpected for there to be a great deal of fluctuation in the amount held by an agency in its debt service reserve fund as amounts therein build up from loan repayments and are used to smooth out revenue flow.

The most important factor in structuring student loan revenue bonds has been the condition of the bond market (i.e., the level of interest rates). When 15–18 year rates on student loan revenue bonds have exceeded the 7 percent base rate on student loans, agencies generally have not been able to market long-term issues because of the possibility that at some future date the special allowance rate (which is directly a function of 91-day Treasury bill rates) will not produce sufficient revenue to cover the portion of the interest rate on the bonds in excess of 7 percent. In such market environments, most issuers have elected to sell short-term bonds secured by Sallie Mae or bank-forward commitments to buy the student loans prior to the maturity of the bonds. While the risk of negative arbitrage still exists in such issues if the bond are sold at rates in excess of 7 percent, the "horizon" is considerably shorter and, in some cases, the forward commitment may be exercised if a negative arbitrage situation develops because of a decline in Treasury bill yields.

An attempt to overcome the so-called 7 percent problem was made by the Nebraska student loan agency in early 1980 through the issuance of "floating rate" bonds. (See Case Study 26.) The fixed portion of the rate on the bonds was set below the 7 percent base loan rate, and the floating portion was tied to the quarterly special allowance. The issue, for a number of reasons, was not well received in the market, and only a few have been attempted by other agencies since them.

Major Risk Factors

In evaluating student loan revenue bond issues, analysts should direct their attention to the following major risk factors:

1. Quality of guarantee
   a. Are loans FISL (no risk) or state guaranteed loans?
   b. What is the size of the guarantee fund as a percentage of loans guaranteed?
   c. Does the trust agreement or state law require maintenance of the guarantee fund at a certain percentage?
   d. What is the historical default rate?
   e. Can the guarantee agency pay operating expenses from guarantee fees or guarantee fund?
   f. What is the relationship with the loan agency (the issuer of the bonds)?
2. Management of loan agency
   a. Are loans originated by the loan agency, or are they purchased from other lenders? If purchased, does the loan agency have recourse for improperly originated loans?
   b. Is servicing of the loans by the loan agency done directly or by an independent servicer? If independent, what is the servicer's record and experience?
   c. What type of automation has the loan agency implemented? What are annual operating expense requirements?
   d. Is the issuer a political subdivision or a nonprofit corporation? If nonprofit, who really controls it? What was the motivation behind creation?

3. Ability to meet operating expense requirements
    a. Is the trust agreement net revenue or split revenue? If split revenue, what operating reserves are required to be maintained? Will adequate loan servicing revenue be available when loans go into repayment?
    b. What is the average account size in the loan portfolio? What portion of the portfolio is presently in repayment?
4. Nonasset bonds
    a. What percent of the issue is nonasset? What provisions exist for recovering nonasset bonds?
    b. Can payment of operating expenses exacerbate the nonasset problem?
    c. Is there protection against parity bonds increasing nonasset bonds as a percentage of outstanding bonds?
    d. Is any "nonbond" funding of reserves or payment of bond issuance expenses required?
5. Reinvestment risk
    a. Are there provisions for unexpended proceeds? Are bonds being issued to provide money to make new loans, or to finance existing loans?
    b. What is the agency's estimated loan volume? How does it compare with the recent past? What are projections of future volume?
    c. What call provisions exist if cash flow from loans is more rapid than projected?
    d. What maturities are allowed for investment of the debt service reserve fund?
6. Risk of fluctuating special allowance
    a. Is the issue being sold at a rate exceeding 7 percent? If being sold as additional parity bonds, what is the weighted average rate of all bonds outstanding, and what are the maturities of prior issues?
    b. If secured by a Sallie Mae or bank-forward commitment, can the commitment be exercised in the event of negative arbitrage?
    c. Is the issue a net revenue or split revenue pledge? If split revenue, what is operating expense risk?
    d. If net revenue, what assurance exists that sufficient net revenues will be produced if the special allowance rate falls?
7. Cash flow risk
    a. What are the assumptions regarding loan repayment? Default? Can the debt service reserve be used to smooth out cash flow without creating a default?
    b. What special allowance rate assumption is used?

    c. Will the issuance of additional parity bonds and the making of additional loans be necessary to create a loan portfolio of sufficient size to cover operating expenses? Is this likely?

8. Takeout risks (applies only to issues secured by forward commitments to purchase loans)

    a. Is "takeout" possible for the entire term of the bond issue or only for a certain period?

    b. What is the takeout price? What average account size is necessary? Are both in-school and in-repayment loans eligible for takeout?

    c. If the takeout price is less than par, what provisions exist for making up the discount?

    d. What is the credit of the takeout entity? If Sallie Mae, does the term of the bonds fall within Sallie Mae's ability to sell federally guaranteed obligations?

FEDERAL LEGISLATION

Effective October 1, 1980, amendments were enacted to federal legislation affecting guaranteed student loans. The major changes relevant to the analysis of student loan revenue bond issues are as follows:

1. The base interest rate on student loans were raised from 7 percent to 9 percent on all loans made on or after January 1, 1980 (except additional loans to students receiving 7 percent student loans prior to January 1, 1980). The special allowance formula was revised so that the total return on student loans remains the same as before. For example, when the base rate was 7 percent, the special allowance rate was 3½ percent less than the average 91-day Treasury bill rate. Now, at a base rate of 9 percent, the special allowance rate is 5½ percent less than the average Treasury bill rate.

The major reason for this change is to lower the cost to the federal government of the guaranteed student loan program by reducing the amount payable by the federal government as special allowances.

2. Special allowance rates to entities which finance their loan activities with funds obtained from the issuance of tax-exempt obligations are to be paid at one half the rate paid to other eligible lenders. These lenders are, however, guaranteed minimum special allowance rates designed to result in a minimum total return of 9½ on loans subject to reduced special allowances.

This change was enacted to reflect the fact that, of those lenders using tax-exempt obligations to finance their programs, most issue fixed-rate, intermediate-term bonds. The necessity for the income earned by such lenders to float up with Treasury bill rates is obviously less, but the necessity for a minimum total return over the life of the loans is greater under such circumstances. The major effect of this change is that student loan agencies will be able to issue bonds at higher rates since loans made under the new legislation are subject to a floor of 9½, instead of 7 percent under the previous legislation. This change will probably increase the volume of student loan revenue bonds and, for issues marketed at rates substantially lower than 9½, improve the credit worthiness of these issues.

3. Sallie Mae's authorization to issue federally guaranteed obligations was extended from June 30, 1982, to September 30, 1984. This change could result in an increase in the volume of issues secured by Sallie Mae forward commitments. The extension of this period to June 30, 1984, in effect permits issues secured by Sallie Mae forward commitments to mature later and is more workable from the issuer's standpoint. Of course, it is very difficult to determine the credit worthiness of an issue that is secured by a Sallie Mae forward commitment to purchase student loans which extends beyond its ability to issue federally guaranteed obligations.

COMMON MISCONCEPTIONS

There are several common misconceptions that should be dispelled regarding guaranteed student loans and student loan revenue bonds. The first, which was created by the tremendous amount of adverse publicity about student loans, is that student loan revenue bonds are especially sensitive to student loan default rates. *This is not true.* As shown in the appendix below, a well-conceived guarantee program should be able to produce income sufficient to cover all but a calamity situation. Moreover, the 100–90–80 sliding federal reinsurance scale reverts back to 100 percent at the beginning of each year. The average default rate for state guarantee agencies (as calculated under the federal law) has consistently been less than 10 percent. Proper servicing can result in an even lower rate. Most student loans do not default because of borrower deceit or adverse personal circumstances. Instead, the great majority of defaults are caused by the lender's loss of contact with the borrower, particularly during the grace period between the time of leaving school and the time repayment begins.

Another common misconception is that projected loan portfolio cash flow is the most important analytical factor in evaluating a student loan revenue bond issue. Revenue uncertainty is a *fact of life* in student loan revenue bonds. The most well-structured financings are those that accommodate the inherent uncertainty through conservative loan repayment projections and appropriate call features to protect against reinvestment risk.

The last major misconception, and perhaps the most irksome, is that the ability of the federal government to continue to pay interest subsidies, special allowances, and reinsurance payments is somehow dependent on legislative renewal of the program. This is absolutely false. Loans made under the existing student loan program qualify for these federal benefits, and the federal government is contractually obligated to pay the benefits whether or not the present legislation is extended.

APPENDIX: DERIVATION OF "BREAK-EVEN" DEFAULT RATE FOR THE VIRGINIA STUDENT LOAN GUARANTY AGENCY

The purpose of this appendix is to show the derivation of the default rate level at which payments by the State Education Assistance Authority (SEAA—the student loan guarantee agency in Virginia) on defaulted loans, net of federal reinsurance reimbursements, would exceed guarantee fees collected by SEAA. SEAA collects a guarantee fee equal to 1 percent of the loan times the number of years to expected graduation plus one year. For example, a loan to a freshman would result in a 5 percent guarantee fee, for a sophomore 4 percent, and so on. On defaulted loans guaranteed by it, SEAA pays 100 percent of the principal and accrued interest. A loan must be delinquent for 120 days before it may be submitted to SEAA. The approximate academic levels of students receiving student loans from the Virginia Education Loan Authority (VELA—the loan agency in Virginia), and guarantee fees to SEAA resulting from such loans, are as follows.

Academic Level	Percentage of Loans	Guarantee Fee
Freshman	25%	5%
Sophomore	17	4
Junior	15	3
Senior	10	2
Graduate 1	18	4
Graduate 2	10	3
Graduate 3	5	2
Weighted average guarantee fee = 3.7%		

It is reasonable to expect that SEAA's average guarantee fee will be somewhat less than the average fee on loans originated by VELA because private lenders are sometimes reluctant to lend to undergraduates. For this analysis, an average guarantee fee of 3 percent will be used. Assuming an average guarantee fee of 3 percent, the default rate which would cause guarantee losses, net of federal reinsurance payments, to exceed guarantee fees collected is derived as follows:

V = volume of loans
guaranteed
X = "break even" default rate

Guarantee fee income	= I	= (3%)(V)
Gross default claims paid	= D	= (V)(X) + (120/360)(7%)(V)(X)
Federal reinsurance receipts	= R	= (100%)(5%)(V) + (90%)(9% − 5%)(V) + (80%)(X − 9%)(V)
At "break-even" default	= I	= D − R

$$X = 19.7\% \text{ "break-even" default rate}$$

This analysis does not take into account any guarantee fees received for deferment periods or any interest earnings which SEAA would realize between receipt of guarantee fees and payment of default claims. Moreover, it does not take into account any permitted withdrawals by SEAA for payment of its operating expenses. The analysis also assumes that the full original principal amount of a defaulted loan is the defaulted amount. It is important to note that this analysis is done at a theoretical equilibrium level of guarantee activity in which the volume of new loans guaranteed is equal in every year and the amount of loans going into repayment status each year is equal to the amount of loans which become fully repaid or go into default during such year.

Water Bonds

CHAPTER **13**

Edward M. Lehr
Originator—Public Finance
Boland, Saffin, Gordon & Sautter

> Water, water everywhere,
> And all the boards did shrink;
> Water, water, everywhere,
> Nor any drop to drink.

The Rime of the Ancient Mariner clearly identifies man's eternal dilemma, and his words are more timely today than they were a century ago. Although the age-old quest for pure water remains prevalent, contemporary public finance and modern innovative technological achievements have provided America's municipalities with reasonable-cost water resources.

Life in colonial times, or even early 19th-century America, was far less complex than today. Water was a commodity which was easily obtained. Demand was localized and generally could be satisfied by drilling another well or tapping the flow of a nearby stream or river. Land development in barren areas was almost unknown, and the bountiful availability of homestead acreage in the West served as an incentive to pass over arid and marginal land.

America changed rapidly in the 19th century. The nation's pastoral economy proved short-lived and was countervailed by an era of dynamic population growth predicated upon the advent of the factory system, industrialization, innovation, the growth of cities, railroading, and westward migration. The net result of America's 19th-century population thrust was a vastly compounded need for pure water.

The financing of water projects, a 20th-century industry based upon more than 100 years of population growth, initially utilized the general obligation debt repayment pledge as a basic security technique. This approach worked well during the 19th century since the cost of financing water facilities was small and could be readily combined with the bonding of other municipal facilities. However, as municipalities faced the continuing need to finance larger and more costly projects, the concept of revenue bond financing, as well as other techniques, evolved.

REPAYMENT PROSPECTS

Water bonds and notes commonly enjoy excellent repayment prospects. Despite varying security elements and repayment covenants, a water financing represents indebtedness incurred for one of man's most basic needs. Advocates stating a case on behalf of water projects are quick to indicate that many of the pitfalls inherent in other types of general obligation or revenue bond financings do not prove problematic when water debt must be serviced. Given circumstances where water bonds reflect one of several types of debt to be serviced from an ailing, tardy, ad valorem tax roll, there exists the likelihood that water operations would command a premium repayment position over less essential public purposes. Likewise, when considered from the aspect of a revenue bond enterprise, water debt would also reflect debt incurred on behalf of an indispensible need requisite to sustaining life. Bearing this in mind, the indebtedness of a water enterprise ranks superior in repayment prospects when compared to other public purpose revenue bond enterprises such as bridges, dormitories, hospitals, or toll roads—all of which fill essential, but elastic needs that may be influenced by general economic or demographic conditions.

DIVERSE SECURITY ASPECTS

Diversity and the absence of a common security pledge characterize the obligations issued on behalf of water projects. Security may vary from the full faith credit and ad valorem tax pledge through a pledge of the revenues of an enterprise. Within this broad spectrum, security may also include payments based upon flow entitlement, actual gallonage consumed, or even the ultimate security of the double-barrel obligation—"the revenues of an enterprise plus the general obligation full faith and credit pledge of the issuer."

The general obligation water bond is one of the oldest and most popular forms of water debt; such bonds are issued by cities, towns, and villages. Their economic strength is drawn in the first instance from the ability to levy ad valorem taxes. Since the ad valorem taxing power serves as the basis for debt repayment, considerations such as management of an enterprise and its revenue-producing ability are secondary. Accordingly, in the case of the general obligation bond, little significance may be ascribed to the debt repayment prospects of the issuer. Experience has demonstrated the general obligation borrowings, particularly the financings of cities and towns with populations in excess of 25,000, to be a very workable method of securing capital. A notable feature of general obligation financing is that it will commonly provide the issuer with one of the lowest borrowing costs (net interest costs) obtainable in the marketplace.

Analytical Considerations

The purchaser of a water bond secured by taxing power should base his repayment prospects on the current and future outlook for tax collections rather than the operating record of the enterprise. Historic tax collection experience as a criterion should approach or exceed 98 percent of levy collections during the levy year, and total collections (current and delinquent) should total 100 percent of levy. The presence of an overlay factor (an increase in the levy to offset anticipated tardiness in collections) is a definite plus factor. The size of the issuer, its administration, overall debt burden, historic repayment record, and overall credit worthiness are also factors warranting review. With respect to community size, there exists a strong preference for the obligations of communities with populations in excess of 50,000, since such communities generally reflect credits with improved bond market access. The population criterion rule of thumb is an arbitrary one and should not rule out commitments in smaller issuers; however, in the case of the smaller municipalities, additional analytical inquiry may be required in arriving at a determination of credit worthiness. (See Chapter 8.)

REVENUE BONDS

Water revenues bonds, whose origins may be traced to early America, were nurtured by industrialization and blossomed in the 20th century. Their widespread acceptance stems from the excellent debt repayment prospects they afford.

The revenue bond bears a twofold purpose. One is the operation of a money-generating, self-sustaining enterprise which transmits the burden of operations and debt service retirement to the users of the enterprise. The second is the circumvention of general obligation debt limitations and the removal of water enterprises from the property tax rolls.

In considering water revenue bonds as possible commitments, it is important to bear in mind that there are security variances, and several types of bonds fall into the revenue bond category. Therefore, a careful review and understanding of the security pledge becomes paramount. Analytical considerations will of course be dependent on the source of revenues pledged. The most common security offered is a pledge of the revenues of an enterprise or system. This pledge is popular among enterprises with distribution systems. Other securing methods call for the payment, by participants, of annual charges or fees either based upon "flow" (gallonage entitlement) or the actual flow drawn. Obligations secured by flow or entitlement are generally issued by wholesalers of water, whose facilities serve as a supply source to a distribution system.

Retail Systems

In evaluating the investment prospects of a distribution system, inquiry into the historic earnings record of the enterprise for the past three to five years is mandatory. The annual net income before depreciation should be consistent from year to year, and in cases where earnings fluctuate, an inquiry into the cause of the fluctuation is recommended. Significant earnings downturns generally suggest abnormal capital construction or extraordinary maintenance problems. Upticks in annual revenues frequently may be ascribed to a change in the rate structure. The annual coverage trend of net income to existing debt service requirements is a helpful barometer, but should not serve as the basis for forming an absolute judgment of credit worthiness. Since water is a vital commodity desired at low cost, water systems will commonly set utility rates at the lowest possible level requisite to sustaining ongoing operations. Accordingly, whereas rates established to provide for the payment of operating costs and 1.5–2.00 times annual debt service charges would be a positive factor, it may also be possible to fix rates and charges at a level to generate a 1.10–1.20 times debt service and retain a very workable financial posture. Given circumstances wherein the enterprise has established stable operating and revenue collection patterns (as well as predetermined operating, maintenance, and expenditures), rates may be set at levels sufficient to produce a minimal net revenues coverage of 1.00 to 1.10 times debt service coverage. A general rule of thumb would be that higher annual net revenues to debt service coverages contain the elements of a superior investment commitment. The coverage test is a limited tool; it provides investors with an indication of historic earning ability but fails to account for current and projected revenue trends. Its chief shortcoming as an analytical tool is the inability of the test to evaluate other vital factors (such as physical condition, growth trends, capital improvements) which also influence credit worthiness.

VARIANCES IN SECURITY

In the event water were universally present at its point of consumption, there would likely be only two methods of securing water indebtedness—the general obligation bond and the revenue bond. Yet this is really not always the case. All too often a city, town, or village serves as the purveyor of water obtained from a distant source. Another problem arises when water is needed, but the service area is rural agricultural and there is no city, town, or local government to perform the service. Given the presence of such circumstances, the traditional methods of financing new facilities with general obligation or revenue bonds become problematic if not wholly impossible. In the case where a city or a larger governmental unit has no access to water resources, the issuance of general obligation or revenue obligations can provide capital but cannot produce water. In the case of a rural area, the problem becomes paramount since the sparsely populated territory fails to enjoy access to the capital market. For example, were the rural area to issue general obligation debt with its limited economic resources, it might well face the inability to retire indebtedness due to its limited ad valorem tax base. Utilization of the revenue bond financing method would also prove highly problematic, because of the issuer's inability to generate adequate cash flow to service operations and indebtedness. Accordingly, the quest for water, especially in rural areas, often require innovative financing techniques. Let us now consider the alternate financing methods available and evaluate them.

Irrigation and Improvement Districts

The formation of an irrigation or improvement district as a financing conduct is one of the innovative alternates to traditional ad valorem and revenue bond approaches. Irrigation and improvement districts are popular in the West and Far West. They endeavor to provide water in a specific territory that is often agricultural or rural—sparsely populated land. The district generally serves as a retailer marketer of water obtained from distant sources. In cases where local resources are abundant, the district may also serve as an originator in addition to its marketing function. District revenues are derived from both water sales and the levy of ad valorem taxes.

The analysis of these districts requires a very detailed study of the basic makeup of the utility's service area. Traditional analytical norms and ratios may not necessarily provide an adequate measure of the district's worth. In this regard, the investor should consider demographics carefully. Identifying the 10 largest taxpayers, their enterprises, and the length of their historic presence in the local economy will prove helpful. Likewise, in the case of a primarily agriculture territory, consideration should be given to the product line. Certainly, high-valued specialty crops with great dollar yield per acre will provide the local farmer with more wealth than abundantly grown grain crops. Simply expressed, an acre of citrus, strawberries, or truck crops in southern California will outstrip corn, rice, or wheat grown in the midcontinent. Accordingly, it is suggested that one of the best methods for appraising the improvement or irrigation district involves, if possible, a personal inspection tour.

Water Wholesalers

Water wholesaler collection systems have developed as a response to satisfying water demand where insufficient resources were available at the point of consumption. The growth of wholesalers is directly attributable to the growth and development of the nation's cities, towns, and villages, which in early America commonly developed at a port of entry, a crossroads of commerce, or a trading outpost. Many major cities that grew notably during the 19th century (New York, San Francisco, and others) were fortunate enough to have developed their own reservoirs and imponding facilities and therefore became less reliant on participating in the purchases or operations of wholesalers. Alternately, the nation's smaller cities, towns, and villages (which were largely products of burgeoning 20th-century industrialization) relied on the joint development of common supply sources as economical and expedient methods of enlarging their water resources. Accordingly was born the concept of developing remote facilities for the benefit of a common geographic area or even an entire region. Examples of joint participation in the development and utilization of wholesale resources may be found throughout the nation.

Some of the many wholesale systems include the Imperial Irrigation District, Lake Texarkana Water Supply Corporation, Lower Nueces River Water Supply District, North Texas Municipal Water District, and the Colorado River Municipal Water District. The creation of a wholesale utility for the development of facilities for the mutual benefit of two or more communities has several distinct ramifications. In terms of a participating local government, it can obtain water from a distant supply source. Moreover, joint project development also permits the undertaking of larger projects that have often proved too expensive or economically unfeasible for the smaller municipality. Additionally, each participant entering into a purchase agreement avoids the problem of the proliferation of facilities development and the possibility of competing with others (municipalities) for watershed area rights and transmission lines. Perhaps the most notable feature of mutual project development is the advantageous financial structure of project development that permits the issuing body (a large wholesaler) to serve as the master borrower on behalf of several smaller entities, which by contractual agreements assume shares of the borrowing authority's operating costs and indebtedness. Another significant feature accruing to the participants of a wholesaler enterprise is the ability of the participant to share in the development of facilities, which can be economically constructed and operated without recourse to incurring the direct general obligation debt of the participant.

Perhaps the foremost feature of the wholesale supply system is the bond market receptiveness enjoyed by the wholesaler systems, which appeal to investors for several reasons. One is the underlying security and economic strength of the wholesaler, whose ultimate security is the municipalities served. The wholesaler's strength rests upon his ability to collect, impound, and deliver water. They will generally bill for a share of flow or flow entitlement with rates and charges fixed somewhat in excess of annual operating debt service and reserve requirements. A second feature of the wholesale system is market identity. The programs of larger, frequent borrowers and the expertise of their management are generally known to the investment community.

The larger water authorities can also generate additional investor appeal. These issuers and their programs are commonly known to investors. As repeated borrowers in the marketplace they have placed debt with investors throughout the nation. Their obligations are more actively traded in the secondary markets, and the presence of a continuing postsale market affords noteholders or bondholders an increased degree of liquidity.

Security is another positive aspect of the wholesaler. The larger systems whose debts are secured by joint agreements draw their strength from the makeup and resources of several underlying communities. Their operations are shielded from daily local governmental operations. Therefore, the wholesaler plays the role of an informal third party, providing borrowing and professional management expertise on behalf of its underlying clients, and serves as the purveyor of service essential to community life, without consideration to the directives and decisions of the political party in office within a community.

Local Water District

Local districts organized for the purpose of constructing, financing, and operating distribution and supply facilities have become increasingly popular in the last 50 years. These districts, whose primary function is chiefly distribution, are commonly found in the West and Far West. Their primary source of revenues is generally derived from the district's ad valorem taxing power. The strength and well-being of a district rests to a large extent upon the property tax base and the stability of the district's collection record. Water sales also serve as a gross income component. In evaluating the performance and outlook for a district, consideration should be given to its financial results and operating record achieved during the last three to five years. Key indicators include water sales trends, which should follow a gradual, general, overall growth pattern. In the event annual variances in sales, income, demand, or net revenues are prevalent, a more detailed examination of operations is required. Specific areas of consideration may include climatic conditions involving above- or below-average rainfall, rate structure changes, changes in the demographics of the community or district's service area, population growth trends, community wealth, and the outlook for orderly community growth.

ANALYTICAL CONSIDERATIONS

The investor seeking to purchase a fixed-income commitment faces two considerations. One involves an investment decision predicated upon the credit, protective covenants, and debt repayment aspects of a commitment. The second involves the rate of return (yield), liquidity, and degree of price erosion or potential for price gain afforded by the investment he has selected. The discussion here relates solely to credit. Market or technical considerations are not regarded. Some of the underlying credit considerations warranting evaluation include the following:

The Rate Covenant

An analytical plus factor is the presence of a covenant to fix and maintain rates in order to pay operating maintenance and provide a cushion in excess of 1.00 times the current annual debt service and reserve requirements. The question of what is an acceptable coverage level is paramount. The incorporation of a rate covenant producing high net revenues may achieve excellent statistical results and debt service coverages but could prove problematic or even a hardship to the customers of a utility system. By the same token, the adoption of an inadequate rate covenant may also prove detrimental to the issuer. Too low a rate covenant leaves little room for budgetary error, collection tardiness, or escalating operating costs prevalent in inflationary times. Experience indicates the incorporation of a rate covenant prescribing the imposition of rates and charges sufficient to cover operations, maintenance, and 1.20 times the annual debt service and reserve requirements will generally provide a workable financial structure. The 1.20-times rate covenant, while a good rule of thumb, should not be viewed as a written-in-stone criterion, for examples of satisfactory system operations utilizing lower rate structures are common. With respect to the question of whether the rate covenant should require revenues greatly in excess of the foregoing norm, both experience and personal opinion suggest such practices are unnecessary and can place an unduly great cost burden upon the current users of a utility system.

Additional Bonding

Utility systems are dynamic, growing enterprises which require periodic enlargements and facilities improvements. A well-structured financing bears this in mind and should contain a protective additional bond covenant which will afford the issuer maximum flexibility in undertaking expansions and renewals in order to meet the ever-changing needs of the service area. The covenants restricting the issuance of additional parity bonds should permit the issuer optimum flexibility. Alternately, the bondholders should enjoy a degree of protection from the issuance of a virtually unlimited amount of additional debt, which could erode their investment position. Therefore, the additional bonds test should actually reflect a compromise, possibly favoring the issuer. However, in order to retain the bondholder's investment position, the additional bond covenant should have a twofold requisite: (1) that the issuer's recent operating progress (last two years) achieve an in-the-black net income equal to or exceeding the requisites prescribed by the rate covenant; and (2) the facilities to be constructed will, after they have been placed on line, sustain or add to the enterprise's net income. The latter requisite can be achieved by requiring the certification and forecast by an independent consulting engineer, as a result of his review of the capital improvements program, that the facilities to be acquired are necessary and workable and, based upon his preparation of a forecast of all system revenues, the future system will at least sustain an operating record equal to or exceeding the provisions of the rate covenant.

Mandatory Connections

The presence of a local community ordinance mandating all water users to connect to a supply system enhances an investor's security position. However, the absence of mandatory connections need not be an investor's compelling consideration. Experience dictates that, save for the presence of overabundant local well water supply sources, there exists a universal need to obtain quality municipal water.

Hence, demand in most cases will eclipse a mandatory directive. Even with the absence of the mandatory connection ordinance, the power of the local board of health can exert extremely strong pressure to force utilization of the municipal supply source. The "clout" of the local board of health may be attributed to water contamination, which is common to most of the nation's urbanized communities. Since each board of health retains the power to prescribe, set, and enforce quality standards, its directives compel individual users to purchase or produce water of a quality equal to that of the municipal enterprise. In view of this concentrated power, a health board directive can equal or exceed the power of the connection ordinance.

External Aid

Federal and state grants-in-aid for water projects are uncommon. The underlying rationale is that water is an essential commodity whose purveyors are private corporate entities, which function for a profit, or municipal corporations performing a service for a common good. Therefore, the grant structures and aid programs found in hospitals, sewers, transit systems, and other public-purpose projects are not a factor in water utility financings.[1] Were the question of the absence of federal and state grants a negative factor detracting from the quality of water obligations to be considered, the author would be inclined to offer the opinion that the highly inelastic demand for the commodity may well countervail the absence of government aid to the water industry.

Customer Billings

An unusual analytical tool is an attempt to evaluate a utility's operating record on the basis of its ability to provide water service at an economically low customer billing charge. This approach requires a study of the average quarterly customer billing for several systems. The billing approach as a tool of analysis is unique and perhaps reflects an oversimplification of many variable factors, but it will provide an investor with a general monitoring of a system's management expertise and operating efficiency. Although variables such as system age, debt posture, borrowing costs, proximity to resources, growth rate, and the character of the service area will account for billing-cost differentials, it is suggested that the utility system capable of providing good customer service commensurate with lower billing charges warrants attention. The underlying rationale is that the lower-cost

---

[1]State of New Jersey's aid to the North Jersey District Water Supply Commission in 1980 reflects an exception to traditional grant policies.

operator may very well be the more efficient enterprise and provide an investment with better debt repayment prospects.

An approach to evaluating operating efficiency based upon consumer billings would be to calculate an average customer's quarterly bill. Assuming a minimum average household consumption of 5,000 gallons for quarter, a quarterly bill ranging from $25 to $40 may be considered reasonable.[2] The investor, in evaluating a utility commitment, may wish to make additional inquiry into the performance of a particular system whose rates substantially exceed these norms.

Operating Capacity

An analytical inquiry into a system's performance should also include an inquiry into the level of system operations in order to determine the relationship of supply capacity and demand. As a general rule of thumb, an investor should consider a healthy system as an operating entity with the capacity to draw and deliver quality water in quantities far in excess of peak demand. In this regard, the operations of water enterprises differ from the operations of other municipally oriented, revenue-producing enterprises—such as electric systems, hospitals, dormitories, and toll roads—where operating levels close to or at full capacity generally provide most beneficial operating results.

In the case of water enterprises, the underlying rationale for less than peak utilization is that water enterprises operating at levels substantially below optimum capacity can serve additional customers and generate higher revenues without necessitating costly expenditures for capital improvements and the ensuing additional bonding costs. Hence, future customer and revenue growth may be applied to already established debt changes and improve the system's net revenues and its ratios of net revenue to debt service coverage. Given the alternate position, that of a system operating at peak capacity, any additional demand should result in the need for enlarged facilities and additional bonding. Under these circumstances the bondholder's investment position would be somewhat eroded because of the need for additional bonding and an increase in the overall debt burden to be serviced.

Special Considerations

In addition to the foregoing analytical criteria, there are special circumstances which warrant investors' consideration. These factors

---

[2]Billing estimates are based upon charges imposed in 1980 by an efficiently operating, established municipal utility. Regional variances in consumption and operation patterns may result in higher minimum demand and utility system operating charges.

are indeed special since they exist only in select geographic areas. They include: (1) the problem of salt water intrusion, (2) the possibility of a sinkhole, and (3) dependency upon multiwell water supply resources.

1. Salt water intrusion is a condition where raw river or well water becomes contaminated by the presence of salted ocean water. The condition is activated by a rapid drawdown of fresh water from its supply sources and the natural intrusion or replacement of the fresh water by seawater. This condition commonly occurs on low-elevation, coastal, flat land and is particularly prevalent in Florida. The problem of salt water intrusion is easily solved by simply reducing the rate at which the fresh water is drawn. This can be achieved by utilizing additional wells or drawing water from additional or more distant water sources. As for the economics involved, both methods require additional financing.

2. The sinkhole, a cave-in of the earth's surface, is a phenomenon common to rock-free, flat terrain. The sinkhole condition is a product of overtaxing subsurface water resources, which in turn results in a fall-in of surface land. The condition can prove detrimental by (a) disrupting portions of a system's operations, and (b) causing costly property damage in cases involving urbanized territory containing high ad valorem rateables.[3]

3. Multiwell water supply sources also warrant investors' special attention. Simply stated, were a system limited to one, two, or a few wells as supply sources and they were to become contaminated or exhausted, the system's ability to deliver water and operate would be impaired. Likewise, in the case of those systems which rely on one or two wells to provide a substantial portion of the system's overall capacity, a similar problem could impair the system's delivery ability.

CONCLUSION

Water bonds and notes are all too often an overlooked ultimate investment. Man's essential, inelastic, insatiable thirst for pure water serves as the basis for this contention. A well-structured water financing will provide investors with the opportunity to participate in an underwriting whose debt repayment prospects may be second to none.

Indebtedness created on behalf of water facilities is essential debt whose repayment prospects are based on uncompromising need. Accordingly, the traditional reasons for the enterprise's poor earnings record and debt repayment abilities are virtually nonexistent. In the

---

[3]In May 1981, the city of Winter Park, Florida, sustained the loss of an entire shopping center, a number of housing units, and several expensive imported cars as a result of a sinkhole.

case of water enterprises, the analyst cannot ascribe declining college enrollment trends, elective surgery, an energy crisis, general economic conditions, inflation, higher fuel prices, or a number of other reasons as the underlying causes of poor financial and operating progress. In brief, well-secured water obligations together with select other types of revenue bonds may be classified as an ultimate investment.

Small-Issue Industrial Development Revenue Bonds

CHAPTER **14**

Steven E. Scheinberg
Financial Consultant

INTRODUCTION

The volatility of the money markets, evidenced by rapid fluctuations in interest rates and capital availability during the past several years, has significantly curtailed the level of industrial and commercial real estate development. This has served to reduce the economic growth of many communities.

The long-term, fixed-rate mortgage which has served as the primary vehicle for financing income-producing projects has, for the most part, become unavailable from traditional lending sources. Additionally, many real estate projects under consideration for development have been postponed because they are not economically feasible at the recent high level of interest rates and construction costs.

Faced with a significant decline in new economic development, many states, counties, and municipalities have created economic development authorities (EDAs) capable of providing a vehicle for tax-exempt financing of projects in an effort to maintain and expand job opportunities and to enlarge the local tax base. These agencies are empowered to issue limited-obligation securities, known as small issue industrial development revenue bonds (IDBs), for the purpose of financing selected industrial and commercial projects. At least 40 states allow bonds to be used for financing commercial facilities; 18 have no restrictions.

Although the EDAs can agree to act as issuers of securities, there is no assurance that investors for these bonds can be found. Historically, projects financed on a tax-exempt basis and secured by real estate have been placed as tax-exempt mortgages that have been purchased by banks and casualty companies on a private-placement basis. At times this has proven to be a relatively thin market.

However, in recent years, individual investor interest in these securities has grown steadily as the rate of return available on them has reached exceptionally high levels. As a result, a capital market of nonrated bonds has developed that, in 1981, accounted for an estimated 7 percent of all municipally issued securities. Further, many regional and national brokerage firms have participated in underwriting these bonds and maintain secondary markets in them.

In general, however, traditional municipal bond research does not apply to these distinct, tax-exempt securities. This is because the bond's fundamental credit worthiness is not dependent upon the issuing community's willingness or ability to pay. Secondly, all tax-exempt, financed, industrial and commercial development projects operate in a competitive marketplace as compared to municipally sponsored projects that have a regional monopoly.

Lastly, the analysis of small issue IDBs is highly specialized and requires the analyst to integrate real estate, equity, and municipal bond research in order to determine the true investment value of a particular bond.

STEP ONE: LEGAL AND STRUCTURAL CONSIDERATIONS

Under present law, all securities sold by a state or political subdivision to finance a self-supporting, revenue-producing project are defined as industrial development bonds. The federal law that governs the issuance of IDBs is Section 103(b) of the Internal Revenue Code as amended in 1954. This portion of the code was subsequently modified by the Revenue and Expenditure Control Act of 1968 which increased the dollar amount and changed the legal requirements under which industrial development bonds could be sold on behalf of an individual project. Today, the code provides for two classes of IDBs: exempt issues and small issues.

The basis for the difference in treatment between exempt and small issue IDBs lies in the nature of the project's direct and indirect benefits to the community in which it will be located. Bonds issued under the portion of the code pertaining to exempt securities are for facilities that provide the greatest and most diverse social benefits, and from which no individual profits financially. Examples of exempt facilities include electric generating plants, mass transit projects, hospitals, and airports.

Conversely, typical small issue IDB projects are sold on behalf of a for-profit corporation or partnership and include factories, hotels, shopping centers, and office buildings. Although these projects benefit the community in that they expand the local economy, increase the property tax base, and produce new employment opportunities, they also provide a direct financial return to the developer. In addition to profit, this may include investment tax credits, depreciation benefits, or other tax advantages.

Whereas a state, city, or town may sell industrial development bonds to finance a profit-making facility, it is rare that any will participate monetarily in the venture. To maintain this distinction, small issue industrial development bonds are legally structured so that the issuer acts as a pass-through without any financial liability for the debt that bears its name.

In the most commonly used legal structure for IDBs, the local economic development authority holds title to the facility and leases it back to the developer(s) for a period that is coterminous with the maturity of the bonds and with annual lease rental payments that are equal to the yearly debt service expense. This permits the developer to retain the collateral financial benefits, obtain lower-cost tax-exempt financing, and provide maximum protection from liability for the issuer. In addition to structuring IDBs in a manner that financially insulates the issuer, bonds authorized under Section 103(b) of the Internal Revenue Code and determined to be small issues must meet a variety of supplemental legal requirements, a violation of which will result in a loss of the bonds' tax-exempt status.

In terms of investment risk, this can be as great a liability as default. Although investors are usually protected by some remedy if the bonds do become taxable, the loss of their exempt status will almost always adversely affect the holder by resulting in an immediate loss of value and liquidity, or an inability to reinvest at an equivalent tax-exempt rate. For these reasons and others, the analysis of small issue IDBs should start with a reading of the legal opinion and a comprehensive review of the terms of the indenture.

Specifically, those issues structured by and with opinions by a nationally recognized bond counsel are most desirable. Also, it is advantageous to the investor that issues have an opinion rendered by a counsel who is knowledgeable in the laws of the state and locality where the project will be constructed.

Among the primary reasons for the use of an experienced, nationally recognized bond counsel is the common use of bond proceeds for construction in order to reduce the total interest expense of developing a commercial real estate project. In these cases, it is primarily the responsibility of the bond counsel, in drafting the indenture, to ensure that the bond proceeds may only be dispersed after proper certification of work completed. Experienced bond counsels will also include in the indenture a variety of other basic safeguards to protect investors prior to the release of any funds. These include the receipt of all environmental approvals and permits, completion of all plans and drafts, obtaining all necessary forms of insurance, and bonding of the construction company. As additional security, the indenture should assign the potential proceeds of any third party to the bondholder.

When reviewing the contents of the indenture and the tax-exempt opinion, analysts should realize that each has, in part, been written to comply with two of the major legal requirements of the IRS code. These are the "capital expenditure rule" and the "substantially all test." Although, to be offered for sale, all issues will initially comply with both regulations, the language of the opinion and, to a greater extent, the obligations of the developer under the indenture, will provide valuable insight in determining the structural quality of the issue. For example, the capital expenditure rule prohibits the developer of a commercial real estate project financed with tax-exempt bonds from making capital expenditures in excess of $10 million within the issuing community's incorporated boundaries in a six-year period that extends for three years prior to and after the sale of the bonds. Therefore, the developers should covenant in the indenture not to make any deliberate expenditure that would result in a loss of the tax-exempt status of the bonds. This is essential, since the failure of bond counsel to include an expense that the IRS ultimately deems to be applicable towards the $10 million limit, or the realization of a necessary expenditure that was not foreseen, may reluctantly force the developers to postpone some other portion of the project in order to remain under the limit.

For this same reason it is also preferable to avoid issues with a par value in excess of, say, $9.95 million, since margin for error will be slight and a significant number of commercial real estate projects experience cost overruns.

The second major concern to analysts and investors involves the application of bond proceeds. Referred to as the substantially all test, this regulation mandates that at least 90 percent of the issue's proceeds must be used to acquire land and depreciable assets. Costs such as issuance expenses, monies held as a reserve, or capitalized interest are all considered neutral and may therefore be deducted from the par value of the issue to determine the total amount of funds applicable under the rule. This is permissible since, without these expenditures, the bond issue could not be sold and the project built.

However, IRS rulings on what other expenditures qualify under the test have failed to produce a comprehensive guideline to what is considered an applicable cost. For instance, the expense of refurbishing or modifying equipment or a building is includable, but not the cost of relocating used equipment, the acquisition of inventory, or the purchase of goodwill.[1] Further, many of the decisions stating what does qualify, especially when a project is completed below cost, have been rendered through private rulings and are considered unclear. Analysts must therefore carefully review the scope of the project and the use of bond proceeds looking for any expenditure that for some reason could not qualify. Also included in the review should be the construction timetable and allowances for overruns.

Lastly, to be considered for investment, the indenture of each issue should provide that, in the event of taxability, either all bonds will be called for immediate prepayment at a substantial premium (preferably 5 percent) or that the coupon rate will be increased to that available on similar taxable investments.

STEP TWO: SMALL ISSUE INDUSTRIAL DEVELOPMENT BOND CREDIT ANALYSIS

Once the analyst is satisfied with the quality of the legal and structural components of the issue, attention should be focused on determining the bonds' financial credit worthiness. For the basis of analysis, all small issue IDBs may be categorized into two groups. These are:

1. *Industrial projects:* secured by a rated or nonrated corporation's full faith and credit, and possibly the facilities constructed with bond proceeds.
2. *Commercial projects:*
   a. Speculative issues, secured by a first lien on the facility and its gross revenues.
   b. Lease rental issues, where a substantial portion of the annual debt service is derived from one or more leases with primary tenants who are rated or nonrated credits.

Despite the similarity in the security elements of these bonds, the analysis of each is substantially different. This is due to a variety of

---

[1]Robert S. Price, *ABCs of Industrial Development Bonds* (Packard Press, 1981), p. 16.

factors that reflect the relative amounts of real estate, equity, and municipal bond analysis necessary to evaluate the credit worthiness of each type of IDB.

Industrial Issues: Analytical Considerations

Historically, most IDB issues have been sold on behalf of a regional industrial company seeking to expand its facilities. The profile of a typical industrial project in this group would include funds for site acquisition, the construction of a new plant, and equipment purchases. Together, it is expected that the investment will enhance the corporation's ability to do business and, thereby, its market share.

The analysis of this group of IDBs should therefore start with a comprehensive review of the company's balance sheet and income statement, both of which should be certified by an established regional or national accounting firm. In these issues, the opinion of an equity analyst is essential. The traditional analytical ratios should all be reviewed as well as an attempt made to assess the company's prospects for growth over the ensuing five years. This is especially necessary for smaller, young corporations.

Analysts should also make year-to-year comparisons to determine the company's financial stability, level of growth, efficiency of growth, and ability to pay. In particular, analysts should attempt to assess the company's overall capacity to incur decreases in sales and meet the annual fixed charges.

To determine the bondholder's true security in an industrial project, one critical area for in-depth analysis is the use of bond proceeds. Special attention should be paid to the amount of funds designated for equipment and machinery as compared to amenities that add little to the bondholder's fundamental security. Of particular importance are the useful life of the equipment, depreciation benefits, and salvage value.

Whereas hotels, shopping centers, and office buildings have limited alternative values, some industrial buildings and certain types of machinery can actually appreciate in value, thereby benefiting the bondholder. Thus, the most desirable industrial bond investments will be issues where the majority of funds will be used to acquire a building and machinery with an extended useful life, high residual or secondary market value, and a diversity of applications.

Another essential factor to consider in the analysis is the company's total operating history. In general, the shorter the company's operating history the more risk to the investor over the long run. Therefore, credit should be given to companies which have been in continuous business in excess of 20 years. Bond issues on behalf of young but successful industrial companies may be acceptable risks if the majority of the proceeds will be used to acquire plant and machinery such as a warehouse in an industrial park.

In this group of bonds, analysts may be selective and should feel comfortable recommending securities with a maturity equal to 1½ times the company's operating life depending upon historical performance.

Commercial Issues: Overview

Since 1977 the amount of IDBs sold to finance commercial real estate projects has increased precipitously.

Unlike bonds sold on behalf of industrial corporations, IDBs issued to finance commercial real estate projects are typically start-up situations in which the developer is constructing a new revenue-producing facility. Although virtually all issues in this category of bonds are secured by a first lien on the project and its gross revenues, for the basis of credit analysis commercial projects may be divided into two distinct groups: (1) purely speculative projects such as hotels or cultural facilities sponsored by a nonprofit charitable organization and (2) lease rental projects where all or a substantial portion of the annual debt service will be derived from leases with one or more primary tenants.

Regardless of the specific type of commercial project being financed, one aspect of the bond's credit worthiness that is essential to consider is the ratio of developer equity to bond funds. Typically, real estate developers will seek to borrow as much of the total project cost as possible, thereby minimizing their potential monetary loss. As a rule, however, the larger the amount of debt the project must repay, the greater the risk to the investor. In response, analysts should require at least 25 percent of the total project cost to be equity, either in the form of developer's capital or a federal, state, or local economic grant. Further, highly leveraged projects should especially be avoided whenever the facility has a limited alternative economic value and its sale, in the case of default, will probably not produce sufficient funds to redeem all the outstanding bonds.

The only instance in which developer equity may not be required is when the bonds are a general obligation of a regional or national chain and are not dependent on the success of the individual project.

Speculative Commercial Projects:
Analytical Considerations

Perhaps the most difficult type of industrial development bond to analyze is that sold to finance purely speculative projects (e.g., hotels). This is because the analyst's principal source of financial information is a feasibility study.

Similar to the importance of bond counsel in determining the issue's tax exemption, analysts should carefully note who performed the feasibility study. When credit worthiness is evidenced with a study by a firm that has little or nominal experience, bond issues will have greater risks to the investor. For this reason it is advantageous to look for issues with feasibility studies by the various accounting and consulting firms that have developed expertise in assessing the viability of specific types of projects.

When reviewing speculative commercial real estate projects, analysts will generally find it helpful to divide their analysis into three parts. First, they should assess the experience and the ability of the developer(s) to construct the facility and to manage it. Second, analysts should examine the legal opinion and the terms of the indenture, as previously outlined, this time also noting the obligations of the developers to maintain and to operate the project. Third, analysts must determine the financial strength of the project by dissecting the feasibility study. Together, these three broad areas of analysis will reveal the issue's true credit worthiness.

Although many developers sign fixed-cost contracts to insulate themselves and bondholders from significant overruns during construction, all sizable real estate projects involve risks that potentially endanger the tax-exempt status and/or investment quality of the bonds. Therefore, with respect to the construction period, it is clearly advisable to avoid issues undertaken by individuals without substantial development experience, especially when the project is unique or highly specialized.

To assess the project's management, particularly in a developer-operated facility, the best guide is to compare the size and the scope of the project to the type and depth of experience of the developer. The safest investments in these bonds will be for projects sponsored by individuals with substantial experience in real estate construction who retain independent professionals to manage the facility once it is completed. This will serve to minimize the risks during construction and help ensure that the project is administered by efficient and cost-effective management.

Almost always, when analyzing speculative real estate projects, the most complex portion of the offering statement to review will be the feasibility study and, in particular, the sections containing the cost/income projections. In this area, some basic guidelines are helpful. First, demand projections based upon the historical performance of similar facilities in the development area are the most reliable. Second, analysts should not expect any facility, albeit brand new, to significantly outperform its competitors unless it has some special feature that is generally unavailable elsewhere. Third, always compare the assumed rate of interest on the bonds in the feasibility study to the actual rate of interest, and adjust the projected debt service coverage to reflect any increase or decrease in the annual interest expense. In some issues this difference can be upwards of 150 basis points. Fourth, projects that are to be built in stages in order to comply with the capital expenditure rule involve the greatest degree of risk. Last, analysts should compare the issuer's demographics as described in the feasibility study to the latest available census data on the community, looking for any substantial differences in such statistics as population, income growth, level of economic activity, assessed valuation, etc.

If not otherwise included in the feasibility study, one final task that is essential for the analyst to perform in order to evaluate a speculative real estate project is a sensitivity analysis. This will reveal the project's ability to withstand decreases in usage and still meet all fixed expenses. Here, analysts should start by varying the income projections and then examine the effect of a 10 percent increase in construction and operating costs on the project's cash flow and debt service coverage. Issues that are truly credit worthy should be able to withstand such increases and still meet the annual debt service expense within a comfortable margin.

Among the other financial factors that are essential for commercial real estate projects to be considered credit worthy are: ample reserves for replacement and repair, sufficient initial operating capital, a debt service reserve fund equal to one year's maximum debt service, and comprehensive insurance coverage pledged as security to bondholders.

Analysts must carefully scrutinize each of these points to ensure that the bondholder's interests are protected. The failure of any particular issue to meet the minimum levels mandated in the feasibility study or by good business practice should be grounds for the analyst's rejection.

Lease Rental Projects: Analytical Considerations

Bonds secured by rents collected under lease arrangements may be issued for both industrial and commercial projects, including shopping centers and office buildings. In these issues the fundamental credit worthiness of the bond should be considered only as strong as the primary tenant(s)' ability to pay.

Credit worthy lease rental bond issues should grant the bondholder a first lien on the facility, its appurtenances, the real estate, and the project's gross revenues. However, in some issues the developer(s) may not own the land but have a leasehold interest that extends significantly beyond the life of the bonds. These are clearly less secure than issues where the developer has a fee-simple interest and the land is further security.

In addition to any income from the primary tenant(s), the pledged revenues should include all other rents from such sources as strip space leased to local merchants in a shopping center or office building, a coffee shop, newspaper stand, or parking garage. In essence, no portion of the project, whether financed with bond proceeds or equity, should be omitted as security for the investor.

Similarly to bonds sold for small manufacturing or industrial companies, the analysis of the primary tenant's financial position should be prepared by an equity analyst. In issues where the principal tenant is a rated corporation (e.g., K mart), the analyst's job will be significantly easier. This is true even if their rent does not fully cover the annual debt service expense. Alternatively, in these issues the credit analysis should focus on the secondary tenants and their ability to pay.

Equally as important, however, are the legal responsibilities of all tenants as defined in the indenture. Triple net leases—those that provide for the tenant to assume all interior and exterior maintenance, including such items as utility costs and snow removal—are the most desirable. In general, bondholders will benefit from less ongoing responsibility to the project by the developer/landlord. This does not include necessary oversight.

During the course of the issue's life, investors should expect changes in the secondary tenants and in some cases the primary tenant(s). This is most likely to occur where the value of the real estate and the level of local business activity have declined. Obviously, when the new occupant is a weaker credit than the previous tenant, the bondholder's security interest will deteriorate. In this respect, analysts should carefully review the procedure, described in the indenture, upon which tenants can be replaced.

Other covenants of the indenture that are required to make the bonds credit worthy include allowances for repairs and improvements, a debt service reserve fund, reasonable conditions for modifications of the project, the disposition of insurance proceeds, general repair expenses, payment of taxes and other potential assessments, and conditions for the sale or transfer of the property.

Finally, for issues sold to finance shopping centers, analysts must check for potential additions to the project that could ultimately violate the capital expenditure rule.

CASE STUDIES

The following case studies are summaries of actual bond issues that were brought to market and placed. Each has been selected because it reflects the salient points outlined in this chapter. In some

issues, a variety of different financing techniques have been combined
and fully illustrate the diverse nature of the small issue IDB market.

Case I

$23,900,000
College Park Business and Industrial
Development Authority, Georgia
Industrial Development Revenue Bonds
Series 1982

of which:

$7,700,000 Airport Hotel Associates #1 LTD Project
$8,300,000 Airport Hotel Associates #2 LTD Project
$7,900,000 Airport Hotel Associates #3 LTD Project

The $23.9 million College Park Business and Industrial Develop-
ment Authority issue was a unique offering that obtained an exemption from the IRS limit relating to capital expenditures by dividing
the project into three independent components with three separate
development groups. The distinct nature of this issue was initially
revealed in the summary of the legal opinion on the cover page of the
offering statement. Here, the emphasis should be on the section of the
official statement entitled "Tax Exemption" where the following language appeared:

> A private letter ruling has been obtained solely for the purpose of ex-
> empting each issue of the Series 1982 Bonds from the Proposed Amend-
> ments of Regulations Section 1.103–7 and 1.103–10 published in the
> Federal Register on October 8, 1981, relating to whether multiple lots
> of industrial development bonds will qualify as separate, exempt, small
> issues or will be treated as a single large issue.

In effect, the three separate development groups were permitted to
mutually offer separate bond issues to finance a single 400-room hotel
adjacent to a new civic center. By doing so, the developers were able
to save substantially on issuance costs.

Case II

$1,900,000
Rutherford County, Tennessee
Industrial Building Revenue Bonds
Series A
(Alton Box Board)

This issue was sold in 1970 to raise funds for the construction of a
manufacturing plant that was expected to create 150 new jobs. Bond

proceeds were used to acquire land ($45,000), construct a building ($880,000), purchase equipment ($865,000), and issue the bonds ($110,000).

Fundamentally, in this issue the bondholder's true security was as strong as the Alton Box Board Company's ability to pay. However, among the conditions specified in the indenture the company was required to:

Lease the building from the county for a period identical to the life of the bonds and with payments in an amount equal to the annual debt service;

Complete the project even if the cost exceeded the total bond proceeds;

Maintain and insure the project over the life of the bonds;

Restructure or repair the building if damaged;

Pay a 6 percent premium to investors if the bonds become taxable.

In addition to these security provisions, all of which served to protect the investor, almost 95 percent of the bond proceeds were to be used to acquire assets that could have some value in the secondary market.

In 1981, the Alton Box Board Company was sold to the Jefferson Smurfit Group of Dublin and is now doing business as the Alton Packaging Company.

Case III

$3,400,000
Schuyler County Industrial Development Agency
Industrial Development Revenue Bonds, 1971
Watkins Glen Grand Prix Project

This issue was sold in 1971 on behalf of the Watkins Glen Grand Prix Corporation to finance improvements to the Watkins Glen Grand Prix track in Schuyler County, New York. It was projected at the time of issuance that the annual Grand Prix race, in addition to other events, would provide new economic opportunities for the community.

In this issue, the Watkins Glen Grand Prix Corporation covenanted to lease the project for a term identical to the bonds, to properly maintain it, and to meet all other supplemental expenses. Of the $3 million in bond proceeds, almost all were used to refurbish the race track and reviewing stands.

To demonstrate the credit worthiness of the bond issue, a feasibility study was performed and was included in the offering statement. According to projections at the time, bondholders could expect a minimum 2.24 times debt service coverage over the 20 years the bonds were to be outstanding. This projection was based on the attendance performance of similar spectator sports and the historical level of usage of the track since the opening of the USA Grand Prix in 1961.

In the past several years, however, the race track has experienced declining attendance as a result of poor weather at the time of the Grand Prix. Further, the International Grand Prix Association has considered eliminating Watkins Glen from the Grand Prix circuit. As a result, there was a default on the bonds in 1981.

Case IV

$9,900,000
Economic Development Corporation
of the City of Battle Creek
RBM Hotel Corporation
Series A

This issue was sold to provide partial financing for a 15-story, 248-room hotel facility with 52,500 square feet of adjacent retail space to be located in the central business district of Battle Creek, Michigan. The project, which was initiated in 1980, is the third phase of a re-development plan designed to revitalize the downtown area.

The total cost of the project was estimated at $17.9 million of which $2 million was developer's equity, $5.5 million an Urban Development Action Grant (with repayment subordinated to bondholders), a $500,000 loan from the Stouffer Corporation, and $9.9 million in bond proceeds.[2] In this issue the debt represented only 55.3 percent of the total project cost and appraised value.

Under the terms of the indenture, the bondholders have a first lien on the project and its revenues, including the rents received under the lease agreement with the retail shops. The facility is to be managed by Stouffer's Corporation, Hotel and Inn Division, and contains two dining rooms, a cocktail lounge, meeting and conference rooms, and recreational facilities.

Title to the project will be held by the issuer, with the developer obligated to make lease payments in an amount equal to the annual debt service. The developers of the project have substantial experience in real estate development and have signed a fixed-cost construction contract. They have also convenanted to maintain the project in good condition including any necessary repairs or modifications, obtain all necessary and reasonable forms of insurance, pay all taxes and liens, fund a debt service reserve fund equal to the maximum

---

[2]Under the present IRS guidelines, projects that have an Urban Development Action Grant may total $20 million of which only $10 million may be derived from bond proceeds.

annual debt service due, and pay an 8 percent premium to investors in the event the bonds become taxable.

Included in the official statement was a copy of the feasibility study that projected the first year's coverage to be 1.5 times based upon a 70 percent occupancy rate in the hotel and a 38 percent usage rate in the retail space.

Construction of the hotel was fully completed in 1981. The shopping space, however, was expected to be completed in 1982–83.

Case V

$5,700,000
College Park Business and Industrial
Development Company, Georgia
Industrial Development Revenue Bonds
Days Inn of America, Inc., Project
Series 1982

The College Park Business issue is an example of a nonrated commercial company that has obtained local tax-exempt financing for a facility. In this issue, the bonds are secured by the full faith and credit of the parent corporation, the Cecil B. Day Company, and a first lien on the facility. The investment quality of these bonds is therefore only as strong as the Cecil B. Day Company's ability to pay.

Since the credit worthiness of the bonds is not directly tied to the success of the project, a feasibility study was not necessary. Instead, a copy of the company's income statement, related financial reports, and a summary of the corporation's day-to-day business was included.

This project is presently under construction.

Case VI

$14,200,000
Intrepid Museum Foundation
A New York Not-For-Profit Education Corporation
16 Percent Gross Revenue Bonds,
Series 1982

The Intrepid Museum Foundation was created in the city of New York to provide financing and management for the drydocking and transformation of the aircraft carrier USS *Intrepid* into a naval museum. The foundation was chartered as a not-for-profit corporation under the IRS Code and was legally empowered to issue tax-free bonds.

The credit worthiness of these bonds is totally dependent upon the success of the museum as a tourist attraction. Included in the official statement was a feasibility study that based the projected demand for the museum upon a wide variety of similar national and citywide tourist attractions.

As a general test of the project's ability to repay the bonds, a sensitivity analysis was included in the study. First the project's total revenue forecast was assumed to be 10 percent less than expected, and second, costs were assumed to be 10 percent more than expected. In the first instance average debt service coverage over the first 10 years of operation was reduced from 1.83 times to 1.46 times. In the second case, on increased costs, debt service coverage was reduced from 1.83 times to 1.64 times. This was exclusive of the payment of subordinated loans.

The Intrepid Museum bonds were fully placed at a 16 percent rate of interest, and the facility opened for business in August 1982.

CONCLUSIONS

The preceding analysis and research formats are intended to provide analysts and investors alike with guidelines to review small issue IDBs. In some cases these bonds will offer investors the opportunity to lock in 150 to 200 basis points more in yield than Baa- or BBB-rated issues. As the market for these securities continues to grow, analysts will become routinely obligated to make recommendations on their credit worthiness.

Although nonrated small issue IDBs have traditionally been perceived as highly risk oriented, in some cases they are very attractive investments. If considered as a tax-exempt mortgage structured into a bond issue for sale to individuals, their record with respect to financial losses has generally been excellent, when chosen on a selective basis. This is evidenced by the investment success of insurance companies and commercial banks, who have historically been the primary source of funding for these projects.

Airport Revenue Bonds

CHAPTER **15**

Alan J. Goldfarb

Investment Officer
The First National Bank and
Trust Company of Oklahoma City

Allan A. Ryan III

Senior Vice President
Smith Barney, Harris Upham & Co., Inc.

The nation's airports play a vital role in providing a transportation network that can quickly move people within a short period of time and at relatively lower cost when compared to all other modes of travel.

Generally, airport revenue bonds are payable from a pledge of all revenues derived from the operation and use of the airport's facilities. Such a pledge traditionally is supported by contractual use agreements with the carriers and concessionaires serving the facility.

Airport revenue bond financing developed as a response to the demand for new and or improved airport facilities following World War II. Commercial air travel had been available, albeit in a limited form, since the 1920s. Technological advances, enhanced by the development of bigger, faster aircraft during the war, provided a base for the rapid expansion of the air carrier industry. The introduction of commercial jet aircraft in the late 1950s caused a further and more explosive growth and with it a renewed demand for appropriate ground facilities.

In the early 1950s, however, the industry was still in its infancy.

A long-established rail system and a traditional reliance in the United States on the automobile, combined with aircraft that were smaller, slower, and less reliable, created a perception in the investment community that bonds supported by revenues derived from the operation and use of an airport should be classified as risky securities. An evaluation of the airline or airlines serving a community was considered the principal means of determining security, not the existing or potential demand for air transportation from the community being served. Investors therefore attached particular importance to the support given to existing or projected revenues by contractual agreements with the airlines.

In the early days of airport revenue bond financing, which took place in the 1950s, commercial airline travel was virtually in its infancy, and the buyers of airline revenue bonds placed particular importance on the support given to projected revenues by agreements with airlines as nationally known commercial enterprises. The financing of Miami International Airport in 1954 by the Dade County Port Authority is an early example of this concept.

Carrying the Miami concept a step further was the financing of Chicago's O'Hare International Airport in 1959 by airport revenue bonds secured largely on the strength of use agreements with the dozen carriers that agreed to serve the proposed airport. (Another major factor, again, was the size of the financing—$120 million—in relation to the market then being served. O'Hare was a new ball game: a facility created by the airlines as the first "connecting hub" and sized well beyond the needs of the Chicago market alone.)

The O'Hare agreements provided for periodic adjustments of landing fees to the extent necessary to cover airport maintenance and operations and revenue bond debt service. In recognition of this commitment by the airlines to support the proposed airport, it was necessary for the public operator to give up certain controls over the airport operation—in particular, decisions regarding future capital improvements.

The financing of new terminal facilities in Tampa in 1968 represented still another variation in the concept of use agreements whereby airline "guarantees" of debt service coverage (through a "residual cost" rate-making approach) did not take effect until after the fifth year of operation of the proposed new facility. The airport operator, the Hillsborough County Aviation Authority, (with the support of the city of Tampa and Hillsborough County) assumed the financial risks of airport operation through the crucial first five years of operation. In the Tampa case, much greater emphasis had to be attached to feasibility studies compared with the reliance on airline credit that existed in the O'Hare airport bonds.

As the air transportation industry has grown and matured, the investment community has come to perceive more and more that the security of an airport revenue bond issue should also include the underlying strength of the local air traffic market. San Francisco sold $143 million of 30-year bonds with a 15-year landing fee agreement that had only a 12-year remaining term. Phoenix and Las Vegas have issued airport revenue bonds with no airline agreements, relying largely on the estimated strength of their growing traffic markets, as projected in their respective feasibility studies, to provide comfort to the investor. Even without deregulation and the current CAB legislative proposals, it was probable that long-term airline agreements, with a term coincident with the amortization period of the bonds, would be used less and less in revenue bond financing at the larger airports.

SIGNIFICANCE OF AIRLINE USE AGREEMENTS

In view of the foregoing, it is important to understand and emphasize the significance of use agreements between airlines and airport operators:

1. They have historically provided strong security: as such, the agreements or airline guarantees have the effect of broadening the market for large bond issues.
2. They are useful to airport operators because they reduce the operators financial risks and ensure a specified level of operating revenues and coverage.
3. They evidence an intent (though not necessarily a legally binding commitment) by the airline corporations to provide service to the community.[1]
4. They establish and provide evidence of the financial and operational relationship between the airline and the airport operator.
5. They give endorsement by knowledgeable commercial interests of the future viability of the planned airport project to be financed with the proposed bond issue.

Not every airport operator wants, needs, or in fact should have use and lease agreements with the airlines. There are many situations, however, where such agreements are necessary for bondholder secu-

---

[1]Many airline leases contain termination provisions which permit an airline to terminate its agreement (upon notice) if its authority to serve an airport is revoked, suspended, or substantially modified by the CAB. (Note that the authority to serve under a CAB certificate is *both* a right and an obligation.)

Under deregulation, an airline can initiate a request to cease service, and the CAB *must* grant that request (and issue the appropriate order) unless continuation of the service is required to maintain "essential air service" at the airport. Thus, at many airports, an airline apparently could terminate a long-term agreement unilaterally, even if that agreement had been used in part to secure a revenue bond offering.

rity, particularly at airports where the magnitude of debt required to finance facilities required by the airline industry is large relative to the size of the market being served.

Airline Use Agreements and Revenue Bond Financing— Case Examples

Phoenix. There has been much discussion among municipal bond analysts and those in the airport industry of the so-called "rate-setting" approach and the relative merit, in terms of credit quality, of financing airports without airline agreements as has been done in Phoenix.

The absence of airline use agreements has certainly not prevented Phoenix from relying on revenue bond financing for capital improvements. Yet, it is important to note that Phoenix has a relatively modest revenue bond debt burden in relation to the traffic market served.

In addition, the Phoenix revenue bonds benefit from the additional debt coverage provided by subordination of substantial airport-related general obligation debt.

Nonetheless, the absence of airline use agreements in Phoenix has not greatly detracted from the credit worthiness of its revenue bonds.

Yet airline use and lease agreements, which perhaps are not "essential" in every case, are important to the credit quality of many other airport revenue bonds—both from a historical perspective (the vast majority of the dollar volume of airport revenue bonds outstanding today are secured in part by long-term airline agreements) and in the new context of a deregulated airline industry.

San Jose. San Jose is a good case in point. In the mid-1970s, the CAB granted to a number of airlines "hyphenated route authority"— the right to provide service to the San Francisco Bay Area at any of three airports. Under this authority, San Jose received significant new air service by new carriers—service that was, in fact, "optional" on the part of the carriers. Thus, San Jose operated in much like a deregulated air service environment even before the passage of the Airline Deregulation Act.

The San Jose use and lease agreement was negotiated in 1977 in light of the knowledge that substantial capital investment (to be financed through airport revenue bonds) would be required over the next 5 to 10 years for terminal, parking, and airfield expansion, and for land acquisition and relocations to accommodate both continuing traffic growth and tight state noise regulations. The total investment is certain to be large in relation to the traffic market served by the airport. An effective long-term financial arrangement between the city and the airlines is therefore essential.

Although the 30-year term of the San Jose agreement indicates a "long-term" contractual relationship between the city and the airlines, each airline has the right to terminate and walk away on 30-days' notice with no lease obligation. The basic goal of the parties was only to establish and document an operational relationship.

Orlando. In Orlando, new terminal facilities will be constructed to meet the stated needs of the new airlines entering the Orlando market under deregulation, but only on the condition that each new airline executes the present long-term use and lease agreement and commits to amortize the cost of the facilities constructed for its benefit. The primary objective of this policy on the part of the airport operator was to transfer to the airlines the financial risk (of underutilization of facilities) inherent in a market dominated by recreation and tourism. There is "open access" to any airline willing to take the risk (the 30-year rental commitment).

The Orlando rate-making formula assures the operator of a substantial annual "profit" (funded debt service coverage) and gives it the flexibility to plan and construct additional capital improvements as necessary following review and consultation with the airlines.

Conclusion on the Use Agreements

The proper conclusion to be drawn from these examples is that different airport bond securities are necessary in different circumstances.

In the past, airline use agreements have played an important role in the financing of this nation's airports, and they will continue to do so in the future. Long-term use agreements should not be sacrificed at the "altar" of the elusive and ill-defined ideal of "open access." Blanket proposals to set aside the prevailing practice of securing bonds with airline use agreements in the interest of possibly solving a problem experienced at only a few of the nation's largest airports should be seen as a major threat to credit quality.

The airlines should have to enter into long-term use agreements where the circumstances appear to be appropriate for providing bond security. Where major investments in facilities are required, the airport operators and the bondholders should not be left holding the bag, particularly in today's climate of uncertainty regarding the economy and availability of fuel.

IMPORTANT FUTURE CONSIDERATIONS IN AIRPORT REVENUE BOND ANALYSIS

Deregulation will bring about changes in the credit and security features of airport revenue bonds. The underlying strength of the air traffic market will be of paramount importance. Long-term airline use agreements will be less common but should continue to be used in appropriate circumstances.

What, then, are the key factors investors should consider in evaluating airport revenue bonds in the future? We suggest that, in addition to the air service market and the traditional financial security factors (reserves, coverage requirements, etc.), there will be:

1. Greater Emphasis on "Managing" Existing Facilities. The first objective must be to obtain the greatest capacity from available facilities through renovation and improvement and through more intensive utilization.[2] Airport operators must be judged in how well they improve the utilization of existing terminal facilities. Where existing long-term use agreements exist, the operator must be able to rely on "jawboning" with incumbent carriers to release or sublet space to new carriers.[3] New use agreements should establish utilization standards and reserve management flexibility to reassign space.

2. More Rigorous Justification of Planned Improvements. Because of deregulation, airport operators will face increased pressure from the airlines (and possibly the federal government) to invest in additional facilities. Investors and analysts should be looking for more rigorous justification of planned improvements in relation to the optimum facility requirements needed for the market being served. Construction of excess capacity, in the absence of specific long-term airline guarantees as written in the use agreements, should be viewed as a very negative credit feature.

3. Greater Importance of Feasibility Studies. Significantly greater reliance should be placed by investors on feasibility studies regarding the traffic potential of the air service area and revenue generating potential of the airport. The added flexibility of airline entry and exit and the diminished reliance on long-term use agreements make these appraisals of future traffic and revenues of paramount importance. The fundamentals of airport revenue bond financing—such as operating characteristics, airport rates and charges, coverage of debt service, flow of revenues, maturity structure, reserves, and various covenants—will still be significant, but the essence of revenue bond security will be the vitality and stability of the local demographic and economic base as substantiated by professional feasibility consultants. Thus, careful evaluations of local area economic trends, air service, traffic forecasts, aircraft operations and

---

[2]With regard to airfield capacity, FAA task force studies of the eight busiest airports, evaluating means of improving capacity and reducing delays, are now nearing completion. These studies may soon be extended to include the 25 to 30 busiest airports.

[3]The sponsor does retain the right of condemnation of a portion of a lease-hold if necessary to assure the availability of facility for new carriers.

landing weight projections will have to be made. In addition, rules of thumb should be developed to compare airport revenues and costs with industry norms.

4. Increased Scrutiny and Appraisal of Management Performance. Because the flexibility of airlines to stay or leave reduces the importance of the obligation previously assumed by the airline corporations, investors should look with increasing scrutiny at the performance of airport management. The added responsibility of airport operators (and potential liability) in a deregulated industry makes it mandatory that the practical judgments regarding current and future needs for air service and required facilities be made by experienced, competent professional managers. Investors and analysts should look more carefully for evidence that critical management and planning decisions are not compromised by local political pressures or considerations. Carefully considered, formally adopted lease and concession policies will be important.

These are uncertain times for the airport operators. The pressures to incur large amounts of long-term debt for airport expansion and development are great. The long-term prognosis for the airline industry is, at best, cautious in light of the cost of new equipment and facilities, upward pressures on fuel prices, and the unpredictable economic outlook.

Changing economics, operations, and resulting investor concerns have created an increasing need to approach the credit analysis of airport bonds on a case-by-case basis. There are significant differences between airport facilities and the credit worthiness of their respective bonds.

WHAT THE ANALYST AND INVESTOR SHOULD LOOK FOR IN THE FEASIBILITY STUDY

An airport feasibility study is a special report prepared by a consultant, and paid for by the bond issuer, which states that the airport being financed by tax-exempt bonds is necessary and will be capable of supporting the debt by revenues generated from the facility.

The typical feasibility report should be divided into several sections:

1. *Current airport system* should describe the present airport facilities, including airport traffic, as to the number of enplaned (boarding) passengers for the past five years and projected for the next five years.
2. *Economic and demographic factors* should describe the area where the airport is located; the employment trend in the area; the type of commercial activities and projected growth in the

area. Also included in this part of the report should be a detailed description of the airport's current and planned facilities. This section also should detail the project being financed, including the status of actual construction, a breakdown of the airlines along with the percentage of the market they serve. *This information is essential for a complete analysis.*

3. *The air trade area* should contain a geographic description of the area served by the airport. This section should include trend analysis, both historical and projected, relating to such items as the population of the service area, general economic indicators; i.e., nonagricultural employment, disposable personal income, tourist activity, air cargo, etc.

4. *Significant factors affecting future airline traffic* is a key section that should be carefully reviewed. Usually included in this portion of the report is information relative to government regulations which could negatively impact the revenues of the airport, possible ramifications of a poor national or international economy, as well as data concerning the profitability of the airline industry.

The actual report prepared by the consultant will almost always appear as an appendix to the official statement. Analysis of a revenue bond financing for an airport requires that the report be carefully scrutinized to ensure that the airport's system is financially and operationally sound. The analyst or investor should be alert to any downward trend in key operation or financial areas, including passenger enplanements, population growth, debt service coverage, etc. The analyst should also keep in mind the effects of the national as well as the local economy on the airport's operations.

In conclusion, the airport consultant is hired by the bond issuer to give their stamp of approval to the tax-exempt financing. A thorough reading and evaluation of this important document can provide insight concerning the viability of the airport system and the resulting credit worthiness of the bonds.

ADDENDUM

The Effect of Airline Deregulation on Airport Bond Security

The Airline Deregulation Act of 1978, enacted and signed into law in October 1978, has ushered in a new era of change and uncertainty in air service at the nation's airports.

Among its many provisions, the act:

Opens up dormant routes (where no more than one carrier is already providing service) to the first applicant willing to initiate service.

Allows each carrier to add one new route per year for the next three years without CAB approval.

Reverses the burden of proof (regarding the "public convenience and necessity" test for new service) from the applicant to the opposing party in CAB route award procedures.

Permits termination or suspension of service at a community upon 90 days' notice.

Allows the carriers significantly greater flexibility to raise or lower fares.

After December 31, 1981, CAB authority over domestic routes was eliminated, and carriers now have total flexibility to provide service on any routes without any application process. Other provisions of the act establish a subsidy program geared to ensure that small communities will receive "essential air service."

Effect of Deregulation on Airline Service and Airport Facility Needs

What does deregulation signal for the future?

The *non-hubs* (and perhaps some of the smaller small hubs) stand to lose a substantial portion of the certificated service now provided by the local service carriers. Small enplanements at the non-hubs limit the ability of these carriers to operate economically with the larger jet aircraft they now have in their fleets. This situation should stimulate the inauguration and growth of new commuter airlines. It is possible, however, that the local service carriers may choose to stay in these markets by expanding their own commuter-type services— such as Southern Airway's use of its Searingen Metro aircraft on some of its present routes.

For the smaller airports, the shift toward reliance on commuter airline services could have a beneficial financial effect. Increased flight frequency by smaller aircraft will mean greater peak spreading, increased utilization of existing airport facilities, and less rapid deterioration of capital expenditure requirements in the future.

On the other hand, most of the *small hubs* and the smaller medium hubs—those with traffic levels generally ranging from 250,000 to 750,000 enplaned passengers annually—should retain significant scheduled airline service but with a higher proportion of flights by regional carriers. These airports will be important elements of the emerging feeder-hub airport system—a system that depends upon extensive feeder service to and from small communities (small and medium hubs). The small hubs will probably lose many of the gains in air service that they have achieved over the past 15 years. Fewer airlines will serve each airport, and they will provide service mostly to the important hub airports (in the southeast, Atlanta and Memphis).

Nonstop service to more distant points will be sharply curtailed. Airlines that now provide only limited service to given airports will probably leave those markets; the established carriers will become more dominant.

Requirements for new facilities at the small hubs should be less severe than at the large airports; greater utilization of existing facilities will be possible as a result of the "consolidation" of air service to fewer carriers. Management attention will shift from long-range planning to interim "maximization planning"—planning designed to maximize the capacity and functional efficiency of existing terminal and airfield facilities.

Yet some small hubs (such as Charleston, South Carolina) will require major investments in the next few years—particularly for new terminals. These airports will represent the most difficult credit risks because of *(a)* uncertain future air service patterns, *(b)* lack of earnings history, and *(c)* extensive investments required relative to the traffic market being served. The small hub airport operator may be caught in a "squeeze"—limited ability to rely extensively on either general obligation bond financing (as a result of the taxpayers' revolt) or revenue bond financing (because of uncertainties regarding earning capacity and air service under deregulation).

Because of this situation, the small airports will have to bridge the gap between general obligation financing and "pure" revenue bond financing by choosing financing approaches that combine features of both. Where possible, the *credit* of the taxpayers may be required (tax pledges for maintenance and operations on debt service) to lower overall borrowing costs, with rates and charge policies designed to recover all airport costs, thereby avoiding the need for taxpayer *dollars.*

At many *medium hubs,* air service patterns should not change very dramatically. (Nashville, for example, has had virtually no changes in air service since passage of the act.) Facility requirements will follow modest trends in traffic growth anticipated at these airports.

At the larger airports (*large hubs* and larger medium hubs), significant new service has been initiated on new and competitive routes by both new and incumbent carriers as a result of the dormant and permissive authority provisions of the act. This new service, coupled with the traffic surge generated by increased fare flexibility and discount fares, is producing (and will continue to produce) severe terminal capacity constraints and, in some instances, increased aircraft delays because of airfield congestion at a number of airports.

The introduction of new airlines and more flights is generating tremendous pressure to build new, exclusive-use terminal facilities and to expand airfield facilities at the large airports. Financing requirements will be substantial at some airports over the next five years, and this will make the exact determination of credit worthiness all the more important.

Single-Family Mortgage Revenue Bonds

CHAPTER **16**

Rhonda S. Rosenberg
Assistant Vice President
Drexel Burnham Lambert Inc.

Eileen Titmuss Austen
Corporate Vice President
Director of Municipal Research
Drexel Burnham Lambert Inc.

Since their inception, tax-exempt single-family mortgage revenue bonds have been widely used and well received. The market for these bonds has grown significantly, as they have comprised an increasingly greater share of total new municipal offerings since 1977. Because of their relatively high yield, generally strong security, and self-supporting nature, these bonds have been popular with politicians, taxpayers, and investors.

From the issuer's viewpoint, single-family mortgage revenue bonds allow the local governmental unit to satisfy a public purpose by increasing the supply of low-cost housing. Housing costs are reduced because the homes are financed from capital raised in the municipal bond market, realizing the interest cost savings associated with tax exemption. In addition, the issuer does not assume any direct or indirect debt liability. Since the bond program is supported by mortgage loan repayments and investment earnings, the debt is considered a self-supporting obligation for which the issuer has no legal responsibility. Consequently, single-family bonded debt is not included as part of an issuer's traditional debt burden.

From the taxpayer's point of view, the bond program can serve to stimulate new construction and therefore jobs, provide new property tax revenues without an increase in tax rates, and stimulate the local housing resale market.

Due to the program's broad-based popularity, billions of dollars of housing bonds have been sold and are actively traded in the secondary market. As the market has been flooded with new issues, underwriters have been hard pressed to develop new security and structural devices to enhance the attractiveness of one program over another. Consequently, analysts have been called upon to evaluate these new techniques and their impact to bondholders. In addition, analysts have been required to provide an ongoing credit assessment of housing bonds especially as changes in interest rates, real estate markets, unemployment rates, and other economic factors impact mortgage repayments and possibly bond security.

This chapter identifies several tools the analyst can use to measure a new issue's credit value, as well as techniques that provide for ongoing credit assessment. The initial sections of the chapter offer a detailed explanation of bond structure and security, and highlight the differences between state and local (counties, cities, towns, villages) programs. The latter half of the chapter focuses on analytical strategies designed to measure an issue's ability to generate a revenue stream of sufficient size to pay program expenses and debt service. Finally, the chapter concludes with a forecast of potential new-issue volume. Because new-issue bond sales will be limited over the near term (for reasons explained later on), we expect that analysts will be increasingly called upon to provide current information on outstanding issues as opposed to credit assessment on new issues. Consequently, we advise the reader to pay particular attention to analytical techniques designed for evaluating established bond programs.

EVOLUTION OF A PROGRAM

Prior to the issuance of tax-exempt housing bonds, low-cost housing was made available primarily through federal, state, and local programs that offered rent subsidies, tax credits or abatements, or loan guarantees. In 1968, Congress passed legislation permitting the use of tax-exempt bonds for housing purposes. This legislation gave states the green light to authorize the issuance of revenue bonds whose proceeds would finance low- and moderate-cost housing. Most state housing finance agencies (SHFAs) were created shortly afterward and sold their first bond issues in the early 1970s. (Local government units did not become tax-exempt housing issuers until 1978.)

The authorization to sell housing revenue bonds gave SHFAs a means by which to increase the amount of money available to finance housing at lower cost, as capital in the tax-exempt market could be raised at below-conventional rates. The authorization to sell revenue bonds gave the agencies the ability to assume a role similar to that of a private lending institution. They were expected to originate mortgage loans at interest rates that reflected their own cost of money, which of course was less than that of a traditional lender.

In an effort to make the state agency programs successful, bond issues were generally tightly constructed to help ensure adequate cash flow and bondholder protection. The extent to which these objectives are realized varies from program to program and is reflected in the credit quality which ranges from medium- to high-grade credit worthiness. The various program arrangements and their impact on bond security are described below; specific risk analysis techniques are outlined in a later section of this chapter.

MORTGAGE PURCHASE BONDS VERSUS LOANS–TO–LENDER BONDS

Although single-family housing bonds have been issued under a variety of names (residential mortgage revenue bonds, home ownership development bonds, single-family mortgage purchase bonds), they have been administered either as loans-to-lender programs or mortgage purchase programs. These two programs have certain similarities. Both share the goal of increasing the amount of low-cost housing. They are structured similarly in that both require the issuer to act as a private lender who lends money at rates at least equal to his cost of raising capital plus operating expenses.

There are, however, notable differences in their implementation, sources of revenue to support debt service, and form of bond security. Mortgage purchase bonds are issued to buy mortgage loans from those lenders who agree to originate loans on behalf of the issuer. Proceeds from a loans-to-lender bond sale, however, are primarily used to make collateralized loans to lending institutions (savings and loans associations and/or banks) who must use the money to originate mortgage loans at a rate above their loan interest cost.

Mortgage purchase bonds are payable from a revenue stream comprised of mortgage loan repayments and investment earnings on reserve funds. (Reserve funds are discussed later in this chapter.) Loans-to-lender bonds however, while sharing with mortgage purchase bonds the feature of revenue deriving from investment earnings on reserve funds, are payable from a revenue stream generated by lender loan payments: loan payments from the lender to the issuer.

Finally, mortgage purchase bonds are secured by a portfolio of mortgage loans purchased with the bond proceeds. Loans-to-lender bonds, however, are secured by collateral which must be pledged to each lender's loan. In the event a lender defaults in its loan repayment obligation, the trustee can liquidate the collateral to rectify the loss and pay debt service on a timely basis. The collateral can take the form of either securities or mortgage loans. When securities are used as collateral, they usually must be direct obligations of the U.S. government or obligations guaranteed by the U.S. government. The amount of collateral required can vary from 100 percent of the principal amount of the outstanding loan up to 150 percent of the outstanding balance, depending upon the investment quality of the collateral.

Loans-to-lender programs have not been used as frequently as the mortgage purchase program by either SHFAs or local issuers. Lending institutions often decline participation in these programs because they are too costly. The cost becomes burdensome because the collateral requirement is valued at the market value of the collateral (this is tied to interest rate cycles) and not at par. Thus, as interest rates rise, lending institutions have to augment the dollar amount of collateral so that the *market value* of the collateral equals the collateral requirement.

THE MECHANICS OF SINGLE-FAMILY BOND PROGRAMS

The single-family bond programs, as they have been established, are essentially modeled after the corporate pass-through method of financing. The pass-through concept as it applies to the single-family program is quite simple. When a SHFA or other issuer, such as county, city, town, or village, borrows money in the tax-exempt market at a rate appreciably less than the current rate of home mortgages, the interest cost savings are passed on to the home buyer in the form of a relatively lower-rate mortgage. After the bond issue closes, the proceeds are used to fund mortgage loans and bond reserve funds, and to pay the costs of bond issuance (trustee fees, underwriters fees, legal fees, etc.)

The proceeds used to fund mortgage loans usually comprise 80–85 percent of bond proceeds. This money is held by the trustee and is invested at a rate above the bond yield until it is needed to finance a loan. The loans are financed through private lenders who, prior to the bond sale, agree to originate and service the loans on behalf of the issuer. Bond issuers rarely originate and service their bond loans because private lenders are considered to be more experienced at mortgage financing, have established credit relationships with constituents in the issuer's jurisdiction, and enjoy increased accessibility to those desiring mortgage financing. (Most lenders have numerous branches, whereas the typical issuer maintains only one office in order to curtail administrative costs.) With the origination of mortgage loans an asset is created—a mortgage loan portfolio—that can generate revenues to pay debt service. Generally, mortgage loan principal is used to pay bond principal while mortgage interest is used to pay bond interest.

The proceeds used to fund reserve funds usually comprise 10–15 percent of total bond proceeds. The two reserves commonly created are a debt service, or capital reserve, fund and a mortgage reserve, or reserve for loan losses, fund. In addition to the mortgage loans, these reserves are used as security for the bonds. Reserve funds must be maintained at minimum amounts that are specified in each program. Usually the debt service reserve fund must be maintained at an amount equal to 10–12 percent of the outstanding bonds or maximum debt service due in any year. The mortgage reserve fund is usually maintained at an amount equal to 1–3 percent of the outstanding principal amount of mortgage loans. Although reserve requirements never change over the life of the bond issue, they can be tapped to prevent a default when revenue shortfalls occur. The reserve funds are invested in medium- to long-term securities at a rate above the bond yield. Along with mortgage interest payments, the investment earnings generated from the reserves are used to pay bond interest. Along with mortgage principal payments, the principal amount of the reserves is used to retire bond principal. (Typically, reserve principal is used to satisfy a portion of the final principal payment.)

The result of using proceeds to pay the costs of issuing bonds creates a gap where initially there is more debt than assets, or nonasset bonds. The existence of nonasset bonds poses a major risk to the program because the bonds (debt) are not secured by an asset (mortgage loans or reserves). Although they are called nonasset bonds, the liability is spread out over the entire issue and affects every bondholder. This gap is covered during the life of the bond issue through arbitrage earnings such as the investment earnings generated from the investment of bond proceeds prior to loan origination. (Arbitrage earnings are a major feature of the majority of issues and will be explained in greater detail later on.)

From the previous description, it would appear that single-family bond programs are similar to bond programs that finance the creation of a new hospital or power supply system. These bond programs are commonly referred to as start-up projects because bond proceeds are used to create an asset and revenue stream where none existed prior to the bond sale. They are often considered speculative, because delays in the creation of the asset can interfere with timely debt service payments.

Unlike hospital and power bond programs, however, the asset created in a single-family bond program is an unknown entity to the investor. For example, the quality of the mortgage portfolio asset cannot be assessed because the mortgage loans are not in place. Furthermore, the bond issuer has no control over the life expectancy of the asset (mortgage loans). In a power or hospital bond program it is possible to structure the debt payment to coincide with the life expectancy or depreciation of the hospital or power plant. While the mortgage loans and the mortgage bonds can be structured to mature at the same time, mortgage loans are often prepaid. The Federal Housing Administration has tracked the average life of its 30-year mortgage portfolio on a state-by-state basis. In general it has been found that 30-year mortgage loans have an average life as short as 10–12 years. It is therefore possible for a housing issuer to have more bonds outstanding than revenue-producing assets, should a significant percentage of loans prepay.

To establish a successful bond program, several factors must be present. First, sound lending criteria must be observed to create a portfolio/asset of investment-grade quality. Second, the asset must always at least equal the outstanding bonds in order to ensure that the revenues generated will be sufficient to meet debt service. An asset of sufficient size must be created in time to generate a revenue stream to meet the first debt service payment. Finally, the program must be tested under various prepayment assumptions to ensure that the program's cash flow can maintain the balance between assets and liabilities. These problems are interrelated and must be resolved by careful planning prior to bond issuance and by requiring, in the bond indenture, rigorous financial management during the life of the program. To a large extent, the method used in resolving these problems determines the program's credit quality.

Creating a Quality Asset

The objective in creating a quality asset is to promote timely mortgage repayment and to discourage mortgage loan default. Establishing the lending criteria prior to the bond sale is critical because it allows one to assess the quality of the asset. To some extent, however, the public purpose of the program limits the quality of the portfolio. This purpose often requires an issuer to reserve its tax-exempt mortgage money for those persons and families of low to moderate income. The income requirement, which is typically defined in the bond's official statement, can restrict bond mortgages to persons who would not qualify for a conventional loan. Within this restriction, an attempt may be made to ensure that a quality asset is created by limiting mortgage loan eligibility and establishing other financial criteria. For example, the purchase price of the property being financed may also be limited. These limitations, defined in the public-offering statement, seek to create a situation where restricted income levels and financing needs are matched.

Quality is further enhanced as each mortgage loan in the portfolio is secured by a first lien on the financed property. In the event of mortgage loan default the issuer, or the loan servicer on the issuer's behalf, has the right to acquire the property through foreclosure proceedings. Acquisition of the property permits property resale, the proceeds of which must be used to pay debt service in place of the scheduled mortgage payments. The value of the first-lien however, can be jeopardized if the property is not maintained. Therefore, in an attempt to protect the value of the first-lien status, two additional requirements should be made. These mandate that an equity contribution or downpayment be provided prior to loan origination and that the mortgage finance a primary or principal place of residence. Private lenders contend that the equity contribution in mortgage financing increases property maintenance over maintenance levels of rentals, where the renter has no equity at stake.

Another lending requirement that attempts to preserve the value of the property is fire and standard as well as special hazard insurance. These two types of insurance are required and monetarily protect the bondholder from property destruction. Insurance proceeds can be used to pay debt service when the property securing the mortgage is destroyed or damaged. If not used to pay debt service, the insurance must be used to repair the property so that it can eventually be resold.

In an effort to achieve a quality portfolio of a high level, issuers require mortgage loan insurance when loan-to-value ratios are high. Loan-to-value ratios are a measure of the equity contribution to a mortgage financing. For example, if a downpayment is made in an amount equal to 10 percent of the purchase price of the property, the loan-to-value ratio will equal 90 percent, reflecting a ratio of 10 percent ownership, 90 percent debt. Most programs permit the financing of mortgages only where the loan-to-value ratio is 80 percent or less. However, if the loan-to-value ratio exceeds 80 percent, the mortgagor is required to purchase one of three types of mortgage insurance: private mortgage insurance, Federal Housing Administration insurance, or Veteran's Administration loan guarantees. In addition, many issues contain provisions for mortgage pool insurance where 100 percent of any loss resulting from a mortgage default is covered for up to as much as 10 percent to 15 percent of the total original amount of the loan portfolio. These types of insurance provide different levels of coverage and different methods of claim payment. These differences can affect bond security and must be evaluated with regard to the quality of the mortgage portfolio and the strength of reserve funds.

FHA insurance provides the greatest amount of coverage against defaults by providing essentially 100 percent of the unpaid principal amount of the loan. Claims submitted to FHA are paid in either cash or FHA debentures. Upon foreclosure of a mortgage the amount of reimbursement is adjusted so that the amount the agency collects after the default (i.e., receipts from the sale of the foreclosed property) is deducted from the total claim. Included in the FHA claim are taxes, insurance, legal fees, and other expenses that the agency has incurred while the loan is in a nonpayment status.

VA guarantees, on the other hand, cover the lesser of 60 percent of the unpaid principal amount of the mortgage or $25,000. This form of insurance is often equated with FHA insurance because of the security both insurers provide. The VA program differs from FHA and private mortgage insurance because no equity contribution is required by the mortgagor. The VA has two options when it is presented with a claim. It can either pay its percentage or minimum liability, or take title to the property and reimburse the bond issuer for the full amount of the loan. Because VA has historically provided full reimbursement, investors have come to view VA guarantees as comparable to the 100 percent reimbursement in FHA insurance.

Coverage provided by private mortgage insurance ranges from 20 percent to 30 percent of the purchase price of the home when combined with the downpayment. The private mortgage insurer has three options open to it to satisfy a claim. It can pay its percentage liability, it can take title to the property and reimburse the bond issuer in full (100 percent of the unpaid principal, accrued loan interest, taxes, and other expenses) or it can authorize the bond issuer or its agent (bond trustee, loan servicer, etc.) to dispose of the property with the understanding that any shortfall in receipts is covered by the insurance up to the dollar limitation of the policy. The determining factor in choosing a method to satisfy the claim is loss reduction. Consequently, the insurer usually pays its percentage liability. Because 70 percent to 80 percent of the loan is uncovered, the issuer is responsible for recouping the remainder of the balance.

The issuer's ability to cover losses depends upon the economy and housing market, as the loss can be recaptured through a resale of the property. If the property can be resold, the issuer can increase its liquidity because the resale price reflects the total value of the property while the remaining loss is only a percentage of value. Thus, in good markets, the agency may be able to generate a profit. However, if the housing market declines, recouping even the loss portion of the loan could be problematic. An additional option may be available to the issuer, if a mortgage pool insurance policy was also secured. The pool policy covers 100 percent of the remaining loss up to a maximum liability of the total pool insurance reserve. (As mentioned above, the liability of this policy is usually limited to 10–15 percent of the total principal amount of the original loan portfolio.)

The use of one form of insurance over another has varied with each program. Some bond issuers only accept FHA-insured or VA-guaranteed loans into their portfolio. Other issuers use a combination in establishing a loan portfolio. Still others only accept privately insured or conventional loans. The type of loans to be originated from bond proceeds is always determined prior to bond issuance and can be regulated by the bond resolution, the issuer's enabling legislation, or by a desire to achieve a certain level of bond security. Traditionally, programs with only FHA-insured or VA-guaranteed loans have been rated higher and have sold at lower yields than programs with only private insurance or a combined insurance plan. Although FHA insurance and VA guarantee programs offer better coverage than private insurance plans, there are disadvantages associated with the government-affiliated policies. These disadvantages, which will be discussed later on, can increase a bond program's risk so that the higher rating (often Aa/AA) associated with an FHA/VA bond sale is not always warranted. Furthermore, privately insured bond issues can be structured to provide a very strong level of protection, thus deserving high-grade bond rating designations which they often do not receive.

In conclusion, the lending criteria of equity contribution requirements—first-lien status, purchase price limits, and property insurance—are typical attempts to promote timely mortgage payments in a population whose income may be low. The various types of default insurance protect the bondholder in the event the foregoing does not create timely mortgage payments.

Satisfying the Asset Test

As previously explained the structure of single-family bond programs (bond issuance costs are paid from bond proceeds) and the lack of control over the life of the asset (mortgage loan prepayments) create a situation where outstanding debt exceeds the value of the asset. This asset/bond imbalance must be closed to ensure bondholder security. Two strategies are available which permit an issuer to control mortgage/bond life expectancy and close the gap created from cost-of-issuance expense. These procedures are relatively standard in every issue, but their success in satisfying the asset test is dependent upon numerous external factors. Consequently, any bond assessment must evaluate not only the procedure but also the ability to implement the procedure.

The first method used to strike the imbalance created from bond issuance expenditures requires the issuer to generate revenues in excess of its annual expenses (trustee fees, administrative costs, etc.). The excess revenues are accumulated with the trustee in a fund known as the surplus fund or residual account. As the excess revenues are accumulated, the asset test is modified, taking new monies into account. This may be thought of as an equation: assets (mortgage loan and reserves) = liabilities (outstanding bonds). The excess revenue, which is called arbitrage profit, is generated from the investment of program assets at rates above the yield on the bonds. For example, if bond interest cost is 7 percent and the program assets are invested at a rate of 8½ percent, a profit of 1½ will be generated. The amount of arbitrage profit that can be earned is limited because of the arbitrage restrictions of the tax code. In addition, the accumulation of excess revenues is limited because a portion of the profit is used to pay program expenses.

Prior to the passage of the 1980 Mortgage Bond Subsidy Act, the issuer could essentially elect to invest his income according to one of three choices: He could:

1. Invest proceeds (as defined by IRS) for a three-year period of unrestricted yield with a ⅛ percent restriction for the remaining life of the issue.
2. Waive the temporary investment period in exchange for a ½ percent yield differential over the entire life of the issue.
3. Qualify as an acquired program obligation (as defined by IRS) which would permit a 1½ percent differential over the life of the issue. (Due to difficulties in meeting the test for this method, few issuers choose to exercise this option.)

Because the lion's share of housing bonds were issued prior to the act's passage, most were structured employing one of the above options. Since the passage of the law, issuers are limited to a 1 percent arbitrage limit.

Prior to mortgage loan origination, bond proceeds are invested in short-term securities that yield, within the arbitrage limit, a return above the rate of the bonds. The interest rate of the mortgage loans is also set at a level above the rate of the bonds, to yield a return within the arbitrage limit. Consequently, the greater the profit margin the higher the interest cost of the mortgage. Finally, reserve funds are usually invested in long-term securities, above the rate of the bonds but also within the permitted arbitrage spread.

Thus, arbitrage profit is used to recoup the nonasset portion of the bond issue. Historically, the issuer could elect to structure its issues with arbitrage rates or profit margins set at low levels which reduce the mortgage rate, or permit arbitrage levels or profit margins set at or close to maximum amounts which rapidly recouped nonasset bonds and, therefore, raised the mortgage interest rate. The issuer's choice must always be assessed in light of the size of the nonasset portion of the issue. In general, from an investor's viewpoint, the selection of high profit margins is preferable because the asset test is satisfied relatively faster. However, if stringent lending criteria are used to originate the mortgage loans and conservative assumptions are used in projecting investment return over the life of the bond issue, then the need for a wide profit margin is reduced.

The second aspect of the asset test, controlling mortgage and bond life expectancies, is also essential to the success of a bond program. Its importance arises from the shortened average life that mortgage loans have historically experienced. A reduction in the average life of a mortgage, which is commonly called a prepayment, occurs when the loan is paid in full prior to its maturity. Mortgage loans are prepaid for numerous reasons such as the sale of the home, a refinancing of the mortgage at a lower interest rate, or a foreclosure on the property which, when sold, generates the funds to retire the mortgage loan. Mortgage loan prepayments affect the asset test because outstanding mortgage loan principal declines faster than outstanding bond principal. The net effect of uncontrolled mortgage loan prepayments is an increase in the asset/bond imbalance initially created from the payment of bond issuance costs.

Two strategies have been used to control the asset/bond ratio. Naturally, the goal of these methods is to have asset and bond average life coincide. This relationship is brought about by either shortening the life of the bond or extending the life of the asset.

The typical procedure used by bond issuers to shorten the life of a bond is to exercise a call feature. A call feature allows the issuer to retire bonds prior to their stated maturity. The call feature used by single-family bond issuers to control asset/bond life is known as "extraordinary mandatory bond redemption." Extraordinary mandatory bond redemptions require issuers to retire bonds at par prior to maturity, as opposed to the more common optional call which is exercised at a premium. When the bond is called through extraordinary redemption, it ceases to earn interest and its full principal value is paid to the investor.

There are several aspects to extraordinary redemption, and all are used to balance the asset and bond life expectancy. For example, nonasset bonds can be recouped through extraordinary redemptions. Nonasset bonds create an asset/bond relationship wherein outstanding mortgage loans and reserve funds are of less value than the value of the outstanding bonds. When surplus revenues are accumulated, this relationship changes because the surplus increases the asset side of the equation. Sometimes, instead of allowing the surplus to accumulate, it is used to retire bonds prior to maturity. This affects the asset/bond equation because the size of the assets remains the same (the surplus is always expended) but the amount of outstanding bonds declines. This procedure is also followed as mortgage loan prepayments are received. Since prepayments cause assets to decline faster than outstanding bond principal, the prepayments are used to retire bonds. This decreases the amount of outstanding bonds by an amount equal to the reduction in assets. Thus the initial asset/bond imbalance is brought under control as the average life of the bonds is made to coincide with the average life of the mortgage loans.

Some investors think that this extraordinary redemption feature weakens the value of housing bonds as an investment. This viewpoint has emerged because the investor cannot control the average life of his own municipal bond portfolio. Frequently, when an investor buys a 30-year bond, he attempts to lock in a certain interest rate for a definite time span. Extraordinary redemptions cast doubt upon this since the bonds can be retired at any time. Therefore, the investor assumes an interest rate risk because, if the bond is called, he may not be able to reinvest his funds at a comparable or higher rate. Another drawback associated with extraordinary redemptions is that the investor is not paid a premium price for his bond. The premium is designed to compensate the investor for his reinvestment risk when attempting to reinvest the retired principal amount of the initial investment. Another difference between extraordinary and optional redemptions is that one is mandatory, the other discretionary.

Optional redemptions do not have to be exercised by bond issuers and are only done so when the redemption assists the issuer in his debt management. Extraordinary mandatory redemptions, however, must be exercised when the monies designated for the redemption are earned. This is true for many single-family bond programs because some indentures mandate the use of mortgage loan prepayments and surplus revenues for bond calls.

Because many investors resist the purchase of securities with an extraordinary call feature, issuers often manage the impact of prepayments on the asset/bond relationship by extending the life of the asset. One way to extend the life of the asset is to use prepayments and surplus revenues to originate new mortgage loans that can also secure the bonds and produce yields above the yield of the bonds but within permitted arbitrage limits. Thus as loans prepay, causing a decline in the program's assets, the principal amount of the prepayment is used to originate a new mortgage loan. Consequently, the asset side of the asset/bond relationship remains relatively constant. When surplus revenues are used to originate new loans, increasing the value of the assets, the amount of nonasset bonds declines.

The flaw in this approach is that the frequency and size of prepayments usually increase as interest rates decline. During such periods the issuer may be unable to reinvest the prepayment monies at an interest rate high enough to support the expenses of the bond program. Furthermore, each time a loan prepays, the issuer loses a certain amount of income from the arbitrage spread which is built into the rate of the mortgage. If a loan prepays, the amount of interest income accruing on the loan either declines or is eliminated, depending on whether or not the loan is paid in full.

Another method used to extend the asset average life is to discourage prepayments. Bond issuers have done this by charging a prepayment penalty, a method most effective on those people who prepay mortgages because they believe they will be able to fund the loan at a lower interest rate. The penalty is similar to a bond premium in that it increases the principal amount of the mortgage loan. For example, if a mortgage loan with an outstanding balance of $50,000 prepays and the prepayment penalty equals 5 percent of the outstanding balance of the loan, then the prepayment price will equal $52,500. The penalty is designed to reduce the interest cost savings that can result from a loan refinancing.

A third procedure used to extend the asset average life allows an issuer to reinvest prepayments and surplus revenues in fixed-income securities whose yield exceeds the yield on the bonds without exceeding the arbitrage limit of the issue.

In general, the method used to satisfy and maintain the asset test is defined in the bond indenture. Some indentures are more flexible than others and permit the issuer to employ any of the above techniques in attempting to reach and maintain the required asset/bond relationships. When several techniques are permitted, the issuer is allowed to assume an investment manager's role. Assuming such a role, however, requires the exercise of cash flow management and investment strategy which may often conflict with an issuer's required role of administering public policy. For example, using prepayments to originate new mortgage loans perpetuates the public purpose of the program. However, if the new mortgage loans are originated 5 years after the inception of the bond program and possess a 30-year maturity, then the asset/bond relationship will again be unbalanced. In this situation the mortgage loans would mature five years after the bond matures. Alternatively, if mortgage loan principal is used instead to retire bond principal, then cash flow difficulties could arise when the bond matures prior to the mortgage loan. Inflexibility in the indenture, on the other hand, can create a different set of problems. For example, when the asset test can only be satisfied by exercising the extraordinary mandatory call, the issuer may be prevented from generating additional surplus revenues. Furthermore, secondary market trading of the bond may be impaired if the issuer demonstrates that the extraordinary call must be used often.

Timing Debt Service Payments with Asset Creation

Timing debt service payments with the creation of the asset securing the bonds is a risk common to all start-up projects. The timing problem emerges because the maturity structure of the bond issue is established at bond sale, prior to the creation or construction of the asset. Thus, the first debt service payment, whether it be an interest payment or a principal and interest payment, must be established based on an anticipated asset creation schedule. Although it is possible to account for construction delays, there is no way to accurately anticipate the extent of the delays.

The timing problem becomes manifest when a debt service payment arises and the asset either has not been created or was not created early enough to generate sufficient revenues. In a single-family bond issue, it will emerge if the maturity schedule of the bonds is finalized prior to any attempt to originate mortgage loans. If the demand for mortgage money is less than the amount of bonds sold, the issuer will be unable to create an asset of equal value to the bonds. Even when mortgage loan demand warrants a bond sale of a specified amount, mortgage loan origination can be impaired due to a decline in conventional mortgage rates immediately following the bond sale. Should this happen, the issuer may have difficulty originating mortgage loans because less costly conventional mortgage money may be available. Of course, an issuer can be allowed an unlimited amount of time in which to originate the loans. The risk, however, then becomes whether or not an asset of sufficient size to support the bond issue can be created in time to meet the first debt service payment. Single-family bond programs have addressed these potential problems by limiting the loan origination period and by calling bonds, if necessary, under the extraordinary mandatory redemption procedure.

There are two time limits imposed in a typical single-family bond program. The first time limit is called the commitment period and usually expires 6 to 12 months after the bond closing date. The commitment period is the time when mortgage loan applications are received and approved for funding. During this time, the mortgage loan applicant is assured that his loan will be funded as soon as the legal technicalities of the mortgage financing are finalized. Once the issuer makes enough commitments to cover the bond issue, it is not required to attempt to originate any additional loans. The actual funding of the loans takes place during the origination period, the second time limit, which usually overlaps and lasts approximately six months after the commitment period.

If a sufficient number of commitments is not received prior to the end of the commitment period, the unused portion of the bond issue is used to call bonds in accord with the extraordinary mandatory redemption feature of the bond issue. As with prepayments and surplus revenues, the extraordinary call is exercised at par and allows the issuer to curtail any growth in the asset/bond imbalance arising initially from the payment of bond issuance expenses. Unlike the call from prepayments, the issuer rarely has any other alternatives in how to expend this money.

Extraordinary mandatory calls occurring after the termination of the origination period are due to an inability to fulfill the obligations incurred during the commitment period. This can happen for instance when a commitment is made to fund a loan for a house that is in the process of being built. Since the mortgage money cannot be used for construction expenses, the mortgage loan is funded after the home is constructed. If construction is delayed, the issuer may be unable to fund the loan prior to the end of the origination period. Consequently, bonds in the amount of the unfulfilled commitment (unexpended bond proceeds) are called prior to maturity. As in the case with bond calls from uncommitted bond proceeds, calls from unexpended bond proceeds are mandatory and are exercised at par.

The establishment of a time limit enables an issuer to accurately determine the completion date of the creation of the asset or mortgage portfolio. Since the time frame for asset creation is established at the same time as the bond sale, the first debt service payment date can be appropriately set, and use of the extraordinary mandatory call with uncommitted or unexpended bond proceeds can maintain the asset/bond relationship at the same ratio as at the time of the bond sale.

To minimize origination difficulties the issuer should demonstrate that there is demand for mortgage money in an amount at least equal to the size of the bond issue. Assessing demand for mortgage money is complex for two reasons. First, the public purpose of the bond program usually restricts the size of the total mortgage market to those persons within a specified income range. Second, the total amount of available property that can be financed is reduced to the extent that the property falls within the purchase price limitations of the program. Consequently, any demand analysis must carefully account for these restrictions.

A demand analysis is usually conducted in one of two ways. One method involves hiring outside consultants with an expertise in real estate to formally measure the potential market. This analysis, commonly called a feasibility study, examines the dollar amount of mortgage loans originated in previous years, the percent of the total population that falls within the income limits of the program, the availability of multi-versus single-family housing, the amount of available property within the purchase price limitations of the program, the amount of new housing construction, the conventional mortgage rate in the area, and other pertinent economic and demographic factors. The result of the study is reported in a dollar amount that is supposed to reflect the demand for mortgage money at an interest rate the consultant assumes the issuer will charge.

The feasibility consultants usually qualify their results with the following statement: "Mortgage demand may increase if the interest rate in the program is less than the rate assumed in the study, or it may decrease if the rate is higher than the one assumed in the study; mortgage demand may be less than predicted in the study if conventional rates decline . . . ." In recognition of this qualifying statement, the results of the study must be evaluated in light of current tax-exempt interest rates which affect the program's mortgage rate, and in light of the date of the study, which could render the results obsolete.

Demand analysis is also conducted in a less formal fashion by the lenders who are expected to originate and service the loans. Private lenders are used to service and originate the loans on behalf of the issuer because, as previously mentioned, they are thought to have more experience at mortgage financing, have established credit relationships with constituents in the issuer's jurisdiction, and have increased accessibility to those desiring mortgage financing. The use of private lenders creates uncertainty because the responsibility for asset creation is transferred from the issuer to the lender. It is the lender who must observe the income restrictions and purchase price limitations of the program, process the loans for special and standard hazard insurance, secure a first-lien status on the property, and observe the origination and commitment time limits. Furthermore, lenders may experience a conflict of interest because their main business purpose may be the origination of mortgage loans.

To encourage lenders to participate in the program, the issuer permits the charging of mortgage origination and servicing fees. To ensure that their best origination effort is used, lenders must often sign a commitment agreement that obligates them to originate a self-determined, specified dollar amount of loans during the origination period. In the event the obligation is not fulfilled, the lender is charged a penalty which is often called a commitment fee. Prudent business practice mandates that the lender guard against overcommitting, especially if the program sets very specific limits on prospective purchases. Therefore, the issuer assumes that lenders are conservative in establishing a commitment amount. Based on these conservative estimates, the commitment amount often becomes the guideline used to measure demand, and when bonds are sold, the size of the issue is usually less than the total amount of commitments received.

Traditionally, commitment agreements have been signed prior to the bond sale. The issuer has the option to accept commitments from several lenders or to assign the entire loan origination responsibility to one lender if the lender is certain it can fulfill the obligation of the commitment. In general, the use of numerous lenders provides the issuer with greater flexibility in ensuring successful loan origination. Using numerous lenders allows the issuer to match commitment amounts with the lender's historical origination capability. Multiple originators also increase the geographic availability of the loans so that the mortgage loans are available to a wider segment of the population and risk is more widely dispersed. Flexibility in loan origination increases as the number of lenders increases because the unfulfilled commitment amount of one lender can be assigned to another lender whose demand for mortgage money is greater than its original commitment obligation.

Loan origination can be further enhanced if an issuer discourages the use of bond proceeds for mortgage loans involving new construction. Often limits are set on the amount of new construction loans lenders can originate. In most bond programs, lenders are permitted to reserve for new construction 10 percent of their total commitment obligation. When bond proceeds are primarily reserved for mortgage loans on existing housing, the impact of potential construction delays on loan origination is reduced.

In most programs the lenders who originate the loans also service the loans. Servicing mortgage loans involves collection of the mortgage payments on a monthly basis, monitoring the timeliness of the mortgage receipts, transfer of the mortgage payments to the bond trustee for debt service payments, and so on. As issuers choose lenders for the loan origination aspect of the program, servicing capabilities should be assessed along with other capabilities. A lender's mortgage loan delinquency rate is an indication of the credit criteria a lender uses in originating loans for its own portfolio and the monitoring and follow-up procedures used while the loan is outstanding.

ANALYSIS OF MORTGAGE REVENUE BONDS

Credit analysis of single-family bonds centers around an assessment of the issue's three critical features noted earlier: asset quality, satisfaction of the asset test, and the timing of asset creation.

Asset quality can be evaluated with the most certainty because the lending parameters are established prior to the bond sale. In addition, the geographic area for loan origination is a known factor, as is the extent of mortgage insurance, the provisions for the insurance payment, and the foreclosure laws of the area. Asset test satisfaction and asset creation are the features of the program most likely to be affected by external factors. For example, conventional mortgage lending rates can decline after the bond sale, reducing the attractiveness of the bond mortgage rate so that loan origination projections are not met. This actually occurred in the second quarter of 1980.

From April to May 1980, approximately 20 local issuers came to market and, subsequent to the bond sale, had difficulty originating their loans. Shortly after their bond sales, interest rates declined dramatically so that conventional lending rates were at or below the bond mortgage rate. By August 1980, half of the programs were predicting that bond calls from unexpended bond proceeds were likely. A problem arose for investors because the decline in interest rates had caused their bonds to trade at a premium. The question became whether to sell the bond at a premium, generating a capital gain, or hold the bond at the risk of a par call from unexpended bond proceeds. In the end, only one issue called bonds. The bond call which occurred on July 1, 1981, comprised almost 30 percent of the issue!

In light of the real possibility of bond calls, analysis of asset test satisfaction and asset creation must involve an evaluation of the assumptions used in developing the debt repayment structure. The assumption used should tell an analyst what funds will be available to pay debt service and expenses. Since debt repayment is structured on an assumed mortgage repayment schedule, a reserve investment rate, and the demand for mortgage money, this analysis is more difficult than the asset quality analysis because the basis of the debt structure is unknown at the time of the bond sale and involves a prediction as to what is most likely to occur.

Analysis of Asset Quality

The main objective in analyzing asset quality is to determine the degree of assurance in the issuer's ability to generate the revenues to pay debt service and expenses. Since debt service and expenses are paid from mortgage repayments, the analysis of asset quality measures the certainty of mortgage repayment. Mortgages are repaid in one of three ways: timely or accelerated mortgage payments, mortgage insurance, and foreclosures.

Mortgage insurance and foreclosure laws are fairly easy to evaluate. The criteria for both are usually clearly defined in the official statement. Investors have generally placed greater value on certain types of insurance (such as FHA insurance or VA loan guarantees) over other types (such as private mortgage insurance). The advantage of FHA and VA insurance is that both are issued by a federal agency. The ability to satisfy an insurance claim appears more certain with FHA insurance or VA guarantees.

However, private mortgage insurance also has its advantages. The requirement for a policy from a private mortgage insurer is usually more stringent that that of either FHA or VA. Private mortgage insurers generally require an equity contribution to the mortgage whereas VA guarantees do not. In addition, the process of foreclosure and claim payment is more rapid with private insurance as opposed to FHA or VA. Acceptance into a federal program is usually contingent upon adherence to certain regulations. Consequently, issuers often revoke some management controls that do not have to be sacrificed in a privately insured program. For example, issuers loose their ability to prohibit mortgage loan assumptions. Compliance with this regulation is often burdensome if the issuer's cash flow is dependent upon a certain level of prepayments. If mortgagors are selling their homes through loan assumption instead of through full prepayment, then the issuer's cash flow may not be sufficient to meet debt service. While prepayments could be promoted by prohibiting loan assumption, the issuer is not permitted, in a FHA or VA loan, to enact this policy.

Foreclosure laws, specifically in terms of instituting the legal proceedings, can vary from issue to issue and from state to state. The preservation of value, the most important aspect of foreclosure, is a function of the issuing community and can be measured by examining growth in assessed and real property values and trends in the general housing market.

Mortgage repayment capabilities are also a function of the area designated for loan origination, especially in terms of a mortgagor's ability to generate an income for loan payments. Consequently, the wealth of the area in terms of growth in bank deposits, employment opportunities and mix, unemployment rate, and area size are all criteria to be considered in much the same way a general obligation credit is evaluated for its ability to collect taxes.

Timely debt service payments are dependent upon timely mortgage receipts, which require rigorous monitoring. It requires prompt recognition of a late payment with a corresponding follow-up response. A servicer's ability to monitor mortgage payments is somewhat apparent by evaluation of the servicer's own delinquency rate. Since most bond program servicers are either the loan originator or the bond issuer, its historic delinquency rate relative to state and national rates can be used to assess its credit judgment and servicing skills.

Analysis of Asset Test Satisfaction

The ability to satisfy the asset test is primarily concerned with assessing the repayment of the nonasset portion of the bond issue. Thus a certain spread is needed and should be reflected in the mortgage rate and investment yield on program funds. Although the spread between the mortgage rate and the bond rate can be set at the bond sale, the ability to invest reserve funds at a sufficient spread over the bond rate is likely to vary over the life of the issue. This is particularly true for the investment of the mortgage reserve fund and program cash flow. These two assets are usually invested in short-term securities and are therefore subject to reinvestment risk. Consequently, it is important that the issuer structure debt repayment assuming a relatively low investment rate.

Nonasset bonds are also recouped from the spread over the mortgage rate. Here, too, uncertainty exists because the average life of the mortgage loan is uncertain. Timely debt service payments should be demonstrated under a range of assumptions, such as zero prepayments and substantial prepayments, in the early years of the program. The guideline used in testing prepayment assumptions is the FHA decrement tables on the historic prepayment rate of 30-year mortgage loans insured under Section 203 of the Federal Housing Act. If the bond issue repayment schedule is structured to assume that no prepayments will occur, then timely debt service payments should be comfortably demonstrated under simulated cash flows incorporating high prepayment assumptions such as 4 times, or 400 percent of, FHA experience in the state of bond issuance. Passage of this high-level test assures that a sufficient amount of arbitrage spread can be earned on the interest portion of the mortgage, even if the mortgage is paid in full prior to maturity, reducing the interest income. The converse is true when debt repayment is structured assuming a certain percentage of the loans will prepay.

In an open-ended program, prepayments increase reinvestment risk. Open-ended programs allow prepayments to be reinvested into new mortgage loans and fixed-income securities, or to call bonds. Risk is increased because variations in interest rate cycles change the investment strategy used. Since bond proceeds are ultimately being used for investment purposes, expertise in investment strategy is required. In most programs either the management of the SHFA or the bond trustee makes the investment decisions. Consequently, the persons responsible should demonstrate a historical ability to make the appropriate investment decision. If rates are declining the best strategy is to secure the highest, relatively long fixed rate possible. This can be done through the origination of mortgages or through the investment of securities. If rates are rising, short investments are usually the best strategy until interest rates peak. Overall, prudent financial management should be observed. This often requires that a certain portion of the program's assets (approximately 30 percent) be held in short-term investments of three to five years. It is important for an issuer to be able to maintain a certain level of liquidity, particularly in open-end programs.

Analysis of the Timing of Asset Creation

This aspect of the analysis is also based on certain cash flow assumptions. The assumptions are important relative to the first debt service payment. Although bonds can be called from unexpended bond proceeds, substantial bond calls early in the program's life can interfere with the issuer's ability to recoup the nonasset bonds since the interest income and, consequently, arbitrage profit will be reduced.

Demand for mortgage money is the critical factor to successful loan origination, and the accuracy of an issuer's demand evaluation must be assessed. Demand varies with changes in interest rates: as rates decline, demand increases. To be accurate, the demand analysis should conservatively estimate the mortgage loan rate of the program. If the projected rate is lower than the program's mortgage bond rate, which can be determined after the bond issue is priced or from housing bonds priced in the secondary market, expected origination should be less that the demand analysis indicates. Conversely, if the rate assumed in the demand analysis is higher than the actual program mortgage rate, demand should be greater than predicted.

To accurately assess demand, the feasibility (or demand) study should measure the size of the population and the amount of property that qualifies under the program's purchase price and income limits. If not accurately measured, demand can be overstated. An example of this occurred in an issue of the Home Finance Authority of Dade County, Florida, Series 1980 program which sold during the second quarter of 1980. Months after the bond sale, loan origination was proceeding more slowly than had been projected in part because the loan interest rate was incompatible with the income limitations of the program. Furthermore, the purchase price limitations were found to be too narrow, so that a sizable portion of the total available property in the county did not qualify for financing under the program.

Since local banks are used to originate the mortgage loans, their capability must also be measured. Historical conventional origination experience should be examined in relation to commitment amounts. The ability of a bank to satisfy its commitment should be questioned when the commitment amount significantly exceeds historical annual origination experience. When several originators are used, this problem can be lessened as one bank's unfulfilled commitment can be designated to another bank. Thus, commitment amounts should be evaluated not solely on a one-to-one basis but also as an overall designation. If some banks have moderately overcommitted themselves, other banks should be undercommitted to compensate. The primary aspect to recognize is gross aberrations in commitment amounts relative to historical experience.

Since the loans are only originated for completed dwellings, origination capability can be deterred when commitments have been designated for new construction. This is often done to promote construction in an area. A problem arises when construction of the dwelling is not completed prior to the end of the origination period. Since the unit is not complete and habitable, the loan cannot be funded. This occurred in a Duarte, California Redevelopment Agency program. Approximately $1.5 million of bond proceeds were reserved for financing loans on a condominium project; since the construction of the project was not completed by the end of the origination period, a bond call was exercised.

As with any bond analysis, the program must be evaluated as a whole and not on the basis of one factor. In general, the greater the diversity, such as a wide geographic area and numerous originators, the lower the risk. Similarly, the more conservative the assumptions used, the lower the risk.

STATE AND LOCAL PROGRAMS

Local governmental units entered the single-family bond market in 1978. One of the first issues was sold by the city of Chicago, Illinois, in the amount of $100 million. The Chicago issue was followed by a Denver, Colorado, issue of $20 million. By the end of March 1978, local units had sold approximately $1.6 billion of mortgage revenue bonds. In 1979, total housing bond sales amounted to $12 billion, an increase of 167 percent over the $4.5 billion sold only by SHFAs in 1978. The large increase in housing bond sales in 1979 was largely due to the increased activity in local mortgage bond sales. During 1978 and 1979, distinct structural differentiations emerged between local housing bond sales and SHFA bond sales. The major difference between the two developed because SHFAs structured their deals to create an ongoing program, while local issuers structured their bond issues to create a finite program that terminates when the last outstanding bond is retired. The distinction became apparent in the bond resolutions used by the SHFAs versus those used by local issuers (county, city, town, village).

In general, SHFAs used an open-ended resolution to create their program. An open resolution permits the issuer to add new mortgage loans to the portfolio through the issuance of additional parity bonds and the reinvestment of prepayments or surplus revenues. A closed-ended bond resolution, however, forbids the issuance of additional parity bonds, and requires that prepayments and surplus revenues be used to retire bonds prior to their stated maturity. Consequently, closed-ended resolutions exercise the extraordinary mandatory call feature more frequently than open-ended resolutions.

The open-ended resolution has allowed SHFAs to exercise greater latitude in satisfying the asset test. The increased flexibility stems from the use of prepayments and surplus revenues for either a bond call at par, the origination of new mortgage loans, or an investment in fixed-income securities. The advantage to an open-ended resolution is that cash flow can be managed in a variety of ways and adjusted to changes in the economy. The disadvantage is that, as the portfolio grows through new loan originations, the life of the asset may ultimately exceed the life of the bonds. The advantage of the closed-ended resolution is that the quality and contents of the loan portfolio are static and more susceptible to ongoing analysis. The disadvantage is that there is no flexibility in cash flow management, a serious problem during the period when the asset bond ratio is imbalanced. In the closed-ended resolution, substantial prepayments result in the termination of the asset before sufficient arbitrage revenues have been earned to recoup the nonasset bonds. Obviously, the size of the spread is more important and should be greater in closed-ended programs than in an open-ended one. Several other structural differences exist between these programs which impact both the quality of the asset and the cash flow of the program.

Asset quality has differed because state programs have historically used a lower range than local issuers in developing purchase price and income limitations. Another difference is that many state programs are secured by a debt reserve fund that enjoys a moral obligation pledge of the state's general fund. This pledge allows the state to appropriate monies to the SHFA for the sole purpose of restoring the debt service or capital reserve fund to its minimum requirement. However, a moral obligation pledge is not as strong as a general obligation pledge. Unlike the full faith and credit pledge, a moral obligation is not a legally enforceable obligation or a legal liability of the state. Nevertheless it does provide a means of maintaining the liquidity and size of an important program asset, the reserve fund.[1]

The cash flow of open-ended and closed-ended programs is different because of the treatment of prepayments and surplus revenues. Many state programs adjusted their debt service schedule on the assumption that a certain percentage of loans prepay prior to their maturity. When prepayment assumptions are used, a cash flow develops requiring annual debt service to be paid, in part, from prepayment receipts. The goal of this procedure is to lower the interest cost of the bonds. The cost is lowered because the bond issue's serial maturities are increased to coincide with the reduced average life of the 30-year mortgage. Similarly, the term bond maturities are decreased in an amount

---

[1]See Chapter 30 for additional information.

comparable to the increase in serial maturities. Bond interest cost is also lowered because serial bonds usually carry a rate that is lower than term bonds.

A problem can arise with this procedure because the receipt of prepayments is related to changes in interest rate patterns. Consequently, prepayment assumptions add an interest rate sensitivity feature to the issuer's ability to pay debt service. As long as interest rates are below the mortgage rate of the program, it is expected that prepayment receipts should be sufficient to satisfy debt requirements. However, when rates are above the level charged by the program, prepayment receipts may decline to levels that are not sufficient to allow timely debt service payments.

This has recently been experienced by several SHFAs. Our in-depth analysis of this situation, conducted in November 1981, revealed that out of 33 agencies 64 percent experienced prepayments at levels less than were required for timely debt service payments. This study also revealed that agencies were handling this shortfall by tapping the surplus revenues that had accumulated. In all cases, the accumulated surplus was sufficient to sustain a shortfall for at least one year. However, the ability to sustain such shortfalls on a long-term basis is a serious threat to bond security, and several techniques have been developed to manage this problem. For example, a new bond issue can be sold with a lower prepayment assumption, which rearranges the debt schedule of the issuer and thus makes it more manageable.

The increased interest rate sensitivity of housing bonds is more common in open-ended programs than in closed-ended ones. Although this can be a problem, especially when prepayment shortfalls are sustained for an extended period, cash flow management involving the accumulation of surplus revenues can be used to offset prepayment shortfalls.

Another difference between closed-ended and open-ended programs is the maintenance and use of surplus revenues. In most closed-ended programs an account is created for the accumulation of surplus revenues. The revenues are held within the account and are used as additional security for the bonds. In an open-ended program, surplus can be removed from the program or resolution and placed into the general fund of the issuer. This is very common in state programs that are additionally secured by a general obligation pledge of the SHFA. The intent of this pledge is to enhance bond security by including, as security, all the revenues of the particular state agency involved, including those generated from multifamily programs. The drawback of this approach is that, when the surplus is removed from the program, the issuer can use it for any public purpose it desires.

Here again, managerial expertise is critical to maintaining bond security, because short- and long-range cash flow patterns must be anticipated.

In general, the differences in these programs have not resulted in a higher level of credit worthiness for one type of issuer over another. The differences have caused moderate distinctions in the analytical method used to evaluate the programs. In addition, investor preferences for state versus local programs have developed for a variety of reasons. Some investors prefer local programs because they are not as susceptible to changes in interest rate climates and because the composition of the loan portfolio will remain static over the life of the bonds. Other investors prefer state programs because they have greater market access than local issues. Market access and an open-ended resolution are important because new debt can be sold to adjust the debt retirement schedule of the agency, bringing it more closely into line with actual experience rather than with pure assumptions.

THE FUTURE OF SINGLE–FAMILY
MORTGAGE BONDS

On April 25, 1979, legislation was introduced into the U.S. House of Representatives that altered the future of single-family bonds. The proposed bill required the termination of the federal tax exemption of mortgage revenue bonds issued after April 25, 1979. The intended impact of the bill was devastating because single-family bonds would not be afforded the tax-exempt status associated with municipal offerings and because the implemetation date of the bill coincided with its proposal date. The bill was prompted because several congressmen believed that the increase in housing bond issuance, especially during 1978 and 1979, had significantly reduced federal revenues by adding to the supply of federally tax-exempt offerings.

There was substantial opposition to this bill from both the investment community and local and state housing bond issuers. Many issuers and underwriters had bond sales scheduled after the April 25 deadline of the bill. Consequently, bond issues with sale dates after April 25 contained a qualified legal opinion. Opposition to the bill was also heard from congressmen because it was considered unfair to introduce a bill that, when passed, would be retroactive in implementation. Consequently, several additional bills were introduced in Congress that also proposed restrictions on housing bond sales, although their implementation dates varied. Two such congressional actions, Senate Resolution 188 and Senate Resolution 455, created additional confusion in the marketplace. Neither resolution had the status or impact of a proposed bill, but instead both expressed the sentiments of the Senate. This sentiment was that housing bonds should be permitted to sell, in unrestricted quantities, until December 31, 1980.

Congress finally determined the fate of Mortgage Revenue Bonds during November 1980. However, during 19 months of uncertainty, several billion dollars in bonds were sold. Because these new issues were selling with an ambiguous tax status, new security and structural devices were implemented to enhance the marketability of the bonds. Additional security was provided through the use of a bank letter of credit, surety bonds, and mortgage loan takeouts by major lending institutions.

Structural and Security Variations in Single-Family Bonds: Letter of Credit

Pima and Pinal counties, Arizona, were two issuers that used the letter-of-credit device.[2] The issues were structured with the standard security features of mortgage loan repayments. They were further secured by a letter of credit in an amount equal to total bond debt service. Thus, if the issuer experienced a revenue shortfall during the life of the issue, the letter of credit could be drawn down. The mortgage loans originated under these two programs have mortgage loan payments which are structured on the basis of a 30-year amortization period. In the 12th year of the bond issue, a large balloon payment is due. At that point, the letter of credit becomes the primary security for the bonds. To meet the balloon debt service payment, the issuer draws down the letter of credit, retires the bonds, and assigns the mortgage loans to the bank. The bank can then decide either to incorporate the loans into its own portfolio or sell them.

Several other advantages associated with this financing accrue to the bondholder, mortgagor, and the bank. The bondholder is offered a very secure bond with a limited risk of having his bonds called. Bond issues secured by a letter of credit generally bear a rating reflecting the bank's credit as opposed to the issuer's credit. (Unlike other single-family issues, these bonds cannot be called from prepayments or excess revenues.) The mortgagor receives a low-interest loan, (tied to the net interest cost on the bonds) for 12 years, after which time the rate has to be adjusted either to 50 basis points above the conventional rate or up to a ceiling of approximately 15 percent. The interest cost of the bonds was controlled because their maturity was approximately cut in half. The bank received a commitment fee for the letter of credit and had an opportunity to acquire mortgage

---

[2]Letter-of-credit–backed bonds are discussed in Chapter 22.

loans with a potentially reduced average life and a reduced loan-to-value ratio.

The Surety Bond

Several local issuers in Kansas sold housing bonds similar to those above but used a surety bond for the provision of additional security. The bonds were sold under a loans-to-lender program. In these financings, the lending institutions themselves were insured for their obligation to repay the trustee on behalf of the issuer. The surety bond guarantees the repayment of principal and interest on each lender's loan. The insurance is effective as long as the insurer's premiums are paid. Premiums are paid from program revenues, on which they have a prior lien over all other program costs, including debt service. As in the Arizona issues, there were no provisions for a prepayment call. However, in the event of lender default, bonds could be called from unexpended or uncommitted bond proceeds and funds received from the surety bond if the insurer decided to pay in full the remaining portion of an outstanding loan. Where a lender does default on its payment to the trustee, the insurer has the option to either prepay the entire loan for the lender or to continue to make to the trustee, on behalf of the lender, the regularly scheduled loan payments.

The Variable Rate Coupon Bond

In addition to shortening the maturity schedule of the bonds, other structural innovations were employed. One such innovation was the use of a variable-rate coupon bond. As with prior issues, variable-rate bonds are secured by and payable in the first instance from mortgage loan payments, and then from the various reserve funds. However, the bond interest rate, which is paid semiannually, varies with each payment date. Sometimes there are a floor and a ceiling that control the extent to which the rate can rise or fall. The interest rate to be paid to the bondholder is calculated seven days prior to the coupon date as the higher of either 75 percent of the long-term Treasury bond rate or 65 percent of the short-term T bill rate. The mortgage loans, however, carry a fixed interest rate. Thus, if the interest to be paid on the bond exceeds the yield on the loan, insurance is used to pay the bondholder the interest rate differential. The interest rate differential occurs, for example, when the interest rate calculation results in a coupon of 11½ percent and the mortgage loans, after program expenses, yield 11 percent. The insurer, therefore, has to pay the bondholder the dollar value of the ½ percent differential. In return for this service, the issuer pays the insurer a premium.

The Put, or Option, Bond

The put, or option, bond was another structural variation implemented to strengthen the marketability of mortgage bonds.[3] Like the balloon payment structure, option bond issues are characterized by a shortened maturity schedule which reduces bond interest cost and lowers the program's mortgage rate. This structure was most effective in stimulating bond issues during a period of relatively high tax-exempt rates because mortgage rates were held to a minimum. Unlike the balloon payment program, the option bond does not add to the mortgage loans a risk of interest rate refinancing. The mortgage loans, in an option bond program, have been structured with a fixed interest rate and a 30-year term.

An option bond is usually a term bond of 20 to 30 years that can be retired at the bondholder's option, after approximately 5 years (the optional redemption date varies with each program). An investor who purchases an option bond receives the right to tender at par all or part of his bonds to the trustee, beginning on a specified date five or six years after the bond sale. More simply, this means that the trustee is obligated to purchase at par all bonds put to him. The put bond creates a situation where bond principal comes due long before mortgage loan principal. Satisfaction of the put obligation is ensured by a letter of credit in an amount equal to the total amount of put bonds sold. Thus, when the total amount of bonds put to the trustee exceeds mortgage principal receipts, the letter of credit is drawn down in an amount equal to the difference. Unlike the letter-of-credit financings previously described, which are secured by a letter of credit and are rated based on the financial strength of the bank, put bonds with a letter of credit are not the same. The letter of credit as well as the put option are only effective as long as the bond program is solvent. If for any reason (such as extensive mortgage loan delinquencies) the bonds enter into default, the option bonds cannot be purchased by the trustee. This restriction is necessary because the bank that provides the letter of credit assumes into its investment portfolio all put bonds repurchased from letter-of-credit draws. The bank then relies on mortgage loan cash flow as security for its investment.

Historically, put bonds have been priced according to their first option tender date. Because the term bond is priced as a shorter bond,

---

[3]Put bonds are discussed in Chapter 21.

the bondholder does suffer a loss in yield. He is compensated for this loss of return by the trustee and letter of credit, which guarantee the existence of a secondary market for the bond.

The Super Sinker Bond

One last structural variation that has emerged is known as the super sinker bond. A super sinker bond program is similar in every respect, except the extraordinary mandatory call, to the typical single-family issue described earlier in this chapter. A difference arises because of a variation in the strip-call aspect of the program's extraordinary mandatory redemption provision.

A strip call requires that redemption monies be applied to the retirement of bonds in each maturity in the same proportion as the total maturity bears to the entire bond issue. This procedure is best explained by the following example. Assume that a $10 million bond issue is structured with three maturities: one for $5 million, one for $2 million, and one for $3 million. Also assume that by the extraordinary call date $1 million in revenues are generated for bond redemption. The $1 million will be used to call bonds according to a strip-call feature. This call feature requires that 50 percent of the call monies be used to retire the $5 million maturity because it comprises 50 percent of the total bond issue. Likewise, 20 percent of the redemption monies, or $200,000, will be used to retire the $2 million maturity and 30 percent of the $1 million, or $300,000, will be used to retire the $3 million maturity. Consequently, bonds are retired in each maturity according to the maturity's proportional weight to the total bond issue.

The typical super sinker issue is characterized by three term maturities. Although super sinker bonds are retired through a strip-call feature, the proportional weight is skewed in the direction of the super sinker maturity to increase the dollar size of the super sinker maturity for redemption calculation purposes only.

This procedure was employed in structuring the $150 million Dade County, Florida, Series 1980 housing bond program. The Dade County issue had term maturities in 2000, 2011, and 2012 in amounts equal to $15 million, $94 million, and $18 million, respectively. Individually the three maturities represent 10 percent, 63 percent, and 12 percent of the total bond issue while the serial bonds equal 15 percent of the total issue. The redemption provisions stipulate that the 2012 maturity should be excluded from the redemption calculation. Thus the calculation is based on a $132 million issue instead of the actual size of $150 million. It further stipulates that term bonds will be retired in a specified order and that, for the purposes of the calculation, the 2000 and 2011 maturities will be combined and counted as one maturity. The order followed requires the trustee to retire the entire 2000 term maturity prior to retiring the 2011 and 2012 maturities. In addition, the 2011 maturity must be fully retired prior to retiring the 2012 maturity. Consequently, if the trustee were to receive $5 million in redemption monies, bonds would be retired as follows: First the trustee would determine that, based on an issue of $132 million, the serial bonds comprise 17 percent of the issue and the combined 2000 and 2011 maturity comprises 83 percent of the issue. Therefore, of the $5 million in redemption monies, $850,000 would be used to retire the serial bonds and $4.15 million would be applied to retire term bonds. Because the provisions mandate that the 2000 maturity be retired prior to the 2011 and 2012 maturities, the $4.15 million in redemption monies are used to call only term bonds scheduled to mature in the year 2000. This amount is far greater than the amount a standard strip call would mandate to the 2000 maturity.

In a standard strip call, the following proportional weights would be observed: 15 percent, 10 percent, 63 percent, and 12 percent for the bonds maturing serially and in 2000, 2011, and 2012 respectively. Consequently, only $50,000 would be designated to term bonds maturing in 2000. The net effect of the super sinker provision is to shorten the life of a term bond, which in our example would mean that the 2000 term could be retired in 4 to 6 years as opposed to 20 years. The advantage of a super sinker bond is that the investor owns a bond that is priced as a long-term security although its expected life is comparable to some serial maturities. The disadvantage stems from the uncertainty surrounding the call. The ability to produce a super sinker's bond call is dependent upon the generation of extraordinary mandatory redemption monies (prepayments and surplus revenues). If an investor needs to receive his principal at a set time, or if he wants to lock in a set rate, the super sinker may be an inappropriate investment. On the other hand, if the investor does not need a guaranteed short-term investment, the super sinker will outperform a serial bond with regard to coupon rate. An analyst should be able to advise an investor as to the likelihood of the shortened bond life based upon the spread built into an issue and historic prepayment rates for the area.

The Residential Mortgage Subsidy Bond Tax Act of 1980

The passage of the Mortgage Subsidy Bond Tax Act, as it is more commonly called, was as important to the single-family bond market as the legislation that created the program. As previously mentioned, it was passed by both houses of Congress in November 1980 and ended a 1½-year period of uncertainty for both single-family bond issuers and underwriters. The purpose of the act was to reduce the dollar volume of new single-family bond sales, to encourage their use for those people evidencing the greatest need for mortgage financing, and ultimately to end the program entirely. These goals were accomplished by imposing several stringent requirements on bond issuance. This has meant that single-family bonds can be marketed only as long as all of the act's requirements are satisfied. The most salient features of the act are:

1. *Residency requirement:*
   a. The recipient of the mortgage loan must reside in the home being financed.
   b. The home must be located within the jurisdiction of the authority leasing the obligation.
2. *Three-year requirement:*
   a. The recipient of a mortgage loan may not have been a homeowner at any time during the three-year period ending with the date that the mortgage is executed.
   b. The three-year requirement does not apply to loans made in a "targeted area," a qualified home improvement loan, or a qualified rehabilitation loan.
3. *Purchase price requirement:* The acquisition cost of a residence cannot exceed 90 percent of the average purchase price of single-family residences (in the statistical area, or SMSA, in which the residence is located) which were purchased during the most recent 12-month period for which data is available.
4. *Amount limitation:*
   a. Mortgage bonds may be issued annually in each state in amounts not to exceed the greater of either 9 percent of the "average annual aggregate principal amount of mortgages executed during the immediately preceding three calendar years for single-family, owner-occupied residences within the state, or $200 million."
   b. The money, based upon a formula which can be changed by state law or by the governor of the state, is divided between the state and the localities. Basically the SHFA is entitled to 50 percent of the limit; the remainder can be divided.
5. *Targeted-area requirements:*
   a. At least 20 percent of the proceeds must be held aside for one year to be used for mortgages on targeted-area residences.
   b. A targeted area is a "qualified census tract," or an area of current economic distress.
6. *Arbitrage limitations:* The effective rate of interest on the mortgages may not exceed the yield on the issue of tax-exempt obli-

gations by more than 1 percent. In addition, the restriction does not permit the fees and costs incurred by a mortgage bond issue to be computed in the arbitrage limit, does not provide for instances of negative arbitrage, and limits the reserve amount on which interest may be earned to 150 percent of the annual debt service on the bonds. The amendment approved by both the House and Senate would simplify arbitrage accounting, allow excess arbitrage earnings to be remitted either to the mortgagors or the U.S. Treasury, and permit the pooling of arbitrage earnings.

7. *Registration:* All bonds issued after December 31, 1981, must be registered.
8. *Tax exemption:* All qualified mortgage bonds must be issued prior to December 1, 1983, in order to be tax-exempt.
9. *New mortgages:* Funds must be used to acquire new mortgages except replacement of construction period loans, bridge loans, or temporary financings.
10. *Assumptions:* Mortgages are assumable only if all the above requirements are met by the new mortgagor. This in effect limits the financing of FHA-insured or VA-guaranteed mortgage loans, for these programs require the free assumption of mortgage loans.
11. *Veteran bond exceptions:* Qualified mortgage bonds do not have to comply with any of the above restrictions to remain tax-exempt. A qualified veterans' mortgage bond is:
    a. Registered after December 31, 1981.
    b. Part of an issue for which all proceeds are used to provide residences for veterans.
    c. One in which payment of principal and interest is secured by a general obligation of the state.
    d. One in which proceeds are used to acquire new mortgages.
12. *Rehabilitation and home improvement loans:* are permissable under the new legislation.

Thus, as can be discerned from a reading of the provisions, the financing of single-family mortgage bonds is far more difficult than it was prior to the act's passage.

The most restrictive aspects of the act are items 2,4,5,6,7, and 8. Item 2 is commonly referred to as the "first-time home buyer" provision and will impact future issues primarily in the timely asset creation phase of the program. If first-time home buyers are the only population subject to loan origination, demand for mortgage money must be further curtailed. In the original program, total demand was reduced by both income and purchase price limitations. In future issues, demand will be further restricted because the segment of the population that meets the income and purchase price limitations will also have to meet the three-year, no home ownership provision.

Item 5, listed above, also effects timely asset creation and increases the probability of an extraordinary mandatory call from unused bond proceeds. Since 20 percent of the proceeds will be reserved for targeted-area financings, bond calls may be warranted when mortgage demand for this type of area is not evidenced.

Item 6, arbitrage limitations, makes it extremely difficult to structure an issue that is marketable and in compliance with the law. Marketability is affected because the issuer is left with a significantly reduced spread and profit margin that reduces the financial cushion usually afforded bondholders. If excess arbitrage is earned, the issuer is required to return it to the mortgagor or the Treasury, even if the program is in default.

Items 4 and 7 were designed to curtail the dollar volume of single-family bonds and should severely impact marketability. The registration requirement is particularly prohibitive because of the increased work involved in trading registered bonds. A registered bond is one where the bondholders's name appears on the face of the bond. Consequently, every bond trade in which ownership changes will require the printing of a new bond with new owner's name, and the destruction of the prior owner's bond.

By far, item 8 above is the most disheartening to issuers and underwriters alike. The construction industry, as well, has balked at this provision. Not much can be said about it except that new tax-exempt, single-family programs will soon be extinct. The only advantage to this provision is afforded to bondholders of outstanding issues. From December 2, 1983, and beyond, the supply of housing bonds will remain constant or diminish as bonds are called and retired.

CONCLUSION

Despite the several limitations placed upon issuers since the passage of the Residential Mortgage Subsidy Bond Tax Act of 1980, many housing issuers have come to the market. Most have found it necessary to contribute money upfront in order to compensate for the smaller profit allowed under the new arbitrage restrictions. Because the new legislation so severely limits issuers, bonds are usually not as well secured. As a result, bonds issued prior to the act are by and large of higher credit worthiness.

If Congress does not extend the legislation permitting this type of financing, then investors will be increasingly more interested in the outstanding bonds. Thus, the analyst would do well to fully understand program cash flows in anticipation of projected bond calls which could fit into any of several portfolio strategies.

Public Power Revenue Bonds

CHAPTER 17

Tifton Simmons, Jr.

Senior Vice President
Smith Barney, Harris Upham & Co., Incorporated

INTRODUCTION

This chapter examines public power revenue bonds beginning with a description of relative size and historic perspective. The nature of electric utility is then discussed in terms of demand and supply of electric power and energy. The demand and supply discussion leads to the recognition of different types of electric utility systems. The latter part of the chapter is devoted to the analysis of historic performance and evaluation of projected future results.

Electric revenue bonds constitute a significant portion of all tax-exempt financing. In 1981, electric revenue bonds accounted for approximately 5 percent of total construction in the United States and over 15 percent of total heavy construction. The entire electric utility industry had a net electric plant investment in 1980 of over $286 billion, making it perhaps the largest industry in the nation.

Capital requirements of the electric industry are very high particularly as compared with other industries such as manufacturing. The current demand for environmental protection will further intensify the capital requirements, causing an even higher capital-to-revenue ratio.

The electric utility industry in the United States consists of four major groups: investor-owned private power companies, public-owned municipal power systems, rural electric cooperatives, and federal power agencies. In terms of relative size, the private investor-owned utilities provided approximately 75.4 percent of kilowatt hour (kwhr) sales in 1980 as compared to 14.7 percent for public-owned municipal systems, 6.5 percent for rural electric cooperatives, and 3.4 percent from the federal power agencies. In terms of the number of systems, however, public-owned systems included over 2,200 separate systems, while private power companies had only 217 companies and rural electric cooperatives had 924.

Public power systems range in size from the Power Authority of the State of New York, which sold 45.6 billion kwhr in 1980, down to very small distribution systems with sales of less than one million kwhrs. The environment the publicly owned municipal systems work in is very similar to those of the other three groups. Essentially, electric systems are either highly regulated, privately owned businesses or nonprofit businesses that operate in a monopoly or oligopoly condition in the area they serve. The systems themselves, on the public-owned side, include small distribution systems; systems that generate, transmit, and distribute power; municipally owned bulk-power suppliers; joint-action agencies; and hybrid types of agencies.

The volume of public power revenue bond issues from 1977 through 1981 has been $5.75 billion, $5.79 billion, $4.6 billion, $4.6 billion, and $6.8 billion, respectively. Most industry projections call for even higher capital requirements for the next five years, to be financed principally from public power revenue bonds.

NATURE OF ELECTRIC UTILITIES

This section deals with the supply and demand constraints of providing the services that electric utility companies provide. It will also look at the peak-demand and capital problems inherent in meeting such supply and demand forecasts.

On the demand side there are generally four categories of demand for electric utility service: residential, commercial, industrial, and sales for resale. Additionally, in certain parts of the country there are such special categories as agricultural pumping and street lighting. Residential demand is subject to climatic conditions, but does tend to exhibit predictable peak load patterns. Commercial users typically operate from 9 to 5 in terms of their peak-load usage, while industrial users in some cases operate continuously around the clock. Such continuous use provides utilities with better load factors. Sales for resale generally apply to surplus capacity and often provide short-term benefits to utilities making such sales.

On the supply side, the generating plants basically take the form of hydroelectric; fossil, consisting of oil, gas, and coal; and nuclear-fueled plants. Hydroelectric plants, of course, have no fuel costs; consequently, they are operated as much as water conditions allow. The year-to-year production is less predictable than other forms of generation because they are subject to water flows which vary from year to year based on rain and snowfall. In the fossil-fueled area, oil and gas plants typically can range from small units that are relatively inefficient but provide good, cheap capacity to meet peak-load periods, all the way up to fairly large base-load types of units. A base-load generating unit is one that is operated as continuously as conditions will allow. Typically, coal units are operated as base-load units. Nuclear units, due to the heavy capital costs and operating characteristics, must be operated as base-load units to be efficient.

In general, the thermodynamic characteristics of larger units enable them to achieve better operating efficiency (better heat rate) than smaller units. For many years it was generally accepted that larger units also achieved better capital cost efficiency. Inflated construction costs, rigorous regulatory approvals, and long construction periods have cast doubt on the capital cost efficiency argument. Additionally, the reliability of capital cost estimates and construction period forecasts is far less than is the case for smaller units. There appears to be great variation from one utility to the next in the ability to build generating units within projected time frames and cost estimates. To evaluate new projects being considered, analysts should look at actual versus projected results of recently constructed plants by a particular utility.

The essential peak-demand problem of the electric utility industry hinges on the fact that demand for electric energy varies both over a 24-hour period and seasonally. Another characteristic of electric energy is that it generally cannot be stored in quantity. Production of energy has to be simultaneous with use. The only significant exception is the operation of some conventional hydroelectric facilities and pumped-storage hydroelectric facilities. Consequently, capacity in the form of generation must be sufficient to provide for predicted peak loads throughout the year plus adequate reserves in the event peak loads exceed projections or certain units are out of operation. To the extent a system has very large generating units, their reserves should be higher. As previously mentioned, generating units are very capital-intensive machines. Thus, in utility service areas where peak loads are far in excess of average loads, capacity goes unused a larger percent of the time. A look at system load factor over a period of a year can give an investor an idea of how much capacity goes unused during the course of the year. Typically, service areas with extreme temperature variation show the lowest load factors. Utilities that serve areas with low load factors can often benefit by employing various load management techniques such as lower off-peak pricing.

Another characteristic of the electric utility industry is the fact that it operates somewhat like a monopoly. This is primarily a consequence of the capital-intensive nature of the industry. Economies of scale of large units and the peak-demand problems mentioned above are exaggerated by duplication of facilities. As a practical matter, electric utilities are not pure monopolies because there is some cross-elasticity of the demand between substitutes, such as gas for electric service. Therefore, electric utilities do not exhibit pure monopolistic pricing characteristics. On the other hand, electric utilities do display decreasing costs and negatively sloped demand curves. Additionally, due to the divisions of demand as indicated above, price differentiation for the product is possible among purchasers. For these reasons, in the private investor-owned utilities sector, most of the industry is heavily regulated. Municipal utilities, for the most part, are not directly regulated at all in terms of the price they can charge for the product because they are nonprofit entities.

TYPES OF MUNICIPAL SYSTEMS

Municipally owned distribution systems typically are smaller, city-owned systems that purchase all of their electrical energy from another supplier: either a municipal agency, an investor-owned utility, or in some cases a rural electric cooperative. Pure distribution systems are not as capital-intensive as those systems that have generation facilities and long transmission lines. Consequently, financial analysis may expect municipally owned distribution systems to exhibit higher debt service coverage and better balance sheet ratios. A particular problem for pure distribution systems is that they tend to be the less profitable customers of investor-owned utilities and something of a problem in rate cases. Consequently, many investor-owned utilities are willing to give up municipally owned distribution systems as customers and concentrate on more profitable users. This can result in uncertain future energy sources for such distribution systems.

A second type of municipal system is the municipally owned generation, transmission, and distribution system. Typically, this type of system would be a larger city that must necessarily provide its own electrical power and energy as well as distribution facilities. Often such generation is located some distance from the city, thus the need for transmission. These fully integrated, municipally owned utility systems are often considered the strongest municipal systems in terms of credit worthiness. City systems such as Los Angeles, Sacramento, Seattle, Lansing (Michigan), Jacksonville and Orlando (Florida), Lafayette (Louisiana), Austin and San Antonio (Texas), generally all benefit from diverse user bases, self-determination in terms of owning their own generation, and competent management staffs.

As an additional element to strengthen their respective credits, many of these large, city-owned systems pay excess revenues from their utilities to the city general fund. Consequently, there is typically a political incentive to keep rates for electric service at such levels to continue to provide excess funds to the city. These excess funds provide relatively high coverage for bondholders of these large city systems.

In terms of economic efficiency, some criticism has been leveled at cities that use the electric system to generate excess funds that are ultimately used for general purposes of the city. Esssentially, the academic argument holds that, by using electric rates to subsidize the general tax base, a city causes underutilization of its electric system due to higher-than-necessary rates. Overall, this produces a misallocation of resources since it distorts the normal pricing that would prevail otherwise. The bondholder does, on the other hand, have additional comfort due to higher debt service coverage. There is an important distinction between an electric system that retains excess funds for system improvement and one that transfers such funds to the city for general improvements. From a credit point of view, the former is preferred.

The third type of municipal systems is the municipally owned bulk-power supplier. Typically this takes the form of a state agency, a joint-action agency, or in some cases a hybrid form of agency: that is, one that is primarily a bulk power supplier, but has some limited distribution as well. The municipally owned bulk-power suppliers have the same purpose; to build large, efficient generating units and supply power to smaller systems either throughout the state or, in the case of joint-action agencies, to the participants in the agency. Politically, there is usually a big difference. The governing boards of state agencies are typically appointed or elected at a state level. Typical joint-action legislation allows two or more cities to get together and form an agency. The governing boards of such joint-action agencies are appointed from the participating cities. Relative to state agencies, they tend to be autonomous in terms of politics. Bulk-power suppliers tend to operate with lower coverages than the fully integrated, municipally owned systems. They are typically secured by "take-or-pay" contracts with the participants or member cities that purchase power from the bulk suppliers.

FINANCIAL STATEMENT ANALYSIS

Balance sheet analysis is intended to show how much capital is invested in the utility, how well those assets earn, what the financial structure of the utility is, and the inherent financial leverage in the utility. As previously mentioned, electric utilities are very capital-intensive. Consequently, balance sheet analysis for a municipal electric utility would certainly be different than balance sheet analysis for other, less capital-intensive businesses.

Utility plant, as defined by the uniform system of accounts, can tell a great deal about a utility, although the numbers alone do not give the full picture. Plant in service must be looked at not only in terms of amount carried on the books (which is done at original cost), but also the time such plant was put in service, since inflation and higher-cost construction have pushed the costs of new plant up significantly in the past several years. Utilities with large successful coal or nuclear plants placed in service in the mid-to-late 1970s now have extremely valuable assets worth far more than the original cost as carried on the books. Conversely, utility systems that are changing from distribution only to generation and distribution are faced with higher cost of capital, higher construction costs, and delays associated with increased regulation. Thus, balance sheet analysis should look at plant in service as of a particular date (with knowledge of the relative age of the assets in service) as well as planned additions to plant in the future. It should also be acknowledged that widely used ratios, such as the ratio of plant per dollar of operating revenue, will vary depending on the type of plant in service. Typically, the lower-capital-cost oil and gas units will have a lower number than the hydroelectric and nuclear-fueled systems.

In general, the debt for municipal electric systems is straightforward. In many cases more than one lien exists although, given the uncertainty of results of municipal bankruptcy, lien status is of questionable value in the final analysis.[1] Additionally, an event of default on a junior lien obligation in and of itself often constitutes an event of default for the senior lien obligation.

Limits on the issuance of debt through the additional bonds test have changed in recent years. The vast additional capital requirements of many electrical utilities have forced them to alter their additional-bonds test either through refunding or issuance of subordinate obligations. Typically, the "old" style of additional-bonds tests required historic coverage of debt service by net revenues. Debt service included outstanding as well as bonds being issued. Historic requirements of 1.5 times were not uncommon. As capital costs of power

---

[1]See the Appendix to this book for a discussion of municipal bankruptcy.

plants increased, few utilities could meet the high historic coverage requirements. The "new" style of additional-bonds tests typically has lower requirements (1.0–1.25 times) and allows for future earnings to be taken into account. Consequently, bond investors have come to place less reliance on limitations for the issuance of debt than has been the case in the past. Many large, integrated systems and virtually all joint-action agencies have very weak additional-bonds tests. The contrary argument to tight additional-bonds tests is that the protection that debt limitations give to the bondholder ultimately result in deteriorated plant and the need to purchase high-cost power from other utilities.

As indicated above, there are vast differences in the types of municipal systems; thus, there are necessarily differences in balance sheet considerations among those types. In many cases the municipally owned distribution system will have high debt service coverage with relatively low debt, while fully integrated systems will necessarily have more debt due to the generation facilities they possess. As pointed out above, many city-owned systems that are fully integrated generate excess revenues which flow to the general fund of the cities. Therefore, they usually exhibit high debt coverage and have high credit worthiness. Bulk power suppliers are often analyzed in terms of their constituents or power purchasers. Joint-action agencies display very low, if any, "real" debt service coverage. Many joint-action agencies, for example, utilize what is known as "Chinese" coverage, whereby the utility will agree to charge rates sufficient to pay operations and maintenance, debt service, and some percentage over debt service, perhaps 10–25 percent. This "10–25 percent Chinese" coverage can then be credited, to the extent it is not used, to the following year's obligation. In many cases the first-year coverage is funded from bond proceeds so that, if everything goes properly, the power purchasers never have to pay more than one times real coverage over the life of the bonds. Therefore, analysis of any sort of debt-to-equity ratio for joint-action agencies would provide the investor with no assurance that he had a good bond. That result is from a balance sheet standpoint. The highly leveraged joint-action agencies and, to some extent, all bulk-power suppliers must necessarily be analyzed in terms of their constituent power purchasers and strength of the contractual arrangement between such purchasers and issuing agency.

The income statement for municipally owned electric utilities should be looked at in terms of the revenue sources, the operating results, coverage of debt service, historic trends, and the historic willingness to pay. As indicated previously, revenues can come from a variety of sources, and rates can be differentiated among those sources. Often, certain types of revenue sources such as heavy industrial users can inflate earnings for municipal utilities in good economic times, and in bad times can overly depress such earnings. Generally speaking, a solid residential base is something to look for in the revenue source. An analysis of operating results should look carefully at purchased power and fuel costs as well as the revenue sources mentioned above. Excess capacity can sometimes mean that relatively large sums of revenue can be earned from sales of excess power to other utilities. On the other hand, large purchases of power from others can signal inflexibility on the part of that utility and the possible need for large capital additions in the future.

Both from the standpoint of revenue sources and operating results, several key ratios should be looked at for the utility being analyzed. Such ratios include operating ratio, interest coverage, debt service coverage, debt service safety margin, and the debt ratio. As previously mentioned, among the three types of municipal systems these ratios will vary. Certain of the ratios become less meaningful for the highly leveraged joint-action agencies. Some attempts have been made to analyze such agencies in terms of the constituents and the power purchasers. The difference between fully integrated, municipally owned systems and bulk-power suppliers is one of relying on operating results versus contractual commitments.

Historic trends and historic willingness to pay are important, particularly from the standpoint of municipally owned distribution systems and fully integrated, municipally owned utility systems. Most state and joint-action bulk-power suppliers are relatively new, and historic trends are much more difficult to gauge. Additionally, since the bulk-power suppliers usually charge no more than a certain minimum coverage, historic trends should provide virtually the same result every year. That would not provide a meaningful test of how the utility is doing during depressed business conditions. Many integrated systems and municipally owned distribution systems have existed for some time, and historic results that go through depressed business cycles can give the investor a sense of willingness and ability to pay on the part of those utilities. Analysis should always include observation of historic willingness to pay, since many municipal systems are controlled by politically sensitive individuals. The willingness of utility systems to raise rates as necessary, during periods of stress from rate payers, should be viewed as a definite positive in the analysis of a particular system.

EVALUATION OF FUTURE RESULTS

There has been a gradual trend for municipal systems to increase their plant in service relative to the amounts of plant in service of investor-owned utilities over the past several years. Thus, the evaluation of future results has become more and more important in the analysis of municipally owned electric systems. In the case of the joint-action agencies, which now account for a significantly high percentage of all electric revenue bonds sold, no historic data is available. Consequently, projections and evaluation of future results are extremely important.

Customer mix is one of the first elements to examine in the evaluation of future results. Basic categories of customer mix have been discussed above. Customer mix includes detailed analysis of the service area territory. Population trends have tended to be one of the largest variables that a utility has to gauge its own future load growth. The nature of industry in commercial development and the goods and service mix are all important in determining the relative merits of the customer mix. Residential revenue has tended to be more predictable and stable during economic swings than industrial revenue. Analysis also includes such ratios as residential revenue per kwhr, sales revenue per kwhr, percent residential of all kwhr sales and percent residential of all sales revenue.

Since the debt incurred relates to power supply, the power supply mix is an important element of analysis of future operating results. The power supply mix not only includes variously sized units but fuel mix as well. Many analysts consider a diversified fuel mix to be positive to an electric utility. As a result of the dramatic change in the nuclear industry and the inability to successfully complete nuclear power plants, nuclear plants under construction have diluted the credit worthiness of many municipally owned utilities as well as investor-owned utilities. (See Case 3.) On the other side of the coin, many utilities (principally in the South, West, and East) that have relied largely on oil- and gas-fired generating units have been hurt during the late 1970s due to the high cost of such fuel. The uncertainty in the long-term cost and supply of oil and gas has forced many utilities to go into nuclear- and coal-fired units.

LEGAL FRAMEWORK

The legal framework for evaluation of public power revenue bonds generally consists of three areas. The first area concerns limitations imposed by state law; the second relates to covenants or promises made in the bond resolution securing the bonds; and the third deals with contractual arrangements with any third-party power purchaser.

The major concerns of state laws, as they relate to electric revenue bonds, deal with flexibility. Since financing electric power projects often involve more than one bond issue, bondholders must be assured of the ability to issue subsequent bonds to finance the project. Many states have limitations in terms of rates; in some cases, legislative

approval is needed for the total amount of bonds issued. Generally,
limitations related to subsequent bond issues are viewed as negatives
in the evaluation of credit. When such limitations exist, a historic
look as to how easily past limitations have been changed can be useful. Other state law limitations include rate commissions, plant siting
commissions, and state environmental approvals. Many states have
laws that limit service areas that can be annexed by municipal utilities. These laws have served to protect service areas of rural electric
co-ops and investor-owned utilities. Another state law consideration
is whether or not the utility has power of *eminent domain.*

In terms of bond covenants, bondholders look to several covenants
that have become almost typical for all public power revenue bond
issues. These covenants include:

1. Covenant to complete construction of projects being financed.
2. Covenant to maintain rates sufficient to pay all costs including
   debt service on bonds plus any debt service coverage.
3. Covenant to maintain all other agreements including power sales
   contracts, if any, so as not to harm bondholders.
4. Covenant against disposition of revenue-earning properties.
5. Covenant to maintain insurance in adequate amounts.
6. Covenant to maintain appropriate books of account.
7. Covenant to retain a nationally recognized, independent consulting engineer.

Bondholders also demand dilution protection through additional-bond
tests that have been discussed before and clearly spelled-out default
procedures and remedies. Bondholders should also look at investment
procedures and the evaluation of investments to make sure their secured funds are protected.

Third-party contractual obligations whereby one party purchases
power and energy from another party and agrees to pay for such
power and energy can take several forms. The two basic forms, utilized a great deal in joint-action agencies around the country, are contracts known as "take-or-pay" contracts and "take-and-pay" contracts.
In a take-or-pay contract, which may have step-up limitations, the
purchaser agrees to pay for power and energy in such amounts as to
cover all requirements of the seller. (See Cases 3 and 25.) These payments are made whether or not the plant is finished and whether or
not any power and energy is delivered. In the case of take-and-pay
contracts, all payments for power and energy are made if any power
and energy is available. If such power and energy is not available,
payments are not required; thus catastrophic avoidance is not inherent in this type of contract. Certain hybrid varieties of these contracts
exist, in many cases to get around state laws and outstanding bond

resolutions. Nevertheless, the essential ingredient for analysis is whether or not the contract guarantees payment.

ENGINEERING REPORT

As previously pointed out, many new projects involve huge capital requirements. In many cases, debt service for these capital requirements cannot be covered by historic earnings. Consequently, the use of capitalized interest has increased and projected earnings become very important in the evaluation of bonds issued to finance such projects. In this case, the opinion of an independent consulting engineer, as well as the opinion of the construction engineer is very important. It should be pointed out that ideally the construction engineer should not be the same firm as the consulting engineer. In the final analysis, the reputation of the consulting engineer is very important in evaluating the engineering report. The report itself should contain projections of demand, projections of sales, projections of revenues, expenses, and overall ability to cover future debt service requirements. Analysis should include a thorough review of assumptions and conclusions of the consulting engineer. Particular attention should be given to any qualifications on the part of the engineer's conclusions.

The opinion of the construction engineer related to the plant construction itself is another important appendix to be examined in an official statement. Special attention should be given to cost projections, while delays and cost overruns should be noted carefully. The track record of the construction managers should be reviewed. The balances between size efficiencies and construction management problems of large plants should be assessed. Adequacy of fuel and transportation of fuel should be evaluated as well.

Overall capital requirements and the ability to access the market are two other considerations in the analysis of future results. Typically, market access has not been a major problem for municipal utilities in this country. Several huge projects, however, have recently brought into focus the question of ability to raise capital in very large amounts in both good and bad markets. Consequently, it is an extremely important item to note for huge, capital-intensive projects.

A final item to review in terms of the overall evaluation of future results is an outlook of the regional economics of the area being served by the utility. In part, this is accomplished by study of the customer mix. However, as regional economics change throughout the states, electric uses have changed as well. These regional economic characteristics should also be evaluated in terms of relative electric rates in one general area versus another general area that could compete for certain large industrial-type users.

SUMMARY

The purpose of this chapter has been to give a general outline of the evaluation of public power revenue bonds. It has looked at the nature of the electric industry, including demand and supply of electric power and energy, and has addressed certain characteristics such as different types of systems. It also addressed financial statement analysis including balance sheet and income statement analysis, and also identified the other critical areas that the analyst should be aware of.

College and University
Revenue Bonds

CHAPTER **18**

John De Jong
Vice President
National Securities and Research Corporation

An investor or credit analyst should view college and universities as
organizations that sell services. Although the service for which they
are most noted is the formal educational instruction known as
"higher education," colleges and universities also sell hotel services
(primarily to those they instruct), research services, and entertainment (for example, sports events). These organizations need large
amounts of money to purchase and maintain such capital assets as
land, buildings, books, and various sorts of expensive scientific equipment.

THE HISTORICAL DEVELOPMENT OF THE COLLEGE
AND UNIVERSITY SYSTEM

The Religious Influence

The first schools of higher education were privately organized and
often connected with some recognized religious denomination. Aspir-
ing clergy and others desirous of the training which might give them
the hallmarks of a gentleman comprised the student body.

Dartmouth College v. *Woodward*

In 1819 Chief Justice Marshall's decision in *Dartmouth College* v. *Woodward* established private colleges as charitable corporations privately controlled for public benefit.[1] The decision effectively delayed the growth of state universities until after the Civil War, thereby strengthening for a time the influence of religion in higher education.[2]

Early Financial Expedients

College financing in those early years was a hand-to-mouth affair. Almost no institutions had significant endowments until after the Civil War. Outside sources of funds included subscriptions in both cash and kind, sewing circles, the American Education Society of the Congregational Church, the sale of perpetual scholarships, and outright grants from various states.[3] Low faculty salaries also contributed to maintaining the precarious financial balance.[4]

Changing Attitudes in the 19th Century

The Morrill Act of 1862. By the middle of the 19th century pressures to secularize and broaden the curriculum were increasing, both in the United States and in Europe. The Morrill Act, passed in 1862, required that the states set aside revenue from public lands specially ceded to them for the support of one or more institutions of higher learning emphasizing agriculture and other practical pursuits. The first user of Morrill Act funds was Yale, which established the Sheffield Scientific School in 1868 over the protests of the classicists.[5] The creation of many public institutions, still known as "land grant" schools, was encouraged.

Changes in Curriculum. By the last quarter of the 19th century, the classical education had given way to a wider outlook. German-trained scholars and increasing endowment income helped the change along.[6] This resulted in the widespread use of the elective

---

[1]Thomas Edward Blackwell, *College Law: A Guide for Administrators* (Washington, D.C.: American Council on Education, 1961), p. 22.

[2]Richard Hofstader and Wilson Smith, eds., *American Higher Education*, vol. I (Chicago: University of Chicago Press, 1961), pp. 149–150.

[3]Frederick Rudolph, "Who Paid the Bills? An Inquiry into the Nature of 19th Century College Finance," *Harvard Education Review* 31, no. 2 (Spring 1961), pp. 146–56.

[4]Ibid., p. 156.

[5]Richard Hofstader and Wilson Smith, eds., *American Higher Education* vol. II (Chicago: University of Chicago Press, 1961), pp. 582–83.

[6]David B. Tyack, "Education and Social Unrest, 1873–78," *Harvard Education Review* 31, no. 2 (Spring 1961), p. 209.

system of courses and the development of the true university offering advanced degrees and involved in research.[7]

Teachers Colleges. To fill the demand for elementary and secondary school teachers, normal schools—or teachers colleges, as they once were known—also appeared in the last part of the 19th century. Traditionally they have instructed their graduates more in the techniques of teaching than in the subject matter to be taught. Although in recent years they have changed their names and taken on some of the characteristics of small liberal arts colleges, they remain an identifiable type.[8]

The Present System

By 1900 most of the important components of the current system of higher education were present. It is important to recognize the basic difference in attitude between the private schools devoted to the liberal arts and the newer class of schools with their more practical bent. Neither type has been able to exist without outside financial aid. It also seems proper to point out that the growth of public institutions coincided with the accelerating pace of American industrial development. In recent years, public two-year colleges have assumed a more important role.

A QUANTITATIVE PICTURE OF THE SYSTEM

It is not difficult for an analyst to begin to build a picture of the higher education industry. The following general discussion draws upon the *1981 Statistical Abstract* published by the Department of Commerce.[9] Data on individual institutions are available from college guides prepared for and sold to prospective students and their parents.

In 1978, there were 2,871 institutions of higher education. This represented an increase of 46 percent from the 1,968 in existence in 1960.

In 1980, degree enrollment amounted to over 10 million. Most of these students were seeking degrees either at the bachelors level or below, and most were enrolled in public establishments. Fewer than half of all high school graduates enroll in college. Enrollment is affected by the level of family income.[10]

---

[7]Allan M. Cartter, ed., *American Universities and Colleges* (Washington, D.C.: American Council on Education, 1964), p. 23.

[8]Ibid., p. 30.

[9]U. S. Department of Commerce, Bureau of the Census, *Statistical Abstract of the United States: 1981,* (Washington D.C.: 1981), Table 266, p. 158.

[10]Ibid., Tables 265, 266, 267, and 269, pp. 158–59.

In 1981 the average tuition charge in private colleges was $3,434. In public schools this figure was $657. For board and dormitory charges, the spread between the two types of institutions was not nearly as great, but private schools, on average, still cost more.[11]

COLLEGE AND UNIVERSITY ACCOUNTING

Colleges and universities use a system of financial reporting based on the same self-balancing fund concept employed by such nonprofit organizations as hospitals and governments. (See Chapters 35–38.) The rules of this sort of accounting were not pulled together until the 1930s and even today are less developed than for profit accounting.[12]

A CONTRADICTION FACING THE ANALYST

An important conclusion to be drawn from the foregoing brief sketch of the higher education system is that its services are of interest to a minority of the population, some of whom cannot afford them. This means that each individual school is in competition for students. Nevertheless, the accounting system used is not set up to measure relative competitive success with one or a few summary measures—a function performed by earnings in the private business sector, for example. In fact, colleges and universities are not generally supposed to generate regular financial surpluses.

Without regular internally generated surpluses, however, the administrators of the school have a difficult time expanding or improving the physical plant on a regular basis. This explains the attraction of the municipal bond market. Adequately secured bonds can be sold to provide predetermined amounts of capital at the administration's option. This is more convenient than sewing circles or waiting for the expectations contained in the will of a wealthy benefactor.

SECURITY FOR HIGHER EDUCATION BONDS

Sources of Revenue

Colleges and universities receive income in many different ways. Tuition, room and board charges, and government grants are generally the largest of these, but user fees can also be substantial. Outside giving and endowment income may be significant.

---

[11]Ibid., Table 275, p. 162.
[12]Edward S. Lynn and Robert J. Freeman, *Fund Accounting: Theory and Practice* (Englewood Cliffs, N.J.: Prentice-Hall, 1974), pp. 926–27.

Creating Bondholder Claims against Revenue

Breaking Up the Revenue Stream. In structuring a pledge of revenue, the institution has the option of breaking up its total income stream into its components and pledging each one against separately secured debt or consolidating and borrowing under a single pledge. For example, a school might secure each dormitory separately or pledge revenue from a system of many dormitories and dining halls.

Consolidation will make the analyst's job less difficult since reporting will be less complex. In addition the analyst will not have to make judgments about relative usage and condition of facility A over facility B.

The "General Obligation" Pledge. It is also possible to carry consolidation to the ultimate degree and make bonds a general obligation of the college. The phrase *general obligation* has a long history of imparting a high level of security to tax exempts, but it is important to remember that colleges and universities do not have the power to tax traditionally associated with the use of these words.

In fact, the use of the balanced fund accounting method assumes that just about every dollar of income is received in connection with some specific service or other. There is no room for discretion in allocation of funds in this scheme of things nor need there be any discretionary income to be allocated if services are to be provided at cost.

Asset Pledges

Nonfinancial Assets. Bondholders might receive a claim against real assets of the school. It is not clear, however, how valuable this claim might be. Depending on type and location, these assets might not have an alternative use and therefore might have no market value.

Financial Assets. Some schools, especially those private foundations that have been in existence a long time, may have investment portfolios, the income from which supports the functioning of the institution. These assets may also be available to secure bonds.

The *Statistical Abstract* indicates that, in 1979, the book value of endowments across the country aggregated $16.8 billion. Of the total, $13.4 billion was in the hands of private colleges.[13] Harvard University's general pooled investments had a value of $1.3 billion in June of 1981,[14] so it is evident that financial assets are not evenly distributed across institutions.

---

[13]*Statistical Abstract,* Table 276, p. 163.
[14]Proposed official statement dated November 24, 1982, for $245,000,000 Massachusetts Health and Educational Facilities Authority Revenue Bonds, Harvard University, Series E, Appendix B, p. B–4.

It is not uncommon to find bond issues of private schools that are collateralized by a pool of assets segregated from the general endowment funds and that serve as bond security.[15]

Value of Asset Pledges. It is clear that asset pledges can be of limited value to the security holder. Therefore, it is very important that the analyst be confident that the institution will continue to exist in substantially its present form.

This is particularly important now for two reasons. Not only are publicly supported schools less expensive to the student by a significant amount, but also the number of people in the 18 to 22 age group will drop by about 25 percent between now and 1994. The decline will be greater in some areas of the country than others.[16] It seems reasonable to assume that some private colleges will find themselves under great financial pressure.

It may be dangerous for the analyst to accept enrollment forecasts at face value. *Forbes* magazine recently reported on a survey of college presidents done for the Association of Governing Boards of Universities and Colleges. According to the survey, 42 percent expected continued growth for their institution, 15 percent expected a drop, and the rest, or another 42 percent, saw steady enrollment. The economist doing the survey, noting the population trends, forecast that, "Private liberal arts colleges, regional state universities and private two-year colleges will be especially hard hit, with schools in the Northeast taking the worst beating."[17]

ANALYZING AN INDIVIDUAL ISSUE

Setting Cost and Resource Benchmarks against which to Measure an Individual School

Barron's Profiles of American Colleges, issued just about every year since the mid-1960s, attempts to show the prospective student what he would be buying if he attends a particular school, how difficult a school is to enter, and what the costs will be. This information can also be used by the bond analyst to gauge a school's competitive position. In Table 1, averages or ranges of various quantitative measures for schools of various types are presented. All measures are

---

[15]Chapter 28 discusses higher education revenue bonds collateralized by financial assets such as common stocks and taxable bonds.

[16]William M. Bulkeley, " 'Baby Bust' Enrollment Drop Seen Having an Uneven Effect," *The Wall Street Journal,* December 14, 1982, p. 33.

[17]"The Shrinking Campus", *Forbes,* November 8, 1982, p. 12.

Table 1
Selected Measures for Three Groups

	Eight Ivy League Schools	*Six Large State Universities*	*Six Schools Rated "Less Competitive" by Bar Guide*
Average percent of Ph.D.s	95%*	67%*	48%†
Range of student faculty ratio	6 to 1–12 to 1	14 to 1–23 to 1	9 to 1–20 to 1
Costs (average): Tuition			
Room and	$7,105	$1,219‡	$2,584
board	2,995	2,370	1,870
Range of library services:			
Books	1,200,000–10,200,000	1,100,000–4,000,000	45,000–885,000
Periodicals	6,000–100,000	4,000–24,475	355–5,502
Incoming students (average):			
Applied			
Accepted	11,011	13,532	2,665
Enrolled	2,738	10,393	2,056
Applied/enrolled	1,518	5,423	1,193
(percent)	7.25%	2.50%	2.20%

*Based on the four that reported this statistic.
†Based on the five that reported this statistic.
‡In-state tuition.
Data taken from *Barron's Profiles of American Colleges*, 13th edition, Volume 1 (Barron's Educational Series, Inc., Woodbury, New York, 1982).

based on data in the 1982 addition of the guide. Explanations of the chosen measures follow.

Quality of Service. A student goes to a college to learn from those who are themselves well-educated. In our society this can be measured by the percentage of the faculty holding doctorates and the student/faculty ratio. If a school is staffed entirely by Ph.D.s and has a low student/faculty ratio, the student will have the opportunity to spend much time with well-trained instructors.

A second major component of service which can be expressed quantitatively is the size of the library. Clearly this statistic will be affected by such factors as the size of the student body and the importance of graduate education, but it still remains an important indicator.

Costs. The importance of this criterion is self-evident and invites comparison across schools in relation to faculty/student ratios and library facilities.

Applications Received, Students Accepted, and Students Enrolled. These three numbers taken together tell the analyst how difficult the school's "product" is to sell. Computation of these numbers over a period of years for individual schools could be quite revealing.

Observations Based on Table 1.   Although it must be admitted at the outset that a far more detailed set of benchmarks could be developed, it is nevertheless the case that even Table 1 reinforces some of the observations made earlier. The "Ivy" schools have a more highly trained faculty and enormous libraries to serve their students than the other schools; but including the trade-off between cost and quality in the argument, the state schools as a group do not come off badly. The appeal of the Ivy League is shown by the fact that these schools received more than seven applications for each student actually enrolled compared to both other types which had a ratio of 2 + to 1.

From Table 1 it appears that the state subsidies affect the cost of instruction more than the cost of housing. The difference between the lowest and highest room and board cost is only $1,125 compared to a $5,886 difference in instruction charges.

The "less competitive" schools appear to be at a disadvantage. Three private and three public schools were included in this category. When the averages were derived, they showed that total costs in this class of school were not much different from the state university average in spite of the fact that resources were significantly less. The highest total cost included in these averages, for example, was $7,050, a figure well above the state university average. This particular school showed a faculty/student ratio of 16 to 1, gave no figures on the level of faculty training, and had a library of 45,000 volumes only. The school is enrolling 1 student for every 2.2 applications it receives. It may well be possible to get a better education for less if one looks around a bit.

Reading the Indenture and Flow of Funds

It is not possible or productive to be very specific about indenture provisions in a limited space. In general, the usual revenue bond considerations apply. The analyst should understand where the bond's claim stands against competing claims and be sure that sufficient care will be given to segregation of income and investment of any available reserve balances in secure assets. The analyst should also be sure that construction funds will be handled carefully.

It is worth repeating that if available revenues are produced from only a single facility, e.g., a single dormitory rather than from a system, it is necessary to reach some conclusions about how important this facility is likely to be to the institution in the future and what kind of condition the facility is in. This information may not be easily obtained.

The Final Investment Judgment

After looking at the school in general and the bond contract and facilities in particular, a credit judgment should be possible. The presence of general obligation pledges and pledged assets may give additional security and comfort.

In view of the importance of having the institution as a functioning entity, it may be valuable for the analyst to form an opinion on how frequently the situation should be reviewed or, to put it another way, for what period in the future the analyst feels comfortable with his judgment. As the case histories given next will show, reviews may need to be fairly frequent, especially for smaller private institutions.

LESSONS FROM PAST PROBLEMS

Colleges and universities do not have major difficulties with enough frequency for these to be the subject of regular reporting in the media. Nevertheless occasional instances can be found. Four have lessons for the analyst and are worth mentioning.

These are the crisis at the University of Pittsburgh in the late 1950s and early 1960s, the demise of John J. Pershing College of Beatrice, Nebraska, in 1971, the closing of Eisenhower College located in New York State in 1982, and the investment troubles of the New York State Dormitory Authority with the firm of Lombard-Wall, Inc. *None of these situations involve bond defaults,* but all demonstrate some aspects of the business risk attached to college operation.

The University of Pittsburgh Crisis[18]

In 1955 the University of Pittsburgh (Pitt) acquired a new chief executive who decided to upgrade the quality of the school by such measures as lowering the student/faculty ratio, tightening admission standards, and improving the level of faculty training by raising salaries to attract better faculty. His plan for doing this included a projection of an increased endowment.

In the event only part of the plan was successful, it was generally agreed that the school's quality had been improved. However, the endowment did not grow fast enough and enrollment did not grow very rapidly either, although operating costs increased about four times in a 10-year period.

Expenditure demands were met by outside borrowing, by consuming endowment, and by an accounting technique called interfund bor-

---

[18]The Pitt crisis was reported in the following articles: Frederick C. Klein, "City College Woes," *The Wall Street Journal,* September 17, 1965, p. 16; Robert H. Terte, "Pittsburgh University Expansion Plans," *New York Times,* July 25, 1965, p. 46.

rowing which allowed the university to move cash around from fund to fund to meet its most pressing outside cash needs. It was reported that the trustees were not being adequately informed.

The Pitt crisis developed very rapidly. The combined account deficit went from zero to $19 million in about five years.

Three important analytical points are demonstrated by the Pitt crisis. The first is the impact of management on the course of events. It is clear that what happened resulted from a deliberate policy change. The second is the speed with which the school's financial situation deteriorated. The third is the importance of interfund borrowing as a danger signal of financial problems. In a fund accounting scheme where just about every incoming dollar is earmarked for a specific function and a growing financial surplus is not a goal, the moving of actual cash from fund to fund to pay current bills is a sign that some part of the overall operating plan is not going well.

The Pitt situation was eventually resolved thanks in large part to the intervention of the state legislature which appropriated substantial sums for the school's use, although it was not required to do so. The school still exists, and, judging by *Barron's* guide, is thriving.

The Closing of John J. Pershing College[19]

John J. Pershing College was located in Nebraska and had 350 students in 1971. That winter it was announced on one Thursday that the school would close at noon the next day because of money troubles. This school does not appear in *Barron's* guide, and it must be assumed that the closing was permanent. The lesson for the analyst is clear; closing can be very rapid indeed.

The Closing of Eisenhower College[20]

Eisenhower College, which had been taken on by nearby Rochester Institute of Technology three years before because of its financial troubles, did not open in September 1982. Enrollment was dropping, and the current account deficit was $5.7 million—a large sum compared with an enrollment of 400.

Although the plant of the school is valued at $45 million on the books, it is currently for sale for about $18 million which, it is reported, will about cover debts and closing costs. Although Eisenhower benefited from a famous name and considerable one-time support for buildings, it had no endowment or alumni body to speak of. Its costs

---

[19]J. Brian Smith, "Displaced Men Students Find a Feminine Haven," *The Evening News* (Newark, N.J.), February 2, 1971, p. 21.

[20]Anne Makay-Smith, The Death of a College Underscores the Plight of Private Institution," *The Wall Street Journal,* December 14, 1982, pp. 1, 20.

at $8,800 per student were not low. The decision to close was made in July of 1982 and was not expected by the staff, although they were aware of problems.

The Eisenhower closing demonstrates again that closings happen very quickly and that there is basis in fact for skepticism regarding enrollment projections. It is also important to note the difference between the reported book value of the plant and the as-yet unattained sale price. The facilities are located in a small town, and a buyer may not be easy to find.

The Lombard-Wall Problem

On August 12, 1982, Lombard Wall, a New York City firm dealing in money market securities, filed for bankruptcy. The New York State Dormitory Authority, which acts as financing agent for college and university construction programs in the state, had invested a large amount of idle funds belonging to several different entities in repurchase agreements with this firm.[21] It was discovered that the agency's investment was not adequately protected. Charges of mismanagement and administrative cover-up have been made, but it looks as if ultimate losses will not be major.[22]

Although, at first glance, the Lombard-Wall situation might seem to be an instance where state involvement has not been helpful, it is important to look not only at the problem but at the response. It is clear that something went wrong, but it is also evident that response from other parts of the state administration have tended to protect the ultimate position of the schools owning the assets in question. Both this situation and the Pitt crisis demonstrate that state governments can act to stabilize difficult situations if they wish. Private colleges can only enter the tax-exempt market through a tax-exempt issuing authority. Such an authority, in addition to providing tax exemption to the school, can also provide some comfort to security holders through outside supervision that bondholders would not otherwise have.

CONCLUSIONS

College and university revenue bonds present the analyst with a set of unique problems not really reflected in the flow of funds through an indenture-created financial structure. When colleges develop financial problems, there may be very little warning; and college administrators may not be expert business managers. Already

---

[21]Repurchase agreements are discussed in Chapter 25.

[22]Gordon Matthews, "Dormitory Officials Charged with Lombard-Wall Cover-Up," *American Banker,* December 17, 1982, p. 3.

visible changes in the age composition of the population indicate that some schools will have a difficult time in the future. Nevertheless, education is a major contributor to the national well-being, and a well-conceived borrowing program should result in securities of acceptable quality. On a relative basis securities from a major state university should be, other things being equal, preferred to others of the class. Ideally, this class of bond should be followed almost like the securities of a private sector business, a task which will be difficult for any owner who does not have available significant analytical resources. Therefore, these bonds may be more suited to institutional rather than individuals' portfolios.

Multifamily Housing Revenue Bonds

CHAPTER 19

Joseph F. Coleman
Municipal Bond Department
Goldman, Sachs & Co.

Judy Wesalo-Temel
Municipal Bond Department
Goldman, Sachs & Co.

INTRODUCTION

During the late 1970s and early 1980s, multifamily housing bonds attracted significantly less attention than their single-family counterparts. While single-family issues have been the focus of such innovations as rapid-paydown assumptions, tender options, super-sinkers, and exotic mortgage instruments, the structure of multifamily financings has remained relatively consistent. The primary, if not sole, exception is the recent introduction of low-coupon or zero-coupon bonds which, in fact, do not greatly change the shape of the issuer's cash flow.

This contrast is also seen in a credit sense. The multifamily issuer has not been subject to sweeping regulatory change, and has had the opportunity to assemble a straightforward package of federal subsidy and insurance programs to provide a high level of security.

Unfortunately for both the issuer and the investor (not to mention the credit analyst), this situation is changing. As this is written, the direction of federal housing policy is undergoing close scrutiny. As a result, two programs critical to multifamily housing, Section 8 and

285

GNMA Tandem, may be facing extinction. For the authors of a how-to guide for credit analysis, this creates another problem. A credit approach focusing on the details of existing federal programs may be of limited utility several years hence, when an entirely different federal role may have emerged. To deal with this problem, this chapter will devote some attention to the currently operative federal programs and will refer to them repeatedly, but will attempt to go beyond them to the basic issues of multifamily finance. The approach taken is to discuss generic issues which will occur in all multifamily bonds, regardless of subsidy, and ways in which they are commonly addressed. By examining the functional role of subsidies and other credit features, regardless of their specific terms, we hope to offer basic tools which the analyst can apply to future financings.

The substance of this chapter is divided into six sections which may be broadly grouped into two categories. The first three sections survey the field of multifamily housing bonds. Areas discussed include the types of obligations sold, current federal programs, and an overview of the types of risks faced by the bondholder. The second three sections detail specific areas of analysis to be considered in any issue. These include fundamental analysis of the assets to be financed, analysis of formal bond security provisions, and financial analysis. The credit problems posed in each of these areas will be affected by the shape of any state or federal programs. The final section of the chapter summarizes our approach and offers some thoughts for the future.

TYPES OF OBLIGATIONS

For our purposes, we may distinguish two broad types of multifamily bond programs: direct-loan programs and loans-to-lenders issues. New-issue Public Housing Authority (PHA) bonds are no longer marketed, and the characteristics of outstanding PHA bonds are identical, in subsidy terms, to project notes discussed elsewhere in the volume. For information on the PHA program see Case 22 of this book.

Direct-Loan Programs

This type of issue is structured so that bond proceeds are used to make a mortgage to a developer for construction and/or permanent financing of multifamily housing. The developer may be a limited-dividend syndicate or a nonprofit organization. Repayment of bonds in this case will be determined by the cash flow provided by mortgage payments, non-mortgage investments (e.g., reserve funds), insurance proceeds, or external credit supports. Aside from external supports such as state moral obligations or letters of credit, the bondholder is exposed to many of the risks of real estate finance—insured or uninsured. A fuller discussion of risks follows in a subsequent section. Direct-loan programs may be issued under the tax exemption afforded under Section 103 of the IRS code or, in some cases, under Section 11(b) of the Housing Act of 1937.

Section 11(b) provides for the tax exemption of securities issued by local public-housing authorities (and state agencies on behalf of PHAs) for subsidized units. These projects may be owned by the PHA or, as is currently more common, mortgaged by a limited-dividend syndicate or non-profit developer. The amount of bonds which may be issued is determined by project cost (based on capitalization of cash flow), reserves, and cost of issuance. Limits on each of these items are prescribed in the section. Mortgages made under 11(b) can be for up to 90 percent of project cost for limited-dividend developers and up to 100 percent for nonprofit sponsors. These financings, which may be insured or uninsured, may be for permanent financing only, and are thus often structured as simultaneous note/bond offerings (a structure now prohibited under Section 103) with Federal Housing Administration (FHA) insurance. In such an issue, timing and insurance endorsement are risks to the Construction Loan Note (CLN) holder, but the bond takeout and insurance provide considerable security. For additional information, see Chapter 33.

The Section 103 exemption is by far the most common legal framework for publicly offered multifamily issuance. Multifamily bonds are subject to restrictions common to all revenue bond issuance and are also subject to certain provisions of the Mortgage Subsidy Bond Tax Act of 1980. In addition to bond registration (the broader application of which is uncertain at this writing), the primary limitation of this act concerns a requirement that all bond-financed multifamily projects must make provision for low- and moderate-income occupancy. Specifically, 20 percent of the units in a development (15 percent in targeted areas) must be rented to or held available for low- and moderate-income individuals. The duration of this reservation is the longest of one half the bond issue, the length of the Section 8 contract, or 10 years after 50 percent occupancy is achieved. Multifamily bonds issued under Section 103 are considered industrial development bonds (IDBs). Their future in connection with recently enacted IDB legislation is also uncertain.

Loans-to-Lenders Programs

In a loans-to-lenders program, bondholder security is completely divorced from the performance of the asset to be financed (except for the income requirements). Bond proceeds are used to make a loan to a financial institution, with the stipulation that the borrower in turn uses the proceeds for lending to a mortgagor. Security for the bond-holder lies in the loan agreement between the issuer and the lender (typically a bank or S&L). The loan must be repaid by the lender regardless of the status of the multifamily development. Ideally, analysis of bond security would require analysis of the lender, which is beyond the scope of this chapter. Short of that, however, three types of additional security have been used to backstop the repayment pledge of the bank.

First, and most commonly used, is a pledge of collateral valued at a certain multiple of the lender loan. The reason for overcollateralization is to protect against a decline in the liquidation level of collateral under adverse interest-rate conditions and to compensate for credit risk. For example, there may be a requirement that the bank pledge 125 percent of loan value in government or agency securities, but 175 percent of single-family mortgages may be required. Given the asset structure of most S&Ls, seasoned single-family mortgages are often used. Risk elements here include lien priorities on the collateral, which can only be addressed by bond counsel, and the valuation question. Most recent programs have called for periodic revaluation of collateral, and a requirement for the lender to offer additional collateral if market value declines.

A second, less frequently used, approach is for the lender to obtain an irrevocable letter of credit on the lender loan from a well-capitalized, credit worthy, money-center bank. This structure assumes the same characteristics as any letter-of-credit financing, and further severs the link to the multifamily use of proceeds.

Third, several recent loans-to-lenders financings have been structured to use bond proceeds to purchase certificates of deposit (CDs) from the lender bank, which uses these funds to make the mortgage or mortgages. The bondholder, by virture of owning a CD, enjoys the benefits of insurance from the Federal Savings and Loan Insurance Corporation (FSLIC) or the Federal Deposit Insurance Corporation (FDIC). (For additional information, see Chapter 27.) The bondholder is insured up to the limits of federal insurance, currently $100,000 per account. The advantage to the lender is that it can participate, even if its balance sheet would preclude the pledge of collateral or a letter of credit, or if it does not wish to pledge collateral. Credit risks are apparently limited to the lender's maintaining its FDIC/FSLIC standing. In larger holdings, the $100,000 limit may represent an additional disadvantage.

Loans-to-lenders programs, then, separate bond security from the operation of the mortgage portfolio. For the balance of this chapter, we will concentrate entirely on direct-loan programs in which the mortgage portfolio is of critical importance to the bondholder.

FEDERAL PROGRAMS

Federal involvement in financing multifamily bonds is twofold. First, the use of federal insurance goes far to minimize the risk of mortgage default. Second, a number of federal subsidy programs enhance the level of cash flow and add stability to cash flows. These functions are discussed individually below.

Federal Insurance

Title II of the National Housing Act is the authorizing legislation behind Federal Housing Administration (FHA) insurance on various types of mortgages. The most widely used programs for bond-funded multifamily programs are Section 221(d)(3) and Section 221(d)(4). The most important difference between the two sections is the maximum loan amount as a percentage of the property financed (loan-to-value ratio). Section 221(d)(3) will insure mortgages for up to 100 percent of project cost, while section 221 (d)(4) will insure mortgages up to 90 percent of project costs, i.e., requiring 10 percent equity by the developer. In practice, given other program requirements, this translates to the general use of 221(d)(3) for nonprofit project sponsors and 221(d)(4) for limited-dividend developers.

Both programs have dollar mortgage limits determined by such things as the size and location of the development, type of project (e.g., new construction versus rehabilitation), and physical plant features. The key factor with both programs is the level of insurance provided. Upon a mortgage default continuing for 30 days, the mortgagee may pursue claim to the title of the property or, more commonly, assign the mortgage to FHA. Assignment to FHA is the more common approach because it avoids the delays associated with foreclosure or other legal means to secure title. If the mortgage is assigned to FHA, and various warranties are made by the mortgagee, insurance should essentially pay 99 percent of the unpaid mortgage and interest at the debenture rate (i.e., the rate set by FHA under which it would issue its own debentures) from the date the mortgage is first eligible for assignment. The timing of payments depends on the status of the loan. Prior to final endorsement of insurance by FHA (effectively meaning project completion), 70 percent of the claim will be paid within 15 days of filing—versus 90 percent on a loan which has received endorsement. The balance is paid after receipt by FHA of financial and legal documentation. Current policy calls for payment of FHA insurance in cash, although it is empowered to issue long-term securities in payment.

The depth of FHA insurance and the liquidity offered by rapid payment and cash settlement provide a great deal of security to the bond-holder, vastly reducing portfolio risk. The issuer could also complement the FHA insurance with features providing full protection which, of course, further strengthens credit worthiness. These include funding the one-month interest foregone prior to assignment, creating a reserve for the uninsured 1 percent mortgage amount, and supplying a cash flow cushion for the period prior to full FHA settlement. Even without these features, however, the FHA insurance as provided is a substantial credit benefit. We should note that there is some risk in construction financing from a project's inability to reach final endorsement for one reason or another. In a bond financing by a major issuer this risk is generally minimal, owing to agency management and mortgage underwriting practices. In an 11(b) note/bond financing, this risk is borne by the noteholder, and is discussed elsewhere in this volume. For additional information, see Chapter 33. In a bond financing, furthermore, this risk cannot be addressed by the analyst from generally available information.

Finally, FHA procedural requirements themselves provide some assurance that prudent lending practices, concerning the selection of projects and developers, as well as the management of construction costs, are followed by the issuer.

Federal Subsidies

In addition, and sometimes in tandem with FHA insurance, subsidy programs are used to construct multifamily housing for low- and moderate-income persons. The popularity of subsidy programs has waned and we will not spend too much time discussing the specifics of each program.

Section 236. New projects built with Section 236 payments have not gone up since 1974, as the program was suspended in the housing moratorium of 1973. However, projects which were built using the subsidy have been sustained, so a brief discussion of Section 236 is necessary if an analyst or investor encounters outstanding bonds of this type of security. Section 236 is basically an interest-rate subsidy to the lender to allow the mortgagor to reduce the monthly payments. This can be combined with federal insurance. The interest-payment subsidy lowers the effective rate of the mortgage to 1 percent. There were program eligibility requirements, including specifying the type of tenant, project rents, mortgage amounts, and rental assistance payments to tenants.

Section 8. 1974 was a critical year for multifamily housing. This was the year that saw the end of Section 236 interest-rate subsidies for new construction and the enactment of the Housing and Community Development Act of 1974. This act introduced the Section 8 program of the U.S. Housing Act of 1937, as amended. Section 8 is essentially a program in which HUD subsidizes the difference between the "fair-market rent" and a percentage of the tenant's income. This percentage has recently been increased to 30 percent from 25 percent.

The subsidies are made via two different contracts. One is the Annual Contributions Contract (ACC) entered into between HUD and the HFA. The ACC obligates HUD to provide funds for the HFA to make housing assistance payments to the developer of a project. The contract between the HFA and the developer is called the Housing Assistance Payment (HAP) contract. The HFA will pay the developer the difference between the total housing expense (or contract rent) after deduction of debt service, escrow, and reserve requirements, and the eligible tenant's contributions. The ACC remains in place as long as the HAP contract is in force. HAP contracts can vary among different HFAs.

The duration of initial HAP contracts and optional extensions have varied. Often these are shorter than the final bond maturity. The analyst or investor should evaluate the conditions under which the extension would not be exercised, and if so, what are the available remedies and cash flow protections for the bondholder.

The total housing expense, or contract rent, is initially based on the fair-market rent of the unit, which is periodically determined by HUD for specific localities. Contract rents over 100 percent of the fair-market rent may be approved by HUD under certain circumstances. There are numerous regulations regarding automatic annual adjustments in the contract rent and also special adjustments to reflect increased expenses.

Eligible tenants for Section 8 assistance must not exceed income limits set by HUD and must meet other criteria. There are also regulations concerning payment of the subsidy if the unit becomes vacant. Section 8 payments are made during the initial rental phase, and a portion continues for up to 60 days in the event of subsequent vacancies. The debt service portion of the subsidy attributable to a vacant unit continues for one year.

In looking at a state HFA issue that is Section 8 assisted, one should check to see if the subsidy is pledged as security for the bonds.

A comparison of Section 8 with Section 236 is revealing in the way housing policy has changed in the United States. Section 236 subsidizes the interest rate down to 1 percent; it provides for no adjustments due to increased operations and maintenance costs. Section 8, on the other hand, provides for a very deep subsidy for these variable expenses. While the security in a Section 8 issue is superior for a bondholder to Section 236, it is exactly the deep subsidy that has

292   *Chapter 19*

caused the federal government to reexamine housing policies and to limit the Section 8 program. At this point it is unclear what direction that will take.

OVERVIEW OF BONDHOLDER RISKS

The purpose of any municipal credit analysis is, of course, to assess the risks present in the loan and the degree to which the bond in question offers protection from those risks. As a background for analysis, therefore, this section identifies general classes of risk to which the bondholder is exposed. With this in hand, specific areas of analysis can be developed to assess each category.

Aside from the market risk faced by the holder of any security, the multifamily bondholder faces two broad classes of credit risk which result from the hybrid nature of the financing. On one hand, because cash flow derives from a pool of mortgages, these bonds share some characteristics of issues based on the arbitraging of financial assets, such as single-family mortgage bonds or student-loan revenue bonds. On the other hand, the bonds face the additional risks inherent in project financings, such as hospitals or electric revenue bonds. This is because the economic viability and physical integrity of assets are critical to income—factors which are typically absent in pure cash flow financings. This second risk category is particularly important in the case of uninsured projects, found most frequently in state HFA issues.

Finally, though each is discussed separately, we emphasize the interrelation of the two categories of credit risk.

Mortgage Portfolio Risks

Multifamily housing bonds are, of course, payable from the receipt of mortgage and investment income by the issuer. Risk factors are those which will impair the timing or adequacy of cash flow. This is true of any bond based on financial assets and, in fact, cash flows from multifamily housing bonds should be very predictable, as discussed in another section. At least three factors, however, distinguish multifamily cash flow risk from, for example, single-family issues.

First, unlike single-family portfolios backed by a large number of undifferentiated loans, the typical multifamily issue offers less diversity, as it is backed by a comparatively small number of large projects. This gives rise to concern over the project itself, discussed separately below, and makes each mortgagor's behavior much more important to the bond's credit worthiness.

Second, the multifamily bond typically carries a much higher public policy content than a single-family issue, as the intent is to provide housing to a deprived client group. This may result in a reluctance by the issuer to enforce its rights in a nonperforming mortgage, lest the tenants be harmed.

Third, the low-income tenant group may, depending on subsidy, make the rent roll relatively inflexible in the face of operating-cost increases, reduced occupancy, or other factors.

While each of these areas can be effectively addressed through the design of subsidy programs, features of the mortgage, bond covenants, insurance, and so forth, they raise the following questions as subjects of analysis:

1. Will effective mortgage rates provide a sufficient spread for debt service, agency costs, and safety margins?
2. To what extent will a small number of mortgage delinquencies or defaults affect the timing or adequacy of cash flow?
3. Are mortgage payments subject to rent-roll pressures from operating-cost increases, rental limits, or other project-related risks?
4. How much reliance is placed on nonmortgage income or other revenue sources? Alternatively, what other sources are available to the issuer, and how reliable are these?

Project Risks

The risks identified above can exist even in a sound, well-operated building. The likelihood of delinquency and default from physical deterioration or rent-roll weakness will be magnified, however, if the project is under-utilized, overly costly, or improperly maintained. These factors, therefore, expose the bondholder to credit risk questions fundamental to any facility. Relevant considerations include:

Construction Risks. Aside from the use of CLN's with a bond takeout, many financings will use bond proceeds for both construction and permanent financing. During construction, the developer has no cash flow and construction delays or cost overruns can affect bond security. Possible consequences include noncompletion or delays that change the timing of cash flow available to meet the fixed-debt service schedule. Cost overruns may also require additional financings, diluting the bondholder's asset protection.

Operating Risks. Depending on the nature of the subsidy program, if any, changes in the operating cost of the building may reduce the security provided by the rent roll as the developer's income is reduced. This recalls our discussion of the differences between the Section 236 and Section 8 programs. Another, related, risk is that of a failure to physically maintain the building, with the result that it ultimately deteriorates or is unable to attract tenants.

Occupancy Risks. Whether subsidized or unsubsidized, rental income is contingent on maintaining occupancy. Occupancy may drop because of physical deterioration of the project or because of a change in the service area of the development. There is, unfortunately, no dearth of low-income individuals, but a change in the demographics of an area or widespread neighborhood deterioration may affect occupancy.

Again, individual bond programs can be designed to minimize each of these risks, and fundamental analysis can assess risk levels.

Having identified several areas of risk, we turn in the balance of this chapter to analytical factors. Analysis of project fundamentals, formal security techniques, and financial analysis, together, will offer insights into the relative exposure of various bond issues.

FUNDAMENTAL PORTFOLIO ANALYSIS

A state housing finance agency exists to provide housing to low- and moderate-income persons. The HFA makes construction and permanent loans to the developer of housing for this segment of the population.

Underwriting Criteria

One key part of the analytical process is determining the HFA's ability to evaluate the prospects for developments it is asked to finance. One typical HFA, for example, takes the following steps for approval of residential developments.

Initial Site and Market Review. When a prospective mortgagor submits a proposal, the HFA does an analysis of the site to determine the need for subsidized rental housing.

Feasibility Review and Approval. Once the site and market approval is granted, the prospective developer must submit specific information to the agency, including architectural and technical plans.

Commitment Review and Approval. The agency performs design and financial analyses before a final commitment is given. Often origination, financing, and other fees are collected at this point.

To assure project viability, an HFA may seek a variety of construction period measures. For a typical state housing finance agency (HFA) these include:

1. Assurance of Completion. The State HFA should require that the developer execute a construction contract in a form that is approved by the Department of Housing and Urban Development (HUD), in order to receive the FHA insurance. To assure the completion, the developer must provide some type of financial security in the form of a performance bond or an irrevocable letter of credit.

2. Cost Overrun Agreement. This addresses which party is responsible for cost overruns.

3. Development Contingency Fund. The HFA should require that each mortgagor provide at the initial closing of the mortgage loan a fund consisting of cash or irrevocable letters of credit or other forms of credit equal to a percentage of the mortgage loan. This is additional security for contingencies that might arise during construction.

4. Monitoring during Construction. Both HUD and the HFA should require and perform regular inspections of the project during the construction period.

One looks to see if the projects will be occupied by families with children, by the elderly, or any other type of group. Projects which are occupied by the elderly may have lower maintenance costs, and the rent roll has more stability.

Once the type of unit is known, the analyst or investor should look at the geographic distribution of projects. Are all of the projects to be financed located in one city or area of the state, or are they spread around? It is not necessarily better if there is geographic diversity just for the sake of that diversity. The location of the project must be carefully thought out to ensure that the project fits in with the environment. To get the best handle on this type of information, the analyst cannot rely solely on the Official Statement that is issued when the housing agency is selling bonds. The analyst must keep current with the agency's annual reports, audits, and anything else that can bring to bear knowledge about the agency.

We have been emphasizing the need to evaluate the management of the state agency. One can start with reading the qualifications of the chief officers in the agency. There should be a balance of people with financial, planning, architectural, and management experience. The investor must feel confident that the management of the agency will be able to spot project problems before they become major, and that they will be able to evaluate new projects and select those that can best fit the needs of the people of the state.

ANALYSIS OF FORMAL SECURITY

The analyst begins the study of the formal security of a multifamily housing bond issue by looking at the types of reserve funds that exist for the benefit of the bondholders. Reserve funds are limited by the IRS to a reasonable amount of reserves, interpreted as 15 percent of the principal amount of the bond issue. The issue often contains a debt service reserve fund equal to maximum annual principal and interest on that series of bonds. If the series of bonds is issued under a closed indenture, then the debt service reserve can only be used for a default of those projects.

Under an open indenture, additional reserve requirements will be added for each series. The reserve fund may be filled from bond proceeds or other agency funds immediately at the time of closing, or the agency may choose to increase the level of the fund over a specified number of months in order to reach the required level.

The bond issue may also contain an additional reserve fund. This fund is usually of a smaller amount and contains highly liquid securities. It is intended to provide cash flow support from sources other than a major default.

After looking at the size and quality of these reserve funds, the analyst then looks at various features of the indenture. First, the flow of funds is analyzed. A multifamily housing bond, like many other types of revenue bonds, is payable from the net revenues of a project. There are some gross-revenue pledges, but they are not very meaningful. The feeling is that if the project is not being operated and maintained properly, then shortly it will become difficult to pay the debt service. The feature the analyst looks for is to see that monies are put aside for debt service after the payment of ordinary operation and maintenance expenses. Ideally, this money is put aside monthly; that is, each month one sixth of their next interest payment and one twelfth of the next annual principal payment will be deposited with the bond trustee. After this is ascertained, the analyst looks to see what other types of funds exist for the benefit of the bondholder or the project. Many times there are contingency funds or other special funds that receive money after payment of debt service.

Another consideration in the flow of funds is disposition of net revenues after meeting the requirements of various accounts. The analyst looks to see whether monies must stay within the indenture or if they can go to the general fund of the agencies.

Here the distinction must be drawn between an open and closed indenture. An open indenture allows additional projects to be added to the portfolio in the future, and to be secured on a parity with the outstanding bonds. A closed indenture will not permit this.

The debt service reserve fund, the mortgage reserve fund, and the indenture features are the main elements in the security of a housing bond. However, the analyst must also look toward external credit supports in order to come up with a complete picture of a state housing agency. First, one ascertains if a particular issue is a limited obligation of the agency or if it is a general obligation of the agency, payable from all of its resources. A limited obligation of a state agency is not as strong legally as a general obligation, as it is secured only from revenues under that indenture. However, this is a grey area of analysis. It is possible that a state agency will not allow a limited obligation to go into default and affect the agency's overall credit.

Another determination is whether the state housing agency is supported by a moral obligation of the state. What this means is the analyst must look to see what procedures are available, if any, for the agency to have its debt service reserve fund filled back up to the required level. A moral obligation is expressed through language stating that the directors of the agency must provide proof that the reserve fund is deficient, and certify this to the governor of the state. The governor must then go to the state legislature and request an appropriation. The legislature does not have to appropriate the money, but is viewed as having a moral obligation to do so. For additional information, see Chapter 30.

FINANCIAL ANALYSIS

Having addressed the fundamental analysis of assets to be financed (corresponding to the concept of project risk), this section deals with the financial analysis that can help assess mortgage portfolio risks. Unfortunately, most of the ideas presented here will be of use only in the case of major-state HFA or big-city issuers with large, ongoing financing programs. This is true for at least three reasons.

First, these issuers are the only entities who can really affect bond security once the bonds are issued. In a small, closed-end 11(b) financing, for example, there is typically neither a substantial staff nor a great deal of discretionary cash to be managed. In a loans-to-lenders program, security is entirely a consequence of the lenders' solvency as well as legal availability, and liquidation value of collateral. If a program is properly structured, any interruption in paydown will be quickly met by the application of reserves and pursuit of foreclosure or assignment insurance, and therefore the analyst should focus intensely on these factors. In open-ended HFA programs, by contrast, new issuance will repeatedly change assets, reserve levels, fee realization, mortgage income, and the behavior of fund balances, to name just a few items. Further, the size of the cash flow here is large enough that it can be affected by professional management.

A second difficulty in the analysis of local programs is that, for the new issue purchaser, key financial information is generally unavailable at the time of the bond sale. During the bond sale it is not possible to provide information about the mortgage rate and spread against bond rates, reinvestment yields, or often even the size of the reserves because these are unknown until the issue is completely finalized. While this is also true for the state issuer, past performance of a prior series or other indentures may provide some comfort, as will excess funds or undesignated fund balances. The local program, having none of these sources, is dependent solely on internal cash flow adequacy.

Third, the availability of information to the holder or secondary market purchaser is very sporadic. Indeed, given the absence of a staff or ongoing organization, GAAP-based financial statements may not exist, and pursuit of project audits can be fruitless.

Each of these factors reinforces the tendency to rely heavily on indenture features and explains the prevalence of FHA insurance among local issuers. That said, the discussion which follows will apply to most issuers—state or local—if full audited statements are available. After a brief discussion of cash flow features, we will review individually income statement and balance sheet analysis.

Cash Flow Characteristics

Theoretically, at the time of bond closing, multifamily cash flows should be almost totally predictable. This is particularly true if proceeds are used solely for permanent financing and not for construction lending. In most issues the project to be financed is known or a pool of potential candidates is identified. Thus, with the bond rate and reinvestment yield in hand, the feasible mortgage and fee structure can be computed to produce the requisite cash flow and non-asset bond coverage. Since the marketing period of the bonds will indicate the feasibility of various mortgage rates, mortgage closing on a completed development can rapidly follow bond closing (or be delayed in order to maximize arbitrage within limits of regulation, reinvestment rate, and developer need). In turn, particularly for small issues with one mortgage, debt service can be scheduled to closely match the combination of reserve earnings and mortgage paydown, effectively eliminating the problem of prepayment estimation. Prepayments (voluntary, as opposed to foreclosure payments) do not offer the same risk as for single-family issues because, in the shortrun, the developer has no interest in doing so. For the limited-dividend developer, tax consequences, including mortgage payments and depreciation, are an important part of the syndication and will not lightly be forgone. While there may ultimately be a desire to convert the units to market-rate occupancy, the duration of contracts, discussed above, will combine with tax reasons and substantial prepayment penalties to delay this behavior beyond the point of non-asset bond concern.

In summary, in our theoretical ideal, all rates are locked-in and there is no risk of mortgage acquisition timing or management of float, delinquency, and prepayments. The remaining risk is one of project viability, meaning that there will be either adequate cash flow or very little at all, requiring foreclosure and/or assignment.

Obviously, if this ideal were met in every issue, analysis of financial statements would be an idle exercise. Factors which change this theoretical scheme include (1) variation in the spread relationships between earnings and costs of funds that will affect asset coverage, (2) the use of bond proceeds for construction financing, which increases timing uncertainties and dependence on nonmortgage investments, and (3) most important, the use of open-ended indentures. This is a two-edge sword, in that sale of successive bond series can have a positive or negative effect on the bond program. It will, however, have some effect (as noted above) on various indicators, thereby repaying the analyst's attention. Combining the use of open indentures with bond funded construction is common in state HFA's, reinforcing our conclusion that this is the most fertile area for financial analysis.

Before turning to the specifics of financial statements analysis, we should discuss one final cash flow note concerning deep original issue discounts. Known variously as zeros, deferred interest bonds, deferred coupon bonds, or capital appreciation bonds, these instruments pay little or no current income. Instead, the investor receives a return through the accretion of principal, or through the compounding to maturity of unpaid interest. The advantages or disadvantages of such a plan to the investor are not within the scope of this chapter, but we should note that there is no necessary credit risk associated with them. While it is sometimes assumed that these instruments represent "balloon" maturities requiring the issuer to provide large amounts of cash, in actuality they are usually accomodated within a level debt service structure. Instead of the typical level debt service solution which shows rising principal and declining interest, the absence of interest due on the zero allows a larger portion of cash flow in early years to be designated for serial principal. Thus, there actually will be level or declining principal due each year in the early years of the serial schedule. Conversely, the initial principal of the zero is small, so that the maturity value approximates that to be paid on a large dollar amount of current coupons. From the standpoint of the issuer's cash flow requirements, the net effect is the same. The issuer simply designates a larger portion of payments as principal in the early years and a larger portion as interest in the later years. While this may have interesting consequences to the issuer, it need have no credit consequences.

Income Statement

In our view, four areas of consideration are important in the analysis of multifamily-program income statements. These are sources of income, treatment of expenses, noncash items, and coverage.

Sources of Income. Cash income in a multifamily program can only derive from one of two sources: mortgage income or the investment of cash balances. Nominal mortgage income in the multifamily case will be typically much closer to the cost of carry than for single-family programs because of heavier discounting, i.e., the use of mortgagor points or fees, and because of narrower spreads used to insure the feasibility of the building. Fees, in turn, may be actually paid or computed in the nominal mortgage amount. In fact, in the early years of the program, interest coverage solely from mortgage returns may be negative. Thus, returns on invested balances and from undrawn proceeds, fees retained, and reserves are a very important component of income. Analyzing sources of revenue is a two-step process: determining the relative importance of nonmortgage resources, and determining their predictability. Dependence on nonmortgage sources is measured most simply by the ratio of nonmortgage revenue to total cash revenue (i.e., excluding noncash items such as the recognition of fees). This information, however, is only useful when it is matched to the sustainability of nonmortgage income. This can be inferred from the amount of cash balances relative to mortgage receivables and their prospect for drawdown. Either in footnote disclosure or on the balance sheet, many issuers will indicate how much of cash and investments carried are required reserves. Netting this amount plus payables and upcoming principal due (again from footnotes) will yield idle cash, which represents either fund balance or monies awaiting mortgage purchase. With knowledge of prevailing interest-rate trends, bond interest coverage, and the arbitrage relationship between mortgage rates and other investments, the analyst can draw conclusions as to the likely direction of revenues and net income. If, for an extreme example, mortgage income covered interest expense together with only slight assistance from nonmortgage investments, and if investments will not shortly flow out to bonds payable, the incremental nonmortgage revenue is clearly positive. If, by contrast, coverage is low with substantial mortgages remaining to be committed at a low rate, the direction is quite different, as this revenue will rapidly be consumed.

Treatment of Expenses. Analysis of expenses on a multifamily-issuer income statement will consider the trend of noninterest expenses, their relation to the status of the issuer's building program, and their sources of payment. The focus here is on noninterest expenses because interest costs are fixed, and their impact will be captured in coverage computation.

The components of noninterest expense include mortgage underwriting and processing, administration of federal program requirements, project budget review, subsidy-adjustment, bond-payment functions, and cash management. Mortgage servicing is not a major item, as it would be for single-family issues, because of the small number of mortgagors. Given the variation in levels of involvement in these functions among issuers, there is no rule of thumb concerning an appropriate level of expenses. More important is the trend of expense to gross revenue or mortgage revenue—a rapid increase in expenses must be reviewed for its potential drain on fund-balance accumulation. Increases in expenses may be related to changes in fixed-cost items such as office space and information systems, or change in personnel expense. In either case, increases in costs should be clearly related to agency operations. For example, increases in expenses will normally occur in growing agencies with ongoing bonding programs and substantial construction in progress. In a mature agency, with most of its portfolio in seasoned mortgages, a sudden change in expenses would be a greater source of concern.

A final note about expenses concerns their treatment in the accounting-funds structure and their source of payment. The two types of treatment are either to include administrative expenses in the statements of the bond funds for which they were incurred or, alternatively, all agency expenses may be accounted for in an agency general fund, with only debt service showing in the bond funds. In the latter case, each bond fund will typically show a transfer to the general fund in the amount of its expenses. Items to keep in mind here include the fact that this format does not usually correspond to the indenture flow of funds. Even if expenses are shown outside bond funds, they may still have claim to bond funds under the indenture prior to debt service. Thus, for analysis of net income and ratios, such a transfer should be considered an expense. Alternatively, if transferred amounts vary greatly from year to year, this may indicate subsidy of one bond program by another—a definite warning sign. Further, the general fund from which expenses are paid may or may not have assets of its own that create earnings to support expenses. Subject to the kind of revenue analysis discussed above, this is a positive feature.

Noncash Items. Three noncash items are often found on the multifamily-issue income statement: deferred-fee income, amortization of bond-issuance expense, and provision for loan losses. Fee recognition varies with agency policy, and income statement treatment is not necessarily related to the timing of payment. If fee income is identified as deferred income, it should definitely be excluded from financial-ratio computation. If it is, in fact, a cash item, the earlier comment about its likely recurrence applies.

Bond-issuance expense may be treated in one of two ways, each of which affect both income statement and balance sheet. One treatment is to carry two liability items on the balance sheet: bonds payable and unamortized bond discount, which are then netted to produce the carrying value of the bonds payable. Both items are reduced proportionally as bonds are retired. Alternatively, the bond carrying value may be before discount, with a deferred asset set up in the amount of unamortized bond discount. In this treatment, the asset is reduced by annually expensing a portion through the income statement, reducing the asset gradually as bonds are paid. The third common noncash item is the provision for loan losses. This item is generally determined solely by the judgment of the agency and/or its auditors, and reflects their expectations concerning ultimate foreclosure losses on loans currently experiencing payment problems or for which problems are anticipated. The accounting treatment is a current-period expense with a corresponding reduction in the value of assets (i.e., mortgages). Problem loans which become current may result in a reversing entry, creating a gain on the income statement.

As with any financial statement analysis, these items must be added back or reduced, as appropriate, in the computation of financial ratios. Substantial fee income, for example, which has already been collected and is held on the balance sheet, will overstate current-period earnings. Asset ratios, as discussed below, should reflect the true dollar value of liabilities and these should be offset solely against earning assets. The treatment of noncash items varies significantly among issuers, and standardization requires careful restatement by the analyst.

Coverage.   Historically, debt service coverage has not been considered a useful analytical construct in reviewing housing bonds. The reason lies in our description of the theoretically ideal cash flow, presented earlier. Since principal is paid from the liquidation of mortgages, and since there is assumed to be a positive effective carry on interest, there is presumably no requirement for additional earnings to cover debt service beyond that associated with non-asset bonds. As long as asset protection is assured and cash flow is timely, $1.0 \times$ coverage is assumed to be adequate.

However, a quick computation of coverage will offer a number of advantages. Coverage will indicate the rapidity of non-asset bond coverage, protection against illiquidity of bond-financed assets, and the spread between earning assets and cost of funds. Two coverage ratios may be computed: interest coverage and principal coverage. Combined coverage is not necessarily useful because the flow of funds may differ, with revenue going first to interest. Interest coverage is defined as:

$$(\text{Interest} + \text{Net income} + \text{Noncash items})/\text{Interest}$$

Principal coverage is defined as:

$$(\text{Mortgage principal paid} + \text{Net income} + \text{Noncash items}) / \text{Principal paid}$$

Net income appears in both because it indicates the margin of interest coverage and because it is available for principal and, indeed, required given the presence of non-asset bonds or variations in principal matching in the earlier years of the loan.

Balance Sheet Analysis

As with any financial entity, the multifamily income statement reflects performance of operations during the year but the balance sheet reflects the degree of protection against adverse circumstances. Areas to be examined include asset protection, liquidity, fund balances, and transfers. Together, these items can provide an indication of the issuers' continued viability (i.e., ability to meet principal and interest) if cash flow is temporarily impaired. Generally, we discount the other use of balance sheet strength, determining liquidation value and non-asset risk in a crash-call scenario, because of the reduced non-origination risk in multifamily programs.

Asset Strength. The broadest measure of balance sheet strength is the asset ratio (assets/liabilities). In the case of a new program this ratio may be below 1.0, reflecting the non-asset bond concept, i.e., the dollar difference between bonds sold and assets acquired. Even most new issuers, however, will not show negative net worth, due to mortgage points and the asset-side treatment of deferred issuance costs, for example. Aside from the non-asset bond case, the asset ratio is an indication of margin of protection against nonperforming assets, such as mortgage delinquencies or investments which, for market reasons, cannot be liquidated at their carrying value. All things being equal, the program with assets of 106 percent of liabilities has more flexibility in raising cash than one with a ratio of just 100 percent. Just as with noncash income items in the coverage computation, asset-ratio calculations can be improved by removing from the balance sheet items which would not be available for bond liabilities. These would include, in addition to deferred issuance cost, such things as cash and investments representing developer escrows and cash amounts equivalent to net payables, if any existed. On the liability side, bonds payable should reflect the full amount outstanding. Thus, the more restrictive asset ratio calculation will generally consider only the following:

(Cash + Investments + Mortgages)/Bonds payable

The cash and investments are adjusted for net payables and other dedicated purposes.

Liquidity. Since we have defined the purpose of balance sheet analysis as measuring availability of resources in the event of reduced cash flow, the ability to turn assets into cash is an important complement to the overall asset ratio. Since it is unlikely that individual mortgages could or would be sold at their carrying value (aside from insurance assignment), the level of cash and investments will distinguish the protection level offered by various programs. This will be affected most by the initial level of reserves, but will also reflect mortgage spread, reinvestment strategy, indenture requirements and agency policy on transfers versus retention of assets. Generally, adjusting once again for net payables and escrows, the ratio of cash and investments to total assets, and its trend over time, will be indicative of relative liquidity. We have, here and above, emphasized the importance of netting payables in evaluating assets. The reason for this is that mortgage receivables, on a monthly cycle, will almost always be less than semiannual interest payables. This is particularly true in the common combination of a June 30 fiscal year and a July 1 bond payment date. Thus, this amount of cash will soon disappear from the balance sheet.

Finally, with respect to liquidity, valuation of reserves is another indication of asset quality. Reserve proceeds in any financing are typically invested in relatively long securities—often as long as the final bond maturities—in order to maximize arbitrage earnings. Since prices for fixed-income securities become more volatile with longer maturities, they are particularly vulnerable to bear markets. In a period of spectacular rises in interest rates, such as most of the 1970s, carrying values of reserve funds (usually valued at the lower of cost or par, and not marked to market) may be substantially above their liquidation value, if needed. Market value of securities is often disclosed in footnotes to the financial statements. This valuation problem is true for all types of revenue bonds, of course, but given the cash flow nature of multifamily financings and the inability to adjust rental revenues, it is especially important for these issues.

Fund Balance. Fund balances are often taken as the quickest and simplest measure of a program's financial health. Often expressed as a percentage of assets or bonds payable, fund balances are important. We discuss them last, however, because they will be influenced by factors already discussed. For example, consider two identical programs, one of which writes down the mortgage portfolio for nonperforming loans. Since fund balance is the asset-liability residual, this write-down will also reduce fund balance, though the two programs are identical in asset strength. Alternatively, the loan-loss reserve may be a separate asset item, in which case fund balance is unchanged. Similarly, consider an agency which has not written down nonperforming mortgages and has had to draw down cash for debt service. Because assets still exceed liabilities, the fund balance is unchanged, but the quality and liquidity of this fund balance is reduced, and it certainly does not represent immediately available resources. Another example is the fact that some programs aggressively transfer fund balance to general reserves where they are still available, though not pledged for the bonds, and others transfer them to other bond programs where they are no longer available to the original bond program. Reserve policies, of course, will also affect the realizable dollar value of fund balances. The point, therefore, is that the fund balance itself can be exceedingly misleading as a measure of balance sheet strength. Its usefulness in expressing accumulated earnings must be carefully hedged by evaluation of other factors.

Overall, particularly for an ongoing open-indenture state program, analysis of the income statement and balance sheet can provide a great deal of information about the condition of the program. This should not overshadow the importance of legal features or external security. Rather, positive financial performance provides an additional cushion against the day when these features will be required, by which time the market may demand an additional risk premium.

CONCLUSION

Multifamily housing bonds have, over the years, provided substantial housing production for the needy and have provided a relatively secure and attractive tax-exempt investment. Because these risk characteristics can be specified fairly thoroughly, issuers and underwriters have been able to devise a variety of ways to address them. We began this chapter by emphasizing the changing nature of federal policy which has provided the underpinnings of these issues. Regardless of future directions in federal subsidy and insurance, the risk elements will remain the same. The purchaser will still require assurance that construction can be completed, that rent roll and investments will be sufficient for expenses and debt service, that cash flow will be timely, and that protection is afforded against major mortgage defaults. We hope that by including the areas of analysis we have discussed, the investor and analyst may better assess relative credit worthiness among the numerous multifamily housing revenue bond issues.

Toll Road and Gas Tax Revenue Bonds

CHAPTER 20

Charles T. Noona

Senior Vice President
L. F. Rothschild, Unterberg, Towbin

Dell H. Stevens

Consultant
L. F. Rothschild, Unterberg, Towbin

Highway revenue bonds can be divided into two security types: toll road revenue bonds and gas tax revenue bonds. The proceeds of the toll road bonds are used to build specific revenue-producing facilities such as turnpikes, bridges, and tunnels. For these bonds, the security is mainly derived from the tolls collected. The second type of highway bond, the gas tax bond, is secured by highway fund revenues, primarily gasoline and other motor fuel taxes, but may also include driver's license fees, vehicle registration charges, and other related revenues.

TOLL ROAD, BRIDGE, AND TUNNEL REVENUE BONDS

Most toll road, bridge, and tunnel revenue bonds are in very excellent, strong financial condition. In many cases, bonds are being retired prior to their original maturity schedule. The reason for the good record is the fact that many of the facilities were financed and constructed in the 1950s and 60s when interest rates and construction costs were much lower than they are now. Also, tolls have generally

306

been raised to offset rising operating and maintenance expenses. In recent years there were only three major toll facilities with interest payments in arrears. (See Cases 8, 9, and 13.) Each one got into difficulty right from the beginning because either competing highways had more of an impact than expected or because construction costs far exceeded the original estimates.

The vast network of the interstate highway system is approximately 95 percent completed, so there is little need for new competing roads to be built. Some toll road authorities plan to sell $100–200 million of bonds over the next few years for various improvements such as new toll barriers, ramps, and widening sections of the roadway.[1] Although some authorities will be refunding their debt, most have no plans to issue additional bonds in the future. With two or three exceptions, the toll road authorities have done a very good job of maintaining their facilities.

It is worth noting that the same cannot be said about the streets, highways, and bridges of the nation in general. Some press reports have indicated that there is a need for $500 billion of construction for highways during the 1980s. Bridge replacement or rehabilitation will require over $40 billion during the period. Despite these indicated needs, highway and bridge construction has been on the decline with $13.3 billion spent in 1980, $11.9 billion in 1981, and $10.95 billion estimated in 1982. The trend should be reversed in 1982–83 with $11.9 billion expected to be spent mainly for repair and maintenance. This increase, however, is hardly keeping up with inflation. Part of the problem has been a reduction in federal spending. By 1984–85, the condition of the nation's toll-free roads and bridges may be such that large sums of money will be urgently needed for maintenance and various other improvements. If these expenditure reductions are not modified, the need to raise this capital may fall upon the state and local governments or upon their toll-charging authorities.

Of the approximately 60 toll road bonds rated by Moody's or Standard & Poor's, only two major bonds are now in arrears on interest payments. Of the balance, many authorities are in very good financial condition with interest coverage of at least three times. In many cases, coverage is even higher, and bonds are being retired prior to their scheduled maturity date, a great improvement from 30 years ago when many toll road bonds were not current on interest payments. There are several reasons for this improved performance.

---

[1]For additional information concerning the 25 major toll road authorities, see Municipal Bond Research Department, *Toll Road Bonds: Is Continued Improvement Likely?* (New York: L. F. Rothschild, Unterberg, Towbin, November 16, 1981).

Favorable Factors

1. With most toll road facilities constructed 20 to 30 years ago, bond financing programs benefited from the low interest rates of those periods. For example, some coupons are as low as 2.50 percent, and many are below 5 percent. Consequently, many of these issues now sell at large discounts, some as low as during the mid -1950s. Therefore, the issuer can obtain huge savings by purchasing the bonds in the market at such big discounts. Many authorities are doing just that.

2. When most toll road projects were being built, the costs for materials and labor were much cheaper also. Therefore, few bonds had to be sold to complete the roadway. As inflation caused the normal costs for operations and maintenance to increase generally, tolls were raised. This resulted in the debt service requirement decreasing as a percentage of total annual revenues. Normal operating expenses are usually not large in relation to total revenues.

3. Despite periodic gasoline shortages and higher prices of fuel, the number of vehicles using toll facilities has increased over the past 10 years. Barring an almost complete shutoff of oil imports, most toll roads should be able to function adequately through another oil crisis.

4. An ongoing maintenance program is of prime importance. Most toll road authorities are continuously maintaining their roads and constantly resurfacing sections of the road. Normally, roads must be resurfaced every 10 to 12 years. If sections are not regularly resurfaced, an extraordinary maintenance reserve should be built up and utilized so that large sums of borrowed money are not needed all at once to resurface the entire turnpike. In some cases, the state maintains the roadway through its highway department. This is the case with the California Toll Bridge Authority which reports especially low operating ratios because it must support only operating expenses and debt service requirements.

Unfavorable Factors

1. Over the years, several toll road facilities have been adversely affected by inability or reluctance to raise tolls adequately. In 1974, the New Jersey Turnpike Authority requested a 37 percent toll increase to help cover an increase in its maintenance reserve requirement of $10 million. Only 15 percent was granted in 1975. This resulted in minimum debt service coverage and required an additional toll increase of 20 percent in 1980. The West Virginia Turnpike Authority did not raise tolls sufficiently when additional bonds were sold to finance the construction of additional lanes not included in the

original plans. This was in agreement with recommendations by the consulting engineers. The bond trustee had a toll study prepared by a new consulting engineer and eventually succeeded in having the tolls raised.

2. Competition from other roads should be closely monitored. The Chicago Calumet Skyway and the Indiana Toll Road were both adversely impacted by completion of Interstate 94 from Michigan, which diverted traffic to a toll-free entrance into Chicago, the Dan Ryan Expressway. Also, the Chesapeake Bay Bridge and Tunnel lost traffic because it was not able to attract traffic from the Maryland Northeast Expressway. (See Cases 9 and 13.)

3. Sometimes the provision for extraordinary maintenance has a prior claim on revenues to bond debt service. This should not be the case because it tends to encourage deferring toll increases. Where defaults have occurred, the practice has been to provide some major maintenance.

4. An open-ended provision is not recommended for additional bonds; instead, junior lien bonds should be issued for expansion and additions. If no additional protection is provided, as in the case of the Chesapeake Bay Bridge and Tunnel Series C bonds, this keeps the overall coverage low. If a project is questionable, junior bonds may make it feasible if they are state guaranteed as in the case of the New York Thruway and the Rhode Island Turnpike and Bridge Authority.

5. The level of truck traffic may be essential to the toll road. There are two points to consider. First, trucks give the road surface a pounding and precipitate more road maintenance than other vehicles. Second, trucks are business vehicles and are more closely tied to the economy than other vehicles. Therefore, in a severe recession, truck traffic is likely to decline more than other vehicles. As a partial offset to these factors, trucks should be charged higher tolls than other vehicles.

New or Unusual Features

In 1981, Delaware began depositing its surplus motor vehicle fuel tax receipts into the operating fund of the turnpike. This is designed mainly to afford additional coverage for its turnpike bonds, with most of the surplus revenues from the fuel tax expected to flow through to the state's general fund. The turnpike bond ordinance has a toll covenant requiring tolls to be set at a level sufficient to produce net revenues equal to 1.25 times debt service.

In the case of the Kentucky Turnpike, annual lease rental payments are made by the Department of Highways to meet debt service requirements. The lease rental is paid out of the transportation fund, which receives the proceeds of motor fuel and usage taxes, license and privilege taxes, toll road revenues, and coal severance taxes. Road maintenance is also paid from this fund. The toll revenues alone are not sufficient to pay for debt service on the bonds. If the lease is cancelled, the bonds would be payable, to the extent available, from taxes collected on motor fuels consumed on the system and from tolls. The idea of a cancelable lease still somewhat limits the saleability of the authority's bonds, but it should be noted that the state supreme court has indicated that the state does not permit its political subdivisions to issue general obligation bonds. The lease rental mechanism is as close to a general obligation as the law allows. No cancelable lease of one or two years' duration has ever been canceled.

In a few rare cases, the federal government has funded 90 percent of the construction costs for some projects. The New York State Bridge Authority only had to pay 10 percent of the estimated $45 million for the new Newburgh-Beacon Bridge which is expected to open in December 1983. The project was financed under the 1929 Old-field Act. Small portions of the New York Thruway were also financed under this act.

Oil Crisis Impact

Prior to 1974 the nation had enjoyed a steady increase in annual vehicle miles driven. The oil crisis of 1974 marked the first decline ever for vehicle miles driven. The bond analyst can no longer assume that each year will result in uninterrupted growth in traffic. Of the 25 major toll authorities in the country, most had well over 20 percent growth in traffic between 1970 and 1980. Some exceeded a 50 percent increase. Only one bridge authority and one toll road department had a traffic decline or growth of less than 1 percent for the period. From 1975 to 1980, the pattern is the same except that the growth rates are lower because they cover fewer years. A point to consider is that during the 1970s many facilities were being completed. Therefore the increase in traffic for many authorities is partially attributable to new roads or bridges being opened.

The traffic results for 1979–80 are different. Three bridge commissions reported slight declines for the period. Furthermore, over half of the major turnpikes showed declines. These declines in traffic were caused by a combination of a soft economy in the area, toll increases, and to a lesser extent higher fuel prices. With an improvement in the economy, traffic should improve. Even if further moderate traffic loss occurs, the interest coverage levels for the large majority of these authorities is such that, with a few exceptions, there should be no problem in meeting principal and interest requirements.

GAS TAX REVENUE BONDS[2]

The gasoline shortages of the 1970s and possible continued short fuel supplies could reduce the amount of highway fund revenues available to many states. This does not necessarily mean that all motor vehicle fuel tax bonds will be significantly weakened in quality. On the contrary, a number of bonds secured by highway funds or gasoline taxes provide a high degree of bondholder protection for the following reasons:

1. Most highway fund issues are secured by a constitutional or statutory pledge of highway funds, gasoline taxes, or a portion of a specific fuel tax. The constitutional pledge offers stronger security in that it requires a vote of the people to change any of the provisions that are capable of being altered. For example, a constitutional first-lien pledge of gasoline taxes would be stronger than a statutory first-lien pledge.

2. The first-lien pledge is especially noteworthy in this case because highway funds are usually dedicated to the state's highway program; therefore, surplus revenues are used for operation and maintenance. The bondholder benefits from leverage with a first-lien pledge. Double-digit inflation has caused operating and maintenance costs to rise rapidly. To offset this, states must either cut back on such expenses and let roadways deteriorate, or increase revenues. If revenues increase, debt service coverage will rise as a benefit of inflation. The leverage factor becomes more important where debt service is less than 50 percent of the highway fund budget which is often the case. Ohio has two issues that are secured by highway revenues. Both are self-supporting with one having a prior lien on such revenues. The junior-lien bond is a general obligation of the state, whereas the senior-lien bonds are not. The state intends to pay both issues from highway revenues, so the first-lien bonds would have more than adequate highway revenues available to pay debt service.

3. Increasing taxes has never been a popular method of raising funds. Gasoline prices were stable until 1973 when the Arab-Israeli war occurred. Wholesale prices rose from 20.9 cents per gallon in November 1973 to 31.45 cents in December 1974. Then they moved with inflation until 1979 when wholesale gasoline prices jumped from 47.16 cents in January to 84.78 cents in January 1980. Prices continued to climb and peaked at $1.23 in March 1981. Since then they have steadily drifted down to $1.15 in January 1982. Raising the state-imposed gasoline taxes by a few cents has less of an impact at

---

[2]For additional information on gasoline tax revenue bonds, see Municipal Bond Research Department, *Underrated Gasoline Tax Issues* (New York: L. F. Rothschild, Unterberg, Towbin, August 6, 1979); and *Gasoline Tax Issues* (New York: L. F. Rothschild, Unterberg, Towbin, January 5, 1981).

current prices then it did when the wholesale price of gasoline was under 20 cents. Over the past few years, a number of states have raised their gasoline taxes. Pennsylvania raised its state tax on gasoline from 9 cents a gallon to 11 cents effective July 1979. Arkansas, Iowa, Montana, Nebraska, and Washington also raised their respective gasoline tax rates from 1 to 1.5 cents in 1979.[3]

4.   The use of blended fuels such as gasohol may become common. This type of fuel is distributed from a pump just like gasoline and can be taxed the same way if necessary. Motor fuel taxes are an important source of state revenues—one the states will not want to lose.

5.   Most states tax gasoline on a per-gallon basis. A number of states tax gas as a percentage of price, which produces higher revenues in periods of rising prices. This method is not as vulnerable to declining volume.

6.   Debt service coverage is high for gas tax bonds. If conservation or high prices act as a deterrent to consumption and volume sales decline even 15 to 20 percent, coverage may also decline but will still be at levels able to support a high-quality rating. For example, in 1981 Ohio's two classes of highway bonds had coverage of 60.9 times and 9.9 times, respectively. Louisiana has two gas tax bonds that had coverage of 4.5 times and 22.5 times. Both Louisiana issues are also general obligations of the state. Washington has some issues that have over 24 times coverage. With such wide protection these issues would be immune from revenue declines caused by any conceivable decline in gasoline consumption.

7.   A highway fund generally derives most of its revenues from gasoline and motor fuel taxes. Additional funds may also be provided by license and registration fees, fines, and penalties, or even a portion of sales tax revenues. The less reliance on gasoline and motor vehicle fuel taxes, the less impact a decline in fuel sales would have on pledged revenues.

Gas tax bonds that are particularly well secured are the Louisiana

---

[3]The following states passed legislation in 1981 to raise their gasoline tax. The rate for states using a percent of the wholesale or retail price method has been converted to a per-gallon equivalent:

Arizona, to 8¢ from 7¢	Ohio, to 10.3¢ from 7¢
California, to 9¢ from 7¢ (effective 1983)	Oregon, to 8¢ from 7¢ (effective 1/1/82)
Colorado, to 9¢ from 7¢	Rhode Island, to 12¢ from 10¢
Delaware, to 11¢ from 9¢	South Carolina, to 13¢ from 11¢
Idaho, to 11.5¢ from 9.5¢	South Dakota, to 13¢ from 12¢
Indiana, to 10.5¢ from 8.5¢	Tennessee, to 9¢ from 7¢
Iowa, to 13¢ from 10¢	Utah, to 11¢ from 9¢
Minnesota, to 13¢ from 11¢	Vermont, to 11¢ from 9¢
Nevada, to 10.5¢ from 6¢	Washington, to 13.5¢ from 12¢;
New Hampshire, to 14¢ from 11¢	back to 12.0¢ from January 1 to
New Mexico, to 9¢ from 8 ¢	June 30, 1982)
North Carolina, to 12.5¢ from 9.5¢	Wisconsin, to 13¢ from 9¢

Long Range Highway Bonds secured by the proceeds of a 4-cent gasoline tax. Coverage in 1980–81 was 22.5 times, and the bonds are also general obligations of the state. The Ohio Highway Improvement Bonds also are examples of strong bonds. They are payable from a constitutional first lien on highway user receipts which include motor fuel taxes, licenses, and registration fees. This is a closed-lien issue with coverage of 60.9 times. The Pennsylvania General Obligation Highway Bonds and Highway and Bridge Authority (not general obligations) also are well protected. They are secured by a constitutional first-lien pledge of the motor license fund which receives the proceeds of registration and license fees, grants, gasoline taxes, and other taxes. Coverage in 1980–81 was 5.0 times; the state increased the gasoline tax 2 cents per gallon in 1979.

Table 1 lists these and other gas tax issues. Double-barreled general obligation highway bonds of prime states such as Texas, North Carolina, and New Jersey are not listed because they are afforded the highest credit worthiness based on the state's own general obligation quality.

Table 1
Selected Gas Tax–Secured Bonds

Issue	*Constitutional Pledge*	*Statutory Pledge*	*General Obligation of State*	*Debt* Service Coverage*
Alabama Highway Authority				
Series O–X	Yes	Yes (1st lien)	No	3.5x
Kansas Highway Authority	No	Yes (1st lien)	Yes	2.3x
Louisiana				
(Act 284 of 1952 Bonds)	No	Yes (1st lien)	Yes	4.5x
(Act 141 of 1955–Long Range Highway Bonds)	No	Yes (1st lien)	Yes	22.5x
(Act 101 of 1961–Long Range Highway Bonds)	No	Yes (1st lien)	Yes	22.5x
Michigan Highway Revenue Bonds (Trunk Line and Grand Rapids Expressway)	Yes	Yes (1st lien)	No	10.6x
Ohio Highway Improvement Bonds				
(closed issue)	Yes (1st lien)	No	No	60.9x
Highway Obligations	Yes (2d lien)	No	Yes	9.9x
Pennsylvania				
G.O. Highway	Yes (1st lien)	No	Yes	5.0x
Highway and Bridge	Yes (1st lien)	No	No	5.0x
Washington Motor Vehicle Fuel Tax Bonds				
Chapters 56, 121, 167, 7	No	Yes (1st and 2d lien)	No	24.3x
Chapters 83, 360, 5	No	Yes (various liens)	Yes (if issued on or after 6/1/73)	5.0x overall

*As of 1981.

Credit Analysis of Hybrid and Special Bond Securities

Section FOUR

Option Tender or Put Bonds

CHAPTER 21

Sylvan G. Feldstein, Ph.D.
Senior Municipal Specialist
Merrill Lynch, Pierce, Fenner & Smith, Inc.

Frank J. Fabozzi, Ph.D., C.F.A.
Professor of Economics
Fordham University

INTRODUCTION

An option tender bond—or put bond, as it is known in the municipal bond industry—is one in which the bondholder has the right to return the bond to the bond trustee prior to its stated long-term maturity. In some instances the bondholder has the right to "put" the bond as early as the first anniversary date of the original issuance. In other instances, the bondholder has to wait up to 10 years before returning the bond. In any event, and unlike other municipal bonds that may be tendered in which the issuer or bond trustee decides whether or not and how much to pay the bondholder, the put bond requires the bond trustee to purchase it from the bondholder at a price of par; that is, the full payment of principal must be made regardless of existing market conditions. Of course, if the bondholder decides not to exercise this put, he can continue to hold the bond to its long-term maturity. However, the issuer still reserves the right to call the bond. For some put bonds, the issuer can call them all on their first puttable dates; for others, mandatory sinking funds begin on the first puttable dates;

317

and for still other put bonds, the first call dates are five years or later after the first puttable dates.

WHY PUT BONDS ARE ISSUED

Since the end of 1979 there have been fewer buyers of long-term municipal bonds than previously. Traditionally, the long municipal bond market has been strongly supported by two types of buyers. High-income, private investors bought municipal bonds because they were reliable sources of tax-free fixed income. Also, institutions with profits to shelter, such as fire and casualty insurance companies, bought them for the same reason. Many private investors as well as insurance companies have at times shifted their buying to shorter maturities in response to their concern over inflation and a desire to remain more liquid. Additionally some companies, faced with reduced profit margins caused by inflation and stronger competition, sometimes stop buying municipal bonds altogether.

As a response to the weak market for long-term municipal bonds, investment bankers have used a number of unique financing mechanisms to allow issuers to raise capital through long-term bonds. The put bonds are one example: The purchaser buys a bond usually with an approximate 30-year stated maturity. While the bondholder can hold the bond to maturity or to the first call date, he also has the right to return the bond to the issuer. In some issues he can return the bond as early as one year after the date of issuance. When he does so, the bondholder receives his full principal back. In return for the right to redeem his bond prior to the stated 30-year maturity, the investor accepts a yield somewhat less than he would receive on a regular long-term bond, but still more than the yield on a serial bond that would mature on the first puttable date. The yields initially have ranged from 75 to 175 basis points less than long-term issues but 25 to 100 basis points more than serial bonds.[1]

The benefit to the issuer is that it has raised money for capital projects at interest rates 75 to 150 basis points below the market rates for long-term bonds. While the bondholder has the right to redeem his bond prior to maturity through the put mechanism, if interest rates decline the put may never be exercised by the bondholder. Instead, he may continue to hold the bond to maturity provided it is not called by the issuer.

The benefit to the bondholder is that, while he has a long-term bond, he also has the right to get his principal back early. If he does so, he will have earned interest (during the time he held the bond) at

---

[1]The economic analysis of the value of a put option is discussed in Chapter 29 of *The Municipal Bond Handbook: Volume I* (Homewood, Ill.: Dow Jones-Irwin, 1983).

a higher rate than if he had held a straight serial bond. For this right of early redemption, he accepts a lower rate of interest than on a straight long-term bond.

TWO TYPES OF PUT BOND SECURITIES

The focus of this chapter is not on the ability of the respective issuers to pay interest to the bondholder after the bond is sold and before it is put; instead it is on the ability of the issuer to pay the principal when the bond is put to the bond trustee by the bondholder. So far, only two types of bonds have been issued: (1) those backed by commercial bank letters of credit in addition to the issuer's cash flow revenues, and (2) those secured entirely by the cash flow revenues of the issuers.

Put Bonds Backed by Commercial Bank Letters of Credit

Between December 1980 and mid-1981, 14 single-family mortgage revenue bonds have come to market with the put options. While the bonds have stated maturities of either 32 or 33 years, the bondholders have the option in either 5 or 6 years (and any year thereafter), upon 60 days' prior written notice, to put the bonds to the respective bond trustees. The bond trustees, in these instances acting as tender agents, are required to purchase the bonds at par and to draw upon— if necessary after exhausting any available funds from mortgage payments and prepayments—letter-of-credit commitments made by commercial banks. All of the single-family mortgage revenue put bonds issued through mid-1981 and backed under this structure have been supported by letters of credit from only one commercial bank, Citibank, N.A. of New York.

Table 1 contains information about the 14 single-family mortgage revenue put bonds outstanding as of mid-1981. Also indicated for each bond is the total amount of the issue, the date of the issue, the coupon of the put bonds, the term maturity of the put bonds, the first date when the put bonds can be given to the bond trustee at par, and the amount of the issue that is puttable at that time. It should also be noted that under normal circumstances, while the put bonds are not callable as a whole, they all have mandatory sinking fund redemption requirements. For all 14 put bonds, the mandatory sinking funds begin on the first puttable dates and continue annually thereafter. The amount of bonds subject to the first mandatory sinking fund requirements is less than 1 percent for each of the 14 put bonds.

In addition to the 14 single-family mortgage revenue put bonds backed by letters of credit from Citibank, N.A. of New York, by mid-1981 one hospital put bond backed by a letter of credit has also been issued.[2] (In this instance the letter-of-credit agreement is with the First National Bank of Saint Paul, St. Paul, Minnesota.) These hospital put bonds are callable by the issuer beginning on June 1, 1988, at a price of 102. Additionally, the put bonds are subject to a mandatory sinking fund beginning on June 1, 2005.

Put Bonds Secured Solely by the Cash Flow Revenues of the Issuers

In this security structure, the put bonds are redeemed at par from monies generated by the respective issuer's normal cash flow revenue security provisions. Through 1981, hospital revenue put bonds, industrial revenue put bonds, and public power revenue put bonds have been issued, the latter by the Washington Public Power Supply System (WPPSS) under two separate security structures. One also has been issued by the South Carolina Public Service Authority.

Table 2 shows the nine hospital put bonds issued between 1976 and 1980 and backed by cash flow. All of them are noncallable. Some of these early put bonds were not issued so much because of investor aversion to long-term bonds as they were to lower the net interest costs and to capture federal reimbursement for debt service on the hospital bonds, at that time allowed for puttable bonds but not for the straight debt. Table 3 includes the names and descriptions of some of the put bonds issued after 1979 backed by cash flow.

OVERALL CREDIT STRENGTHS AND WEAKNESSES

In assessing the investment quality of a put bond, the analyst or investor should answer certain questions concerning the financial and legal structure of the overall put bond security. The focus should be on those factors which may either strengthen the put bond security or, conversely, prevent a bond issuer from being able to redeem the bond at par if it is tendered on the first puttable date. The credit quality ranges all the way from put bonds redeemable with absolute certainty, as in the case of put bonds issued in 1982 by the Massachusetts Health and Education Facilities Authority on behalf of Harvard

---

[2]The issue referred to is the New Castle Area Hospital Authority, Pennsylvania, Hospital Revenue Bonds, Series 1981.

Total amount of issue: $13,445,000.
Date of issue: June 1, 1981.
Put coupon: 12.50 percent.
Put term maturity: June 1, 2011.
Date of first put: June 1, 1986.
Amount of first put: $8,215,000.

The foregoing information was culled from the issue's official statement.

Table 1
Citibank, N.A., Letter-of-Credit–Backed Put Bonds

Name of Issuer	Total Amount of Issue	Date of Issue	Put Coupon	Put Term Maturity	First Put Date and Amount
Barton County, Kansas, Single-Family Mortgage Revenue Bonds, 1981 Series A	$ 23,205,000	4/1/81	9.20%	7/1/2013	7/1/86 $ 22,775,000
Brevard County Housing Finance Authority, Florida, Single-Family Mortgage Revenue Bonds, Series 1980B	150,000,000	2/1/81	9.00	2/1/2013	2/1/86 146,450,000
City of Baltimore, Maryland, Single-Family Mortgage Revenue Bonds, 1981 Series	100,000,000	7/1/81	10.00	7/1/2013	7/1/87 97,980,000
Denton County Housing Finance Corporation, Texas, Single-Family Mortgage Revenue Bonds, Series 1980	24,655,000	11/1/80	9.50	12/1/2013	12/1/85 23,895,000
Hutchinson, Kansas, Single-Family Mortgage Revenue Bonds, 1981 Series A	18,845,000	4/1/81	9.25	7/1/2013	7/1/86 18,480,000
Johnson County, Kansas, Single-Family Mortgage Revenue Bonds, 1981 Series A	64,715,000	6/1/81	9.90	7/1/2013	7/1/87 63,395,000
Louisiana Public Facilities Authority 1981 Single-Family Mortgage Purchase Bonds	200,000,000	4/1/81	9.20	10/1/2013	10/1/86 196,125,000
Orange County Housing Finance Authority, Florida, Single-Family Mortgage Revenue Bonds, Series 1980	130,000,000	5/1/81	9.50	8/1/2013	8/1/87 126,545,000
Pueblo County, Colorado, Single-Family Mortgage Revenue Bonds, 1981 Series A	105,000,000	3/1/81	9.00	6/1/2013	6/1/86 103,005,000
Pulaski County Residential Housing Facilities Board, Arkansas, Single-Family Mortgage Revenue Bonds, 1980 Series	24,800,000	12/1/80	9.50	12/1/2013	12/1/85 24,150,000
Pomona Redevelopment Agency, California, Residential Mortgage Revenue Bonds, 1980 Series C	118,500,000	4/1/81	9.40	4/1/2014	4/1/87 114,585,000
Shawnee County, Kansas, Single-Family Mortgage Revenue Bonds, 1981 Series A	25,000,000	6/1/81	9.75	7/1/2013	7/1/87 24,460,000
Tom Green County Housing Finance Corporation, Texas, Single-Family Mortgage Revenue Bonds, Series 1980	23,465,000	11/1/80	9.50	12/1/2013	12/1/85 22,815,000
Williamson County Housing Finance Corporation, Texas, Single-Family Mortgage Revenue Bonds, Series 1980	24,595,000	12/1/80	9.50	12/1/2013	12/1/85 23,955,000

Source: Official statements of the various issues.

Table 2
Put Bonds Solely Secured by the Cash Flows of the Issuers (issued 1976–1979)

Name of Issuer	Total Amount of Issue: ($000s)	Date of Sale	Put Coupon	Put Term Maturity	First Put Date and Amount ($000s)	Call Date and Price
Centre County Hospital Authority, Pennsylvania Centre Community Hospital	$ 6,935	6/7/79	6.25%	7/1/2011	7/1/89 $2,040	7/1/89 at par
Chester County Hospital Authority, Paoli Memorial Hospital	6,885	1/27/77	5.85	2/1/2003	2/1/87 1,445	2/1/87 at 102
Erie County Hospital Authority, Hamot Medical Center of Erie, Pa.	43,690	4/22/77	5.75	1/1/2006	1/1/87 3,335	1/1/87 at 102
Illinois Health Facilities Authority, Northwestern Memorial Hospital	71,065	10/26/77	5.20	5/1/2005	5/1/87 6,935	Not callable
Sayre Borough Hospital Authority, Pa., Robert Packer Hospital	23,680	7/26/76	7.00	11/1/2005	11/1/86 5,000	11/1/85 at 103
Sayre Borough Hospital Authority, Pa., Robert Packer Hospital	25,055	12/15/77	5.50	11/1/2005	11/1/87 5,000	11/1/87 at 102
The Hospital Authority of Philadelphia, Thomas Jefferson University Hospital	98,660	12/14/76	5.90	7/1/2000	7/1/86 8,475	Not callable
The Hospital Facility Authority of Portland, Oreg. Good Samaritan Hospital and Medical Center	36,300	8/4/77	5.00	7/1/2009	7/1/87 5,000	Not callable
The Ind. Development Authority of Maricopa County, Ariz., St. Joseph's Hospital and Medical Center	85,750	11/6/78	6.20	11/1/2011	11/1/88 6,865	11/1/87 at 101

Source: Data provided by Kidder, Peabody & Co. Inc., copyright © 1980, reproduced with permission.

Table 3
Put Bonds Solely Secured by the Cash Flows of the Issuer (issued 1980–1981)

Name of Issuer	Total Amount of Issue ($100s)	Date of Issuer (Date of Sale)	Put Coupon	Put Term Maturity	First Put Date and Amount ($000s)	Call Date and Price
Chester County Hospital Authority, Pa., Coatesville Hospital	$ 24,500	(3/31/80)	10.25%	7/1/2010	7/1/90 $ 1,000	7/1/90 at par
Escambia County Health Facilities Authority, Fla., Life Care of Baptist, Inc.	22,000	(5/13/80)	9.75	7/1/2010	7/1/85 6,365	7/1/90 at par
Jacksonville Health Facilities Authority, Fla., St. Vincent's Medical Center;	23,620	7/1/80	6.80	1/1/2005	1/1/90 5,000	1/1/200 at par
St. Catherine Laboure Manor	3,130	7/1/80	7.50	1/1/2005	1/1/90 595	1/1/2004 at par
Louisiana Offshore Terminal Authority, Deepwater Port Revenue Bonds, First Stage Series	100,000	5/1/81	9.50	9/1/2009	9/1/86 16,500	9/1/91 at 103
Maine Health, & Higher Education Facilities Authority, Eastern Maine Medical Center Issue, Series 1981	19,515	6/1/81	10.50	10/1/2000	10/1/91 5,000	10/1/91 at 102
Shelby County, Tenn., Hospital Revenue Bonds, Series 1981	91,350	6/1/81	10.00	6/1/2011	6/1/91 15,000	6/1/91 at 103
South Carolina Public Service Authority, Electric System Expansion Revenue Bonds, 1981 Series B	200,000	6/1/81	10.50	7/1/2021	7/1/91 50,000	7/1/91 at 103
WPPSS, Nuclear Project #1 Revenue Bonds, Series 1981C	40,000	4/1/81	10.25	7/1/2015	7/1/91 40,000	7/1/91 at par
WPPSS, Nuclear Projects #4 and #5 Revenue Bonds, Series 1980E	50,000	12/1/80	11.75	7/1/2010	7/1/90 50,000	7/1/95 at 103
WPPSS, Nuclear Projects #4 and #5 Revenue Bonds, Series 1981B	30,000	3/1/81	11.00	7/1/2009	7/1/91 30,000	7/1/96 at 102

Source: Data from official statements of the various issues.

University, to the put bonds issued in 1980 and 1981 by the Washington Public Power Supply System for its nuclear projects #4 and #5.[3] While in some instances if all else fails hard-pressed issuers could attempt to redeem their put bonds with proceeds from new refunding bond issues, the focus in this chapter is on the underlying credit strengths and weaknesses as derived from the original put bond indentures.

The Puttable Letter-of-Credit–Backed Bonds

While the conventional purpose of the letter-of-credit agreement with a commercial bank is to provide additional standby liquidity to the borrower if unforeseen circumstances arise, in the case of the 14 puttable single-family mortgage revenue bonds it could become the underlying security for the bondholders. If, in an adverse interest-rate environment, the bondholders all decide to put their bonds to the trustees prior to the stated term maturities, the letters of credit will have to be used to pay the put bondholders for their bonds. This is particularly the case since it is expected that if all the puttable bonds are presented on the first put dates, the issuers' normal cash flows (made up of mortgage repayments and prepayments) would by themselves be insufficient to pay the principal on all the put bonds tendered.

As an example, while the 14 put bonds issued by mid-1981 are puttable five to six years after their respective issuances, available information on mortgage prepayment experiences for the various counties and areas involved suggest that prepayments will not be sufficient. Of course, in a higher interest-rate environment than existed when the put bonds were issued, the prepayments might be expected to become even less than the historical experience would indicate. Therefore, the bond issuer—on the one hand facing put bondholders who want their principal, and on the other hand having insufficient revenues generated through normal mortgage prepayments and repayments—will face a cash flow risk once all the various program reserves are exhausted. In this worst-case situation, the letter-of-credit agreement becomes in effect, the security for the bondholder.

In light of this it must be noted that the letter-of-credit agreement is not ironclad. There are circumstances under which the commercial bank does not have to honor its commitment. While it does not appear likely at this time that these circumstances would occur, the analyst or investor should be aware of even the potential risks involved.

First, the letter-of-credit agreement states that it does not have to be honored by the bank if the issuer has already defaulted on the

---

[3]The WPPSS case is discussed in Case 3.

payment of interest and principal (including sinking fund payments) prior to the puttable dates.[4] Therefore, the analyst must assess the ability of each respective issuer to meet cash flow needs prior to the first puttable date.[5] Strongly secured single-family housing revenue bonds usually have the following five characteristics:

1. The home loans must be insured by the Federal Housing Administration (FHA), Veterans Administration (VA), or an acceptable private mortgage insurer, or have a loan-to-value ratio of 80 percent or less.
2. All conventional loans should also be covered by a 10 percent mortgage pool insurance policy.
3. There should be special reserves including a debt reserve which has an amount equal at least to maximum annual debt service, as well as a mortgage reserve which has an amount equal at least to 1 percent of the bonds outstanding.
4. The issuer should be in a region of the country which has sound economic growth as indicated by steady real estate valuation, personal income, and retail sales growth, as well as a low unemployment rate and a relatively low tax burden.
5. No project financing is involved.

Of the 14 single-family mortgage revenue put bonds issued, 13 were substantially well secured in terms of the above criteria. The 14th put bond, issued by the Pomona Redevelopment Agency in California, was the weakest primarily because there was no mortgage pool insurance and project financing was involved.

Even if the bonds are not in default prior to the puttable date, a second potential concern for the analyst is the future legality of the letter-of-credit agreement with the bank, which for all 14 bonds is with Citibank. The office of the U. S. Comptroller of the Currency regulates national banks and has had under review certain aspects of the letter-of-credit device primarily to see if it is in accordance with safe and sound banking practices. Evaluating the letter-of-credit device from the point of view of bank participation in the financial futures and forward placement markets was not the focus of the review.[6] It must be noted that only a major financial crisis could prevent Citibank from being able to meet its obligations under the

---

[4]Letter-of-credit agreements are discussed in Chapter 22.

[5]Single-family mortgage revenue bonds are discussed in Chapter 16.

[6]It was reported in Shirley Hobbs Scheibla, "Wall Street's Hottest Issue: Should Commercial Banks Be Allowed to Underwrite Revenue Bonds?" *Barron's* February 23, 1981, that the U. S. Comptroller of the Currency was reviewing the device to determine if it was a financial future, and thus in violation of Treasury banking rules. According to an interview held June 29, 1981 with Patrick Doyle of the legal department of the Office of the Comptroller, the review of the letter-of-credit device was limited to deciding whether or not it placed a financial hardship on the bank.

letter-of-credit agreement. As of December 31, 1979, Citibank was the second largest privately owned commercial bank in the world in terms of total assets.[7]

While Citibank's counsel, Shearman & Sterling, is of the opinion that under current law and regulations the letter of credit is legally binding on Citibank, it must also be noted that the use of a letter of credit as security for puttable municipal bonds is new.[8] Since the put bond is a new structure there is little or no regulatory guidance in this area.

The one hospital put bond secured by a letter of credit was the First National Bank of Saint Paul (New Castle Area Hospital Authority, Pennsylvania, Hospital Revenue Bonds, Series 1981). It has a somewhat similar letter-of-credit structure, though there also are significant security differences. First, the letter-of-credit agreement is with the First National Bank of Saint Paul, Minnesota, not with Citibank. While the former is a respectable regional bank, Citibank is a major international bank with many more assets. Secondly, the St. Paul bank does not have to purchase the put bonds if the bonds are already in default in paying debt service or if the hospital is in default in making certain other rental payments. Third, for a hospital bond, the possible imposition of wage and price controls by the state and federal governments and the reduced need for the hospital, as the result of future competition from neighboring health facilities or of changes in medical treatment methods, could significantly reduce patient revenues available for debt service and thereby bring about a default prior to the first puttable date. Though it is projected to be 88.4 percent in 1986, in fiscal 1980 (ending June 30) the occupancy rate was only 73.1 percent. Of all the original 15 letter-of-credit–backed put bonds, this one clearly was the weakest.

Hospital Revenue Put Bonds

Since 1976 several hospital revenue put bonds have been issued that are secured by the issuers' cash flows. Representative issues include the Illinois Health Facilities Authority (Northwestern Memo-

---

[7]The Citicorp annual report for 1979.

[8]A typical legal opinion by Shearman & Sterling states that: "Shearman & Sterling, counsel to the bank, have pointed out that the use of a letter of credit for the purposes described herein is new and has not been the subject of any court decision, nor has it been passed upon by the Comptroller of the Currency. It is the opinion of Shearman & Sterling that under current law and regulations the letter of credit constitutes the legal, valid, and binding obligation of the bank, enforceable against the bank in accordance with its terms except as limited by applicable insolvency, reorganization, liquidation, readjustment of debt, or other similar laws affecting the enforcement of creditors' rights and by general principles of equity." From the official statement of the $200 million Louisiana Public Facilities Authority, 1981 Single-Family Mortgage Purchase Bonds (March 13, 1981), page 9.

rial Hospital of Chicago Revenue Refunding Bonds, Series 1977), the Jacksonville Health Facilities Authority (St. Vincent's Medical Center Revenue Bonds, Series 1980, and St. Catherine Laboure Manor Revenue Bonds, Series 1980,), and Shelby County, Tennessee, Health and Educational Facilities Board (Hospital Revenue Bonds, Series 1981). The two Jacksonville put bonds are "joint and several" obligations—i.e., each issuer is also responsible for the other's obligation if necessary.

The overall security structures for the hospital put bonds are generally the same. In effect, the issuer establishes a special fund at least three years prior to the first put date. Specified annual amounts from hospital and patient care revenues are required to be deposited in the fund so that, by the first put date, monies already in the fund will be sufficient to pay the principal on the put bonds. Usually the required amounts equal the depreciation monies. Once these reserves become fully funded as required on the first put dates, they in effect become escrowed accounts. The put bonds also have access to the debt reserves.

Public Power Revenue Put Bonds

Put bonds issued by public power authorities are primarily secured by the issuers' cash flows. Additionally, the issuer's debt reserves can also be used, if necessary and available, to retire the put bonds. It must be noted, however, that these debt reserves are also pledged to the issuer's straight revenue bonds as well. If the issuer is experiencing significant financial problems prior to the first put date, the monies in the debt reserve may have already been used. Usually the put bondholder is required to notify the issuer six months prior to when he plans to put the bond back to the issuer. This six-month period allows the issuer time to adjust his electric service billings to reflect the increased debt service requirements, which the issuer is legally obligated to meet. It must be noted that these put bonds are a form of bond anticipation note since the issuers can be expected to issue new bonds to retire the put bonds instead of raising electricity rates. However, since the amount of put bonds issued by any one power authority represents such a small percentage of its total bonds outstanding, the redemption of the put bonds, even if the entire issue is put at the same time, should not significantly impact the power authority's cash flow.

In the case of the $50 million put bonds issued by the South Carolina Public Service Authority (Electric System Expansion Revenue Bonds, 1981 Series B), the bonds also have access to a reserve account. The authority has a strong operating history. In fiscal 1980, debt service coverage was 2.14 times, and in fiscal 1983, it is expected to be 1.85 times. Also, it generates most of its electricity by coal-fueled units. Analysts, however, should be aware of the fact that the authority will have to issue additional bonds to complete its construction projects. Additionally, while the put bondholder has the right to tender his bond at par on July 1, 1991, the issuer also has the right under normal circumstances to call the bonds at the same time at 103. If interest rates decline significantly by then, the issuer may elect to call the put bonds.

In the case of the Washington Public Power Supply System, put bonds have been issued under two separate security structures. Under one security structure (for Projects #4 and #5) the bonds are secured by the net revenues of the proposed generating facilities under take-or-pay agreements.[9] Under the second security structure (for Project #1), in addition to the net revenue security the put bonds are secured by the pledge of the Bonneville Power Administration to pay the bondholders if necessary.[10]

Concerning the put bonds for Projects #4 and #5, all the electrical generating facilities that were under construction have been terminated. There is no historical cash flow record for the analyst to review. The analyst has to rely upon the legality of the pledge of the issuer to charge rates to its participating 88 municipalities and electric cooperatives, among others, that are sufficient to meet (along with other expenses) its debt service obligations including the put bonds.

The put bonds issued for Projects #4 and #5 (with 11 percent and 11.75 percent coupons, respectively) are not to be confused with the one put bond issue of WPPSS's Project #1 (with 10.25 percent coupons). These latter put bonds are secured by the net revenues of these proposed generating facilities, under take-or-pay agreements with the participants, as well as by the legal obligation of the U. S. Department of Energy, acting through the Bonneville Power Administration, to pay if necessary the total annual costs of Project #1 including debt service on the put bonds whether or not the project is completed and generating electricity. On April 21, 1981, U. S. Representative James Weaver of Oregon (Democrat) stated that Bonneville does not have the legal authority to make cash payments; in the opinion of bond counsel, special counsel to WPPSS, and Bonneville's general counsel, Mr. Weaver's contention was without merit.[11]

Unlike the WPPSS Projects #4 and #5, put bonds which are only

---

[9]For additional information about WPPSS, see Case 3.

[10]According to Brendan O'Brien, Esq., of Wood & Dawson, New York, N. Y., the put bonds have been specifically approved by the Bonneville Power Administration. Interview with one of the authors, held April 21, 1981.

[11]Congressman Weaver's remarks were reported in *The Bond Buyer,* April 27, 1981, page 1. The legal opinions are in the official statements for the WPPSS bonds.

callable five years after the first puttable dates and at premiums of 103 and 102, respectively, the WPPSS Project #1 put bonds can be called by the issuer at par at the same time that they are puttable by the bondholder. Therefore, if interest rates decline dramatically, these put bondholders may have their bonds called for redemption by the issuer on the first puttable date.

Industrial Development Revenue Put Bonds

An industrial revenue bond with a put feature is part of a bond issue of the Louisiana Offshore Terminal Authority (LOOP INC. Project Deepwater Port Revenue Bonds, First State Series C). The put bonds in the first instance are secured by tariffs and revenues derived from the offshore superport. There also is a deficiency makeup agreement, which is a several but not joint obligation of five oil companies—Ashland Oil, Inc., Marathon Oil Company, Murphy Oil Company, Shell Oil Company, and Texaco, Inc. There is no debt reserve for the issue. The put bondholders do not have a mortgage or any security interest in the project. Being a several but not joint obligation, each oil company is only legally responsible for its agreed-upon share of the project. If the security were joint *and* several they would be responsible for each other's obligations as well. Since the put bonds are several but not joint, the credit assessment has to be made on the basis of the weakest oil company. Because of the credit worthiness of the shipper-owners, the put bonds are of investment grade quality.

While these bonds are puttable on September 1, 1986, they are not callable by the issuer until September 1, 1991, and then at 103.

CONCLUSIONS

In this chapter we have explained the characteristics of and credit considerations in analyzing puttable bonds. As noted in this chapter, credit risks range all the way from absolute safety to great uncertainty. It is hoped that this chapter will provide the analyst or investor with the analytical tools for making the necessary distinctions.

Letters-of-Credit– Backed Bonds

CHAPTER **22**

Cadmus M. Hicks, Ph.D.
Research Analyst
John Nuveen & Co., Incorporated

DESCRIPTION

Letters of credit (LOCs) are increasingly being used to enhance security and marketability of municipal debt obligations. An LOC is a commitment by a bank to pay principal and interest on municipal notes, commercial paper, or bonds in the event that the issuer is unable to do so. A complementary reimbursement agreement obligates the issuer to pay the bank for any amounts drawn under the LOC. In order to obtain an LOC from a bank, an issuer typically pays an annual commission of approximately 0.3 percent to 1.5 percent of the principal amount of the LOC. In exchange, the issuer hopes to improve the credit worthiness of its debt obligations and to obtain a correspondingly lower interest cost on its borrowings.

Generally, the LOC authorizes the bond trustee to draw from the bank an amount equal to the principal amount of the bonds plus interest (seven months' interest is a common allowance). The trustee is required to draw upon the LOC promptly in the event of default under the bond indenture or under the obligor's reimbursement agreement with the bank (such as a failure to pay the annual commitment fee). Since any default under the reimbursement agreement gives the bank the right to terminate the LOC within a certain time (usually 60 days), such a default necessitates using the entire LOC to call the bonds. Otherwise only the amount necessary to make the current payment is drawn. Partial drawdowns must be promptly restored by the obligor in order to prevent default under the reimbursement agreement.

LOCs are frequently used by commercial paper and other short-term issuers, although it is not uncommon to find LOCs which mature in as long as 10 years (the maximum length of LOCs issued by federal banks). Often, LOCs are used to support industrial development revenue bonds issued on behalf of nongovernmental corporations whose lease rental or installment sales payments constitute the principal security for the bonds. LOCs are also frequently used for housing bond programs.

RENEWABLE LOCs, PUTS, AND FLOATING RATE BONDS

In some financings, the LOC may expire prior to the maturity of the bonds. To protect the bondholder from the fundamental alteration of the security of his bonds which would result from the expiration of the LOC, provision should be made in the bond indenture for the issuance of a new LOC, either by the original bank or one of comparable quality, prior to the expiration of the old LOC. There should also be the stipulation that if a new LOC is not obtained, the trustee must use the existing LOC to purchase the bonds of all holders who do not want to retain those securities in the absence of LOC support.

LOCs are frequently used for bonds that have put options (more properly, "demand for payment" options) which allow a bondholder to tender his bonds to a trustee or a remarketing agent at par plus accrued interest. (See Chapter 21.) If not remarketed, the bonds are eventually delivered by the trustee to the bank, where they continue to represent outstanding debt of the obligor until the obligor repays the amount drawn on the LOC. Until such repayment is made, the obligor must pay interest on any amounts drawn on the LOC. Of course, bonds which are not backed by LOCs can also have demand options, but in such cases bondholders must rely solely on the liquidity of the obligor. A put option is usually exercisable on a given date (typically five years after issuance), or it may be exercisable periodically, in some cases with as little as five business days' notice.

Bonds with put options often have floating interest rates, which are designed to facilitate marketing bonds at par both in the primary and secondary markets. It is for this type of bond that remarketing agents are sometimes used. The interest rate for floating- or variable-rate bonds and notes is adjusted periodically on the basis of some recognized index or is calculated as a percentage of a specific bank's prime rate. Such revisions are usually made semiannually, monthly, or whenever the prime rate changes.

In recognition of the fact that floating-rate, demand bonds are treated as commercial paper despite their nominal long-term maturity dates, the analyst should apply dual credit risk ratings: a long-term debt rating and a commercial paper rating. Both ratings should be based on the strength of the bank—the long-term rating reflecting the bank's commitment to pay debt service in the event of default by the obligor, and the commercial paper rating reflecting the LOC's capacity to provide liquidity for the put option.

CONDITIONAL "IRREVOCABLE" LETTERS OF CREDIT AND OTHER CURIOSITIES

In connection with put bonds, a distinction must be made between LOCs that back the bonds and LOCs that support only the put option. The latter type of LOC may be conditional even though the LOC may be termed *irrevocable*. An LOC that backs only the put option is usually no longer valid if the bonds go into default. For example, the preliminary official statement for a recent bond issue announced on the cover page that "the trustee's obligation to purchase the tendered option bonds is supported by an *irrevocable letter of credit* issued by (the bank)" (emphasis added). However, further in the document we read, "Option term bondholders shall have *no right to tender* and the bank shall have no obligation under the letter of credit, *if at the time of tender the option term bonds are in default* as to payment of principal or interest" (emphasis added). Clearly the LOC, in this case, merely ensures operation of the put option, it does not guarantee payment of the bonds themselves.

Another important distinction is between a letter of credit and a line of credit. Since this distinction may not be universally recognized in the language of official statements, the specific terms of each credit arrangement should be scrutinized. However, as the terms are generally used in municipal financings, a *line* of credit is a commitment by a bank to lend money to an issuer and is invalid in the event of default by the issuer. A *letter* of credit is a commitment by a bank to pay money to a trustee for the benefit of bondholders and is designed to protect the bondholders against default (except LOCs backing put options as discussed above). Lines of credit (sometimes called revolving bank loans) are often used to provide liquidity to issuers of commercial paper and bonds with put options. The use of both letters of credit and lines of credit to back municipal commercial paper increased dramatically in the first half of 1982 to the point of covering about half of all such issues.[1]

Like letters of credit used to support put options, lines of credit may also be referred to as irrevocable, but this does not change their conditional nature. None of the irrevocable letters of credit which have been issued to provide additional security for bonds (as opposed to backing a put option) are conditional upon the obligor not being in default.

LETTERS OF CREDIT AND BANKRUPTCY[2]

The new federal bankruptcy law poses a peculiar danger to the holder of LOC-backed bonds: if the obligor were to declare bankruptcy within 90 days after retiring a bond issue, such payments could be construed as "avoidable preferences"—attempts to benefit one group of unsecured creditors at the expense of the other.[3] Under these circumstances, a judge could order the former bondholder to return the principal and interest he had received. The greatest danger in this situation is that repayment might be demanded after the termination of the LOC (which would be likely if the LOC were to terminate at the maturity date of the bonds).

The simplest way to protect bondholders from having to pay back principal and interest in bankruptcy proceedings after the LOC has expired is a requirement that the issuer make payments to the trustee at least 91 days prior to the due date. This way, if the obligor were to file for bankruptcy within the next 90 days, the LOC would still be good. And if bankruptcy were declared after 90 days, the payment to the trustee would not constitute an avoidable preference since it was made before the critical 90-day period. Alternatively, the duration of the LOC may be extended to at least 91 days beyond the maturity date of the bonds. (Since bankruptcy may be declared within 90 days after the payment of a coupon but prior to the maturity date of the bonds, the size of the LOC may need to include at least 300 days' interest: six months to cover the coupon, 90 days to cover the preferential period, and 30 days to allow time for redemption of the bonds prior to maturity.)

---

[1]See the special report "Municipal Commercial Paper," May 1981, issued by John Nuveen & Co. Incorporated for more information.

[2]For additional discussions of this issue, see Standard & Poor's *Creditweek,* January 25, 1982, pp. 1933–36; *Fixed Income Investor,* June 21, 1980, pp. 553–54; and James E. Spiotto, *Bonds: Defaults and Remedies* (New York: Practicing Law Institute, 1982), pp. 163–66.

[3]In a recent case in Pennsylvania *(In re Copter, Inc.),* the court decided to recognize the state's own preferential payment period of 120 days rather than the federal period of 90 days. This decision may require the framers of LOC agreements in certain states to provide more extensive protection to bondholders.

Holders of municipal commercial paper maturing in less than 45 days enjoy a different form of protection. Since payments of obligations incurred in the debtor's and creditor's normal course of business and paid within 45 days cannot be avoided as preferential, payments of notes with terms of less than 45 days, in the opinion of various law firms, should also be free from the threat of court-ordered repayment.

Another problem is that a bankruptcy trustee might use a temporary restraining order (TRO) to block payment under an LOC in order to prevent a secured creditor (the bank) from being substituted for an unsecured creditor (the bondholder). This problem exists when the bank holds deposits of the obligor, which can be offset by amounts due to the bank under the reimbursement agreement. This was the basic issue in the *Twist Cap* case which became a key element in LOC law.[4] The precedent of the *Twist Cap* decision, however, has since been effectively overruled by a recent U.S. district court decision.[5] Nevertheless, to avoid the possibility of any problems resulting from reliance on an LOC from a bank which is a secured creditor of the obligor, bond indentures should require either that the LOC bank waive any right of offset or that the bonds be purchased by an agent (such as a third-party depository) which is unsecured with respect to the obligor.

Since none of these techniques for avoiding the dangers inherent in bankruptcy proceedings has yet been tested in court, prospective purchasers of LOC-backed, tax-exempt paper should obtain a legal opinion from competent nationally recognized counsel regarding provisions to protect bondholders.

THE RATING OF LOCs

When municipal obligations supported by LOCs were first offered for sale, there was considerable uncertainty regarding certain aspects of the recently passed bankruptcy code. At that time, legal counsel would only render guarded opinions. However, since then the legal community has become more confident regarding interpretations of bankruptcy law as it applies to LOCs, and "clean" legal opinions are now being given for many issues.

In cases, where bond counsel has opined that there is no reasonable danger of avoidable preference problems or TROs, the credit worthiness of the issues can be determined primarily on the basis of the

---

[4]*Twist Cap, Inc.* v. *Southeast Bank of Tampa, 19 Bankruptcy Reporter* 284 (D. Fla. 1979).

[5]*Westinghouse Credit Corporation* v. *Virginia E. Page,* No. 81-3172 (D.D.C. March 30, 1982).

strength of the bank. In situations where the LOC terminates before bond maturity, the credit risks of credit worthiness are valid only as long as the LOC is in place. Of course, when an LOC is used only to provide liquidity for a put option, the ratings credit risks should be on the obligor's credit worthiness.

Bank Strength

Since most municipal analysts are not familiar with the intricacies of bank credit analysis, they are apt to have difficulty determining the strength of the security provided by even the most well-known institutions. In view of this lack of specialized knowledge, reports issued by the commercial rating companies will probably be the most convenient source of this type of information for many analysts. Ratings of bank debentures and commercial paper may be useful in the event that ratings of the LOC-backed municipal securities are not available since LOCs, like debentures, constitute unsecured obligations of the bank.

As might be expected, in evaluating a bank and its LOCs, credit risk is based upon, among other things, the extent of the bank's contingent liabilities under its outstanding LOCs (which do not appear on the balance sheet but must be included in the footnotes). Banks are not required to maintain reserves to cover their LOCs, nor are there any limitations on the aggregate amount of contingent liability a bank may incur under its LOCs. However, a standby LOC is subject to the limitations placed on the amount a bank can lend to any single borrower.[6] In these respects, LOCs are inferior to municipal bond insurance which is subject to strict reserve requirements and limits on the volume of business as determined by the industry's regulatory authorities.

This situation may present a potential for abuse. For example, in 1981 one nationally recognized bank more than doubled the amount of its standby LOCs to the point where its contingent liability under LOCs was equivalent to 16.4 percent of its total loans. Other banks have also increased their LOC business considerably in the past year. Recently, however, several of the banks which have been most active in writing LOCs for municipal debt have indicated that they will curtail their participation in this line of business.

---

[6]12 *USC* 84 and 12 *CFR* 7.1160. A study of corporate and municipal LOCs issued in 1978 (Peter R. Lloyd-Davies, "Survey of Standby Letters of Credit," *Federal Reserve Bulletin*, September 1979, pp. 716–19) reveals that losses under LOC programs have been extremely low: only 2.03 percent of the total dollar amount of the LOCs was ever drawn down, and only 0.03 percent was not immediately restored. This compares to a reserve for losses rate of 0.41 percent on the banks' conventional loans.

THE INVESTOR'S PERSPECTIVE

Three factors argue against relying totally on LOCs for security:

1. The bankruptcy problem.
2. The liquidity risks of the banks issuing LOCs.
3. The difficulty of assessing the risks of bankruptcy and liquidity.

At the very least, the presence of a weak obligor raises questions about the judgment of the bank making the LOC commitment. The lack of limitations on the aggregate amount of LOCs that may be written by any one bank may tempt some banks to overextend themselves, particularly in those cases where the banks also have a role in underwriting the bonds or in servicing mortgage loans made with housing bond proceeds.[7] Furthermore, there is always the possibility that bond counsel may have misjudged how future bankruptcy cases will be decided. Therefore, the first line of security, the credit worthiness of the issuer, remains a very important factor; and LOCs should be regarded as an enhancement to, rather than a substitute for, credit worthiness. As such, they can significantly improve the security and marketability of intrinsically sound debt obligations.

---

[7]See the article on this subject by Tim Carrington in *The Wall Street Journal*, February 11, 1982, pp. 1, 44.

Refunded Municipal Bonds

CHAPTER **23**

Sylvan G. Feldstein, Ph.D.
Senior Municipal Specialist
Merrill Lynch, Pierce, Fenner & Smith, Inc.

INTRODUCTION

While originally issued as either general obligation or revenue bonds, municipals are sometimes "refunded." A refunding occurs when the original bonds are escrowed or collateralized by either direct or indirect obligations or by those guaranteed by the U.S. government. The maturity schedules of the securities in the escrow fund are such so as to pay when due bond, coupon, and premium payments (if any) on the refunded bonds. Once this cash flow match is in place, the refunded bonds are no longer secured as either general obligation or revenue bonds. They now have a new security: the escrow fund. Such bonds, if escrowed with U.S. government securities, have little if any credit risk. They are the safest municipal bond investments available.

In this chapter refunded bonds are discussed in terms of (1) the general structure of an escrow fund, (2) the reasons why bond issuers refund their bonds, (3) the two major types of refunded bonds, and (4) how the analyst or investor should determine the degree of insulation from adversity of an escrow fund—and thereby, the credit worthiness of the refunded bonds.

337

Pure versus Mixed Escrow Funds

An escrow fund is an irrevocable trust established by the original bond issuer with a commercial bank. Government securities are deposited in an escrow fund which will be used to pay debt service on the refunded bonds. A "pure" escrow fund is one in which the deposited securities are solely direct obligations of the U.S. government, whereas a "mixed" escrow fund is one in which the deposited securities are not 100 percent direct U.S. government securities. Other securities that have been placed in mixed escrow funds include federal agency bonds, certificates of deposit from commercial banks, indirect U.S. government obligations, and even state general obligation bonds.

REASONS FOR REFUNDINGS

Removing Restrictive Bond Covenants

Many refunded municipal bonds were originally issued as revenue bonds. Revenue bonds are usually secured by the fees and charges generated by the completed projects, such as toll roads, water and sewer systems, hospitals, airports, and power generating plants. The specific security provisions are promised by the bond issuer in the bond trust indenture before the bonds are sold. The trust indenture describes the flow-of-funds structure, the rate or user-charge covenant, the additional-bonds test requirements, and other covenants. Many refundings occur because an issuer wants to eliminate restrictive bond covenants such as rate charge covenants, additional-bonds tests, or mandatory program expenditures. A refunding eliminates, or defeases, the earlier covenants since the bonds are deemed to have been paid once they are refunded and cease to exist on the books of the issuing jurisdiction.

Changing the Debt Maturity Schedule

Some bonds are refunded in order to change the issuer's debt maturity schedule—either to make the yearly debt service payments more level or to stretch out the maturity schedule. An example of the latter are certain bonds of the New York State Municipal Assistance Corporation for the city of New York (MAC).

Saving Money for the Bond Issuer

Still another reason for issuers to refund municipal bonds is to reduce their interest payment expenses. Typically, substantial interest cost savings can occur when interest rates decline approximately 200 to 300 basis points from the levels when the bonds were originally issued. By refunding the outstanding bonds with a new issue, the bond issuer in effect is refinancing the loan at a lower interest rate. Additionally, based upon certain interpretations of Internal Revenue Service arbitrage procedures, some refundings that save money for the issuer can even take place in an interest-rate environment that has not dramatically declined.

TWO TYPES OF REFUNDED BONDS

The escrow fund for a refunded municipal bond can be structured so that the refunded bonds are to be called at the first possible date as was established in the original bond indenture. The call price usually included a premium of from 1 to 3 percent above par. This type of structuring usually is used for those refundings which either reduce the issuer's interest payment expenses or change the debt maturity schedule.

While many refunded bonds are to be retired at the first callable date, some escrow funds are structured differently. In these refundings, the maturity schedules of the escrowed funds match the regular debt service requirements on the refunded bonds as originally stated in the bond indenture. This type of structure usually is used when the objective is to defease any restrictive bond covenants.

Refunded bonds can be called by the issuer before the first call date and prior to the stated maturity of the bond if there is a mandatory sinking fund provision in the original bond indenture. As an example, in 1977 the state of Massachusetts refunded an issue of 9 percent general obligation bonds that had been issued in 1976 and were to mature on June 1, 2001. Under the refunding, the bonds—now fully secured by U.S. government securities—are to be called on June 1, 1987, at 104 percent. However, under the original sinking fund provisions, each June 1 from 1978 to 1987 the state of Massachusetts must call at par a preset portion of the outstanding 9 percent bonds.

DETERMINING THE SAFETY OF
THE REFUNDED BONDS

Refunded municipal bonds are generally the safest investments because they are the most insulated from adversity, provided that the escrow funds have only direct U.S. government securities, or those backed by the U.S. government—i.e., that they are pure escrows. Specific questions for the analyst to ask are:

1. Have sufficient monies been deposited in an escrow fund at a commercial bank or a state treasurer's office to pay the bondholder?

2. Has the bond issuer signed an escrow agreement naming the bank or state treasurer as the irrevocable trustee for the escrow fund?

3. Have certified public accountants reviewed the contents of the escrow fund to determine if it consists of either direct U.S. government obligations (U.S. Treasury notes, state and local government series) or obligations unconditionally guaranteed by the U.S. government? Examples of the latter would include: obligations of the Government National Mortgage Association (Ginnie Mae), Federal National Mortgage Association (Fannie Mae), obligations which have a Ginnie Mae guarantee, Farmers Home Administration (FmHA) Insured Notes, and export-import bank obligations, among others.

4. Have the certified public accountants also certified that the cash flow from the escrow fund will provide sufficient revenue to pay the debt service as required in the refunding?

5. Has a qualified, nationally recognized attorney reviewed the complete transaction and given an opinion that no federal, state, or local laws have been violated, including arbitrage limitations in Section 103 of the Internal Revenue Code of 1954, as amended?

6. What size commercial bank is involved? Preferably a large bank which is well-capitalized should be used so as to minimize the impact if an embezzlement of funds or other irregularity should ever occur.

Zero-Coupon Bonds

CHAPTER 24

Sylvan G. Feldstein, Ph.D.
Senior Municipal Specialist
Merrill Lynch, Pierce, Fenner & Smith, Inc.

Frank J. Fabozzi, Ph.D., C.F.A.
Professor of Economics
Fordham University

INTRODUCTION

A zero-coupon bond is one in which no interest coupons are paid to the bondholder. Instead, the bond is usually purchased at a very deep discount and matures at par. The difference between the original issue discount price and par represents a specified compounded annual interest rate on the bond. There is no reinvestment risk as with regular coupon bonds, since the compound annual interest is virtually assured provided the bondholder keeps the bond to maturity and the issuer is financially able to make the payment at the time of the issue's maturity.[1] Variations of the zero-coupon, compound-interest concept are municipal bonds marketed and sold as municipal multipliers, capital accumulators, capital appreciation bonds, or compound interest bonds. (Chapter 25 of Volume I provides a more detailed discussion of zero-coupon bonds and their variants.) The advantage to the investor of purchasing zero-coupon bonds is that reinvestment

---

[1]See Chapters 5 and 34 in *The Municipal Bond Handbook: Volume I* (Homewood, Ill.: Dow Jones-Irwin, 1983), for a discussion of reinvestment risk.

risk is eliminated. Because of this, the investor should be willing to purchase the issue at a somewhat lower yield than comparable issues with regular coupon payments. The lower interest cost should also be attractive to the issuer. Additionally, since there are no semiannual interest payments to be paid, the issuer has to pay out no cash until maturity. It should also be noted that, since the zero-coupon bonds do not bear interest on a semiannual basis, the administrative costs should be reduced for the issuer as well.

The risk for the issuer is primarily an increased interest cost risk. Unlike full-coupon municipal bonds where the issuer only pays annual interest, the zero-coupon bond issuer eventually has to pay the bondholder compounded annual interest. While the issuer may enjoy a yield give-up for providing the investor with this compounded annual interest rate, if interest rates substantially decline by the time the zero-coupon bonds come due, the issuer may have been better off having paid annual (noncompounded) interest instead.

CREDIT ANALYSIS OF ZERO–COUPON BONDS

Zero-coupon bonds present a unique credit risk for the investor. On the one hand, if interest rates substantially decline during the time horizon when the zero is outstanding and the zero matures in a relatively low interest-rate environment, the buyer of such a bond will have made a good decision—from an interest-rate perspective—to have bought the zero. On the other hand, if interest rates do substantially decline, it may not have been a very prudent decision for the issuer to have sold the compound interest bonds. A lower interest-rate environment could present financial problems—particularly for weaker revenue bond issuers—in generating sufficient monies to pay the zero-coupon bondholders as well as annual operating and routine maintenance expenses.

In determining the relative credit worthiness of specific zero-coupon bonds, there are at least three areas of concern. They are:

1. If the zero-coupon bond is issued as part of a revenue bond issue, the zero-coupon portion should not be a balloon maturity. That is, the issuer's financial plan for its funded debt should be characterized by level debt service.

2. If the interest-rate environment does substantially decline after the zero-coupon bonds are issued, the indenture should provide the issuer with the flexibility to call the bonds prior to maturity at a price substantially below par; that is, as a percentage of the bond's compound accreted value. While weak protection from an early call is not an attractive feature to the investor, from the analyst's point of view zero-coupon bonds with early call provisions do provide the issuer with greater financial flexibility. Of course, if a 30-year zero-

coupon bond is callable after 10 years, the investor should review the bond for investment in terms of its compound annual yield to the first call date and not to its maturity date.

3. Since the time horizon for the maturity of some zero-coupon bonds ranges up to 30 years, the bond issuers could be expected to undergo various economic cycles which could negatively affect their ability to make the final debt payments. Clearly, the more insulated the issuer is from financial adversity at the time when the zero-coupon bond is issued, the stronger it should be—to cushion adverse economic stresses. Therefore, the most attractive zeros are those of the highest credit worthiness when issued, whether they are state general obligation bonds, or well-secured revenue and hybrid bonds.

CONCLUSION

Zero-coupon bonds are new forms of municipal bonds. There are three major credit risk considerations of which, perhaps, the most important is the underlying credit quality of the zero-coupon issuer. Generally, zero-coupon bonds of high-quality issuers are substantially the more attractive.

Repurchase Agreements, or Repos

CHAPTER **25**

Sylvan G. Feldstein, Ph.D.

Senior Municipal Specialist
Merrill Lynch, Pierce, Fenner & Smith, Inc.

INTRODUCTION

This chapter discusses the analytical factors to be considered in determining the credit worthiness of repurchase agreements, or "repos" as they are known in the capital markets and municipal finance industry. Increased concern about repos developed in August 1982 when a New York City–based firm—Lombard-Wall, Inc., which was principally engaged in the business of arbitraging and trading government obligations and other money market instruments—filed for reorganization relief under Chapter 11 of the Federal Bankruptcy Code. At the time of the bankruptcy, Lombard had repos outstanding across the country with over 50 municipal bond and note issuers or their designated bank trustees including state agencies as well as local governments. Several issuers were dependent on the repos to finance ongoing construction and related activities. In many of the bond and note security structures, repos had been used as part of the financing plan.

WHAT IS A REPO?

A repo is a contractual agreement between a municipal issuer (or its bank trustee) and a commercial bank, brokerage firm, or other
344

government bond dealer. In the transaction, the repo issuer (such as a government bond dealer) receives cash and, in turn, usually provides interest-bearing U.S. government securities to a municipal issuer as collateral for the cash, with the contractual commitment to repurchase the securities at predetermined dates and prices. Often, long-term bond proceeds, construction loan note proceeds, and even cash flow revenues are invested through repos until the money is needed to pay either debt service or construction expenses associated with the specific projects. Over the years, investment bankers and municipal issuers have found repos to be attractive short-term investment vehicles since they can match the maturity of the repo to their specific cash flow needs.

WHAT IS THE CREDIT RISK?

Repos were not considered pressing credit concerns until the summer of 1982 when a few modestly capitalized government bond dealers that had repos outstanding experienced severe financial stress. These firms were Drysdale Securities Corporation, Comark Securities, Inc., and Lombard-Wall, Inc. On August 12, 1982, as noted above, Lombard-Wall filed for court protection under the Federal Bankruptcy Code. Under the automatic-stay provisions of section 362 (a) of the code as well as a temporary restraining order issued on August 17 by the judge at the request of Lombard-Wall, no bond or note trustee could sell the collateral securing a Lombard-Wall repo without court approval. In effect, the collateral was frozen.

As an example of the severity of this freeze on individual credit worthiness, one hospital bond issuer had $43.34 million, or 37 percent of its bond proceeds, invested with Lombard-Wall. Another issuer had its total debt reserve fund invested with Lombard under a 30-year repo. Several construction loan note issuers also had whole note issue proceeds invested with Lombard-Wall.

The credit risks for the holders of the bonds and notes involved were substantially increased because:

1. The bankruptcy court's restraining order on August 17 prevented the sale or disposition of securities received from Lombard-Wall under repurchase or investment agreements without court approval.
2. Several of the bond and note issuers were dependent upon these securities to finance construction and related activities.
3. It was not possible to determine future court actions in these areas.[1]

---

[1] This is based upon the author's observations, at the time of the court proceedings, as well as upon interviews that he had with various lawyers involved in the litigations.

Additionally, in an oral opinion by the bankruptcy judge in September 1982 concerning the Dauphin County Hospital Authority of Harrisburg, Pennsylvania, it was held that the repo collateral belonged to Lombard-Wall.[2] That is, the court considered the collateral used in the repos to be "secured loans" to Lombard-Wall and *not* "sales-repurchase contracts." Before the collateral could be liquidated, both Lombard-Wall and the judge would have to agree on the terms of the liquidation and who was to receive the proceeds.

THE THIRD-PARTY ISSUE

In the Lombard-Wall case, the judge also refused to release the collateral which had been borrowed by Lombard-Wall from a third party. At least three Texas bond issuers—the Lubbock Housing Finance Corporation, the Abilene Housing Finance Corporation, and the Baytown Housing Finance Corporation—received approval to sell only two thirds of their collateral, as the other third had been borrowed by Lombard-Wall from a third party.

It should be noted that after the court's decision, the trustee for the three bond issues—the First Interstate Bank of California—decided to use its own resources to remedy the losses resulting from the Lombard-Wall investments.[3]

EVALUATING REPO AGREEMENTS

While the great bull bond markets of August and September 1982 helped to bail out Lombard-Wall, at the time over 50 municipal bond and note issuers faced serious financial problems as the result of the bankruptcy. Therefore, if repos are used in financial transactions, the analyst should consider the following factors:

1. Are construction funds, any other bond proceeds, or project enterprise revenues invested through repos? If so, to what extend is the bond or note issuer dependent on the repo monies? Clearly, construction loan note proceeds, debt reserve funds, mortgage loan repayments, and grant receipts invested in repos are of greater concern to the analyst than are idle funds.

2. Are the repos with well-capitalized, established government

---

[2] "Sale Barred of Lombard-Wall Bonds Used in Repo for Hospital Authority," *American Banker,* September 20, 1982, p. 2. According to the counsel for Dauphin, before the Judge's oral decision was typed and signed, the parties involved settled their dispute. Interview with James A. Moyer, Esq., of LeBoeuf, Lamb, Leiby & Macrae, October 4, 1982.

[3] "3 Texas Agencies Will Be Repaid Lombard Funds," *The Bond Buyer,* September 9, 1982, p. 3. It should also be noted that it was reported that the third party involved was the trust department of Bankers Trust, in *The Bond Buyer,* September 7, 1982, p. 1.

bond dealers, brokerage firms, or banking institutions? Repos should not be with small, government-securities arbitrage and trading firms. Inclusion on an approved trading list of the Federal Reserve Bank is not sufficient evidence of credit worthiness.

3.   Are the repos fully secured with collateral independently held, and are the bank trustees identified in the repo agreements as having "bought" the securities they hold as collateral? Title to the collateral should at all times be with the trustee.

4.   The collateral should only include:

a.   Direct general obligations of, or obligations the payment of the principal and interest of which are unconditionally guaranteed by, the United States of America.
b.   Bonds, debentures, or notes issued by any of the following federal agencies: Federal Home Loan Banks, Federal Land Banks, Bank for Cooperatives, Federal Financing Bank, or Federal Home Loan Mortgage Corporation (including participation certificates).
c.   Public housing bonds, temporary notes, or preliminary loan notes fully secured by contracts with the United States of America.

5.   Because the vagaries of the bond markets impose the risk that the fair market value of the collateral may substantially decline at any time, the collateral should be valued at least monthly. The fair market value of the securities, as stated in the repo agreements, should mean the bid prices as they appear in the "Composite Closing Quotations for Government Securities," published by the Federal Reserve Bank of New York.

6.   If the value of the collateral decreases below the levels agreed upon under the repurchase agreements and are not replenished within three business days, then the bond or note trustees should have the right to sell the respective securities. If the repo issuer defaults in an interest payment for three business days, or one business day after notice, the bank trustee should have the option to declare the repo agreement terminated.

7.   The repo agreements should state that third parties are not owners of any of the collateral, and they are free of all liens.

CONCLUSION

Repos perform necessary timing functions in many financial transactions. For bond and note issuers their use is widespread and beneficial in keeping financing costs as low as possible. Therefore, there is nothing conceptually wrong with having repos in bond and note security features, provided they are of relatively short duration and are structured along the lines noted in this chapter.

"FHA-Insured Mortgage" Hospital Revenue Bonds*

CHAPTER **26**

Sylvan G. Feldstein, Ph.D.
Senior Municipal Specialist
Merrill Lynch, Pierce, Fenner & Smith, Inc.

INTRODUCTION

Administered by the U.S. Department of Housing and Urban Development and the Department of Health and Human Services, the Federal Housing Administration (FHA) hospital mortgage insurance program began in 1968 under Section 242 of the National Housing Act, as amended. Since the program began about 200 hospitals have participated; however, only a few issued tax-exempt bonds. The Atlantic City Medical Center bonds of the New Jersey Health Care Facilities Financing Authority and the Buffalo General Hospital bonds of the New York State Medical Care Facilities Finance Agency are examples of tax-exempt hospital revenue bonds that are secured in part by

---

*Data for this chapter are drawn from: Interview with a representative of the Merrill Lynch Capital Markets Health Care Financing Department. Date: January 25, 1983; Official Statement for $107,275,000. New Jersey Health Care Facilities Financing Authority Revenue Bonds, Atlantic City Medical Center Issue (FHA Insured Mortgage), Series A, dated: November 1, 1982; and Official Statement for $210,160,000. New York State Medical Care Facilities Finance Agency, Buffalo General Hospital Insured Mortgage Hospital Revenue Bonds, 1982 Series A, dated: October 8, 1982.

FHA-insured mortgages. By 1982 only three hospitals, all involving special non-operating reasons, have received insurance benefits.

This chapter describes the security features provided by this program and outlines the questions the analyst should ask when determining the credit worthiness of hospital bonds with FHA-insured mortgages. (Chapter 11 discusses hospital revenue bonds.) It should be noted that these security structures are very complex and in this short essay are only identified the general areas to be addressed by the analyst.

WHAT IS FHA HOSPITAL MORTGAGE INSURANCE?

Under the FHA hospital mortgage insurance program, once a hospital defaults on its mortgage payment, the bonding authority or the trustee files a claim for the FHA mortgage insurance. The claim can be paid in debentures in an amount equal to 99 percent of the outstanding mortgage balance. The debentures would be due 20 years from the date of the mortgage default, but could be redeemable at par by the U.S. government on any debenture interest date. The payment dates are January 1 and July 1 of each year. After the trustee files a claim, FHA issues a debenture, though the timing of its doing so is at its discretion. It is reasonable to assume that debenture issuance may take no longer than twelve months, but no time period is guaranteed.

WHAT IS THE CREDIT RISK?

Several features of the FHA hospital mortgage insurance program could present impediments to the timely payment of debt service if there is a mortgage payment default by the particular hospital involved. These potential problems result because of the following provisions:

1. The FHA insurance covers only 99 percent of the outstanding mortgage balance when the mortgage payment default occurs.
2. The claim is almost certainly to be paid in 20-year, interest-bearing debentures, not cash.
3. The U. S. government is not required to issue the debentures within a specific time period, and debt service on the bonds could become due before the debentures are issued. It should be noted, however, that FHA should be able to process the claim and issue debentures within twelve months.
4. Thirty days' interest on the bonds is not covered by the FHA insurance. This occurs because insurance claims bear interest from the date of default (non-payment) and a missed payment would include interest for the month prior to the payment date.

Of course, these credit features are in addition to the traditional security features of a hospital revenue bond. In the first instance, it is expected that debt service will be paid from hospital revenues. Briefly, the factors to consider include determining the range and quality of health care provided, (i.e., primary, secondary, and tertiary), whether the hospital is a start-up or ongoing facility, the historical and projected annual hospital occupancy rates, the degree of dependency of patient day revenues derived from medicare and medicaid, and the hospital's operating ratio among other ratios and financial health indicators.

It should be noted however, that a hospital using the FHA insurance program usually is of far lower credit quality than other hospitals, or it would not go to FHA. Even so, the analyst or investor should still determine if the hospital is of at least "bare bones" investment quality, i.e., it has the basic financial viability and cash flow to pay debt service.

WHAT IS THE "PRUDENT MAN" EVALUATION APPROACH?

While the FHA hospital mortgage insurance does not, by itself, provide complete backup security to the bondholders, it does (when properly supplemented by special debt and reserve fund structures) provide a high degree of safety. For any particular hospital revenue bond that has FHA mortgage insurance, the investor or analyst should be concerned about the following:

1. Is there a reserve fund (which is often called a mortgage reserve fund or collateral account), that contains an amount at least equal to the sum of the 30 days of bond interest which is not covered by the FHA insurance, as well as the difference between the principal amount of the bonds outstanding and 99 percent of the mortgage balance? If this reserve is backed by a letter of credit, it must be irrevocable and from a well-capitalized commercial bank.

2. Is there a debt service reserve fund containing an amount at least equal to maximum annual interest? If repurchase agreements (repos) are used, they must be overcollaterized with direct or indirect U.S. government guaranteed securities; evaluated periodically with prompt makeup provisions and remedies given to the trustees; and provided by well-capitalized credit worthy financial institutions.

3. The structure of the bond issue is very important because the debentures that would be issued by the U.S. government mature 20 years after the date of the mortgage default, and because the hospital bonds generally have maturities of much longer periods. Should a mortgage default occur when less than 20 years remain for ultimate bond maturity, or any intermediate maturity, the debenture interest

received should be sufficient to provide for all bond principal and interest payments. Should a mortgage default occur when more than 20 years remain for ultimate bond maturity, the semiannual debenture interest and maturing principal (due 20 years after the date of the default) should be able to provide for bond principal and interest requirements. This is usually accomplished if the bonds are amortized at a more rapid rate than is the mortgage—that is, in general the mortgage and debenture interest rates should be fixed at higher rates than the interest rates of the municipal bond. Consequently, over time as the amount of bonds is reduced the FHA insurance—which covers 99 percent of the outstanding mortgage—covers more and more bonds outstanding. This structure, along with the mortgage reserve fund and the debt service reserve fund, should provide strong security to the issue.

4. Since HUD could redeem the debentures in cash prior to their stated 20-year maturities, the projected cash flows, if available in the official statement, must demonstrate the ability to retire the outstanding bonds in case of early debenture redemptions.

5. Because of the possible need to draw upon them, the investments in the mortgage reserve and debt service reserve funds must be of high quality and be liquid. Additionally, the investments must be controlled by the trustee.

It should also be noted that since the FHA hospital mortgage insurance is a remedy for a mortgage default, obviously the stronger the hospital is on its own merits, the more attractive the overall credit worthiness of the bond issue.

Bonds Secured by Federal Savings and Loan Insurance Corporation (FSLIC) Insured Certificates of Deposit

Sylvan G. Feldstein, Ph.D.
Senior Municipal Specialist
Merrill Lynch, Pierce, Fenner & Smith, Inc.

INTRODUCTION

This chapter discusses the analytical factors that should be considered in determining the credit worthiness of municipal bonds that are secured by Federal Savings and Loan Insurance Corporation insured certificates of deposit. This is a new financing structure that was introduced to investors in the fall of 1982. An example of one such bond is the Canadian County Home Finance Authority, Oklahoma, $9.175 Million Loans-to-Lenders Revenue Bonds—Savers Federal Savings and Loan Association Projects.[1]

SECURITY FOR THE BONDS

In this security structure, the proceeds of a bond sale are deposited in a savings and loan association which, in turn, issues a certificate of deposit (CD). The CD is insured by the Federal Savings and Loan

---

[1]From the preliminary official statement for the bond issue, dated November 16, 1982.

Insurance Corporation up to a limit of $100,000 of combined principal and interest for each bondholder. The savings and loan association uses the money to finance low- and moderate-income rental housing developments.

THE FEDERAL SAVINGS AND LOAN INSURANCE CORPORATION

The Federal Savings and Loan Insurance Corporation (FSLIC) was created under the National Housing Act of 1934, as amended, and is supervised by the Federal Home Loan Bank Board. The Federal Savings and Loan Insurance Corporation insures individual accounts in FSLIC-insured savings and loan associations up to a maximum of $100,000, inclusive of principal and interest. On December 31, 1981, FSLIC had approximately 3,800 member federal- and state-chartered savings institutions as members with aggregate insurable accounts of over $500 billion. FSLIC had an aggregate primary and secondary reserve of approximately $6.3 billion.[2]

It should also be noted that while the FSLIC's obligations are not legally backed by the "full faith and credit" of the United States, on March 16, 1982, the House of Representatives with the Senate concurring passed a nonbinding concurrent resolution (H. Con. Res. 290) stating that "deposits up to the statutorily prescribed amount in federally insured depository institutions are backed by the full faith and credit of the United States."[3] It should also be noted that FSLIC is authorized to borrow from the U.S. Treasury up to $750 million for insurance purposes.

EVALUATING THE BONDS

In determining the degree of credit worthiness of an FSLIC-backed bond, the analyst or investor should consider the following eight factors:

1. The final maturity date of the certificate of deposit with the savings and loan association should be concurrent with the principal maturity of the bonds.

2. There should be a reserve fund that can pay debt service on the bonds if a default occurs on the certificate of deposit. The amount of money in the fund should equal at least 60 days of interest on the bonds. Since interest on the certificate of deposit is not insured by FSLIC after the date of default, this fund can be used to pay up to 30

---

[2]Information reported in the Federal Home Loan Bank Board 1981 Annual Report.
[3]This is reported in the official statement for the $42.2 million Panhandle Regional Housing Finance Corporation, Texas, bond issue, p. 11.

days of accrued but unpaid interest on the CD prior to the default. It also can be used to pay up to 30 days' interest on the bonds from the time a default on the CD occurs to the date on which FSLIC pays the insurance claim. While FSLIC is not under any legal obligation to pay its claims within any specified time period, a recent default by an insured association was covered by payment of 90 percent of all insured claims within 12 business days.[4] Of course, future experience may require a longer period to be covered in the reserve fund.

   3. The reserve fund monies should be under the control of the trustee and governed by an investment agreement which provides for high liquidity. If repurchase, or repo agreements are used, they should conform to the guidelines discussed in Chapter 25.

   4. Because the holder of the CD does not have a security interest in the specific assets financed by the bond proceeds, and FSLIC has no taxing power and its obligations are not backed by the full faith and credit of the U.S. government, the analyst should determine if the particular savings and loan association involved is well-established, in an economically stable region of the country, and has retained earnings well above the amount required by the Federal Savings and Loan Insurance Corporation.

   5. The bond trustee must have established procedures for determining the aggregate principal amount of bonds owned in excess of $100,000 by any one bondholder. The trustee should accept for registration only bonds owned by the following entities, and should be provided all of the following information:

a. An individual (including joint ownership): with name, address, and social security number for each owner;

b. A corporation: with name, address, and tax identification number.

c. A partnership: with name, address, and tax identification number.

d. A trust: with trustee's name and address, name of the settlor of the trust, the trust's tax identification number, and, if known, the settlor's social security or tax identification number.

Also, the trustee should be required to notify the transferee and transferor if the transfer causes a bondholder to own bonds in an amount in excess of FSLIC insurance limits.

   6. The bond trustee must also have procedures for promptly ap-

---

[4]As reported in the Federal Home Loan Bank Board 1981 Annual Report, on May 18, 1981, the Economy Savings and Loan Association of Chicago, Illinois, was placed in receivership. This action was requested by the state of Illinois, and required payment by FSLIC of the insured deposits. The Economy Savings and Loan Association had over 8,000 accounts and $74 million in deposits. FSLIC reopened the savings and loan association five days following the default date and began paying the insured depositors. Within 12 days following the default, over 90 percent of all insured savers had been paid.

plying for FSLIC insurance on behalf of the specific bondholders should a CD default occur. Failure to promptly apply could cause the loss of FSLIC insurance coverage for the bondholders.

7.   Under current federal tax law, 20 percent (15 percent for housing projects located in targeted areas) of the housing rental units financed by the bond proceeds must be occupied by low- or moderate-income tenants. If rental units are not available for occupancy on a continuing basis for low- and moderate-income tenants, the bonds can lose their tax-exempt status as of the date of issuance of the bonds. This could occur 60 days after the noncompliance is first discovered. Because of this possibility, the developer should be required through formal documentation to comply with these requirements at all times. Sometimes a special warranty deed can be filed in the real-property records of the county where the project is located; it can be a restrictive covenant binding upon and running with the title to the project.

8.   There should be a legal opinion by a nationally recognized bond attorney that FSLIC insurance is applicable for the specific bonds involved.

CONCLUSION

While the FSLIC insurance security concept initially appears clear-cut, the above eight concerns indicate the high degree of investigation that must be undertaken in the analysis. While these bonds do have the potential of being high-quality investments, they also require careful analysis.

Higher Education Revenue Bonds Collateralized with Common Stocks and Taxable Bonds

Sylvan G. Feldstein, Ph.D.
Senior Municipal Specialist
Merrill Lynch, Pierce, Fenner & Smith, Inc.

INTRODUCTION

A new municipal bond credit risk has developed over the last few years as the result of the changing nature of the equity and taxable-bond markets. Specifically, the unprecedented volatility in these capital markets has required the analyst to view the stability of stored wealth—which common stocks and fixed-income debt are supposed to be—much more cautiously than in the past. This is particularly so when they are used as collateral to provide security to municipal bondholders.

THE NEW VOLATILITY FACTORS

As examples of the volatility of the equity markets, the Dow Jones Industrial Average dropped from 918 to 730 between February and March 1980. This represented a loss in value of 20 percent over a two-month period. Also, in 1981, the Dow dropped from a high of 1031 in April to a low of 807 in September, for a drop of almost 22 percent.

Volatility has racked the fixed-income capital markets as well. In the U.S. Treasury bond market long-bond yields jumped from a low of 9.75 percent in June 1980 to a high of 12.35 percent the following December. If the "govies" had been bought at par at the 9.75 percent yield rate, they would have declined in market value by almost 20 percent in less than six months. Similar volatility has occurred in the corporate bond market. Between September 1979 and March 1980, for example, yields on long high-grade corporate bonds jumped from approximately 9.70 percent to 13.50 percent. That is, collateral that had been priced at par in September was worth one fourth less if it had to be liquidated six months later in March 1980.

VOLATILITY AND MUNICIPAL BONDS

Increased volatility in the capital markets has required the analyst to further refine the credit risk criteria as related to collateralized debt. The volatility factor has weakened the degree of insulation from adversity of those municipal bonds collateralized by portfolios of stocks and bonds—primarily those issued for private colleges and universities and secured in part with separately collateralized securities funds. Under this financing arrangement, which first became popular in the 1970s, investment securities of a college were deposited in a collateral or debt service reserve fund held by the bond trustee, to be used, if necessary, to pay debt service on the bonds. Private colleges and universities with ample, unrestricted endowment funds found this security structure an attractive way of reducing their interest costs through the improved credit worthiness which the collateralized bonds brought about.

In determining the degree of insulation from adversity, or margin of protection, of these bonds, analysts previously looked for the securities used as collateral to be limited only to being readily marketable. If the basic criterion was met, and if the college or university had the financial ability to replenish the collateral in the event of any deficiency and was itself of good credit quality, generally one could feel very comfortable with the security structure.

INDICATORS OF CREDIT WORTHINESS

Indicators of good credit quality for a private institution of higher education usually include the following:

1. High levels of endowment. Generally, an endowment of at least $10,000 to $15,000 per student in 1983 dollars is desirable.
2. A trend, over at least the last three years, of favorable operating-

fund end-of-year balances—that is, no operating deficits and strong financial controls.
3. Stable student enrollments.
4. Selective admission standards.

In a volatile market such as existed in the late 1970s and early 1980s, however, the standard of readily marketable securities was too broad even for colleges of good credit quality. Under this standard, eligible collateral funds could include primarily lower-quality or very volatile securities.

A fundamental consideration is the composition and level of the collateral: eligible investments should only include U.S. governments, corporate bonds, preferred stock, and common stock of corporations whose bonds are of high credit worthiness. The required collateral amount usually should vary from 100 percent to about 120 percent of the par value of the bonds outstanding. If the collateral is not all of high quality, additional coverage such as 150 percent of total debt service may be desirable. Another security feature would be for the annual cash flow from the collateral to cover debt service at least 1.5 times.

In addition, the frequency of evaluation is important. The trustee should be required at least quarterly, if not on a more regular basis, to evaluate the collateral to determine that its market value equals the amount required in the indenture. While the norm for evaluating the collateral has varied from a monthly to a quarterly requirement, the former time frame is preferred.

There should also be provisions for replenishment by the institution if necessary. An institution must be required by a covenant to replenish the fund within a specified time horizon. For some of the older outstanding issues, this has ranged up to six months, whereas a two-week deadline is most desirable.

Of course, the strongest secured collaterized bonds would be those in which the collaterized securities are limited to prime quality; that is, only in direct obligations of the U.S. government, such as treasury bonds, and those in which the maturing principal and coupon payments roughly match the debt service schedule on the outstanding municipal bonds. An example is the collaterized issue of the Minnesota Higher Education Facilities Authority on behalf of Carleton College: Revenue Bonds, Series Two-E. It should be noted that other issues of Carleton College—Revenue Bonds, Series O (1975) and Revenue Bonds, Series T (1977)—are of weaker credit quality for two reasons. First, the cash flow structure of the collateralized securities and the debt service on the municipal bonds do not match. Second, the permitted collateral can be of less than prime quality. While the credit characteristics of the college are strong, the pledged collateral provides limited credit strength.

CONCLUSION

In addition to an evaluation of the institution's credit quality, careful attention also should be given to the quality of collateral and the coverage and replenishment provisions.

Municipal Bonds
with Warrants

CHAPTER **29**

Sylvan G. Feldstein, Ph.D.

Senior Municipal Specialist
Merrill Lynch, Pierce, Fenner & Smith, Inc.

Frank J. Fabozzi, Ph.D., C.F.A.

Professor of Economics
Fordham University

In this chapter we discuss the concerns that the investor or analyst should have when determining the credit quality of "warrants."[1] Warrants allow their holders to buy bonds from the issuer at par and at predetermined coupon rates during a specified time period—usually two years.

The first time a municipal bond with a warrant was issued was in January 1981 when the Municipal Assistance Corporation (MAC) sold $100 million of 10⅝ percent coupon bonds due in 2008 along with two-year warrants allowing their holders to purchase another $100 million at the same coupon rate and due in 2007.[2] The warrants could be detached from the bonds and did trade in the secondary market in ways similar to "options" in the stock market. This financing arrangement was used by the issuer since the use of the warrants

---

[1]It should be noted that these warrants are not the same as tax warrants issued by state and local governments. The latter are usually short-term notes issued in anticipation of taxes. The term *tax warrant* is just another name for tax anticipation notes. The credit analysis of such notes is discussed in Chapter 32.

[2]For information on the security structures of the various MAC bonds, see Case 21.

360

allowed it to price its bonds at a lower coupon rate than would normally be the situation. In the example above, MAC saved approximately 75 basis points in its initial borrowing costs by issuing warrants.

CREDIT CONSIDERATIONS

Warrants are issued in high interest-rate environments as a way to reduce interest costs for a bond issuer. If interest rates dramatically decline before the warrant's expiration date and the warrantholders exercise their warrants, the issuer then will have to issue bonds with coupon interest rates substantially above the current market levels. As an example, MAC in November 1981 also sold bonds with two-year warrants to buy $59,505,000 in bonds with 12¾ percent coupons. When yields declined during the fall of 1982, investors began to exercise their warrants.[3] While MAC saved approximately $295,000 to $443,000 a year through the reduced interest on the original 12¾ percent issue, it will have to pay $1 to $1.2 million more annually on the 12¾ percent bonds that have been issued to the warrantholders.[4] This is because they were issued at a time when the market for MAC bonds was approximately 11 percent.[5]

POTENTIAL FINANCIAL BURDEN ON THE ISSUER

Of the two major credit quality considerations, the first credit concern is to determine how many warrants have been issued and the additional revenues required by the issuer for debt service if all the warrants are converted into bonds. Clearly, an issuer who sells substantial amounts of warrants at just the peak of a high interest-rate/inflation cycle could be exposing itself to substantial financial pressures in a lower interest-rate/stable-price environment. For a revenue bond issuer such a development could substantially reduce the net revenue coverage figures and thereby the credit worthiness of the underlying bonds. Because of this, in evaluating the credit worthiness of a warrant, the analyst should determine the financial impact on the issuer if—in a worst-case scenario—all the outstanding warrants are exercised. If the exercise of the warrants results in substantially

---

[3]Municipal Assistance Corporation for the City of New York, *First Quarter Report Ending September 30, 1982*, Note 8—Commitments, dated November 4, 1982.

[4]"Some Gimmicks Used to Sell Bonds Sour as Rates Fall, Inflation Slows," *The Wall Street Journal*, December 14, 1982, pp. 33, 43. Of course, it should also be noted that MAC saved investment banking fees since holders exercised their warrants and bought additional bonds directly through the warrant agent, the United States Trust Company of New York.

[5]Interview with MAC bond trader in the Municipal Bond Department of Merrill Lynch, Pierce, Fenner & Smith, Inc., January 3, 1983.

reduced credit worthiness, the attractiveness of the warrant clearly
becomes less so.

Again turning to MAC, while (as noted above) the issuer did have
to pay increased debt service as the result of its 12¾ percent bond
warrants, it has averaged out its interest costs by selling warrants during various stages of the interest-rate cycle. Some warrants have become worthless to their purchasers, which of course is
what the issuer wanted to see occur. These would be for many
of the 10⅝ percent bond warrants which expired in January 1983.[6]
Additionally, the amount of MAC warrants outstanding represented
a very small percentage of MAC total debt.[7] Clearly, if warrants are
issued, it is desirable to see them issued at various stages of the interest-rate cycle and in amounts of relatively modest size.

LEGALITY CONCERN

The second concern for the analyst or investor in evaluating the
investment quality of a warrant is its legality. There must be a legal
opinion rendered by a nationally recognized municipal bond attorney
that the issuance and performance of the warrant will not violate any
existing state and local governmental laws. This is particularly important since warrants are new to municipal finance and have not
been directly addressed in state constitutions.

CONCLUSIONS

Warrants are relatively new in municipal finance with only one
issuer, MAC, having issued them. Guidelines for the investor or analyst to use in evaluating their credit worthiness are twofold: First,
what is the financial impact on the issuer's revenues if all the outstanding warrants should be exercised, and concurrently, has the issuer sold warrants during various stages of the interest-rate cycle so
as to average out its interest-rate-exposure? Second, is there a legal
opinion by a nationally recognized municipal bond attorney clearly
indicating that the issuer can issue and execute the warrants?

----

[6]While the detachable warrants for the 10⅝ percent bonds were for $100 million
in additional bonds, warrants were exercised for $31,590,000 of the 10⅝ percent
bonds. Municipal Assistance Corporation, *Third Quarter Report Ending March 31,
1983.*

[7]Ibid. As of September 30, 1982, the amount of warrants issued as a percentage of
outstanding MAC liabilities was 0.01 percent, i.e., $159,505,000 versus $7,754,854,119.

Moral Obligation Bonds

CHAPTER **30**

Walter D. Carroll

Vice President
Merrill Lynch, Pierce, Fenner & Smith, Inc.

Sylvan G. Feldstein, Ph.D.

Senior Municipal Specialist
Merrill Lynch, Pierce, Fenner & Smith, Inc.

In several states, state agencies have issued revenue-type bonds that carry a potential state liability for making up deficiencies in their one-year reserve funds, should any occur. In most cases if a drawdown of the reserve occurs, the state agency must report the amount used to the governor and state budget director. The state legislature, in turn, may appropriate the requested amount, though there is no legally enforceable obligation to do so. Bonds with this make-up provision are the so-called "moral obligation" bonds.

Below is an example of the legal language which explains this procedure and which is usually enacted into law by the particular state legislature involved:

> In order to further assure the maintenance of each such debt reserve fund, there shall be annually apportioned and paid to the agency for deposit in each debt reserve fund such sum, if any, as shall be certified by the chairman of the agency to the governor and director of the budget as necessary to restore such reserve fund to an amount equal to the debt reserve fund requirement. The chairman of the agency shall annually, on or before December first, make and deliver to the governor

363

and director of the budget his certificate stating the sum or sums, if any, required to restore each such debt reserve fund to the amount aforesaid, and the sum so certified, if any, shall be apportioned and paid to the agency during the then current state fiscal year.

Since 1960 over 20 states have issued bonds with this unique revenue deficiency make-up feature. The first state was New York State with its housing finance agency (HFA) moral obligation bonds. This feature was developed by a well-known bond attorney, John Mitchell, who had extensive experience and knowledge of state constitutions and laws.

In the history of moral obligation financing, most of this debt has been self-supporting—no state financial assistance has been required. However, in most of the instances where the moral pledge was called upon, the respective state legislatures responded by appropriating the necessary amounts of monies. This occurred in Pennsylvania with the bonds and notes of the Pennsylvania HFA; in New Jersey with the bonds of the South Jersey Port Authority; and in New York State with the bonds and notes of the UDC and with housing bonds of the HFA.

In terms of credit quality, while the "moral obligation" is not legally enforceable by the bondholders, it does indicate legislative support. Of course, while the general obligation pledge provides the highest degree of legal comfort to the bondholder, a moral obligation does provide some comfort as well—though certainly not on the same level and not legally enforceable.

The credit evaluation of the moral obligation pledge varies widely among analysts and investors. To those who place a high degree of emphasis upon legal protections in their credit analysis, the moral obligation pledge is given no weight whatsoever in the credit evaluation of the issue since it involves no legally binding obligation upon the governmental unit to replenish the reserve fund; i.e., the bond is rated solely upon the evaluation of the initial source of payment. To those analysts and investors who place a high degree of emphasis upon ability and willingness to pay, rather than legal protections, the moral obligation pledge is viewed as almost equal to the general obligation pledge.

Despite the nomenclature of the financial mechanism, the bondholder is not relying upon the "morality" of future legislatures but rather upon their practicality. The governmental unit may be expected to replenish the debt reserve fund because the cost of doing so is viewed as less severe than the increased costs associated with the bond market penalizing the governmental unit for not replenishing the fund. The increased costs would arise from the higher interest rates which the governmental unit making the moral obligation pledge (and even related units of government) would have to pay on future issues of its own debt.

There are certain factors which the analyst or investor should investigate when evaluating a particular moral obligation bond.

1. *Essentiality of purpose.* What is the purpose for which the moral obligation bond is being issued? A future legislature is more likely to make the necessary appropriation to replenish a debt reserve fund if the issue was sold to finance a governmental building or low-income housing than if it was sold to finance a sports stadium. In the latter case, the legislature being asked to make the appropriation to replenish the reserve fund might seriously question the appropriateness of the actions taken by the legislature which made the moral obligation pledge.

2. *Feasibility of project.* Is the project one which has a strong probability of being self-supporting from its planned source of payment? Even if the project should not attain full self-supporting status, the smaller the amount of the shortfall, the less controversy should result over an appropriation to replenish a reserve fund shortfall. The debate about the appropriation could be much more heated if such support is so sizable and continuous as to raise concern that the project should never have been undertaken.

3. *History of moral obligation support.* Clearly, the bondholder can take more comfort in the moral obligation pledge if the particular state has a demonstrated track record of replenishing a debt reserve fund when necessary, as is the case in New York, New Jersey, and Pennsylania.

4. *Debt burden and amount of moral obligation debt.* Even the moral obligation bulls would prefer a general obligation bond in a worst-case economic and financial scenario. Thus, careful consideration should be given to the debt burden and budgetary operations of the governmental body making the moral obligation pledge, including both its direct debt and the amount of moral obligation debt.

Life Care Bonds

CHAPTER 31

Michael Kluger
Associate
Merrill Lynch White Weld Capital Markets Group

Richard M. Gerwitz
Associate
Merrill Lynch White Weld Capital Markets Group

The inherent high risk of "life care" bonds limits their universal acceptance by investors. However, a careful examination of credit quality may warrant limited investor participation in this traditionally high-yield sector of the tax-exempt market. This chapter attempts to familiarize investors with life care bonds and the criteria which should be used in their evaluation.

A typical life care (or continuing care) community consists of condominium apartments specifically designed for use by the elderly, and a health care center with traditional nursing home beds and services. A community building—where residents can receive their meals, participate in recreational activities, and receive ambulatory medical services—as well as landscaped areas and other supportive living arrangements are also generally included as part of a continuing-care community project. Entering residents sign a lifetime residency agreement, which entitles them to occupancy in a condominium unit and medical and nursing care on the premises if such services are needed. The agreement also guarantees the ability of residents to permanently transfer to the skilled or intermediate nursing care facility at no additional cost. For this package, residents agree to pay a one-time entrance fee, typically in the range of $15,000 to $75,000, and a monthly maintenance fee of $350 to $1,500. Occupancy of a unit by more than one resident generally does not increase the entrance fee, but does result in a higher monthly maintenance fee. Actual entrance and monthly maintenance fees reflect a variety of factors including: the size and relative desirability of the condominium units; the rate structure of the individual community (some require high entrance fees and low monthly fees, while others require just the opposite); the costs a community faces in providing the services guaranteed to residents in the lifetime contract; and the costs associated with expected mortality and morbidity (illness) events for male and female residents at various ages as determined by an actuarial study.

The general description of life care communities outlined above is subject to wide variation. Some communities offer their life care residents comprehensive medical services (i.e., physical therapy, X-ray and psychiatric services) at no extra charge, while other communities bill their residents for all but the most basic medical services. Similarly, there is wide variation among life care communities in the general services they offer to residents. Life care communities may or may not offer such services as condominium housekeeping, maintenance, gardening, carpets, and linen. Management must determine the appropriate level of free service a community is capable of providing. Too little free service will leave a community unable to attract new residents, while too much free service creates the possibility of financial strain.

Life care communities may be managed by an inhouse staff or by a contract management firm. Start-up facilities tend to utilize contract managers because they offer the initial development and marketing expertise that is so important to the future success of a community. The contract manager's fee is usually legally subordinate to debt service and other required community payments.

FINANCIAL CHARACTERISTICS

The primary sources of revenue for life care communities are monthly service fees, earned entrance endowments, and health center revenues. Interest on community funds and accounts is also an additional, sometimes substantial source of nonoperating revenue. For the purpose of illustrating dependence on the various sources of revenue, this section utilizes statistics gleaned from the forecasted financial statements of five start-up facilities that issued bonds during 1980 and early 1981.

The majority of operating revenues for life care communities come from monthly maintenance fees. Reliance on these fees averaged 51.0

percent and ranged from 49.2 percent to 62.8 percent for the five projects reviewed. Life care community management should be able to periodically adjust these fees for both existing and new residents in response to increasing costs of operation. As a general rule, communities will not automatically terminate a resident contract solely because of the resident's inability to pay the monthly service fees. A community will usually waive monthly fees if such action will not impair its ability to operate the facility, and if it has been determined that the resident's inability to pay is a result of forces outside his or her control. In fact, some communities have established separate funds from which monies can be used to defray waived monthly fees. A thorough review of the financial standing of prospective residents prior to entry, however, should help to minimize such events.

Earned entrance endowments supplied an average of 26.3 percent, and ranged from 18.8 percent to 40.3 percent of annual revenues of the communities reviewed. Communities generally receive an entrance endowment deposit when a residency agreement is signed, and the balance no later than when the unit is occupied. The funds are placed in a separate entrance endowment account, and are recorded as a liability of the community to provide future services. This deferred revenue is drawn down and recognized as earned income over the period of time which it is expected the resident will occupy the unit. The period over which the entrance endowments will be amortized is determined through the use of an actuarial study or from past experience. Actuarial studies may be accomplished for the resident population as a whole or, more conservatively, for each individual upon entry. Should a resident die before the actuarially determined drawdown period is over, the bond indenture may specify: that the funds be drawn down as scheduled without interruption; that the remaining funds be recognized as earned during the year in which the resident dies; or that a specified amount of the remaining funds be refunded to the resident's beneficiaries. Determining the period over which the entrance endowments will be drawn down is crucial to the success of the community. A particular danger is that the entrance endowments will be drawn down too quickly. If endowments are exhausted before a regular rate of turnover is attained, the community will be unable to secure new entrance endowments and will likely suffer from cash flow difficulties. In general, the estimated average age of entering residents is 75 and their life expectancy, and the draw down period, is 12 years.

Residents may terminate their contract and receive entrance endowment refunds within certain restrictions. Communities which allow refunds will often require that a new resident be secured for the vacating occupant's apartment before determining the proportion of the entrance endowment to be kept. In any event, a community will usually keep at least 1 or 2 percent of the endowment per month of occupancy, subject to a stated minimum percentage.

The third major source of revenue is derived from the health center. This source accounted for 10.4 percent to 25.7 percent of operating revenues for the five projects. The average was 18.4 percent. Health center revenue comes from both resident and nonresident facility use. During the first few years of operation of a start-up facility, residents are not expected to utilize the health center to the extent that they will as they age. For this reason, nonresident health facility use is particularly significant and desirable during this time period. Such revenues may be an important component of a community's cash flow in the initial years. As residents are transferred from their apartments to the health facility, their monthly service fees become revenues of the center and their apartments are made available to new residents. Certain patients, both residents and nonresidents, may be covered by medicare while staying in the health facility. The same rules covering medicare hospital reimbursement apply to life care community reimbursement.

Other than gifts and donations, which are generally insignificant for life care communities, interest income on community funds and accounts is the major source of nonoperating revenue. In our sample, nonoperating income as a percentage of *total* revenue ranged from 10.4 percent to 25.7 percent, and averaged 18.4 percent. Bond indentures require that money held in the various funds be invested in government obligations, certificates of deposit, or time deposits of any bank or trust company which conforms to certain requirements.

Like most government operations, life care communities segregate their revenues and expenditures into various fund accounts depending on their source and ultimate use. Typically, a revenue fund, construction fund, bond fund, and a continuing care endowment trust fund for the deposit of entrance endowment fees are established. A depreciation and maintenance fund, or some similar vehicle, should also be set up to provide for future improvements and maintenance of the facility, since maintaining an attractive and well-operating facility should contribute to the ability of a community to compete for new residents in future years.

CREDIT EVALUATIONS

While most of the country's 600 life care communities are proprietary institutions, an increasing number are organized as nonprofit 501(c)(3) corporations that can issue tax-exempt revenue bonds through state and local development authorities or other similarly empowered public entities. In addition to industrial development authorities (IDAs), health facility authorities have been occasional issuers of life care bonds. Issuers generally advance the net proceeds of a bond issue to the community via a loan, installment sale, or leasing agreement. The community agrees to make periodic payments to the issuer in amounts sufficient to meet debt service on the bonds and other incidental issuer costs. To secure the payment to the issuer, the community generally pledges its gross revenues and grants a first mortgage lien on its facilities. All rights under the various community agreements are assigned to, and all funds flow through, the trustee.

Life care communities have had tax-exempt revenue bonds issued on their behalf to finance start-up facilities as well as additions to existing communities. As a result of the availability of historic financial and operating information, the evaluation of the credit quality of an ongoing community obviously presents less of a problem than the analysis of a completely new facility. Therefore, while investors should approach the whole area of life care financing with caution, an extra degree is required when evaluating new communities because of the reliance on the accuracy of utilization and revenue forecasts. In either case, however, *the analysis of credit quality focuses on the strength of the issue's security provisions, the adequacy of project management, the community's financial and operating characteristics, and an assessment of future demand.* Investors should also be aware of the potential risks associated with the life care industry before making purchase decisions.

Most of the above information can be obtained from an examination of the official statement. Like hospital bond official statements, most continuing care statements are divided into two parts: (1) that which provides the basic information concerning the life care community, the project, the parties involved, and the bonds and their security provisions; and (2) that which contains the feasibility study. A well-constructed feasibility study is one of the best tools that investors have at their disposal. If executed by a recognized accounting or management consulting firm, the feasibility study should provide a wealth of information in a concise and logical format. We would recommend that investors begin their review with this section of the official statement and, if satisfied with its conclusion, review the other areas of concern.

SECURITY PROVISIONS

The basic security provisions of a continuing care issue are similar to those commonly found in other revenue bond financings. A debt service reserve equal to maximum annual debt service, rate covenants, and an additional-bonds test should be provided for in the indenture. Projects should also carry loss and damage, as well as use and occupany, insurance.

MANAGEMENT

Capable management may be the single most important variable contributing to the ultimate success of a life care community. Unfortunately, it is difficult to assess the intangible qualities that characterize capable management. As a result, the analysis of this aspect of continuing care must rely on a review of management experience as evidenced by successful involvement in other similar communities or, if already in operation, the track record of the community. A life care community run by a management team that has little or no historical basis for evaluation should be viewed with a healthy dose of skepticism.

While we have come across a number of communities in our review that operate with an in-house staff, the majority utilize consultants with previous experience in the industry. Consultants are often involved in the planning, development, and marketing of the project, as well as day-to-day management. Management fees vary, but generally take the form of either an annual fee or an annual base fee plus a fee on the number of occupied units. Provisions are usually contained in the management contract for the annual adjustment of fees based on changes in the consumer price index. These fees should always be subordinate to the payment of debt service.

FINANCIAL AND OPERATING ANALYSIS

Since most life care community financings coming to market are for start-up facilities with no operating history, analysts and investors, in order to gauge the prospects of a community, must rely on the adequacy of the pledged security, the accuracy of the feasibility study, and an assessment of the abilities of the project management. If the financing is for the expansion of an ongoing community, a review of historic operating and financial information should provide a good indicator of credit quality. As is the case with hospital bonds, the use of ratio analysis to accomplish this review is particularly useful. However, due to the infancy of this sector, comparative industry medians have not yet been compiled. Historic analysis for life care, therefore, focuses more on trends evidenced by the individual community over time. Communities should exhibit a consistent trend of positive financial results as reflected by such statistics as the operating margin, operating ratio, net takedown, and debt ratio. Occupancy levels should be high, and a current waiting list for approximately 20 percent of the units is desirable.

The Feasibility Study

Feasibility studies provide the investor with an independent opinion concerning the ability of a community to generate revenues sufficient to meet operating expenses and make required debt service payments. Of course, the value of the feasibility study is contingent upon the ability and experience of the person who writes it. Typically, these studies will cover a period of five years, including estimates for three full fiscal years after project completion. Each report is generally divided into three parts: (1) a cover letter indicating the scope of the review, the methodology used, and the conclusion reached; (2) a set of forecast financial statements including a statement of revenues and expenses, changes in fund balance, and balance sheet; and (3) a section detailing the assumptions used to construct the forecast financial statements. The assumptions relating to the forecast financial statements contain useful descriptive information for the investor. Usually included are: a description of the life care community; the construction program and financing; and the critical variables related to future assumptions regarding community revenues and expenses. This is followed by a delineation of the primary geographic market area and an estimate of the number of potential life care residents residing therein. By estimating market penetration, the feasibility consultant can project revenue forecasts which are critical to the development of the financial statements. A well-constructed feasibility study will also contain a sensitivity analysis indicating how the forecast will change should certain key variables, such as resident demand, significantly differ from expectations.

In general, the primary market area is considered to be potentially weak unless at least 20 percent of those aged 65 or older can afford the community's entrance fee. Industry standards also dictate that the community should not have to draw more than 5 percent of the financially and demographically eligible service area residents to maintain full occupancy of the facility. A service area resident is generally considered income eligible who has an annual income equal to twice the monthly maintenance fee. It is also assumed that any homeowner is able to afford the life care community entrance fee, since the average price of a home (assuming most elderly persons selling homes will have little or no mortgage liability remaining) is more than enough to meet most entrance fee requirements.

Investors should also pay close attention to the competitive market environment within which the community is being established. While many life care communities are located in areas where they are the only such facilities, continued industry growth will probably alter this situation. In addition, these communities face competition from nursing homes and other forms of long-term care and housing for the elderly. Since a successful community is predicated on the maintenance of a certain level of occupancy, a determination of the current and projected level of competition is an important part of the credit analysis.

Bondholder Risks

Bondholder risks associated with tax-exempt life care bonds focus on three areas of concern: unanticipated economic events, errors in pricing decisions, and increased government regulation. Adverse events in any of these areas could cause financial deterioration which will be reflected by a deteriorated credit condition, with subsequent decline in market price of the bonds held or, in extreme cases, the inability of the community to make required debt service payments. Unanticipated economic events could render incorrect both the revenue and expenditure assumptions upon which a project's viability is based. While feasibility studies assume a given rate of inflation, and indicate what reduced demand for residential units would mean in terms of project revenues, extreme economic downturns could cause financial strain. Most feasibility studies utilize sufficiently conservative alternate occupancy assumptions so as to preclude all but the most severe economic events from causing debt repayment difficulty. Those communities will initially assume 95 percent to 99 percent occupancy, and test debt service coverage using occupancy levels ranging from 80 percent to 85 percent. However, our review of a number of feasibility studies includes situations where alternative "distress" occupancy level tests have not been employed. Investors should carefully examine the margin of debt service coverage in these cases.

While life care communities have the ability to raise entrance and monthly fees in response to increased costs of operation, the fact that most residents are living on fixed incomes can make it difficult to pass such increased costs on to current residents. According to regulation 72–124 of the Internal Revenue Code, a tax-exempt 501(c)(3) corporation must continue to provide services to residents, under certain circumstances, *even if they can no longer pay their bills*. As we have noted before, a number of communities have established resident reserve funds which offer subsidies to those in financial need. We regard their availability as a positive factor. Inflation can also threaten the financial standing of a community by eroding the real value of escrowed funds. This is particularly true of communities that rely heavily on the entrance endowments relative to monthly fees.

Management pricing decisions also loom large as a potential element of bondholder risk. Competitive and nonprofit considerations put pressure on management to keep entrance and monthly fees at a minimum; at the same time, ethical considerations dictate that quality care be provided regardless of cost. Within the context of problems created by the pricing paradox, there are many factors which can impact the financial condition of an existing life care community. Management's key pricing tool is the study conducted by a recognized actuarial consultant. The actuarial study is helpful to management because it predicts turnover and health liability patterns over time for significant population groups. Using the study to make pricing decisions can be risky, however, because expected levels of turnover and health liability may not be realized for a specific period of time or for small population groups.

The potential for increased regulation is another source of bondholder risk. Compared with the hospital industry, the life care industry currently operates in an environment of little regulatory review and pressure. Federal involvement is limited to the standard medicare and medicaid certification processes. The continuing care industry has escaped excessive regulation in the past because it has been a relatively small segment of the health care industry. If industry growth projections prove accurate and life care communities begin to play a more prominent role in providing the elderly with long-term care and housing, there is likely to be an increase in regulatory pressure. Concern arises because a change in the regulatory environment of life care communities is likely to impact, directly and indirectly, net revenues available for debt service payments. An area of direct regulatory vulnerability is that portion of continuing care revenues which come from third-party payers (medicare, medicaid, Blue Cross). Life care vulnerability to third-party revenue limitations is minimized because the major sources of revenue are monthly maintenance and entrance fees. However, third-party revenue does flow to communities as reimbursement for residents who have been transferred to intermediate (all third-party payers provide reimbursement except medicare, in most states) or skilled (all third-party payers) nursing facilities. The percentage of nursing revenue which comes from third parties in a community varies widely. In a new community which opens its nursing facility to the general public, the percentage can be in excess of 60 percent. In contrast, an older facility which has been in existence for 9 or 10 years will generally receive less than 20 percent of its nursing revenue from third parties. There are several proposals at the federal and state level which would reduce medicare and medicaid reimbursement payments to health care institutions. To this extent, an established and ongoing community is less vulnerable to the enactment of reimbursement limitations than a similar but newer community.

Regulations may also be enacted which limit the creation and expansion of life care communities. Currently, all communities which have a skilled and/or intermediate care nursing facility are subject to planned project review and approval under Public Law 93–641, the National Health Planning and Resources Development Act of 1974. This act has also been interpreted to include provisions for appropriateness review of existing programs by planning officials. Appropriateness review requires an ongoing evaluation of the need for nursing services provided by a life care community. If these services are found to be inappropriate, a community could lose its medicare/medicaid eligibility. Selective regulation of various aspects of life care communities has also been carried out at the state level. To the extent that these and any future regulatory actions at any level of government limit community flexibility in establishing fees for services, or impact the level of services delivered, bondholder risks could correspondingly increase.

CONCLUSION

Availability of the substantial yield advantage offered investors in life care bonds should be viewed in light of the risks associated with this class of securities. In our opinion, investors who do their homework and select bonds which have been issued to finance viable and feasible ongoing or start-up projects should benefit from the current lack of market and credit guidelines.

Credit Analysis of
Municipal Notes

Section FIVE

Tax, Revenue, Grant, and Bond Anticipation Notes

CHAPTER **32**

Sylvan G. Feldstein, Ph.D.
Senior Municipal Specialist
Merrill Lynch, Pierce, Fenner & Smith, Inc.

Frank J. Fabozzi, Ph.D., C.F.A.
Professor of Economics
Fordham University

Notes are temporary borrowings by states, local governments, and special jurisdictions to finance a variety of activities.[1] Usually, notes are issued for a period of 12 months, though it is not uncommon for them to be issued for periods of as short as 3 months and for as long as 3 years. There are two general purposes for which notes are issued—to even out cash flows and to temporarily finance capital improvements. Each is explained below.

TWO MAJOR PURPOSES OF NOTES

Evening Out Cash Flows

Many states, cities, towns, counties, and school districts, as well as special jurisdictions sometimes borrow temporarily in anticipation

---

[1] Information on the note issues discussed in this chapter is derived from the official statements of the various issues. General analytical concepts are from Luther Gulick, "Debt Administration," in *Municipal Finance,* ed. A. E. Buck in collaboration with other staff members of the National Institute of Public Administration and the New York Bureau of Municipal Research (New York: Macmillan, 1926).

of the collection of taxes or other expected revenues. Their need to borrow occurs because, while payrolls, bills, and other commitments have to be paid starting at the beginning of the fiscal year, property taxes and other revenues such as intergovernmental grants are due and payable after the beginning of the fiscal year. These notes—identified either as tax anticipation notes (TANS), revenue anticipation notes (RANS), or grant anticipation notes (GANS)—are used to even out the cash flows which are necessitated by the irregular flows of income into the treasuries of the states and local units of government. In some instances, combination tax and revenue anticipation notes (TRANS) are issued, which usually are payable from two sources.

Temporarily Financing Capital Improvements

The second general purpose for which notes are issued is in anticipation of the sale of long-term bonds. Such notes are known as bond anticipation notes (BANS). There are three major reasons why capital improvements are initially financed with BANS.

First, because the initial cost estimates for a large construction project can vary from the construction bids actually submitted, and since better terms are sometimes obtained on a major construction project if the state or local government pays the various contractors as soon as the work begins, BANS are often used as the initial financing instrument. Once the capital improvement is completed, the bills paid, and the total costs determined, the BANS can be retired with the proceeds of a final bond sale.

Second, issuers such as states and cities that have large, diverse, and ongoing capital construction programs will initially issue BANS, and later retire them with the proceeds of a single, long-term bond sale. In this instance, the use of BANS allows the issuer to consolidate various, unrelated financing needs into one bond sale.

The third reason why BANS are sometimes issued is related to market conditions. By temporarily financing capital improvements with BANS, the issuer has greater flexibility in determining the timing of its long-term bond sale and possibly avoiding unfavorable market conditions.

SECURITY BEHIND TAX AND REVENUE ANTICIPATION NOTES

Tax anticipation notes are generally secured by the taxes for which they were issued. For counties, cities, towns, and school districts, TANS are usually issued for expected property taxes. Some governmental units go so far as to establish escrow accounts for receiving the taxes and use the escrowed monies to pay noteholders.

Revenue anticipation notes and grant anticipation notes are also usually, but not always, secured by the revenues for which they were issued. These revenues can include intergovernmental grants and aid as well as local taxes other than property taxes. In one extreme case, and as the result of the New York City financial crisis in 1975, RANS issued by New York City for expected educational aid from the state of New York provide for the noteholder to go directly to the state comptroller and get the state aid monies before they are sent to the city's treasury, if that is necessary to remedy a default. Most RANS just require the issuer itself to use the expected monies to pay the noteholders once they are in hand. Additionally, it must be noted that most TANS, RANS, and GANS issued by states, counties, cities, towns, and school districts are also secured by the *general obligation pledge,* which is discussed latter in this chapter.

INFORMATION NEEDED BEFORE BUYING TAX OR REVENUE ANTICIPATION NOTES

Before purchasing a TAN, RAN, or GAN, the investor or analyst should obtain information in five areas in addition to what is required if long-term bonds are being considered for purchase. The five areas are:

1. Determining the reliability of the expected taxes and revenues.
2. The dependency of the note issuers on the expected monies.
3. The soundness of the issuers' budgetary operations.
4. The problems of "rollovers."
5. The historic and projected cash flows by month.

Each area is discussed below.

1. Determining the Reliability of the Expected Taxes and Revenues

If a TAN is issued in anticipation of property taxes, a question to ask is: What were the tax collection rates over the previous five years? Tax collection rates below 90 percent usually indicate serious tax collection problems. Additionally, if the issuer is budgeting 100 percent of the tax levy while collecting substantially less, serious problems can be expected.

If a RAN or GAN is issued in anticipation of state or federal grant monies, the first question to ask is if the grant has been legislatively authorized and committed by the state or federal government. Some

RAN issuers, which included New York City prior to its RAN problems in 1975, would issue RANS without having all the anticipated grants committed by the higher levels of government. This practice may still be used by other local governments that are hard-pressed to balance their budgets and obtain quick cash through the sale of RANS. A safeguard against this is to see if the issuer has in its possession a fully signed grant agreement prior to the RAN or GAN sale.

2. Dependency of the Note Issuers on the Expected Monies

One measure of the credit worthiness of the TAN or RAN issuer is the degree of dependency of the issuer on the temporarily borrowed monies. As examples, some jurisdictions limit the amount of TANS that can be issued in anticipation of property taxes to a percentage of the prior year's levy that was actually collected. The state of New Jersey, which has one of the most fiscally conservative local government regulatory codes in the country, limits the annual sale of TANS and RANS by local governments to no more than 30 percent of the property taxes and various other revenues actually collected in the previous year. Many other states are more permissive and allow local governments to issue TANS and RANS as high as 75 to 100 percent of the monies previously collected or even expected to be received in the current fiscal year.

3. Soundness of the Issuers' Budgetary Operations

Another critical element of the TAN or RAN issuer's credit worthiness concerns determining whether or not the issuer has an overall history of prudent and disciplined financial management. One way to do this is to determine how well the issuer, over the previous five fiscal years, has maintained end-of-year fund balances in the major operating funds.

4. Problems of Rollovers

Key indications of fiscal problems are revealed when issuers either retire their TANS and RANS with the proceeds of new issues or issue TANS and RANS to be retired in a fiscal year following the one in which they were originally issued. Such practices are known as "rollovers," and are sometimes used by hard-pressed issuers to disguise chronic operating budget deficits. To leave no doubt as to the soundness of their budgetary operations, many states, local governments, and special jurisdictions have established, either by statute or by administrative policy, that all TANS and RANS issued in one fiscal year must be retired before the end of that fiscal year. While such a policy reduces the flexibility of the issuer to deal with unexpected emergencies that may occur, it does help provide protection to the noteholders against TANS and RANS ever being used for hidden deficit financing.[2]

It must be noted that in some circumstances RANS and GANS can be properly issued for periods greater than 12 months. For an example, RANS of the Alabama Federal Aid Highway Finance Authority were issued in July 1981 and were due 2½ years later on January 1, 1984. These RANS are in anticipation of the authority's receiving the federal share of its costs of certain interstate highway construction projects. The Federal Highway Administration has established a 36-month reimbursement schedule. Therefore, in this instance the RANS must be outstanding for a period greater than 12 months.

5. The Historic and Projected Cash Flows by Month

The last area for investigation by the investor or analyst is the TAN or RAN issuer's cash flow history and projections. Initially, what is required here is a monthly accounting, going back over the previous fiscal year, which shows the beginning fund balances, revenues, expenditures, and end-of-month fund balances. In the analysis of this actual cash flow, the investor should determine how well the issuer has met its fiscal goals by maintaining at least a balanced budget and meeting all liabilities, including debt service payments. Table 1 is a historic monthly cash flow summary for RANS that were issued by Buffalo, New York.

The second cash flow table to review is the one on the projected monthly cash flows for the fiscal year in which the TANS or RANS were to be issued. Here, the investor should look to see if the issuer has included in the projections sufficient revenues to retire the TANS or RANS, and if the estimated revenue and expenditure amounts are realistic in light of the prior fiscal year's experience. Table 2 is a projected monthly cash flow summary for RANS that were issued by Buffalo, New York.

---

[2]It should be noted that this approach toward rollovers is contrary to the position of the late Jackson Phillips, former head of Moody's municipal department, who wrote in August 1975 that "the ability to refinance (rollover or renew) a maturing note has been regarded as a valuable backstop to notes of the revenue-anticipation type. . . . Evaluation of a note must, therefore, consider . . . the availability of refinancing through market rollover. . . ." "Liquidity of Temporary Loans," *Moody's Municipal Credit Report*, August 1, 1975. However, this policy statement was made before the New York City general obligation note crisis of 1975—which occurred largely because the use of the rollover mechanism had allowed the city to avoid retiring its notes and, instead, to annually increase its short-term debt until it had become unmanageable.

Table 1

CITY OF BUFFALO
CASH RECEIPTS AND DISBURSEMENTS
(Combined City and Board of Education General Funds)
July 1, 1981 — June 30, 1982 (Actual)
(000's Omitted)

	July 1981	August 1981	September 1981	October 1981	November 1981	December 1981	January 1982	February 1982	March 1982	April 1982	May 1982	June 1982	Totals
Beginning Cash and Investments	$23,378	$27,661	$24,879	$21,334	$65,262	$50,112	$39,212	$49,854	$43,622	$34,166	$18,291	$27,240	
CASH RECEIPTS:													
Property Taxes(1)	25,445	17,023	1,443	1,461	1,646	12,008	25,566	1,402	3,567	1,348	1,468	467	92,844
State and Federal Aid(2)	4,805	867	2,866	14,044	682	6,171	4,578	16,084	3,872	1,694	26,529	57,111	139,303
Erie County Sales Tax(3)	1,537	2,049	2,030	4,847	2,191	2,138	3,538	—	5,772	6,336	556	2,204	33,198
Other Income	1,854	3,593	4,534	3,392	4,431	3,391	2,888	6,278	6,240	4,154	3,892	10,435	55,082
Temporary Loans				50,000				19,000					69,000
TOTAL CASH RECEIPTS	$33,641	$23,532	$10,873	$73,744	$8,950	$23,708	$36,570	$42,764	$19,451	$13,532	$32,445	$70,217	$389,427
CASH DISBURSEMENTS:													
Operations	$21,026	$26,314	$14,418	$29,816	$24,100	$29,715	$25,928	$23,996	$28,907	$29,407	$23,496	$28,873	$305,996
To Capital Debt Service Fund	8,332					4,893							13,225
Temporary Loans Repaid								25,000				44,000	69,000
TOTAL CASH DISBURSEMENTS	$29,358	$26,314	$14,418	$29,816	$24,100	$34,608	$25,928	$48,996	$28,907	$29,407	$23,496	$72,873	$388,221
Ending Cash and Investments	$27,661	$24,879	$21,334	$65,262	$50,112	$39,212	$49,854	$43,622	$34,166	$18,291	$27,240	$24,584	

(1) Property taxes received in fiscal year 1981-82 exceed those projected to be received in fiscal year 1982-83 mainly due to the amount of taxes in arrears, including demolition assessments, paid by the City to the City Treasurer in 1981-82 as a result of acquisition of property by the City through "in rem" foreclosure proceedings.

(2) State and Federal Aid received in fiscal year 1981-82 is less than that projected to be received in fiscal year 1982-83 as a result of $13.7 million of overburden aid due in June 1982 but received on July 2, 1982, plus $9 million of additional aid to education expected to be received in fiscal year 1982-83.

(3) Erie County Sales Tax receipts are lower in fiscal year 1981-82 than projected for fiscal year 1982-83 as a result of a payment of approximately $3.0 million expected to be received in June 1982 but actually received in July 1982.

Source: Official statement for $50 million Buffalo, New York, RAN sale of August 5, 1980.

Table 2

CITY OF BUFFALO

CASH RECEIPTS AND DISBURSEMENTS
(Combined City and Board of Education General Funds)

July 1, 1982 — August 31, 1982 (Actual)
September 1, 1982 — June 30, 1983 (Projected)
(000's Omitted)

	July 1982	August 1982	September 1982	October 1982	November 1982	December 1982	January 1983	February 1983	March 1983	April 1983	May 1983	June 1983	Totals
Beginning Cash and Investments	$24,584	$39,547	$36,991	$26,553	$77,680	$63,131	$46,843	$55,206	$51,410	$40,019	$23,945	$32,730	
CASH RECEIPTS:													
Property Taxes(1)	19,526	23,114	1,302	1,302	1,475	11,194	23,863	1,302	3,297	1,215	1,302	867	89,759
State and Federal Aid(2)	20,574	1,133	3,380	14,437	3,953	3,838	3,395	13,948	6,324	2,662	28,872	73,609	176,125
Erie County Sales Tax(3)	4,839	2,237	2,147	5,138	2,287	2,252	3,730	3,906	2,182	6,686	563	2,344	38,311
Other Income	833	5,218	4,235	3,147	2,938	5,333	3,155	2,828	6,386	3,138	3,828	5,249	46,288
Temporary Loans				60,000									60,000
TOTAL CASH RECEIPTS	$45,772	$31,702	$11,064	$84,024	$10,653	$22,617	$34,143	$21,984	$18,189	$13,701	$34,565	$82,069	$410,483
CASH DISBURSEMENTS:													
Operations	$22,262	$34,258	$21,502	$32,897	$25,202	$34,097	$25,780	$25,780	$29,580	$29,775	$25,780	$33,880	$340,793
To Capital Debt Service Fund	8,547					4,808							13,355
Temporary Loans Repaid												60,000	60,000
TOTAL CASH DISBURSEMENTS	$30,809	$34,258	$21,502	$32,897	$25,202	$38,905	$25,780	$25,780	$29,580	$29,775	$25,780	$93,880	$414,148
Ending Cash and Investments	$39,547	$36,991	$26,553	$77,680	$63,131	$46,843	$55,206	$51,410	$40,019	$23,945	$32,730	$20,919	

(1) Property taxes received in fiscal year 1981-82 exceed those projected to be received in fiscal year 1982-83 mainly due to the amount of taxes in arrears, including demolition assessments, paid by the City to the City Treasurer in 1981-82 as a result of acquisition of property by the City through "in rem" foreclosure proceedings.

(2) State and Federal Aid received in fiscal year 1981-82 is less than that projected to be received in fiscal year 1982-83 as a result of $13.7 million of overburden aid due in June 1982 but received on July 2, 1982, plus $9 million of additional aid to education expected to be received in fiscal year 1982-83.

(3) Erie County Sales Tax receipts are lower in fiscal year 1981-82 than projected for fiscal year 1982-83 as a result of a payment of approximately $3.0 million expected to be received in June 1982 but actually received in July 1982.

Source: Official statement for $50 million Buffalo, New York, RAN sale of August 5, 1980.

THE SECURITY BEHIND BOND ANTICIPATION NOTES

BANS are secured principally by the ability of the issuers to have future access to the municipal bond market so as to retire the outstanding BANS with the proceeds of long-term bond sales. Additionally, it must be noted that most BANS issued by states, counties, cities, towns, and school districts are also secured by the general obligation pledge, which is discussed latter in this chapter.

INFORMATION NEEDED BEFORE BUYING BOND ANTICIPATION NOTES

Two factors determine the ability of the issuers to gain market access. Therefore, the BAN investors should obtain information in these areas:

1. The credit worthiness of the issuers.
2. Expected future market conditions and the flexibility of the issuers.

Each is discussed below.

1. Credit Worthiness of the Issuers

Since the outstanding BANS are to be retired with the proceeds of long-term bond sales, the credit worthiness of the BANS are directly related to the credit worthiness of the underlying bond issuers. Therefore, the investor must obtain the same credit information on the BANS that he would if long-term bonds were being issued. In general, the stronger the bond credits, the greater are the abilities of the BAN issuers to successfully complete their respective long-term bond sales. Additionally, the investor or analyst should also make a determination as to the probable market access and acceptance of the BAN issuer. That is, in the past how well have the bonds of the issuer been received in the marketplace? Has the issuer had to pay interest costs substantially higher than other bond issuers that were of similar credit worthiness? Answers to these questions will determine the credit risks involved when purchasing the BANS.

2. Expected Future Market Conditions and the Flexibility of the Issuers

While it is not possible for the BAN investor to know in advance the condition of the market when his BANS come due, it is safe to conclude that, if the issuer's credit worthiness is at least of investment-grade quality, there should usually be a market for that issuer's bonds. Of course, the weaker the credit worthiness and the larger the amount of BANS to be retired, the higher the rate of interest would have to be.

If the BANS come due at a time when the municipal bond market is experiencing rising interest rates, the BAN issuer should have the flexibility to retire the maturing BANS with a new new BAN issue instead of issuing long-term bonds. Most state and local government finance regulations recognize this need for allowing BANS to be retired from new BAN issues. Also, the ability of the issuer to refund, in the municipal market, the maturing BANS with new BANS is directly related to the credit quality of the issuer. It should also be noted that, unlike most TANS and RANS, BANS can be refunded— i.e., rolled over—into new BANS. However, prudent issuers usually are limited by local laws to having their BANS outstanding for no longer than five to eight years. If there is no limit as to how long the BANS can be outstanding, the temptation is great for the BAN issuer to avoid funding out the BANS with a bond issue.

SECURITY BEHIND THE GENERAL OBLIGATION PLEDGE

Many TANS and RANS issued by states, cities, towns, counties, and school districts, are secured by the general obligation pledge. What this means is that the issuers are legally obligated to use, if necessary, their full taxing powers and available revenues to pay the noteholders. Therefore, if a tax anticipation note is issued by a city secured by property taxes as well as by the general obligation pledge, and if the city's property tax collection rate that particular year does not generate sufficient taxes to pay the noteholder, the city must use other resources to make the noteholder whole, including available monies in its general fund. Of course, the importance of the general obligation pledge is directly related to the diversification of the issuer's revenue base and lack of dependence on note sales, as well as on the soundness of its budgetary operations. Many BANS are also secured by the general obligation pledge of the issuer. If the overall credit quality, revenue structure, and market image of the underlying general obligation issuer are stronger than those of the agency or department that has issued the BANS, then the general obligation pledge would be a positive factor since it would strengthen market access either for a rollover of the BANS or for retiring them with the proceeds of a long-term bond sale.

CONCLUSION

While the credit analysis of notes has certain similarities to the analysis of long-term bonds, note analysis presents some additional challenges for the analyst or investor. In the above discussion, the more important areas of concern are identified. They should be explored in detail for determining the degree of insulation from adversity of any particular note.

Construction Loan Notes

CHAPTER 33

R. Scott Richter

Vice President
Ehrlich-Bober Advisors, Inc.

INTRODUCTION

In recent years, construction loan notes have taken on an important role in providing short-term financing for construction projects, particularly in the area of multifamily housing. The incentives to obtain the lower cost of financing availed through the sale of construction loan notes are clear. However, the complexities involved with the security mechanism and the structuring of a construction loan note financing is not often quite as self-evident. To understand a construction loan note financing, an analyst must be familiar with cash flow analysis, mortgage financing, Federal Housing Administration insurance, and (as applicable in multifamily housing projects) the Department of Housing and Urban Development (HUD) rental assistance payments made pursuant to its Section 8 program. In this chapter, a framework has been developed to assist in providing analysts with a basic understanding of the security pledged to noteholders, as well as a depiction of the financial flows required to assure a solvent construction loan note security.

389

PURPOSE

Construction loan notes have been sold to provide short-term (usually securities which mature within three years) construction financing for multifamily housing projects. These housing projects, which enjoy the benefits of relatively low-cost, tax-exempt financing, are tenantable by low- to moderate-income people defined as those persons who qualify for rent subsidy payments under the Department of Housing and Urban Development's Section 8 assistance program.

Hospitals and nursing homes have also used construction loan notes as a source of financing. However, the amount of financing underwritten for these purposes pales in comparison with the volume of notes sold to finance construction for multifamily housing projects. Therefore, to satisfy the major thrust of questions concerning construction loan note financing, this chapter concentrates on short-term financing for multifamily housing projects.

INCENTIVES FOR CONSTRUCTION LOAN NOTE FINANCING

Construction loan notes are used as a source for financing because they usually avail lower-cost funds. Issuers of notes are generally able to capture a lower rate of interest than the cost of borrowing incurred in the long-term market. Even though long-term financing eventually becomes a cost factor in the project, the use of notes defers the higher costs of long-term financing at least until the project is completed. These lower financing costs enable the note issuer to generate more arbitrage earnings, thereby improving on the security of the investment. Pursuant to Internal Revenue Service regulations, the proceeds of tax-exempt borrowers can be invested in "unrestricted-yield, taxable securities" for a specified period sometimes extending up to three years.[1] This unique relationship—where tax-exempt borrowers are allowed to reinvest note proceeds into considerably higher-yielding taxable securities for temporary periods—provides an additional source of income which enhances the security. *Analysts should check the note indenture to make sure these arbitrage earnings are pledged to the noteholders.*

APPROACHES TO CONSTRUCTION LOAN NOTE FINANCINGS

Essentially, construction loan notes have taken on two forms: first, the construction loan note (CLN) which usually ties FHA mortgage

---

[1]Frederic L. Ballard, Jr., *ABCs of Arbitrage,* rev. ed. (Packard Press, 1981), p. 1. See Chapter 15 of *The Municipal Bond Handbook: Volume I* (Homewood, Ill.: Dow Jones-Irwin, 1983) for a discussion of arbitrage restrictions.

insurance into its security blanket; second, turnkey project notes which do not typically resort to FHA insurance but rather incorporate a layer of payment and performance bonds in combination, at times, with a letter of credit approximating 25 percent of the project as additional protection.

The construction loan note approach shifts the weight of the construction risk primarily onto the back of the FHA mortgage insurance component. This mortgage insurance protects against construction problems such as delays caused by soft foundations, defective materials, nonconformity with building codes, building supply problems, labor disputes, inclement weather, and many other unpredictable events. The importance of the FHA mortgage insurance is that it affords noteholders the prospect that their interest and principal payments will be met in spite of problems encountered in the construction phase.

In the event the construction project is completed in a timely manner, as in a great majority of cases, the notes are generally repaid by one of two methods. First, long-term bonds can be used as a source of financing to pay the notes at maturity or appropriate call date after the construction is completed. Bonds are sold at the time of the note sale to assure the availability of long-term financing and to lock in the cost of capital. The second approach incorporates a note takeout from the Government National Mortgage Agency (GNMA). The GNMA takeout provides the substantial amount of moneys needed to redeem the notes and thereby is the source for the long-term financing of the project.

Turnkey project notes recently have become more plentiful as housing authorities have chosen this method to produce more cost-effective public housing projects. Essentially, turnkey project notes are sold to finance construction of a housing project; and the housing authority, backed by HUD's pledge of full faith and credit, enters a contract to purchase the completed project. The HUD purchase provides the takeout for the notes, but only if the completed project conforms with HUD's standards. Technically, if there is a failure by the developer/contractor to meet HUD requirements, the final buyout does not have to occur. If HUD does not purchase the project, noteholders must look to the payment/performance bonds and/or the letter of credit which developers should have pledged as additional security. Obviously, the need for reliable and experienced contractors is even more imperative when turnkey construction is involved.

As presented, construction loan notes and turnkey project notes differ in the type of protection extended to investors. With the FHA insurance, the CLN security structure is more direct than that of turnkey project notes, which incorporate a more complex security mechanism. In many other respects, however, these note structures face similar hurdles in their security and cash flow designs. To assist

analysts in their understanding of construction loan note alternatives, a typical security statement has been dissected in a step-by-step
approach in the following sections of this chapter. Furthermore, it
should be understood that, while only one approach is exemplified
here, there are countless ways to structure these note financings, and
analysts must always be on the lookout for shifts in security and
structure so that a proper understanding of the note structure is in
hand.

BASIC COMPONENTS FOR SECURITY INVESTMENT

In order for the analyst to assess the ultimate investment question
of whether or not an issuer can meet interest when due as well as
maturing principal, the security pledged to the noteholders must be
understood. The following is from a recent official statement setting
forth the note security which is typical of many construction loan
note financings for multifamily housing. Essentially, there are three
aspects of the note security which an analyst must come to grips with:
(1) determining which assets are pledged to the noteholders; (2) ascertaining how these assets are protected during the vulnerable
stages of construction; and (3) knowing how these pledged assets generate cash to meet the interest and principal requirements on the
notes.

Security

The notes will be special obligations payable solely from and secured
by a pledge of the following revenues and assets to the extent deposited
or to be deposited in the construction loan account: (1) unexpended proceeds of the notes; (2) payments representing principal or interest due
under the construction loans; (3) proceeds from the assignment or sale
of construction loans to GNMA or others; (4) proceeds from or on account of the deposit agreement and the yield-maintenance agreement,
as hereinafter defined; (5) any amounts received by the corporation as
a result of proceedings taken in the event of a default on a construction
loan, including proceeds of federal mortgage insurance; (6) any income
derived from the investment of the foregoing; (7) proceeds of any obligations of the corporation issued to pay or renew the notes; and (8)
amounts with respect to proceeds of any deposit of cash, letters of credit,
or promissory notes for the GNMA discount.[2]

A description of the note obligation and the eight components of security pledged in the above example are explained in more detail below.

---

[2]Official statement for $75,775,000 of New York City Housing Development Corpo-
ration—Construction Loan Notes, 1981 Series A, January 20, 1981, pp. 4–5.

Note Obligation

The analyst's first step in understanding the security statement is to recognize the type of obligation that is presented. The nature of the notes is spelled out in the opening statement of our example in that they are special obligations of the issuing agency. This begins to set the stage for further research in determining the inherent security extended to the special obligation pledge.

The bond analyst will usually run into two forms of note obligations—the special obligation and the general obligation. Usually, a special obligation pledge limits an investor's claim to the revenues and assets related to the project financed by the notes. A general obligation pledge commonly avails all the unencumbered assets of the issuing agency. Obviously, from the investor's viewpoint, a general obligation pledge has more meaning if the issuer has other assets generating surplus revenue which, if needed, would be available to the noteholders.

The usefulness of a general obligation pledge is exemplified when linked to a state housing finance agency which has demonstrated a favorable track record and may have accumulated surplus revenues from previous projects. Analysts, however, should look beyond the bottom line to determine the likelihood that any surplus funds will remain. The first check should be directed to ascertaining the amount of outstanding general obligations in relation to any surplus. Today's surplus may be needed tomorrow by those agencies which might experience cash flow shortages because of overestimating mortgage prepayments in their single-family mortgage programs and/or rising mortgage delinquencies. Also, during periods when states face federal cutbacks in aid or imminent contraction in other state tax revenues, any large surplus built up by the state's housing finance agency may be looked upon as a potential source of funds and, in some instances, can be reappropriated by the state.

The special obligation pledge is usually limited to the assets financed by the particular issue. Local housing authorities (cities, towns, counties) tend to incorporate the special obligation pledge into their programs. This approach enables the authority to keep the project revenue separate from any other programs, allowing the simplification of bookkeeping and the clean passing of certain financial management and oversight responsibilities to the trustee.

It should also be recognized that a special or general obligation pledge does not imply the ability to impose a tax. For the most part, state and local housing authorities are not granted the ability to tax. Some state housing agencies, however, have been granted access to certain forms of tax revenues through the moral obligation pledge pertaining to debt service reserve fund makeup provisions. (See

Chapter 30.) One example would be the Idaho State Housing Finance Agency, whose debt service reserve fund is indirectly tied to state sales tax revenues.[3]

Note Proceeds

The unexpended proceeds of notes (refer to item (1) of the above excerpt) should be pledged to noteholders as a component of the note security. The availability of unexpended proceeds to noteholders is important, particularly when the project is not completed or construction costs are overestimated. These excess funds are then available to meet debt service requirements.

Construction Loan Payments

Construction loan payments (refer to item (2) of the security excerpt) are a necessary ingredient in the security of the notes. As note proceeds are apportioned to the contractor to pay for construction, a construction loan rate on these distributions must be established at a level sufficient to cover the interest cost of the notes. The rate typically is set at least 1 to 2 percent above the cost of the note borrowing.

It is important to recognize that the interest to be paid by the contractor on the construction loan is generally capitalized in the mortgagable amount. This eliminates any concern that a contractor or developer will not be able to meet its interest payment requirements under the construction loan agreement. However, the issue of timely completion is still a critical element in any construction financing. To satisfy investor concerns over the prospect of noncompletion, construction insurance is generally required to cover noteholder obligations in the event of damages to the project or construction delays. In construction loan note financings, insurance provided by the Federal Housing Administration should be required in the bond indenture. As discussed in more detail in the section on FHA insurance, projects constructed under the umbrella of federal insurance are stipulated to have each construction loan advance insured by FHA. This protects the investor against loss of principal and interest income in the event ensuing problems are encountered and the project cannot be completed in a timely manner.

In those note financings, typically turnkey project notes which do not rely upon FHA insurance, the analyst should look for a strong performance and payment bond (surety bond) and/or a letter-of-credit pledge amounting to 25 percent of the total loan. The 25 percent

---

[3]Official statement for $16,220,000 of Idaho Housing Agency—Insured Section 8 Assisted Housing Bonds, 1980 Series A, September 5, 1980, pp. 8–9.

level, which now appears to have become the norm, seems to have been established as an acceptable level to both the issuers and investors. As an adjunct to a letter of credit, collateral in the form of mortgages or securities may be stipulated in the bond indenture to be posted by lenders, which provides additional security protection.

The presence of a surety bond places the developer's assets at risk in the event the projects are not completed in a timely manner. The surety is provided by a surety bond company which issues bonds to assure completion of construction. There are usually two types: a payment bond and a performance bond. The payment bond assures payment of subcontractors in the event the developer fails. The performance bond relates to timeliness of the project. In the event the project is behind schedule, the surety bond company can appropriate the developer's assets and spend those funds to get the project back on schedule. A deficiency in disclosure in most offering official statements to investors appears to be that the surety bond companies are not mentioned by name. Although the great majority are financially sound, knowing which insurance company or companies are involved would heighten the investor's awareness of the strength of his downside protection.

It is also important for analysts to review the developer's capability and previous experience in regard to completing similar projects. Although the past is not always prologue in the construction industry, there is some comfort in knowing if the contractor has participated in similar-sized construction projects. Relying upon proven contractors helps to avoid the possibility of taking on a neophyte contractor who may unwittingly experience developmental problems and, in turn, cause unscheduled delays and potential cash flow problems. This is particularly important in turnkey construction projects where HUD can elect *not* to accept the project if it is completed in a manner which does not conform with its standards.

Incentives for Contractor's Performance

Contractors carry out their obligations for two main reasons: first, their own capital is at risk; second, if a project is not completed, there will be no profit for them. In very general terms, an FHA 221(d)(4) insured housing project is insured for approximately 90 percent of its total requirement costs. The remaining 10 percent is equity provided by the developer in two forms. About one fifth of a developer's equity is cash and letters of credit, expended first on project costs. This places the developer's funds on the line, serving as an element of risk to the developer in the event the project is not completed. The remaining four fifths of the developer's equity is mortgagable by HUD and therefore is apportioned into the total cost of the project.

Upon completion, the developer sells the project to limited partnerships while usually retaining a ½ of 1 percent equity interest and the management rights in the project. The sale of the project enables the developer to liquidate its majority interest in the project and realize the projected gains. These limited partnerships have been easy to sell as tax shelters because of the generous tax benefits and cash flow which they provide to investors in high tax brackets. Tax losses accrue from the depreciation of the housing project and other special tax benefits made available to low-income new/rehabilitation housing projects. The cash flow is derived from any surplus rental income. If the developers do not perform, they do not realize any profit and face the likely prospect of not participating in any future public housing projects.

Permanent Financing Mechanism

Permanent financing (item (3) of the above excerpt) must be in place in order to provide for the timely redemption of the construction loan notes. (Turnkey project notes rely upon HUD, acting through the local authority, to purchase the project after completion.) Since a housing project is generally geared to a 20–40 year payout period, funding of short-term construction loan notes by longer-term financing is imperative. In the past, there have been two forms of long-term financing utilized to fund notes.

Regulations promulgated by HUD and the IRS, for the most part, shape the kind of long-term financing which is used. On the local level, such as a city or county project, bonds can be sold simultaneously with the notes to secure the cost of capital and to assure the availability of the long-term financing. This approach falls under the purview of HUD's Section 8–11(b) regulations. (Interest requirements on the long-term financing are met by investing bond proceeds in higher-yielding taxable securities, during the construction period as permitted by IRS arbitrage regulations.)

When a simultaneous note/bond financing is being reviewed, analysts should also ascertain the timing as to when bond proceeds are made available to noteholders. As outlined in the FHA insurance discussion below, there is typically a 6- to 12-month period (usually 8 months for tax-exempt financings) before the FHA insurance is processed and the proceeds availed to pay the claim. In most note/bond financings, bond proceeds are not available to pay noteholders until the final FHA insurance endorsement is obtained. However, in some cases, the bond indenture may permit bond proceeds to fund noteholders if a claim to the FHA has been filed within six months of the maturity date of the notes. This provision is aimed at eliminating any snags that may occur late in the development stages, particularly with the timing of note payments. Another potential revenue source, if pledged to Section 8–11(b) noteholders, can come from surplus arbitrage earnings obtained from the investment of the long-term bond proceeds. In order to determine if such a pledge is made, analysts may have to review the documentation in the bond official statement in addition to the note official statement.

On the state level, it is customary to provide the long-term financing with GNMA takeout or by an agency bond issue. Essentially, a GNMA takeout provides 97.5 percent of the total amount of the financing required to meet the maturing notes. The remaining 2½ percent, which analysts should make sure is available, is usually provided by developers in the form of a letter of credit which is pledged to noteholders in the event other income sources, such as investment income, have not covered this differential.

Locking up long-term financing at the inception of the project is important in that it not only eliminates the risk that there will be no permanent financing available when the notes mature but it also sets the cost of that financing. This assures project owners and investors that permissible HUD rent levels under Section 8 will provide sufficient rental income to cover debt service and expected operating costs of the project.

Investment Agreement

The investment agreement (item (4) of the excerpt) relates to the investment of note proceeds prior to the disbursement of the construction loan advances. This agreement should be arranged to yield a rate of return which is higher than the interest cost of the notes. With the IRS allowing unrestricted yield investment (tax-exempt note proceeds temporarily invested in taxable securities) for certain specified periods sometimes extending up to three years, obtaining a positive rate of return has not been difficult for issuers of CLNs. This agreement should be signed prior to the sale of the notes in order to avoid taking the chance that subsequent market fluctuations may result in lower-than-expected arbitrage earnings.

Once a project is completed under GNMA financing, it usually takes about two to three months until the GNMA takeout occurs. With the GNMA interest rate set at a subsidized level (currently at 7.5 percent), this rate may not cover the interest rate on the notes (as depicted in the cash flow example later in this chapter where the interest rate on the notes is 10 percent). Calculations must be made to determine whether sufficient earnings will be obtained to close any interest gap during the period after the GNMA takeout and the maturity of the notes. As an additional layer of security, a 2 percent working-capital letter of credit may be required to be supplied by the developers in order to offset any potential shortfalls.

Federal Housing Administration Insurance

The multifamily housing projects financed by the construction loan notes may be insured under FHA insurance Section 221(d)(4) (item (5) of the excerpt). The major reason for incorporating FHA insurance is that notes tend to be unsalable when mortgage insurance or strong performance and payment bonds are not present. Risks in uninsured construction are great—delays are incurred, foundations sink, and developers default. Under 221(d)(4), these risks are not the investors' concerns but rather HUD's problems to the extent that HUD insures each construction loan advance so that the investor is assured that his money eventually will be returned.

In the event of a default, the question of timeliness in the receipt of FHA insurance benefits must be considered. Under Section 221(d)(4), notice to HUD should be filed 30 days after default. It is the responsibility of the project manager and/or trustee to report any default to HUD. If the management/trustee is remiss and notification is delayed beyond the 30-day waiting period, the project's cash flow may be impaired. After the 30-day period, the authority (mortgagee) can either assign the mortgage to HUD or go through foreclosure, which means the authority must take title to the project and then pass that title along to HUD. For investors, it is desirable to see the authority covenant to assign the mortgage to HUD because foreclosure can be a complicated and time-consuming process. Any snags encountered during foreclosure proceedings can increase the chance that any insurance payments will not arrive in time to redeem the notes when due.

When assigning a defaulted mortgage to HUD/FHA pursuant to Section 207 of the National Housing Act, a 1 percent assignment fee is required. When reviewing a state 103(b) note financing which falls under the purview of Section 207 of the National Housing Act, analysts must make sure that provisions have been made to cover the interest which will accrue over the 30-day waiting period before HUD is notified of the default, and check to see that resources are available to meet the 1 percent assignment fee. Under Section 8–11(b), HUD does not require an assignment fee, thus the analyst only has to address the 30-day waiting period.

To put these factors into perspective, on a 9 percent loan the 1 percent assignment fee and the 30-day filing period which equals $\frac{1}{12}$ of the interest requirement would amount to about 1.75 percent of the total loan for a CLN financing sold under Section 103. Usually the 2.0–2.5 percent working-capital letter of credit posted by the developers is sufficient to offset these contingencies. The analyst will recall that this letter of credit can double as a backup for any interest rate differential between the GNMA loan rate and the interest cost of the notes.

Timing of FHA Insurance Payments. Under HUD regulations, HUD must pay 70 percent of the insurance claim within 15 days and the balance, after audit, within 3 to 12 months.[4] However, HUD has given certain assurances that tax-exempt financings will be processed for insurance in six months or less, provided HUD is notified that the project is being financed with tax-exempt funds.[5]

HUD Debenture Rate. The HUD debenture rate is the rate of interest which is paid on the outstanding balance of the mortgage. Interest starts to accrue on the insured loan balance at the time HUD is notified of a default (after the 30-day assignment period), and interest continues to accrue until the final insurance payment is received. The HUD debenture rate as of January 1982 was set at 12¾ percent. Since this rate is adjusted to reflect current market conditions, the analyst must make sure the debenture rate (an interest-only payment) is at least equal to the interest cost of the notes in order to assure a positive cash flow.

Noteholder's Right to Income Derived from Assets

The noteholder's right (item (6) of the excerpt) to any income derived from the investment of the assets pledged under the indenture includes interest income, rental income, letters of credit, and fees, among other items.

Section 8—Rent Assistance. Since the projects are geared to low- to moderate-income families in areas where a need for subsidized housing exists, demand for the projects generally is not a problem, particularly when the tenant is required to pay only 15 to 30 percent of his adjusted income on rent when comparable quality housing is available only at significantly higher cost levels. The difference between the fair-market rent, as established by HUD, and the tenant's contribution is paid by HUD under its Section 8 rent subsidy program. If vacancies exist, HUD rental assistance continues for 60 days at a level equal to 80 percent of the vacant unit's rent. After 60 days, vacancy assistance can continue for up to 12 months but at an adjusted level to reflect only the apartment's apportioned share of the debt service cost.

---

[4]Official statement, New York City Housing Development Corporation, p. 9.
[5]*Revised Rating Criteria for Securities with FHA Multifamily Mortgage Insurance* (New York: Standard & Poor's, May 1980).

Renewal Notes

The noteholder's right to the proceeds of any renewal notes (item (7) of the security excerpt) gives the issuer more flexibility in the event the outstanding notes must be refinanced or refunded. If the project is not completed in a timely manner, renewal notes may be sold to redeem the original notes and to provide the additional time necessary for project completion.

Letters of Credit—Cash Deposits

Any moneys available for cash deposits, letters of credit, or promissory notes for the GNMA discount (item (8) of the security excerpt) are pledged to noteholders to cover the gaps for the GNMA spread and the FHA insurance workout (30-day lag and 1 percent assignment fee). In addition, these deposits/letters of credit provide more incentive for the developers to perform, as their capital is tied to these security enhancements.

Project Substitutability

Many agencies, particularly those that are involved with numerous projects such as the state agencies, have the flexibility to substitute projects. Analysts should not be too concerned with this apparent agility in that project substitution can only be effectively dealt with early on, prior to any investment in bricks and mortar. Once a project is started, those funds expended are generally irretrievable. Projects that cannot be finished must have adequate insurance or alternative protection, such as a letter of credit and/or pledged payment and performance bonds to meet investors' claims.

CASH FLOW

Now that the analyst has had a chance to review the basic components of the security pledged to noteholders, the next section will delve into how the elements of the note security interact and generate cash flow to meet the requirements of interest when due and principal as it matures for the notes.

The cash flow illustration below depicts a financially successful project. In order to assure a financially solvent project, certain protective measures must be incorporated. These backstops must cover the expenses related to the selling of the notes, the possible need of recouping the amount of money equal to one month's interest cost, and the 1 percent assignment fee when applicable under a state 103(b) FHA-insured financing. Depending on the size of the financing, the costs of issuance can run 1.5 percent to 3 percent of the loan. Taking the midpoint (2.25 percent) and adding the other factors—one month's interest plus the 1 percent assignment fee, which approximates 1.75 percent—you have a differential of 4 percent which must be covered by various combinations.

To offset this 4 percent differential, issuers rely upon (1) positive arbitrage earnings on the investment agreement; (2) an irrevocable letter of credit or a promissory note which is obtained from the developers; (3) in the case of a state agency, the agency itself, which can set aside surplus funds that can be obtained by state appropriation; (4) equity contributions from developers; and (5) the sale of premium bonds, in that the developer essentially subsidizes the loan by paying a higher loan rate on advances for construction.

The following pages contain a cash flow breakdown for a typical local housing project financed with notes under Section 8–11(b). It should be mentioned that in the cash flow statement, for simplicity, semiannual construction disbursements have been assumed while in reality these disbursements are generally made on a monthly basis.

In the Section 8–11 (b) model, it is assumed $1 million of 10 percent notes dated January 1, 1980, maturing on January 1, 1983, and callable on January 1, 1982 at 100, have been sold to finance a 20-unit, multifamily project. The notes will be paid after the project is finished in two years from proceeds of the bond sale which typically occurs simultaneously with the note sale.

The note sale produces $980,000 after deducting $20,000 for issuance costs, of which $232,500 is earmarked for the first construction loan advance. The remainder, $747,500, is temporarily invested pursuant to the investment agreement. As the construction loan advances are drawn down, the investment income earned from the temporary investments decreases. However, this reduction in cash flow is substantially replaced by the interest income earned on the construction loan. Interest income on the construction loan is usually capitalized from note proceeds, as construction loan interest is considered a mortgagable expense by HUD. Also capitalized from note proceeds is a portion of the interest expense on the notes.

After the project is completed, the issuer can use the bond proceeds to call the notes at par. In other instances, the notes will remain outstanding until maturity if the bond proceeds can be reinvested in a way to cover the interest cost of the notes. (Sometimes the notes are noncallable.) These investments are often prearranged as a part of the investment agreements.

As seen in Exhibit 1, rental income begins after the project is completed. Usually, apartment rental income is the main revenue source to pay debt service on the bonds; but while the notes remain outstanding, rental income is generally pledged to noteholders. To offset unexpected costs, funds in the surplus account, as well as Section 8 vacancy assistance payments, may be used as a resource.

Exhibit 1
Cash Flow Illustration for a Note Financing Issue under Section 8–11(6) ($1 million of notes sold resulting in $980,000 of proceeds after issuance costs; $000)

	1-1-80	7-1-80	1-1-81	7-1-81	1-1-82	7-1-82	1-1-83
Note proceeds in temporary investments	$747.5	$515.0	$282.5	$ 50.0	$ 0	—	—
Investment income at 14 percent[a]	—	52.3	36.0	19.8	3.5	—	—
Construction loan advance	232.5	465.0	697.5	930.0	980.0	—	—
Interest income at 12 percent[b]	—	14.0	27.9	41.8	55.8	—	—
Rental income	—	—	—	—	—	$30.0[d]	$60.0[ef]
Total income	—	$ 66.3	$ 63.9	$ 61.6	$ 59.3	—	—
Total interest expense	—	50.0	50.0	50.0	50.0[g]	—	—
Surplus funds[c]	—	16.3	13.9	11.6	19.3	—	—
Accumulated surplus balance	—	16.3	30.2	41.8	51.1	—	—

[a]Short-term temporary investments made pursuant to prearranged agreements.
[b]Construction loan—interest on this loan is usually capitalized from note proceeds.
[c]Surplus fund not reinvested in this example, but in actuality it is.
[d]$500/month/unit × 6 months × 50 percent vacancy during rent-up (assumption) = $30,000.
[e]$500/month/unit rent = approximately $125 tenant contribution + $375 HUD rental assistance/unit basis.
[f]$500/month/unit × 6 months = $60,000 rental income.
[g]Notes assumed to be called at par on 1-1-82.

The cash flow is substantially the same for a 103(b) note financing as it is for a Section 8–11(b) note issue, with two caveats. First, sufficient reserves must be generated to cover the two- to seven-month period between the time the project is completed and the GNMA takeout is effected. Second, these reserves must cover any negative interest-rate spread between the net interest cost of the notes and the GNMA rate of 7.5 percent during the period the notes remain outstanding after the GNMA takeout occurs. Keep in mind that rental income and Section 8 vacancy assistance may also be used as other sources of income, and that capitalized construction loan income and capitalized note interest may also be available.

MARKETABILITY OF CONSTRUCTION LOAN NOTES

Construction loan notes sold by established state housing finance agencies tend to command lower rates than local agencies involved in one or two projects. Furthermore, turnkey project notes usually trade at higher yield levels relative to their FHA-insured counterparts. Secondary market transactions generally parallel the behavior of the primary market pricing for these notes on both the bid side and the offered side of the market.

CONCLUSION

Construction loan notes and turnkey project notes, if properly structured, can offer investors a well-secured investment alternative in the short maturity range of one to three years. Investors will achieve comfort from those CLNs which have the sponsorship of an experienced state housing finance agency. With an established background in multifamily developments, state housing agencies have demonstrated their capability of completing successful projects. Furthermore, a general obligation pledge from a healthy state agency gives an investor the knowledge that other resources and the tacit approval of a state provide additional means and flexibility in confronting any snags encountered along the construction process.

In turnkey project notes, construction risk is amplified, and the role of management is even more critical in the absence of FHA insurance. It is imperative that analysts investigate the experience of the developers/contractors. The surety bonding company providing the performance and payment bonds must be of acceptable quality. Additional security such as a letter of credit or similar credit enhancement (i.e., collateral) should be posted in order to have the investment safeguarded. Furthermore, a clear statement for action in the event of default should be available, as the local housing authority in conjunction with HUD has the final say on whether or not a completed project is acceptable.

Turnkey project notes benefit in the same manner as CLNs when a strong state agency is the issuer, as more construction experience and financial resources may be at hand in the event problems are encountered. The local agency, particularly the nonprofit agency without a city or county sponsor, may be more susceptible to payment delays in the event construction problems are encountered, as their alternatives for remedy are less. Given this, analysts and investors can expect to see increased credit enhancements for local-agency, turnkey project notes, such as a stronger letter-of-credit backing or other forms of collateral.

There is no doubt that construction loan notes are complicated both in structuring and in their security provisions. To assure a successful financing from the credit worthiness point of view, all the pieces must be there, and only after checking for those particulars can an intelligent investment decision be made.

Tax-Exempt Commercial Paper

CHAPTER **34**

James J. Goodwin II

Director
Division of Bond Finance
State of Florida

INTRODUCTION

Since the advent of tax-exempt commercial paper in 1973, this instrument has attracted ever-increasing interest on the part of institutional investors as well as prospective issuers. Since 1980, many of the problems associated with the initial offering of such a vehicle have been solved, and many investors have become more comfortable with the concept which includes various levels of security or credit "backstops" for the benefit of the investor. This chapter traces the evolution of traditional commercial paper, some legal questions indigenous to tax-exempt commercial paper, the relative integrity of the credit support behind the issuers, and some observations on the future of its market.

EVOLUTION OF COMMERCIAL PAPER

Commercial paper is generally defined as short-term, continuously offered, negotiable debt instruments issued by businesses, and includes all bills, notes, and acceptances arising from the normal conduct of business.[1] The term is better understood to represent the short-term, unsecured, discount obligations of recognized, well-established businesses and corporations issued in large dollar amounts for various periods ranging to 270 days.

Commercial paper is no neophyte to the American financial scene. Its origins are found about the time of the Revolutionary War; in several locales, commercial paper was accepted as a stronger medium of exchange than the then fledging currencies of the separate colonies. During that period, no universal system of monetary interchange had been agreed to, and the majority of currencies issued were variously influenced by British demand for specie.

Since its inception, commercial paper has played an ever-expanding role in trade and banking. At the end of 1962, approximately $6 billion was outstanding. Year-end 1969 witnessed $32.6 billion outstanding, an increase of 443 percent. By the end of 1974, this amount surged to $53.3 billion, up 63 percent from only five years before. This represents an average annual growth of nearly 66 percent for the 12-year period ending December 1974.[2] Market growth was somewhat moderate to flat from 1974 to 1977, when year-end outstandings reached $65.1 billion. Since then, however, the market has virtually exploded, as indicated in the following seasonally adjusted outstandings:[3]

Month End	Billions
12/78	$ 83.4
12/79	112.8
12/80	125.1
12/81	162.8
12/82	166.5

The market depth has been clearly demonstrated. Some of this phenomenal growth is attributed to stronger corporate cash management practices instituted in the mid-70s and the willingness of banks to provide backstop funding facilities in tight money market conditions. The latter enabled investment bankers to offer the very short corporate debt with assurances that a fickle market acceptance could be offset by the bank funding. The institutional investor imputed a higher order of security to such an arrangement and eagerly sought to commit idle short-term funds to such investments, which offered rates higher than other alternatives such as repurchase agreements.[4]

---

[1]David M. Brownstone and Irene M. Frank, *The VNR Investors' Dictionary* (New York: Van Nostrand Reinhold, 1980), p. 70

[2]David M. Durst, *The Complete Bond Book* (New York: McGraw Hill, 1975) pp. 180–215.

[3]*Federal Reserve Bulletin,* August 1981, p. 327.

[4]In a repurchase agreement, the holder of securities sells these securities to another party, with an agreement to repurchase the securities at a fixed price on a specified date. The security buyer in effect lends the seller money for the period of the agreement, and the terms of the agreement are structured to compensate the lender. See Chapter 26.

Indeed, several issuers found the market so active that they started issuing the obligations directly instead of through their investment banker. As of this writing, over 1,000 issuers participate in the market, and indicators project continued growth both in outstandings as well as issuers.

The mid-70s saw some changes take place in the tax-exempt market as well. The Urban Development Corporation default, quickly followed by the New York City general obligation note defaults, caused a great deal of general concern in the investment community, in the short-term market in particular.[5] Aside from the then more prevailing queries about the future of our older urbanized centers, decreasing tax bases, and emigration to the Sun Belt, serious questions were raised concerning debt management. For a number of years, politicians had relied upon the short-term debt markets under the guise of "cash flow" or "bridge loan" necessity and had vectored some borrowed funds into purposes other than those intended by the borrowing. They became entrapped in problems of high interest rates, market reception, revenue shortfalls, "rollovers," and workout financings, and, in some cases, were forced to surrender their financial autonomy to oversight control boards.

During 1974–76, the investing public learned to its dismay that the general obligation pledge was something less than what it was represented and what they had understood it to be. The investor became more discriminating and demanded a higher order of security to protect his investment. Issuers employed various security devices such as funds impoundment, third-party depositaries for pledged revenues, and oversight boards; but Buffalo was the first to use a commercial banking consortium to "backstop" its general obligation, short-term, revenue anticipation notes in 1975. (The "backstop" concept will be addressed later in this chapter.) The financing was well received given the tenor of the market at that time.

THE FIRST ISSUES

If tax-exempt commercial paper is defined as continually offered, flexible maturity, short-term, tax-exempt debt, then the first such issue was the Virginia Electric & Power Company's (VEPCo's) $38 million pollution control offering of December 1972. This financing was underwritten by Lehman Brothers and maintained by them for approximately two years at which time VEPCo funded the outstanding into the long-term market. The issue carried a standby line of bank credit backstopping the issue. The paper was issued at par with inter-

---

[5]See Case 1.

est accruing on an actual/365 basis instead of being discounted as was the custom with taxable commercial paper.

VEPCo II was the second tax-exempt commercial paper offering. This $27 million issue in 1977–78 was for another pollution control financing, and was also maintained by Lehman for approximately two years until it was funded by the issuance of bonds.

The third occurrence was more typical of that which we see today. The VEPCo issues were of such size that the underwriter essentially could privately place them and, in fact, directed the issues to corporate purchasers of conventional commercial paper, giving them a taxable equivalent yield equal to what they would receive in the conventional market. The third issue, a $50 million offering for the Government Development Bank for Puerto Rico (GDB), brought in late 1977, required additional marketing skill. At that time, the commonwealth's agencies and authorities had experienced some difficulty in market access caused to some extent by a "flight to quality" resulting from the New York City situation. GDB's purpose was to supply funds to these agencies and authorities through loans so as to bridge those periods when the direct issuers encountered financing difficulty. The issue was guaranteed by the commonwealth and further backstopped by a formal lending agreement with Manufacturers Hanover Trust Company of New York. For this facility, GDB paid a fee which covered both principal and interest on the outstanding paper. The issue was subsequently sized to $75 million and two years thereafter to $150 million. At the time of this writing, Manufacturers Hanover still remains behind the issue exclusively and has not syndicated the exposure.

The fourth issue was the $53 million Illinois Educational Facilities Authority program issued on behalf of Loyola University of Chicago in June 1980. This offering was also brought by Lehman Brothers and carries a backstop provided by the First National Bank of Chicago. The authorizing act of the Illinois legislature contains no restrictions on the number of times debt issued under it may be refinanced.[6] Thus, although the facility contemplates a date beyond which paper will not be issued (excluding so-called bank bonds), the financing might be "evergreen" (that is, an issue continuing to be offered for an open-ended period). This financing incorporates a unique feature of providing not only a backstop to the issuer but also a standby credit facility to the beneficiary, Loyola University.[7] The standby facility provides extra liquidity to the university in the event it cannot otherwise refund the commercial paper. It allows the uni-

---

[6]Annual official statement (1980–1981) of Illinois Educational Facilities Authority Short-Term Revenue Bond Program, October 21, 1980, p. 2.

[7]Ibid., p. 6.

versity to draw on the standby to the extent that the commercial paper and standby outstandings do not exceed $60 million. This drawdown matures in mid-1983 and is recast to a three-year term loan amortizing quarterly.

It should be noted that a number of the issues encountered while researching this chapter provide for maturities out to 360 days. In practice, little if any issuance is found between the 270–360 period. This seems to be by reason of a conservative interpretation of Section 3(a)(3) of the Securities Act of 1933, which in part provides that registration of commercial paper public offerings is required when the original maturity exceeds nine months. Tax-exempt commercial paper is doubly exempt inasmuch as municipal issues are exempt from registration.

The fifth entry in the marketplace was the Salt River Agricultural and Improvement District which offered a large $225 million package through Goldman Sachs and Co. in August 1980. This issue signaled the advent of the large public power issuers in the market referenced earlier. Although Salt River enjoyed facile market access by virtue of its bond ratings, it had determined that such a facility was cost-effective when compared to its traditional bank line arrangements given the virtually insatiable appetite for such paper by the newly organized short-term, tax-exempt funds. The Salt River issue was backed by a banking consortium providing a takeout which could reduce if not periodically renewed and thus require the utility to regularly enter the long-term market. Experience to date has indicated that Salt River has been able to issue its paper at a blended rate below that available through the banks in their backstop, even after having experienced some upwards yield adjustment caused by the effect of Economic Recovery Tax Act of 1981 upon the funds and the all-savers certificates.

At this writing, there are 47 issuers in the tax-exempt commercial paper market, accounting for approximately $3.7 billion of an authorized $3.9 billion. In early 1983, Goldman Sachs estimated that the market would approximate $6.5 billion by year-end 1983, by virtue that several more states are about to enter the market.[8]

BACKSTOP FACILITIES

All tax-exempt commercial paper issued to date has included one of several types of banking facilities which provide additional comfort to the investor. They include: an irrevocable letter of credit, a revolving credit agreement, and a line of credit.

---

[8]Discussion with S. Michael McCarthy and Phylis Esposito, Vice Presidents, Goldman Sachs & Co., New York, September 22, 1981 and March 29, 1983.

The irrevocable letter of credit is typically governed by the provisions of the Uniform Customs and Practices for Documentary Credits, 1974 Revision, and Article V of Uniform Commercial Code as adopted by the state where the issuer is located. The irrevocable letter of credit offers the highest order of security backstop. This facility essentially permits for no exculpation on the part of the issuing bank and requires the bank to pay, upon proper notices being given, the amount necessary up to the limits of the letter. One is cautioned to determine, as with other facilities, whether the backstop extends only to defaulted principal or whether it includes principal and interest through the date of default.

The revolving credit agreement is a formal facility entered into between the commercial paper issuer and the bank, for the resulting benefit of the paper holder. Although the terms of the facility are generally all-encompassing, one must examine the specifics to determine if there are exculpatory provisions (such as certain time frames) to be met which may release the issuer from performance responsibilities, or "no material adverse change" clauses which may give rise to a release of responsibility. If such language is not evident, one may fairly presume that the credit integrity of this facility is akin to that of the letter of credit.

The line of credit must be regarded as the third level of backstop, given the fact that these facilities typically provide for a wide range of release clauses which might give the issuing bank a reason not to provide funds when required. To date, no issuers have opted to use this type of backstop, although its possible usage may be foreseen by general obligation issuers with high credit integrity and market identification.

Regardless of the type of facility used, they generally provide for a period of time, after an event of default, during which the holder must assert his claim in order to benefit from the facility. These periods may run as long as 30 days following an event.

In smaller issues, it is not unusual to find one bank backstopping the facility although, partially caused by the perceived novelty of tax-exempt commercial paper, even small issues are typically syndicated among several banks. In order to garner an A1 or P1 credit rating, the backstop is usually issued by an AAA-rated institution or syndicated among a number of AAA-rated banks or otherwise similarly regarded financial institutions.

FEE AND CHARGES

Depending upon the type of backstop facility utilized, banks charge anywhere from 1/4 to 1 percent per annum with the norm ranging between 3/8 and 3/4 of 1 percent. Usually, the first year's fee is paid in advance and is not refundable. The rate attached to borrowings extended under the facility are ordinarily based on a floating percentage of the prime rate or other definitive interest-sensitive funding vehicle. These rates have spanned 60–70 percent of prime except for the rather unique pricing mechanism incorporated in the Loyola backstop issued by First National Bank of Chicago.[9]

On the distribution side, the investment bankers normally charge ⅛ of 1 percent of the balance except in pollution control issues, where the fee is somewhat higher. So far, the structure of the issue and the size do not readily lend themselves to underwriting syndication and

---

[9]Annual official statement (1980–1981), pp. 5–6. The unique pricing mechanism for this issue is described as follows:

Bank Bond Purchase Agreement. The university, the authority and the bank have entered into a bond purchase agreement dated as of May 1, 1980 . . ., pursuant to which the bank has agreed to purchase bonds having final maturities not later than 60 months from their respective dates of issuance (the bank bonds) subject to certain conditions precedent set forth therein. The purpose of the bank bond purchase agreement is to provide the university and the authority with a measure of liquidity in the event short-term bonds cannot be sold to refund previously issued short-term bonds. The bank bonds will bear interest at a rate of interest equal to the lesser of (1) 18 percent or (2) 75 percent of the base rate (defined therein) if the aggregate principal amount of bank bonds outstanding is not in excess of $30 million, and 80 percent of the base rate if such aggregate outstanding principal amount exceeds $30 million. The base rate . . . is defined as the greater of (1) the corporate base rate (as announced by the bank from time to time) or (2) one half of 1 percent plus 115 percent of the latest three-week moving average of secondary market morning offering rates in the U.S. money market banks. The bank bonds will bear interest quarterly, and principal will be payable in quarterly installments commencing June 25, 1985, with a final maturity in each case not later than 60 months from the respective dates of issuance of such bank bonds. The bank bonds are prepayable at any time and may be converted into short-term bonds 120 days after issuance pursuant to, and in accordance with, the bank bond purchase agreement.

Standby Credit Agreement. The university and the bank have entered into a standby credit agreement dated as of May 1, 1980 . . ., for the purpose of providing the university with a measure of liquidity in the event that all or any portion of the short-term bonds or the bank bonds could not be sold to finance the project or cannot be sold to refund the short-term bonds. The standby credit agreement provides for the bank to loan the university up to $60 million reduced by the amount of loans made thereunder and the principal amount of outstanding bank bonds, subject to certain conditions which are similar to the conditions precedent to the issuance of bank bonds. Loans made under the standby credit agreement will be evidenced by a revolving credit note bearing interest at the base rate and maturing June 1, 1983. The revolving credit note may be converted at the option of the university to a term loan bearing interest at the base rate plus one fourth of 1 percent per annum and maturing in 12 substantially equal quarterly installments of principal beginning June 25, 1985, and ending March 25, 1988.

Conditions to Bank's Obligations. The bank bond purchase agreement contains certain covenants and agreements of the university, the compliance with which is a condition precedent to the obligation of the bank to purchase bank bonds thereunder. Included are covenants of the university requiring the maintenance of certain ratios and restricting the issuance of additional indebtedness. The obligation of the bank to make loans under the standby credit agreement is also conditioned on the compliance with certain of such covenants.

thus do not have the regular takedown and concession provisions associated with other traditional tax-exempt underwritings.

In 1981, the Municipal Bond Insurance Association (MBIA) commenced offering insurance to various issuers of short-term municipal debt. This insurance has been extended to select general obligation issuers without bank backstops, and it is undetermined at this embryonic stage whether such a device might be used in association with a tax-exempt commercial paper offering. It appears clear, however, where the issue is revenue-based versus general obligation, that some type of bank backstop facility would be required. Further, the magnitude of some of the current offerings, when coupled with that in the pipeline, may be of such individual size as to make insurance impractical. If insurance were to be utilized behind tax-exempt commercial paper, one would have to examine the cost effectiveness, given the 30 to 50 basis-point charge for the insurance, in addition to the cost associated with that facility extended by the bank or banks.

THE PREFERENCE PROBLEM

The changes in the bankruptcy act effected in the 1979 code present some interesting questions relative to the use of letters of credit and revolving credit agreements backstopping paper issuers.

Under previous bankruptcy law, a trustee was permitted to cause the reversal of payments made to an unsecured creditor during a specific period immediately preceding the filing in bankruptcy. The period usually covered the 90 days preceding the filing of the petition. The purpose was to protect the corpus of the debtor for the general benefit of all unsecured creditors, and the law granted the trustee the power to cause payment reversal when it could prove that the benefiting creditor had reason to believe the debtor's insolvency at the time the payment was made. The theory was to preclude the debtor from making specific arrangements with one of few creditors to the exclusion of the others when those few creditors perceived a technical insolvency anticipatory to the bankruptcy filing.

Section 547 of the 1979 bankruptcy act now provides that the trustee need not prove such knowledge of insolvency during the preceding period, but enables it to cause the reversal of payments anyway for the benefit of the general class of unsecured creditors.[10]

Under the current law, should an issuer file in bankruptcy, a paper holder having a maturity 90 days or less from such a filing, and having been "paid" via a rollover of the paper, could be forced to repay to the trustee that paid to him even though he did not have awareness

---

[10]M. Douglas Watson, *Bank-Supported Commercial Paper—A Risk Analysis,* (New York: Moody's Investors Service, 1981).

of the impending insolvency of the issuer. In this situation, the creditor might not have recourse to the bank issuing the backstop if a payment had been made or if the backstop facility had expired. Conversely, until more definitive rulings are made, a question exists as to whether a bank must make payments to all paper holders having maturities during the 90-day period preceding filing, regardless of the number of times the paper had been "rolled." Theoretically, at least, if a bank were backstopping $20 million of paper which was renewed twice during the 90-day period, and assuming notice provision to the bank was met, one could mount a case (except for the passage of time) that the bank would be liable for up to three times its agreed upon indemnity (that is, $60 million).

CONCLUSION

It appears as though tax-exempt commercial paper shall increase in its popularity for both issuers and purchasers in the future. For the issuer, it provides an alternative financing vehicle to more traditional bond, note, or bank loan credit extensions and gives the issuer maximum flexibility. These attractions will be modified somewhat by a steeply inverted yield curve which might exert more pressure on the banks to carry the issuers for short to intermediate periods.

The most important effect of tax-exempt commercial paper is yet to be realized. It is whether its growth and acceptance will create a major adjustment in the municipal marketplace through the compression of debt. Even if the system is not abused, the absolute dollars invested in commercial paper will proportionately increase issuers' reliance upon the marketplace for continued access. The ability of the market to accomodate massive size for taxable issuers has been well demonstrated. The viability of tax-exempt commercial paper shall only be tested in an environment of extremely tight money, steeply inverted yield curves and attendant pressures last seen in 1975–76.

Municipal Accounting and Financial Reporting

Section SIX

Corporate Accounting versus Municipal Accounting: The Economic Factors—Efficiency and Equity*

CHAPTER **35**

Abraham J. Simon, Ph.D., CPA

Professor of Accounting and Information Systems
Queens College, City University of New York

Periodic income is not an effective tool of financial planning or control. This conclusion seems to accord ill with the fact that income measurement has long been a central theme of accounting and the main preoccupation of the accounting profession. Yet this fact need not impress us. The practice of medicine once consisted largely of bloodletting.[1]

What is municipal accounting? Is it similar to or different from corporate accounting? In certain respects, municipal accounting is quite different from commercial accounting for a profit-seeking company.

*I would like to thank in particular for their review and helpful comments on this chapter Bradley Benson of Ademco, Leonard E. Berry of Georgia State University, A. Wayne Corcoran of Baruch College—CUNY, Peter Eilbott and Harry I. Greenfield of Queens College—CUNY, Felix Pomeranz of Coopers & Lybrand, and Michael Shamosh of Marks, Allen & Co. I would also like to thank my wife, Marilyn S. Simon, for her proofreading and editing of the materials in the chapter. Of course, any remaining defects in form or substance are my responsibility.

[1]David Solomons, "Economic and Accounting Concepts of Income," *Accounting Review,* July 1961, pp. 382–83. The Solomons quote is to alert the unwary to the existence of an extensive body of studies that have criticized rather severely the traditional accounting calculation of the net income of a commercial enterprise.

In other respects it is rather similar. Why are there differences between municipal and corporate accounting? What are the differences? What are the similarities? This chapter provides a framework for understanding *why* there are differences between municipal and commercial accounting. In this and the following three chapters we shall be describing the differences and the similarities. Our ultimate aim is to provide you with an understanding of municipal accounting and municipal financial reporting.

OVERVIEW OF FACTORS THAT LEAD TO DIFFERENCES BETWEEN MUNICIPAL AND CORPORATE ACCOUNTING

The traditional view of accounting for a corporation is that it supplies information that is expected to be useful for economic decision making.[2] This view applies also to accounting for a municipality. However, accounting for government entities, such as municipalities, is seen also as generating information expected to be useful for legal, social, and political decision making.[3]

Over time the basic purposes of accounting for profit-seeking organizations have become somewhat broader and more like those for governmental entities. Thus, even businesses have been expected to

---

[2]Discussions of the basic function or purpose of accounting can be found in: Accounting Principles Board, *APB Statement No. 4*, "Basic Concepts and Accounting Principles Underlying Financial Statements of Business Enterprises" (New York: American Institute of Certified Public Accountants, 1970), para. 21; Committee to Prepare a Statement of Basic Accounting Theory, *A Statement of Basic Accounting Theory* (Evanston, Ill.: American Accounting Association, 1966), p. 2; *FASB Statement of Financial Accounting Concepts No. 1*, "Objectives of Financial Reporting by Business Enterprises" (Stamford, Conn.: Financial Accounting Standards Board, 1978), para. 9; Study Group at the University of Illinois, *A Statement of Basic Accounting Postulates and Principles* (Urbana: University of Illinois, Center for International Education and Research in Accounting, 1964), p. 2; and Study Group on the Objectives of Financial Statements (the Trueblood Committee), *Objectives of Financial Statements* (New York: American Institute of Certified Public Accountants, 1973), p. 13.

[3]Discussions of the function of accounting for governmental entities can be found in such sources as: National Committee on Governmental Accounting (old NCGA), *Governmental Accounting, Auditing, and Financial Reporting* (Chicago: Municipal Financial Officers Association, 1968), pp. 1–2; American Accounting Association, Committee on Accounting Practice of Not-for-profit Organizations, "Report of the Committee on Accounting Practice of Not-for-Profit Organizations," *Supplement to Volume XLVI of the Accounting Review*, 1971, pp. 83–84; American Institute of Certified Public Accountants, Committee on Governmental Accounting and Auditing, *Audits of State and Local Governmental Units (ASLGU)*, 2d ed. (Industry Audit Guide) (New York: American Institute of Certified Public Accountants, 1974 and 1979), pp. 6–7; National Council on Governmental Accounting (new NCGA), *NCGA Statement 1*, "Governmental Accounting and Financial Reporting Principles" (Chicago: Municipal Finance Officers Association, March 1979), pp. 4–5; and Municipal Finance Officers Association, *Governmental Accounting, Auditing, and Financial Reporting (1980 GAAFR)*, (Chicago: MFOA, 1980), pp. 3–4.

supply accounting information useful in meeting social and other objectives as well as purely economic ones.[4] Still, the basic purpose of commercial accounting remains firmly focused on providing information useful in predicting return and risk arising from business activities. This information is generated for such users as business managers, creditors, investors, investment analysts, and others.

Investors in such public sector securities as municipal bonds are also interested in forecasting return and risk on these investment instruments. However, the public sector raises the major portion of its resources not from borrowing but from taxes. Municipal accounting should supply information not only to investors in municipal securities and to public sector managers, but also to taxpayers and to their legislative representatives. The same taxpayers who provide the bulk of the financial resources to finance the operation of a municipal entity are also the prime consumers of municipal goods and services.

In the long run, a business must supply goods and services on which it earns a profit resulting in a return attractive to investors at an acceptable level of risk. One could say that it is ultimately the consumers of the products and services marketed by a business corporation who finance its operation. However, the interest of consumers in the activities of companies that supply private sector (marketable) goods and services is very different from the interest of taxpayer-consumers in the activities of governmental entities which supply governmental goods and services. This difference arises largely because of the nature of the economic characteristics of pri-

---

[4]Examples of discussions or studies of corporate social reporting are as follows: David F. Linowes, "An Approach to Socioeconomic Accounting," *Conference Board Record,* November 1972, pp. 58–61; American Accounting Association, Committee on Environmental Effects of Organizational Behavior, "Report of the Committee on Environmental Effects of Organization Behavior," *Supplement to Volume XLVIII of the Accounting Review* 1973; Study Group (Trueblood Committee), *Objectives,* pp. 53–55; National Association of Accountants, Committee on Accounting for Corporate Social Performance, "Report of the Committee on Accounting for Corporate Social Performance," *Management Accounting,* February 1974, pp. 39–41; Ralph W. Estes, "A Comprehensive Corporate Social Reporting Model," in *Social Accounting: Theory, Issues, and Cases,* ed. Lee J. Seidler and Lynn L. Seidler (Los Angeles: Melville Publishing, 1975), pp. 185–204; American Accounting Association, Committee on Social Costs, "Report of the Committee on Social Costs," *Supplement to Volume L of the Accounting Review,* 1975, pp. 50–89; American Accounting Association, Committee on Accounting for Social Performance, "Report of the Committee on Accounting for Social Performance," *Supplement to Volume LI of the Accounting Review,* 1976, pp. 38–69; Marc Epstein, Eric G. Flamholtz, and John McDonough, *Corporate Social Performance: The Measurement of Product and Service Contributions* (A study for the National Association of Accountants) (New York: National Association of Accountants, 1977); and Stephen L. Buzby and Haim Falk, "Social Responsibility Reporting: A Note of Caution," in *Collected Papers of the American Accounting Association's Annual Meeting,* August 21–25, 1979, Honolulu, Hawaii (Sarasota, Fl.: American Accounting Association, 1979), pp. 278–94.

vate (marketable) goods and services as opposed to public (nonmarketable) goods and services. An example of a private good would be automobiles; while national defense would be an example of a public good. Note that the term *economic goods* is understood to cover both tangible goods and intangible services.

The differences in these economic characteristics also lead to differences in the types of organizations that supply the different types of goods. Market goods are supplied, for the most part, through business corporations and other profit-seeking entities, while public goods are supplied by nonprofit entities in the form of governmental organizations.

Significant differences between accounting for a business corporation and accounting for a governmental organization can be seen to rest to a great degree on three interrelated factors:

1. Differences in the economic characteristics of market goods as against public goods.
2. Differences in the interests of consumers of market goods as against taxpayer-consumers of public goods.
3. Differences between the types of organizations that supply market goods and those that supply public goods.

Each of the three factors will be discussed in this chapter. The most fundamental of the three factors—differences in the economic characteristics between market and public goods—will be explored in some depth. Rounding off this chapter will be a discussion of how these factors, particularly the market versus public goods issue, help explain some of the significant differences between business and municipal accounting.

THE ECONOMIC CHARACTERISTICS OF MUNICIPAL GOODS AND SERVICES THAT ARE PUBLIC GOODS AND SERVICES

Municipal Goods and Services and Pure Public Goods

Governmental entities such as municipalities provide their citizens and taxpayers with a wide range of goods and services. A vital distinction in the type of goods (and services) provided by governmental units would be between those goods which should be supplied *without* a direct user charge to consumers and those for which user charges *should* be levied against consumers. This distinction is basic toward understanding some of the significant differences between business and governmental accounting. Our discussion of the existence of public goods for public sector accounting is based partly and builds on a study by A. J. Simon, "Fiscal Accountability and Principles and Mechanisms of Disclosure for Major Local and State Governments in a Democratic Society."[5]

Public goods, described in greater detail subsequently, *should not* be subject to user charges. Market goods *should* be subject to user charges. This does not mean that in practice all public goods are supplied by minicipalities without a user charge. Although the major portion of public goods do seem to be supplied without these charges, there are public goods which are supplied subject to user charges.[6]

Municipalities also supply market goods. Basically these goods are subject, for the most part, to user charges. However, the user charges set by municipalities will not necessarily be equal to what a private enterprise would charge for such goods. Some user charges set by municipalities will be significantly below the price that would be charged by a profit-seeking private company; and in some cases the user charges will be zero.[7] Our discussion of the economic characteristics of public goods concentrates on what it is about such goods that results in their being supplied for the most part without user charges. An understanding of just why certain goods are supplied without user charges is essential to understanding the nature of the accounting differences between business enterprises and governmental organizations.

The services of a municipal electric or municipal transportation company are examples of services supplied by a municipality on a user charge basis. These services are supplied also by private companies. The accounting for a municipal utility or transportation company would be relatively similar to business accounting used by a private sector company in the same line of business. Goods (and services) which can be supplied through the market, and paid for in

---

[5]*Collected Papers of the American Accounting Associatino's Annual Meeting,* August 20–23, Denver, Colo.(Sarasota, Fl.: American Accounting Association, 1978), pp. 794–831.

[6]A. A. Walters describes rural and interurban roads, when they aren't congested, as pure public goods. See his *The Economics of Road User Charges* (Baltimore, Md.: The John Hopkins Press, 1968), pp. 16–17. Interurban roads in the form of toll roads would be an example of a public good supplied to a user charge. In a municipal area, a bridge that's uncongested during off-peak hours and which is subject to a toll charge would be another example of a public good supplied subject to a user charge. The economic characteristics of public goods which suggest when roads and bridges should be considered public goods will be discussed later on.

[7]Werner Z. Hirsch cites public hospitals, public libraries, and school lunches as examples of goods or services for which users charges aren't used or are significantly below the prices that would be charged if the goods were supplied by private, profit-seeking enterprises. See Hirsch's *The Economics of State and Local Government* (New York: McGraw-Hill, 1970), p. 34.

terms of user charges by consumers, are called market or private goods. The accounting for a municipality's activities which produce market goods should be quite similar to the accounting by a business corporation producing the same kinds of goods.

Municipal accounting becomes distinctively different from business accounting when it has to account for activities which generate goods and services which are not paid for on a user charge basis. Even in this case there are a great many similarities with business accounting, but there are also significant differences which need to be understood. Examples of services supplied by a municipality without a user charge would be police protection, fire protection, streets, street lighting, traffic control devices and traffic control, sidewalks, and most bridges. Let's look at certain of these examples a little more closely to see why there are no user charges.

In American society, the citizen as pedestrian assumes that he or she has the right to move about easily and freely in public places. Normally, one doesn't ask why there are no user charges for the services rendered by such public areas as public sidewalks, public streets, and the like. One simply walks along sidewalks, streets, etc., and does not think about an obligation to pay directly for the benefits being received. However, it does cost money (more importantly, real resources are used) to construct and maintain public streets, sidewalks, etc., and someone has to pay and bear the cost of real-resource use. But, paying for the cost or maintenance of a public sidewalk or public street is not the same thing as paying a user charge for the pedestrian use of such public areas. The actual users of public areas, such as pedestrians, are the real beneficiaries, while those who pay for the construction and maintenance of such areas may or may not be the prime beneficiaries of the services rendered by such areas.

In the case of a market good, there tends to be a more or less close correlation between the benefits received by consumers of the market good and the amounts that these same consumers pay to cover the costs of supplying such a good. This is because the consumers of market goods pay user charges for the use of the goods, and the user charges tend to approximate the *incremental* costs of supplying such goods. However, in the case of a nonmarket good such as a public sidewalk, the user of the sidewalk, who receives benefits from using it, is not necessarily the same individual who pays for the cost of constructing and maintaining the sidewalk.

The cost of building and maintaining sidewalks, curbs, and streets is often borne in good part by the owners of the properties adjoining such public areas. If a property owner who bore the entire cost of building and maintaining a sidewalk were the only user of the sidewalk, then as the only consumer of the sidewalk's services that property owner's payments would (over the life of the sidewalk) correlate with the benefits from the use of the sidewalk. However, those who pay for the building and maintaining of public areas such as sidewalks are not the only users of such public areas. Many users of public areas—in fact, all of those who use public areas—receive benefits for which they do not pay directly in the form of user charges. In the broadest sense, a user of a public area can be thought of as anyone who receives benefits from its existence.[8]

There are advantages to having consumers pay user charges under the appropriate circumstances. In the case of market goods supplied through relatively competitive markets, one tends to find that the user charges (i.e., the market prices) paid by consumers approximate in monetary terms the benefits which consumers expect to receive from the consumption of such goods. At the same time, the user charges cover approximately the incremental costs of producing the goods. Consumers pay directly through user charges for the incremental costs of the benefits that they receive. The market mechanism tends to match incremental benefits and incremental costs. The matching of incremental benefits and incremental costs through competitive markets tends to lead to an efficient use of society's resources. The quantities of market goods tend to be maximized for a given quantity of resources used in the production of such goods. Another way of stating this is that the cost of producing market goods will be minimized under adequate competition.[9]

A word of caution is in order. Although it might sound like relatively competitive markets should lead to a fair distribution of market goods to consumers, this is not necessarily the case. Competitive markets do not assure us that an equitable distribution of goods and services will be made to consumers. There is no guarantee that the distribution will be equitable or inequitable. Truly competitive markets are neutral on this question of equity. Other considerations, such as the distribution of income and wealth in the society and the society's notions about equity, are among the major factors that will help to determine whether or not a particular distribution of market-type goods or services is or isn't equitable. Markets which are not adequately competitive are *not* likely to be neutral with respect to an

---

[8]In later discussion, we shall see that *access* to public areas can be described as a pure public good. In this case, the user of a public area would be anyone who benefits from its existence.

[9]A demonstration of the static efficiency of perfect competition can be found in a textbook such as James M. Henderson and Richard E. Quandt, *Microeconomic Theory: A Mathematical Approach* (New York: McGraw-Hill, 1958). pp. 202–208.

equitable distribution of market goods and services. Such markets tend to generate inequities.[10]

If competitive markets tend to be efficient (though not necessarily equitable), then why is it that public areas such as sidewalks and streets, that are for the use of pedestrians, are not supplied through the market? Why is it that there are no user charges for the use of public areas? Unfortunately, the services rendered by public areas such as sidewalks do not result in the kind of economic good that can be marketed so that one can take advantage of the efficiencies generated by competitive markets. Why is that?

In order to market an economic good, one has to be able to charge a fee per unit of the good used by a consumer and, at the same time, be able to exclude consumers who do not pay the fee from enjoying the benefits of the good. Excluding those who do not pay from the benefits of an economic good is known as the "exclusion principle" in public sector economies. If a person cannot be excluded from the benefits of an economic good—i.e., the exclusion principle cannot be applied—then that person does not have an incentive to voluntarily pay for benefits received. If there is no incentive to pay, then it is highly likely that no voluntary payment will be forthcoming.

An economic good which generates benefits which consumers desire, but for which there are not likely to be voluntary payments, is not the kind of good that a private business would want to produce and market. Such a good would generate costs, but little or nothing in the way of sales receipts. The services rendered to pedestrians by

---

[10]With respect to equity considerations in terms of the distribution of goods and services to consumers, the neutrality of perfectly competitive markets is generally an implicit assumption of any analysis of such markets. See, for example, the discussion on efficiency and economic institutions in David N. Hyman, *The Economics of Governmental Activity* (New York: Holt, Rinehart & Winston, 1973), pp. 30–36. However, William J. Baumol in his textbook, *Economics Theory and Operations Analysis* (Englewood Cliffs, N.J.: Prentice-Hall, 1961), tells us that "we shall see that the marginal optimality rules are either silent or prejudiced on the question of income distribution and are, therefore, necessarily incomplete or unsatisfactory even on questions where distribution is not the primary issue" (p. 248). What this means is that any analysis that tells us that perfectly competitive markets are efficient and that such efficiency is optimal contains a hidden assumption in favor of the status quo income distribution, whatever that income distribution happens to be. The "marginal optimality rules" to which Baumol refers, and which are used to demonstrate the efficiency of perfectly competitive markets, are "prejudiced" in a sense toward the status quo income distribution, since the rules are unable to warn us as to whether we have a "good" or "bad" income distribution. Baumol is concerned with income distribution because the distribution of income is one of the factors that determines the distribution of spending by consumers on goods and services. If the distribution of income is considered inequitable, then it is likely that the distribution of spending also will be inequitable. This means that some consumers will be getting an unfair share of the goods and services produced in the society. Baumol also included the distribution of wealth in his caveat about the fact that competitive markets favor the status quo whether it is equitable or inequitable status quo.

public areas such as sidewalks and streets are an example of an economic good which generates benefits which consumers want but
would not generate voluntary payments of a fee per unit of service
because the exclusion principle cannot be applied properly. Why is
this so?

Public areas such as sidewalks and streets render their services in
an indivisible fashion to consumers as pedestrians. In order for a sidewalk or a street to provide a pedestrian with a service that satisfies
a right to move about freely, easily, and in an incognito fashion (i.e.,
with relative privacy) in a public area, it must remain an undivided
whole. Unlike a market good which can be subdivided into small
units and sold to consumers on an individual basis, streets and sidewalks cannot be divided up into small units and at the same time
satisfy the right of consumer-pedestrians to move about easily, freely,
and incognito over certain areas. If an economic good cannot be divided up and sold to consumers on an individual basis, then the exclusion principle cannot be applied.

Why is it that the use of public areas cannot be divided up into
marketable units and sold to consumers as a marketable good? (If you
think that this crucial point could bear a bit more elaboration, then
study the discussion in Appendix A to this chapter.) The benefits of
the services rendered through the use of public areas is a prime example of what has been called a "public good" to distinguish this kind
of good from a market good which has been called a "private good."
Public goods have the characteristic that an additional unit of consumption, or use, of the good can be had at zero marginal cost. Another way of describing this characteristic is that there is a lack of
rivalry in the consumption of a public good. This means that if I consume one unit of a public good, I do *not* use resources which could
have been used to produce another unit of the public good for someone
else to consume. Someone else and I can each consume one unit of the
public good at the same time without impairing each other's consumption of the good. In fact, both another person and myself can
each consume one unit of the public good, and there is still no less of
the public good for a *third* person to consume. In the case of a private
or market good, once I consume one unit of the good, there is actually
one unit of the good less than before, so that my consumption of one
unit of a market good can take away from someone else's potential
consumption of that good. In the case of private or market goods,
there is *rivalry in consumption:* more consumption for me can mean
less consumption for you from a given quantity of the good. In the
case of a public good, the *lack of rivalry in consumption* means that
more consumption for me does not necessarily mean less consumption
for you out of a given quantity of the good.

In the case of a public area, one does find circumstances where there is rivalry in consumption. (Appendix B to this chapter discusses that topic.)

While one does not find tolls charged to pedestrians for the use of public areas, the same does not hold true in all cases for automobiles and other vehicles. In the case of streets, automobiles are not normally charged a fee for street use; but one does find the selective use of tolls as user charges in the case of highways and bridges. However, a single trip by a typical automobile normally causes little or no wear for many types of thoroughfares.

Assuming travel during uncongested periods, the marginal or incremental cost of a single trip over a certain type of highway or bridge would be close to and perhaps even equal to zero. Where the tolls for highway or bridge use are significantly above marginal cost, we would not have efficient allocation of resources, but instead have a misallocation of resources.[11] We would also have the added cost and inconvenience of operating the toll collection systems. This type of selective mispricing does not seem to occur with regard to pedestrian use of public areas.

Access to public areas is a public good supplied by governmental units such as municipalities because it is a nonmarket good which private businesses could not supply profitably. This type of good has been called also a "collective consumption" good, because it cannot be divided up into single units and sold to consumers on an individual basis.[12] Unlike, for instance, phonograph records (which are a divisible market good which can be sold in individual units to individual consumers), public areas cannot be divided up into small units and sold to consumers on an individual basis if they are to function effectively to satisfy an individual's need to be able to move about easily and freely.[13]

---

[11]Price greater than marginal cost causes a misallocation of resources, not only because there has been too great a discouragement of the use of the bridge or highway. There is also the problem that too much money has been placed in the hands of a public sector entity. The collector of the user charges will be a bridge or highway authority that has been set up to administer the operation of the bridge or highway. There is no particular reason to believe that the bridge or highway authority will spend the excessive revenues wisely, and there are many reasons to believe that excessive revenues will lead to wasteful spending.

[12]A discussion of public goods can be found, for example, in the textbook by Bernard P. Herber, *Modern Public Finance: The Study of Public Sector Economics,* 3d ed. (Homewood, Ill.: Richard D. Irwin, 1975), pp. 53–59). A pure public good as distinguished from a quasi-public good (to be discussed later) is also called a collective consumption good; see also James M. Buchanan and Marilyn R. Flowers, *The Public Finances: An Introductory Textbook* (Homewood, Ill.: Richard D. Irwin, 1975), pp. 25–27). Carl S. Shoup, in his *Public Finance* (Hawthorne, N.Y.: Aldine Publishing, 1969), pp. 66–67, prefers to describe publicly supplied, pure public or collective consumption goods as group consumption goods.

[13]Division of a public area does not necessarily mean actually physically breaking it down into small units, but can mean simply erecting physical barriers to control access. Hirsch, *Economics of State,* pp. 43, observes that one could use electronic devices to monitor and measure the use of public areas but that one then has the disadvantage of public invasion of privacy.

We have assumed that access to public areas is considered a right to which all citizens of American society feel themselves entitled. We can also assume that citizens consider themselves entitled to equality of opportunity in their exercise of a right such as access to public areas. Another way of putting this is that the benefits that any particular citizen can expect to enjoy from access to public areas should be equal to the benefits that any other citizen can expect to enjoy from this right.

We have now spelled out the major economic characteristics of a pure public or collective consumption good. My enjoyment or consumption of the benefits of such a good does not take away from any other consumer's enjoyment or consumption of the benefits of that public good. My enjoyment or consumption of the benefits of a pure public good can be equal to any other consumer's consumption of the benefits of such a good. The marginal or incremental cost of consuming or enjoying incremental benefits of a pure public good is zero. The benefits generated by pure public, or collective consumption, good are indivisible, so that the exclusion principle cannot be applied with the expected economic consequences of an efficient allocation of society's resources. If the exclusion principle cannot be applied, then pure public or collective consumption goods cannot be marketed.

Access to public areas by pedestrians seems to fulfill the requirements of a pure public good supplied at the level of municipal government. A table summarizing the pertinent characteristics of a pure public or collective consumption good is shown in Exhibit 1.

Municipal Goods and Services, Impure Public or Quasi-Public Goods, and Externalities

Pure public goods are a special case which illustrate what should be called the ideal type of governmental good that cannot be supplied through the market mechanism. However, most goods supplied by governmental entities without user charges are not pure public or collective consumption goods but are better described as "impure public" or "quasi-public" goods.[14] Quasi-public goods have certain of the economic characteristics of pure public goods but can have also some of the characteristics of market or private goods.

Certain types of goods and services generate benefits not only for those consumers who purchased and paid for these goods and services, but also for third parties who have not paid for the benefits. Take, for example, elementary and secondary school education. Elementary and secondary school education provides benefits not only for those being educated but also for the rest of the community. Elementary

---

[14]Discussions of impure public, or quasi-public, goods can be found in such sources as Buchanan and Flowers, *The Public Finances,* pp. 31–32; Herber, *Modern Public Finance,* pp. 57–59; and Hyman, *Economics,* pp. 85–90.

Exhibit 1
Pertinent Economic Characteristics of a Pure Public or Collective Consumption Good

1. A good (includes a service) whose benefits are available to any and all citizens who desire them. If the good is supplied at all, then all citizens are considered entitled to enjoy the benefits of consuming the good.*
2. The good or service generates collective benefits so that the exclusion principle cannot be applied to promote efficient allocation of resources. Benefits are indivisible in consumption. The inability to apply the exclusion principle means that voluntary user charges cannot be used to finance the supply of the quantity of the good or service desired by citizens.
3. If benefits are completely indivisible in consumption, then this means that there is a lack of rivalry in consumption. A lack of rivalry in consumption means that the incremental cost of a unit of consumption is equal to zero.†
4. The good is assumed to be available to all citizens in such a manner that they have the opportunity to enjoy equal benefit levels from consuming a good of given quality.

---

*Once a pure public good such as national defense is supplied, then all citizens in the society are considered to have a right to enjoy the benefits of this good.

†Public goods are not necessarily the only types of goods for which incremental (or marginal) cost may be zero. Take the case of attending a sports or theatrical event. As long as there are no congestion costs, then the marginal cost of admitting one more fan to a sports arena (or another theatergoer to a play) will be zero. However, sports events and plays can be and are supplied normally through the market mechanism, even though the marginal cost of one more unit of consumption is zero. The reason for this is that the exclusion principle can be applied easily in a cost-effective manner. An excellent discussion distinguishing marketable goods with zero marginal cost from nonmarket goods with zero marginal cost can be found in Carl S. Shoup, *Public Finance* (Hawthorne, N.Y.: Aldine Publishing, pp. 66–74. Note that Shoup prefers a somewhat different terminology from the usual publicoods terminology found in other discussions.

and secondary school education is provided both through the public sector in public schools and also as a market or private good subject to user charges in the private sector through private schools. Why is it that we have *both* public sector elementary and secondary school education without direct user charges, and private sector forms which do have these charges?

Education generates both current and future benefits. The current benefits of education can be considered a consumption good. A child enjoys the developing ability to read and write. Here we have the direct beneficiary of an elementary school education reaping the benefits of that education currently as a consumption good. Children do not pay directly for their education; rather their parents bear the costs either in the form of taxes to support a public school system, or through user charges to finance a private education for their child. If we view the family as the primary consumption unit rather than the child, then the family is enjoying the benefits of an elementary school education for its children as a current consumption good. Certainly, parents take great pleasure in seeing their offspring master the art of reading and writing, etc.

However, elementary and secondary school education also generates future benefits. Goods which generate future rather than current benefits are investment rather than consumption goods. Once a student has attained literacy, that talent can be exercised both today for present benefits and tomorrow for future benefits.

Elementary and secondary school education, as both a consumption and an investment good, will generate benefits not only for those being educated and their immediate families, but also for unrelated third parties. The community-at-large benefits in general from the existence of a literate population. The indirect benefits of elementary and secondary school education can be called the "external benefits" or the "externalities" resulting from education.[15] How do externalities in the form of benefits arise?

If education were what has been called a pure private (or pure market) good, then all of the benefits of education would accrue entirely to those who pay for education. Those who pay for education would be the sole beneficiaries, and those who do not pay would be completely excluded from the benefits. If education were a pure private or pure marketable good then the exclusion principle could be applied perfectly. The benefits of education would be perfectly divisible so that those who do not pay for the benefits could be excluded completely from enjoying those benefits. But education, particularly at the elementary and secondary school levels, is not a pure private or pure market good. We can benefit from someone else's literacy without ever having necessarily contributed directly to the financing of their education.

In the case of a pure private good, by definition, all of the benefits of such a good accrue only to the party who pays for the good. All other parties are completely excluded from enjoying any of the benefits if they haven't paid for these benefits. If all benefits are fully paid for by those enjoying the benefits, then market prices should reflect fully the benefits and costs of the goods passing through the market. If there are some people who partake of the benefits from certain goods without ever paying user charges for these benefits, then market prices will not reflect all of the benefits being consumed for these goods. If the market price for a good reflects fully all of the costs and all of the benefits, then all of the costs and benefits will have been *internalized* through the market mechanism. Sellers will realize revenues from all of the benefits accruing to buyers because of the perfect application of the exclusion principle. All of the costs of producing and selling a good will be reflected fully in the market price of the good if there are no *externalities* on the cost side—external costs that producers and sellers can shift to third parties. If a producer or a

---

[15]A discussion of externalities appears in John F. Due and Ann F. Friedlaender, *Government Finance: Economics of the Public Sector,* 5th ed. (Homewood, Ill.: Richard D. Irwin, 1973), pp. 77–96. See also Herber, *Modern Public Finance,* pp. 36–41; and Hyman, *Economics,* pp. 43–66.

seller generates costs for which that producer or seller does not have to pay, then such a producer or seller can be described as a "free rider." If there are no external costs or no free riders on the cost side, then all costs will have been internalized into the market price. This occurs when the exclusion principle operates perfectly for producers and sellers of goods and services, as well as for consumers of such goods and services.

If there are no costs that escape the market mechanism (i.e., no external costs) then the costs of producing and marketing, which is called the "private cost," to an individual firm is also the cost to society. The cost to society of producing and marketing a good would be called its "social cost." If there are external costs (such as pollution) which an individual firm imposes on unrelated third parties, then its private costs will be less than the social costs of producing and marketing its products.

Similarly, on the benefit side, if there are no benefits that escape the market mechanism (i.e., no external benefits and no free rider consumers), then the benefits of consuming a good by an individual or by a family—the *private benefits*—will be equal to the benefits to society—the *social benefits*. However, if there are third-party effects in terms of external benefits and free riders, benefits for which consumers do not pay, then social benefits will exceed private benefits. Remember that private benefits are the benefits for which consumers have paid.

External benefits and external costs are benefits and costs that are called external because there has been no payment for these benefits or costs so that they have not been internalized directly into market prices. The external benefits and external costs are external to the market mechanism. Once you have significant external benefits or costs, market prices no longer serve necessarily as adequate signaling devices for the efficient allocation of society's resources.

There are external benefits when social benefits exceed private benefits. There are external costs when social costs exceed private costs. Social benefits are composed of both private benefits and external benefits. Social costs are composed of both private costs and external costs.

In the case of a pure public (or collective consumption) good, consumers do not pay user charges for any of the benefits from the good. It is in the nature of a pure public good that the payment of user charges would not lead to an efficient allocation of resources. For a pure public, or collective consumption, good all of the social benefits are necessarily of the external variety. This means that, for such a good, marketable private benefits are equal to zero. The benefits of a pure public good are completely indivisible so that the exclusion principle cannot be applied appropriately, and it is this situation that generates all external benefits and no private benefits.

A good or service that has a mixture of both private and external benefits in consumption can be supplied either as a nonmarket good through the public sector or as a private good through the market mechanism. If the good or service has very significant external benefits relative to private benefits, then it does not pay a private firm to supply the good through the market mechanism. Instead the good is supplied through the public sector, and such a good would be called an impure public or quasi-public good. If, on the other hand, the good or service generates many private benefits relative to external benefits and does so at a level profitable enough to be supplied through the market mechanism in the private sector, then such a good or service would be called an impure *private* or quasi-*private* good.

Elementary and secondary school education is supplied both in the public and private sectors. When such education is being supplied through the public sector not on a user charge basis, then it would be considered a quasi-public or impure public good. When elementary and secondary school education is supplied in the private sector and financed in a good part through user charges, then we have an example of a quasi-private or impure private good.

Education at the elementary and secondary school levels is a major example of a quasi-public or impure public good that is supplied on a nonuser charge basis by local governmental units such as municipalities. Even when elementary and secondary school education is provided in the private sector, it is normally supplied not through profit-seeking business enterprises but through nonprofit entities. A table showing the pertinent economic characteristics of an impure public, or quasi-public, good appears in Exhibit 2.

Nonmarket Municipal Goods, User Charges, and Distinctive Features of Municipal Accounting

Municipalities not only supply goods on a nonuser charge basis, but also supply goods subject to significant user charges. In many instances the public sector supplies goods subject to significant user charges while the same types of goods are also supplied by profit-seeking private enterprises. Major examples of municipal corporations and the types of market goods that they supply are municipal electric companies, municipal gas companies, and municipal transportation companies.

Some discussions of those goods supplied by governmental units and subject to significant user charges tend to lump such goods together with goods that are not subject to significant user charges (or are subject to no user charges). These discussions combine all of these goods and services into the category of quasi-public or impure public goods.

Thus far, we have dealt with goods supplied by governmental units

Exhibit 2
Pertinent Economic Characteristics of an Impure Public or Quasi-Public,
Consumption Good

1. All citizens are considered to be entitled to enjoy the benefits of consuming the good, once it is supplied.

2. All citizens are *not* considered to be entitled to equal benefit levels or equality of consumption in terms of units of the good or service (of a given quality) available to be consumed.

3. There is rivalry in consumption: i.e., one citizen's consumption of a quasi-public good can take away from another citizen's ability to consume the good. The incremental, or marginal, cost of consuming one more unit of the good is greater than zero.

4. Private benefits do not equal social benefits. The good or service generates external benefits of a sufficient quantity so that private, profit-seeking enterprises will not supply the *quantity* of the good *desired* by citizens. The exclusion principle cannot be applied effectively and voluntary user charges cannot be used to finance the desired supply of the good or service.

primarily on a nonuser charge basis. The reason for this is that we wished to set out the economic basis for the existence of nonmarket public goods supplied by governmental units. It is the need to supply such goods that leads ultimately to the distinctive differences between governmental (and municipal) accounting and business (and corporate) accounting. When municipalities supply what essentially are market goods, then the accounting for such goods can be, for all practical purposes, largely the same as accounting for market goods supplied by private, profit-seeking companies.

The distinction between nonmarket goods supplied on a no-user-charge basis and market goods supplied on a user charge basis is fundamental to understanding the basic differences between public sector (and municipal) accounting and business (and corporate) accounting. We turn next to this chapter's second major topic area which covers differences in the interests of consumers of market goods vis-à-vis the interests of taxpayer-consumers of public goods.

PUBLIC GOODS AND THE INFORMATION NEEDS OF TAXPAYERS AND OF INVESTORS IN MUNICIPAL SECURITIES

Municipal Governments as Trustees of the Funds that They Receive from Taxpayers

A taxpayer makes payments in the form of taxes which are required by law to finance the provision of public goods by governmental units. These payments are required to be made regardless of the types, quantities, or qualities of public goods being supplied by the governmental unit and consumed by taxpayers. The reason for this state of affairs has already been discussed. The benefits generated by public goods are indivisible, so that voluntary user charges would not normally generate the types, quantities, and qualities of public goods desired by consumers on an individual basis. At the national level, the archetypical public good is national defense. Can one imagine a pure public good such as national defense being financed through voluntary payments and being supplied to each consumer "one unit" at a time? At the level of municipal government, pedestrian access to public areas has properties similar to national defense as a pure public good. Pedestrian access to public areas is not financed through the use of voluntary payments by consumers. Other municipal public goods such as fire protection and police protection also are not financed through voluntary payments.

Public goods whether at the national, state, or municipal levels are financed through *involuntary* payments (from the individual's point of view) which are unrelated to the actual consumption of the public good by individual taxpayers. Because the payments are involuntary, governmental units can be viewed as holding these payments in *trust* for taxpayers to be used for the purposes spelled out in the laws that govern the spending of taxes and the supplying of governmental goods. As trustees, governments have an obligation imposed through law to spend moneys that they receive from taxpayers in accordance with the appropriate legal requirements.[16]

In the case of market goods, there is not the kind of trust relationship and arrangement between consumers and suppliers that one finds between taxpayers and governmental suppliers of public goods. In the case of a marketable good, a consumer makes a voluntary payment that is related to the type, quantity, and quality of the good acquired. The consumer gives up consideration in the form of a monetary payment, and the enterprise supplying the good or service gives up consideration in the form of the good or service. The consumer receives the good or service and the business enterprise receives the monetary payment. Value has been exchanged for value and there is no need for a continuing trust arrangement between the parties.[17]

In sharp contrast to market goods, taxpayers make involuntary payments which are held in trust for them by governmental units. There has been no exchange of value for value at the time that taxes are paid. There is a continuing interest on the part of taxpayers that they in fact do and will receive the types, quantities, and qualities of goods and services for which they have paid taxes.

---

[16]In old NCGA, *1968 GAAFR,* p. 1, we are told that citizens and taxpayers are "vitally concerned with" among other things, "the stewardship . . . of both elected and appointed public officials in administering the government's financial transactions." This point of view stresses the trust relationship between taxpayers and governments.

[17]In the case of those marketable products for which sellers provide such services as warranty repairs, there will be a continuing relationship between buyer and seller.

The idea that governmental units hold funds in trust for taxpayers has had a significant impact on the nature of accounting and reporting that one finds for governmental units such as municipalities compared to that for business enterprises. Governmental units cannot raise or spend moneys unless the authority to tax or to spend is embodied in some law. Governmental accounting utilizes budgetary and fund accounting in a way that differs significantly from that found in business accounting. This will be discussed subsequently.

Municipalities as Monopolistic Suppliers of Public Goods

In earlier discussions of the efficiency of markets in the supplying market-type goods and services, it was stressed that efficiency presumes sufficient competition. Whenever there is one supplier of a good or service (a monopolist) or a few suppliers (oligopolists), then the chances are rather great that the efficiencies due to adequate competition will be missing. Now it may well be the case that there are mass-production efficiencies (internal economies of scale), due to great size and high-volume sales, which justify to some degree the existence of one or a few sellers. However, it is not at all clear that the efficiencies due to mass production will not be partially or entirely offset by the inefficiencies due to insufficient competition.

The same difficulties are present when a good is supplied through the public sector. Since public goods by their nature tend not to be supplied through the market mechanism, one can then argue that the public sector is more efficient in supplying such goods. However, if there are few close market alternatives for a particular public good or service, this means that the governmental unit supplying that good is in the position of a monopolist or an oligopolist.[18] The lack of competition will almost inevitably lead to a tendency toward waste and inefficiency in the public sector probably at least as severe as that of a private sector monopolist or oligopolist.

The fact that municipal governments can exercise monopoly- or oligopoly-like power over their citizens and taxpayers is a significant added factor justifying the view that governmental units should be viewed as trustees of the funds which they receive from taxpayers. The fact that taxpayers must make involuntary payments to governmental entities, and that such entities can exercise monopoly-like power over taxpayers, helps to explain why legal requirements loom so large in shaping public sector accounting and reporting.

***

[18]Hirsch, *Economics of State,* p. 35, notes the monopoly position that governmental entities may enjoy in the case of goods and services supplied through user charges. This adds to the monopoly position of governmental entities with respect to public goods. See also the discussion "Involuntary Resource Providers and Largely Monopolistic Services" in MFOA, *1980 GAAFR,* p. 2.

Taxpayers as Involuntary Investors

The trustee relationship between a government and its taxpayers finds its analogue in the private sector in the fiduciary relationship between investors and the companies in which they invest their funds. Investors place their funds in a variety of investment instruments: savings accounts, certificates of deposit, corporate bonds, corporate common stock, and corporate preferred stock are only a few of the wide variety of investment instruments. A trustee or fiduciary relationship arises between an investor and the organization or company which has issued the investment instrument.

Accounting and reporting for private, profit-seeking companies has been influenced significantly by the concept that there is a trust relationship between such companies (their officers and their directors) and those who invest or will invest in the companies. Financial reporting for private sector, profit-seeking companies is geared to the information needs of investors in these companies, which have been entrusted with investors' funds in order to invest these funds in profitable ventures that are expected to generate target rates of return on investment at levels of risk expected to be acceptable to the investors.

Taxpayers can be considered, in a sense, as investors in public sector activities.[19] However, there are critical differences between private sector investors and taxpayers as investors. Investors in private sector securities and other private sector investment instruments can decide voluntarily on an individual level whether to spend their money now on consumption goods or postpone consumption and place their funds in investment instruments. Taxes are involuntary payments from the individual point of view. Investors can acquire and dispose of their investments voluntarily. If the management of a particular company is not generating the kind of profit and risk performance that a particular investor desires or expects, then there are generally other ready buyers available to whom to sell the investment. Taxpayers cannot get their money back if they don't like the types, quantities, or qualities of public goods being provided.[20] If tax-

---

[19]The Trueblood report (Study Group, *Objectives*, p. 49) describes briefly some of the similarities between the payment of taxes by taxpayers and the decision to invest in securities by investors.

[20]Taxpayers ultimately can move from a community if they are dissatisfied with the services provided and/or the local tax burden. The idea of taxpayers "voting with their feet" is discussed in a pioneering study by Charles M. Tiebout, "A Pure Theory of Local Expenditures," *Journal of Political Economy* 64 (October 1956), pp. 416–24. There are costs associated with voting with one's feet. From a short-term frame of reference, it is a good approximation to assume that taxpayers are relatively immobile and therefore would tend to have less flexibility as compared to investors in private sector securities. The Tiebout article is discussed in such books as Wallace E. Oates, *Fiscal Federalism* (New York: Harcourt Brace Jovanovich, 1972), and Hirsch, *Economics of State*.

payers are to be viewed as analogous to investors, then they must be viewed as involuntary investors. This means that the fiduciary or trust relationship between a taxpayer and a governmental unit is even more critical than that between an investor and the organization that issues a marketable investment instrument. Recall also the earlier discussion about the monopoly or oligopoly position of a governmental entity with respect to its taxpayers, and one can begin to appreciate the critical nature of the trust relationship between a government and its citizens and taxpayers.

In a very real sense, accounting and reporting in the public sector has a greater burden to bear than accounting and reporting in the private sector. Private sector investors have more options available to them in the case of private sector market investments than do public sector taxpayers who have contributed involuntary payments to governmental organizations. This difference helps account for the pervasive character and importance of law on the activities and accounting of governmental entities.

Municipal Accounting and Reporting as a Public Good

Governments receive, hold, and use tax moneys in trust for taxpayers. As trustees, governments have an obligation to report to taxpayers on the way that taxpayers' moneys are used. The obligation is discharged through financial and other kinds of reporting on how tax moneys are spent. Financial reporting by governmental units is generally required by law. Accounting and financial reporting by governmental units does not seem to be a marketable good for individual taxpayers as in the case of accounting and financial reporting by business enterprises.

In the private sector, accounting and reporting for private, profit-seeking entities can be considered basically a marketable good. Accounting for managerial purposes is a necessary ingredient in the operation of a business enterprise. Companies find it worthwhile to buy the resources necessary to produce the information that they need for managerial accounting purposes. In addition, external financial reporting by private companies also can be considered a marketable good. Private, profit-seeking companies find it worth their while to bear the costs of financial reporting to their current creditors and stockholders. The same external financial reporting generates benefits also for future creditors and investors.

In fact, there are a number of specialized profit-seeking companies which can be considered in the business of producing financial information. Credit rating agencies, investment advisers, financial analysts, journals and newspapers dealing with financial matters, certified public accounting firms which function as independent auditors and in other capacities, and others are part of a system of information producers who sell marketable services.

Creditors, equity investors, and the companies in which investments are made all appear willing to pay for the services of the information specialists. However, in the public sector we do not find for taxpayers a similar system of information production about the activities of public sector entities. Taxpayers do not seem willing to pay on an individual basis for information about the finances and activities of governmental units.[21] Why is there this difference between the willingness of private investors to pay for investment information about private sector investments, and the unwillingness of taxpayers to pay for analogous information about public sector activities of entities such as municipal governments?

Private sector investors believe that investment information will help them make better investment decisions. The private incremental benefits of private sector investment information must be greater than the private incremental costs for individual private sector investors to be willing to purchase such information. However, taxpayers have no such incentive with respect to information about public sector activities. Taxpayers have no choice about the payment of their taxes. Whether a taxpayer is more or less informed about the activities of the government will have no immediate or short-term impact on the amount of taxes paid.[22] Note also that, since public goods generate benefits which are largely indivisible or are composed largely of external benefits, an individual taxpayer varying his or her level of consumption will really have no perceptible impact on the level of governmental output and governmental expenditures. The benefits of

---

[21]Newspapers are a source of information on activities, abuses, etc. by governmental units. Taxpayers are willing to pay for the purchase of newspapers, so that this could be an example of taxpayer willingness to purchase information about public sector activities. However, newspapers provide a wide variety of different types of information far beyond being simply transmitters of news about government. Jerold L. Zimmerman contends that the demand for newspapers is largely of the entertainment variety. The question raised by Zimmerman is whether taxpayers really would be willing to purchase newspapers in as large quantities as they do if newspapers carried no other information except news about governments. He thought not. See J. L. Zimmerman, "The Municipal Accounting Mazes: An Analysis of Political Incentives," *Studies on Measurement and Evaluation of Economic Efficiency of Public and Private Nonprofit Institutions: 1977.* Supplement to *Journal of Accountancy* 15 (1977, p. 121.

[22]In the long run, taxpayers (in democratic settings) can have an impact on the level of taxes that they pay. Examples of dramatic voter impact on taxes would be the passage of Proposition 13 in California and the passage of Proposition 2½ in Massachusetts. The *New York Times* (March 28, 1981, p. 8, col. 3–5), reports on the suspension by Moody's of its bond ratings for Boston and 36 other Massachusetts local governmental units. The suspension of the bond ratings is attributed to the fiscal stress resulting from adjustments by local governmental units to the anticipated effect of Proposition 2½ once it becomes effective. Of course, such suspensions are not permanent if governmental units are perceived as able to adjust adequately to the impact of fiscal restraints.

governmental accounting and reporting, from the point of view of the individual taxpayer, are indivisible and inure to the community as a whole. Individual taxpayers cannot capture the benefits of accounting and reporting by governmental entities. This means that accounting and reporting by governmental and, therefore, municipal entities should be considered a public good.[23]

Is municipal accounting and reporting also a public good for investors in municipal securities? Investment in municipal securities is a voluntary activity of an investor, in contrast to the payment of taxes which is involuntary from the point of view of the individual taxpayer. An investor can vary his or her holdings of municipal securities as a result of information that affects that investor's expectations about the return and risk associated with those securities. This is in sharp contrast to the ability of a taxpayer to vary the amount of taxes paid in the short run in response to information concerning municipal activities. Individual investors in municipal securities can capture the incremental benefits of information stemming from accounting and reporting by municipalities. Investors in municipal securities utilize investment information generated by such information-producing firms as municipal bond rating agencies. These information-producing firms are in turn dependent for the production of investment information on accounting and reporting by municipalities. Therefore, investors in municipal securities do have the ability to capture incremental private benefits from investment information generated from municipal accounting and reporting.

Does this mean that, for investors in municipal securities, municipal accounting and reporting should be considered a marketable good? Investors may pay for investment information generated by investment information producing firms, but this does not make municipal accounting and reporting a marketable good. The investment information from the private information-producing firms can be considered a marketable good when it is paid for by investors. However, municipal accounting and reporting is being sold neither to investment information producing firms nor to investors in municipal securities, so that it remains a public good for these parties as well as for taxpayers.

The Objectives of Municipal Accounting and Reporting for Taxpayers and Investors

Given the distinctive differences between the kinds of goods and services supplied by municipalities as compared to those supplied by

---

[23]See Simon, "Fiscal Accountability," p. 800. Zimmerman, "Municipal Accounting Mazes," also treats information about the public sector as a public good.

business corporations, what should be the basic objectives guiding municipal accounting and reporting?[24] Municipal accounting and reporting should generate information that helps taxpayers and investors answer certain fundamental questions. What are some of these fundamental questions?

Is the municipality supplying the types, quantities, and qualities of public goods for which taxpayers have entrusted their money? Are these public goods being supplied at minimum cost? The first two questions refer, respectively, to the effectiveness and efficiency of municipal operations with respect to the supply of public goods. Is the municipal government supplying the appropriate mix of public and marketable goods? This question is addressed to the composition of the basket of goods and services provided by the municipality. Is the municipal government undertaking too many activities? In other words, is the size of the public sector too large? Do municipal activities, quite apart from the supply of public goods, have any unintended side effects on taxpayers, citizens, businesses, and other organizations? Are citizens, taxpayers, businesses, and other organizations getting their fair share of public goods produced by the municipality? That is, is there equity in the distribution of public goods by the municipality? Is each taxpayer paying his or her fair share of taxes required to finance municipal activities? Is there equity in the distribution of tax costs borne by taxpayers? Is the expected rate of return on a particular municipal security adequate to compensate an investor for the expected level of risk to which he or she will be exposed by investing in that security? What level of risk should an investor expect to be exposed to when investing in a particular municipal security?

These fundamental questions led A. J. Simon in his study, "Conceptual Problems in the FANO Study by the FASB with Respect to

---

[24]Robert N. Anthony, in a study for the Financial Accounting Standards Board, *Financial Accounting in Nonbusiness Organizations* sets out the objectives of financial reporting by nonbusiness organizations (including governmental units) in terms of "user needs." Anthony tells us that users desire information on (1) financial viability, (2) fiscal compliance, (3) management performance, and (4) the cost of services provided. See Anthony *Financial Accounting in Nonbusiness Organizations: An Exploratory Study of Conceptual Issues (FANO)*, Research Report (Stamford, Conn.: Financial Accounting Standards Board (FASB), 1978), pp. 48–52. William W. Holder, in a study for the National Council on Governmental Accounting, also adopts the Anthony fourfold framework. See Holder, *A Study of Selected Concepts for Governmental Financial Accounting and Reporting*, an NCGA Research Report (Chicago: National Council on Governmental Accounting: 1980), p. 21. Abraham J. Simon formulates the objectives of governmental accounting and reporting in terms of the classic economic approach to such matters. See Simon, "Conceptual Problems in the FANO Study by the FASB with Respect to Public Sector Accounting and Disclosure," *Proceedings of the American Accounting Association's Mid-Atlantic Regional Meeting*, April 5–7, 1979, College Park, Maryland, ed. A. J. Stagliano (College Park: University of Maryland, 1979), pp. 42–54.

Public Sector Accounting and Disclosure," to set out a series of objectives for public sector disclosure.[25] This work was based on an earlier study of his cited previously in this chapter.[26] In his 1979 study, Simon tells us that:

> Since voters are sovereign, their disclosure needs must be sovereign. These disclosure needs and *the objectives of public sector disclosure* can be summarized in terms of reporting on goal attainment in the following 11 areas of public sector achievement with respect to: (1) the type, (2) quantity, and (3) quality of public goods; (4) the level of the public sector output relative to the private sector, and (5) the composition of the public sector output; efficiency in the allocation of resources (6) in the public sector, and (7) in the impact of public sector activities on the private sector; equity in the distribution of (8) the benefits of public sector activity, and (9) the costs of public sector activity; and in the case of investment in the public sector, (10) the return associated with such investment and (11) the risk associated with such investment. The first nine areas of disclosure are primarily the concern of taxpayers and consumers of public goods, while the last two areas are primarily the concern of investors (Simon, 1978).[27]

The 11 objectives of accounting and reporting for a municipality provide us with a concise overview of the basic information needs of taxpayers and investors with respect to municipal activities.[28]

Does municipal accounting and reporting actually address itself to meeting the 11 fundamental objectives in order to provide information to answer the fundamental questions? Later on in this chapter and over the course of the three following chapters, we shall describe municipal accounting and reporting as required by current standards. Once you have had a chance to study these standards, then you will be better able to answer this question.

PUBLIC GOODS AND DISTINGUISHING CHARACTERISTICS OF MUNICIPAL ORGANIZATIONS VERSUS BUSINESS CORPORATIONS

The Exclusion Principle and Private Ownership

The basic distinction on which we have been focusing throughout our discussion is that between marketable private goods and nonmar-

---

[25]Ibid., p. 44.

[26]Simon,"Fiscal Accountability," pp. 802–803.

[27]Simon, "Conceptual Problems," p. 44. The (Simon, 1978) study referred to at the end of the quote is the same one cited in the previous footnote.

[28]We have cited propositions 13 and 2½ as dramatic examples of voter sovereignty.

ketable public goods.[29] Differences between these two types of economic goods can lead to differences between the kinds of organizations that supply each type of good. The differences in certain characteristics between organizations such as municipalities (which supply nonmarket public goods) and business corporations (which supply marketable private goods) can help to explain some of the most important differences between corporate business accounting and reporting and municipal accounting and reporting.

The existence of marketable private goods means that there are economic goods that can be provided on a voluntary basis to individual private buyers and consumers. It means also that private manufacturers and sellers can be organized by individuals on a voluntary basis to supply such goods. In fact, the existence of such goods means not merely that private companies supplying marketable private goods can be formed voluntarily but, more importantly, that private companies without public prodding *will* be formed to supply such goods. One does not need special legislative acts to force people to form business corporations to supply marketable private goods. As long as a marketable good is sufficiently profitable, private individuals will form private businesses on a voluntary basis to supply such a good. The exact form of business organizations may be regulated by law—e.g., proprietorships or partnerships as against corporate forms of organization—but one does not need a law to encourage people to form businesses to exploit opportunities to supply profitable and marketable private goods. The structure of economic rewards and penalties will tend to affect the form of organization that private business ventures will take. However, common to all of the different forms of private business organization is private ownership of the business venture. This means that ownership interest in a private business is itself marketable. Regardless of the form of organization, owners can sell all or a part of their interests in a private business on a voluntary basis to other willing investors.

The original real economic good or service being supplied is marketable because the benefits of the good are divisible and may be enjoyed by prospective consumers only if these consumers are willing to pay for the good. The exclusion principle applies in the case of mar-

---

[29]One should note that there are nonmarketable private goods as well as nonmarketable public goods. An accounting framework for nonmarketable private consumer goods can be found in two studies by Abraham J. Simon. These are "An Economic and Macroaccounting Framework for Household Nonmarket Production and Its Uses: The Output Side," *International Journal of Accounting Education and Research* 12, no. 2 (Spring 1977), pp. 143–68; and "A Macroaccounting Framework for the Value-Added and Saving Side of Household Nonmarket Production," *International Journal of Accounting Education and Research* 13, no. 1 (Fall 1977), pp. 93–129.

ketable real economic goods, whether these goods are real consumer goods or real producer goods used in the production of consumer goods. The right to supply a marketable good will itself be a marketable property right only if its benefits are also subject to the exclusion principle.[30]

What are the benefits that flow from the right to supply a marketable private good? The monetary benefits are the net cash proceeds that an investor expects to be able to utilize to the exclusion of all other parties. An investor expects to be able to ultimately convert the monetary benefits into real benefits in terms of consumer goods. Investors expect to receive, and do receive net cash proceeds which they can use exclusively for themselves and to which third parties will have no claims. The exclusion principle does operate with respect to the right to supply a marketable good or service. Not only must the exclusion principle operate, but also the investor must expect to receive sufficient net future cash proceeds relative to his or her investment to meet at the least the desired rate of return on such investment at an acceptable level of risk. This leads us to the obvious and most significant characteristic of organizations that supply marketable private goods—that is, that such organizations will tend to be of the profit-seeking variety.

Public Goods and Public Sector Organizations Such as Municipalities

Now let us contrast the organizations that supply marketable private goods on a voluntary basis with the organizations that supply nonmarket goods in a democratic society. Private individuals will not voluntarily form profit-seeking, privately owned organizations in order to supply nonmarket public goods. The right to supply a nonmarket public good does not generate the profit-making opportunities that will induce private individuals to form voluntarily private, profit-seeking organizations. Instead, through a predominant political process rather than through a predominant economic process, the community will have to create nonprofit, public sector organizations such as municipalities to supply nonmarketable public goods at the municipal level. These public sector organizations are not subject to

---

[30]This is a necessary but not sufficient condition. Not only must the benefits be subject to the exclusion principle, but potential organizers of a business must expect sufficiently profitable results from operations at acceptable levels of risk. Earlier, the problem of external benefits and costs that bypass the market mechanism was discussed. Ways of internalizing such externalities and improving the operation of the market have been studied in the context of a market for property rights. Two such studies are Harold Demsetz, "The Exchange and Enforcement of Property Rights," *Journal of Law and Economics,* October 1964; and J. H. Dales, *Pollution, Property, and Prices* (Toronto: University of Toronto Press, 1970).

individual private ownership. There are no ownership interests in such organizations which can be bought and sold in a market.

The fact that public sector organizations such as municipalities will not receive voluntary payments to finance the supply of public goods leads to other distinguishing characteristics relative to business corporations. If no voluntary payments are forthcoming, then these public sector organizations will have to have the power to raise revenues themselves in an other than voluntary manner in order to finance their activities. In a democracy such as the United States, the raising of revenues will take place through a predominant political process. In the United States, the raising of revenues to finance public sector activities is subject to legislative action, executive concurrence, and judicial review. The power to raise involuntary payments is hedged in all sorts of checks and balances which operate at times quite well, and at other times rather less well than is intended.

A private company does not need a specific law to permit it to raise a particular type of voluntary payment from its customers. Of course, one assumes that both the seller and buyer are operating in general within the law so that the seller is supplying a legally permitted good, and the buyer is not trying to obtain the good through illegal means such as theft.

Not only is the revenue or receipts side of a public sector organization such as a municipality subject to specific laws, but so is the spending side. Municipalities do not have the power to engage in any activities other than those authorized in specific legislative acts which have passed through a legislative process and are subject to judicial review. Further, the authority to spend money to carry out particular types of authorized activities is itself subject also to specific legislative acts. In the case of resources which have been raised through law by involuntary payments, these resources cannot be used unless in accordance with specific laws authorizing such use. A municipality's authority, both to raise resources and to use those resources, must be spelled out in specific legislative acts. The exercising of the revenue-raising and spending authorities is subject also to judicial review.

A private business, on the other hand, does not need a specific legislative act to enable it to raise voluntary payments for its goods and services, nor does it need another legislative act to authorize it to spend moneys on the activities which enable it to supply goods and services. A business corporation does not need a specific legislative act to permit it to raise resources from creditors and equity investors, although these fund-raising activities are subject to particular regulations or laws. The resources raised from creditors and equity investors are done so on a voluntary basis.

The fact that business corporations and other private business organizations are profit-seeking entities, and that municipalities are not profit-seeking entities, has had a significant impact on the kind of accounting and reporting that one finds for these organizations. The fact that municipalities can only raise and spend resources obtained on an involuntary basis through legislative processes, and that business corporations are not subject to such specific legal constraints, also has had an impact on accounting for corporations versus accounting for municipalities.

THE IMPACT OF MUNICIPAL PUBLIC GOODS ON MUNICIPAL VERSUS CORPORATE ACCOUNTING

Turning now to the final topic of this chapter, we will explore some specific differences in accounting principles as between corporate and municipal accounting that result from the fact that municipal organizations (and other government organizations) tend to be best suited to supply nonmarket public goods, while business corporations (and other business organizations) tend to be best suited to supply marketable private goods. Before we actually compare corporate and municipal accounting principles, it would be useful to have an idea of the circumstances under which business accounting principles have been and are developed for corporate accounting.

Generally Accepted Accounting Principles for Corporate Financial Reporting

Earlier, we noted that a basic purpose of business accounting (as well as nonbusiness accounting) is to provide information useful for economic decision making. Accountants tend to approach business accounting and thus corporate accounting from two major perspectives. One perspective accountants call "financial accounting"; the other is called "managerial accounting." The difference between the two is in terms of the users at which the accounting information is directed. Financial accounting is supposed to generate information that is expected to be useful to and used by parties who are primarily external to the business enterprise. In the case of corporations, financial accounting produces information that is expected to be useful to and used by creditors, shareholders, potential future investors (of both the creditor and shareholder variety), financial analysts, governmental agencies, financial intermediaries, information-producing firms, and other parties external to the corporation.

Managerial accounting produces information that is internally oriented. The information is expected to be useful to and used primarily by users who are directly affiliated with the corporation, such as its managers and board of directors. Managerial accounting supplies information to be used for planning and control purposes by corporate management. Of course, there are areas of overlap between financial and managerial accounting and also between external and internal users of each type of accounting information. We will be concerned primarily with corporate financial accounting. We are concerned with the kind of accounting information that is directed primarily at parties who are external to the corporation.

While it true that corporate financial accounting is concerned with information that is expected to be useful to external parties in decision making, this is really not the whole story. Financial accounting has not only been thought to produce information useful for economic decision making but it has also been and still is seen as performing a "custodial" function. In fact, it seems that the custodial function of financial accounting has tended to dominate the "information for decision making" function. W. H. Beaver describes the shift in emphasis, over time, from the custodial function of accounting to the function of information for economic decision making in his *Financial Reporting: An Accounting Revolution*.[31] If one is to understand certain features of business accounting as applied to corporations, one must keep in mind that financial accounting (as distinct from managerial accounting) has been subject to at least two different objectives which at times are not necessarily compatible with each other. Other forces which have been in operation on financial accounting will be described shortly.

The custodial point of view stresses that investors (both creditors and shareholders) have entrusted funds to the corporation, and that it is the function of accounting to provide these investors with a monitoring system in the form of historical records that show how the managers of the business have cared for these funds. The custodial function tends to be backward looking. It tends to view investors as somewhat locked into their investments. Also this approach appears to be more appropriate for the creditor investor than for an equity investor.

The function of information for economic decision making, on the other hand, tends to be forward looking. This approach treats investors as forward looking and not locked into their investments. It stresses that investors of both the creditor and equity variety are interested in predicting *future* corporate profitability and the *future* risk prospects of the corporation. Historical information is useful primarily if it helps in the prediction of future return and risk for a particular investment. Information on the custodial performance of corporate management is useful if it helps in the prediction of future

---

[31](Englewood Cliffs, N.J.: Prentice-Hall, 1981). The "financial accounting revolution" has found its way into the textbooks. A recent textbook by George Foster, *Financial Statement Analysis* (Englewood Cliffs, N.J.: Prentice-Hall, 1978), reflects the impact of the attempts to subject financial accounting to economic analysis in the context of corporate finance and econometric measurement.

management performance with respect to corporate profitability and risk.

The custodial approach to accounting tends to stress the kind of information that would be considered useful to investors *after* they have made an investment decision and committed their funds. The information for economic decision making tends to stress the information required by investors *before* completing investment decisions. There are areas of overlap between these two approaches and often it is difficult to decide whether a particular type of information is more suited for one approach than the other. However, broadly speaking, keeping these two approaches in mind will help to some degree in understanding some of the basic features of corporate financial accounting.

The basic instruments generated by corporate financial accounting for external reporting purposes are the three basic financial statements that one normally finds in the corporate annual reports prepared by management for the benefit of the stockholders. The basic financial statements are considered to be prepared by, and the responsibility of, corporate management—as is true for the rest of the corporate annual report. The basic financial statements along with appended notes to these statements are usually subjected to audit by independent, certified public accounting firms. The independent auditors certify the information contained in the basic financial statements and the appended notes to these statements. The other parts of the corporate annual report, other than the basic financial statements and their notes, are not subject to independent verification by external auditors.

This independent certification represents an evaluation as to whether the basic financial statements (and their notes) present "fairly" three frames of reference of the activities of the corporation. One frame of reference stresses the financial position of the corporation. A second frame of reference stresses the results of the operations of the corporation. The last frame of reference tries to capture certain items that may have not been fully disclosed by the first two frames of reference. It stresses changes in the financial position of the corporation. Each frame of reference has its own basic financial statement. The three basic financial statements are: (1) the statement of financial position, (2) the income statement, and (3) the statement of changes in financial position.[32] The three basic financial statements

---

[32]Each of the basic financial statements has been and is known by more than one name. For example, the statement of financial position is most often called the balance sheet. It is also called a statement of financial condition. The income statement is also called the statement of earnings, or the results of operations. Earlier, the income statement was called the profit and loss statement. The statement of changes in financial position is also called a statement of changes in financial condition. Earlier this statement had been known as the statement of source and application of funds, or simply as the funds statement.

are supported by a set of explanatory notes that are intended to clarify and elaborate particular items appearing in the financial statements. The notes are intended also to provide pertinent additional disclosures covering significant items that do not appear directly in the basic financial statements.

What does "fairly present" mean in terms of the auditor certification of the three basic financial statements (and their notes)? It seems to mean that the three basic financial statements (along with their notes) have been prepared in accordance with generally accepted accounting principles (usually abbreviated as GAAP) which have been applied in a consistent fashion from one year to the next. Generally accepted accounting principles are the accounting rules to be used for external financial reporting purposes.[33] The accounting principles are described as generally accepted because there are major interest groups which believe themselves affected by accounting principles and appear to participate actively in the formulation of modifications of old GAAP and the introduction of new GAAP.[34] The support of the major interest groups (or at least not their active opposition) is required in order for accounting principles to be generally acceptable.

The major interest groups involved in the formulation of GAAP have been primarily (but not solely): (1) independent certified public accounting firms acting individually and (2) through their professional association, the American Institute of Certified Public Accountants (AICPA); (3) business clients of the independent auditors acting on their own and (4) through their various trade associations and organizations; (5) the Securities and Exchange Commission (SEC); and (6) the investment community in its various facets. From time to time, the Internal Revenue Service and even the U.S. Congress have had an impact on the formulation and acceptance of GAAP.[35]

---

[33]A description of the notion of generally accepted accounting principles may be found in *AICPA Professional Standards, vol 3, Accounting* (New York: Commerce Clearing House for the AICPA, 1981) AC Section 1022, Para. .19 to .23. These paragraphs are taken from *APB Statement 4,* Chap. 12, para. 27–31, as amended.

[34]The idea that a political process leads to the modification and introduction of accounting principles is discussed, for example, in Charles T. Horngren, "The Marketing of Accounting Standards," *Journal of Accountancy,* October 1973, pp. 61–66; and in David Solomons, "The Politicization of Accounting," *Journal of Accountancy,* November 1978, pp. 65–72.

[35]Until 1973 the Accounting Principles Board (APB), a committee of the AICPA, was considered the primary private sector body concerned with the process by which GAAP was formulated and accepted. In 1971, the APB circulated a document which proposed to eliminate a conflict between two different accounting methods to account for the investment tax credit. Glenn A. Welsch, Charles T. Zlatkovich, and Walter T. Harrison tell us that the APB "lost the battle in the political arena when business executives pressured Congress to insert a provision in the Revenue Act of 1971 which legally permitted choice of either method of accounting for the investment credit." See Welsch, Zlatkovich, and Harrison, *Intermediate Accounting,* 5th ed. (Homewood, Ill.: Richard D. Irwin, 1979), p. 497. Homer A. Black also describes the congressional action which effectively prevented the APB from modifying GAAP. See Black, "Accounting for Corporate Income Taxes," in *Handbook of Modern Accounting,* 2d ed., eds. Sidney Davidson and Roman L. Weil (New York: McGraw-Hill, 1977), chap. 36, p. 36.

The development of GAAP has been the result of a loose kind of political interaction between the various major interest groups and other parties. Currently, the rule-making body in the private sector through which the development and acceptance of GAAP is focused is the Financial Accounting Standards Board (FASB). The FASB is the most recent private sector compromise among the various major interest groups, and has the primary responsibility for the formulation and modification of GAAP, and also for the process to obtain acceptability of GAAP.

In order to ensure that financial statements do in fact fairly present financial position, results of operation, and changes in financial position in conformity with GAAP, independent CPA firms perform auditing activities in conformity with what are called "generally accepted auditing standards (GAAS)." The professional association of independent CPAs and independent CPA firms, the AICPA, has the primary responsibility for the formulation and modification of GAAS as well as ensuring that GAAS achieves general acceptability. The purpose of GAAS is to establish and maintain the level of quality of audits performed by external CPA auditors. There is also the significant impact of the legal liability that auditors can incur when they do not meet what are considered to be acceptable levels of auditing work. One should note that the economic penalities arising from successful lawsuits against the auditing profession have also acted as a force in improving GAAS.[36]

Acceptance for changes in GAAP appears over the years to have involved significantly more controversy and a much greater reaction from business enterprises than have changes in GAAS. Changes in GAAS are perceived basically as part of the tool kit of the professional auditor. Auditing is essentially a marketable service supplied by auditing firms to their clients. Any benefits or costs involved with respect to changes in GAAS appear to be internalized through the market mechanism. However, business enterprises do *not* seem to behave as though all of the benefits and costs that result from changes in accounting principles are purely private benefits and private costs. We have noted in the prior discussion that achieving acceptability for GAAP involves political interaction among a number of major interested parties. As soon as one observes the presence of political interaction, then one begins to suspect the existence of external benefits and external costs which bypass the market mechanism. Business en-

---

[36]A discussion of an independent auditor's legal liability may be found in a typical auditing textbook such as Howard F. Stettler, *Auditing Principles,* 4th ed. (Englewood Cliffs, N.J.: Prentice-Hall, 1977), pp. 34–39. See also the monograph by Denzil Y. Causey, *Duties and Liabilities of Public Accountants* (Homewood, Ill.: Dow Jones-Irwin, 1979).

terprises behave as if there are external benefits and external costs associated with changes in GAAP.[37]

Thus, the generally accepted accounting principles which help determine the form and content of the three basic financial statements (and their notes) are the result of a political process in which the participants act to protect what they perceive to be their economic interests. The end result seems to have been a mélange of accounting principles which may or may not be consistent with the two fundamental functions of accounting discussed above: the custodial function and the function of information for economic decision making.

Despite the fact that changes in business GAAP and therefore changes in business accounting are subject to a political process, certain major differences between business accounting and municipal accounting rest to a striking degree on the fact that businesses supply primarily marketable private goods, and that one of the major classes of goods supplied by municipalities is nonmarketable public goods. We turn next to an examination of some major differences between business (and corporate) accounting and municipal accounting.

The Income Statement: Marketable Private Goods and Accrual Accounting

The supplying of marketable private goods will be undertaken if perceived as sufficiently profitable. This means that in all probability the most important informational feature of accounting for a business corporation is the accounting for and reporting of profit. In fact, the entire focus of accounting and reporting for business corporations can be characterized as profit-oriented. The major task of external financial accounting and reporting for businesses is to provide information to enable investors to judge where the most profitable opportunities are likely to be found, and to assess the level of risk-taking likely to be associated with each profit opportunity. As a result, one finds that one of the major basic financial statements that private sector business (and corporate) accounting generates is the income statement, which reports on corporate profits and losses.

---

[37]William H. Beaver concluded that the empirical studies that he reviewed do not support the contention that changes in accounting principles have had significant economic effects. He also concluded that the empirical evidence that he reviewed did not support a need for governmental regulation of financial disclosure by profit-seeking enterprises. A major characteristic of the studies that Beaver reviewed is that they are essentially empirical statistical correlation studies which try to measure the impact of change in accounting principles and the effect of government regulation (via the Securities and Exchange Commission) on observable market prices of equity securities of private companies. One of the major limitations of such studies is that they would not detect the existence of significant externalities which do not pass through the market mechanism and would not exercise a directly observable impact on the market prices of the securities being studied. See Beaver, *Financial Reporting,* p. 202.

The income statement is intended to be essentially an historical document of what has happened to corporate profits and losses. However, be forewarned that all sorts of forecasts may be embedded in the typical corporate income statement. Accountants would argue that financial statements (including the income statement) are based, by and large, on objective historical data. Nevertheless, a close examination reveals that what may have begun as largely historical in nature turns out to contain a significant amount of data manipulation which is pure forecasting.[38]

The fact that business corporations supply marketable private goods affects how accountants account for and report on the activities of such enterprises. It also affects how accountants calculate corporate profitability reported on through the income statement. Generally accepted accounting principles favor a method known as "accrual accounting" as the preferred way to estimate the net income (or loss) reported as the measure of corporate profitability in the income statement. Accrual accounting is a particular kind of "accounting basis." An accounting basis refers essentially to the time at which one recognizes a particular type of economic event in the financial accounting records of a business. The accrual basis uses, for the most part, the delivery of goods and services as the time at which one records revenues or expenditures for a business enterprise.

Under certain circumstances, the effect of an economic event should be recorded in the accounting records even though goods or services have not been delivered. For example, a significant loss on the purchase of merchandise at a firm price under a noncancelable purchase agreement should be recognized, even though title to the goods has not passed to the buyer.[39] In this case, the buyer should

---

[38]Depreciation and amortization accounting, which purports to measure the consumption of long-lived tangible and intangible fixed assets in the operation of a business, gives us examples of forecasting estimates which enter into the figures shown in the basic financial statements. The estimate for uncollectible accounts receivable is essentially also a forecasted figure which shows up in the basic financial statements. In fact, *FASB Statement No. 5*, "Accounting for Contingencies" (Stamford, Conn.: FASB, 1975) is entirely about items whose recognition in the financial accounting records and the financial statements require forecasting. Other examples of particular accounting requirements which contain significant elements of forecasting can be found in Accounting Principles Board *APB Opinion No. 8*, "Accounting for the Cost of Pension Plans" (New York: AICPA, 1966); *FASB Statement No. 35* "Accounting and Reporting by Defined Benefit Pension Plans" (Stamford, Conn.: FASB, 1980); *Audits of Fire and Casualty Insurance Companies* (New York: AICPA, 1966); and *Audits of Stock Life Insurance Companies* (New York: AICPA, 1972).

Note that an "FASB statement," which is a pronouncement of the Financial Accounting Standards Board, also may be called a "statement of financial accounting standards."

[39]This requirement, under generally accepted accounting principles, appears in Chapter 4 ("Inventory Pricing") of *Accounting Research Bulletin No. 43*, "Restatement and Revision of Accounting Research Bulletins" (New York: AICPA, June 1953). In that chapter, the requirement to recognize a loss on a purchase commitment appears

record a loss prior to the actual receipt of the goods. As a second example, consider the case of a company that extends a warranty on the products that it sells. As of the end of a fiscal period, there may be customer warranty claims that have not yet reached the company. Ultimately, the company will incur servicing costs relating to these warranty claims. Title for the goods or services associated with the cost of servicing the warranty claims has not passed, but an estimated liability should be recognized under the accrual basis of accounting.[40] In both these examples, it was not the passing of title for goods and services that triggered the accrual basis, but a contractual commitment associated with market-type goods or services.

The accrual basis of accounting can be used by private business precisely because they supply marketable private goods. Such goods are divisible so that they can be contracted for on an individual basis. The accrual basis is not feasible for nonmarket public goods. These goods render their benefits in an indivisible way, from the individual point of view, so that one cannot track delivery of divisible units of such goods from individual sellers to individual buyers. In the case of marketable private goods, due to the divisibility of their benefits and the ability to apply the exclusion principle, one can use the delivery of goods or services (or under certain circumstances, contractual commitments) as the economic events that would trigger when one would recognize in the financial accounting records the revenues, expenditures, expenses, assets, and liabilities of a business enterprise—ultimately for purposes of financial reporting.

Under the accrual basis, net income for a business (and a business corporation) is defined as revenues less expenses. Note that expenses are not expenditures. Expenditures under the accrual basis refer to the use of financial resources. Expenses refer to the consumption of real goods and services in the operation of a business. Expenditures would result from the use of financial resources to acquire, for example, real assets. Expenses are estimates of the consumption of real assets (both tangible and intangible) in the operation of a business.

---

as "Statement 10" on inventory pricing and is discussed further in paragraph 17. This requirement is still in force, since it appears in the 1981 edition of *AICPA Professional Standards, vol 3, Accounting,* AC Section 5121, Statement 10 and para. 17.

This recognition of a loss on a purchase commitment is recognized also in intermediate accounting textbooks such as Welsch et al., *Intermediate Accounting,* pp. 368–69; and Donald E. Kieso and Jerry Weygandt, *Intermediate Accounting,* 3d ed. (New York: John Wiley & Sons, 1980), pp. 387–88.

[40]The accrual of an estimated liability as a result of warranty obligations is discussed in *FASB Statement 5,* Appendix A, para. 24–26. Note that an estimated liability that is to be based on expected warranty claims must be based on claims that are believed to have arisen prior to the end of a fiscal period and, of course, for which no liability has been recognized. Warranty claims arising in future fiscal periods beyond the current one are not to be the basis for the accrual of an estimated liability.

In the nonprofit area, financial resources are often used directly to carry out the operating activities of the organization. Where financial resources are used directly in operations rather than for the acquisition of real resources, then such expenditures would be considered also expenses.

In contrast to the accrual basis of accounting, one could use the cash basis of accounting to recognize transactions in the financial accounting records of an enterprise. Under the cash basis, one does not recognize revenues when goods or services are delivered but when cash is collected from the sale of the goods or services. Under the cash basis, expenses do not represent the estimated consumption of goods and services in the operations of the business, but rather cash expenses represent payments of cash for goods and services that *have been or will be* consumed in the operations of the business. Under the cash basis, one uses the time at which receipts from and disbursements of cash, as a result of operations, take place as the time to be used to record operating transactions in the financial accounting records. Accrual-basis net income is accrual-basis revenues less accrual-basis expenses. Cash-basis net income would be cash-basis revenues less cash-basis expenses.

Strictly speaking the term *cash-basis expenses* is not really an ideal term, since expenses usually refer to the consumption of goods and services, not to payments of cash for goods and services. Payments of cash for goods and services are a use of financial resources for the acquisition of goods and services which are expenditures but not expenses. Unfortunately, this difficulty of terminology pervades the concept of cash-basis accounting. There are really several versions of cash-basis accounting but these subtleties are not of major concern to us.[41]

Generally speaking, the accrual basis of accounting is the preferred accounting basis under GAAP. The cash basis is acceptable only as long as it gives results which are essentially the same as the accrual basis.[42] The accrual basis, because it is linked to the delivery of goods and services (or under certain circumstances to contractual

---

[41]See, for example, the definition of the "modified cash basis" which appears in S. Davidson, J. S. Schindler, C. P. Stickney, and R. L. Weil, *Accounting: the Language of Business,* 2d ed., (Glen Ridge, N.J.: Thomas Horton & Daughters, 1977), pp. 34–35. There are also various modifications of the accrual basis used in business accounting. See Arthur L. Thomas, "Revenue Recognition," in Davidson and Weil, *Handbook,* chap. 12, for a full discussion of various bases of accounting used in business accounting.

[42]In 1934 the membership of the American Institute of Accountants (AIA), the predecessor professional organization to the AICPA, adopted six rules with respect to financial accounting and reporting. One of these rules tells us that the preferred basis for revenue recognition is the accrual basis. This rule states among other things that "profit is deemed to be realized when a sale in the ordinary course of business is effected, unless the circumstances are such that the collection of the sale price is not reasonably assured." The rule tells us to record a receivable and thus to accrue revenue

commitments), is compatible with the recording in the financial accounting records of activities associated with the supplying and acquiring of marketable private goods. This basis of accounting is not compatible with the recording in the financial accounting records of activities associated with the production and consumption of nonmarket public goods due to the indivisible nature of these goods. The cash basis of accounting, on the other hand, because it is linked with the payment and receipt of cash is compatible with the recording in the financial accounting records of activities associated either with the supply and demand of marketable private goods or the production and consumption of nonmarket public goods.

Public Goods and the Modified Accrual Basis— the Revenue Side

When a municipality supplies market-type goods, then the recommended accounting basis is the accrual basis. However, when a municipality supplies nonmarket public goods, then the recommended accounting basis is the "modified accrual basis." The modified accrual basis is used particularly to account for nonvoluntary payments in the form of taxes which are used to finance those activities that generate nonmarket public goods.

The *modified accrual basis* (on the revenue side) does not use the delivery of goods or services as the event when one should record revenues from taxes in the financial accounting records. Pure public and quasi-public goods generate relatively indivisible benefits to which the exclusion principle does not apply, and therefore are not subject to user charges. One cannot identify easily on an individual-user basis precisely which taxpayers are getting measurable benefits from particular public goods at any particular time. One has the problem that there are free riders who are receiving significant external benefits. As a result, there is no way to pinpoint in a cost-efficient manner on a one-to-one basis the delivery of goods and services with the recognition of revenues. Instead of voluntary user charges, we have involuntary tax payments from the individual point of view.

On the revenue side, the accrual basis as applied in the private

---

for a credit sale unless collection is not likely. This rule has been kept a part of current GAAP. The rule was originally incorporated into *Accounting Research Bulletin No. 1* issued in 1939 by the Committee on Accounting Procedure (CAP), a committee of the AIA. The CAP lasted from 1938 to 1959; it was succeeded by the Accounting Principles Board (APB). The APB lasted from 1959 to 1973, at which time it was replaced by the Financial Accounting Standard Board (FASB). We noted earlier that the APB was a part of the AICPA, but that the FASB is organized to be an independent entity. Even though *ARB No. 43* was issued by the CAP, the FASB has designated pronouncements of its predecessor organizations to be a part of GAAP, so that those parts of *ARB No. 43* which have not been amended or superseded are still a part of GAAP.

sector for market-type private goods just doesn't work in the case of nonmarket public goods. Instead, the basis of accounting for recognizing revenues from involuntary tax payments is called the modified accrual basis, which uses the cash basis of accounting to record revenues for certain types of taxes, and a type of accrual accounting to record other types of taxes in the financial accounting records of the municipality.

We have already described the cash basis as a method for recognizing or recording revenues in the financial accounting records. Revenues are recognized when cash is collected from customers. In the case of municipal accounting for nonmarket public goods, you don't have cash coming in from voluntary payments of user charges, but cash is coming in from involuntary payments of taxes. Certain types of municipal taxes are recognized as revenues when cash is collected; other types of municipal taxes may be recognized as revenues before cash is collected.

If all types of municipal taxes were recognized as revenues when cash was collected, then all taxes would be on the cash basis. However, certain types of taxes may be recognized as revenues prior to cash collections. This is why the accounting basis is called the modified accrual basis. Recognizing revenues prior to cash collections is one of the basic features of an accrual-type basis of accounting. However, for nonmarket public goods, one cannot use the delivery of goods or services as the way to accrue revenues prior to cash collections. Instead, for nonmarket public goods the accrual of revenues must be based on events other than the delivery of goods and services.

In the case of property taxes, the event used to accrue revenues due from property taxpayers is generally the date on which their properties have been assessed for the current year's property tax. On that date, property tax owners are considered legally liable for the property tax.[43] In order to accrue revenues under the modified accrual basis, they have to be measurable and available.[44]

The property tax is accruable under the modified accrual basis be-

---

[43]See, for example, MFOA, *1980 GAAFR,* p. 39, for a discussion of the accrual of property taxes on the assessment date.

[44]See, for example, AICPA, *ASLGU,* p. 14, for a discussion of "measurable" and "available" as criteria for the accrual of taxes. In June 1981, the National Council on Governmental Accounting issued *NCGA Interpretation 3,* "Revenue Recognition—Property Taxes." This was an attempt to further refine the concept of "availability." Also, certain types of resources received by a governmental unit are not recognized as revenues until spent. The resources are usually in the form of grants. If the conditions of the grant are not met, then the grantee is required to return the resources to the grantor. This version of the modified accrual basis is discussed in *NCGA Statement 2,* "Grant, Entitlement, and Shared Revenue Accounting and Reporting by State and Local Governments," issued by the National Council on Governmental Accounting (Chicago: Municipal Finance Officers Association, 1979).

cause there is a particular date, the assessment date, on which the amount of the property tax is "measurable." The taxpayer's liability for the property tax is measurable because it is quantifiable on a particular date. "Available" means that one expects the cash proceeds from a particular tax to be received in time to be used to pay for the items of expenditure appearing in the current fiscal year's budget. Property taxes are normally assessed so that their cash collection is expected to be received in time to be used to finance the current year's budget activities.

Taxes, other than property taxes, do not normally satisfy the measurability criterion. For example, take the case of sales taxes. One cannot pinpoint, at nominal cost at a particular moment during a fiscal year, taxpayer liability for sales taxes. The liability for a sales tax arises at the time of consummation of a sale of a good or service that is subject to the sales tax. Strictly speaking, for the usual sort of sales tax, the liability for the sales tax at the moment the sale is consummated is transferred from the consumer to the merchant making the sale. The merchant assumes the role of a tax-collecting agent for the governmental unit authorized to receive the sales tax proceeds. The governmental unit could accrue sales tax revenue when sales subject to sales taxes are consummated, since the tax is both measurable and available at that moment. However, this is not done because it would require an extensive reporting system by merchants to governmental units. The cost of accruing the sales taxes at the moment that taxable sales are consummated is considered prohibitive and not worth the benefits. Instead, sales taxes are recognized in the financial accounting records as revenues on a cash basis when merchants file their sales tax returns and pay the amounts of the sales tax liabilities calculated on these returns.[45]

Thus, we see that whether we are dealing with taxes which are accruable or with taxes which are recognized on the cash basis, in either case the delivery of nonmarket public goods cannot be used as a basis to accrue tax revenues.[46]

---

[45]Note that taxes such as sales taxes, which are recognized normally on the cash basis, may be accrued under certain circumstances. AICPA, *ASLGU,* p. 14, tells us that, where taxes have not been received in the form of cash by the usual date for such tax payments and if the amounts are material, then a receivable for such unpaid taxes should be recorded, which means that revenue will be accrued prior to the receipt of cash. Of course, an estimate for uncollectible amounts should be deducted from the amount to be recognized as revenue.

[46]Note that using the sales of marketable private goods as a potential basis for the accruing of sales tax revenues is not the same thing as using the delivery of nonmarket public goods as a basis for accrual. If one could measure delivery of nonmarket public goods to consumers, then one would be able to measure use of public goods and exact user charges for such goods. The sale of marketable private goods is not related in any causative fashion to the use of nonmarket public goods.

The Budget, the Modified Accrual Basis, and the Expenditure Side

In the case of a municipality, the modified accrual basis applied to the expenditure side is distinctively different from this basis applied to the revenue side. In order to appreciate this difference, let us first review how the accrual basis is applied to expenditures by business corporate enterprises. Ultimately, in business accounting one is concerned not so much with expenditures as with expenses. Recall that business net income is calculated by subtracting expenses (not expenditures) from revenues. Earlier, expenses were distinguished from expenditures. Expenses represent an attempt to estimate the consumption of real resources (goods and services) used up in the operation of the business. Expenditures refer to the use of financial resources.

Expenditures by a business enterprise cover both expenditures in the form of voluntary user charges for the acquisition of marketable private goods and services, and expenditures which represent taxes to pay for nonmarket public goods and services. The tax expenditures are not voluntary user charges for the acquisition of divisible private goods and services. According to business GAAP, expenditures should be recorded on the accrual basis. This means that expenditures for marketable private goods and services should be recorded generally on the accrual basis. Expenditures for marketable private goods and services become expenses within the time period during which these goods and services are estimated to have been consumed in operations. Tax expenditures are recognized during that period when the liability for taxes is considered to have been incurred. Where the payment date for a particular tax comes after its liability date, that tax is accrued as an expenditure as of its liability date. If the payment date and the liability date coincide for a particular tax, then the tax expenditure is recorded when paid.

However, unlike expenditures for marketable private goods and services, tax expenditures are not incurred as user charges. Thus, the accrual of tax expenditures where the liability for a particular tax precedes its payment is not based upon the delivery of goods and services. Tax expenditures do not result from the acquisition of divisible goods and services where these taxes are supposed to pay for the supply of nonmarket public goods and services. Tax expenditures for nonmarket public goods and services represent ultimately involuntary payments (from the individual point of view) to help finance public sector activities whether or not these activities are estimated to provide specific benefits to the enterprise. Tax expenditures tend to be treated as expenses as they are incurred.[47]

---

[47]Accounting for income taxes in the basic financial statements is relatively involved, according to current GAAP. Accounting Principles Board, *APB Opinion No.*

Thus, one can see that the accrual basis of accounting affects both the revenue and the expenditure side in business accounting. The effect of the accrual basis on business expenses, however, is less clear-cut. This is due to a number of rather complex and somewhat arbitrary procedures which are used to transform expenditures for real goods and services into expenses (the estimated consumption of such goods and services).[48]

When we turn to the expenditure side of governmental accounting, what we discover is that where a government acquires marketable private goods and services then the recommended accounting basis is, for the most part, the accrual basis. The reason that the modified accrual basis for the expenditure side of a governmental unit is, by and large, really the accrual basis stems from the fact that the expenditures in question are largely for the acquisition of divisible market-type private goods and services.[49] This means that, just as in business accounting, one can use the delivery of such goods and services as the event on which one can base the recognition of a liability and a matching expenditure. Of course, where the governmental unit is receiving benefits from nonmarket public goods and services, one cannot use an accounting basis that depends on the delivery of goods and services. Generally, governmental units do not pay taxes to each other for nonmarket public goods and services. Thus, tax expenditures which are a relevant type of expenditure in business accounting generally do not apply in governmental accounting.

Even though the accrual basis applies, for the most part, to governmental accounting for expenditures, there are still some significant modifications to it that one does not find in business accounting. Cer-

---

11, "Accounting for Income Taxes" (New York: AICPA 1967), sets out the basic GAAP in this area. The complications dealt with in *APB Opinion No. 11* have to do with how to report income tax expense in the basic financial statements when accounting income shown in these statements differs from taxable income shown in the tax return for the enterprise. As a result of the accounting recommended in *APB Opinion No. 11,* tax expenditures as calculated from the liability on the income tax return will not necessarily be equal to tax expenses reported in the basic financial statements. These accounting methods are beyond the scope of the present discussion.

[48]There is a substantial accounting literature covering a wealth of research that deals with the very many problems encountered in the estimation of net income. Probably a good starting point in introducing oneself to the work done in this area would be to look at textbooks dealing with accounting theory. Two such textbooks are Eldon S. Hendricksen, *Accounting Theory,* 3d ed. (Homewood, Ill.: Richard D. Irwin, 1977); and Kenneth S. Most, *Accounting Theory* (Columbus, Ohio: Grid, 1977).

[49]Even though the modified accrual basis is the recommended basis of accounting for state and local governmental units, one finds quite frequently that they use cash-basis accounting. Therefore, in looking at financial statements for state and local governmental units, one must be careful to be sure of the accounting basis used in the financial statements. The issue of the divergence between recommended accounting principles for municipalities and actual practice in financial reporting for such entities is beyond the scope of the current and the following three chapters.

tain of the major modifications have to do with the fact that governmental spending must take place within a framework of legally enacted budgets. The enacted budget of a governmental unit provides it with the authority to spend. This means that no expenditures should be recorded into the financial accounting records unless these have been authorized in the enacted budget. As a result, there are certain types of expenditures which would be accrued in the case of business accounting, but are not accrued in governmental and municipal accounting.

For example, in business accounting, interest is accrued on long-term debt with the passage of time.[50] This is not so in governmental accounting. Interest on long-term debt, in governmental accounting, is shown as an expenditure only when that interest is due and payable and has been provided for in the governmental unit's budget.[51] Another example has to do with personnel costs. In business accounting, if employees have rendered services and have not been paid as of the end of a fiscal period, then an accrual for wages and salaries earned but not paid is recorded in the financial accounting records. In governmental accounting, if at the end of a fiscal period employees have rendered services but have not been paid because there is no provision in the current fiscal period's budget, then there will be no accrual of expenditures for wages and salaries earned but not paid. Instead, employees will be paid out of the next fiscal year's budget, and expenditures will be recognized as part of that year's authorized spending. Further discussion on this point will be found in Chapter 36.[52]

Another pecularity of the expenditure side in municipal accounting

---

[50]The accrual of interest on debt is an example of accrual accounting which uses the passage of time, rather than the delivery of goods or services at a particular moment in time, as the basis for recognizing a transaction in the financial accounting records of a business enterprise. In the case of interest expense from the point of view of the borrower in connection with debt (interest revenue from the point of view of the lender), the interest is assumed to have been incurred (or earned) through the passage of time. See, for instance, the discussion in Thomas, *Revenue Recognition,* pp. 12–7 and 12–8.

[51]The long-term debt in question is called general long-term debt. In *NCGA Statement 1,* p. 9, *general* long-term debt is distinguished from *fund* long-term liabilities. General long-term debt is normally in the form of general long-term bonds which are not a specific liability of a particular fund, but are a general liability usually subject to the full faith and credit of the governmental unit. On the other hand, fund long-term liabilities are an obligation of a particular fund of the governmental unit. They may also be guaranteed by the governmental unit as a whole.

[52]Other examples of differences in accounting for expenditures between the accrual basis of accounting and the modified accrual basis of accounting can be found, for example, in AICPA, *ASLGU,* pp. 16–17. For example, we are told that prepaid expenses do not have to be recorded. This means that an insurance policy that extends over several years would be charged in its entirety as an expenditure in the initial year of the policy. In business accounting, under the accrual basis, the insurance expense from a multiyear policy is allocated over the life of the policy. Remember that accrual basis expenses attempt to measure the consumption of goods and services, not the acquisition of goods and services. Another example involves inventory-type items. According to

has to do with the use of fund accounting. At this point no attempt will be made to explain how fund accounting works. That will be done in the next chapter. However, because of fund accounting, one finds that the maturing of certain types of long-term debt results in the recording of expenditures. The maturing of long-term debt in business accounting would not be recorded as an expenditure.

In business accounting, expenditures are transformed into expenses for purposes of estimating net income. Remember that businesses supply marketable private goods. These private goods are divisible and can be supplied to individual buyer-consumers on a per-unit basis subject to user charges. These circumstances lead private companies to try to estimate costs on a per-unit basis and compare such costs with per-unit user charges to determine product profitability on a per-unit basis. Ultimately, the desire to estimate profitability on a per-unit basis, as well as to estimate net income, leads to the stress on expense estimation for private profit-seeking companies. This same motivation is absent in the case of nonmarket public goods. Such goods generate largely indivisible and nonmarketable benefits.

Governmental budgets covering activities for the supply of nonmarket public goods are put together in terms of expenditures. These budgets function as control instruments over the use of financial resources. Governmental budgets are designed to control the *acquisition* rather than the *consumption* of real resources. This means that governmental financial accounting is concerned with expenditures rather than expenses as a basic financial accounting and reporting category in the case of those activities dealing with nonmarket public goods.

CONCLUSION

The economic distinction that is fundamental to understanding the difference between corporate and municipal accounting is that be-

---

ASLGU, inventory-type items may be treated as expenditures either at the time of purchase or at the time of consumption. In business accounting, inventory items (where material) are accounted for as expenses either by being matched against sales as cost of goods sold, or when consumed in operations if matching against sales is not a relevant consideration.

In *Statement of Position 75–3,* "Accrual of Revenues and Expenditures by State and Local Governmental Units" (New York: AICPA. 1975), pp. 7–8, we are told that the liability for sick leave and vacation pay for governmental employees need not be recorded as an expenditure as incurred. Instead, expenditures for sick leave and vacation pay may be recorded on the cash basis. A statement of position (SOP) such as *SOP 75–3* is a modification or amendment to an audit guide such as *Audits of State and Local Governmental Units.* The method of accounting for and reporting of vacation, sick, and other leave benefits has been modified by the issuance of National Council on Government Accounting, *NCGA Statement 4,* "Accounting and Financial Reporting Principles for Claims and Judgments and Compensated Absences" (Chicago: new NCGA, August 1982). This pronouncement, if followed, should have a tendency to improve somewhat the reporting of certain types of liabilities.

tween marketable private goods and nonmarketable public goods. If a municipality supplies goods and services of the marketable variety which are subject to user charges, then the accounting and financial reporting for such activities will be quite similar to that of a business corporation. However, if a municipality supplies nonmarket public goods, then the characteristics of such goods and services lead to significant differences between municipal and corporate financial accounting and reporting.

If the characteristics of nonmarket public goods play an important role in explaining major differences between municipal and corporate financial accounting and reporting, then it is important that one gets a good grasp of these characteristics. When you have a good understanding of the differences between nonmarket public goods and marketable private goods, then you can look at particular municipal accounting principles and see how and why these differ from their counterpart accounting principles for corporations. In particular, the accrual basis of accounting for corporations is contrasted with the modified accrual basis of accounting for municipalities. This discussion provides us with a foundation for a description of municipal accounting and financial reporting principles, which is the main thrust of the next three chapters.

APPENDIX A

Why the Exclusion Principle Cannot Be Applied to Public Areas for Pedestrian Use

In order to apply the exclusion principle and force a consumer-pedestrian of sidewalk services to surrender a voluntary fee for the use of the sidewalk, you would have to interfere with the right of that citizen-pedestrian to move about easily and in a private fashion. The owner of the sidewalk, in order to apply the exclusion principle, would have to erect barriers around the sidewalk and charge a toll for the use of the sidewalk. The erecting of the barriers would transform a public area such as a sidewalk into a divisible good. However, this would interfere with a citizen-pedestrian's right to be able to move about easily and freely. That right can be exercised effectively only if public areas such as sidewalks and streets are treated as indivisible goods for which the exclusion principle will not be applied against pedestrians.

The treatment of public areas as nonmarket goods for which pedestrians are not to be subjected to user charges rests, so far, on the idea that citizens are entitled to move about freely, easily, and privately as pedestrians. However, suppose one felt that perhaps the advantages of being able to treat the use of public areas as a market good outweighed the advantages of treating it as a nonmarket good. The basic advantage of competitive markets would be that they are efficient in their use of society's resources.

Truly competitive markets generate an efficient allocation of resources only if, in each market, we find the price paid by consumers equal to the marginal cost of producing that good. When price is not equal to marginal cost (the incremental cost of producing an additional unit of a good or service), then it can be shown that either too much or too little of a particular good is being produced and costs of production have not been minimized.[53] Now, how would this work in the case of public areas such as sidewalks?

If the exclusion principle were applied to the use of a sidewalk and a fee charged per unit of use, then that fee or price for sidewalk services should be set equal to the marginal cost of using the sidewalk. The marginal cost of using a sidewalk would be the incremental or extra cost of a single pedestrian using a prescribed area of the sidewalk a single time. Assuming a normal-sized pedestrian carrying the usual load for such a pedestrian over a sidewalk constructed of standard material, then the incremental cost of using a sidewalk a single time is going to be exactly zero.[54] It is very doubtful that there is any "measurable" wear and tear on a sidewalk, resulting from a single use by the typical pedestrian. The major source of wear and tear on sidewalks is likely to be the effect of the elements (changing weather and its components), rather than the wear and tear of pedestrian traffic. Even if pedestrian traffic does have some cumulative long-term impact on a sidewalk, certainly the immediate effect of a single use by a typical pedestrian is simply not measurable. The marginal, or incremental, cost of pedestrian use of sidewalks is zero.

If the incremental cost of pedestrian use is zero, then this means

---

[53]Baumol, *Economics Theory,* pp. 252–56, demonstrates how price must be equal to marginal cost for each commodity if the proper quantity of each commodity is to be produced, resources allocated optimally, and costs minimized. This is one of a number of marginal optimality rules which are discussed in Baumol. He warns us also to beware of the hidden assumption concerning the status quo distribution of income and distribution of wealth which are taken as given, and permit certain consumers to cast unfairly too many money votes in the purchase of goods and services. This causes the ultimate distribution of goods and services, which consumers can enjoy, to be itself inequitable.

[54]Walters, *Economics of Road,* pp. 9–13, contains an analysis of the relevant elements of incremental cost with respect to the use of a road or highway by an automotive vehicle. His analysis can be adapted to a description and investigation of the incremental cost of pedestrian use of public areas. Whereas, for automotive vehicles, incremental cost of the use of even uncongested roads may be greater than zero under certain circumstances (according to Walters), this is highly unlikely in the case of pedestrian use of uncongested public areas.

that a pedestrian's single use of a sidewalk results in no "extra" cost to society. No extra cost means literally that society does not have to allocate any resources at all in order for pedestrians to use sidewalks. This does not mean that it does not cost anything to construct sidewalks. This does not mean that it does not cost anything to maintain sidewalks. Society has to allocate resources to construct and maintain sidewalks, but society does not have to allocate any resources for the actual use of the sidewalks. Well, if society doesn't have to allocate any resources for the use of sidewalks, then the major economic reason for charging a user fee for the use of sidewalks is gone.

The major reason for a user fee for the use of a sidewalk would be that the user charge or price would lead to an efficient allocation of society's resources. The user charge or price for one unit of use has to be equal to the marginal or incremental cost of one unit of use for an efficient allocation of resources in the use of sidewalks to take place. In the case of a sidewalk, since the incremental cost of one unit of pedestrian use is equal to zero, then the user charge itself has to be equal to zero.

If there were a user charge for using a sidewalk, then some pedestrians would be discouraged from using the sidewalk as frequently as if there had been no user charge.[55] This means that some consumers would be discouraged from consumption of a good even though it costs society nothing for that consumption. The consumers who are discouraged from using the sidewalk are worse off, and nobody else in society is better off. In fact, by lowering the user charge to zero, the result would be that consumption of sidewalk services would be greater at no additional cost to society, so that some people (the additional consumers of sidewalk services) would be better off and no one else would be worse off given that the marginal cost of using a sidewalk is zero. Society is therefore better off if no tolls are charged for sidewalk use than if tolls are charged.

Actually, the case against tolls is not simply that people are discouraged from using sidewalks even though there is no cost to society from such use; but the imposition of tolls actually would use additional resources with no incremental benefits. Charging tolls would require blocking off access to sidewalks and creating some sort of toll-collecting system. The blocking off of sidewalks lowers the quality of services rendered by sidewalks, and the toll-collecting system would require the use of society's resources. Therefore a toll system can cre-

---

[55]This assumes that pedestrian demand for the use of public areas is *not* perfectly inelastic with respect to price, i.e., not perfectly unresponsive to the costs imposed by user charges. The number of times that pedestrians use public areas is quite likely to be affected by the existence of user charges.

ate costs where there weren't any required costs in the first place. The costs of a toll system consist partly of lower-quality service and partly of the use of resources to build and run the toll collection system.

Of course, there is no denying that there is a cost (use of society's resources) involved in building and maintaining a sidewalk. Regardless, an attempt to pay for the costs of constructing and maintaining sidewalks through the medium of so-called user charges would not lead to an efficient allocation of society's resources. This is because user charges must be equal to the marginal cost of use, and in the case of pedestrian use of sidewalks, the marginal cost of use is equal to zero.

Therefore, even if one wished to treat pedestrian access to public areas as a market good rather than as a nonmarket good, one could not base this treatment on the economic grounds that user charges for pedestrian use of public areas would lead to a more efficient allocation of society's resources. However, consumer-pedestrians are *not* charged fees for the use of public areas, not only because it is just not economically rational to do so but also because American society appears to view the freedom to move about easily and without impediments as a fundamental right for its citizens. Once we grant that such a right exists, the services rendered by public areas such as sidewalks and streets become a public good, which is to be supplied in a nonmarket mode. But it is also true that the incremental or marginal cost of supplying this public good is zero, so that from an economic point of view the appropriate user charge should be zero. For these reasons, the costs of building and maintaining sidewalks (and other public areas for pedestrian use) are not paid for through user charges, but through taxes either on those presumed to be the prime beneficiaries of sidewalk services, or on the taxpaying population in general, or on both groups. The taxes are not in the form of user charges per unit of use, but in the form of property taxes or other taxes. If the taxes were really in the form of user charges per unit of use (i.e., in the form of tolls), then we would have the consumption-discouraging effect and the lowering-of-quality-of-services effect discussed earlier.

Because the application of the exclusion principle (through the use of user charges) does not make either good social or economic sense in the case of the use of public areas by pedestrians, therefore the services rendered by such public areas cannot be treated as a market-type good. The absence of user charges means no sales receipts from which a private business could recoup the costs of operating sidewalks and streets and make a profit. In the case of new developments of towns or parts of towns, one can cite examples of sidewalks and even streets being included in the price of a new home.[56] In already developed areas, the replacement and maintenance of existing streets (and curbs and even sidewalks) requires governmental intervention to ensure that these public areas meet some common minimum standard of maintenance. In neither case do we have an example of user charges for the use of sidewalks when these are considered public areas.

APPENDIX B

Rivalry in Consumption for Public Areas

The lack of rivalry in consumption for a public good, such as a public area, can have a limit to it. Let's take the case of a sidewalk. If one assumes that the sidewalk is uncongested, my use of the sidewalk would not take away from someone else's use of the sidewalk. For an uncongested sidewalk there is a lack of rivalry in consumption and zero marginal cost of using the sidewalk. Should the sidewalk get more and more crowded, however, the addition of another pedestrian will take away from the quality of someone else's use of the sidewalk. Crowded sidewalks generate congestion costs, so that the marginal cost of an additional use of the sidewalk is no longer zero and there is rivalry in consumption. The presence of congestion costs could be used to justify tolls during those periods of extreme crowding. However, it would seem as if the inconvenience and costs of maintaining a toll collection system far outweigh any benefits to be expected for the relief from congestion that would be achieved as a result of the tolls.

When public areas become congested, this means that users are

---

[56]Shoup, *Public Finance,* pp. 12–26, contains a discussion of streets as an example of a good that generates services of a type which governmental entities supply. Shoup points out that streets are an example of a good that generates services for which it is not feasible to charge pedestrians tolls for the use of the service. Shoup notes also that, often, streets are produced and sold by private firms when entire towns or parts of towns have been developed by private builders. However, he notes also that the more competition among builders the less likely it is that builders will provide streets along with the homes that are being built. While Shoup is basically discussing streets, a similar analysis would apply to sidewalks. However, sidewalks, more than streets, are likely to be constructed along with a home in a new development. In already developed towns where new homes are placed on empty lots or replace old homes, then generally the home purchaser will have the responsiblity for improving already existing sidewalks. Nevertheless, whether a private builder or homeowner assumes initial responsibility for the construction or improvement of a sidewalk, users of sidewalks will not be charged fees for their use.

generating some incremental costs for each other. Still, it is not customary to institute user charges on pedestrians to relieve crowding. Instead, it is normal to let consumers decide for themselves the amount of congestion costs they wish to endure.[57]

---

[57]Where crowds cause extreme congestion at public and civic events, physical barriers (rather than monetary user charges) are normally utilized for crowd control. So that even where congestion costs are positive, monetary user charges are not used to ration pedestrian access to public areas.

The Principles of Municipal Accounting*

CHAPTER **36**

Abraham J. Simon, Ph.D., CPA

Professor of Accounting and Information Systems
Queens College, City University of New York

Anyone familiar with fund accounting will agree that if accountants had been commissioned to create a system of accounting to induce a maximum of obscurity into the affairs of men, they would have invented fund accounting.[1]

SOURCES OF FINANCIAL ACCOUNTING AND FINANCIAL REPORTING PRINCIPLES FOR MUNICIPALITIES

MAP versus MGAAP

This chapter looks at some specifics of municipal accounting principles, which we will abbreviate as MAP. The term *municipal* will be used in its broad (rather than narrow) meaning to cover both state

---

*I would like to thank Bradley Benson of Ademco and A. Wayne Corcoran of Baruch College—CUNY for their review and comments on this chapter. I would also like to thank my wife, Marilyn S. Simon, for her proofreading and editing of the materia'ls in the chapter. Of course, I assume responsibility for any remaining defects either in form or substance.
[1]Kenneth S. Most, *Accounting Theory* (Columbus, Ohio: Grid, 1977), p. 283.

and local governmental units.[2] One could speak of municipal generally accepted accounting principles (MGAAP) but there is a reluctance among accountants to subdivide the notion of generally accepted accounting principles (GAAP) into sets of specialized subspecies.[3] However, there are peculiarities of municipal financial accounting and financial reporting which set it off from business financial accounting and financial reporting, so that it is useful to refer to the set of financial accounting principles that apply to municipal (i.e., state and local) governmental units as municipal accounting principles (MAP).

Now there are organizations that have tried to achieve some sort of uniformity and consistency in financial accounting and financial reporting for state and local governmental units. However, these organizations have not been successful for the most part. While they have produced a set of accounting principles which can be called MAP, these are not generally accepted by state and local governmental units in the same sense as business GAAP are for profit-seeking enterprises. GAAP for business organizations play an important role in financial reporting for private sector companies, particularly those that are publicly held or require certified financial statements for obtaining credit or other purposes. The same cannot be said for the MAP that have been produced by organizations hoping to achieve uniformity and consistency in municipal financial reporting. This situation has begun to change in recent years, particularly since the fiscal crisis of New York City in 1975. There have been forces at work to achieve sufficient uniformity and consistency in municipal financial reporting so that, at some point, one may be able to refer to MAP as MGAAP. However, we have not yet reached that point. Before we delve further into the specifics of MAP, it would be useful to review briefly the history of organizations that have tried to achieve this uniformity and consistency.

A Brief History of Organizations Generating MAP

The major professional group behind the generation of municipal accounting principles (MAP) for state and local (municipal) govern-

---

[2]Municipal Finance Officers Association, *Governmental Accounting, Auditing, and Financial Reporting (1980 GAAFR)* (Chicago: MFOA, 1980), Appendix B, ("Terminology"), p. 67.

[3]See, for example, *FASB Statement of Financial Accounting Concepts No. 4,* "Objectives of Financial Reporting by Nonbusiness Organizations" (Stamford, Conn.: Financial Accounting Standards Board, December 1980), para. 1. The FASB tells us that it "has concluded that it is not necessary to develop an independent conceptual framework for any particular category of entities (e.g., nonbusiness organizations or business enterprises)." A statement of financial accounting concepts is not a source of GAAP, but this indicates the general attitude of the FASB toward any proliferation of specialized kinds of GAAP.

mental units has been the Municipal Finance Officers Association of the United States and Canada (MFOA). The MFOA has been the moving force for almost five decades behind a series of bodies, once known as committees but now called a council, through which MAP have been formalized, updated, and revised. Davidson, Green, Hellerstein, Madansky, and Weil tell us that the Great Depression of the 1930s led to the formation of the first of the MFOA committees.[4] The first committee was called the National Committee on Municipal Accounting (NCMA) and was organized in 1934. The successor to the NCMA was named the National Committee on Governmental Accounting (old NCGA) in 1949.[5] Both the NCMA and the old NCGA were not continuing bodies, but were ad hoc groups brought to life from time to time to update and revise MAP.

The NCMA and the old NCGA were not internal committees of the MFOA, even though the MFOA is seen as the prime moving force leading to their creation. The NCMA and the old NCGA were composed of representatives from a wide variety of professional and institutional associations. These various associations had rather divergent interests in MAP as such. To get an idea of the diversity of the kinds of groups represented on a typical committee, let us look at the makeup of the old NCGA that produced a 1951 manual, *Municipal Accounting and Auditing (MAA)*. That committee had representatives on it from professional accounting groups such as the American Accounting Association, the American Institute of Accountants (the predecessor to the American Institute of Certified Public Accountants), and the National Association of Cost Accountants (now called the National Association of Accountants). There were representatives from professional groups employed in the governmental sector, such as the International City Managers Association; the National Association of State Auditors, Comptrollers, and Treasurers; and the National Association of State Budget Officers. Of course, the Municipal Finance Officers Association also was represented. There were institutional representatives from the American Municipal Association and the National Municipal League. In addition to the representatives from the professional and institutional associations, there were representatives in a liaison capacity from the Association of School Business Officials, the dominion of Canada, and the U.S. federal government.[6] This gives some idea of the diverse interest groups that

---

[4]Sidney Davidson, David O. Green, Walter Hellerstein, Albert Madansky, and Roman L. Weil, *Financial Reporting by State and Local Government Units* (Chicago: University of Chicago, 1977), p. 4.
[5]National Council on Governmental Accounting (new NCGA), *NCGA Interpretation No. 1*, "GAAFR and the AICPA Audit Guide," (Chicago: Municipal Finance Officers Association, April 1, 1976), p. 6.
[6]National Committee on Governmental Accounting (old NCGA), *Municipal Accounting and Auditing* (Chicago: Municipal Finance Officers Association, 1951), pp. viii-x.

were represented on the old NCGA which authored that 1951 manual.[7]

Muncipal Accounting and Auditing updated and revised earlier publications of the NCMA and became a major source of MAP for the next 17 years.[8] It was replaced in 1968 by the last major publication of a reconstituted old NCGA, *Governmental Accounting, Auditing, and Financial Reporting* (usually referred to as *GAAFR*).[9] We will refer to it as *1968 GAAFR,* because there is now a 1980 publication also called *Governmental Accounting, Auditing, and Financial Reporting.*[10] We will refer to the 1980 publication as *1980 GAAFR.* The important point to remember is that, while *1968 GAAFR* was considered a source of MAP, *1980 GAAFR* is *not* considered a source of MAP. Later on, we will describe the current source of MAP. Note that *1968 GAAFR* (also called GAAFR or the Blue Book) was authored by a reconstituted old NCGA which made it a source of MAP.[11] However, *1980 GAAFR* was authored by the MFOA, so that it is not considered a source of MAP.

From 1934 until 1974, the manuals produced by the NCMA and the old NCGA constituted the basic and largely unchallenged source of MAP for state and local governments. However, in 1974, the American Institute of Certified Public Accountants (AICPA) published *Audits of State and Local Governmental Units (ASLGU),*[12] which contained an explicit reference to *1968 GAAFR* to the effect that "Proper use of this guide requires thorough knowledge of *Governmental Accounting, Auditing, and Financial Reporting . . .*"[13] *ASLGU* is primarily an audit manual for independent CPAs and CPA firms who are members of the AICPA.

ASLGU also contains some accounting principles applicable to state and local governmental units (i.e., MAP) which affect independent CPAs and CPA firms (who belong to the AICPA) when they audit and certify financial statements of state and local governmental

---

[7]Ibid.

[8]The old NCGA followed up the 1951 *Municipal Accounting and Auditing* with *A Standard Classification of Municipal Accounts* (Chicago: Municipal Finance Officers Association, 1953).

[9]National Committee on Governmental Accounting (old NCGA), *Governmental Accounting, Auditing, and Financial Reporting (1968 GAAFR)* (Chicago: Municipal Finance Officers Association, 1968); known also as the Blue Book of municipal accounting.

[10]MFOA, *1980 GAAFR.*

[11]The reconstituted old NCGA which authored *1968 GAAFR* was a diverse body similar to the earlier old NCGA which produced the 1951 and 1953 manuals. The American Municipal Association is not shown as represented on the reconstituted old NCGA but the Canadian Institute of Chartered Accountants, the National Association of County Officials, and the National League of Cities were represented. The National Association of Accountants provided a liaison representative.

[12]American Institute of Certified Public Accountants, Committee on Governmental Accounting and Auditing, *Audits of State and Local Governmental Units (ASLGU)* 2d ed. (Industry Audit Guide) (New York: AICPA, 1974).

[13]Ibid., p. xi.

units. There were some differences between the accounting principles contained in *ASLGU* and the MAP contained in *1968 GAAFR*. Thus, for a period of time there appeared to be two separate sources of MAP for those state and local governmental units that require their financial statements to be certified by independent CPA firms.[14] The disposition of these differences in MAP as between *ASLGU* and *1968 GAAFR* will be discussed shortly.

In 1974 the National Council on Governmental Accounting (new NCGA) was established as a quasi-independent body under the sponsorship of the MFOA. The new NCGA was set up as a continuing body in contrast to the earlier NCMA and old NCGA.[15] On April 1, 1976, the new NCGA issued *NCGA Interpretation 1*, "GAAFR and the AICPA Audit Guide," as its initial effort.[16] *NCGA Interpretation 1* disposed of most of the differences in MAP between *ASLGU* and *1968 GAAFR* simply by treating most of the recommended accounting principles of *ASLGU* where they differed from *1968 GAAFR* as acceptable alternative accounting principles.

However, the *major* task undertaken initially by the new NCGA was not just to write a limited intepretation of MAP. The major initial task was to revise and update *1968 GAAFR*. In March 1979, the new NCGA issued *NCGA Statement 1*, "Governmental Accounting and Financial Reporting Principles," to which we shall refer as *NCGA Statement 1*.[17] We are told in *NCGA Statement 1* that it "constitutes a modest revision to update, amplify, and reorder GAAFR. . . . An important objective is to incorporate pertinent aspects of *Audits of State and Local Governmental Units (ASLGU)*. . . ."[18] We are told also that "*NCGA Statement 1* supersedes *NCGA Interpretation 1*. . . ."[19] As of June 30, 1980, the

---

[14] At one time only individual CPAs could belong to the AICPA. Now, CPA firms also can be members of the AICPA. For purposes of our discussion, when we refer to independent CPA firms as auditing financial statements we also mean to include individual CPAs that constitute one-person CPA firms.

[15]*NCGA Interpretation 1, p. 6.*

[16]Ibid.

[17]National Council on Governmental Accounting (new NCGA), *NCGA Statement 1*, "Governmental Accounting and Financial Reporting Principles" (Chicago: Municipal Finance Officers Association, March 1979a). Note that at the time that the new NCGA issued *NCGA Statement 1*, it also issued *NCGA Statement 2*, "Grant, Entitlement, and Shared Revenue Accounting and Reporting by State and Local Governments" (Chicago: MFOA March 1979b). NCGA Statement 2 is considered an application and clarification of the accounting principles set out in *NCGA Statement 1* to the area of grants, entitlements, and shared revenues received by state and local governments. The new NCGA has issued also *NCGA Interpretation 2*, "Segment Information for Enterprise Funds" (Chicago: NCGA, June 1980). This is an interpretation of the accounting principles set out in *NCGA Statement 1*, having to do with the presentation of segment information for enterprise funds in the financial statements of state and local governmental units.

[18]*NCGA Statement 1*, p. 1.

[19]Ibid.

AICPA issued an amendment to *ASLGU* in the form of a Statement of Position (SOP).[20] *SOP 80–2*, "Accounting and Financial Reporting by Governmental Units," tells us "that *Audits of State and Local Governmental Units* be amended throughout to refer to *Statement 1* rather than *GAAFR*. Accordingly, financial statements presented in accordance with *Statement 1* are in conformity with generally accepted accounting principles."[21]

By the way, now that you have been introduced to such publications as *1968 GAAFR* and *ASLGU,* we can draw upon *ASLGU* to reinforce a point made earlier. At the beginning of the chapter it was argued that accountants are reluctant to subdivide GAAP into specialized areas. This is confirmed in *ASLGU* where it is argued that "GAAFR's principles do not represent a complete and separate body of accounting principles, rather are a part of the whole body of generally accepted accounting principles which deal specifically with governmental units. Except as modified in this guide, they constitute generally accepted accounting principles" (p. 9). However, as you will see, there are sufficiently distinctive features in regard to accounting principles applied to governmental units that referring to these at least as municipal accounting principles makes it a lot easier to talk about them.

In summary, one can say that *NCGA Statement 1* replaces *1968 GAAFR,* supersedes *NCGA Interpretation 1,* absorbs *ASLGU,* and now is recognized as the basic source of MAP. One could even say, according to *SOP 80–2,* that *NCGA Statement 1* is a source of generally accepted accounting principles for state and local governmental units, at least from the point of view of independent CPA firms. Of course, whether there is really sufficiently uniform financial reporting by state and local governments in accordance with *NCGA Statement 1* to justify the assertion that it is a source of GAAP (or, as we might call it, MGAAP) applied to state and local governmental units is an empirical question. At the least, one can say that *NCGA Statement 1* is a source of MAP.

There are several issues that will not be dealt with in this chapter. One issue is the gap between MAP and actual financial accounting and financial reporting by state and local governmental units. This issue deals with the degree to which state and local governmental units actually do follow MAP as set out in *NCGA Statement 1*. A second issue is the gap in MAP. This issue deals with potential shortcomings in the version of MAP described in *NCGA Statement 1*. A third issue deals with the concern as to whether the new NCGA

---

[20]AICPA Committee on State and Local Governmental Accounting, *Statement of Position 80–2*, "Accounting and Financial Reporting by Governmental Units" (Amendment to AICPA Industry Audit Guide, *ASLGU*) (New York: AICPA, June 30, 1980).
[21]Ibid., p. 4.

should continue to be the organization charged with the updating or revision of MAP or whether this task should be assigned to the Financial Accounting Standards Board or to an entirely new organization.[22]

In the balance of this chapter we will be concerned primarily with setting out an overview of MAP according to *NCGA Statement 1* and as illustrated in *1980 GAAFR*. Remember that *1980 GAAFR* is not a source of MAP in the same sense as *NCGA. Statement 1 is; but according to 1980 GAAFR* it can provide "detailed guidance to the effective application of *Statement 1* principles to the accounting and financial reporting activities of state and local governments" (p. 1).

THE BASIC PRINCIPLES OF MAP ACCORDING TO *NCGA STATEMENT 1*

The Relationship between *NCGA Statement 1* and *1980 GAAFR*

NCGA Statement 1 sets out 12 basic principles of financial accounting and financial reporting for state and local governmental units. These basic principles are part of what we call MAP. In the language of *Audits of State and Local Governmental Units* as amended by *SOP 80–2,* these 12 basic principles are a part of the whole body of what accountants (particularly independent CPAs) would call generally accepted accounting principles. The 12 basic principles are that part of GAAP that is applicable to governmental units.

The 12 basic principles of *NCGA Statement 1* are explained in

---

[22]See, for example, the discussion in the report issued by the Governmental Accounting Standards Board Organization Committee, "Exposure Draft: Report of the Governmental Accounting Standards Board Organization Committee," dated February 16, 1981. The Governmental Accounting Standards Board Organization Committee was an ad hoc working committee formed in April 1980 as a result of consultations between the AICPA, Financial Accounting Foundation (FAF), MFOA, National Association of State Auditors, Comptrollers, and Treasurers (NASACT), General Accounting Office (GAO), and the new NCGA. These six groups were represented on the committee, which was headed by an academic, Professor Robert K. Mautz of the University of Michigan. In addition, representatives of seven other organizations participated in the deliberations that led to the report issued on February 16, 1981. These other organizations were: Council of State Governments, International City Management Association, National Association of Counties, National Conference of State Legislatures, National Governors Association, National League of Cities, and U.S. Conference of Mayors. The report of the Governmental Accounting Standards Board Organization Committee is an unpublished report. The Committee held public hearings on May 4 and 5, 1981, in Philadelphia, Pennsylvania in order to obtain responses from interested groups and individuals to its report. A summary of the proposed structure of the Government Accounting Standards Board (GASB) appears in the *Public Sector Section News,* 7, no. 1, Fall, 1982, p. 1. A special committee of the Financial Accounting Foundation has become responsible for the organization of the GASB (*Journal of Accountancy,* March 1983, pp. 14–15). The Financial Accounting Foundation has financing and oversight responsibility for the Financial Accounting Standards Board.

fairly general terms in that statement. But, even after you have read *NCGA Statement 1* you would not necessarily really understand exactly how one does municipal accounting. *NCGA Statement 1* is just not that detailed. In contrast, *1968 GAAFR* did provide sufficient detail so that one could get a good grasp on how to do municipal accounting and apply the basic principles that appeared in that manual. However, now you have to turn to *1980 GAAFR* for the details of exactly how to apply the 12 basic principles.

The 12 basic principles of financial accounting are also principles of financial reporting. In its broadest meaning, financial accounting also covers financial reporting. *NCGA Statement 1* contains quite a few illustrative financial statements which purport to show how the 12 basic principles are to be applied in the financial reporting sense. However, the illustrative financial statements of *NCGA Statement 1* do not exhaust entirely the kinds of financial statements that one can expect in municipal accounting and reporting. The illustrative financial statements of *NCGA Statement 1* represent *minimum* required financial reporting for state and local governmental units. *NCGA Statement 1* also describes financial reporting beyond the minimum required. However, you would have to turn to *1980 GAAFR* for actual illustrative examples of financial statements beyond the minimum financial statements required by *NCGA Statement 1*.

Thus, for detailed guidance in this area, both *NCGA Statement 1* and *1980 GAAFR* might be considered a part of MAP. However, as far as independent CPA firms are concerned, only *NCGA Statement 1* contains generally accepted accounting principles applicable to state and local governmental units.

The Basic Principles of Financial Accounting and Financial Reporting

The 12 basic principles of financial accounting and financial reporting of *NCGA Statement 1* did not suddenly spring up full-blown when *NCGA Statement 1* was written. The 12 basic principles are an evolution of basic principles that appeared in earlier manuals of governmental financial accounting and financial reporting. In *1968 GAAFR,* there were 13 basic principles of financial accounting and financial reporting. In the 1951 *Municipal Accounting and Auditing,* there were 14 basic principles of financial accounting and financial reporting. The basic principles of financial accounting and financial reporting relevant to state and local governments according to the manuals prepared by the NCMA, the old NCGA, and the new NCGA have been remarkably similar. The 12 basic principles of financial accounting and financial reporting of *NCGA Statement 1* are shown in Appendix A to this chapter.

Let us look a little more closely at the 12 basic principles. *NCGA Statement 1* sets out 12 *areas* covered by the 12 basic principles. The 12 areas dealt with by the 12 basic principles are shown in Exhibit 1. The 12 areas of *NCGA Statement 1* are condensed further into 7 *categories* by the *Statement*. Both the 12 areas and the 7 categories are shown in Exhibit 1, with the 12 areas arranged in the same order as the 12 basic principles are set out in *NCGA Statement 1*. The 1st area is for the 1st principle, the 2d area is for the 2d basic principle, and so on until the 12th area for the 12th basic principle.

The first basic principle describes a minimum standard of "capability" for a governmental accounting system.[23] Capability has two facets to it: (1) An accounting system has to be able to provide the right kind of information to enable a governmental unit to produce a proper set of financial statements. The standard of quality for financial statements is that they should present fairly and disclose fully the financial position and the results of operations of the funds and account groups of a governmental unit. The terms *fund* and *account group* will be described later on. The key to properly prepared financial statements is fair presentation and full disclosure. (2) The accounting system has to perform a custodial function by making it possible to determine that laws are being complied with and that contractual and other obligations are being met.

Exhibit 1
The Basic Principles of *NCGA Statement 1* in Terms of Areas and Categories

Areas	*Categories*
1. Accounting and reporting capabilities	1. Generally accepted accounting principles and legal compliance
2. Fund accounting systems	2. Fund accounting
3. Types of funds	
4. Number of funds	
5. Accounting for fixed assets and long-term liabilities	3. Fixed assets and long-term liabilities
6. Valuation of fixed assets	
7. Depreciation of fixed assets	
8. Accrual basis in governmental accounting	4. Basis of accounting
9. Budgeting, budgetary control, and budgetary reporting	5. The budget and budgetary accounting
10. Transfer, revenue, expenditure, and expense account classification	6. Classification and terminology
11. Common terminology and classification	
12. Interim and annual financial reports	7. Financial reporting

---

[23]Appendix A, basic principle I, to this Chapter.

In a sense, the remaining 11 basic principles are designed to ensure that the governmental financial accounting system has the accounting and financial reporting capabilities required by the first basic principle. For example, there are three basic principles which deal with fund accounting.[24] There is no counterpart to fund accounting in business accounting. This is a pretty complex part of governmental accounting. A "fund" is defined as a separate accounting and fiscal entity. A fund may also be a separate legal entity. A fund will have its own set of self-contained accounting records. There are eight basic types of funds and there are also subtypes of one of the basic types. One of the three basic principles even tells us that the number of funds should be minimized, as one can see in examining the fourth basic principle shown in Appendix A. The basic purpose of the fund accounting approach to a governmental accounting system is to satisfy the custodial function of governmental accounting. Davidson et al., consider fund accounting to be, in a sense, a "cookie jar" approach to discharging the governmental unit's custodial obligations.[25] Because fund accounting is such an integral and central part of governmental accounting and reporting, it will be covered in some detail.

There are three basic principles (see Appendix A, basic principles V, VI, and VII) that describe how to account for fixed assets. One of these basic principles (Appendix A, basic principle V) also describes how to account for long-term liabilities. Some types of fixed assets and long-term liabilities are accounted for through funds. Others are accounted for in separate accounting entities called "account groups." An account group is simply an accounting entity with its own self-contained set of accounting records. It differs from a fund in that it is not a fiscal entity, i.e., it does not carry financial resources. It is usually not a separate legal entity.

There is a separate basic principle (Appendix A, basic principle VIII) that describes the basis of accounting in terms of both the modified accrual basis and the accrual basis. In the prior chapter, the distinctive features of both the modified accrual basis and the accrual basis of accounting were contrasted with each other. One basic principle (Appendix A, basic principle X) describes such concepts as revenue, expenditure, and expense, and how these concepts fit into governmental accounting. This basic principle also deals with the concept of transfers, which are uniquely a fund-accounting phenomenon. The basic principle dealing with the basis of accounting interacts with this basic principle, which deals with such concepts as revenue, expenditure and expense.

There is a basic principle (Appendix A, basic principle IX) that

---

[24]Appendix A, basic principles II, III, and IV.
[25]Davidson et al., *Financial Reporting,* p. 23.

treats the use of budgetary accounts directly in the financial accounting system of a governmental unit. This is unique to governmental financial accounting. In business accounting, budgeting is considered a tool of managerial accounting; it is not considered a part of the financial accounting system. One purpose of integrating budgeting information directly into the financial accounting records is so that such budgetary information ultimately is reported directly in the financial statements. In business accounting, budgetary information is not reported directly in the basic financial statements. However, in governmental accounting the budget is integrated directly into the financial accounting records so that it can be reported directly in the governmental unit's financial statements. Given the vital and central role of the budget in the life of a governmental unit, there will be, later on, a more comprehensive discussion of how the budget fits into a governmental accounting system.

There is also a basic principle (Appendix A, basic principle XI) that stresses that the terminology used throughout the governmental budget, in its financial accounting records and in the governmental financial statements, be uniform and consistent for the sake of comparability and to avoid ambiguities. The final basic principle (Appendix A, basic principle XII) describes the interim and annual financial statements required of a governmental unit to meet minimum financial reporting standards. Because of the system of fund accounting used in governmental accounting, it will be necessary to discuss governmental financial statements in some depth.

FUNDS AND FUND ACCOUNTING

Governmental Funds

A governmental accounting system is organized around the basic accounting entity known as the fund. The fund concept is also used in business accounting, where a fund is "an asset or group of assets set aside for a specific purpose."[26] An example of assets segregated for a particular purpose would be a sinking fund required by a bond indenture. However, in governmental accounting, a fund is not simply assets put into special accounts but is, in fact, a fiscal and accounting entity with its own self-contained set of books.

In governmental accounting, "fund accounting" means that system of accounting which uses funds as self-contained fiscal and accounting entities. A business corporation is a single legal entity and, at the

---

[26]Sidney Davidson, James S. Schindler, Clyde P. Stickney, and Roman L. Weil, *Accounting: the Language of Business,* 3d ed. (Glen Ridge, N.J.: Thomas Horton and Daughters, 1977), p. 26.

same time, a single fiscal and accounting entity. In a sense, the legal and the fiscal and accounting entities coincide. A governmental unit is a single legal entity but, in the accounting sense, it will be made up of a number of fiscal and accounting entities which may themselves also be separate legal entities. The legal entity that represents a particular governmental unit will not coincide with the fiscal and accounting entities that are used to account for the various activities of that governmental unit.

Why do governmental units use funds and fund accounting? In the preceding chapter, we discussed the fact that governmental units are perceived as custodians or trustees of those resources which they obtain from their constituents as a result of involuntary payments (involuntary from the individual viewpoint). It was observed also that governmental units are often able to exercise monopoly-like powers in their activities. Funds and fund accounting are part of a mechanism by which constituents hope to ensure that governments spend the moneys they have raised for the purposes for which the moneys were intended.

How does one try to make sure that taxes raised for specific purposes are used just for those purposes? A number of devices are used. First, the law which empowers the governmental unit to levy taxes can itself contain language that spells out the purposes for which the taxes are being raised. When this is the case, such taxes are described as earmarked taxes. For example, suppose the property tax that a local governmental unit levies is made up of two parts: one part to be used for general operating purposes and a second part, the earmarked part, to be used for the financing of the local library system. This means that the property tax will generate two types of financial resources for the local governmental unit. One type would be the unrestricted financial resources from that part of the property tax that is levied for general operating purposes. The second type would be restricted financial resources from that part of the property tax that has been earmarked by law to be used only to finance the activities of the local library system. This leads to a second device used to make sure that the moneys will be spent properly.

The second device is fund accounting. In order to account for the receipt and use of the two types of financial resources—the unrestricted financial resources and the restricted financial resources—the local governmental unit should use several types of funds, according to *NCGA Statement 1*.

The *general fund* is used to account for the receipt and use of unrestricted financial resources destined for "general governmental operating purposes"—those activities of a governmental unit that result in the supply of nonmarket public goods and services. A *special revenue fund* would be used to account for the receipt and use of restricted financial resources which have been earmarked for a "particular" general governmental operating purpose. The part of the property tax which can be used for any general governmental operating purpose would be accounted for through the governmental unit's general fund. The part of the property tax that has been earmarked to be used only for the operations of the local library system would be accounted for through a special revenue fund set up for the purpose of accounting for the operating activities of the library system. The general fund of the governmental unit would be a separate legal entity, and also a fiscal and accounting entity with its own self-contained set of accounting records. The special revenue fund set up to account for the activities of the library system would be a second and separate legal entity, and also a fiscal and accounting entity with its own set of self-contained accounting records. The general fund and the special revenue fund are separate legal, fiscal, and accounting entities within the same governmental unit.

There is only one general fund, according to *NCGA Statement 1,* but there can be more than one special revenue fund. Both the general fund and special revenue funds would be what are called operating funds. These are funds that account for resources received by a governmental unit to be used for general operating purposes. The general fund is used to account for unrestricted financial resources to be used for *unspecified* general governmental operating purposes; special revenue funds account for restricted financial resources to be used for *specified* general governmental operating purposes.

Governmental units raise financial resources not only for current operating purposes, but also for the acquisition of capital assets to be used in the general governmental operations. One method of financing the acquisition of major capital assets (either through purchase or by construction) is through long-term borrowing. Such long-term borrowing can take the form of the issuance of general obligation (full faith and credit) bonds. The authority to issue general obligation bonds is normally derived from voter approval of such bond issues. The financial resources raised from the sale of general obligation bonds would be earmarked financial resources, in which case (in a fund accounting system) it would be logical to set up a special revenue fund to account for the receipt and use of the restricted resources raised from the proceeds of the sale of the general obligation bonds. However, *NCGA Statement 1* (and its predecessor, *1968 GAAFR*) does not recommend a special revenue fund; instead it recommends what is called a *capital projects fund.* A capital projects fund is used to account for the receipt and use of restricted financial resources which are to be used for the acquisition of major capital assets. The capital assets acquired by purchase or construction through restricted financial resources accounted for in a capital projects fund usually are major capital assets to be used in general governmental operations.

Thus, the proceeds from the sale of general obligation bonds to be used to acquire major capital assets would be restricted financial resources to be accounted for in a capital projects funds. Actually, a capital projects fund can be thought of as a specialized kind of special revenue fund. Both types of funds account for restricted financial resources. A special revenue fund accounts for the receipt and use of restricted financial resources to be used for current general governmental operating purposes. A capital projects fund accounts for the receipt and use of restricted financial resources used to acquire major capital assets where the capital assets themselves are to be used in general governmental operations.

Some words of warning or observations are in order at this point. Capital projects funds account for restricted financial resources used to acquire major capital assets, but do *not* account for the major capital assets that have been acquired. The acquired major capital assets are to be accounted for through a separate accounting entity, according to the recommendations of *NCGA Statement 1*. This separate accounting entity, a general fixed assets account group, will be discussed in a bit more detail later on.

As part of our words of caution, note also that capital projects funds do not account for the long-term liability to the governmental unit that results from the issuance of the general obligation bonds. The general long-term liability to the governmental unit is to be accounted for through a separate accounting entity according to the recommendations of *NCGA Statement 1*. This separate accounting entity is called a general long-term debt account group. It will be discussed in somewhat more detail later on. The capital projects fund accounts only for the restricted financial resources which arise from the sale of the general obligation bonds, not for the long-term liability of the bonds.[27]

So far, three types of funds have been discussed, the general fund, special revenue funds, and capital projects funds. All of these funds belong to the category of "governmental funds," a category which was introduced by *NCGA Statement 1*. In terms of the analysis of the preceding chapter, governmental funds cover all of the fund types which are used to account for unrestricted and restricted financial resources

---

[27]Note that prior to *1968 GAAFR* (i.e., according to the 1951 *Municipal Accounting and Auditing*), the proceeds from general obligation bonds would be accounted for through bond funds. The bond funds of 1951 *Municipal Accounting and Auditing* performed the same function for proceeds of general obligation bond issues as do the capital projects funds of *1968 GAAFR* and *NCGA Statement 1*.

which are used to finance those governmental activities that lead to the supply of nonmarket public goods and services.

The governmental funds category also covers two other types of funds. The fourth type of governmental fund is called a *debt service fund*. Debt service funds account for the receipt and use of restricted financial resources used to pay interest and principal on general long-term debt. The general long-term debt may be in the form of general obligation bonds, or it may take other forms. As noted earlier, one could use a special revenue fund for restricted resources to repay interest and principal on long-term debt. However, *NCGA Statement 1* recommends the use of a debt service fund. Again, as in the case of a capital projects fund, one can say we have another example of a specialized kind of special revenue fund.[28]

The fifth and last type of governmental fund is a *special assessment fund*. This type of fund is a bit more complex than the prior types of governmental funds that have been discussed. First, a special assessment fund accounts for the receipt and use of restricted financial resources. This makes it similar to a special revenue fund. Second, the restricted financial resources are earmarked for capital improvements. This makes this type of fund similar to a capital projects fund. Thus, the question arises as to why there is a need for still another type of fund?

The capital improvements covered by a special assessment fund are different from the capital improvements covered by a capital projects fund. The latter are to be used in general governmental operations which are presumed to result in public goods that benefit the citizenry as a whole. The benefits are relatively indivisible and individual beneficiaries cannot be easily identified. The capital improvements covered by a special assessment fund (call these special assessment capital improvements) are assumed to benefit an identifiable group within the general population of constituents. For example, the repairing and maintenance of sidewalks and streets represent capital improvements of a type where, it is argued, a group of major beneficiaries can be identified in a general way. It is argued that the properties (and the owners of these properties) that adjoin the sidewalks and streets being repaired or maintained are an identifiable group of major beneficiaries.

---

[28]Prior to *1968 GAAFR* (i.e., according to 1951 *Municipal Accounting and Auditing*), the specialized fund type to be used to pay interest and principal on general obligation terms bonds would be called a "sinking fund." The sinking funds of 1951 *Municipal Accounting and Auditing* performed the same function for general obligation term bonds as the debt service funds of *1968 GAAFR* and *NCGA Statement 1* perform for general long-term debt. Note that the sinking-fund type of governmental accounting is a self-contained fiscal and accounting entity which is quite different from the concept of sinking fund in commercial accounting which is simply a segregation of assets in accordance with the requirements of a bond indenture.

If it is the case that an identifiable group of major beneficiaries of certain types of capital improvements can be located, then such beneficiaries should be charged for their fair share of the cost of the capital improvement. In fact, in the case of the cost of repairing and maintaining sidewalks and streets, property owners are levied property taxes on their properties to pay for the cost of maintaining and repairing sidewalks and streets adjoining their properties. In many instances in the case of sidewalks, the property owners themselves maintain these directly without the need for the use of property taxes. Where property taxes are used, this type of property tax is called a special assessment to distinguish it from general property taxes. Special assessment property taxes are earmarked taxes on properties where the earmarked tax is to be used only for capital improvements that are assumed to benefit the property on which the special assessment is levied.

Note that, in the prior chapter, sidewalks and streets are discussed in some detail as examples of pure public goods that are collectively consumed and whose benefits are indivisible. If that is the case, then how can one argue that the beneficiaries can be identified (as was argued above for special assessments) if the benefits are indivisible and collectively consumed? It is true that the services rendered by sidewalks and streets are indivisible and collectively consumed. It is also true that the properties (and their owners) that adjoin the sidewalks and streets that are to be maintained and repaired are among the *potential* beneficiaries of such capital maintenance and improvement. Clearly, they are not the only potential beneficiaries. The *actual* beneficiaries are all of the citizens entitled to access to public areas as a pure public good supplied by a particular governmental unit (see the discussion in the preceding chapter, including the appendixes). Owners of properties adjoining public areas simply are easily identified potential and actual beneficiaries for purposes of levying taxes for special assessment capital improvements. Strictly speaking, the usual argument that one finds for the special assessment on a property is that it is the property adjoining the special assessment capital improvement that is assumed to benefit from that improvement. Normally, however, the property will have an owner, so that benefits to the property can be assumed to be conferred on the owner. In any case, the question is whether special assessment taxes violate the economic notion of efficiency that user charges are not appropriate in the case of nonmarket public goods and services? The answer seems to be that such taxes do not violate efficiency notions because normally they are not in the form of user charges. Rather, special assessment property taxes are based on an equity principle in taxation: the benefit principle.

Actually, from an accounting standpoint we have not really spelled

out all of the complexities of special assessment funds as contrasted
with the other four governmental fund types. Special assessment levies may not necessarily be used directly to pay for the cost of constructing a special assessment capital improvement as it is being
built. Instead, the cost of building a major special assessment capital
improvement may require long-term financing. If long-term financing
is required, then the financing usually takes the form of special assessment bonds. Special assessment bonds are a direct liability of a
special assessment fund. The special assessment fund will be a separate legal and fiscal and accounting entity. Special assessment bonds
may carry also an additional guarantee of the payment of interest
and principal by the governmental unit in case the resources of the
special assessment fund prove inadequate to this task. Such an additional guarantee need not be present for a particular issue of special
assessment bonds. However, whether or not special assessment bonds
carry an additional guarantee from the governmental unit, the payment of interest and principal is normally made out of the resources
raised from special assessment property tax levies. This means that
when long-term financing is used for a special assessment capital project, then special assessment property tax levies will be used to pay
interest and principal on the special assessment bonds rather than
being used only to pay for the immediate cost of constructing the capital improvement. This leads to still a third major characteristic of
special assessment funds, that such funds also can be used to receive
financial resources that will be used to pay interest and principal on
long-term debt. This makes a special assessment fund similar in certain respects to a debt service fund.

Finally, special assessment funds have another major characteristic that the four other governmental fund types do not. Special assessment funds carry special assessment bonds as a direct liability of
such funds. This means that special assessment funds perform the
same function for special assessment bonds as the general long-term
debt account group performs for the general long-term debt of the
governmental unit.

As a result of all of the special circumstances associated with special assessment capital improvements, special assessment property
tax levies, and special assessment bonds, *NCGA Statement 1* recommended a specialized fund, the special assessment fund. This fund
type accounts for the receipt and use of restricted resources raised
from special assessment tax levies which are used for special assessment capital projects and for the payment of principal and interest on
special assessment bonds, and it carries the long-term liability for
such bonds.[29]

---

[29]The five types of governmental funds are described in the third basic principle of
NCGA Statement 1 shown in Appendix A.

Proprietary Funds

Governmental units supply not only nonmarket public goods and services but they also supply goods and services on a user charge basis. As discussed in the prior chapter, goods and services that can be supplied on a user charge basis must be of the marketable variety. The "proprietary fund" category of *NCGA Statement 1* refers to a fiscal and accounting entity (it may also be a legal entity) that is used to account for those governmental activities that result in the supply of marketable goods and services to be financed largely on a user charge basis. There are two types of funds recommended in *NCGA Statement 1* that fit into the proprietary fund category. The two types of funds are *enterprise funds* and *internal service funds.*

The difference between enterprise funds and internal service funds is that the former type supplies marketable goods and services to members of the public as well as to governmental units. Internal service funds, on the other hand, are set up as separate fiscal and accounting entities to supply market-type goods and services only to governmental units (i.e., only to its own or to other governmental units). Internal service funds are not set up to supply goods and services to the general public.

Both enterprise funds and internal service funds normally supply their goods and services subject to user charges. This means that fund types such as these should not be used to account for activities that result in a supply of nonmarket public goods and services. It also means that governmental-type funds should not be used to supply market-type private goods and services on a user charge basis. Such fund types should be used basically to account for governmental activities that result in a supply of nonmarket public goods and services.

Actually, *NCGA Statement 1* does not appear to carry out fully the distinction between funds used just to account for the supply of nonmarket public goods and services and those funds that are to be used just for the supply of market-type private goods and services. This is because the general fund, which is a governmental fund, is defined also as the fund "to account for all financial resources except those required to be accounted for in another fund."[30] This means that the general fund can function not only as a governmental fund but it can function also as the residual fund, which accounts for financial resources and activities not accounted for through some other fund. It is possible, then, to find the general fund accounting for commercial-type activities as well as public goods activities. The commercial activities for which the general fund accounts should be minor in na-

---

[30]See the description of a general fund which appears as the first type of fund in basic principle III in Appendix A.

ture if the recommendations of *NCGA Statement 1* are being followed properly. If there are any major commercial-type activities undertaken by the governmental unit, then according to *NCGA Statement 1,* either an enterprise fund or an internal service fund should be used.

If a municipality operates a utility company, then that utility company would normally be organized as a legal entity separate from the municipality itself. According to *NCGA Statement 1* (and the earlier manuals), the fiscal and accounting entity to be used to account for the resources, liabilities, and activities of the municipal utility company would be an enterprise fund. Utility services are a market-type private good; they would be supplied normally on a user charge basis.[31] A municipally operated transportation company would be another example of an activity to be accounted for through its own enterprise fund. Separate enterprise funds would be used for a municipal utility company and a municipal transportation company, if a municipality supplied both types of services.

In order to manage the use of its own automotive equipment more efficiently, a governmental unit will set up the equivalent of its own automotive rental service. Such a governmentally run automotive rental service which provides motor vehicle services to the other departments or agencies of the governmental unit (and perhaps even to other governmental units) would be called a "central garage and motor pool." The resources, liabilities, and activities of a central garage and motor pool should be accounted for through a separate internal service fund according to *NCGA Statement 1.* The same recommendation appeared in the earlier manuals except that the terminology was somewhat different. In *1968 GAAFR,* this fund type would have been called an intragovernmental service fund. In 1951 *Municipal Accounting and Auditing,* the name would have been working capital fund.[32] The other departments or agencies of the governmental unit are expected to pay user charges for the services of the central garage and motor pool. The user charges are expected to cover the cost of the services received including the cost of operating the central garage and motor pool. Central purchasing and stores departments as well as central printing and duplicating departments would be other examples of activities that should be accounted for through their own internal service funds.[33]

---

[31]Utility companies have been such an important activity of municipal governments that, in the 1951 *Municipal Accounting and Auditing,* enterprise funds were called "utility or other enterprise funds."

[32]According to 1951 *Municipal Accounting and Auditing* (p. 42), working capital funds were also called revolving funds or rotary funds.

[33]The two types of proprietary funds are described in the third basic principle of *NCGA Statement 1* shown in Appendix A.

Fiduciary Funds

The eighth and final type of fund, according to *NCGA Statement 1,* is called *trust and agency funds.* This final type of fund coincides also with the third and last category of funds: *fiduciary funds.*[34] A fiduciary fund (or trust and agency fund) accounts for those resources, liabilities, and activities which place a governmental unit in the position of a trustee or custodian. It was pointed out earlier (and in the previous chapter) that, from one point of view, a governmental unit can be considered in a trustee relationship with citizens and taxpayers in general with respect to all of its activities. However, this general notion of trusteeship is less specific than the notion of trusteeship or custodianship which underlies fiduciary, or trust and agency, funds. The notion of trusteeship which underlies fiduciary funds is that the resources held in such funds by a governmental unit are actually held in trust in accordance with specific legal or contractual arrangements which provide for the creation of a trust, and result in a trust or agency relationship. Thus, the resources received into the general fund or into a specific revenue fund are received in general in trust for all of the citizens and taxpayers. However, there is no specific legal or contractual requirement that specifies that the resources are actually to be held in trust for a particular, identifiable party. The resources to be accounted for through a trust or agency fund are resources held for other parties who can be identified on an individual basis. The trust arrangement, between the governmental unit and specifically identifiable third parties, is formalized through a particular law or contract which usually requires the use of a trust or agency fund.

NCGA Statement 1 provides for a four-way breakdown of the category of fiduciary funds. There are (1) expendable trust funds, (2) nonexpendable trust funds, (3) pension trust funds, and (4) agency funds. *Expendable trust funds* account for resources where both the trust principal (known as the corpus of the trust) and trust income can be spent for the purposes spelled out in the trust arrangement. According to *1980 GAAFR, NCGA Statement 1* recommends that "the use of Expendable Trust Funds should generally be limited to instances where legally mandated, or where a formal legal trust relationship exists. Amounts currently available for expenditures for general governmental operating purposes generally should be accounted for in the general fund or in special revenue funds" (p. 69).

---

[34]The term *trust and agency funds* is a carry-over from *1968 GAAFR* and also from 1951 *Municipal Accounting and Auditing.* It is not clear why *NCGA Statement 1* needs two different terms, *fiduciary* as well as *trust and agency,* for the same type of fund. Probably, this occurred because the statement tries to distinguish between fund categories and fund types.

Nonexpendable trust funds account for resources where trust fund principal must be kept intact and cannot be spent. Trust fund income may be of the kind that can be spent, or it can become a part of fund principal.

Pension trust funds are a special kind of expendable trust fund. In fact, in *1968 GAAFR*, trust funds were broken down into expendable and nonexpendable, with pension trust funds treated simply as part of the expendable trust funds.

Agency funds are distinguished from trust funds by the fact that agency funds are intended normally to hold resources in a custodial capacity for other parties on a short-term and temporary basis. Agency funds normally show all of their assets owed to outside parties so that liabilities equal assets and a zero fund equity balance results.

A typical example of a trust arrangement that calls for the use of a nonexpendable fund is an endowment given by a private donor who stipulates that endowment principal is not to be spent. Such an endowment, called a permanent endowment, may provide that income can be spent or that income must also be maintained intact. An example of a permanent endowment whose income can be spent is one which provides that endowment income may be used for scholarships for students attending colleges or universities.[35] Note that where endowment income can be spent, the recommended accounting procedure is to transfer the resources received as a result of the endowment income to a separate, expendable trust fund. The separate, expendable trust fund will be used to account for the actual spending of the endowment income. An example of a permanent endowment where both endowment principal and endowment income are to be maintained intact is an endowment where the donor specifies that the endowed resources are to be used for making loans which are expected to be repaid.[36]

Pension trust funds are used to account for public employee retirement systems. This type of fund is by far the most important type of trust fund for state and local governmental units. Because of the importance of pension trust funds and also because of the special accounting problems associated with accounting for pensions, this type of trust fund is treated separately from other expendable trust funds.

A typical example of an agency fund is a tax agency fund. Use of such a fund is warranted when one governmental unit is collecting a tax not only for itself; but in fact, a part of the tax is due to other governmental units. Sales taxes collected by a state government for

---

[35]MFOA, *1980 GAAFR*, p. 69.
[36]Old NCGA, *1968 GAAFR*, p. 75.

itself and for local governments would be accounted for through a tax agency fund.[37]

It appears that fiduciary funds may be used to account both for activities that result in market-type goods and services and for activities that result in nonmarket public goods and services. Thus, we have a situation where other than governmental funds may be used to account for activities that result in the supply of nonmarket public goods and services. Moreover, we also have a situation where a fund type other than proprietary funds may be used to account for activities that result in the supply of market-type goods and services. Recall that the general fund, a governmental fund, also could be used to account for activities that result in market-type goods and services.

Nonexpendable trust funds and pension trust funds are the most likely types of fiduciary funds that will be used to account for activities resulting in marketable goods and services. The type of fiduciary fund most likely to be used to account for activities that will result in nonmarket public goods and services would be an expendable trust fund.

Accounting Basis and Expendable, Modified Expendable, and Nonexpendable Funds

In the discussion of fiduciary funds, the distinction between expendable and nonexpendable trust funds was introduced. This distinction between expendable and nonexpendable funds can be applied to all of the funds of a governmental unit.

An expendable fund is a fund that receives financial resources that are to be spent for specified purposes. The spending of the financial resources is to take place either over a specified time period or until a specified purpose has been accomplished. The financial resources received by an expendable fund do not represent a form of permanent capital for that fund. Rather, the financial resources of such funds represent short-term or nonpermanent capital (if of the longer-term variety) to be used for the activities being accounted for by the expendable fund. Governmental funds such as the general fund, special revenue funds, and debt service funds are all expendable funds because they receive short-term capital in the form of financial resources to be used for specified purposes during a specified time period. Governmental funds such as capital projects funds and special assessment funds are expendable funds because they receive nonpermanent capital in the form of financial resources to be used for spec-

---

[37]A description of fiduciary funds in terms of a four-way breakdown is contained in the third basic principle of *NCGA Statement 1* shown in Appendix A.

ified capital improvements or other capital projects or capital acquisitions. The period of time over which the capital improvements are to be accomplished is not necessarily specifiable in the same terms as the time periods of such governmental funds as the general fund, special revenue funds, and debt service funds.

Nonexpendable funds receive resources—both financial and real—in the form of permanent capital. The permanent capital or principal received initially by a nonexpendable fund is assumed to be maintained intact and is to be replenished out of the operations and activities accounted for by the fund. The proprietary funds, both enterprise and internal service funds, are nonexpendable funds. In addition, nonexpendable trust funds are a nonexpendable fund type because the initial fund capital is to be held intact.

The fact that expendable funds are not intended to maintain a permanent fund capital, and nonexpendable funds are intended to maintain the initial fund principal intact, leads to a difference in the accounting basis for these two different classes of funds. *NCGA Statement 1* recommends the modified accrual basis for all of the governmental funds as well as for expendable trust funds and for agency funds. That is, all of the fund types that we have described as expendable funds are subject to the modified accrual basis of accounting. This basis, as well as the accrual basis, were both described in some detail in the prior chapter. *NCGA Statement 1* recommends the accrual basis of accounting for such nonexpendable funds as enterprise funds, internal service funds, and nonexpendable trust funds.

Recall that the modified accrual basis uses the concept of expenditures rather than expenses to account for the using up of resources. Expenditures represent a using up of financial resources. The expendable funds account essentially for financial resources and not real resources. With regard to the revenue side, the expendable funds derive their revenues mostly from sources that do not involve user charges. Remember the discussion of the preceding chapter covering revenues from taxes and the modified accrual basis. The modified accrual basis appears to be the appropriate accounting basis for expendable funds.

The nonexpendable funds account for both real and financial resources. Since there is an objective for nonexpendable funds—to maintain initial fund capital intact—one needs to distinguish at the end of each period between the initial permanent fund capital and additions to or subtractions from fund capital that result from operations. The accrual basis of accounting is considered as better suited to determining whether or not fund capital is being maintained from one time period to the next. Instead of using expenditures to account for the using up of financial resources, the accrual basis uses expenses. Expenses are an attempt to estimate the using up of real resources. The use of the accrual basis and the use of expenses to estimate the using up of real resources means that, in the case of a nonexpendable fund, one is trying to estimate the extent to which the using up of real resources is impairing the fund capital.

In the case of the nonexpendable funds, revenues tend to be from user charges. Therefore, from the revenue side, the accrual basis is better suited than the modified accrual basis to account for the activities of a nonexpendable fund. Note that revenues being from marketable goods which are divisible in nature enables expenses to be matched against revenues in order to estimate the degree to which costs are being covered during each period of operations. So one can see, from both the revenue and expenses sides, the rationale behind the *NCGA Statement 1* recommendation that the accrual basis applies to proprietary funds and to nonexpendable trust funds. These being nonexpendable funds, the accrual basis is considered to be appropriate for accounting for the activities of such funds.

The one fund type that has not been discussed so far (or should it be called a fund subtype?) is the pension trust fund. In *1968 GAAFR,* pension trust funds were considered an example of expendable trust funds. However, *NCGA Statement 1* treats pension trust funds separately from expendable trust funds. In *1968 GAAFR,* the accrual basis of accounting was recommended for all of the trust fund types, both expendable and nonexpendable. Since pension trust funds were included in the subtype of expendable trust funds, this meant that the accrual basis was recommended also for pension trust funds under *1968 GAAFR.* Under *NCGA Statement 1,* expendable trust funds are separated from pension trust funds. The modified accrual basis is recommended for expendable trust funds, but the accrual basis continues to be recommended for pension trust funds. The question then becomes whether a pension trust fund should continue to be considered an expendable fund.

In answer, it seems that pension trust funds have some of the characteristics of expendable funds and some of the characteristics of nonexpendable funds. On the one hand, under the appropriate circumstances, the initial fund capital of a pension trust fund could be expended to pay pension benefits as required by the pension plan. In addition, the resources of a pension trust fund are essentially financial resources. Thus, we have a fund type whose resources are financial and wholly expendable. These are characteristics of an expendable fund. On the other hand, where pension trust funds are maintained on an actuarial basis, there is a need to distinguish between the capital of the trust fund and additions and subtractions from that capital that result from earnings and contributions and from pension payments. Pension trust funds of governmental units that are maintained on an actuarial basis essentially render services similar to a private pension plan. The services rendered are of the marketable variety. Accounting for the activities of a pension trust fund which provides for marketable pension services to the benefici- aries of the pension plan normally calls for the accrual basis of ac- counting. The accrual basis of accounting as well as these character- istics that call for such a basis means that in these respects a pension trust fund has certain characteristics similar to a nonexpendable fund. Given that the pension trust fund seems to be a hybrid fund with characteristics of both an expendable and a nonexpendable fund, this fund will be described as a modified expendable fund.

A classification of the various fund types into expendable, modified expendable, and nonexpendable is shown in Exhibit 2. Also shown in this exhibit is the accounting basis that applies to each type of fund.

Exhibit 2
Expendable, Modified Expendable, and Nonexpendable Funds and
Accounting Basis

Category and Type	Maintenance of Fund Capital	Accounting Basis
Governmental:[1]		
General fund	Expendable	Modified accrual
Special revenue funds	Expendable	Modified accrual
Capital projects funds[2]	Expendable	Modified accrual
Debt service funds[3]	Expendable	Modified accrual
Special assessment funds	Expendable	Modified accrual
Proprietary:		
Enterprise funds[4]	Nonexpendable	Accrual
Internal service funds[5]	Nonexpendable	Accrual
Fiduciary (also called trust and agency funds):[6]		
Expendable trust funds	Expendable	Modified accrual
Nonexpendable trust funds	Nonexpendable	Accrual
Pension trust funds	Modified expendable[7]	Accrual
Agency funds	Expendable	Modified accrual

[1]The classification into governmental, proprietary, and fiduciary funds categories is new with *NCGA Statement 1*.

[2]Called bond funds in 1951 *Municipal Accounting and Auditing*.

[3]Called sinking funds in 1951 *Municipal Accounting and Auditing*.

[4]Called utility, or other enterprise, funds in 1951 *Municipal Accounting and Auditing*.

[5]Called working capital funds in 1951 *Municipal Accounting and Auditing*, and intragovern- mental service funds in *1968 GAAFR*.

[6]The explicit breakdown of the trust and agency funds (now also called fiduciary funds) into four separate fund types was implied in the prior treatment of such funds both in 1951 *Municipal Accounting and Auditing* and in *1968 GAAFR*.

[7]In *1968 GAAFR*, pension trust funds were classified as expendable funds. However, under *NCGA Statement 1*, pension trust funds are separated from expendable trust funds. Unlike other types of expendable funds, the accrual basis of accounting applies to pension trust funds. In the case of such funds there is an attempt to distinguish between earnings of a pension trust fund and its original capital. This makes this type of fund similar to a nonexpendable fund such as a propri- etary fund. However, under appropriate circumstances the original capital of a pension trust fund is expendable for pension purposes. In this sense, a pension trust fund can be considered an ex- pendable fund. As a result, such funds are described as modified expendable.

Additional Features of the Modified Accrual Basis on the Expenditure Side

There are certain features out of the modified accrual basis on the expenditure side, as set out in *NCGA Statement 1,* that were not discussed in the prior chapter, but with which one should be familiar. Two features were discussed there: First, unpaid interest on long-term debt of the governmental unit does not have to be recorded in the financial accounting records and reported in the financial statements (i.e., accrued) as an expenditure and a liability.[38] Second, unpaid wages which have been earned for services rendered may not be accrued as an expenditure and a liability.[39]

Recall that interest on general long-term debt of a governmental unit is shown as a liability only when due and provided for in the current fiscal year's budget. In commercial accounting, under the accrual basis, interest on long-term debt is accrued as a liability simply with the passage of time, whether or not the interest is due and payable as of the end of the fiscal period. This showing of interest as an expenditure and a liability only when due and provided for in the budget is applicable only to the modified accrual basis of accounting which is relevant for the expendable funds. In the case of the nonexpendable funds, the accrual basis of accounting applies, so that interest on long-term debt would be accrued simply as a function of time.

Under the modified accrual basis of accounting applicable to the expendable funds, wages earned but not paid and not provided for in the current fiscal year's budget would not necessarily be accrued as an expenditure and a liability. This exception is not explicitly stated in *NCGA Statement 1.* Instead one must look closely at illustrations that appeared in *1968 GAAFR* and also in *NCGA Statement 1.* In *1968 GAAFR,* there is a specific account which is called accrued wages payable. Its purpose is to account for and report on wages earned before the end of a fiscal period but not paid by the end of the fiscal period. In *1968 GAAFR* in the "List of Balance Sheet Accounts" (Appendix B, p. 181) we find that the accrued wages payable account is shown as applying to an enterprise fund but not to the general fund or special revenue funds. In addition, in the specific chapters for accounting by the general fund and special revenue funds, we do not find an example of a transaction involving accrued wages payable. However, in the chapter covering accounting for enterprise funds, we do find sample transactions and accounting entries for accrued wages payable. If you couple these illustrations for the handling of accrued

---

[38]*NCGA Statement 1,* p. 12.

[39]This is not an exception of *NCGA Statement 1;* it is a possible interpretation of *1968 GAAFR.* However, see the later discussion.

wages payable in *1968 GAAFR* with the tendency for governmental units (where they actually do utilize the modified accrual basis of accounting for the expendable funds) to record and report only expenditures provided for in the budget, then it is not unreasonable to expect that wages earned but not paid would not be accrued as accrued wages payable under the modified accrual basis in the expendable funds. In *1980 GAAFR,* in the specific chapters for the general fund (and special revenue funds) and for the enterprise funds, as before, there are no illustrative transactions for accrued wages payable for the general fund (and special revenue funds); but there are illustrative transactions for this account for the enterprise funds. However, in the "List of Balance Sheet Accounts" (Appendix C, p. 100) we have the accrued wages payable account; and it is shown as relevant not only for the proprietary funds such as the enterprise and internal service funds, but also for the general fund and special revenue funds. This means that there should be no exception for the accruing of wages earned but not paid and not provided for in the budget. Even though this liability has not been provided for in the budget, under *NCGA Statement 1* it should be accrued for financial reporting purposes. Whether the liability and matching expenditure will be accrued, even when not provided for in the budget, is something to be looked at in terms of whether MAP per *NCGA Statement 1* is actually being followed.

Note that under the accrual basis of accounting (relevant to commercial accounting) applicable to the nonexpendable funds, there should be no question concerning the need to accrue the expense and liability for wages earned but not paid.

Under *NCGA Statement 1,* a liability and an expenditure for unpaid interest for past periods on special assessment bonds need not be accrued in the financial accounting records and for the financial statements, if the amount of the liability to be accrued is approximately equal to the amount of interest revenue (covering past periods) to be accrued as a receivable on unpaid installments of special assessment property taxes.[40] There is nothing exactly analogous in business finance to the special assessment bonds of municipal finance. However, if one thinks of special assessment bonds as another type of long-term debt, then under the accrual basis a liability and an expense for accrued interest would be recognized in the financial accounting records and in the financial statements. Note that under the present value approach to estimating the amount of a liability, the accrual for interest covers interest for past periods. Unpaid interest for future periods beyond the date of the financial statements would not be consid-

---

[40]*NCGA Statement 1,* p. 12.

ered a liability. Unpaid interest for future periods is a contingent liability until these periods have become past periods.

According to *1980 GAAFR* (pp. 14–15), unpaid accumulated vacation pay benefits need not be accrued as a liability and an expenditure under the modified accrual basis in the expendable funds. Also, sick pay which has been accumulated by employees in the form of payable benefits need not be accrued as a liability and an expenditure under the modified accrual basis in the expendable funds. In addition, *1980 GAAFR* (pp. 14–15) sets out "other employee benefits" (without specifying the benefits), which have been accumulated as due but unpaid, as another category of benefits which need not be accrued as a liability and an expenditure under the modified accrual basis.

This exception dealing with accumulated employee benefits and set out in *1980 GAAFR,* is based on a recommendation in *NCGA Statement 1* stating: "Material vested amounts of employee benefits (such as vacation and sick leave) arising from activities financed through the governmental funds should be disclosed in the notes to the financial statements if the total amount exceeds a normal year's accumulation and is not presented in the financial statements."[41] This position of *NCGA Statement 1* is in accord with *SOP 75–3* which is an amendment of *Audits of State and Local Governmental Units.*[42] We are told in *NCGA Statement 1* that, if a liability is not shown in the financial statements themselves, then under certain circumstances the amount of the liability has to be disclosed in the notes to the financial statements. If a liability and the matching expenditure are not shown in the financial statements themselves, this means that the liability has not been accrued even though it is disclosed as part of the notes to the financial statements.

One of the objectives of the accrual basis of accounting and, similarly, for the modified accrual basis is that of fair financial reporting. As part of fair financial reporting, liabilities should not be understated. Therefore, if *NCGA Statement 1* permits exceptions to the accrual of liabilities, that would result in an understatement of liabilities and would not be in accord with the objective of fair financial reporting. Disclosure of liabilities in the notes to the financial statements for those liabilities that have been omitted from the financial statements themselves would overcome the problem, as long as the

---

[41]Ibid., p. 9.

[42]AICPA Subcommittee on State and Local Governmental Auditing, *Statement of Position 75–3,* "Accrual of Revenues and Expenditures by State and Local Governmental Units" (Amendment to AICPA Industry Audit Guide, *Audits of State and Local Governmental Units),* (New York: AICPA, July 31, 1975). *NCGA Statement 1* has been modified by *NCGA Statement 4* on the matter of accounting and reporting for vacation and sick leave benefits as well as on other accounting matters. See footnote 52 of Chapter 35.

disclosure is sufficiently adequate so that an external user of the financial statements could, by using the disclosure and nothing else, adjust the financial statements so as to properly incorporate the full impact of the omitted liability. Disclosures are not always so adequate that an external user can adjust the financial statements to show the full impact of the omitted liability throughout all of the financial statements.

Fund accounting introduces special kinds of complexities into governmental financial reporting. A user of governmental financial statements, due to fund accounting complications, may face a difficult burden if forced to rely on disclosures in the notes to the financial statements in order to adjust these financial statements for omitted liabilities and other omitted items. Besides, it seems an unnecessary exercise to force a statement user to go through if the amounts of omitted items from financial statements are going to be disclosed in any case in the notes to the financial statements. Why not just accrue them directly into the financial statements in the first place? A discussion in *1968 GAAFR* (pp. 12–13) seems to provide one of the major reasons behind this practice.

The reason that certain liabilities might not be reported directly in the financial statements seems to be based on budgetary considerations. If an item of expenditure is not authorized directly in the budget, then it is not necessary to accrue the expenditure for an incurred liability to be shown directly in the financial statements. We find in *1968 GAAFR* "that budgetary compliance is a paramount consideration in governmental accounting and must take precedence over the basis of accounting *per se*" (p. 12). This means that if an item of expenditure is not authorized directly in the current fiscal year's budget, then it is not necessary to accrue an expenditure and the liability that has been incurred. The reason for this position in *1968 GAAFR* rests on a principle that appears in this manual to the effect that, when there is a conflict between legal requirements and the accounting principles required for fair financial reporting, then legal requirements take precedence and, in a sense, fair financial reporting must take a back seat. In fact, the supremacy of legal requirements over fair financial reporting was enshrined as the second basic principle in *1968 GAAFR* (p. 4). Essentially, the same basic principle appears in 1951 *Municipal Accounting and Auditing* (p. 1), also as the second basic principle. A discussion in *1968 GAAFR* tells us:

> The existence of legal provisions which differ from and conflict with sound accounting principles is unfortunate because such provisions can hamper the effectiveness and adequacy of financial information produced by the accounting system. Nonetheless, so long as legal provisions of this type exist, they must be accorded a precedence over the accounting principles or practices with which they differ. (p. 5)

However, *NCGA Statement 1* abandoned the approach of the second basic principle of 1951 *Municipal Accounting and Auditing* and *1968 GAAFR*. Legal requirements no longer take precedence over fair financial reporting. Even though *NCGA Statement 1* has abandoned the principle of legal precedence over fair financial reporting, it still permits certain liabilities to be omitted from being reported directly in the financial statements. Instead, under certain circumstances, the omitted liabilities will be disclosed in the notes to the financial statements. We have observed already that disclosure in the notes to the financial statements may not be an adequate substitute for accrual directly in the financial statements themselves. The greater the number of substitutions of disclosures for accruals, the more likely it is that a user of financial statements will have neither the information nor the know-how to adjust the financial statements for the multifaceted impact of the omitted liabilities. There is also the possibility that information relative to an omitted variable may not be required to be disclosed in the notes to the financial statements. There is really no good reason for legitimate and significant liabilities to be omitted from the financial statements, even if the omissions are only a few specified exceptions to the general accounting principle of accruing material liabilities.

There are two types of current assets that *NCGA Statement 1* treats under the modified accrual basis as exceptions from the usual treatment found under the accrual basis. One such current asset is prepaid expenses.[43] The other type of current asset is inventory.[44]

Prepaid expenses, such as prepaid insurance, do not have to be shown as an asset under the modified accrual basis in the expendable funds.[45] If, however, prepaid expenses are shown as part of the assets, then at the same time, a part of the fund equity equal to the amount of the prepaid expenses has to be identified directly in the financial statements as "reserved for prepaid expenses." Prepaid expenses do

---

[43]*NCGA Statement 1*, p. 12.

[44]Ibid.

[45]Current assets are defined as "cash and other assets or resources commonly identified as those which are reasonably expected to be realized in cash or sold or consumed during the normal operating cycle of the business." This definition is taken from the AICPA Committee on Accounting Procedure, *Accounting Research Bulletin (ARB) No. 43*, "Restatement and Revision of Accounting Research Bulletins" (New York: AICPA, June 1953), chap. 3, para. 4. *ARB No. 43* is considered a source of GAAP for business accounting. In it we are told also that if there is more than one operating cycle within a year, then the year will be assumed to be the minimum operating cycle for purposes of defining current assets. Note that prepaid expenses do not exactly fit the definition of a current asset since some prepaid expenses can have lives extending significantly beyond the normal operating cycle of a business. However, by convention, that portion of prepaid expenses which is a current asset is not separated from that portion which is noncurrent. This neglect of a proper breakdown of prepaid expenses into a current and noncurrent portion is usually defended on the ground that the neglect does not result in a significant distortion of financial statements.

not represent the typical asset of an expendable fund since such assets are supposed to be financial resources available to be spent to finance the activities accounted for by the fund. Nevertheless, *NCGA Statement 1* permits prepaid expenses to be reported directly in the financial statements if an appropriate reserve is shown in the fund equity. The purpose of reserving a part of the fund equity equal to the amount of the prepaid expenses—if such an item is shown as an asset—is so that the unreserved part of the fund equity will be equal to the amount of the assets that represent financial resources of the spendable variety.

Under *NCGA Statement 1,* all material amounts of inventory items must be reported as an asset directly in the financial statements. Inventory-type items like prepaid expenses are not a financial resource of the spendable variety. Note, when the term *inventory* or *inventories* is used, the items covered by this term are real resources of the physical variety. Thus, *NCGA Statement 1* requires also that an amount equal to the amount of the inventory (shown as an asset) be shown in the fund equity directly in the financial statements as "reserved for inventory." This means that the unreserved part of the fund equity will represent only financial resources of the spendable variety.

The concept of spendable resources is not relevant to the accrual basis of accounting. This means that identifying a part of the retained earnings of a business corporation as reserved for prepaid expenses or reserved for inventory would serve no purpose.

There is also a feature peculiar to the treatment of expenditures associated with inventory-type items. We are no longer talking about assets, but about expenditures associated with assets. This particular type of treatment would not occur under the accrual basis of accounting since expenditures do not play the same role in accounting for nonexpendable funds and accounting for business enterprises. *NCGA Statement 1* permits expenditures associated with inventory-type items to be accounted for under either the purchases method or the consumption method.[46]

Under the purchases method, all inventories acquired during a particular fiscal period would be shown as expended during that same period, regardless of the actual amount of physical inventories on hand at the end of the fiscal period. The purchases method is consistent with the notion that expenditures are a use of financial resources. The fact that some of the inventories purchased during a fiscal period remain unused at the end of the fiscal period does not change the amount of financial resources used in the acquisition of such inventories. As observed earlier, *NCGA Statement 1* requires

---

[46]*NCGA Statement 1,* p. 12.

that inventories be reported as an asset directly in the financial statements of an expendable fund such as the general fund, even though the inventory-type items have been treated as fully expended. Because the inventory items are treated as expended, the amount of inventories shown as an asset has to be matched by a reserve for inventories amount to be shown in the fund equity. The amount of inventories shown as an asset would be equal to the physical amount of unused inventory items valued at the lower of original cost or market.[47]

Under the consumption method, the amount of inventory items shown as expended during a particular time period is equal not to the amount purchased during that period but to the amount of inventory items used during the period. Expenditures for inventory-type items under the consumption method will not necessarily be equal to the expenditures for inventory items under the purchases method. Under the purchases method, expenditures for inventory items are equal to the amount of financial resources used for the acquisition of these items. Under the consumption method, "expenditures" for inventory-type items no longer represent the using up of financial resources but instead represent an estimate of the using up of real resources. The consumption method of accounting for expenditures for the acquisition of inventory-type items is, in fact, not compatible with the notion that an expenditure represents a using up of financial resources.

Note that under either the purchases or the consumption method of accounting for expenditures, the amount of inventories shown as an asset would be the same. Of course, this means that the amount shown as reserved for inventories, in the fund equity, would be the same under either method. It is the amount of expenditures that is reported under the consumption method that would differ from the amount of expenditures under the purchases method. There is no particular justification for the use, under the modified accrual basis, of the two different methods of accounting for expenditures as permitted by *NCGA Statement 1,* especially in view of the fact that one of the methods is inconsistent with the usual definition of expenditures.

The two exceptions discussed with respect to the current assets need not have occurred under *NCGA Statement 1.* Inventories and prepaid expenses need not be shown directly in the financial statements as part of the financial resources of an expendable fund. Instead, where it is believed that information on the amount of inventories and prepaid expenses might prove useful to financial statement users, this information could be disclosed in the notes to the financial

---

[47]See, for example, illustrative notes to the financial statements in *1980 GAAFR,* Appendix D, p. 136 — in particular note (1)–G, "Inventory." Note (1) sets out a "Summary of Significant Accounting Policies," and the accounting principle with respect to the valuation of inventory appears in G. of this note.

statement rather than reported directly in the statements themselves. The end result would be that the financial statements of an expendable fund would show only financial resources of the expendable variety; yet the desired information would be at the disposal of the financial statement user. Similarly, there is no need for two methods of accounting for expenditures for inventory-type items. Instead, the purchases method, which is compatible with the concept of expenditures as a use of financial resources, should be used to report expenditures directly in the financial statements. The consumption method, which produces an estimate of inventory-type items consumed, could be used as part of a disclosure in the notes to the financial statements. As a result, the expenditures figure shown in the financial statements would represent the using up of financial resources rather than a mixture of the using up of financial resources and the using up of real resources.

Note that the exceptions discussed above are acceptable to independent CPA firms who could be responsible for auditing and certifying state and local governmental financial statements. This is the case because *SOP 80–2,* to which we referred earlier, amended the industry audit guide, *Audits of State and Local Governmental Units,* so that it conforms to *NCGA Statement 1.* Remember that *ASLGU* and, by virtue of *SOP 80–2,* also *NCGA Statement 1* are considered sources of GAAP (for state and local governmental units) for independent CPA firms.

Budgeting and Fund Accounting

Earlier, it was observed that there are a series of control mechanisms to ensure that resources obtained from taxpayers by governmental units are used for the purposes for which the resources were raised. Legal requirements pervade governmental activities as one such control mechanism. It is easy for those whose experience is largely in the private sector not to appreciate fully the advantages of having the "rule of law" rather than man pervade public sector activities. Fund accounting is another control mechanism. A third and quite essential control mechanism is budgeting. In the governmental sector, budgeting and law are blended together to produce a comparatively sensitive instrument to control governmental spending. All of these control mechanisms are needed because of the absence, on the output side of governmental activities, of the kind of competitive market forces that serve as control mechanisms with respect to private goods and services.

The governmental budget process and the budget document that emerges from this process represent the mechanism by which the political process allocates resources into and within the public sector.

Moak and Hillhouse in their *Concepts and Practices in Local Government Finance* provide us with a series of specific management and other objectives of the budgeting process.[48] These objectives are shown in Appendix B to this chapter. A review of these objectives should give one a sense of the vital role played by the budgeting process and the governmental budget.

Governmental budgeting in the United States, at the state and local governmental levels, reflects the division of powers and functions between the legislative and executive branches. A new governmental budget normally begins life within the executive branch, while that branch is carrying out normal governmental activities to supply non-market public goods and services. The executive budget, when completed, is normally submitted to the legislative branch for review, revision, and approval. Once a budget has been approved by the legislative branch and agreed to by the chief executive official, it is converted from an executive budget to an adopted budget. It is the adopted budget that is actually entered into the financial accounting records of a governmental unit.

How is the adopted governmental budget entered into the financial accounting records? First, we look at the spending side. Prior to the enactment of a governmental budget, one can describe budgeted spending as representing planned spending. Once the budget is enacted into law, then budgeted expenditures would be described as appropriations. Governmental appropriations represent the legal authority for the various branches of a governmental unit to spend the resources expected to be raised to finance the budgeted activities. In governmental financial accounting, the amounts of the governmental appropriations are entered in total into a control account called "appropriations," and also into a series of subsidiary appropriation accounts for each category of authorized spending. There is nothing equivalent to appropriations in the financial accounting records of a business corporation.

In order to help in the prevention of overspending of the governmental budget, the financial accounting records track not only governmental spending through a control account called expenditures (along with appropriate subsidiary accounts), but also track contractual commitments. A contractual commitment of the governmental budget is called an "encumbrance." Encumbrances differ from expenditures in that expenditures are recorded only when goods and services have been received, but encumbrances are recorded when there is a contract for goods or services. Expenditures are recorded when liabilities are incurred, while encumbrances are recorded when con-

---

[48]Lennox L. Moak and Albert M. Hillhouse, *Concepts and Practices in Local Government Finance* (Chicago: Municipal Finance Officers Association, 1975), pp. 81–82.

tingent liabilities are incurred—i.e., contracts are signed or purchase orders are issued.

For example, if a governmental unit enters into a contract to purchase equipment out of unrestricted operating resources, then at the time that the contract is signed, an encumbrance is recorded in the financial accounting records to show that part of the appropriation has been used up. Actually, a particular appropriation category which authorizes the purchase of the equipment would have been used up, either in part or in whole. When the equipment is received, the encumbrance is removed from the appropriation category authorizing the acquisition and replaced with an expenditure. The expenditure represents the using up of financial resources. The encumbrance represented a contractual commitment of the budget. The category which tells us the object of the authorized spending is used also for the encumbrance and the expenditure.

Encumbrances are recorded in the financial accounting records of state or local governmental units in an account also called "encumbrances." The control account for encumbrances records total encumbrances, while the subsidiary accounts for encumbrances record the various categories of encumbrances. The encumbrance categories correspond to the associated appropriation categories. Just as for appropriations, there is no equivalent in the financial accounting records of a business in which to record encumbrances.

The appropriations account, which tracks budget authority to spend, is to be contrasted with the expenditures account, which tracks actual spending. The account that records actual spending is called a "proprietary account." Proprietary accounts are accounts in the financial accounting records that are used to record actual transactions. "Budgetary accounts" account for the budget authority to spend. The appropriations account which represents budget authority to spend would be considered a budgetary account. What about the encumbrances account? This account does not represent a budget amount—e.g., budget authority to spend—nor does it represent necessarily the actual amount spent. Encumbrances *do* deal with actual transactions. The actual transactions are the initiation of actual contractual relationships. Nevertheless, *1968 GAAFR* treats encumbrances as a budgetary account.[49] However, *1980 GAAFR* seems a bit ambivalent on this issue. On the one hand, it shows illustrative transactions in which encumbrances continue to be treated as a budgetary account.[50] On the other hand, encumbrances are described explicitly as an "actual" account, and actual accounts are distinguished from budgetary

    [49]See the definition of "budgetary accounts" which appears in *1968 GAAFR,* Appendix A ("Terminology"), p. 55.
    [50]See the illustrative entries which appear in MFOA, *1980 GAAFR,* chap. 4 ("General and Special Revenue Funds"), p. 4.

accounts.[51] Since encumbrances have been treated usually as a budgetary account, and continue to be treated in this fashion (even though, strictly speaking, they show actual contractual commitments) we shall follow customary usage and classify encumbrances as a budgetary account.[52] Now, assuming that one treats encumbrances as a budgetary acount, then we can say that budgetary accounts are not usually found in the financial accounting records of business enterprises, but proprietary accounts are to be found there.

The revenue side of an adopted governmental budget is recorded also in the financial accounting records of the governmental unit. The account which tracks anticipated or expected revenues is called "estimate revenues." It is considered a budgetary account. There would be no equivalent account in the financial accounting records of a business enterprise. The account called estimated revenues is a control account, and there also would be subsidiary estimated revenues accounts to provide a detailed breakdown of the control figures. The account that tracks actual revenues in the financial accounting records is called "revenues." What else! It is a control account that would be supported by subsidiary accounts. It is considered a proprietary account. Business enterprises would have analogous accounts for revenues in their financial accounting records. These business revenue accounts would be known under a variety of names. Note that business revenues represent voluntary payments for market-supplied goods and services, while governmental revenues can represent involuntary payments (from taxes) for nonmarket public goods and services.

When we speak of the financial accounting records of a governmental unit, we must remember that there is not really one set of financial accounting records but separate sets of financial accounting records for each fund of the governmental unit. There are also separate sets of financial accounting records for the account groups. (We will discuss the account groups later on.) The general fund has its own

[51]See the discussion in MFOA *1980 GAAFR,* chap. 2 ("Principles of Governmental Accounting and Financial Reporting"), p. 17.

[52]A review of some standard textbooks in governmental accounting reveals the continued treatment of encumbrances as a budgetary account. See, for example, Leon E. Hay, *Accounting for Governmental and Nonprofit Entities,* 6th ed. (Homewood, Ill.: Richard D. Irwin, 1980), p. 43; Leon E. Hay and John H. Engstrom, *Programed Learning Aid: Self Review in Accounting for Governmental and Nonprofit Entities* (Homewood, Ill.: Learnings Systems Company, a division of Richard D. Irwin, 1980), p. 18; Emerson O. Henke, *Introduction to Nonprofit Organization Accounting* (Boston: Kent Publishing, a division of Wadsworth, 1980), p. 120. Another standard textbook in governmental accounting is Edward S. Lynn and Robert J. Freeman, *Fund Accounting: Theory and Practice* (Englewood Cliffs, N.J.: Prentice-Hall, 1974). Lynn and Freeman (p. 139) treat encumbrances as a "memorandum" account. A memorandum account is not a proprietary account, so that one can infer that Lynn and Feeman consider encumbrances somewhat like a budgetary account. An updated version of the Lynn and Freeman book became available at the end of 1982.

self-contained set of financial accounting records. Additionally, each of the individual special revenue funds will have a set of self-contained financial accounting records. In other words, each individual fund or account group of a governmental unit has its own self-contained set of financial accounting records.

The governmental budget does not apply to all of the funds of a governmental unit. Budgetary accounts would be incorporated into each set of financial accounting records for each fund to which the governmental budget applies. There are at least two ways of looking at the adopted annual operating budget of a governmental unit. One view of the adopted budget is that it is composed of a collection of adopted annual budgets for each of the funds of the governmental unit that require governmental budgetary control. A second view of the governmental budget is as a comprehensive and unified legal planning and control mechanism for the activities of the governmental unit that supply primarily nonmarket public goods and services.[53] Basically, the governmental budget covers more than one fund, and there should generally be only one overall adopted governmental budget for each fiscal period. The governmental operating budget is usually of the annual variety.[54] Depending on a particular jurisdiction, governmental budgets may be modified through supplemental appropriations.

The annual operating budget for a governmental unit applies primarily to the general and special revenue funds. *NCGA Statement 1* requires formal budgetary accounts in the financial accounting records for the general fund, special revenue funds, and similar governmental-type funds.[55] *NCGA Statement 1* does not require formal budgetary accounts in the financial accounting records for the capital projects or special assessment funds, unless these funds are accounting for numerous construction projects that require detailed and explicit budgetary control.[56] However, if these funds are accounting for a few large capital improvement projects, then formal budgetary accounting may not be necessary. Similarly, debt service funds do not usually need formal budgetary accounting in their financial accounting records.

The most frequent type of budget is called the "line item" or "objective of expenditure" budget. This classification refers to the spending side of the budget. In particular, it refers to the kind of spending categories around which the budget is organized. An object-of-expenditure (or should we say planned or authorized expenditure) category tells us what is to be purchased; i.e., it emphasizes the object to be

---

[53]See, for example, the discussion in MFOA *1980 GAAFR,* p. 16.
[54]According to *NCGA Statement 1,* p. 13, some states have biennial fiscal periods.
[55]*NCGA Statement 1,* pp. 13–14.
[56]Ibid., p. 14.

acquired with budgetary resources. The objects of expenditure become subsidiary accounts in the financial accounting records. These subsidiary accounts are arranged to tell us the amount of an appropriation for a particular object of expenditure, the amount of the appropriation that has been encumbered in the form of encumbrances, and the amount of the appropriation that has been expended in the form of expenditures. Examples of objects of expenditures to be used to classify planned and actual spending would be for the acquisition of personnel services, heating, and telephone. The object-of-expenditure approach concentrates on the inputs being purchased to be used in the operations of the governmental unit.

NCGA Statement 1, as part of its discussion of expenditure classification, provides for categories other than the object-of-expenditure category by which to organize the governmental budget. In *NCGA Statement 1,* we are told that the "function," or "program," classification provides information on the overall purposes or objectives of expenditures. Functions group related activities that are aimed at accomplishing a major service or regulatory responsibility. Programs group activities, operations, or organizational units that are directed to the attainment of specific purposes or objectives."[57] The function, or program, approach to classifying expenditures focuses on the outputs rather than the inputs of governmental activities. Of course, we are actually measuring the outputs themselves not in terms of the benefits perceived by citizens, but in terms of expenditures. Examples of function categories are public safety, health, and education.

The integration of the budgetary accounts into the financial accounting records of a governmental unit not only serves the primary function of managerial control, but it also facilitates external financial reporting to taxpayers and citizens. *NCGA Statement 1* requires a comparison between budgeted (and authorized) expenditures and actual spending to be shown directly in the financial statements of a state or local governmental unit.[58] Such comparisons for purposes of financial reporting normally are also required by the statutory law governing the activities of the state or local governmental unit.

The required comparison, between budget figures accounted for in the budgetary accounts and the actual figures accounted for in the proprietary accounts, requires not only a consistent and compatible terminology between the budget and the accounting system, but it also requires that the same accounting basis be applied to both. In order to handle the problem of comparability between the budget and actual results, *1980 GAAFR* tells us:

---

[57]Ibid., p. 16.
[58]See basic principle IX in Appendix A to this chapter.

> Under Statement 1, it is a GAAP *requirement* that governmental
> GAAP financial reports include comparisons of approved budgeted
> amounts with actual results of operations *on the budgetary basis ac-*
> *tually used to control operations.* If the budget is prepared on a basis
> other than GAAP, a separate reporting of actual results of operations
> in conformity with GAAP is necessary in addition to such required
> budgetary comparisons. Such comparisons are required for the general
> and special revenue funds and other governmental funds for which an-
> nual budgets are legally adopted. (p. 7)

In other words, if the governmental budget for its governmental-
type activities is prepared on the cash basis (perhaps due to legal
requirements), then a comparison between the governmental budget
and the actual figures, for the activities, requires that the actual figures also be on the cash basis for the comparison to be meaningful.
In addition, where the comparison between budgeted and actual activity figures is on the cash basis, then there must be a separate financial statement showing the actual figures for activity on the modified accrual basis. The activity figures would refer to budgeted
figures for planned and authorized expenditures and expected revenues, and to actual figures for actual expenditures and actual revenues. Of course, the authors of *NCGA Statement 1* would prefer that
the budget be prepared in accordance with MAP as set out in the
Statement. In the case of the governmental funds to which the governmental budget applies, the budget should be prepared on the modified
accrual basis. If the budget were prepared on the modified accrual
basis, there would be just one financial statement which would compare the budgeted activity figures with the actual activity figures,
both on the modified accrual basis. In this case, there would be no
need for an additional financial statement to report the actual activity figures on the modified accrual basis.[59]

In *1980 GAAFR,* there are several illustrations of budgets that
are prepared on a basis that is not in conformity with the requirements of *NCGA Statement 1.* For example, *1980 GAAFR* (p. 29)
shows budgetary comparisons for the general fund and for the special
revenue funds, where budgeted expenditures are defined so that encumbrances that are outstanding at the end of the fiscal period (un-
filled purchase orders, etc.) are treated as expenditures of that period.
NCGA Statement 1 (p. 14) tells us that "Encumbrances outstanding
at year-end do not constitute expenditures or liabilities." This means
that a budget that contains expenditure figures that treat encum-

---

[59]See *NCGA Statement 1,* pp. 23–24, for the discussion which requires that the
comparison between budgeted and actual figures be made with the actual figures adjusted to the actual basis used for the legally adopted budget.

brances as though they are expenditures would not be prepared on a basis that is in conformity with the modified accrual basis described in *NCGA Statement 1*. Even though the legally adopted budget is prepared on a basis not completely consistent with the modified accrual basis, *NCGA Statement 1* nevertheless requires actual expenditures to be adjusted to the same basis as the budgeted expenditures. Actual figures for expenditures have to be adjusted to include outstanding encumbrances so that a meaningful comparison can be made between the budget and the actual figures.[60]

CONCLUSION

The heart of state and local governmental accounting as practiced at present rests on three interrelated mechanisms: legal requirements, the adopted budget, and fund accounting. The importance of and the special role played by these three mechanisms for the public sector rests on the fact that governments supply, by and large, non-market public goods, and that this activity is not fully subject to the rigors of a competitive market mechanism. The intricacies of fund accounting have been explored in some detail because this is a feature of governmental accounting that contrasts rather sharply with commercial accounting.

In addition, one can view fund accounting as a kind of superstructure for both governmental financial accounting and governmental financial reporting. This will lead, in the next chapter, to a further discussion of the kinds of assets and liabilities accounted for by each of the different fund types. Also, from the balance sheet perspective, general fixed assets and general long-term debt are not accounted for through the funds of the governmental unit. Accounting for such assets and liabilities must be understood in the context of fund accounting. Discussion of fund assets and fund liabilities and general fixed assets and general long-term liabilities will serve to build a foundation for a discussion of municipal financial reporting.

---

[60]Note that the comparison between budget and actual figures to which our discussion refers has to do with a financial statement called the "Combined Statement of Revenues and Expenditures—Budget (Budgetary Basis) and Actual—General and Special Revenue Fund Types for the Year Ended December 31, 19X2," (see *1980 GAAFR*, p. 29). In *NGA Statement 1* (p. 24) we are told that if individual fund statements are presented in addition to the "combined" statements, then a comparison between budgeted figures which differ from the modified accrual basis with actual figures adjusted to the budgetary basis, would be done in a separate schedule rather than directly in the financial statements for the individual fund. The distinction between combined financial statements and financial statements for individual funds will be discussed in the next chapter.

APPENDIX A

The Basic Principles of Financial Accounting and Financial Reporting According to *NCGA Statement 1**

I. ACCOUNTING AND REPORTING CAPABILITIES

A governmental accounting system must make it possible both: (a) to present fairly and with full disclosure the financial position and results of financial operations of the funds and account groups of the governmental unit in conformity with generally accepted accounting principles; and (b) to determine and demonstrate compliance with finance-related legal and contractual provisions.

II. FUND ACCOUNTING SYSTEMS

Governmental accounting systems should be organized and operated on a fund basis. A fund is defined as a fiscal and accounting entity with a self-balancing set of accounts recording cash and other financial resources, together with all related liabilities and residual equities or balances, and changes therein, which are segregated for the purpose of carrying on specific activities or attaining certain objectives in accordance with special regulations, restrictions, or limitations.

III. TYPES OF FUNDS

The following types of funds should be used by state and local governments:

Governmental Funds

1. The General Fund. To account for all financial resources except those required to be accounted for in another fund.

2. Special Revenue Funds. To account for the proceeds of specific revenue sources (other than special assessments, expendable

---

*Adapted and reproduced from the "Summary Statement of the Principles" with permission from National Council on Governmental Accounting, Statement 1, *Governmental Accounting and Financial Reporting Principles* (Chicago: Municipal Finance Officers Association of the United States and Canada, 1979), pp. 2–4. © Copyright 1979 by the Municipal Finance Officers Association of the United States and Canada.

trusts, or for major capital projects) that are legally restricted to expenditure for specified purposes.

3. Capital Projects Funds. To account for financial resources to be used for the acquisition or construction of major capital facilities (other than those financed by proprietary funds, special assessment funds, and trust funds).

4. Debt Service Funds. To account for the accumulation of resources for, and the payment of, general long-term debt principal and interest.

5. Special Assessment Funds. To account for the financing of public improvements or services deemed to benefit the properties against which special assessments are levied.

Proprietary Funds

6. Enterprise Funds. To account for operations (a) that are financed and operated in a manner similar to private business enterprises—where the intent of the governing body is that the costs (expenses, including depreciation) of providing goods or services to the general public on a continuing basis be financed or recovered primarily through user charges; or (b) where the governing body has decided that periodic determination of revenues earned, expenses incurred, and/or net income is appropriate for capital maintenance, public policy, management control, accountability, or other purposes.

7. Internal Service Funds. To account for the financing of goods or services provided by one department or agency to other departments or agencies of the governmental unit, or to other governmental units, on a cost reimbursement basis.

Fiduciary Funds

8. Trust and Agency Funds. To account for assets held by a governmental unit in a trustee capacity or as an agent for individuals, private organizations, other governmental units, and/or other funds. These include (a) expendable trust funds, (b) nonexpendable trust funds, (c) pension trust funds, and (d) agency funds.

IV. NUMBER OF FUNDS

Governmental units should establish and maintain those funds required by law and sound financial administration. Only the minimum number of funds consistent with legal and operating requirements should be established, however, since unnecessary funds result in inflexibility, undue complexity, and inefficient financial administration.

V. ACCOUNTING FOR FIXED ASSETS AND LONG–TERM LIABILITIES

A clear distinction should be made between (a) fund fixed assets and general fixed assets and (b) fund long-term liabilities and general long-term debt.

1. Fixed assets related to specific proprietary funds or trust funds should be accounted for through those funds. All other fixed assets of a governmental unit should be accounted for through the general fixed assets account group.
2. Long-term liabilities of proprietary funds, special assessment funds, and trust funds should be accounted for through those funds. All other unmatured general long-term liabilities of the governmental unit should be accounted for through the general long-term debt account group.

VI. VALUATION OF FIXED ASSETS

Fixed assets should be accounted for at cost or, if the cost is not practicably determinable, at estimated cost. Donated fixed assets should be recorded at their estimated fair value at the time received.

VII. DEPRECIATION OF FIXED ASSETS

1. Depreciation of general fixed assets should not be recorded in the accounts of governmental funds. Depreciation of general fixed assets may be recorded in cost accounting systems or calculated for cost finding analyses; and accumulated depreciation may be recorded in the general fixed assets account group.
2. Depreciation of fixed assets accounted for in a proprietary fund should be recorded in the accounts of that fund. Depreciation is also recognized in those trust funds where expenses, net income, and/or capital maintenance are measured.

VIII. ACCRUAL BASIS IN GOVERNMENTAL ACCOUNTING

The modified accrual or accrual basis of accounting, as appropriate, should be utilized in measuring financial position and operating results.

1. *Governmental fund* revenues and expenditures should be recognized on the modified accrual basis. Revenues should be recognized in the accounting period in which they become available and measurable. Expenditures should be recognized in the ac-

counting period in which the fund liability is incurred, if measurable, except for unmatured interest on general long-term debt and on special assessment indebtedness secured by interest-bearing special assessment levies, which should be recognized when due.

2. *Proprietary fund* revenues and expenses should be recognized on the accrual basis. Revenues should be recognized in the accounting period in which they are earned and become measurable; expenses should be recognized in the period incurred, if measurable.

3. *Fiduciary fund* revenues and expenses or expenditures (as appropriate) should be recognized on the basis consistent with the fund's accounting measurement objective. Nonexpendable trust and pension trust funds should be accounted for on the accrual basis; expendable trust funds should be accounted for on the modified accrual basis. Agency fund assets and liabilities should be accounted for on the modified accrual basis.

4. *Transfers* should be recognized in the accounting period in which the interfund receivable and payable arise.

IX. BUDGETING, BUDGETARY CONTROL, AND BUDGETARY REPORTING

1. An annual budget(s) should be adopted by every governmental unit.

2. The accounting system should provide the basis for appropriate budgetary control.

3. Budgetary comparisons should be included in the appropriate financial statements and schedules for governmental funds for which an annual budget has been adopted.

X. TRANSFER, REVENUE, EXPENDITURE, AND EXPENSE ACCOUNT CLASSIFICATION

1. Interfund transfers and proceeds of general long-term debt issues should be classified separately from fund revenues and expenditures or expenses.

2. Governmental fund revenues should be classified by fund and source. Expenditures should be classified by fund, function (or program), organization unit, activity, character, and principal classes of objects.

3. Proprietary fund revenues and expenses should be classified in essentially the same manner as those of similar business organizations, functions, or activities.

XI. COMMON TERMINOLOGY AND CLASSIFICATION

A common terminology and classification should be used consistently throughout the budget, the accounts, and the financial reports of each fund.

XII. INTERIM AND ANNUAL FINANCIAL REPORTS

1. Appropriate interim financial statements and reports of financial position, operating results, and other pertinent information should be prepared to facilitate management control of financial operations, legislative oversight, and, where necessary or desired, for external reporting purposes.
2. A comprehensive annual financial report covering all funds and account groups of the governmental unit—including appropriate combined, combining, and individual fund statements; notes to the financial statements; schedules; narrative explanations; and statistical tables—should be prepared and published.
3. General purpose financial statements may be issued separately from the comprehensive annual financial report. Such statements should include the basic financial statements and notes to the financial statements that are essential to fair presentation of financial position and operating results (and changes in financial position of proprietary funds and similar trust funds).

APPENDIX B

Objectives of the Annual Budget Process*

1. To provide for comprehensive involvement of departmental and sub-departmental units of the government in planning the programs to be executed during the ensuing year; the quantification of requirements for personnel, materiel, contractual and other services; and the resolution of these into current dollar requirements.
2. To require the executive branch of the government to produce a program of operating expenditures (including debt service re-

---

*The materials in this appendix are adapted and reproduced with the permission of the Municipal Finance Officers Association of the United and Canada from Lennox L. Moak and Albert M. Hillhouse, *Concepts and Practices in Local Government Finance* (Chicago: Municipal Finance Officers Association of the United States and Canada, 1975), pp. 81–82. © Copyright 1975 by the Municipal Finance Officers Association of the United States and Canada.

quirements) which can be balanced by the recommended revenue program.

3. To provide to each successive level of management—and especially to the chief executive or administrative officer—the means by which competing requirements for limited resources can be effectively evaluated.

4. To provide a system for measuring the objectives expected to be attained within the fiscal period and to facilitate the scheduling of work and the coordination of nonpersonal service requirements with the personal services intended to be engaged.

5. To facilitate understanding by the governing body and the body politic of the proposed plan of operations for the year and to allow revision of the proposed plan prior to legislative approval.

6. To provide a basis for the enactment of the annual appropriation ordinance and such accompanying revenue measures as may be required.

7. To provide a basis upon which planned activities for the ensuring year may be adjusted to conform to appropriations.

8. To provide a basis for financial audit and, hopefully, for performance audit, both during the fiscal year and after the close of the fiscal year.

Municipal Financial Reporting: Part I*

CHAPTER **37**

Abraham J. Simon, Ph.D., CPA

Professor of Accounting and Information Systems
Queens College, City University of New York

INTRODUCTION

In this chapter, we shall look at municipal financial reporting as viewed through the eyes of *NCGA Statement 1.*[1] Earlier, it was stated that the gap in GAAP would not be a topic to which attention would be directed. Rather, the emphasis would be on spelling out the current state of municipal accounting principles (MAP). However, in describing MAP we have, from time to time, permitted ourselves the luxury of a critical observation here and there. Similarly, in describing municipal financial reporting according to *NCGA Statement 1,* we will include some critical observations. The purpose of these critical observations is not really to set out a systematic critique of MAP

---

*I would like to thank Bradley Benson of Ademco and A. Wayne Corcoran of Baruch College—CUNY for their review and comments on this chapter. I would also like to thank my wife, Marilyn S. Simon, for her proofreading and editing of the materials in the chapter. The responsibility is mine for any remaining defects in form or substance.

[1]National Council on Governmental Accounting (new NCGA), *NCGA Statement 1,* "Governmental Accounting and Financial Reporting Principles" (Chicago: Municipal Finance Officers Association, March 1979a).

in terms of either the accounting or the reporting guidelines, but through such observations to try to deepen your understanding of the particular approach to municipal financial accounting and reporting taken by *NCGA Statement 1* and in the explanations of that statement by *1980 GAAFR*.[2]

In this chapter, a number of illustrative hypothetical balance sheets taken from *1980 GAAFR* will be used as the initial type of financial statement to be studied. Prior to the examination of a particular illustrative balance sheet for a particular fund or fund type, there will be a discussion of the types of assets and liabilities accounted for by a specific type of fund that belongs to a particular fund category.

The discussion in this chapter will concentrate on a description and examination of individual fund balance sheets and combining balance sheets. A *combining* balance sheet brings together in a single balance sheet the assets, liabilities, and fund equities of the individual funds of a particular fund type. The discussion of the first two levels of balance sheets—the individual level and the combining level—will lay the groundwork for a third-level balance sheet, called a *combined* balance sheet. It brings together all of the assets, liabilities, and equities of all of the funds and account groups of a governmental entity in a single balance. The combined balance is part of a group of combined financial statements that provide an overview of the assets, liabilities, activities, etc., of the governmental unit. The third-level financial statements will not be described and reviewed until the next chapter. In addition, the other types of financial statements, at each of the three levels of presentation, will be discussed in the next chapter to complete the review of municipal financial reporting.

FUND ASSETS AND LIABILITIES

Governmental Funds

The expendable funds of a governmental unit carry essentially expendable financial resources to be consumed to finance the activities accounted for by the fund. In the case of a *governmental fund,* its financial resources are to be received and used up during the fund's budgetary period. The budgetary period is normally a year, though *NCGA Statement 1* (p. 13) observes that some states have a biennial budgetary period. Assets of the *general fund* normally have a life of one budgetary period, usually one year. In commercial accounting, assets that last for one operating cycle (where the minimum operat-

---

[2]Municipal Finance Officers Association, *Governmental Accounting, Auditing, and Financial Reporting (1980 GAAFR)* (Chicago: MFOA, 1980).

ing cycle is taken to be not less than a year) are classified as "current assets." In other words, the general fund holds primarily current assets. If the assets of a fund tend to be of the one-year duration variety, it is likely that fund liabilities will be of the one-year or current variety. Since the general fund does not carry long-term liabilities, its liabilities would be classified as "current liabilities."

We have dealt already with two exceptions to the rule that the general fund carries essentially financial resources. One exception is prepaid expenses, and the other is inventory. Earlier it was explained that if a general fund did carry these two types of nonfinancial resources, then the fund would show in the fund equity two reservations (or segregations) of fund equity in amounts equal to the amount of the prepaid expenses and the amount of inventory. Both inventory and prepaid expenses are customarily treated as current assets. We did note earlier the inconsistency present in the classification of prepaid expenses entirely as a current asset. Nevertheless, the assets of the general fund—at least the ones discussed so far—are primarily of the current variety. We have not discussed the possibility that the general fund might carry a certain type of noncurrent asset and still be within the recommendations for such a fund spelled out in *NCGA Statement 1*.

Well, there is a possibility that the general fund might account for a noncurrent asset. This can arise if the general fund has made a long-term advance of financial and other resources to some other fund of the governmental unit. The advance is viewed as a long-term receivable, where there is the intention that the general fund is to be repaid by the other debtor fund. An example of this would be an "advance to [the] internal service fund" by the general fund in order to provide that fund with its initial stock of operating resources. In this instance, we have the general fund holding a long-term asset, a receivable due from the internal service fund. It is expected that the latter fund will repay the general fund over future periods out of its operations. Where such an advance is shown as an asset of a general fund, we have a noncurrent asset which is an example of a resource not available for spending during the current budgetary period. As with prepaid expenses and inventory, the general fund would have to set up an amount equal to the amount of the long-term advance as "reserved for advance to internal service fund." That amount would be considered a reduction of the unreserved part of the fund equity. The purpose of this reserve (or segregation) is so that the amount of the unreserved part of the fund equity of the general fund would represent financial resources of the expendable variety available to be spent.

Special Revenue Funds are similar to the general fund. These are expendable funds in that they carry financial resources of the spendable variety. The resources are received and used over the budgetary period for these funds. The budgetary period for the special revenue funds would conform to that of the general fund, which is typically a year. This means that the assets of the special revenue funds are current assets. Similarly, the liabilities of these funds are current liabilities. Typically, special revenue funds are not shown as carrying either noncurrent assets or noncurrent liabilities.

Note that the operating cycle for an expendable fund such as the general fund is not quite the same concept as that found in commercial accounting. In commercial accounting, an operating cycle, from the short-term point of view, is thought of as starting out with a pool of cash which is converted through a production and marketing process ultimately back into cash form. The operating cycle is viewed as self-renewing for the profitable firm. The concept of current assets and current liabilities defined in terms of a potentially self-renewing operating cycle is a useful commercial accounting concept for financial analysis.

Now when we turn to the expendable funds of a governmental unit, we find that these funds account for governmental operations in a fragmented sort of way. The general and special revenue funds account for the financial resources that finance, by and large, governmental production of nonmarket public goods. The *debt service funds* account for financial resources used to service debt. The *capital projects funds* account for financial resources used for the acquisition of major capital assets or improvements. The *special assessment funds* account for financial resources used both for the financing of major capital improvements and/or the servicing of debt. The reasoning behind this fund-accounting division of labor has been discussed earlier. In order to apply the distinction between current and noncurrent assets and liabilities, we need something analogous to the self-renewing operating cycle of a commercial enterprise. The operating cycle of a governmental unit is not to be found by looking at its funds, because of the functional division of labor between the different types of funds, but by looking at the governmental unit itself and the processes by which it undertakes its activities.

Governmental units in terms of their public goods activities do not obtain their financial resources by selling marketable goods and services and receiving voluntary payments in return. The governmental operating cycle and the financing of this cycle revolves around the periodic and cyclic renewal of its budget. The period is usually a year. Therefore, we will use the governmental adopted budget period and the periodic and repetitive renewal of that budget as the core of the governmental unit's operating cycle. For a governmental unit, the distinction between current and noncurrent assets and liabilities of the governmental-type funds will be based on the governmental unit's budgetary period.

The governmental-type funds account for assets in the form of expendable financial resources. The current assets of a governmental-type expendable fund are those assets that are expected to be used up during the governmental unit's budgetary period. The noncurrent assets of a governmental-type expendable fund are those expendable financial resources that are not expected to be used up during the governmental unit's budgetary period. The current liabilities of an expendable fund are those liabilities that are expected to be liquidated through the use of the fund's current assets. The noncurrent liabilities of an expendable fund are those liabilities that are not expected to be liquidated during the governmental unit's budgetary period.

The earlier discussion concerning the breakdown of the current and noncurrent assets and liabilities of the general and special revenue funds is consistent with the definitions for current and noncurrent assets and liabilities that we have adopted for the expendable funds of a governmental unit. How do the assets and liabilities for such fund types as debt service funds, capital projects funds, and special assessment funds break down as between current and noncurrent? We turn to this topic next.

A capital projects fund itself does not seem to have an operating cycle. It isn't an operating fund, as such, for the governmental unit. The life of such a fund is tied to the lives of the capital projects for which the fund accounts. A capital projects fund will last as long as it takes to complete the last of the capital projects for which it accounts. Thus, from the frame of reference of the fund itself, it really doesn't make any sense to distinguish between current and noncurrent assets and liabilities. There is no operating cycle, from the point of view of the fund, on which one can peg the distinction between current and noncurrent. However, when we shift from the perspective of the capital projects fund to the perspective of the governmental unit, we do have a discernible and sensible operating cycle.

From the frame of reference of the governmental unit, a capital projects fund can be considered as accounting for both current and noncurrent assets. If the life of a capital project accounted for by a capital projects fund extends beyond the current budget period, then all of the financial resources accounted for by the fund and expected to be used in future budgetary periods for the capital project would be noncurrent assets. All of the expendable financial resources expected to be used up during the current budgetary period on the capital project would be classified as current assets. Depending on the construction period of the capital projects for which it accounts, a capital projects fund can carry both current and noncurrent assets.

The liabilities incurred by a capital projects fund tend to be liquidated, by and large, within one budgetary period after the date incurred. As a result, capital projects funds are considered to carry basically current liabilities.

In *1980 GAAFR* (pp. 46–48), we find illustrations showing the capital projects fund accounted for on an annual fiscal basis. In addition, in that publication we are told that "*Statement 1* shifted the GAAP accounting and financial reporting for Capital Projects Funds to a strictly annual period–oriented basis. The accounting records must contain, however, sufficient information to permit both: (1) GAAP reporting on an annual period basis; and (2) supplementary data and/ or special purpose reporting on a project length basis" (p. 47). This means that capital projects funds will have two types of financial reporting. One type is based on a reporting period of one year, and the other type has a reporting period that conforms to the project period of the capital projects fund in question.

The special assessment fund type has three facets to its accounting when trying to classify assets and liabilities as current and noncurrent. First of all, it accounts for capital projects so that it can carry current and noncurrent assets for the same reasons as a capital projects fund. A second facet was discussed earlier, that having to do with accounting for "special assessment property tax levies." Special assessment levies are property tax levies, just as general property tax levies are. The receivable for a special assessment tax levy would be recognized on the same basis, the modified accrual basis, as the receivable for a general property tax levy. (The modified accrual basis was discussed in the prior chapter.) However, special assessment tax levies, unlike general property tax levies, may be collectible in installments over a number of budgetary years. This means that the installments collectible in future budgetary years would not be available to be expended during the current budgetary year.

Thus, future installments of a special assessment property tax levy are treated as deferred revenues (per the modified accrual basis of *NCGA Statement 1,* in particular pp. 11–12), and shown in the balance sheet of a special assessment fund as "special assessments receivable—deferred." This deferred receivable would be considered a noncurrent asset. The special assessment property tax installment expected to be collected during the current budgetary period would be classified as a current asset, and the tax revenues from the current installment would be treated as revenues of the current budget period. Thus, based both on the length of a construction period and on the existence of future installments from special assessments, we have two sources for the classification of the assets of a special assessment fund into current and noncurrent.

The liability side of a special assessment fund is quite distinctive from that of the other governmental-type expendable funds. Where a special assessment capital project is financed through the use of long-term special assessment bonds, there we have a long-term liability that would appear on the balance sheet of an expendable fund. The part of the special assessment bond issue which is expected to be liquidated during the current budgetary period would be treated as a current liability. The part of the special assessment bond issue that is expected to be liquidated in future budget periods would be considered a noncurrent liability.[3]

Debt service funds can be broken down into two subtypes. Though they are not usually shown this way, for purposes of applying the current and noncurrent distinction to such funds, it is useful to distinguish between two fund subtypes. First, there are debt service funds that account for financial resources to service long-term serial general obligation bonds. Second, there are debt service funds that account for the financial resources to service term general obligation long-term bonds. The first subtype of debt service funds will be called "serial debt service funds." The second subtype will be called "term debt service funds." Serial bonds are bonds whose principal is scheduled to mature in a series of regular or irregular installments over the life of the bond issue. Term bonds are bonds whose principal matures at a single future date, the maturity date of the entire issue. Serial bonds are the most common type of bond issue for general obligation debt of the long-term variety.

At one time, term general obligation bonds were rather common, but at the present time, this form of long-term general obligation debt has been pretty well phased out. However, where such debt still remains to be liquidated, one should be aware of the fact that term debt service funds are operated as sinking funds. This is done to accumulate sufficient financial resources over the life of a term debt issue so that at maturity date there are sufficient expendable resources available to liquidate the entire principal amount of the bond issue then due. This means that while term debt service funds are still active, they will be composed of noncurrent assets until the budget year when the entire bond issue matures, at which time the noncurrent assets will become current assets.

A term general obligation issue is shown as a general long-term liability in the general long-term debt account group up until the budget year when the bond issue matures. In the budget year when the bond issue matures, it becomes a liability of the term debt service fund that has been accumulating resources for the repayment of the principal of the debt issue. This means that term debt service funds carry only current liabilities and no long-term debt.

---

[3]A brief discussion of special assessment bonds appears in Lennox L. Moak and Albert M. Hillhouse, *Concepts and Practices in Local Government Finance* (Chicago: Municipal Finance Officers Association, 1975), pp. 324–25. Moak and Hillhouse remind us of the significant defaults in the 1920s and 1930s of this type of debt. This kind of history significantly raised people's risk perceptions with respect to this type of debt. Additional guarantees of repayment by the governmental unit itself have been needed to overcome these adverse perceptions with respect to special assessment debt. Still, this type of debt is no longer as widely used as at one time.

Serial debt service funds generally receive the financial resources used to service such debt in the budget year when the debt issue becomes due. This means that serial debt service funds carry basically current assets. On the liability side, long-term serial general obligation debt is shown as a liability of the general long-term debt account group up until the year when it matures. When such debt matures, it becomes a liability of the serial debt service fund that is to service it. This means that serial debt service funds, like term debt service funds, carry only current liabilities.

The governmental funds, being expendable funds, are not supposed to account for real resources. However, as we noted earlier, *NCGA Statement 1* does provide for inventory-type items and prepaid expenses to be shown on the balance sheet of the general fund. Since these are not expendable financial resources, reservations of fund equity also must be shown. Inventory-type items and prepaid expenses would be classified as current assets. We have noted earlier that there is some inconsistency in treating prepaid expenses wholly as a current asset. The major noncurrent assets acquired through the use of the expendable resources of the governmental funds are capital assets such as buildings and equipment. Such capital assets are described in accounting terminology as fixed assets. Fixed assets are not to be accounted for in the balance sheets of the governmental expendable-type funds. Accounting for such assets will be discussed subsequently.

An analysis of the types of assets, both current versus noncurrent and financial versus real resources, and the types of liabilities, current versus noncurrent, is shown in Exhibit 1. This analysis of the types of assets and liabilities to be accounted for in the balance sheets of the governmental funds assumes that these funds are as described in *NCGA Statement 1*.

A Hypothetical Balance Sheet for the General Fund

The balance sheet for the general fund is an individual fund financial statement that shows the assets and liabilities of the general fund as of a particular date. One can think of such a balance sheet in terms of an equation which has a left-hand side (LHS) and a right-hand side (RHS). On the LHS of the equation, one would list the various assets of the general fund and assign values to these assets. The value assigned to an asset usually represents the acquisition cost or historical cost of the asset. The RHS of the equation covers two classes of items. One class represents the liabilities of the general fund. Liabilities are shown as the amounts incurred and generally are to be settled at maturity. The difference between the assets and liabilities is the fund equity, called the fund balance. The fund balance represents the governmental unit's equity in the assets of the

Exhibit 1
Analysis of the Types of Assets and Liabilities to be Accounted for on the Balance Sheets of the Governmental Funds of NCGA Statement 1

Fund Types	Assets				Liabilities	
	Financial Resources[1]		Real Resources			
	Current[2]	Noncurrent	Current[5]	Noncurrent[3]	Current[2]	Noncurrent
General	Yes	No[4]	No[5]	No	Yes	No
Special revenue	Yes	No	No	No	Yes	No
Debt service—serial[6]	Yes[8]	No	No	No	Yes	No
Debt service—term[7]	Yes[8]	Yes[8]	No	No	Yes	No
Capital projects	Yes	Yes	No	No	Yes	No
Special assessment	Yes	Yes	No	No	Yes	Yes

[1]The financial resources are of the expendable variety.

[2]The distinction between current and noncurrent is from the frame of reference of the governmental unit. The governmental unit's operating cycle is considered to be tied to the budgetary financing cycle in terms of the basic adopted budget period. The budget period is usually on an annual basis. Current assets of the expendable funds are expendable financial resources that are expected to be used up during the budget period. Noncurrent assets are expendable financial rsources that are expected to be available for use in future budgetary periods. Current liabilities of the expendable funds are those liabilities expected to be liquidated with current assets. Noncurrent liabilities are not expected to be liquidated during the budget period. Note that despite the application of the modified accrual basis to governmental-type expendable funds, certain of these funds account for noncurrent assets.

[3]Noncurrent real resources include what are called "fixed assets." General fixed assets of a governmental unit are not to be accounted for on the balance sheets of the governmental expendable funds according to the recommendations of *NCGA Statement 1*.

[4]The general fund basically does not carry noncurrent assets, but there is an exception to this general situation. Under certain circumstances the general fund will advance to another fund, such as an internal service fund, resources to be used by that fund as an initial pool of operating resources. The advance from the general fund can take the form of a long-term receivable which is expected to be repaid by the internal service fund out of its operations.

[5]The general fund should not normally account for real resources on its balance sheet since it is supposed to be an expendable fund. However, *NCGA Statement 1* provides for inventory-type items and prepaid expenses to be shown on the balance sheet of the general fund. Neither would be considered expendable financial resources. Note that each of these real resources is to be offset with matching reservations of the fund equity.

[6]For purposes of the current analysis, debt service funds are broken down into two subtypes.

[7]General obligation term bonds, by and large, have been phased out as a long-term financing instrument for state and local governmental units. General obligation serial bonds are the major long-term financing instrument used in place of term bonds. However, where term bonds have not been liquidated in their entirety and are still outstanding, there will be term debt service funds still active to service these bonds.

[8]The sinking fund assets of a term debt service fund are considered noncurrent as long as the term bonds have not matured. Once the general obligation term bonds have matured, then such assets would be classified as current assets.

Exhibit 2
Illustrative Hypothetical Balance Sheet for the General Fund

A-1

NAME OF GOVERNMENT
GENERAL FUND

COMPARATIVE BALANCE SHEET

December 31, 19X2 and 19X1

	19X2	19X1
Assets		
Cash	$255,029	$184,600
Investments, at cost	65,000	—
Receivables (net of allowances for estimated uncollectibles):		
Taxes, including interest, penalties, and liens	61,771	45,200
Accounts	8,300	4,600
Accrued interest	50	—
Due from other funds	12,000	14,000
Due from other governments	30,000	25,500
Advance to Internal Service Fund	55,000	65,000
Inventory, at cost	7,200	5,700
Total assets	$494,350	$344,600
Liabilities and Fund Balance		
Liabilities		
Vouchers payable	118,261	81,100
Contracts payable	57,600	22,000
Due to other funds	24,189	36,000
Deferred revenue	49,500	3,000
Total liabilities	249,550	142,100
Fund balance		
Reserved for encumbrances	38,000	37,500
Reserved for inventory	7,200	5,700
Reserved for advance to Internal Service Fund	55,000	65,000
Unreserved		
Designated for subsequent year's expenditures	50,000	50,000
Undesignated	94,600	44,300
Total fund balance	244,800	202,500
Total liabilities and fund balance	$494,350	$344,600

See accompanying notes to financial statements

Source: Municipal Finance Officers Association, *Governmental Accounting, Auditing and Financial Reporting (1980 GAAFR)* (Chicago: MFOA, 1980), Appendix D, p. 144.

general fund. The fund balance is also a residual figure that ensures that the balance sheet accounting equation is always in balance; i.e., the LHS and the RHS of the equation are always equal.[4] Exhibit 2 is a hypothetical balance sheet taken from *1980 GAAFR*.

The illustrative balance sheet in Exhibit 2 is in comparative form. It shows the financial condition of the general fund as of the end of the current and prior fiscal years. For each year, the LHS of the bal-

[4]The equation applied to the balance sheet of the general fund is known in commercial accounting as the fundamental accounting identity, the fundamental accounting equation, or simply the accounting equation. The equation is Assets = Liabilities + Owners' equity. For the general fund, the fundamental accounting identity would be Assets = Liabilities + Fund balance.

ance sheet is equal to the RHS. For example, for the current fiscal year as of December 31, 19X2, the value of the total assets at $494,350 is equal to the sum of the value of the total liabilities at $249,550 plus the value of the fund balance at $244,800.

The assets for the general fund are basically expendable assets. Two of the assets which do not represent expendable financial resources are "advance to internal service fund" shown at $55,000 as of December 31, 19X2, and "inventory" at $7,200 as of the same date. Since both of these assets are not available for the financing of the activities of the general fund, one finds the types of reservations of the fund equity discussed earlier. One such reservation is "reserved for advance to internal service fund" shown at $55,000, which is exactly the amount of the nonexpendable asset. Similarly, a "reserved for inventory" shown at $7,200 is exactly equal in amount to the associated nonexpendable asset.

There is a third reservation of the fund balance, that wasn't discussed earlier—the *"reserved for encumbrances"* shown at $38,000. What does such a reserve for encumbrances represent? Remember that in the prior chapter encumbrances are described as contractual commitments of the adopted budget. These commitments represent contracts for the purchase of goods or services where the goods have not yet been received nor the services rendered. At the time a contract is signed, accountants record in the financial accounting records of the general fund (assuming that the contract affects the general fund budget) an amount that represents both a commitment of the budget and a reservation of the general fund balance. When the goods or services are received, then the commitment of the budget in the form of an encumbrance is replaced with an expenditure and the reservation of the fund balance is replaced with a liability. The $38,000 shown as reserved for encumbrances represents contingent liabilities in the form of executory contracts on which goods or services are expected to be received after the date of the balance sheet, December 31, 19X2.[5] The contracts were entered into as of or prior to the bal-

---

[5]One expects an appropriation that has been encumbered—i.e., it is subject to a contractual commitment—to continue to constitute spending authority even beyond the end of a budget period. However, there are governmental jurisdictions in which an encumbered appropriation lapses—i.e., it will not continue to be spending authority after the end of a budget period, given that the contracted goods or services have not been received by the end of the budget period. *NCGA Statement 1* (p. 14) provides that governmental entities that treat outstanding contractual commitments on lapsed appropriations as still valid are to account for such commitments either *(a)* as a reservation of the fund balance, or *(b)* as a disclosure in the notes to the financial statements. Of course this means that, in the next budget period, the new budget must include new spending authority in the form of appropriations to cover outstanding encumbrances (i.e., contractual commitments) of prior periods.

ance sheet date.[6] The $38,000 shown as reserved for encumbrances is separate and apart from any amounts shown as liabilities.

In addition to the reserved part of the fund balance, there is the unreserved part, which represents the amount of expendable net financial resources expected to be available to finance future budgeted activities of the general fund. The unreserved part of the fund balance is itself broken into two parts, according to the illustrative balance sheet. One part of the unreserved fund balance is identified as "designated for subsequent year's expenditures" in the amount of $50,000. The other part is identified as "undesignated."

In NCGA Statement 1, we are told that "Fund balance *designations* may be established to indicate tentative plans for financial resource utilization in a future period, such as for general contingencies or for equipment replacement. Such designations reflect tentative managerial plans or intent and should be clearly distinguished from reserves" (p. 17). In other words, a "designation" of the unreserved part of the fund balance does not represent a legal commitment of any sort. Frankly, it is not clear precisely what purpose is served by this particular device for an accounting entity such as the general fund of a governmental unit. If there is a desire and a need for the provision of information on future spending plans, then one would think that a well-conceived note to the financial statements would be significantly more informative than the description "designated for subsequent year's expenditures." The designated amount shown in the illustrative balance sheet both for the current and prior fiscal years is $50,000. In neither case is there an accompanying note to the financial statements explaining clearly and precisely just what the "subsequent year's expenditures" are, nor how the $50,000 was calculated.

Finally, one should note that the illustrative balance sheet does not classify assets and liabilities into current and noncurrent categories. As we have already noted, the general fund should be composed primarily of current assets and current liabilities. However, the advance to internal service fund, in the amounts of $55,000 and $65,000 respectively for the current and prior fiscal years, is a noncurrent asset. How much of the advance to the internal service fund as of the end of the current fiscal year (December 31, 19X2), in addition to the

---

[6]In some governmental jurisdictions, there are limits on the amount of contractual commitments that can be incurred against uncommitted appropriations as the end of a budget period approaches. Systematic control over the rate of spending of a budget over the course of a budget period can be formalized through an allotment system. An allotment represents that part of an appropriation that can be expended during a given allotment period. Allotment periods are generally on a quarterly basis during a budget period. Allotments are the means by which the executive branch controls its own rate of spending out of appropriations.

$55,000 noncurrent asset of that date, is included in the current assets? One should note that the advance did fall by $10,000 between the ending balance of $65,000 of the prior fiscal year and the ending balance of $55,000 as of the end of the current fiscal year. This means that $10,000 of the advance to the internal service fund has been reclassified as a current asset due from the internal service fund as of December 31, 19X2. Later on, as we look at the balance sheet of the internal service fund we will find a current liability in the amount of $10,000 owed to the general fund.

Interestingly enough, the advance to the internal service fund is not the only noncurrent asset to be found among the assets of the general fund. It seems that according to *1980 GAAFR* (the source for the illustrative balance sheet), the receivables also contain a noncurrent component. The receivables cover a number of different types. The receivables for taxes in the amount of $61,771 cover delinquent property taxes, interest, and penalties on such delinquent taxes, and also delinquent taxes that have been converted to tax liens against the properties on which the original tax assessments were levied. The $61,771 is made up of $72,650 of gross receivables of various types associated with property taxes less $10,879 for allowances for uncollectible amounts which represent estimates for uncollectible delinquent property taxes receivable, uncollectible interest and penalties receivable on such delinquent taxes, and uncollectible property tax liens receivable.[7] The $61,771 is an amount of receivables associated with property taxes that is net of amounts expected not to be collected, so that this is an amount expected to be collected but not necessarily within the next fiscal period. In other words, the $61,771 appears to have both current and noncurrent components.

Actually, a clue to the noncurrent component of those receivables associated with property taxes can be found by looking at the liabilities side of the general fund balance sheet. The liabilities of the general fund should be basically of the current variety. However, even here we have a noncurrent component. Unfortunately, one would not know about this noncurrent component from an examination of the financial statements or the notes to the financial statements. Rather, one has to look at the discussion concerning accounting for the general fund to be found in *1980 GAAFR,* according to which the noncurrent portion of the liabilities can be found in the "deferred revenue" shown at $49,500 as of December 31, 19X2.[8] Deferred revenue is made up of two parts. One part of deferred revenue represents property taxes collected in advance in the amount of $15,000. Taxpayers

---

[7]Accounting for the general fund is discussed in *1980 GAAFR,* chapter 4 ("General and Special Revenue Funds").
    [8]Ibid.

paid their property taxes in advance of the period to which such property tax assessments would apply. Thus, the $15,000 are *prepaid* property taxes that are to be treated as revenue, not during the fiscal year ending December 31, 19X2, but during the following fiscal year, which is assumed to be the year when the associated property taxes are assessed. The prepaid property taxes or property taxes paid in advance are accounted for as part of the deferred revenue and are considered a current liability.

The remaining $34,500 of deferred revenue ($49,500 less $15,000) represents property taxes assessed and due either in the current fiscal year or in prior fiscal year but not expected to be collected within the next fiscal year. In fact, in *1980 GAAFR* (p. 39) we are told explicitly that this component of deferred revenue would represent noncurrent receivables. It seems that $34,500 of deferred revenue is associated with at least $34,500 of receivables that have arisen as a result of property taxes. This means that the receivables of $61,771 covering delinquent property taxes as well as interest, penalties, and tax liens associated with delinquent property taxes, would have a component in the amount of $34,500 which would be classified as a noncurrent receivable.

A Closer Look at Deferred Revenue

"Deferred revenue," which appears on the balance sheet of the general fund, has been described as basically a liability composed of current and noncurrent component parts. Deferred revenue has been treated as a liability in our discussion because that is consistent with the approach of *NCGA Statement 1*. It is consistent also with the usual treatment of deferred revenue in commercial accounting. However, there does seem to be a question of whether the entire amount of deferred revenue of $49,500, shown in the hypothetical balance sheet for the general fund, should be treated as a liability.

The question arises because there is a qualitative difference between two parts of deferred revenue. One part is the $15,000 of property taxes paid in advance. These taxes have been paid by taxpayers prior to the date on which the taxes are actually assessed and the liability for the taxpayer established. Now it could happen that when the actual tax liability is established, that it might turn out to be significantly less than the amount of the taxes paid in advance. Between the date that the taxes are paid in advance and the date that the assessment of the taxes is made and the liability established, intervening events (for example, (1) a change in the assessed value of the property, (2) a change in the tax rate to be applied against the property's assessed value, (3) a constitutional limit on property taxes, or (4) a combination of these events) could lead to an actual tax liability that is significantly lower than the amount paid in advance. In that case, the governmental unit would be liable for the excess amount paid in advance over the actual tax liability. Thus, it would seem that the property taxes of $15,000 paid in advance during the fiscal year ending December 31, 19X2, and included in deferred revenue should be treated as a liability because this advance payment fits the usual notion of what is meant by a liability. Assuming that the property tax assessment associated with the advance payment is to take place in the next fiscal year, then the $15,000 would be considered as a current liability. This agrees with the conclusion of the prior discussion of this item.

The other part of the deferred revenue in the amount of $34,500 represents a receivable due from property taxes that have already been assessed, and the receivable is expected to be collected in future fiscal years beyond the next fiscal year. The receivable is therefore classified as a noncurrent asset. Revenue is not to be recognized until those future periods when it is considered available to be used as an expendable financial resource. Therefore, it is treated as deferred revenue similar to the taxes paid in advance. However, the $34,500 is not a liability in the same sense as the $15,000. Unlike the $15,000 of taxes paid in advance for which the actual tax assessments are to be made in a future period, the $34,500 represents already assessed taxes and the liability for the taxpayer is clearly established. The governmental unit would under no circumstances owe any taxpayer any amount out of the $34,500 either in terms of some money refund or in terms of services to be rendered in the future. In other words, the $34,500 does *not* represent an IOU in the sense that the governmental unit has to use any of its resources to satisfy some sort of obligation that is owed by the general fund to anyone internal or external to the government unit.

The $34,500 amount is treated as a deferred revenue under the modified accrual basis as interpreted by *1980 GAAFR* (under *NCGA Statement 1*), and it is not recognized as revenue for the current fiscal year ending December 31, 19X2, because it is not considered as available expendable financial resources. Well, if the $34,500 is not actually a liability, then why has it been classified as one in the illustrative balance sheet for the general fund taken from *1980 GAAFR?* The reason for this classification is because the $34,500 has been included in the deferred revenue; and in commercial accounting, deferred revenue is normally classified as a liability.

In order to decide whether a particular item is or isn't a liability, one needs to have some concept of what a liability is supposed to be. Actually, to some degree, accountants seem to have evolved some rather strange notions about what to include in liabilities. The best way to see this is to look at the definition of liabilities that appears in a generally used source of accounting concepts such as *APB State-*

ment No. 4. According to this statement produced by the Accounting Principles Board, liabilities are defined as "economic obligations of an enterprise that are recognized and measured in conformity with generally accepted accounting principles. Liabilities also include certain deferred credits that are not obligations but that are recognized and measured in conformity with generally accepted accounting principles."[9] From this definition it seems that liabilities can be economic obligations, but liabilities also can cover items that are not economic obligations. Unfortunately, the definition seems so open-ended (or one might say circular) that liabilities can be whatever accountants want liabilities to be.

Given the rather open-ended definition of liabilities used in commercial accounting, one can see the basis for treating the $34,500 as a liability even though it does not actually represent an economic obligation. As an alternative approach to including the $34,500 in deferred revenue, one could deduct this item directly from the receivables representing property taxes. By deducting the $34,500 from the $61,771 of receivables associated with the property taxes, one would then obtain a net receivables figure that represents a current asset of expendable financial resources. The net receivable amount would then represent only current assets. If this approach were not acceptable for some reason, then an alternative to treating the $34,500 as deferred revenue and part of liabilities would be to show the $34,500 in the reserved part of the fund balance, since the associated assets are noncurrent assets. The net result would be that deferred revenue would include only the $15,000 which is an economic obligation. Neither deferred revenue nor liabilities would then be a mixed bag of items to confuse the financial analyst.[10]

A Hypothetical Combining Balance Sheet for the Special Revenue Funds

While there should be only one general fund for a governmental unit, there might be more than one special revenue fund. This means that, for special revenue funds, one can have not only individual bal-

---

[9]Accounting Principles Board, *APB Statement No. 4*, "Basic Concepts and Accounting Principles Underlying Financial Statements of Business Enterprises" (New York: American Institute of Certified Public Accountants, 1970), para. 132.

[10]According to *APB Statement No. 4*, para. 58, "economic obligations of an enterprise at any time are its present responsibilities to transfer economic resources or provide services to other entities in the future." In commercial accounting, the problem of including items that are not economic obligations in liabilities arises for the following reasons. Commercial accountants have been ambivalent toward certain types of deferred credits as to whether these are supposed to be part of the liabilities or part of the owners' equity. These deferred credits generally have arisen because of the use of what is known as the "matching principle" in commercial accounting. This principle is used in the allocation of historical costs over time in the determination of the periodic accounting net income of a business enterprise.

Exhibit 3
Illustrative Hypothetical Combining Balance Sheet for the Special Revenue Funds

NAME OF GOVERNMENT
SPECIAL REVENUE FUNDS

COMBINING BALANCE SHEET

December 31, 19X2
with Comparative Totals for December 31, 19X1

	Parks	State Gasoline Tax	Motor Vehicle License	Parking Meter	Juvenile Rehabilitation	Totals 19X2	Totals 19X1
Assets							
Cash	$39,525	$22,460	$ 5,420	$16,260	$17,720	$101,385	$ 69,935
Investments, at cost	16,200	—	—	15,000	6,000	37,200	46,524
Receivables:							
Taxes—delinquent (net of allowance for estimated uncollectibles)	2,500	—	—	—	—	2,500	—
Accounts (net of allowance for estimated uncollectibles)	3,300	—	—	—	—	3,300	2,700
Accrued interest	25	—	—	—	—	25	—
Due from state government	—	47,250	28,010	—	—	75,260	62,400
Inventory, at cost	1,100	990	702	1,066	1,332	5,190	5,190
Total assets	$62,650	$70,700	$34,132	$32,326	$25,052	$224,860	$186,749
Liabilities and Fund Balances							
Liabilities:							
Vouchers payable	8,604	11,220	4,260	3,220	5,150	32,454	18,073
Contracts payable	12,500	4,000	—	1,800	—	18,300	12,300
Judgments payable	2,000	—	—	—	—	2,000	—
Due to other funds	2,000	—	—	—	—	2,000	4,220
Deferred revenue	1,396	—	—	—	—	1,396	1,121
Total liabilities	26,500	15,220	4,260	5,020	5,150	56,150	35,714
Fund balances							
Reserved for encumbrances	14,000	16,500	10,000	500	5,500	46,500	12,550
Reserved for inventory	1,100	990	702	1,066	1,332	5,190	5,190
Unreserved—undesignated	21,050	37,990	19,170	25,740	13,070	117,020	133,295
Total fund balances	36,150	55,480	29,872	27,306	19,902	168,710	151,035
Total liabilities and fund balances	$62,650	$70,700	$34,132	$32,326	$25,052	$224,860	$186,749

See accompanying notes to financial statements

Source: Municipal Finance Officers Association, *Governmental Accounting, Auditing, and Financial Reporting (1980 GAAFR)* (Chicago: MFOA, 1980), Appendix D, p. 152.

ance sheets for each fund, but also a financial statement that brings together all of the separate balance sheets. The financial statement that brings together individual fund balance sheets for the same fund type is called a combining balance sheet in the language of NCGA Statement 1.[11] In Exhibit 3 is shown a hypothetical combining balance sheet taken from *1980 GAAFR*.

The combining balance sheet for the special revenue funds does not contain any special features that have not been discussed already in connection with the balance sheet for the general fund. This is because the accounting for a special revenue fund is quite similar to that for the general fund. The basic difference is that the general fund can be a more complex accounting entity, since it is defined as the residual fund of a governmental entity that accounts for those activities not accounted for through the other funds.

Hypothetical Combining Balance Sheet for Special Assessment Funds

Among the governmental funds, the other fund type that has a number of special features not usually encountered in the case of the general fund is a special assessment fund. In fact, as noted earlier, a special assessment fund is a combination of a number of different accounting entities. It shares a number of characteristics, in an accounting sense, with such funds types as capital projects funds, debt service funds, and special revenue funds, as well as with the general long-term debt account group. Exhibit 4 shows a hypothetical combining balance sheet for special assessment funds, also taken from *1980 GAAFR*.

The special assessment fund, unlike the other governmental funds, carries significant amounts of noncurrent assets, and noncurrent liabilities owed to parties external to the governmental unit. The receivables for this fund are composed of both the current and the noncurrent varieties of special assessment property taxes receivable. In the earlier discussion of special assessment property taxes, it was observed that such taxes may be paid by taxpayers in a series of installments over a number of years. The current installment of the special

---

[11]In *1968 GAAFR* (p. 30), the combining balance sheet for the special revenue funds was called a combined balance sheet. However, the caption to this statement, shown in *1968 GAAFR* (p. 33) titles this financial statement simply as a balance sheet. This created a certain ambiguity when referring to the various types of financial statements of *1968 GAAFR*. In order to remove this ambiguity, *1980 GAAFR* calls this statement, which brings together the individual balance sheets for the same fund type, a combining balance sheet, and the caption of the statement also calls it a combining balance sheet. The source of the ambiguity can be found in part in National Committee on Governmental Accounting (old NCGA), *Governmental Accounting, Auditing, and Financial Reporting (1968 GAAFR)* (Chicago: MFOA, 1968), p. 33.

Exhibit 4
Illustrative Hypothetical Combining Balance Sheet for the Special Assessment Funds

NAME OF GOVERNMENT
SPECIAL ASSESSMENT FUNDS

COMBINING BALANCE SHEET

December 31, 19X2
With Comparative Totals for December 31, 19X1

	Improvement District Number			Totals	
	77	79	80	19X2	19X1
Assets					
Cash	$ 50,340	$ 87,750	$ 94,095	$ 232,185	$ 307,540
Receivables:					
Special assessments:					
Current	31,000	25,000	15,000	71,000	55,000
Delinquent	2,400	14,000	500	16,900	—
Deferred	271,200	125,000	160,000	556,200	407,035
Liens	935	1,000	—	1,935	—
	305,535	165,000	175,500	646,035	462,035
Accrued interest	25	300	25	350	200
Total assets	$ 355,900	$ 253,050	$ 269,620	$ 878,570	$ 769,775
Liabilities and Fund Balances					
Liabilities:					
Vouchers payable	4,000	14,500	2,100	20,600	4,200
Contracts payable	20,000	25,000	5,000	50,000	35,067
Judgments payable	7,500	2,700	1,000	11,200	9,500
Accrued expenses	6,400	800	3,500	10,700	7,933
Deferred revenues	271,200	125,000	160,000	556,200	407,035
Bonds payable	320,000	60,000	175,000	555,000	420,000
Total liabilities	629,100	228,000	346,600	1,203,700	883,735
Fund balances:					
Reserved for encumbrances	—	—	75,000	75,000	150,000
Reserved for debt service	(273,200)	25,050	(151,980)	(400,130)	(263,960)
Total fund balances (deficits)	(273,200)	25,050	(76,980)	(325,130)	(113,960)
Total liabilities and fund balance	$ 355,900	$ 253,050	$ 269,620	$ 878,570	$ 769,775

See accompanying notes to financial statements

Source: Municipal Finance Officers Association, *Governmental Accounting, Auditing, and Financial Reporting* (1980 *GAAFR*) (Chicago: MFOA, 1980), Appendix D, p. 180.

assessment property taxes, as shown in the illustrative combining balance sheet for all of the special assessment funds, is $71,000. This is the installment as of the end of the current fiscal year that is expected to be paid in the coming fiscal year. The current installment, as of the end of the fiscal year, is therefore a current asset. The installments due beyond the current installment are treated as deferred special assessments receivable. These installments are shown in total amount for all of the special assessment funds as of December 31, 19X2, to be $556,200 in the illustrative combining balance sheet. The deferred special assessments receivable would be a noncurrent asset.

The other receivables shown in the illustrative combining balance sheet are also associated with the special assessment property taxes.

On the liability side, one finds a major noncurrent liability, "bonds payable," in the amount of $555,000 for all of the special assessment funds as of the end of the current fiscal year, December 31, 19X2. The bonds payable are special assessment bonds issued to finance special assessment capital projects. Thus, the special assessment fund is the only governmental-type fund that accounts for long-term debt owed to parties external to the governmental unit on its balance sheet.

Also, on the liability side, one finds classified as a liability "deferred revenue" in the amount of $556,200 for all of the special assessment funds as of December 31, 19X2. The deferred revenue is associated with the noncurrent asset, deferred special assessments receivable. One can see that this noncurrent asset and the deferred revenue are equal in amount. What does deferred revenue in the case of the special assessment fund represent? Earlier it was observed that the deferred special assessments receivable represent future years' installments due on special assessment property taxes. Taxpayers are liable for the entire special assessment—both the current and deferred parts—at the time that the special assessment property taxes are levied. However, where the special assessments represent significant amounts, taxpayers are permitted to pay their special assessment tax liability off over a period of years in annual installments. Given the earlier discussion concerning deferred revenue in the case of the general fund, it can be seen that whenever one encounters deferred revenue, especially the significant amounts shown for the special assessment funds, one needs to look at this item rather closely. The question is, does deferred revenue in this case represent a liability in the sense of an economic obligation, or does it represent something else?

The $556,200 of deferred revenue is associated with $556,200 of future years' installments of special assessment property taxes already considered a liability of the taxpayer. Given that the $556,200 is a liability of the taxpayer to the special assessment funds of the governmental unit, then it cannot be simultaneously a liability of the special assessment funds to taxpayers. The $556,200 represents simply an accounting treatment or method which assigns revenues arising from deferred special assessments receivable to those future periods in which the special assessment installments will be considered current expendable financial resources, and will have become available to finance debt service. Therefore, such deferred revenue cannot be considered an economic obligation of the special assessment funds.

Prior to *1980 GAAFR,* the deferred installments of special assessment property taxes receivable would not have been treated as deferred revenue. Instead, in the year when the special assessment taxes were levied, the $556,200 would have been credited directly to the special assessment fund balances according to the accounting for such funds set out in *1968 GAAFR*.[12] In fact, the *1980 GAAFR* use of deferred revenue (where deferred revenue is classified as a liability) has created a problem separate and apart from the problem that the deferred revenue is not a liability in the economic obligation sense. The additional problem created by the use of deferred revenue for the deferred installments is that, in the case of many special assessments funds, these funds will show continual deficits in their fund balances in the early years of their operations.

The problem of deficits in the fund balance of a special assessment fund created by the methods introduced by *NCGA Statement 1* is recognized in *1980 GAAFR,* wherein we are told the following:

> Since most Special Assessment Fund expenditures take place in the early stages of a project, the *Statement 1* accounting described above generally results in operating deficits in the early years of special assessment projects. . . . Many government finance officers have expressed concern that this deficit creates a potential for misleading inference relative to the financial condition of Special Assessment Funds. The NCGA has recognized this problem and has placed on its technical agenda a project to reconsider the nature and purpose of Special Assessment Funds.[13]

One might hope also that the NCGA would clarify the matter of what it purports to show as liabilities for its accounting entities. Accounting for the $556,200 *not* under liabilities but in the *reserved* part of the fund balance would solve both problems at once. The liabilities of the special assessment fund would then represent economic obligations and not some hybrid assortment of items to puzzle the financial analyst. At the same time, the problem of deficits in the fund balances of the special assessment funds would be resolved. This does not mean that special assessment funds would never show deficits, but their deficits would not be the result of an accounting method that classifies as liabilities certain amounts that are not really economic obligations. Note that the $556,200 would be shown in the reserved part of the fund balances of the special assessment funds because the associated asset is a noncurrent asset.

The treatment of the deferred installments of the special assessment taxes as deferred revenue creates a deficit in the fund balances of the special assessment funds. This can be seen in the illustrative hypothetical combining balance sheet shown in Exhibit 4. Two of the three special assessment funds are shown with deficits in their fund balances. For example, the special assessment fund identified with

[12]Old NCGA, *1968 GAAFR,* chap. IX.
[13]MFOA, *1980 GAAFR,* pp. 49–50.

district number 77 shows a hypothetical deficit in its fund balance of $273,200. The special assessment fund identified with number 80 is shown with a hypothetical deficit of $76,980 in total for the two parts of its fund balance. This special assessment fund balance shows two parts: One part covers a "reserved for encumbrances" at $75,000, and the second part covers a *"reserved for* [future] *debt service"* at $151,980. The reserved for encumbrances part of a fund balance was discussed earlier. The reserved for [future] debt service shows the deficit figure of $151,980 for the special assessment fund numbered 80. The $151,980 is simply a balancing figure after taking account of the need to provide for a $75,000 reserved for encumbrances.

The use of a "reserved for [future] debt service" for all of the special assessment funds means that whatever balance remains in the fund balance (after taking account of current contractual commitment regarding the construction of the capital project by using a "reserved for encumbrances" is earmarked for the servicing of principal and interest on special assessment bonds payable. If the deferred installments of the special assessment property taxes were included in the reserved part of the fund balances rather than being treated as deferred revenue, then the deficits for the total fund balances would be largely eliminated. For example, in the case of the special assessment fund numbered 77, the total fund balance deficit would be reduced from $273,200 to $2,000. In the case of the special assessment fund numbered 80, the total fund balance deficit of $76,980 would be transformed into a positive figure of $83,020.

If the deferred installments of the special assessment property taxes are included in the reserved fund balance, it becomes appropriate to identify these separately. This can be done by showing the deferred installments as "revenue to be recognized." If this were done, for example, in the case of the special assessment fund numbered 77, then the reserved part of the fund balance for that fund would state a reserved for revenue to be recognized in the amount of $271,200. This is the amount of the deferred installments for this fund. The overall fund balance would show a deficit of $2,000. This means that one would continue to show, as before, in the reserved part of the fund balance, a reserved for debt service with a deficit figure in it of $273,200. The reason that the reserved for debt service shows the same deficit figure as earlier is because revenue in the amount of $271,200 remains to be recognized. If the revenue had been recognized in its entirety immediately upon the levy of the special assessment taxes (even though part of these were to be paid in future periods), then the reserved for debt service would show only a deficit of $2,000 and there would be no reserved for revenue to be recognized. In Exhibit 5 is shown "The Effect on the Special Assessment Fund Balance Account of Reclassifying Deferred Special Assessment In-

Exhibit 5
The Effect on the Special Assessment Fund Balance Account of Reclassifying Deferred Special Assessment Installments from Deferred Revenue to Fund Balance*

	Improvement District Number			Totals	
	77	79	80	19X2	19X1
Fund Balances					
Reserved for encumbrances	—	—	$ 75,000	$ 75,000	$150,000
Reserved for revenue to be recognized	$271,200	$125,000	160,000	556,200	407,035
Reserved for debt service	(273,200)	25,050	(151,980)	(400,130)	(263,960)
Total fund balances (deficits)	$ (2,000)	$150,050	$ 83,020	$231,070	$293,075

*The reclassification of the deferred special assessment installments from deferred revenue to the fund balance is prompted by two considerations. First, the deferred special assessment installments are liabilities of the taxpayers and not of the governmental unit. Second, excluding the special assessment installments from the fund balances unnecessarily throws these balances into deficit positions.

stallments from Deferred Revenue to Fund Balance." The assumption underlying this approach is that revenue from the deferred special assessment installment is not to be recognized immediately as revenue upon the levy of the special assessment, nor is it to be treated as deferred revenue and a liability.

Let us return to the long-term liability that is a liability for special assessment bonds. The combining balance sheet for such bonds provides us essentially with the amounts of the bonds payable for each of the three special assessment funds. Additional disclosures with respect to such liabilities are usually to be found in the notes to the financial statements. An illustrative set of such notes (taken from *1980 GAAFR*) is shown in Appendix H to the next chapter. In particular, note (5) in that appendix provides additional disclosures with respect to bonds payable in general. Special assessment bonds are one of the types of bond issues produced by the governmental unit that are discussed in this note. The special assessment bonds for each of three special assessment funds are described in a bit more detail. However, to get a full appreciation of the complexities and characteristics of these and other types of bonds, one must examine and analyze the respective bond indentures for each of the bond issues.

The Fiduciary Funds

The four subtypes (or shall we say types) of fiduciary funds are expendable trust funds, pension trust funds, nonexpendable trust funds, and agency funds. Three of the four types carry basically expendable financial resources: the fourth type, nonexpendable trust funds, can carry both financial and real resources.

Expendable trust funds should be accounted for in the same way as governmental-type funds, according to *NCGA Statement 1*.[14] This means that expendable trust funds, like the governmental funds, would carry current assets and current liabilities on their balance sheets. The distinction between current and noncurrent would be based on the governmental unit's budget period. If an expendable trust fund had assets whose lives were expected to extend beyond that of a budgetary period, then such assets would be classified as noncurrent. Similarly, if an expendable trust fund incurred liabilities which were not expected to be liquidated within one budgetary period, then these liabilities would be considered of the noncurrent variety. This means that expendable trust funds can be visualized as carrying both current and noncurrent assets and liabilities. However, these assets

---

[14]See basic principle VIII in Appendix A of the prior chapter.

and liabilities should be primarily of the current variety, as in the case of governmental funds. The illustrations in *1980 GAAFR* which show accounting for expendable trust funds do not contain examples where such funds carry real resources. This means that fixed assets acquired through trust agreements and which are considered restricted resources should be accounted for through nonexpendable trust funds.

Pension trust funds are a hybrid type of fund that has been described earlier as a cross between an expendable and a commercial type of fund. This fund type was classified as a modified expendable type of fund. Pension trust funds are organized essentially to provide retirement benefits to government employees. This means that the financing of the activities of these funds is tied to the governmental budgetary cycle. Thus, the distinction between current and noncurrent, for this type of fund, will be based also on the governmental unit's budget period. From this point of view, pension trust funds would carry both current and noncurrent assets on their balance sheets. Liabilities also would be of the current and noncurrent variety. Noncurrent liabilities would arise whenever retirement benefits become vested for certain classes of employees. This type of fiduciary fund would carry essentially expendable financial resources. Ordinarily, it would not account for real resources, either of the current or noncurrent variety.

Agency funds are simply custodial arrangements that hold expendable financial resources in trust for specific third parties. The resources should be held on a temporary and short-term basis. Therefore, this type of fund would account only for current assets and current liabilities.

Nonexpendable trust funds are accounted for in essentially the same way as commercial enterprises. Such funds would carry financial resources of both the current and noncurrent variety. The fund may carry also real resources. The real resources can be both of the current and noncurrent variety. Nonexpendable trust funds would be the one type that would carry fixed assets on their balance sheets. This type of fund also would be considered suitable by *NCGA Statement 1* to carry liabilities both of the current and noncurrent variety. So far, only special assessment funds, pension trust funds, and now nonexpendable trust funds would carry long-term liabilities owed to parties external to the governmental unit.

An analysis of the types of assets and liabilities to be accounted for in the balance sheets of the fiduciary funds is shown in Exhibit 6. The analysis assumes that the funds carry the kinds of assets and liabilities appropriate for fiduciary funds, as described in *NCGA Statement 1*.

Exhibit 6
Analysis of the Types of Assets and Liabilities to be Accounted for on the Balance Sheets of the Fiduciary Funds of *NCGA Statement 1*

	Assets				Liabilities	
	*Financial Resources**		*Real Resources*			
Fund Types	*Current†*	*Noncurrent*	*Current*	*Noncurrent‡*	*Current*	*Noncurrent*
Expendable trust	Yes	Yes§	No	No	Yes	Yes§
Pension trust	Yes	Yes	No	No	Yes	Yes
Nonexpendable trust	Yes	Yes	Yes	Yes	Yes	Yes
Agency	Yes	No	No	No	Yes	No

*The financial resources are of the expendable variety with regard to the expendable trust funds, pension trust funds, and agency funds. However, the concept of expendable financial resources would not be appropriate for the nonexpendable trust funds.

†For expendable trust funds and agency funds, the distinction between current and noncurrent would be similar to the distinction defined for the governmental-type funds shown in exhibit 1 (see note 2 of Exhibit 1). The current-versus-noncurrent distinction, using the budgetary period as the basis for the distinction, would be applicable also to pension trust funds. In the case of the nonexpendable trust funds, the current-versus-noncurrent distinction would be closer to the commercial accounting version.

‡Noncurrent real resources include fixed assets.

§Even though circumstances can be imagined under which expendable trust funds could be visualized as carrying noncurrent assets and liabilities, nevertheless, their assets and liabilities should be primarily of the current variety.

Hypothetical Combining Balance Sheet for the Fiduciary Funds

An illustrative hypothetical combining balance sheet for fiduciary funds is shown in Exhibit 7. There are no new significant special accounting characteristics to this combining balance sheet that would call for an extended discussion. One should note that this combining balance sheet, as did the earlier combining balance sheets, contains total columns in which to aggregate the assets, liabilities, and fund balances of the fiduciary funds covered by this statement. The total columns provide aggregate comparative figures for the assets, liabilities, and fund balances of the fiduciary funds for the current and prior fiscal years. The total column for the current fiscal year contains figures that will appear ultimately in another financial statement to be discussed later on.

The illustrative financial statement in Exhibit 7 shows the pension trust fund with a significant balance identified as "fund balance reserved for employees' retirement system." At the same time, this trust fund shows hardly any liabilities at all. Note (8) of the notes to the financial statements, shown in *Appendix H* of the next chapter, contains additional disclosures with respect to the public employee retirement system. This note is reproduced in Exhibit 8 for ease of reference.

According to note (8), the amount shown at $1,426,201 in the fund balance reserved for employees' retirement system is actually composed of four separate reserves. We should take a closer look at these four reserves of the fund balance to get a somewhat better idea of their functions. The first reserve is identified as "fund balance reserved for employee contributions." This reserve is made up of at least two parts. One part of the reserve represents amounts contributed by employees towards their pensions for which the employees have not yet earned vested pension benefits. If such an employee leaves that job before having his contributions tied into vested benefits, then generally such an employee has the right to withdraw such contributions. In fact, two amounts are shown for refunds of employee contributions: one amount of $5,495 for employees who have terminated employment through death, and the second amount of $20,250 for employees who terminated employment through resignations. Thus, it would seem that employee contributions that are not yet tied into vested benefits would constitute the kind of economic obligation of the pension trust fund that should be considered a liability of the trust fund. The second part of this reserve represents employee contributions which are associated with vested benefits. If employees have become entitled to vested benefits, then we have another example of a liability type of economic obligation of the pension trust fund.

Exhibit 7
Illustrative Hypothetical Combining Balance Sheet for the Fiduciary Funds

NAME OF GOVERNMENT
FIDUCIARY FUNDS

COMBINING BALANCE SHEET

December 31, 19X2
With Comparative Totals for December 31, 19X1

	Pension Trust Fund — Employees' Retirement System	Nonexpendable Trust Funds — Endowment principal	Nonexpendable Trust Funds — Revolving loan	Expendable Trust Funds — Endowment revenues	Expendable Trust Funds — Scholarship	Agency Funds — School district tax	Agency Funds — Hospital medical services	Total 19X2	Total 19X1
Assets									
Cash	$ 76,171	$ 2,450	$10,450	$ 680	$20,950	$100,800	$5,200	$ 216,701	$ 119,690
Investments, at amortized cost	1,099,360	131,150	4,550	—	4,200	—	—	1,239,260	1,070,000
Receivables:									
School district taxes	—	—	—	—	—	580,000	—	580,000	182,735
Loans from employees	—	—	35,000	—	—	—	—	35,000	35,000
Accrued interest	1,181	1,400	50	—	35	—	—	2,666	4,080
Due from other funds	10,189	—	—	1,000	—	—	—	11,189	8,620
Total assets	$1,186,901	$135,000	$50,050	$1,680	$25,185	$680,800	$5,200	$2,084,816	$1,420,125
Liabilities and Fund Balances									
Liabilities:									
Vouchers payable	—	—	—	—	—	—	5,200	5,200	7,600
Accrued expenses	3,700	1,000	—	—	—	—	—	4,700	6,070
Due to other taxing districts	—	—	—	—	—	680,800	—	680,800	200,000
Total liabilities	3,700	1,000	—	—	—	680,800	5,200	690,700	213,670
Fund balances:									
Reserved for loans	—	—	50,050	—	—	—	—	50,050	45,100
Reserved for endowments and scholarships	—	134,000	—	1,680	25,185	—	—	160,865	119,035
Reserved for employees retirement system	1,426,201	—	—	—	—	—	—	1,426,201	1,276,150
Unreserved—undesignated	(243,000)	—	—	—	—	—	—	(243,000)	(233,830)
Total fund balances	1,183,201	134,000	50,050	1,680	25,185	—	—	1,394,116	1,206,455
Total liabilities and fund balances	$1,186,901	$135,000	$50,050	$1,680	$25,185	$680,800	$5,200	$2,084,816	$1,420,125

See accompanying notes to financial statements

Source: Municipal Finance Officers Association, *Governmental Accounting, Auditing, and Financial Reporting (1980 GAAFR)* (Chicago: MFOA, 1980), Appendix D, p. 198.

Exhibit 8
Illustrative Disclosure with Respect to a Public Employee Retirement System in the Notes to the General Purpose Financial Statements of a State or Local Government

(8) Retirement Commitments

The City sponsors and administers the Employees' Retirement System. It is accounted for as a separate Pension Trust Fund. It covers all City elementary employees except the school teachers, who are eligible for the State Teachers Retirement System, and employees of the Enterprise and Internal Service Funds, who are members of the XYZ Union administered retirement system. The total pension contribution for the year was $89,243, which includes amortization of an unfunded accrued liability of $243,000 over a 17-year period. All administrative costs of the system are borne by the General Fund.

Changes in Fund Balance Reserve for Employees' Retirement System during the year were as follows:

	Total Reserved Fund Balance	Fund Balance Reserved for Employee Contributions	Fund Balance Reserved for Employer Contributions	Fund Balance Reserved for Membership Annuities	Fund Balance Reserved for Undistributed Interest Earnings
Balance, January 1, 19X2	$1,276,150	$461,725	$493,362	$319,496	$1,567
Additions:					
Employee Contributions	64,274	64,274	—	—	—
Employer Contributions	96,412	—	96,412	—	—
Interest Earnings	28,460	10,330	7,730	8,159	2,241
Total Balance and Additions	1,465,296	536,329	597,504	327,655	3,808
Transfers:					
Annuities Awarded	—	(3,547)	(10,639)	14,186	—
Actuarial Adjustments:					
Current Annuities	—	—	1,287	(1,287)	—
Future Annuities	7,650	—	7,650	—	—
Total Revised Balances	1,472,946	532,782	595,802	340,554	3,808
Deductions:					
Expenditures—Annuities	21,000	—	—	21,000	—
Refunds—Deaths	5,495	5,495	—	—	—
Refunds—Resignations	20,250	20,250	—	—	—
Total Deductions	46,745	25,745	—	21,000	—
Balance, December 31, 19X2	$1,426,201	$507,037	$595,802	$319,554	$3,808

The City also contributed $29,447 this year to the State Teachers Retirement System as its share of elementary school teachers' contributions. The City has no further liability to this system. Future deficits would be financed by the state. Data concerning the actuarial status of the system are not available.

The City also contributed $11,313 to the XYZ Retirement System, a union administered plan which covers all City employees paid from the Enterprise and Internal Service Funds. This is a defined contribution (money purchase) plan.

Source: Municipal Finance Officers Association, *Governmental Accounting, Auditing, and Financial Reporting (1980 GAAFR)* (Chicago: MFOA, 1980), Appendix D, p. 140.

The liability of the trust fund for vested pension benefits would be certain, though the amount would be uncertain and must be estimated. Basically, it would seem that the reserve for employee contributions is really a liability of the pension trust fund.

The next reserve is the "fund balance reserved for employer contributions." One part of this reserve would be associated with vested employee benefits. This part would represent the kind of economic obligation of the pension fund that usually should be considered a liability. The other part of the employer contributions would be associated with unvested employee benefits. This part of the reserve would not represent a liability type of economic obligation until the benefits become vested. Therefore we have a contingent liability which should be a part of a fund balance reserve.

The third reserve is the "fund balance reserved for membership annuities." These are fully vested annuities for which retired employees are actually receiving pension payments. In fact, in note (8), annuity expenditures are being deducted from this reserve in the amount of $21,000 for the current fiscal year. Again we have a liability rather than merely a reservation of a fund balance account.

The last reserve of the fund balance is identified as "fund balance reserved for undistributed interest earnings." This represents interest earnings that have not as yet been allocated to the other three reserve accounts. Part of this account would be a liability if it is to be distributed to a reserve or a part of a reserve that would be considered a liability. The other part of this fourth reserve would not be a liability.

All of the reserves or parts of reserves that would be considered liabilities would be classified as noncurrent liabilities when one applies the current-versus-noncurrent distinction to them.

The above analysis of the various fund balance reserves, which indicates that they should be treated as liabilities, certainly would not find a consensus among accountants. If such a consensus existed, then these reserves or parts of reserves already would be accounted for as liabilities and not as reserves.

In note (8), we are told also that there is an unfunded accrued liability of $243,000. According to *1980 GAAFR*, the unfunded accrued liability "represents the deficiency in contributions made by the governmental unit as employer" (p. 83). It is an "actuarial deficiency." The disclosure tells us that this actuarial deficiency is being amortized over a 17-year period. Each year, the employer's pension contribution (including the current fiscal year's) would make up a part of the deficiency over the 17-year period. There is a discussion in *1980 GAAFR* (p. 72), which argues that the actuarial deficiency is not an accounting liability but an "actuarial liability." The distinction that seems to be implied in that discussion is that actuarial liabilities are simply estimates and thus are not precise enough to be accounting liabilities. However, the question is not the uncertainty of the amount but whether there is, in fact, an economic obligation. If there is an economic obligation from the employer to the retirement system, then we have an accounting liability. The noncurrent portion of such a liability would be reflected in the general long-term debt account group of the governmental entity. That account group will be discussed in the next chapter.

Since the employer is making up the deficiency on a year-by-year basis, there should be a current portion to the liability if it is determined that the employer does have an economic obligation to the pension system. The pension system is being accounted for through a pension trust fund. Thus, the general fund should show a current liability to the pension trust fund for the current portion of the deficiency being made up and treated as a liability, and the pension trust fund should show a current receivable due from the general fund. All of this presupposes that a determination has been made that the actuarial deficiency or part of the actuarial deficiency is an economic obligation so that it should be recognized as a liability.

Again, we have a stituation where there does not appear to be a consensus among accountants that certain types of economic obligations should be treated as liabilities. Given this ambivalence, we find in the illustrated note to the financial statements a disclosure about the "unfunded accrued liability," but nothing appears in the general long-term debt account group for the noncurrent portion of such a liability. The amortization of an unfunded accrued liability of $243,000 over a 17-year period results in an annual amortization of $14,294. If the unfunded accrued liability is determined in whole or in part to be an economic obligation, then the $14,294 will be either in whole or in part the current part of that economic obligation and therefore a current liability. There is nothing to assure us that any part of the $14,294 which is a current economic obligation, is a part of the current liability of the general fund to the pension trust fund.

In summary, one should be aware of the fact that significant economic obligations owed by pension funds to current, former, and retired employees relative to pension benefits will *not* be shown as liabilities of these funds. In addition, economic obligations of governmental units owed to pension trust funds also will *not* necessarily be shown as liabilities of the governmental unit's general fund for the current portion of that liability, nor will the governmental unit's general long-term debt account group necessarily show the noncurrent portion of the liability.

Note (8) shows an illustrative disclosure with respect to a public employee retirement system (PERS) that would appear in the financial statements and accompanying notes of a state and local governmental unit, as interpreted by *1980 GAAFR* in applying *NCGA Statement 1*. However, there is an entirely separate discussion in *1980 GAAFR* regarding disclosures for a PERS. According to *1980 GAAFR,* a comprehensive annual financial report for a PERS should be prepared in addition to and separate and apart from the comprehensive annual financial report prepared for the state or local governmental unit. We are told in *1980 GAAFR* that "MFOA has published *Guidelines for the Presentation of a Public Employee Retirement System Comprehensive Annual Financial Report* which includes detailed discussions and illustrations. . ." (p. 74).

This means that, if in fact a comprehensive annual financial report is prepared for a PERS and if the disclosures in such a report are adequate, then one can make the necessary estimates concerning (1) the liabilities of the pension trust fund to PERS beneficiaries and (2) the liabilities of the governmental unit to the PERS (i.e., to the pension trust fund itself).

Unfortunately, the illustrative financial statements and their notes do not seem to contain any reference to a comprehensive annual financial report for the PERS accounted for by the pension trust fund of Exhibit 7.

Proprietary Funds

The proprietary funds are the basic fund types that, according to *NCGA Statement 1*, should account for those activities of the governmental unit that result in the supply of market-type goods and services. The accounting principles appropriate to these funds are quite similar to those of commercial accounting. Therefore, the assets and liabilities carried on the balance sheets of these fund types will be similar to the assets and liabilities carried on the balance sheets of a commercial enterprise. However, there is a basic difference between the two proprietary funds types—internal service funds and enterprise funds—in accounting for certain kinds of liabilities, that should be described.

The *internal service fund* is set up basically to supply its goods and services to its own governmental unit. Under certain circumstances, such a fund supplies services to other governmental units. This means that, by and large, the fund receives its revenues from its own government unit's agencies and departments that are responsible for the supply of nonmarket public goods. These agencies and departments are financed through the governmental budget process. Therefore, the internal service fund's financing of its goods and services is tied also into the governmental budget cycle. The distinction between current and noncurrent for the internal service fund, just as for the governmental funds, becomes tethered to the governmental unit's budget process and budget period. The current assets of the internal service fund, like the current assets of the governmental funds, represent those assets that are expected to be used up during the budget period. However, one should note that an internal service fund will carry both financial and nonfinancial resources, so that its current assets will be composed of both kinds of resources.

Noncurrent assets of an internal service fund have lives expected to extend beyond the budget period. Noncurrent assets for such a fund will be composed of both financial and real resources. The real resources of an internal service fund include fixed assets such as buildings, equipment, and other capital assets used in the operations of the fund. Remember that the expendable governmental funds do not account for fixed assets in their balance sheets, according to the recommendations of *NCGA Statement 1*. Neither do such fiduciary funds as expendable trust funds, pension trust funds, and agency funds. The only fiduciary fund that is considered suitable for accounting for fixed assets from the balance-sheet point of view would be the nonexpendable trust fund. This does not mean that all nonexpendable trust funds necessarily carry fixed assets. Internal service funds are the second type of fund that would be expected to account for fixed assets in their balance sheets. Typical internal service funds do use fixed assets in their operations, so that these funds will account for such noncurrent real resources on their balance sheets.

On the liability side, one expects internal service funds to carry basically current liabilities on their balance sheets. By and large, such funds would not be expected to incur noncurrent liabilities. The only kind of noncurrent liability that would be consistent with the recommendations of *NCGA Statement 1* for such a fund would be a long-term payable owed to the general fund. Such a long-term payable was discussed earlier from a receivable perspective when describing the possibility for the general fund accounting for a noncurrent asset. As observed earlier, the general fund could provide the initial resources to set up an internal service fund. This provision of the initial resources could be in the form of a repayable long-term advance. The internal service fund would have a long-term payable to be repaid out of the revenues generated by its operations. This long-term payable would be an example of a noncurrent liability compatible with the recommendations of *NCGA Statement 1* for this fund. However, note that this noncurrent liability is owed to the general fund which is a part of the same governmental unit. What one would *not* expect to find in the case of the internal service fund is a long-term liability owed to a party external to the governmental unit.

An *enterprise fund* supplies its goods and services to the general public and also to governmental units. Enterprise fund accounting parallels that for commercial enterprises in the same line of business as that which the enterprise fund is providing in the public sector. The current-versus-noncurrent distinction for the assets and liabilities of an enterprise fund would be similar to the distinction for the parallel commercial business. That is, this distinction would tend to be based on the operating cycle natural to the activities of the enterprise fund. However, where enterprise funds tend to run continual and significant deficits, there one would expect to find the budgetary process for the governmental unit intruding upon the financing cycle of such funds. Since it will be the general governmental budget that will be called upon to make up the deficits of the enterprise fund, it is not surprising that this will impact on the financing cycle of that fund and on the current-versus-noncurrent distinction appropriate to the fund. Nevertheless, the current-versus-noncurrent distinction for this fund should still be based in part on the parallel distinction for commercial enterprises supplying close substitutes. The degree to which the governmental budgetary process also affects the current-versus-noncurrent distinction will depend on the individual circumstances of each enterprise fund.

Enterprise funds, like their commercial counterparts, carry both financial and real resources. The financial resources will be of the current and noncurrent variety. The real resources also will be of the current and noncurrent variety. Enterprise funds will, by and large, depending on the nature of their activities, use fixed assets such as land, buildings, equipment, and other capital assets in their operations. Like internal service funds and certain of the nonexpendable trust funds, the noncurrent assets of an enterprise fund will include fixed assets.

On the liability side enterprise funds, like commercial enterprises, carry both current and noncurrent liabilities from the balance sheet perspective. The only fund types discussed earlier that carried long-term debt owed to parties external to the governmental unit were special assessment funds, pension trust funds, and nonexpendable trust funds. Not all nonexpendable trust funds necessarily carry long-term debt owed to external parties. All pension trust funds are likely to have incurred long-term liabilities owed to external parties. Special assessment funds involved in major capital improvements are likely to be involved in special assessment bond financing. Enterprise funds are another fund type considered suitable by *NCGA Statement 1* to account for long-term debt owed to external parties from a balance sheet point of view. Such long-term debt would be classified as a noncurrent liability. A typical long-term debt incurred by an enterprise fund would be in the form of long-term revenue bonds issued by the fund to be repaid out of its operating revenues.[15]

An analysis of the types of assets and liabilities carried by proprietary funds is shown in Exhibit 9. The analysis assumes, as earlier, that the funds are those fund types described in *NCGA Statement 1* and the types of assets and liabilities are consistent with that description.

---

[15]Enterprise revenue bonds are discussed briefly in Moak and Hillhouse, *Concepts and Practices,* pp. 323–24. Revenue bonds normally have a lien on enterprise funds revenues. However, there are instances of such bonds with additional mortgage liens against the properties financed by the bond issues. Moak and Hillhouse warn us that, in actual practice, revenue bonds come in a wide variety of forms, so that one must be careful not to describe these debt instruments in an overly simple fashion.

Exhibit 9
Analysis of the Types of Assets and Liabilities to be Accounted for on the Balance Sheets of the Proprietary Funds of NCGA Statement 1

	Assets				Liabilities	
	Financial Resources		Real Resources			
Fund Types	Current*	Noncurrent	Current	Noncurrent†	Current	Noncurrent
Internal service	Yes	Yes	Yes	Yes	Yes	No‡
Enterprise	Yes	Yes	Yes	Yes	Yes	Yes

*The financing of internal service fund activities is tied to the governmental budget so that the appropriate current-versus-noncurrent distinction for this fund type should be tied to the budget period. In the case of the enterprise fund, the current-versus-noncurrent distinction would be similar to that for a commercial enterprise. However, it should be noted that when enterprise funds experience continual and significant deficits which are subsidized through the general governmental budget, then the budgetary cycle will have an impact on the financing cycle for the enterprise fund. Under these circumstances, the current-versus-noncurrent distinction will become dependent also on the governmental unit's budgetary period.

†Real resources include fixed assets.

‡Normally, the internal service fund does not carry noncurrent liabilities in its balance sheet. However, as we noted earlier in Exhibit 1, note 4, the general fund could provide the initial resources to start up an internal service fund. The provision of the initial resources could be in the form of a long-term repayable advance from the general fund to the internal service fund. Such an advance would be, for the general fund, a long-term receivable. From the point of view of the internal service fund, we would have a long-term payable to be paid from the operations of the internal service fund. Thus, the internal service fund would have a noncurrent liability. However, note that this long-term liability is owed to another part of the same governmental unit; it is not a long-term liability owed by the governmental unit to an outside party.

Hypothetical Balance Sheets for the Proprietary Funds

The internal service fund and the enterprise fund, both proprietary funds, have balance sheets similar to that of a commercial enterprise. The next two exhibits are illustrative hypothetical balance sheets for each type of proprietary fund. These are not combining balance sheets such as are shown for governmental fund types like the special revenue funds and the special assessment funds. A combining balance sheet was shown also for the fiduciary funds. The balance sheets shown for the internal service fund and the enterprise fund are individual fund balance sheets set up in a comparative format covering the current and prior fiscal years. In Exhibit 10 we have a hypothet-

Exhibit 10
Illustrative Hypothetical Balance Sheet for an Internal Service Fund

NAME OF GOVERNMENT
CENTRAL GARAGE INTERNAL SERVICE FUND

COMPARATIVE BALANCE SHEET

December 31, 19X2 and 19X1

	19X2	19X1
Assets		
Current assets:		
Cash	$ 29,700	$ 50,000
Due from other funds	12,000	20,000
Inventory, at cost	40,000	26,000
Total current assets	81,700	96,000
Property, plant, and equipment:		
Land	20,000	20,000
Buildings	60,000	55,000
Improvements other than buildings	15,000	15,000
Machinery and equipment	25,000	23,000
	120,000	113,000
Less accumulated depreciation	16,900	12,450
Net property, plant, and equipment	103,100	100,550
Total assets	$ 184,800	$ 196,550
Liabilities and Fund Equity		
Current liabilities:		
Vouchers payable	15,000	20,000
Current portion of advance from general fund	10,000	10,000
Total current liabilities	25,000	30,000
Long-term liabilities:		
Advance from General Fund	65,000	75,000
Less current portion	(10,000)	(10,000)
Total long-term liabilities	55,000	65,000
Total liabilities	80,000	95,000
Fund equity:		
Contributed capital—General Fund	95,000	95,000
Retained earnings	9,800	6,550
Total fund equity	104,800	101,550
Total liabilities and fund equity	$ 184,800	$ 196,550
See accompanying notes to financial statements		

Source: Municipal Finance Officers Association, *Governmental Accounting, Auditing, and Financial Reporting (1980 GAAFR)* (Chicago: MFOA, 1980), Appendix D, p. 194.

ical comparative balance sheet for an internal service fund. Exhibit 11 shows a hypothetical comparative balance sheet for an enterprise fund. Both hypothetical balance sheets are taken from *1980 GAAFR*.

In looking at the governmental and fiduciary funds, we used the current–noncurrent distinction in order to get a better understanding of the kinds of assets and liabilities accounted for by these fund types on their balance sheets. We did this even though *1980 GAAFR's* illustrative balance sheets for the governmental and fiduciary funds do not group assets and liabilities into current and noncurrent classes. In the illustrative balance sheet in Exhibit 10 for the internal service fund, however, we do find the current–noncurrent distinction provided.

The current–noncurrent distinction applied to the liability side for the internal service fund also clears up something of an ambiguity that we encountered when we examined the balance sheet of the general fund (Exhibit 2). The general fund shows an "advance to internal service fund" in the amount of $55,000 among its assets for the current fiscal year, as of December 31, 19X2. When we discussed this advance, we wondered as to the amount of the advance, if any, that is included in the current assets of the general fund. Now when we examine the illustrative balance sheet of Exhibit 10 for the liabilities of the internal service fund, we find among the current liabilities of the internal service fund an item described as "current portion of advance from general fund" in the amount of $10,000. The *noncurrent* portion of the advance from general fund is shown in the long-term liabilities in the amount of $55,000 as of December 31, 19X2. This amount agrees with the amount shown in Exhibit 2 as an advance to internal service fund by the general fund.

We do not find among the assets of the general fund a "current portion of advance due from internal service fund" in the amount of $10,000. One would not expect to find such a description since *1980 GAAFR* does not provide for an explicit current–noncurrent distinction to be built into the balance sheet of a fund such as the general fund. Where is the $10,000 due from the internal service fund? In the case of the general fund, it turns out that the current portion of the advance to the internal service fund is included in the asset account "due from other funds." This account shows a balance of $12,000—not $10,000. It seems that at the end of the fiscal year, December 31, 19X2, a special revenue fund called the Parks Special Revenue Fund owed the general fund $2,000. The $2,000 owed by the Parks Special Revenue Fund plus the $10,000 of the current portion of the advance to the internal service fund make up the $12,000 shown as due from other funds. Thus, the current–noncurrent distinction incorporated into the presentation of assets and liabilities of the internal service fund has helped resolve an ambiguity present in the balance sheet of the general fund.

Exhibit 11
Illustrative Hypothetical Balance Sheet for a Proprietary Fund

NAME OF GOVERNMENT
WATER AND SEWER ENTERPRISE FUND
COMPARATIVE BALANCE SHEET
December 31, 19X2 and 19X1

Assets

Assets	19X2	19X1
Current assets		
Cash	$ 279,296	$ 137,760
Receivables		
Accounts (net of allowance for uncollectibles)	24,130	35,800
Notes	2,350	1,250
Due from other funds	2,000	8,000
Inventory, at cost	23,030	11,780
Prepaid expenses	1,200	740
Total current assets	332,006	195,330
Restricted assets, cash, and investments		
With fiscal agent	—	9,000
Customer deposits	64,060	55,500
Revenue bond construction account	—	145,643
Revenue bond current debt service account	117,888	113,150
Revenue bond future debt service account	109,822	82,990
Revenue bond contingency (renewal and replacement) account	14,983	10,985
Total restricted assets	306,753	417,268
Property, plant, and equipment		
Land	211,100	211,100
Buildings	447,700	420,700
Improvements other than buildings	3,887,901	3,372,200
Machinery and equipment	1,841,145	1,525,500
Construction in process	22,713	556,606
	6,410,559	6,086,106
Less accumulated depreciation	640,800	496,700
Net property, plant, and equipment	5,769,759	5,589,406
Total assets	$6,408,518	$6,202,004

Liabilities and Fund Equity

Liabilities and Fund Equity	19X2	19X1
Liabilities		
Current liabilities (payable from current assets)		
Vouchers payable	$ 116,471	$ 44,000
Contracts payable	26,107	414,357
Accrued general obligation bond interest	14,000	14,100
Other accrued expenses	2,870	4,710
Current portion of general obligation bonds	50,000	50,000
Total current liabilities (payable from current assets)	209,448	527,167
Current liabilities (payable from restricted assets)		
Construction contracts	—	145,643
Matured revenue bonds	—	8,000
Matured revenue bond interest	139	1,000
Accrued revenue bond interest	64,749	66,150
Current portion of revenue bonds	48,000	44,000
Deposits	64,060	55,500
Total current liabilities (payable from restricted assets)	176,948	320,293
Long-term liabilities		
Revenue bonds (net of current portion)	1,798,000	1,846,000
General obligation bonds (net of current portion)	650,000	700,000
Total long-term liabilities	2,448,000	2,546,000
Total liabilities	2,834,396	3,393,460
Fund Equity		
Contributed capital		
Municipality	450,000	450,000
Customers	50,000	50,000
Subdividers	870,666	220,000
Total contributed capital	1,370,666	720,000
Retained earnings		
Reserved per revenue bond indentures	129,155	96,975
Unreserved	2,074,301	1,991,569
Total retained earnings	2,203,456	2,088,544
Total fund equity	3,574,122	2,808,544
Total liabilities and fund equity	$6,408,518	$6,202,004

See accompanying notes to financial statements

Source: Municipal Finance Officers Association, *Governmental Accounting, Auditing, and Financial Reporting* (1980 GAAFR) (Chicago: MFOA, 1980), Appendix D, p. 188.

Note that the Parks Special Revenue Fund is shown in the combining balance sheet for the special revenue funds in Exhibit 3. In that exhibit, one can see that the Parks Special Revenue Fund does show among its liabilities an item described as "due to other funds" in the amount of $2,000 as of December 31, 19X2. This little exercise should begin to give one an appreciation of some of the complexities one encounters in the interrelationships among the fund accounting entities of a governmental unit.

The noncurrent assets of the internal service fund shown in Exhibit 10—the Central Garage Internal Service Fund—are basically of the fixed assets variety in the form of land, buildings, etc. A governmental fund may carry noncurrent assets (even though not classified this way in their balance sheets), but none of these assets would be fixed assets. Fixed assets represent real rather than financial resources. The internal service fund, on the other hand, can account for real resources as well as financial resources in its balance sheet. Only one type (or is it subtype?) of fiduciary fund—the nonexpendable trust fund—could be considered suitable, under the guidelines of *NCGA Statement 1,* to account for fixed assets. This does not mean that every nonexpendable trust fund will carry fixed assets in its balance sheet. Rather, when a trust arrangement provides that a governmental entity has been given fixed assets as part of a nonexpendable trust, then such fixed assets would be accounted for through a nonexpendable trust fund.

One should be aware of the fact that, for an internal service fund, the difference between the fund assets and the fund liabilities is not to be described as the fund balance but rather as the fund equity for the internal service fund. This is shown in the illustrative balance sheet of Exhibit 10. The fund equity for this internal service fund is subdivided into two parts. One part of fund equity covers the initial capital contributed to set up the internal service fund. This is shown as "contributed capital—general fund" in the amount of $95,000 both for the current and prior fiscal years. This amount represents resources contributed by the general fund in the form of permanent capital to set up an internal service fund.

Note that the contributed capital of an internal service fund may appear to be somewhat analogous to the paid-in capital of a commercial enterprise. However, there is a difference in the way the capital is raised. In the case of a commercial firm, the paid-in capital represents the voluntarily invested capital of private investors. The contributed capital of an internal service fund represents governmental resources raised through taxation, with these resources allocated by the governmental unit (for purposes of management efficiency) to a fiscal and accounting entity called an internal service fund.

The second part of the fund equity for an internal service fund is called retained earnings. Again, we have an item described in accounting language so as to make it seem analogous to a private sector counterpart. But it should be pointed out that the retained earnings of a private business enterprise are the result of private investment decisions concerning reinvestment in the enterprise. The retained earnings of an internal service fund are not the result of private investment decisions. The retained earnings of an internal service fund appear to arise because the fund calculated the user charges for its goods and services so that it would be able to generate revenues in excess of the costs that accountants assign to the operations of the fund.

An enterprise fund, like the Water and Sewer Enterprise Fund which is shown in Exhibit 11, also has its assets and liabilities separated into current and noncurrent classes like those for the internal service fund. However, a further distinction has been introduced for the enterprise fund. Not only are assets grouped into current and noncurrent classes, but there is also a distinction between unrestricted and restricted assets. This distinction results from certain contractual provisions. In fact, it is the unrestricted-assets class that has been separated into current and noncurrent groupings. The restricted assets are segregated from the unrestricted assets but they have not been grouped into current and noncurrent classes. However, separating the restricted assets into current and noncurrent groupings is not difficult at all, as will be shown subsequently. In the illustrative balance sheet for an enterprise fund in Exhibit 11, there are three classes of assets: (1) unrestricted current assets, (2) unrestricted noncurrent assets, and (3) restricted assets.[16]

The unrestricted noncurrent assets shown for the Water and Sewer Enterprise Fund are basically fixed assets such as land and buildings. The noncurrent assets are essentially real resources used in the operations of the fund. The restricted assets are financial resources which are earmarked for certain liabilities. The unrestricted current assets are composed of both financial and real resources.

On the liability side, there is also a threefold breakdown. Liabilities are separated into current and noncurrent groupings. The cur-

---

[16]In commercial accounting, the restricted assets shown on the balance sheet of an enterprise fund are referred to as "funds." Remember that in commercial accounting a fund is a segregation of the assets of an enterprise due to contractual or administrative requirements. However, in governmental accounting a fund is a self-contained fiscal and accounting entity. In order to avoid confusion by using the term *fund* in two different ways for purposes of governmental accounting, *1980 GAAFR* tells us that "Revenue bond indentures often refer to these accounts as 'funds.' However, they are merely mandatory asset segregations and not funds in the sense of fiscal and accounting entities with self-balancing sets of accounts. Whenever possible, they should be referred to as accounts rather than funds to minimize any potential for misleading inference on the part of financial report users" (p. 60).

rent liabilities are subdivided further as between current liabilities
that are to be serviced from current unrestricted assets, and current
liabilities that are to be serviced from current restricted assets. The
noncurrent liabilities are composed of long-term liabilities owed to
parties external to the governmental unit.

One can observe certain accounting linkages between restricted assets and current liabilities to be serviced from restricted assets. These
accounting linkages are the result of bond indenture and other contractual provisions. For example, one can see that the restricted-as-
sets account "customers deposits," for the current and prior fiscal
years in the respective amounts of $64,060 and $55,500 has an associated matching account among the current liabilities to be serviced
by restricted assets. The associated liability account called "deposits"
shows identical balances with the asset account for the respective
years. There is also a restricted asset described as "revenue bond construction account" which had in it a balance of $145,643 for the prior
fiscal year. This restricted asset is matched with an associated current liability to be serviced from restricted assets called "construction
contracts" with exactly the same balance in it.

In the prior fiscal year, there is a restricted asset with a balance of
$9,000 representing cash "with [the] fiscal agent," who is used to ad-
minister the servicing of the revenue bonds. The associated current
liabilities to be paid from this restricted asset by the fiscal agent are
liabilities for (1) matured revenue bonds at $8,000 and (2) matured
revenue bond interest for $1,000. The last restricted asset that has
associated current liabilities is the "revenue bond current debt service account" with current and prior-year balances respectively of
$117,888 and $113,150. These balances for the restricted assets are
just a bit more than the sum of the balances for each fiscal year for
the related liabilities. For the current fiscal year, these current liabilities total to $112,888 and are composed of liabilities (1) to the
fiscal agent at $139 (2) for accrued revenue bond interest at $64,749
and (3) for the current portion of revenue bonds at $48,000. For the
prior fiscal year, these liabilities total to $110,150 and are composed
of liabilities for (1) accrued revenue bond interest at $66,150 and (2)
the current portion of revenue bonds at $55,500. Thus, by looking at
the current liabilities to be serviced by restricted assets, one can
pretty well decompose the restricted assets into current and noncurrent parts.[17]

---

[17]Stating that the restricted assets exceed their related liabilities by "just a bit
more" is somewhat vague. For the current fiscal year, the restricted assets of $117,888
exceed the associated liabilities of $112,888 by $5,000. This excess, as shall be seen,
will be the subject of a reservation of the retained earnings of the enterprise fund. The
reservation of retained earnings will be discussed subsequently. Similarly, for the prior
fiscal year, the restricted assets of $113,150 exceed the related liabilities of $110,150
by $3,000. As noted, this excess is also subject to a reservation of the retained earnings
of the enterprise fund.

The balances in the noncurrent portion of the restricted assets also are accumulated in accordance with revenue bond indenture provisions. Such bond indentures generally call for additional assets to be accumulated in the early years of a revenue bond issue to provide additional resources to make up any possible deficiencies that might arise in the servicing of such bonds over their life. Assuming that such deficiencies do not occur, then these additional noncurrent restricted resources will be available to service the bond issue near the end of its life, as the last of the serial bonds mature.[18]

The long-term liabilities are composed not only of revenue bonds but also of general obligation bonds. Even though these are called general obligation bonds in the sense that they are full faith and credit instruments, they have been issued with the intention that the primary servicing of this issue will be out of the revenues of the Water and Sewer Enterprise Fund. However, they were issued as general obligation bonds without the sort of lien on enterprise revenue that characterizes the revenue bonds shown for the Water and Sewer Enterprise Fund. Therefore, these bonds will be serviced, not out of restricted resources but out of unrestricted resources. This explains why the current portion of the general obligation bonds for each fiscal year is shown among the current liabilities payable out of unrestricted resources, rather than among the current liabilities payable out of restricted resources.

Additional disclosures with respect both to the revenue bonds and the general obligation bonds serviced out of the revenues of the Water and Sewer Enterprise Fund can be found in the notes to the financial statements. Earlier, in our discussion of special assessment bonds, we referred to the illustrative notes to the financial statements set out in Appendix H to the next chapter. Note (5) contains additional specific disclosures with respect to the two types of bonds shown as long-term debt of the enterprise fund. The general obligation bonds in the amount of $700,000 (both current and noncurrent portions) are included as part of the description of all types of general obligation bond issues of the governmental unit. The revenue bonds are described separately. As observed earlier, in order to get a fuller understanding of the characteristics and complexities of each of these bond issues, one must study and analyze the bond indentures associated with each issue.

The fund equity of the Water and Sewer Enterprise fund contains two major components described in a fashion similar to that of the internal service fund. First, we have the component described as "contributed capital," shown from three sources: municipality, customers, and subdividers. As observed earlier, for the internal service fund,

---

[18]State and local governmental long-term general obligation bond issues are basically serial bonds.

the capital provided by the governmental unit is not invested capital resulting from private investment decisions, even though the enterprise fund is providing basically a marketable-type service. Therefore accountants, rather than describing the capital as paid-in capital (as for a private enterprise), call it contributed capital. If the term *contributed* has a private, voluntary connotation then perhaps some other terminology should be used. In the case of the municipality, the capital might more appropriately be described simply as "allocated."

The "subdividers" part of the contributed capital appears to be not a contribution but rather a tax, similar to special assessment taxes, on developers and subdividers when a public enterprise such as a public utility is not expected to be able to cover the cost of its capital facilities fully out of its own operating revenues.[19] The same circumstances hold for contributions from "customers."[20]

The second component of the fund equity of an enterprise fund is represented by what is described as "retained earnings." The retained earnings represent the excess of the enterprise fund revenues (generated from user charges) over the expenses of operating the enterprise fund up to the date of the balance sheet, less any transfers of past earnings to the governmental unit. The user charges which generate the revenues are generally the result of monopoly-type pricing practices as set by the public enterprise fund in the supply of its goods or services. "Retained earnings" itself is subdivided into "reserved" and "unreserved" parts. Generally, bond indentures can provide that retained earnings be earmarked in amounts equal to certain of the restricted assets.

---

[19]Moak and Hillhouse, *Concepts and Practices,* state:

> The financing of extensions to provide needed service in new localities within the service area of a public enterprise calls for a well-defined policy designed to keep the system self-supporting and to be fair to existing, as well as new, customers. In defining such a policy, a basic question is the extent to which new customers or the developers should be required to aid in financing the cost of the extension. For regulated enterprises, it is a fundamental legal principle that, when the revenues anticipated from an extension are sufficient to cover operating expenses and support the enterprise's investment, the extension should be made without any special charge; but when the anticipated revenues indicate a deficiency in such coverage, the enterprise may remedy the deficiency by such means as requiring contributions to aid construction, refundable advances, or guaranteed rates in excess of the so-called established rate schedules.

In other words, when so-called contributions from developers (or subdividers) are part of the fund equity of an enterprise fund, then these contributions are in the nature of a tax to subsidize the enterprise.

[20]Contributions from customers may arise in the same fashion as contribution from developers or subdividers. In that case, the contributions from the customers are also in the nature of a tax to subsidize the operations of the enterprise fund. In addition, certain charges to customers are not charges for services as such, but special charges that are treated by the utility as additions to its fixed assets. In that case, we also have a customer being "taxed" to finance capital additions. See the discussion of these special charges contained in *1968 GAAFR* (p. 53) which, however, does not recognize the tax nature of the special charges.

In the illustrative balance sheet for the Water and Sewer Enterprise Fund, the reserved part of retained earnings is described as "reserved per revenue bond indentures." According to *1980 GAAFR,* the reserved per revenue bond indentures shown on the balance sheet normally covers all or part of the following types of restricted assets: (1) all of the "revenue bond future debt service account" shown at $109,822 and $82,990, respectively for the current and prior fiscal years; (2) all of the "revenue bond contingency (renewal and replacement) account" shown at $14,983 and $10,985, respectively for the current and prior fiscal years; and (3) part of the revenue bond current debt service account at $5,000 for the current fiscal year and at $3,000 for the prior fiscal year.[21]

CONCLUSION

In this chapter, we have gone through an exposition of the types of assets and liabilities accounted for by the eight basic fund types of *NCGA Statement 1.* In addition, one type of financial statement—the balance sheet, both of the individual fund type and of the combining balance sheet type—was described and explained for the governmental, fiduciary, and proprietary funds. The balance sheet described is one that would be compatible with municipal accounting principles (MAP) as set out in the major source of such principles, *NCGA Statement 1.* Also, the interpretations of *NCGA Statement 1* by *1980 GAAFR* are a basis for our explanation of the balance sheets (both individual fund and combining) that are compatible with MAP.

A number of illustrative balance sheets were examined and discussed. These sample balance sheets were taken from *1980 GAAFR.*

---

[21]According to the illustrative balance sheet for the enterprise fund, the "reserved per revenue bond indentures" part of retained earnings shows a balance of $96,975 in it for the prior fiscal year. This reserve applies to all or part of the three restricted asset accounts that have been described. The three restricted asset account are: (1) revenue bond future debt service account at $82,990; (2) revenue bond contingency (renewal and replacement) account at $10,985; and (3) revenue bond current debt service account, with $3,000 of the balance associated with the reserve. The total of these three figures is $96,975 and that is exactly the amount shown in the retained earnings reserve for the prior fiscal year. By the way, the $3,000 comes from the fact that the restricted assets in the revenue bond current debt service account (at $113,150) exceed by $3,000 the related liabilities (which total $110,150).

Now what about the current fiscal year? Does the calculation work out for the current fiscal year? If one adds up the respective restricted asset accounts at $109,822 plus $14,983 plus $5,000, then the total is $129,805. The $5,000 results from the fact that the restricted assets in the revenue bond current debt service account (at $117,888) exceed by $5,000 the related liabilities (which total $112,888). Unfortunately, one finds that the balance shown in the retained earnings reserve is not $129,805 but $129,155. The difference is $650. A close examination of the materials in *1980 GAAFR* (p. 64) reveals a $650 error that resulted in an overstatement of *unreserved* retained earnings by $650 and an understatement in the *reserved* part of retained earnings by $650. Once the retained earnings reserve is corrected for its understatement by $650, then in fact one obtains the appropriate balance of $129,805.

So far, given the complexity of municipal financial reporting in comparison with financial reporting for a business enterprise, we have only scratched the surface of such reporting. However, the discussion of financial reporting at the level of an individual fund balance sheet, and also at the level of a combining balance sheet for all funds of the same type, is necessary in order to lay a foundation for financial reporting that brings together all of the fund types for a particular fund category. In the next chapter, the overall financial statements as described in *NCGA Statement 1* and *1980 GAAFR* will be discussed and reviewed.

Municipal Financial Reporting: Part II*

CHAPTER **38**

Abraham J. Simon, Ph.D., CPA

Professor of Accounting and Information Systems
Queens College, City University of New York

INTRODUCTION

This chapter begins with an examination of the financial accounting and reporting of the *general* fixed assets and *general* long-term debt of a governmental unit, which have not been reviewed thus far. The accounting for these assets and liabilities is very unlike what one would encounter in commercial accounting. For this reason you need to become fairly familiar with the accounting for such assets and liabilities in order to better appreciate the financial statements of *NCGA Statement 1*.[1] In addition, this accounting has a number of facets to it that involve certain of the governmental-type funds. This means that one needs to be exposed initially to accounting and re-

*I would like to thank Bradley Benson of Ademco and A. Wayne Corcoran of Baruch College–CUNY for their review and comments on this chapter. I would also like to thank my wife, Marilyn S. Simon, for her proofreading and editing of the materials in the chapter. Any remaining defects in form or substance are my responsibility.

[1]National Council on Governmental Accounting (new NCGA), *NCGA Statement 1*, "Governmental Accounting and Financial Reporting Principles" (Chicago: Municipal Finance Officers Association, March 1979a).

porting of governmental funds before attempting to get a grip on accounting for general fixed assets and general long-term debt. The review of the prior chapters concerning accounting and reporting by the various fund types of the governmental unit should provide the required foundation.

In the preceding chapter, the financial statement concerned with financial position—the balance sheet—was reviewed. Both the individual fund balance sheet and the combining balance sheet were discussed and described. Each type of balance sheet deals with financial position but from a different point of view. In this chapter, two other types of financial statements will be discussed, the first of which is concerned with reporting on operations. Its precise name varies somewhat depending on which fund's operations are being reported, but essentially it provides information on such items as estimated and actual revenues, budgeted and actual expenditures or expenses (whichever is the more appropriate), and changes in fund balances or fund equity or retained earnings (whichever is the more appropriate). As is the case for the balance sheet, this statement may be prepared either for an individual fund or it may be prepared in the combining form for all of the funds of a particular fund type. Another type of financial statement will be discussed that reports on changes in financial position. This is the "statement of changes in financial position" and it is prepared for proprietary funds, nonexpendable trust funds, and pension trust funds, but not for the other types of funds (i.e., the expendable funds) of the governmental unit. This financial statement also comes in the individual fund as well as combining fund format.

NCGA Statement 1 provides for still a third frame of reference from which to prepare financial statements in addition to the individual fund level and combining level financial statements. This third level of financial statements, called "combined financial statements," is intended to report on the governmental unit, both its financial position and its operations, from an overall point of view. These financial statements are also called the general purpose financial statements (GPFS). These financial statements plus the individual level and combining level financial statements all are brought together in what is called the comprehensive annual financial report (CAFR). The CAFR also contains a statistical section, along with other items to be described. The discussion of the various elements of the CAFR will complete the review of municipal financial reporting according to the municipal accounting principles of *NCGA Statement 1*. Illustrative examples of financial statements, as well as other elements of CAFR, will be drawn from *1980 GAAFR*.[2]

---

[2]Municipal Finance Officers Association, *Governmental Accounting, Auditing, and Financial Reporting (1980 GAAFR)* (Chicago: MFOA, 1980).

ACCOUNTING FOR GENERAL FIXED ASSETS AND GENERAL LONG-TERM LIABILITIES

Accounting for General Fixed Assets— the Balance Sheet Perspective

A state or local governmental unit, if it follows the recommendations of *NCGA Statement 1,* accounts for its assets from the balance sheet point of view either through its funds or through an account group. The types of assets accounted for on the balance sheets of the individual funds of a state or local governmental unit have already been described. The one class of assets not accounted for through the funds, from the balance sheet point of view, is general fixed assets. Certain of the funds of the governmental unit, from a balance sheet point of view, do account for fixed assets. *NCGA Statement 1* (p. 8) calls such assets "fund fixed assets." The fund types that carry fixed assets on their balance sheets are enterprise funds, internal service funds, and nonexpendable trust funds, according to the recommendations of *NCGA Statement 1.* However, there are fixed assets not accounted for, in the balance sheet sense, by a particular fund. Such fixed assets are called, by *NCGA Statement 1,* "general fixed assets."

One should note the usage of the term *fixed assets* in commercial accounting, where they are distinguished from what might be called circulating assets. An example of the latter would be merchandise that a business sells to its customers. The fixed assets of a commercial enterprise are "fixed" in the sense that they are not sold to customers, but are used in the operations of the business. Fixed assets may be broken down into two categories: tangible and intangible. Tangible fixed assets refer to such physical capital assets as land, buildings, furniture and fixtures, manufacturing machinery and equipment, automotive equipment, and natural resources. Intangible fixed assets refer to fixed assets that do not have physical substance, such as patents, copyrights, trademarks, brand names, and franchise rights. We have noted earlier that the funds that account for fixed assets on the fund balance sheets are the enterprise funds, internal service funds, and nonexpendable trust funds (following the guidelines of *NCGA Statement 1*). The fixed assets of these funds are known as fund fixed assets, and would cover both tangible and intangible fixed assets. Fund fixed assets are used in those activities of the governmental unit that result in the supply of market-type goods and services.

The general fixed assets of the governmental unit are used, by and large, in the activities of the governmental unit that result in the supply of nonmarket public goods and services. The general fixed assets covered in *NCGA Statement 1* are basically tangible fixed assets. The tangible physical assets of a governmental unit are basically assets of the marketable variety and nonmarket public goods. The non-market public goods are called "public domain", or "infrastructure", general fixed assets.

The general fixed assets are accounted for through an accounting entity called an account group. The account group is called the "general fixed assets account group" in *NCGA Statement 1*. In *1968 GAAFR*, the account group was called the "general fixed assets group of accounts."[3] Prior to that, in 1951 *Municipal Accounting and Auditing*, the account group was called the "general fixed assets—self-balancing group of accounts". Over a period of almost 30 years, the account group has retained pretty much the same name, though it has been simplified a bit. The basic purpose of the account group has also remained the same—i.e., to account for the general fixed assets from the balance sheet point of view of a governmental unit.

An account group, such as the general fixed assets account group, is simply a self-balancing set of accounts. In order to understand that, let us think of an account group in terms of a simple equation. The equation has two sides, as equations are prone to do. Let's look at the left-hand side and denote it as LHS. The other side, the right-hand side, we will denote as RHS. Self-balancing means simply that the LHS for the equation is always equal to the RHS. The LHS of our equation for the general fixed assets account will have the different classes of general fixed assets accounted for by the account group. On the RHS we have the sources of the financial and other resources used in the acquisition of general fixed assets. The values recorded for each of the different classes of general fixed assets are the original acquisition costs of these assets. The total of the values on the RHS of the equation will be equal to the total of the historical costs of the different classes of general fixed assets on the LHS of the equation. The way in which depreciation accounting would enter into the equation will be discussed later on.

Whenever a general fixed asset is acquired, both the LHS and RHS of the equation must be increased equally. The amount of the increase is equal to the acquisition or historical cost of the general fixed asset acquired. On the LHS of the equation, a particular class of general fixed assets will reflect the addition of the new asset. On the RHS of the equation, we have the source of the financial resources (where such resources are involved) used to acquire the general fixed assets. The amount of the resources used will be equal to the acquisition cost of the general fixed asset acquired.

The classes of general fixed assets used to account for such assets in *NCGA Statement 1* (p. 30) are: land, buildings, improvements other

[3]National Committee on Governmental Accounting (old NCGA), *Governmental Accounting, Auditing, and Financial Reporting (1968 GAAFR)* (Chicago: MFOA, 1968).

than buildings, machinery and equipment, and construction in progress. Strictly speaking, construction in progress is not in the nature of a fixed asset until construction is complete and the fixed asset resulting from the construction is actually being used in the operations of the governmental unit. The same classes of general fixed assets appear in *1980 GAAFR* (p. 55). The sources of financial resources or other resources used in the acquisition of general fixed assets are shown in *1980 GAAFR* (p. 53) as: general fund revenues, special fund revenues, special assessments, and (from the capital projects funds) general obligation bonds, federal grants, and state grants. We also find in *1980 GAAFR* (p. 53) two additional sources described as private gifts and other sources.

Not all general fixed assets need to be reported upon. *NCGA Statement 1* (p. 9) permits optional financial reporting of those general fixed assets that are called public domain, or infrastructure, general fixed assets. Public domain general fixed assets cover such capital assets as roads, bridges, curbs, gutters, streets, sidewalks, drainage systems, lighting systems, and other similar immobile assets. *NCGA Statement 1* (p. 9) argues that such infrastructure assets are only of value to the governmental unit. This is a strange assertion. One assumes that these assets are of value to the ultimate consumer of the services rendered by the assets. I suspect that what the authors of *NCGA Statement 1* intended to say was that these public domain general fixed assets are not marketable assets. We have noted earlier that these assets are nonmarket public goods.

According to *NCGA Statement 1,* infrastructure general fixed assets can be accounted for through the general fixed assets account group. However, *NCGA Statement 1* also permits these assets not to be accounted for through this account group. This means that the financial accounting records need not reflect such assets in the financial accounts, and such assets need not be reported in the financial statements prepared from these records. However, whether or not infrastructure general fixed assets are reported in the financial statements, the notes to the financial statements have to disclose to the reader of such statements the precise accounting policy with respect to such assets. *NCGA Statement 1* (p. 9) recommends that, whether or not infrastructure general fixed assets are included in the financial accounting records, managerial accounting records—including such records as deeds, maps, and listings of assets—should be maintained for management and accountability purposes. It is interesting to note that *1980 GAAFR* (p. 53) actually recommends that public domain general fixed assets be accounted for in the financial accounting records in the general fixed assets account group, but that such assets be segregated from the other general fixed assets that are not of the public domain variety.

Accounting for the Acquisition of General Fixed Assets

While it is correct, following the guidelines of *NCGA Statement 1,* that the various fund types of a governmental unit do not account for general fixed assets from a balance sheet perspective, certain of these fund types will be involved in accounting for the resources used for the acquisition of general fixed assets. The fund types that were discussed earlier as accounting for the financial resources that are used for the acquisition of capital assets (general fixed assets) were the capital projects funds and the special assessment funds. However, these are not the only governmental fund types whose financial resources can be used for the acquisition of general fixed assets. Both the financial resources of the general fund and the special revenue funds can be used for the acquisition of general fixed assets.

The capital projects funds account for certain types of restricted resources that are specially earmarked for the acquisition of capital assets. The restricted resources accounted for by a capital projects fund would arise from such sources as the proceeds from the issuance of general obligation bonds, federal grants, and state grants. One assumes that the purpose of the issue of general obligation bonds was the financing of the acquisition of general fixed assets. Similarly, the federal grant was earmarked for the acquisition of general fixed assets. And, in the case of a local government receiving a grant from a state government, the state governmental grant was earmarked for the acquisition of general fixed assets. When the proceeds from the general obligation bonds and the receipts from the federal and state grants are all earmarked for the acquisition of general fixed assets, then the appropriate fiscal and accounting entity to account for such restricted resources would be a capital projects fund.

The special assessments fund accounts for restricted financial resources from special assessment property tax levies and/or from the proceeds of special assessment bond issues. These restricted resources are normally involved in the financing of the construction of special assessment capital improvements that will ultimately be accounted for as general fixed assets, once construction is complete and the capital improvements are rendering their services.

Unrestricted financial resources from general property taxes or sales taxes, etc., that are budgeted to be used for the acquisition of general fixed assets would be accounted for through the general fund. In addition, restricted financial resources—e.g., earmarked general property taxes normally accounted for by a special revenue fund— would also be accounted for by such a fund as long as such resources are not budgeted in major amounts to be used for the acquisition of general fixed assets. Thus, one has examples of both the general fund and special revenue funds accounting for financial resources budgeted to be used for the acquisition of general fixed assets.

Note that the acquisition of a general fixed asset by a governmental unit will involve two types of accounting entities. For example, assume a general fixed asset is acquired through the use of the financial resources of the general fund. At the time of the delivery of the general fixed asset, one will find that the net financial resources of the general fund will decrease by the acquisition cost of the asset. At the same time, the general fixed asset will be recorded in the accounts of the general fixed assets account group. From the point of view of the governmental unit as a whole, actually what has happened is that financial resources have been converted into real resources.

Accounting for Depreciation of General Fixed Assets

For purposes of financial reporting in commercial accounting, accountants go through an exercise of allocating the historical cost of a fixed asset over its estimated useful life. The allocation of a historical cost to a particular time period is considered a conversion of historical costs into expired costs. Expired costs are also called expenses. Where the fixed asset is a tangible fixed asset but not a natural resource, the allocation of historical cost over estimated useful life is called "depreciation." When dealing with natural resources, the allocation of historical cost is called "depletion." If the fixed asset is an intangible asset, then the allocation of historical cost is called "amortization." An asset such as land is considered neither a depreciable nor depletable asset so that its historical cost is not allocated over a future estimated life. The future estimated life of land is considered indeterminate.

NCGA Statement 1 sets aside an entire basic principle to the subject of accounting for depreciation of both general fixed assets and fund fixed assets.[4] Depreciation of fund fixed assets is to be recorded and reported in the appropriate nonexpendable fund that carries fund fixed assets in its balance sheet. Suitable nonexpendable funds for the carrying of fund fixed assets have been noted to be the enterprise funds, internal service funds, and nonexpendable trust funds. However, depreciation of general fixed assets is not to be shown in any of the various fund types. In particular, the governmental funds are not to record in their accounts any depreciation expense for the depreciation of general fixed assets. Recall that the acquisition of general fixed assets—using the resources of expendable funds such as the general fund, special revenue funds, and capital projects funds—resulted in a decrease in the net financial resources of these funds. Depreciation expense is not a use of financial resources. Thus, depreciation expense should not be deducted from the financial resources of an expendable fund because (a) the resources of such funds are reduced

---

[4]See basic principle VIII in Appendix A of Chapter 36.

when assets are acquired and (b) an expense is not necessarily an expenditure.

Depreciation of general fixed assets may be shown in the general fixed assets account group. This is optional and not required. If depreciation of general fixed assets is shown in the general fixed assets account group then it is recorded in an account called "accumulated depreciation." The depreciation expense recorded in this account is deducted from the historical cost shown for the general fixed assets to arrive at a net figure for these assets. Historical cost less accumulated depreciation is called the "book value" of a fixed asset in commercial accounting.

NCGA Statement 1, in basic principle VII, also provides that depreciation may be recorded in cost accounting systems for purposes of cost analysis. It is not clear why basic principle VII concerns itself with the managerial accounting aspects of depreciation. From a managerial accounting standpoint, depreciation calculations appear to be a relatively useless exercise. Allocating the historical cost of a fixed asset over its estimated useful life appears to serve no useful decision-making purpose. In fact, a very well-known introductory textbook in managerial accounting by C. T. Horngren tells us that "The most widely misunderstood facet of replacement analysis is the role of the book value of the old equipment in the decision. The book value, in this context, is sometimes called a *sunk cost,* which is really just another term for historical or past cost. All historical costs are always irrelevant to choosing among alternative courses of action."[5]

Some 20 years earlier, a French textbook on managerial economics also dealt with depreciation accounting as part of a class of problems which the author, J. Lesourne, called "economic pseudoproblems in accounting." Lesourne uses the term *amortization* to cover all intertemporal historical cost allocations whether these be of the depreciation, depletion, or amortization variety as defined earlier. Lesourne tells us that where "expenditures are fixed, their allocation among different departments is arbitrary and useless from the economic standpoint since the decisions to be taken are independent of these expenditures. . . . Later . . . the problem of allocating fixed charges among various years will be considered as part of the amortization problem. Here again the problem of allocation will not bear on the problem of decision-making. . . ."[6]

One should note that the critics of the traditional methods of de-

[5]Charles T. Horngren, *Introduction to Management Accounting,* 5th ed. (Englewood Cliffs, N.J.: Prentice-Hall, 1981), p. 124.

[6]Jacques Lesourne, *Economic Analysis and Industrial Management,* trans. Scripta Technica, Inc. (Englewood Cliffs, N.J.: Prentice-Hall, 1963), p. 235. The book is based on the French edition, *Technique Economique et Gestion Industrielle,* 2d ed. (Paris: Dunod Press, 1960).

preciation accounting methods which allocate historical costs in some arbitrary fashion over estimated useful life, do recognize the significance of depreciation in the area of taxation. Since the tax authorities permit the deduction of depreciation, depletion, and amortization for tax purposes, these methods of allocating historical cost over time will have an economic impact on an enterprise because of tax consequences. However, one should note that no such claim can be made for depreciation accounting by state and local governmental units since they are not subject to the tax laws to which commercial enterprises are exposed.

Accounting for the Disposition of General Fixed Assets

The last facet of accounting for general fixed assets deals with the disposition of such assets, and also with any financial resources obtained from the disposal. When general fixed assets are disposed of, they are simply removed from the general fixed assets account group. If no depreciation has been recorded in this account group, then accounting for the disposition of general fixed assets means simply decreasing both the LHS and RHS of the equation for the general fixed assets account group by the amount of the original acquisition cost (historical cost) of the disposed asset. If depreciation has been recorded in the general fixed assets account group, then one removes not only the historical cost from a particular fixed asset account in which such costs are recorded, but also the amount of the accumulated depreciation on such an asset, recorded in an associated accumulated depreciation account. In effect, the book value of the disposed asset is being removed from both the LHS and RHS of the equation for the general fixed assets account group.

When a general fixed asset is disposed of and financial resources are obtained from the disposal, then such resources are normally accounted for in the general fund. The disposition of a general fixed asset can affect two types of accounting entities: the general fixed assets account group and the general fund. In commercial accounting, the disposition of a fixed asset will affect the single accounting entity used to account for the activities of the enterprise. This single accounting entity will show the removal of the fixed asset and associated accumulated depreciation from its books, and also show on the same books any resources obtained from the disposal of the fixed asset.

The various facets of accounting for general fixed assets is shown in Figure 1. This figure shows the fiscal and accounting entities involved in the acquisition and disposition of general fixed assets. The figure also shows the accounting entity that accounts for general fixed assets from the balance sheet perspective—i.e., while these assets are held and used as assets of the governmental unit.

Figure 1
Accounting for General Fixed Assets*

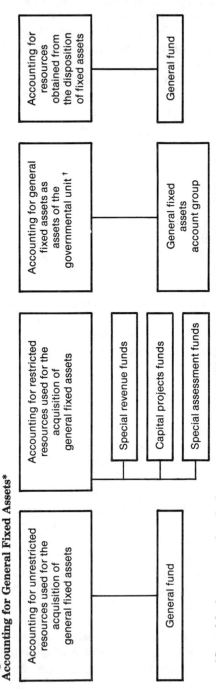

*General fixed assets cover those fixed assets not accounted for as fund fixed assets under the guidelines of *NCGA Statement 1.*
†The general fixed assets account group is used not only to account for general fixed assets, but also to account for depreciation on such assets. Under *NCGA Statement 1,* depreciation accounting for general fixed assets is optional.

Illustrative Disclosures with Respect to General Fixed Assets

Financial reporting and other disclosures with respect to the general fixed assets of a governmental unit are shown in five places in the illustrative financial report of *1980 GAAFR*. First, the general fixed assets are reported in the combined balance sheet—an overall financial statement covering all of the fund types and account groups of the governmental unit. Appendix G to this chapter contains a set of illustrative combined financial statements. These are the general purpose financial statements (GPFS). The notes to the GPFS are considered an integral part of the statements. The notes are shown in Appendix H.

The illustrative combined balance sheet appears as Exhibit 1 in Appendix G. In the illustrative combined balance sheet, the general fixed assets are shown at a cost of $6,913,250 as the single asset category of the general fixed assets account group. The general fixed assets account group has its own column in the illustrative combined balance sheet. In the column for this account group, one will find no amount shown under "liabilities" because the account group carries no liabilities. However, in the same column under "fund equity," one finds the amount $6,913,250 identified as "investment in general fixed assets," which is simply a balancing account which records the sources of financing for general fixed assets equal in value to the asset side of the general fixed assets account group.

The second place for disclosure about the general fixed assets is in the notes to the financial statements. In the illustrative combined balance sheet, one finds next to the asset account "fixed assets *(net of accumulated depreciation)*" a cross-reference to note (4). Thus, we must look at note (4) of the notes to the financial statements for further information concerning the general fixed assets. Note (4) to the illustrative combined balance sheet is shown in Appendix H as part of all of the illustrative notes to the financial statements. Note (4) provides a breakdown of the general fixed assets by major fixed asset category such as land and buildings. At the beginning of the current fiscal year, total cost for all of the general fixed assets is shown at $5,174,250. Additions to and disposals of general fixed assets by major fixed asset categories is shown so that ending balances are disclosed for each major category. The ending total balance for the general fixed assets is $6,913,250, which ties into the figure reported in the illustrative combined balance sheet. The note also provides summary financial information on construction in progress. For the financial resources used to finance the construction on the three capital projects covered by the construction in progress, accounting is being done through two capital projects funds and one special assessment fund.

For some unexplained reason, note (4) is identified as "changes in general fixed assets," when in fact the note discloses information about fund fixed assets carried by the enterprise and internal service funds. The figures shown for the fund fixed assets in note 4 for the two types of proprietary funds agree with the figures for fund fixed assets (net of accumulated depreciation) in the combined balance sheet.

The third place that one finds a disclosure with respect to the general fixed assets is also in the illustrative notes to the financial statements in Appendix H. In this case, note (1) is the pertinent note. Note (1) is usually the note which summarizes significant accounting policies used in the preparation of the financial statements. Note (1)B discusses accounting policies with respect to both the general and fund fixed assets and with respect to both general and fund long-term liabilities.

In note (1)B the difference between accounting for fund fixed assets versus general fixed assets is described briefly. The major categories of fixed assets are named. For this particular hypothetical governmental unit, public domain (infrastructure) general fixed assets are accounted for in the financial accounting records in the general fixed assets account group. Recall that *NCGA Statement 1* provides an optional financial accounting treatment for public domain general fixed assets. Such assets need not be accounted for in the financial accounting record, although other types of records are to be kept for these assets for managerial planning and control purposes. The valuation basis for the fixed assets is stated to be historical cost and approximations to historical cost when these are necessary.

Note also that for this particular governmental unit no depreciation is recorded in the financial accounting records for the *general* fixed assets. Depreciation is recorded for the *fund* fixed assets. If that is the case, then the identification shown in the combined balance sheet could be somewhat misleading. In that financial statement, we have the general fixed assets described as fixed assets (net of accumulated depreciation)—note (4). "Net of accumulated depreciation" applies to the fund fixed assets carried by the proprietary funds, but does not apply to the general fixed assets carried in the general fixed assets account group. This is a good example of why it is important to read the notes to the financial statements very carefully in order to avoid carrying away potentially misleading impressions that could be conveyed by confining oneself to a superficial examination of the statements.

The fourth place where one finds a disclosure with respect to the general fixed assets is in an illustrative supporting schedule to the financial statements. Such a hypothetical schedule, taken from *1980 GAAFR,* is shown in Exhibit 1. The schedule in Exhibit 1 shows sim-

Exhibit 1
Illustrative Hypothetical Schedule for Reporting the General Fixed Assets and Their Sources of Financing

NAME OF GOVERNMENT

SCHEDULE OF GENERAL FIXED ASSETS —
BY SOURCES

December 31, 19X2

General Fixed Assets:	
Land	$1,259,500
Building	2,855,500
Improvements other than buildings	1,036,750
Equipment	452,500
Construction in progress	1,309,000
Total general fixed assets	$6,913,250
Investment in General Fixed Assets from:	
Capital Projects Funds:	
General obligation bonds	$3,540,850
Federal grants	1,000,000
State grants	300,000
County grants	625,000
General Fund revenues	562,400
Special Revenue Fund revenues	309,500
Gifts	175,500
Special assessments	400,000
Total Investment in General Fixed Assets	$6,913,250

Source: Municipal Finance Officers Association, *Governmental Accounting, Auditing, and Financial Reporting (1980 GAAFR)* (Chicago: MFOA, 1980), Appendix D, p. 203.

ply the historical costs accumulated for each major fixed asset category without any reduction for estimated accumulated depreciation. As noted earlier, depreciation accounting based on historical cost appears to serve no known useful decision-making purpose. In the governmental area, where public goods are supplied, the usual arguments in favor of depreciation accounting are even more irrelevant since the traditional arguments are set in a commercial marketable goods environment.

There is a *fifth* location in the financial statements that contains some discussion with respect to the general fixed assets. In Appendix D to this chapter there is "An Illustrative Finance Director's Letter of Transmittal that Functions as an Introductory Section for a Comprehensive Annual Financial Report." This letter of transmittal contains a very brief discussion of the general fixed assets. The discussion provides one additional bit of information to the effect that "the original cost of the assets . . . is considerably less than their present value."

Information Relevant with Respect to the General Fixed Assets

The basic information relative to the general fixed assets shown in the financial report from *1980 GAAFR* concerns the historical cost of these assets and a single year's additions and dispositions. The information is highly condensed summary financial information. That the information is highly condensed and in summary form is not the only problem. A more basic problem seems to be that the most valuable kinds of information with respect to the general fixed assets are not shown. The finance director provides us with a judgment that the original costs of the general fixed assets are significantly less than their present value as of the date of the financial statements. This is a very interesting bit of information, but we are not provided with the basis for the judgment. Note also that, since this judgment does not appear anywhere in the general purpose financial statements verified by independent auditors in the example from *1980 GAAFR,* therefore the finance director's judgment is not subject to independent auditor verification.

What does the finance director mean by "present value"? Does present value represent the market value of the general fixed assets if the governmental unit chose to dispose of them as of the date of the balance sheet? Or, does present value refer to the replacement cost that the governmental unit would have to incur were it to desire or need to replace all of its general fixed assets, as of the balance sheet date, with new assets of identical types and qualities as the original assets? Or, does present value mean something else?

There are certain kinds of summarized information with respect to the general fixed assets that would be useful to a financial analyst studying the financial condition of a governmental unit and its financing needs. For example, is there information available on the general state of repair or disrepair of the general fixed assets? For general fixed assets for a given level of performance, are acquisition and maintenance costs minimized? How well have the general fixed assets performed relative to performance goals for such assets? What are the utilization rates for different types of general fixed assets? What are the governmental unit's spending plans with respect to the maintenance, upgrading, or replacement of its general fixed assets over the next 1, 2, 5, and 10 years? Does the governmental unit's accounting system generate any information that would help answer any of these questions? A financial analyst would be interested in capital spending plans relative to capital needs over different future time horizons. Neither *NCGA Statement 1* nor *1980 GAAFR* seems to address either of these financial information needs of users of governmental external financial reports.

General Long-Term Liabilities— Evolution in Reporting Standards

NCGA Statement 1 distinguishes between *general* and *fund* long-term debt. Fund long-term debt is owed to parties outside the governmental unit, and it is primarily a liability of a particular fund of the governmental unit. Such debt may also be a contingent liability of the governmental unit itself. For example, special assessment bonds are long-term debt of a special assessment fund. Such bonds may carry an additional guarantee that the governmental unit will be responsible for the payment of interest and principal if the resources of the responsible special assessment fund prove inadequate. Even if special assessment debt carries an additional guarantee from the governmental unit, it will nevertheless be shown as a liability of the special assessment fund. Any additional guarantees are to be disclosed in the notes to the financial statements. Certain nonexpendable trust funds and pension trust funds may incur long-term debt owed to parties external to the governmental unit. Such debt, along with special assessment long-term debt, would be considered fund long-term debt per *NCGA Statement 1*. Finally, enterprise funds can incur long-term debt which also would be classified as fund long-term debt.

General long-term debt represents long-term debt owed to parties external to the governmental unit and *not* considered debt of the fund types just described as carrying fund long-term debt. The classic example of general long-term debt would be general obligation bonds which represent a lien on future governmental tax revenue in terms of the full faith and credit of the governmental unit. General obligation bonds, at present, are in the form of serial bonds. In earlier periods, such bonds came in the form of term bonds. Each type has been discussed earlier. General long-term debt can include formal debt instruments such as bonds, warrants, and notes which are not a direct liability of a particular fund and are of the long-term variety. In addition, *NCGA Statement 1* (p. 9) includes in general long-term debt other kinds of noncurrent liabilities—such as long-term lease purchase agreements—that are to be financed through the resources of the governmental funds, but are not considered liabilities of such funds. Long-term lease purchase agreements are the only explicit example of "other kinds of noncurrent liabilities" set out in *NCGA Statement 1* that should be included in general long-term debt.

With regard to other kinds of noncurrent liabilities we might have thought that *NCGA Statement 1* would have included in general long-term debt, the *Statement* appears ambivalent. Earlier, we noted that significant vested amounts of various kinds of accumulated unpaid employee benefits (such as vacation pay and sick leave) only have to be disclosed in the notes to the financial statements if such noncurrent liabilities (normally to be paid from the governmental funds) exceed a normal year's accumulation and are not shown directly in the financial statements. In other words, these types of long-term debt can be shown in the general long-term debt account group; but, if not reported there, then under certain circumstances disclosure in the notes to the financial statements is required. In earlier chapters (35 and 36), we noted that accounting and reporting for vacation pay and sick leave benefits has been modified somewhat by *NCGA Statement 4*. It is not clear why *NCGA Statement 1* would permit underreporting of liabilities in the financial statements when disclosure is required in the notes to the financial statements once the liability passes a certain threshhold. Earlier, we discussed some of the disadvantages of reporting liabilities solely as a disclosure in the notes to the financial statements rather than directly in the financial statements. The preferred approach is to report a liability directly in the financial statements with additional useful and appropriate explanations set out in the notes.

NCGA Statement 1 (p. 27), in a footnote, informs us that accounting and reporting "of pension plan liabilities related to activities financed through governmental funds, is under study by the FASB, the AICPA State and Local Governmental Accounting Committee, and the NCGA."[7] Again, we have an ambivalence concerning a general long-term liability. In *1980 GAAFR* (p. 57), examples of noncurrent liabilities (in addition to formal debt instruments) are lease-purchase agreements, installment purchase contracts, judgments and claims, unfunded pension obligations, and accumulated unpaid vacation, sick pay, and other employee benefits. Well, some of these examples are required to be included in the general long-term debt account group and general long-term liabilities, and some are not. For example, *1980 GAAFR* (pp. 14–15) repeats the alternative accounting and reporting treatments of *NCGA Statement 1* with respect to accumulated unpaid vacation, sick pay, and other employee benefits. This means

---

[7]The study of pension accounting by the Financial Accounting Board resulted in a publication called *Discussion Memorandum: Employers' Accounting for Pension and Other Postemployment Benefits* (Stamford, Conn.: Financial Accounting Standards Board, February 1981). Discussion memorandums can be an initial stage of a major revision of existing generally accepted accounting principles covering a particular area of financial accounting and reporting. The second stage in revising GAAP for pension plans has been reached with the issuance of an exposure draft by the new NCGA (see footnote 31 of this chapter).

that, even though this item is shown in *1980 GAAFR* as an example of a noncurrent liability to be recorded in the general long-term debt account group, it doesn't have to be recorded if an exception or ambivalence about the matter appears in *NCGA Statement 1*. Of course, this makes sense since *1980 GAAFR* cannot amend *NCGA Statement 1*. So we are left with pension liabilities as another example of a general long-term liability on which *NCGA Statement 1* does not take a clear and unambiguous stand.

This discussion should give something of an awareness as to the differences between the recording and reporting of certain types of liabilities for governmental entities as contrasted with the accounting principles that apply to business enterprises. Market forces do have a tendency, though this does not operate perfectly, to penalize those business enterprises that show a reluctance to be entirely candid about their liabilities. However, the private sector has its own problems concerning proper reporting of liabilities, particularly with respect to pension liabilities. See, for instance, the discussion in an intermediate accounting textbook by Davidson, Stickney, and Weil, or in an article by Lucas and Hollowell, "Pension Accounting: The Liability Question."[8]

One should note in fairness to the public sector that, even though standards of reporting liabilities have been criticized, the standards—i.e., municipal accounting principles (MAP)—of *NCGA Statement 1* are nevertheless an improvement over its predecessor manuals. For example, in *1968 GAAFR*, the examples of liabilities to be recorded, in what was known at that time as the general long-term debt group of accounts, were long-term formal debt instruments in the form of general obligation bonds, time warrants, and notes.[9] Prior to *1968 GAAFR*, in 1951 *Municipal Accounting and Auditing*, we have the general bonded debt and interest—self-balancing group of accounts.[10] This account group accounted only for general obligation bonds, hence its name of "general bonded debt." Moreover, here was

---

[8]Sidney Davidson, Clyde P. Stickney, and Roman Weil, *Intermediate Accounting: Concepts, Methods, and Uses* (New York: Dryden Press, 1981). The authors argue that "We suspect that the reason supplemental actuarial values are not shown as liabilities is in part political. . . . The potential increase in liabilities is so unpalatable . . . the promulgators of accounting principles are pressured both by labor and by management not to require immediate recognition of liabilities for supplemental actuarial value" (p. 19–10, footnote).

Timothy S. Lucas and Betsy Ann Hollowell, "Pension Accounting: the Liability Question," *Journal of Accountancy,* October 1981, pp. 57–66. The authors conclude that: "Based on our work to date, we are not convinced by the arguments against recording a liability when a pension plan is established or amended. We believe that an accounting liability does exist and that including it with other liabilities in the balance sheet will significantly improve the usefulness of financial statements" (p. 66).

[9]Old NCGA, *1968 GAAFR,* p. 101.

[10]National Committee on Governmental Accounting (old NCGA), *Municipal Accounting and Auditing* (Chicago: MFOA, 1951), p. 136.

recorded, as a liability, all of the future value of interest on bonds. It is not clear why the future value of interest was recorded initially as a liability, since one normally records the present value of a bond at the time it is issued and the future value of interest is not a liability.

Thus, it would seem that the types of liabilities to be reported by state and local governmental units as general long-term debt have increased over time as municipal accounting principles evolved gradually toward a fuller reporting and disclosure of general long-term liabilities. But, as we have seen, municipal accounting principles still have a way to go toward a truly complete reporting and disclosure of governmental liabilities.

Accounting for General Long-Term Debt in the Illustrative Financial Statements and Other Disclosures

Accounting for general long-term debt has a number of complicated facets to it, given the fund accounting approach of governmental accounting. These facets should be understood in order to get a sense of how state and local governmental units report their liability for such debt. In order to understand how general long-term debt is accounted for and reported on, it will be useful to use as working examples a number of the illustrative financial statements taken from *1980 GAAFR* as well as the notes to these financial statements.

We will have to look in a number of different places in the illustrative financial report in order to become familiar with the financial statements, notes to the financial statements, and other disclosures. This will help us become comfortable in working with the financial report. The starting place in looking for disclosures about liabilities— in particular, general long-term liabilities—would be the combined balance sheet for the governmental unit as a whole. The illustrative combined balance sheet is shown in Appendix G to this chapter. In the combined balance sheet, we need to look at the column identified as the general long-term debt account group. Under liabilities and in this column, we find $1.7 million shown for general obligation bonds. Next to the description for general obligation bonds, we are directed to a second place for further disclosures, to note (5) of the notes to the financial statements in Appendix H.

Note (5) is identified as "changes in long-term debt," and begins with a summary of the beginning-of-the-year balances for general obligation bond liabilities, revenue bond liabilities, and special assessment bond liabilities. In addition, the summary shows new issues of long-term debt, and retirements of old issues of long-term debt. As a result, end-of-the-year balances are shown for liabilities with respect to general obligation bonds, revenue bonds, and special assessment bonds. At this point, our interest is focused on the general obligation bonds.

The balance of the general obligation bonds as of the end of the current fiscal year is shown at $2.4 million. However, the ending balance shown in the combined balance sheet for general obligation bonds accounted for in the general long-term debt account group is $1.7 million. The difference between the two figures is $700,000. In the column for the enterprise fund we find $700,000 shown for general obligation bonds. Recall that when the assets, liabilities, and fund equity shown in the individual balance sheet for the Water and Sewer Enterprise Fund were reviewed, it was observed that the fund carried $700,000 of general obligation bonds as a fund liability. Under the municipal accounting principles (MAP) of *NCGA Statement 1,* the $700,000 of general obligation bonds to be serviced out of enterprise fund revenues will not be accounted for through the general long-term debt account group.

Under the MAP of *1968 GAAFR,* that preceded *NCGA Statement 1,* the $700,000 of general obligation bonds serviced out of the revenues of the enterprise fund would appear as a liability in two places in the financial statements: the Water and Sewer Enterprise Fund and the general long-term debt account group (called a group of accounts in *1968 GAAFR*).[11]

The summary in note (5) also shows that during the current fiscal year, two new issues of general obligations bonds were sold. The two issues are shown at $700,000 and $200,000 in the summary. The proceeds from the two issues will be accounted for in two capital projects funds, because each issue is for the financing of a general governmental construction project. One project is related to a civic center, the other to a recreation center.

In Exhibit 2 is shown an illustrative combining statement of revenues, expenditures, and changes in fund balances taken from *1980 GAAFR*. Up until now we have discussed and reviewed one basic type of financial statement—the balance sheet. The balance sheet is supposed to show financial condition for a fiscal and accounting entity such as a fund or for a number of funds taken together. The financial statement shown in Exhibit 2 is a statement of revenues, expenditures, and changes in fund balances. It reports in financial terms on the financial activities and/or real operations accounted for by a fiscal and accounting entity or entities such as a fund or group of funds. The particular statement shown in Exhibit 2 is a combining statement that brings together the financial and real activities accounted for by all of the funds of a given fund type. In this instance, the combining statement brings together the fiscal activities (receipts and uses of financial resources) and real activities (capital construction projects financed by the financial resources) accounted for by all of the funds that are capital projects funds. Capital projects funds are

---

[11]Old NCGA, *1968 GAAFR,* p. 101.

Exhibit 2
Illustrative Hypothetical Combining Statement of Revenues, Expenditures, and Changes in Fund Balances for the Capital Projects Funds

NAME OF GOVERNMENT
CAPITAL PROJECTS FUNDS

COMBINING STATEMENT OF REVENUES, EXPENDITURES, AND CHANGES IN FUND BALANCES

Year Ended December 31, 19X2
With Comparative Totals for Year Ended December 31, 19X1

	High School Auditorium	Storm Sewer System	Civic Center	Mill Street Bridge	Richard Craddock Memorial Recreation Center	Totals 19X2	19X1
Revenues:							
Intergovernmental	$ —	$ —	$1,250,000	$ —	$ —	$1,250,000	$300,000
Miscellaneous	—	—	3,750	—	—	3,750	20,000
Total Revenues	—	—	1,253,750	—	—	1,253,750	320,000
Expenditures - capital projects:							
Construction contracts	210,000	15,000	940,500	70,000	189,000	1,424,500	717,428
Engineering and other	17,000	—	153,500	5,000	25,500	201,000	27,834
Total expenditures	227,000	15,000	1,094,000	75,000	214,500	1,625,500	745,262
Excess (deficiency) of revenues over expenditures	(227,000)	(15,000)	159,750	(75,000)	(214,500)	(371,750)	(425,262)
Other financing sources:							
Proceeds of general obligation bonds	—	—	702,500	—	200,000	902,500	—
Operating transfers in	—	—	50,000	—	14,500	64,500	87,000
Total other financing sources	—	—	752,500	—	214,500	967,000	87,000
Excess (deficiency) of revenues and other sources over expenditures	(227,000)	(15,000)	912,250	(75,000)	—	595,250	(338,262)
Fund balances at beginning of year	229,350	18,000	—	110,000	—	357,350	695,612
Fund balances at end of year	$ 2,350	$ 3,000	$ 912,250	$ 35,000	$ —	$ 952,600	$ 357,350
See accompanying notes to financial statements							

Source: Municipal Finance Officers Association, *Governmental Accounting, Auditing, and Financial Reporting (1980 GAAFR)* (Chicago: MFOA, 1980), Appendix D, p. 171.

expendable funds, so that the statement of revenues, expenditures, and changes in fund balances essentially shows sources and uses of financial resources.

In Exhibit 2, under the description "other financing sources," we find the proceeds of $702,500 and $200,000 that resulted from the sales of $700,000 and $200,000 worth of par values of two general obligation bond issues. The difference between the par value of the larger bond issue and the proceeds realized from that issue represents a $2,500 premium from the sale of the bonds. In commercial accounting, from the balance sheet point of view, long-term bonds are recorded initially at their present value. This would mean that if the new issue of general obligation bonds had been a liability of the enterprise fund rather than general long-term debt, then, as a liability of a fund accounted for by commercial generally accepted accounting principles (commercial GAAP), the bonds would be recorded at their initial present value of $702,500.

However, in governmental accounting, the liability for general obligation bonds would be recorded at par value (also the maturity value) as general long-term debt. In Exhibit 2, the $2,500 premium is included in the proceeds from the bond issue. This accounting treatment for the premium will be discussed later on. In commercial accounting applicable to an enterprise fund, for example, the premium would be amortized over the life of the bond issue to be included as part of the income of the enterprise. In governmental accounting in the case of general long-term debt, a premium or a discount is not accounted for separately and amortized over the life of a bond issue.

In the summary at the beginning of note (5), we also have the general obligation bonds being reduced by $110,000 during the current fiscal year. Remember that general obligation bonds come in two varieties in the illustrated examples to which we refer. One of the issues of general obligation bonds is considered fund long-term debt since it is serviced out of the revenues of the enterprise fund. Earlier, when the balance sheet for the Water and Sewer Enterprise Fund was reviewed, it was observed that the liability for the general obligation bonds was composed of both current and noncurrent components. In the illustrative combined balance sheet in Exhibit 1 of Appendix G, the distinction between current and noncurrent has been dropped. In the illustrative individual balance sheet for the Water and Sewer Enterprise Fund in Exhibit 11 of Chapter 37, for both the current and prior fiscal years, $50,000 of the general obligation bonds are classified as current liabilities. This means that during the current fiscal year $50,000 of such bonds should have been retired. Therefore, of the $110,000 of bond retirements shown in the summary at the beginning of note (5), $50,000 applies to the retirement of the general obligation bonds treated as a fund long-term liability. Thus, the remaining $60,000 would apply against general obligation bonds accounted for through the general long-term debt account group. Such general obligation debt normally would have been retired by the use of resources accounted for through debt service funds.

In Exhibit 3, we show an "Illustrative Hypothetical Combining Statement of Revenues, Expenditures, and Changes in Fund Balances for the Debt Service Funds," taken from *1980 GAAFR*. In this statement, you should observe expenditures in the amount of $60,000 described as "principal retirement" in the debt service fund set up to service the 1969 Street, Bridge, and Drainage general obligation bonds. Back in note (5) in Appendix H in information following the summary at the beginning of the note, these same bonds are described as serial bonds maturing in annual installments of $60,000 to $80,000.

There are two debt service funds shown in the combining statement of revenues, expenditures, and changes in fund balances. In fact, there seems to be a missing debt service fund. If one returns to note (5) in Appendix H, then one will find in the information follow-

Exhibit 3
Illustrative Hypothetical Combining Statement of Revenues, Expenditures, and Changes in Fund Balances for the Debt Service Funds

NAME OF GOVERNMENT
DEBT SERVICE FUNDS

COMBINING STATEMENT OF REVENUES, EXPENDITURES, AND
CHANGES IN FUND BALANCES

Year Ended December 31, 19X2
With Comparative Totals for Year Ended December 31, 19X1

	1969 Street, Bridge and Drainage	1979 Civic Center	Totals	
			19X2	19X1
Revenues:				
Taxes	$49,362	$ —	$49,362	$48,329
Intergovernmental	41,500	—	41,500	39,900
Miscellaneous	—	2,500	2,500	—
Total revenues	90,862	2,500	93,362	88,229
Expenditures:				
Principal retirement	60,000	—	60,000	60,000
Interest and fiscal charges	25,800	—	25,800	27,600
Total expenditures	85,800	—	85,800	87,600
Excess (deficiency) of revenues over expenditures	5,062	2,500	7,562	629
Fund balances at beginning of year	5,010	—	5,010	4,381
Fund balances at end of year	$10,072	$ 2,500	$12,572	$ 5,010

See accompanying notes to financial statements

Source: Municipal Finance Officers Association, *Governmental Accounting, Auditing, and Financial Reporting (1980 GAAFR)* (Chicago: MFOA, 1980), Appendix D, p. 167.

ing the initial summary, a description of four separate issues of general obligation bonds. Two of the issues were outstanding at the beginning of the current fiscal year. One of the two issues is serviced by the Water and Sewer Enterprise Fund. The other issue is serviced by the 1969 Street, Bridge, and Drainage Debt Service Fund shown in the combining statement of Exhibit 3. There are two new issues, but only one debt service fund is shown. There is no debt service fund shown for the issue of general obligation bonds to finance construction associated with a recreation center. As of the end of the fiscal year, no resources were received to be used to service this long-term debt issue, so that no financial statements are shown for a debt service fund set up to service this issue.

The debt service fund set up to service the new issue of bonds to finance the construction associated with a civic center shows miscellaneous revenues of $2,500 for the current fiscal year. It is not quite clear just what would be the source of such resources to be accounted for as revenue. At this point it will be useful to look at the "Illustrative Combining Balance Sheet for the Debt Service Funds" shown in Exhibit 4 and taken from *1980 GAAFR*.

In the combining balance sheet of Exhibit 4, the 1979 Civic Center

Exhibit 4
Illustrative Combining Balance Sheet for the Debt Service Funds

NAME OF GOVERNMENT
DEBT SERVICE FUNDS

COMBINING BALANCE SHEET

December 31, 19X2
With Comparative Totals for December 31, 19X1

	1969 Street, Bridge and Drainage	1979 Civic Center	Totals 19X2	19X1
Assets				
Cash	$ 8,389	$ 2,500	$10,889	$ 4,305
Receivables (net of allowances for estimated uncollectibles):				
Taxes, including interest, penalties, and liens	3,528	—	3,528	2,500
Total assets	$11,917	$ 2,500	$14,417	$ 6,805
Liabilities and Fund Balance				
Liabilities:				
Deferred revenues	$ 1,845	$ —	$ 1,845	$ 1,795
Fund balance:				
Reserved for debt service	10,072	2,500	12,572	5,010
Total liabilities and fund balance	$11,917	$ 2,500	$14,417	$ 6,805

See accompanying notes to financial statements

Source: Municipal Finance Officers Association, *Governmental Accounting, Auditing, and Financial Reporting (1980 GAAFR)* (Chicago: MFOA, 1980), Appendix D, p. 166.

Debt Service Fund is shown with a single asset of $2,500 in "cash" balanced by $2,500 in the "Fund balance—reserved for debt service." There are no assets in this debt service fund that would appear to be able to generate any revenues. Thus, the $2,500 must have been received by the fund from external sources not related to any fund assets. The amount is identical to the $2,500 of premium shown as part of the proceeds of $702,500 from the civic center bond issued accounted for by a capital projects fund. Now, if the $2,500 had not been shown as part of the proceeds of a bond issue in the capital projects fund but had been accounted for separately, then it would be clear that the $2,500 of revenue in the debt service fund is in fact the $2,500 of premium. In fact, a premium on a general obligation bond issue normally would be accounted for in the debt service fund set up to service that issue. So it would seem that the capital projects fund should have recorded, as proceeds from the bond issue to be accounted for in that fund, some $700,000 rather than $702,500. It all depends on whether the bond indenture for the general obligation bonds authorizes a premium to be spent on the construction project or whether, as is normally the case, the premium is earmarked to be used to service the debt.

Let us return to note (5) in Appendix H once more. At the same time, let us introduce an illustrative statistical table in Exhibit 5 as another type of disclosure in the financial report taken from *1980 GAAFR.*

In the statistical table shown in Exhibit 5, we have information on past annual debt service payments on the one old outstanding general obligation bond issue that is accounted for through the general long-term debt account group. The table attempts to provide us with a measure of debt burden in terms of the annual debt service relative to total expenditures through the general, special revenue, and debt service funds.

In note (5) in Appendix H, there is information disclosed on future debt service with respect to all of the different types of long-term debt outstanding at the end of the current fiscal year. Instead of a single general obligation bond issue outstanding as of the end of the current fiscal year and accounted for through the general long-term debt account group, there are now three issues outstanding. The annual debt service on these three issues would constitute a significant rise over the annual debt service on a single bond issue. The calculation of annual debt service for the general obligation bond issues for the year 19X3 is shown in Exhibit 6, which shows the annual debt service on the general obligation bonds accounted for through the general long-term debt account group separately from the annual debt service on the general obligation bonds serviced through the Water and Sewer Enterprise Fund.

Exhibit 5
Illustrative Statistical Table with Respect to Past Annual Debt Service for General Obligation Bond Issues Outstanding as of the End of the Current Fiscal Year, Relative to General Governmental Expenditures

NAME OF GOVERNMENT

RATIO OF ANNUAL DEBT SERVICE EXPENDITURES FOR GENERAL BONDED DEBT TO TOTAL GENERAL EXPENDITURES

Last Ten Fiscal Years

Fiscal Year	Principal	Interest	Total debt service	Total general expenditures(1)	Ratio of debt service to total general expenditures
19W3	$60,000	$42,000	$102,000	$1,304,100	7.8%
19W4	60,000	40,200	100,200	1,430,700	7.0
19W5	60,000	38,400	98,400	1,533,200	6.4
19W6	60,000	36,600	96,600	1,625,600	5.9
19W7	60,000	34,800	94,800	1,689,800	5.6
19W8	60,000	33,000	93,000	1,798,000	5.2
19W9	60,000	31,200	91,200	1,951,300	4.7
19X0	60,000	29,400	89,400	2,113,900	4.2
19X1	60,000	27,600	87,600	2,219,280	3.9
19X2	60,000	25,800	85,800	2,403,350	3.6

Note:
(1) Includes General, Special Revenue, and Debt Service Funds.

Source: Municipal Finance Officers Association, *Governmental Accounting, Auditing, and Financial Reporting (1980 GAAFR)* (Chicago: MFOA, 1980), Appendix D, p. 216.

Exhibit 6
Calculation of Annual Debt Service for Fiscal Year 19X3 for General Obligation Bonds

General Obligation Bonds	Balances 12/31/19X2	Interest Rates	Annual Debt Service		
			Interest	Principal	Total
Street, bridge, and drainage improvements	$ 800,000	3%	$24,000	$ 80,000	$104,000
Civic center	700,000	4	28,000	35,000	63,000
Recreation center	200,000	5	10,000	10,000	20,000
General long-term debt	1,700,000		62,000	125,000	187,000
Waterworks	700,000	4	28,000	50,000	78,000
General Obligation	$2,400,000		$90,000	$175,000	$265,000

Balancing Accounts for the General Long-Term Debt Account Group

Let us look once more at the illustrative combined balance sheet shown as Exhibit 1 in Appendix G and at the general long-term debt account group shown therein. The liability side of this account group has been examined in some detail. However, the balancing accounts have not as yet been reviewed.

There are two balancing accounts shown under "assets" in the general long-term debt account group in the combined balance sheet. Even though these two accounts are listed in the assets section, neither account, in fact, represents an *asset* as that term is usually defined. The two accounts are: (1) "amount available in debt service funds" with a balance of $12,572 at the end of the current fiscal year and (2) "amounts to be provided for the retirement of general long-term debt" with a balance of $1,687,428 as of the end of the current fiscal year. The two figures in these accounts total to the liability figure of $1.7 million for the general long-term debt account group. The two accounts are *not* asset accounts, but are simply *balancing* accounts so that the general long-term debt account group would be a self-balancing set of accounts.

The balance of $12,572 shown in amounts available in debt service funds is, in fact, equal to the total amount shown in the reserved fund balances for the two debt service funds. This can be checked out by looking at the illustrative combining balance sheet for the debt service funds shown in Exhibit 4. This means that the two balancing accounts in the general long-term debt account group will show simply the financial resources available to service general long-term debt that have been accumulated in debt service funds and the amount of financial resources that remain to be accumulated to service general long-term debt. Thus, one is forewarned to scrutinize any combined balance sheet for a governmental unit so as to be sure of the meaning and content of any of the so-called asset, liability, or equity accounts that appear in such a financial statement. Later on, we shall take a closer look at the combined balance sheet that appears in Appendix G.

An Overview of Accounting for General Long-Term Debt

In view of the relatively complex methods of accounting for general long-term debt, it might be useful to have an overview of accounting for such debt. Earlier, in Figure 1, an overview of accounting for general fixed assets was provided. Now, in Figure 2, there is an analogous overview of accounting for general long-term debt.

FINANCIAL STATEMENTS FOR FINANCIAL AND REAL ACTIVITIES

Resource Inflow and Outflow Concepts

The basic financial statement that has been subjected to major review and discussion so far, with a few exceptions, has been the balance sheet that reports on financial condition as of a given date. In the case of the expendable funds, there is a second basic financial

Figure 2
Accounting for General Long-Term Debt*

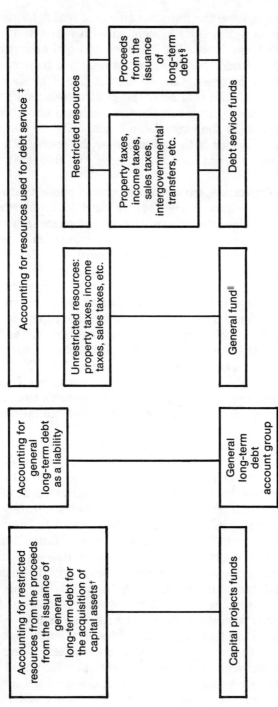

*General long-term debt does not include fund long-term debt. Fund long-term debt covers long-term debt of special assessment funds, enterprise funds, pension trust funds, and nonexpendable trust funds. In the language of *NCGA Statement 1*, fund long-term debt refers to long-term debt owed to parties external to the governmental unit and accounted for by a fund of that unit.

†"Acquisition of capital assets" covers both capital assets acquired by purchase and capital assets constructed by or for the governmental unit.

‡Debt service covers the payment of interest and principal.

§Refers to refunding issues of general long-term debt.

‖According to *1980 GAAFR* (p. 43), *NCGA Statement 1* permits the direct payment of interest and principal of general long-term debt out of unrestricted resources to be accounted for through the general fund. This is stated to be a change from the accounting procedure set out in *1968 GAAFR*.

statement, which reports on the financial effects of real activities and on financial activities not directly associated with real activities accounted for through these funds. The financial and real activities are reported on over the course of a fiscal period from one balance sheet date to the next balance sheet date. Thus, the financial statement that reports on financial and real activities can be seen as a kind of link between one balance sheet and the next balance sheet. *NCGA Statement 1,* in the case of the expendable funds, calls the statement that reports on the activities of these funds over the course of a fiscal period the "statement of revenues, expenditures, and changes in fund balance."

The statement of revenues, expenditures, and changes in fund balance tracks financial resource inflows and outflows for an expendable fund. There are four major categories of financial resource inflows and outflows for an expendable fund. Two of these categories appear in the title of the statement: revenues and expenditures. *Revenues,* a major financial resource inflow category, is defined in *1980 GAAFR* (Appendix B) for an expendable fund as "increases in governmental fund-type net current assets from other than expenditure refunds and residual equity transfers. Under *NCGA Statement 1,* general long-term debt proceeds and operating transfers-in are classified as 'other financing sources' rather than revenues" (p. 72). *Expenditures* is a major financial resources outflow category. In *1980 GAAFR* (Appendix B), it is defined as "decreases in net financial resources. Expenditures include current operating expenses which require the current or future use of net current assets, debt service, and capital outlays" (p. 62).

The second major category of financial resources inflows for an expendable fund is *other financing sources.* This category is defined in *1980 GAAFR* (Appendix B) as "governmental fund general long-term debt proceeds, operating transfers-out, and material proceeds of fixed asset dispositions. Such amounts are to be classified separately from revenues" (p. 69). The definition should have referred to "operating transfers-in" rather than to "operating transfers-out." Since "other financing sources" is a major financial resource inflow category, it would follow that *other financing uses* would be a major financial resources outflows category. In *1980 GAAFR* (Appendix B), this category is defined as "governmental fund operating transfers-out. Such amounts are classified separately from expenditures" (p. 69).

In the definitions of the four major categories of financial resources inflows and outflows, the concepts of operating transfers-in and operating transfers-out show up repeatedly. In order to understand those concepts, one needs to get a sense of the concepts associated with the different types of transfers between funds. The concept of transfers between funds was not incorporated explicitly into the fund accounting framework of *1968 GAAFR*. In fact, the notion of different types of transfers between funds appears in the audit (and accounting) manual discussed in earlier chapters, *Audits of State and Local Governmental Units*.[12] Under the impetus of the audit manual, *NCGA Statement 1* introduced the notion of transfers between funds in a number of different guises. The motivation behind the need to account separately for various kinds of transfers between funds appears to reside in a desire to distinguish between those transactions which are, in a sense, internal to a governmental unit and those that are between the governmental unit and external parties.

Interfund transactions are defined in *1980 GAAFR* as "transactions between funds of the same government. They include (1) quasi-external transactions, (2) reimbursements, (3) residual equity transfers, and (4) operating transfers."[13] Each of these different types of interfund transactions should be defined in turn. Quasi-external transactions are defined as "interfund transactions that would be treated as revenues, expenditures, or expenses if they involved organizations *external* to the governmental unit—e.g., payments in lieu of taxes from an enterprise fund to the general fund; internal service fund billings to departments; routine employer contributions from the general fund to a pension trust fund; and routine service charges for inspection engineering, utilities, or similar services provided by a department financed by one fund to a department financed from another fund—should be accounted for as revenues, expenditures, or expenses in the funds involved."[14] Reimbursements are defined as "(1) repayments of amounts remitted on behalf of another party; (2) interfund transactions which constitute reimbursements of a fund for expenditures or expenses initially made from it which are properly applicable to another fund—e.g., an expenditure properly chargeable to a special revenue fund was initially made from the general fund, which is subsequently reimbursed. They are recorded as expenditures or expenses (as appropriate) in the reimbursing fund and as reductions of the expenditure or expense in the fund that is reimbursed."[15]

Residual equity transfers are defined as "nonrecurring or nonroutine transfers of equity between funds—e.g., contributions of enterprise fund or internal service fund capital by the general fund, subsequent return of all or part of such contribution to the general fund,

---

[12]American Institute of Certified Public Accountants, Committee on Govermental Accounting and Auditing, *Audits of State and Local Governmental Units (ASLGU)*, 2d ed. (Industry Audit Guide) (New York: AICPA, 1974 and 1978).

[13]MFOA, *1980 GAAFR,* Appendix B, p. 65.

[14]Ibid., p. 70.

[15]Ibid., p. 71.

and transfers of residual balances of discontinued funds to the general fund or a debt service fund."[16] Finally, we have the definition of operating transfers as "all interfund transfers other than residual equity transfers—e.g., legally authorized transfers from a fund receiving revenue to the fund through which the resources are to be expended, transfers of tax revenues from a special revenue fund to a debt service fund, transfers from the general fund to a special revenue fund or capital projects fund, operating subsidy transfers from the general or a special revenue fund to an enterprise fund, and transfers from an enterprise fund other than payments in lieu of taxes to finance general fund expenditures."[17] Note that operating transfers refer to all interfund transfers other than residual equity transfers. We have defined interfund transactions, but we have not defined interfund transfers. In *1980 GAAFR,* interfund transfers are defined simply as "see residual equity transfers and operating transfers."[18] Well, it seems that there is a bit of circularity in the definitions of operating transfers and interfund transfers. However, if one concentrates on the examples given for operating transfers, then one gets a sense of the nature of this concept. In addition, a review of the other types of interfund transactions such as quasi-external transactions, reimbursements, and residual equity transfers will help one get a better idea of what operating transfers are and are not.

Expendable Funds—Illustrative Financial Statements

Now that we have had a chance to review various inflow and outflow concepts used in the financial statements covering real and financial activities for the expendable funds, we should look at illustrative financial statements using these concepts. In Exhibit 7, we have an illustrative hypothetical statement of revenues, expenditures, and changes in fund balance, for the general fund, with a comparison between a GAAP basis budget and actual.

Into the illustrative financial statement in Exhibit 7, one sees incorporated the basic concepts for the inflow and outflow of resources. This statement functions not only to report on actual resource inflows and outflows, but on expected inflows and planned outflows. The comparison between budgeted and actual for the general fund satisfies requirement 3 of basic principle IX in *NCGA Statement 1.*[19] Remember that the general fund accounts basically for the receipt and use of unrestricted financial resources.

---

[16]Ibid., p. 72.
[17]Ibid., p. 69.
[18]Ibid., p. 65.
[19]In Appendix A of Chapter 36.

Exhibit 7
Illustrative Hypothetical Statement of Revenues, Expenditures, and Changes in Fund Balance, with a Comparison between a GAAP Basis Budget and Actual: The General Fund

NAME OF GOVERNMENT
GENERAL FUND

STATEMENT OF REVENUES, EXPENDITURES, AND
CHANGES IN FUND BALANCE—BUDGET (GAAP BASIS) AND ACTUAL

Year Ended December 31, 19X2
With Comparative Actual Amounts for Year Ended December 31, 19X1

	19X2			19X1
	Budget	Actual	Variance—favorable (unfavorable)	Actual
Revenues:				
Taxes	$ 848,000	$ 846,800	$ (1,200)	$ 790,965
Licenses and permits	125,500	103,000	(22,500)	96,500
Intergovernmental	234,500	186,500	(48,000)	166,110
Charges for services	90,000	91,000	1,000	88,980
Fines and forfeits	32,500	33,200	700	26,300
Miscellaneous	19,500	18,000	(1,500)	14,256
Total revenues	1,350,000	1,278,500	(71,500)	1,183,111
Expenditures:				
General government	129,000	121,805	7,195	134,200
Public safety	277,300	258,395	18,905	257,260
Highways and streets	84,500	85,400	(900)	62,286
Sanitation	50,000	56,250	(6,250)	44,100
Health	47,750	44,500	3,250	36,600
Welfare	51,000	46,800	4,200	41,400
Culture and recreation	44,500	40,900	3,600	47,981
Education	541,450	509,150	32,300	509,960
Total expenditures	1,225,500	1,163,200	62,300	1,133,787
Excess (deficiency) of revenues over expenditures	124,500	115,300	(9,200)	49,324
Other financing sources (uses):				
Operating transfers out	(74,500)	(74,500)	—	(87,000)
Excess (deficiency) of revenues over expenditures and other uses	50,000	40,800	(9,200)	37,676
Fund balances at beginning of year	202,500	202,500	—	240,176
Increase in reserve for inventory	—	1,500	1,500	—
Fund balances at end of year	$ 252,500	$ 244,800	$ (7,700)	$ 202,500

See accompanying notes to financial statements

Source: Municipal Finance Officers Association, *Governmental Accounting, Auditing, and Financial Reporting (1980 GAAFR)* (Chicago: MFOA, 1980), Appendix D, p. 145.

The financial inflows derive from such tax sources as property taxes, income taxes, sales taxes, and taxes on gross business receipts. Other revenue sources are intergovernmental revenues, licenses, permits, fines, etc. The revenue sources that stem from nonuser charges are designed to generate financial resources to finance the real activities of a governmental unit in the form of nonmarket public goods.[20]

---

[20]See the discussion of the characteristics of nonmarket public goods in Chapter 35 and in appendixes A and B of that chapter.

Real activities of a governmental unit also result in the supply of market-type goods and services which should be accounted for primarily through proprietary funds.

However, it appears that some market-type goods and services are supplied by the government and accounted for through the general fund. This can be seen from the revenue category "charges for services." The category covers some charges that would be considered user charges and other charges that are not user charges but really taxes. A true user charge would constitute a price for a marketable good or service to someone who purchases the good or service voluntarily. Specifically, the user purchases a clearly identified number of units of the good or service. Some of the charges for services are really analogous to the special assessment taxes discussed earlier. These are not user charges, but taxes that are based on the benefit principle of taxation. See the earlier discussion on municipal nonmarket public goods.[21]

A major outflow category is expenditures. Expenditures are classified by broad "functional" categories. Expenditures could also be classified by "object of expenditure." Both concepts were discussed earlier.[22] These expenditures cover financial outflows associated with real activities of the governmental unit. In the case of the general fund, the real activities involve the supply of nonmarket public goods.

In addition to the two major inflow–outflow categories of revenues and expenditures, the illustrative statement shows also the other two major inflow–outflow categories: other financing sources and other financing uses. These two categories are shown together and actually reduce to the single outflow category, other financing uses, since the item described under the category is "operating transfers-out." The amount of the operating transfers-out is $74,500. Where did the $74,500 go? Operating transfers-out are an interfund transaction— i.e., a transaction internal to the governmental unit. The general fund has transferred financial resources to other funds, but which other funds?

We can clear this matter up by looking at another statement of revenues, expenditures, and changes in fund balance, but not from the point of view of the individual fund. We will look not at a combining statement, which brings together different funds of a particular fund type into one statement, but at the combined financial statement. The combined financial statement at which we need to look is the "Combined Statement of Revenues, Expenditures, and Changes

---

[21]Ibid.

[22]In the section on "Budgeting and Fund Accounting" in *Chapter 36,* is a discussion of: (1) broad "functional" categories for the classification of budgeted and actual expenditures and (2) "object of expenditure" categories for the classification of budgeted and actual expenditures.

in Fund Balances—All Governmental Fund Types and Expendable Trust Funds" shown as Exhibit 2 in Appendix G. Sure enough, one finds $74,500 of transfers-in in the combined statement to match the $74,500 of transfers-out from the general fund. The transfers-in are shown in the amount of $64,500 for the capital projects funds, and $10,000 for the special assessments funds.

There is one other item that appears in Exhibit 7 separate and apart from the four categories of resources inflows and outflows. Near the bottom of this statement we find in the actual column $1,500 described as "increase in inventory" being added to the actual fund balance of the general fund. Recall that, in an operating expendable fund such as the general fund, inventory (which is not an expendable financial resource) nevertheless is shown among the assets of the fund. In order that the unreserved fund balance show *net* financial resources, the fund balance has to be reserved in an amount equal to the amount of the inventory shown as an asset. The increase in this reserve by $1,500 must mean that the associated asset account—inventory—must have increased by $1,500 for the year. This can be seen in the illustrative comparative balance sheet for the general fund shown earlier.[23]

Earlier in this chapter, we referred also to other examples of the statement of revenues, expenditures, and changes in fund balance. These earlier examples were combining statements that bring together all of the funds of a given fund type into a single financial statement. The earlier combining financial statements to which we referred were for capital projects funds (Exhibit 2) and debt service funds (Exhibit 3). The capital projects funds account for financial resources associated with *real* activities. The debt service funds account for basically financial resources associated with *financial* activities. The inflow and outflow categories used for the general fund also appear in the statements for the capital projects and debt service funds.

Sources and Uses Financial Statements

The general fund accounts basically for current assets and current liabilities. This means that the unreserved part of its fund balance essentially represents net current assets in the form of expendable financial resources. This means that the statement of revenues, expenditures, and changes in fund balance is essentially a statement that tracks changes in current assets and current liabilities, and the current assets are basically expendable financial resources. Thus, "revenues" represents certain kinds of sources for financial resources; "expenditures" represents certain kinds of uses of financial resources.

---

[23]Exhibit 2 of Chapter 37.

The other two major categories of resource inflows-outflows are also sources and uses. In effect, the statement that accounts for and reports on the activity of the general fund over a fiscal period is nothing but a "sources and uses of financial resources" statement. In commercial accounting, this would be known simply as a "sources and uses of funds financial statement"; however, that name would be confusing for governmental accounting because the notion of "funds" refers to fiscal and accounting entities.

In fact, all of the expendable fund types account essentially for expendable financial resources, so that the statement of revenues, expenditures, and changes in fund balance for these fund types would be considered a sources and uses of financial resources financial statement. By the way, the statement of revenues, expenditures, and changes in fund balance could just as easily have been called the statement of revenues, expenditures, other financing sources and uses, and changes in fund balance, which would have made it relatively clear that one was dealing with a sources and uses financial statement. The alternative name was not chosen, I assume, because of its length; the basic name is long enough.

Proprietary Funds and Other Nonexpendable Funds

In the case of expendable funds, there was one basic statement to report on the activities of the fund over the course of a fiscal period. In the case of proprietary funds, pension trust funds, and nonexpendable trust funds, there are two basic types of financial statements to report on the activities of these fund types over the course of a fiscal period. These fund types account both for real and financial resources. One of the basic financial statements primarily tracks the real activities of the fund over the course of the fiscal period. This statement is called the "statement of revenues, expenses, and changes in retained earnings" for the proprietary funds. For the pension trust and nonexpendable trust funds, the statement is called the "statement of revenues, expenses, and changes in fund balances." In Exhibit 8, we have a statement of revenues, expenses, and changes in retained earnings for the Water and Sewer Enterprise Fund in comparative format. This statement is prepared from the point of view of an individual fund. In Exhibit 9, we have a combining statement of revenues, expenses, and changes in funds balances for pension trust and nonexpendable trust funds. This statement is a type of combining statement for all of the fiduciary funds that are subject to the accrual basis.

The basic financial statements shown in Exhibits 8 and 9 are not statements that report on sources and uses of financial resources. Instead of *expenditures,* these statements use *expenses.* While expenditures represent a use of financial resources, expenses are an estimate

Exhibit 8
**Illustrative Hypothetical Statement
of Revenues, Expenses, and
Changes in Retained Earnings for
an Enterprise Fund**

NAME OF GOVERNMENT
WATER AND SEWER ENTERPRISE FUND

COMPARATIVE STATEMENT OF REVENUES,
EXPENSES, AND CHANGES IN RETAINED EARNINGS

Year Ended December 31, 19X2 and 19X1

	19X2	19X1
Operating revenues—		
charges for services	$ 672,150	$ 603,563
Operating expenses:		
Personal services	247,450	219,718
Contractual services	75,330	67,614
Supplies	20,310	15,629
Materials	50,940	47,644
Heat, light, and power	26,050	21,475
Depreciation	144,100	129,010
Total operating expenses	564,180	501,090
Operating income	107,970	102,473
Nonoperating revenues (expenses):		
Operating grants	55,000	50,000
Tap fees	22,000	20,000
Interest	3,830	3,200
Rent	5,000	5,000
Interest and fiscal charges	(78,888)	(122,408)
Total	6,942	(44,208)
Net income	114,912	(58,265)
Retained earnings at beginning of year	2,088,544	2,030,279
Retained earnings at end of year	$2,203,456	$2,088,544

See accompanying notes to financial statements

Source: Municipal Finance Officers Association, *Governmental Accounting, Auditing, and Financial Reporting (1980 GAAFR)* (Chicago: MFOA, 1980), Appendix D, p. 189.

of the consumption of real resources used in operations during a fiscal period. The goods and services supplied are of the marketable variety. This means that revenues are generated from user charges. It also means that the accrual basis of accounting, rather than the modified accrual basis, is relevant to the recognition of revenues.[24] The subtraction of expenditures from revenues, in the case of an expendable fund, measures increases or decreases in financial resources. The subtraction of expenses from revenues of a nonexpendable fund supplying market-type goods and services is a measure of the net income

---

[24]See the discussion of the accrual basis of accounting versus the modified accrual basis in the context of nonmarket public goods versus marketable goods in Chapter 35.

Exhibit 9
Illustrative Hypothetical Combining Statement of Revenues, Expenses, and Changes in Fund Balances for Pension Trust and Nonexpendable Trust Funds

NAME OF GOVERNMENT
PENSION TRUST AND NONEXPENDABLE TRUST FUNDS

COMBINING STATEMENT OF REVENUES, EXPENSES,
AND CHANGES IN FUND BALANCES

Year Ended December 31, 19X2
With Comparative Totals for Year Ended December 31, 19X1

| | Pension Trust Fund | | Nonexpendable Trust Funds | | | |
| | Employees' Retirement System | | Endowment principal | Revolving loan | Totals | |
	19X2	19X1			19X2	19X1
Operating revenues:						
Interest	$ 28,460	$ 23,973	$ 2,530	$ (50)	$ 2,480	$ 2,145
Contributions	160,686	144,670	—	—	—	—
Gifts	—	—	40,000	5,000	45,000	—
Total operating revenues	189,146	168,643	42,530	4,950	47,480	2,145
Operating expenses:						
Benefit payments	21,000	12,000	—	—	—	—
Refunds	25,745	13,243	—	—	—	—
Total operating expenses	46,745	25,243	—	—	—	—
Income before operating transfers	142,401	143,400	42,530	4,950	47,480	2,145
Operating transfers (out)	—	—	(2,530)	—	(2,530)	(2,120)
Net income	142,401	143,400	40,000	4,950	44,950	25
Fund balances at beginning of year	1,040,800	897,400	94,000	45,100	139,100	139,075
Fund balances at end of year	$1,183,201	$1,040,800	$ 134,000	$ 50,050	$ 184,050	$ 139,100

See accompanying notes to financial statements

Source: Municipal Finance Officers Association, *Governmental Accounting, Auditing, and Financial Reporting (1980 GAAFR)* (Chicago: MFOA, 1980), Appendix D, p. 199.

generated from the supply of such goods and services. "Net income" is an attempt to measure the impact of real operating activities on the equity of a nonexpendable fund when such a fund carries both financial and real resources.

Nonexpendable funds carry fixed assets, where such assets are used in the operations accounted for by the fund. If fixed assets are used in operations, then depreciation expense is taken on such fixed assets. Earlier we had noted difficulties associated with depreciation accounting.[25] In any case, net income as shown in the financial statements in exhibits 8 and 9 is essentially what one would expect in commercial accounting.

One of the nonexpendable trust funds shown in the financial statement of Exhibit 9 does not quite fit the mold of a commercial activity.

---

[25]There is a considerable accounting literature on the difficulties associated with the estimation of net income. The quotation at the start of Chapter 35 is intended to forewarn the unwary.

The major part of what are described as revenues were derived by the nonexpendable endowment trust fund from gifts and *not* from user charges. Gifts are shown in the amount of $40,000. The interest earned of $2,530 from the investments of this fund would represent revenue from user charges. The user is the party that has the use of the invested funds, and the user charge is the interest paid for the use of the invested funds.

Total revenues from gifts and interest income amount to $42,530. No expenses are shown, but the $2,530 is shown as deducted from revenues as an operating transfer-out. The nonexpendable fund is shown with what is described as net income, in the amount of $40,000, which is simply the revenues from gifts. Where has the $2,530 gone? Why has it gone? Why aren't any expenses deducted in arriving at net income?

The justification for transferring the $2,530 of financial resources realized from the interest earnings would have to be found in the trust agreement that established the nonexpendable endowment trust fund. One can speculate; but it would seem that, while the principal of this particular trust arrangement is nonexpendable, the agreement must provide that the income from principal is expendable. Of course, this could only be confirmed if a disclosure in the financial statements specified that income from the nonexpendable endowment trust fund is to be treated as expendable. The illustrative financial statements are assumed to have been subjected to independent audit, so that one would assume that the auditors have confirmed the proper handling of endowment investment income as an expendable resource.

If the endowment investment income is expendable, then one should expect an expendable trust fund to show an operating transfer-in of $2,350. This information would most likely appear in the combining statement of revenues, expenditures, and changes in fund balances for the expendable trust funds. Such a statement has not been included. However, with some luck, the same information might also appear in the "Combined Statement of Revenues, Expenditures, and Changes in Fund Balances—All Fund Types and Account Groups" shown as Exhibit 2 in Appendix G. This assumes that the figure shown as operating transfers-in for the expendable trust funds shows just the $2,530 and that the $2,530 has not been merged together with some other operating transfers-in. Sure enough, we do find in the combined financial statement in Exhibit 2 in Appendix G that operating transfers-in for the expendable trust funds is shown at $2,530.

One can also answer the question as to why no expenses are shown in the nonexpendable endowment trust fund. The principal of each endowment in that fund must be kept intact. Expenses will be charged against expendable endowment income. That income is accounted for in a separate expendable trust fund; therefore, expenses will be charged in that fund against the endowment income that has been transferred to that fund. In the expendable trust fund, expenses will be described as expenditures because expendable financial resources are used.

One should note that the contributions shown as revenue in the pension trust fund in Exhibit 9 do not refer to contributions in the sense of gifts or donations. In nonprofit accounting, contributions refer to gifts or donations; but in pension fund accounting, contributions refer to payments by both employers and employees to help finance employee retirement benefits. Thus, contributions used in pension accounting represent payments in exchange for expected retirement benefits. Retirement benefits are a marketable good, and the payments for such benefits would be in the nature of user charges.

One can argue that the statements shown in Exhibits 8 and 9 are similar to a statement of net income and retained earnings for a commercial enterprise, so that this name could have been used for these statements. However, it can also be argued that the activities accounted for by proprietary funds, nonexpendable trust funds, and pension trust funds are not organized to be primarily profit seeking and profit maximizing, but instead can be viewed in that indeterminate zone between profit-seeking enterprises and not-for-profit entities. This may be the reason that the authors of *NCGA Statement 1* did not call the statements of Exhibits 8 and 9 a statement of net income and retained earnings, but adopted the strategy of calling them a statement of revenues, expenses, etc.

There is still a third type of basic financial statement applicable to the proprietary funds, pension trust funds, and nonexpendable trust funds. This is the statement that reflects sources and uses of financial resources resulting from both real and financial activities. In Exhibit 10 we show a statement of changes in financial position for an enterprise fund from the point of view of an individual fund. In Exhibit 11 we have a combining statement that brings together those fiduciary funds that are subject to the accrual basis of accounting. The statement of changes in financial position does not introduce any new concepts from governmental accounting that have not been covered earlier.

GENERAL PURPOSE FINANCIAL STATEMENTS

The financial statements that are intended to provide an overview of the financial condition and the real and financial activities of a state or local governmental unit, according to *NCGA Statement 1*, are called "general purpose financial statements" (GPFS). In fact, the

Exhibit 10
Illustrative Hypothetical Statement of Changes in Financial Position for an Enterprise Fund

NAME OF GOVERNMENT
WATER AND SEWER ENTERPRISE FUND

COMPARATIVE STATEMENT OF CHANGES
IN FINANCIAL POSITION

Year Ended December 31, 19X2 and 19X1

	19X2	19X1
Sources of working capital:		
Operations:		
Net income	$ 114,912	$ 58,265
Item not requiring working capital—depreciation	144,100	129,010
Working capital provided by operations	259,012	187,275
Contributions by subdividers	650,666	—
Net decrease in restricted assets	110,515	743,386
Total sources of working capital	1,020,193	930,661
Uses of working capital:		
Acquisition of fixed assets	324,453	841,812
Decrease in long-term general obligation bonds payable	50,000	50,000
Decrease in long-term revenue bonds payable	48,000	44,000
Net decrease in current liabilities payable from restricted assets	143,345	4,318
Total uses of working capital	565,798	940,130
Net increase (decrease) in working capital	$ 454,395	(9,469)
Elements of net increase (decrease) in net working capital:		
Cash	$ 141,536	$ 576,361
Receivables (net)	(10,570)	2,396
Due from other funds	(6,000)	(11,323)
Inventory	11,250	5,286
Prepaid expenses	460	520
Vouchers payable	(72,471)	(46,087)
Contracts payable	388,250	(525,400)
Accrued general obligation bond interest	100	200
Other accrued expenses	1,840	(11,422)
Net increase (decrease) in working capital	$ 454,395	$ 9,469

See accompanying notes to financial statements

Source: Municipal Finance Officers Association, *Governmental Accounting, Auditing, and Financial Reporting (1980 GAAFR)* (Chicago: MFOA, 1980), Appendix D, p. 190.

GPFS are intended by *NCGA Statement 1* to be able to stand on their own, separate and apart from the individual fund statements or the combining statements. The GPFS are supported by a set of notes to the financial statements, considered to be an integral part of the GPFS; the GPFS would be considered incomplete without the accompanying notes.

The GPFS focus primarily on the combined financial statements, which bring together in a single financial statement the combining and/or individual fund financial statements for the different fund types. In the case of one of the combined financial statements, even the account groups are included in the statement. There are six com-

Exhibit 11
Illustrative Hypothetical Combining Statement of Changes in Financial Position for Pension Trust and Nonexpendable Trust Funds

NAME OF GOVERNMENT
PENSION TRUST AND NONEXPENDABLE TRUST FUNDS

COMBINING STATEMENT OF CHANGES IN FINANCIAL POSITION

Year Ended December 31, 19X2
With Comparative Totals for Year Ended December 31, 19X1

| | Pension Trust Fund | | Nonexpendable Trust Funds | | | |
| | Pension Retirement System | | Endowment principal | Revolving loan | Totals | |
	19X2	19X1			19X2	19X1
Sources of working capital:						
Operations—net income	$ 142,401	$143,400	$ 40,000	$ 4,950	$ 44,950	$25
Investments maturing	25,000	20,000	—	—	—	—
Total sources of working capital	167,401	163,400	40,000	4,950	44,950	25
Uses of working capital—						
Purchase of investments	145,360	131,000	—	—	—	—
Net increase in working capital	$ 22,041	32,400	40,000	4,950	44,950	25
Elements of net increase (decrease) in working capital:						
Cash	$ 20,121	$ 28,619	$ (690)	$ 5,000	$ 4,310	$25
Investments	(2,019)	821	40,550	(50)	40,500	—
Receivables	—	—	520	—	520	—
Due from other funds	2,189	2,100	—	—	—	—
Vouchers payable	1,750	860	—	—	—	—
Accrued liabilities	—	—	(380)	—	(380)	—
Net increase in working capital	$ 22,041	$ 32,400	$ 40,000	$ 4,950	$ 44,950	$25

See accompanying notes to financial statements

Source: Municipal Finance Officers Association, *Governmental Accounting, Auditing, and Financial Reporting (1980 GAAFR)* (Chicago: MFOA, 1980), Appendix D, p. 200.

bined financial statements. A list of the six combined financial statements that make up the GPFS appears at the beginning of Appendix G. The six statements will be reviewed and discussed as appropriate.

Combined Balance Sheet

The first and most comprehensive of the GPFS is the "combined balance sheet—all fund types and account groups." This balance sheet brings together in a single financial statement the assets, liabilities, and fund equities of all of the different fund types and also the account groups of a governmental unit. Recall that an account group has, on one side, a set of balancing accounts rather than assets, liabilities, or fund equities. The combined balance sheet for all of the fund types and account groups is shown as Exhibit 1 in Appendix G.

One can actually trace figures appearing in the combined balance sheet back to the place where these same figures would appear: (1) in a particular individual fund balance sheet if there is only one fund for a particular fund type or (2) in a particular combining balance sheet if there is more than one fund for a particular fund type. For example, in the case of the general fund, the total assets figure shown in the column for the general fund in the combined balance sheet of Exhibit 1 of Appendix G is $494,350. Now, if we return to the individual fund balance sheet for the general fund in Exhibit 2 of Chapter 37, we will find the same total assets figure of $494,350. One can trace each of the asset figures appearing for the general fund in its column in the combined balance sheet back to the individual balance sheet for this fund. The same matching of figures from the combined balance sheet can be traced back to the individual fund balances for the liabilities and components of fund equity (the fund balance) of the general fund.

The various types of assets, liabilities, and components of the fund balance (fund equity) of the general fund were discussed earlier. There is no need to repeat that discussion. However, one should remind oneself of some of the problems noted with respect to the assets, liabilities, and components of the fund balance. Assets and liabilities are not classified as between current and noncurrent. Even though the general fund carries basically current assets and current liabilities in its balance sheet, if you don't apply this distinction between current and noncurrent to this fund in the combined balance sheet, then you won't be able to apply the distinction to the other fund types that do carry significant amounts of noncurrent assets and noncurrent liabilities, and where the separate presentation of current from noncurrent assets and liabilities would be useful. Real resources such as prepaid expenses and inventory can appear as assets even though the general fund is an expendable fund composed of expendable financial resources. Investments are shown at cost with no provision for an additional disclosure for their market value.

Liabilities for the noncurrent portion of accumulated unpaid employee benefits such as vacation and sick pay are not reported directly as part of general fund liabilities. A separate disclosure in the notes to the financial statements is required when the accumulated unpaid benefits pass a threshold amount. Earlier, we noted that accounting and reporting for vacation pay and sick leave benefits has been modified somewhat by *NCGA Statement 4*. The current portion of the economic obligation of the governmental unit for accumulated pension fund benefits is not necessarily shown in its entirety as a liability from the general fund to the pension trust fund that accounts for a public employee retirement system. The amount shown in Exhibit 2 of Chapter 37 and Exhibit 1 of Appendix G for "deferred revenue" at $49,500 is partially composed of a part that can be considered an economic obligation, but the other part is not an economic obligation at all. Part of deferred revenue is a liability, and part of it is something else again. This issue was considered in detail earlier.

In the case of the special revenue fund, we have a number of such

funds, so that one matches the figures in the combining balance sheet
for this fund type with the figures in the combined balance sheet. For
example, the total for the assets for the special revenue funds in their
column in the combined balance sheet is $224,860. In Exhibit 3 of
Chapter 37, we have a combining balance sheet for the special revenue funds. The total assets figure appearing in the total column as of
the end of the current fiscal year is once again $224,860. We have our
match. Each of the asset, liability, and fund balance figures that appear in the total column (for the current fiscal year) in the combining
balance sheet match up with the figures appearing in the combined
balance sheet in the column for the special revenue funds. Once
again, we have a deferred revenue item shown for the special revenue
funds. Whether or not it contains any amounts that are not economic
obligations is not disclosed.

In Exhibit 4 of Chapter 37, we have a combining balance sheet for
the special assessment funds. The same matching of assets, liabilities,
and components of fund equity (the fund balance), between the combined balance sheet and the combining balance sheet, can be done for
this fund type as for the fund types already discussed. One should
mention that, on the combined balance sheet, the asset for special
assessments receivable is a single figure that is made up of four separate figures for these receivables appearing in the combining balance sheet. Special assessments receivables, unlike other types of receivables, are not reduced for the amount estimated to be
uncollectible. Uncollectible special assessments receivables, if not recovered from liens against the properties subject to the special assessments, normally would be made up by the governmental unit out of
general revenues if additional resources are needed to cover such
items as construction costs or debt service on special assessment
bonds.

As noted for the general fund, and applicable also to the special
revenue funds, etc., there is no classification as between current and
noncurrent assets or liabilities for this fund even though noncurrent
assets and noncurrent liabilities are quite significant. The amount
shown as deferred revenue is *not* a liability since it isn't an economic
obligation of the special assessment fund, but is in fact an economic
obligation of taxpayers and their properties subject to the special assessments. The major liability of the noncurrent variety for this fund
is represented by special assessment bonds. Discussed earlier were
the problems of interpretation and of the deficit position in the overall
fund balance created by the accounting and reporting treatment of
the deferred special assessment installment as deferred revenue. Assuming the modified accrual basis of accounting for this fund, alternative accounting and reporting treatments also were discussed earlier.

At this point, we should note that some accountants would recognize all of the special assessments, deferred or current portion, as revenue as of the date that the special assessments are levied. This implies that the accrual basis of accounting, rather than the modified accrual basis, should be applied to the special assessment fund. The net effect of each of these alternatives to the approach set out in *1980 GAAFR* would be to avoid treating the deferred installments as though they were liabilities. Also eliminated would be the problem created by showing the fund balance in deficit position in the early years of the fund.

In Exhibit 4 we have a combining balance sheet for the debt service funds. Again assets, liabilities, and components of the fund balance can be matched from the combined balance sheet back to the combining balance sheet. Illustrative balance sheets have been shown for four of the five types of governmental funds (not for the capital projects funds).

In Exhibit 7 of Chapter 37, a combining balance sheet is shown for the fiduciary funds. Once again assets, liabilities, and the components of the fund balances can be traced from the combined balance sheet back to the combining balance sheet. The problems associated with the accounting and reporting treatment of the liabilities of the pension trust fund have been discussed extensively. These problems also spill over into an understatement of the associated current parts of certain liabilities associated with a public employee retirement system (PERS). And in addition, long-term liabilities of the governmental unit associated with a PERS also may be understated in the general long-term debt account group. As for certain other fund types, an appropriate classification between current and noncurrent assets and liabilities for the fiduciary funds could prove useful. Note should be taken also of the fact that there should be a disclosure of whether or not a comprehensive annual financial report (CAFR) is prepared for a PERS.

In Exhibits 10 and 11 of Chapter 37 are individual fund balance sheets for, respectively, an internal service fund and an enterprise fund. The assets, liabilities, and fund equities for each fund can be traced from the combined balance sheet to the individual fund balance sheets. The different types of assets, liabilities, and components of fund equities for these fund types have been reviewed in some depth. On the individual fund balance sheets, assets and liabilities are classified as between current and noncurrent; however, when we turn to the combined balance sheet, this distinction has been lost.

There are some considerations that affect all of the fund types included in the combined balance sheet. For example, investments are carried at cost with no provision for a separate disclosure for market value. There are also various kinds of disclosures in the notes to the financial statements, referred to within the combined balance sheet, that should be reviewed by a user of the general purpose financial statements. For example, information is provided on the additional amount by which property taxes may be raised within legal requirements, usually subject to constitutional limits. Information is provided also with respect to commitments and contingent liabilities.

Lastly, we turn to the two account groups shown in the combined balance sheet. The major significance of the way the two account groups have been included in the combined balance sheet is that each account group has a set of balancing accounts. The balancing accounts introduce a significant distortion into the combined balance sheet. The balancing accounts for the general long-term debt account group are not assets, even though shown as part of the combined assets. These are simply accounts which provide information on the amount of resources that have been accumulated and remain to be accumulated to service the general long-term debt. In a similar vein, one must state that the balancing accounts for the general fixed assets account group are not equity accounts per se. These accounts just provide information on the sources of financial resources used to finance the acquisition of the general fixed assets. This information was set out in the schedule for reporting the general fixed assets and their sources of financing shown in Exhibit 1.

The problem with the meaning of the balancing accounts for the two account groups helps explain in part why the total columns for the current and prior fiscal years in the combined balance sheet are labeled "memorandum only." In fact, under item K of note (1) in *Appendix H,* we find a discussion concerning the total columns in the combined balance sheet. Eliminations of interfund receivables and payables, and interfund transactions in general, are not required by *NCGA Statement 1.* The figures in the total columns in the combined balance sheet are not comparable from one year to the next, nor from one governmental entity to the next.

Could a meaningful set of total columns be produced for the combined balance sheet so that it could be transformed into a consolidated balance sheet? There are a number of accountants who believe that consolidated financial statements are both feasible and desirable for a governmental unit.[26] In *1968 GAAFR,* there was an explicit position against consolidated financial statements for state or local governmental units.[27] *NCGA Statement 1* neither encourages nor discourages consolidated financial statements; it simply does not include

---

[26]See for example, the discussion in Sidney Davidson, David O. Green, Walter Hellerstein, Albert Madansky, and Roman Weil, *Financial Reporting by State and Local Governmental Units* (Chicago: University of Chicago, 1977).

[27]Old NCGA, *1968 GAAFR,* p. 111, argues that "a consolidated balance sheet similar to one for a private business corporation is not satisfactory" in the case of a governmental unit.

them as an explicit part of the financial statements that it does recommend. It encourages "research and experimentation" in the matter of designing financial statements appropriate for state and local governmental units.[28] However, it is not a purpose of this chapter to argue the advantages of significant changes in municipal accounting principles for accounting and reporting.

In any case, it must be stressed that the total "assets" figures that appear in the columns for the current and prior fiscal year in the combined balance sheet cannot be considered meaningful, since they include such items as the figures shown in the balancing accounts for the account groups. In addition, interfund receivables and payables have not been eliminated.

Hypothetical Combined Financial Statements on Real and Financial Activities over the Course of a Fiscal Period

Four of the five other illustrative financial statements taken from *1980 GAAFR* that make up the illustrative GPFS are combined financial statements that report on the real and financial activities of the governmental unit over the course of a fiscal period. In Exhibit 2 of Appendix G, all of the expendable funds have been brought together in a single financial statement that reports on the financial effects of real activities *and* on financial activities. As in the case of the combined balance sheet, the figures appearing in this combined financial statement can be traced back to individual fund or combining financial statements, whichever is appropriate. For example, the individual fund statement in Exhibit 7 of this chapter contains both budgeted and actual figures for revenues, expenditures, and other financing sources (uses) for the general fund. The actual figures for the various revenues, expenditures, etc., can be traced from the combined statement in Exhibit 2 of Appendix G to the combining statement in Exhibit 7.

The budgeted figures for revenues, etc., appearing in the individual fund statement of Exhibit 7 can be matched to figures appearing in still another, third combined financial statement: the "Combined Statement of Revenues, Expenditures, and Changes in Fund Balances—Budget (GAAP Basis) and Actual—General, Special Revenue, and Capital Projects Fund Types," shown in Exhibit 3 in Appendix G. The budget *and* actual revenue, etc., figures that appear in the combined statement in Exhibit 3 can be matched against the figures in the statement in Exhibit 7.

The combined financial statements appearing in Exhibits 2 and 3 of Appendix G can be interpreted to be sources and uses of financial resources statements, which is what they are, for the expendable funds. This interpretation was discussed earlier. Notice also that the combined

---

[28]*NCGA Statement 1*, p. 26.

financial statement of Exhibit 2 has its total columns for the current and prior fiscal years marked "memorandum only," as was done for the combined balance sheet of Exhibit 1. Again we are warned that the total columns for the current and prior fiscal years are not to be interpreted as containing consolidated figures, since appropriate eliminations of intercompany transactions have not been made and are not required to be made by *NCGA Statement 1*. The combined financial statement in Exhibit 3 does not contain total columns.

In Exhibit 5 in Appendix G, we have the "Combined Statement of Revenues, Expenses, and Changes in Retained Earnings/Fund Balances—All Proprietary Fund Types and Similar Trust Funds." This statement brings together in a single combined statement the proprietary funds, the pension trust funds, and the nonexpendable trust funds. As for all of the combined statements, the figures appearing in this combined statement can be matched against figures appearing in individual fund or combined financial statements, whichever is appropriate. Again, the total columns for the current and prior fiscal years are marked "memorandum only."

The combined statement in Exhibit 5 of Appendix G is a statement that matches expenses against revenues so that it is analogous to a net income statement in commercial accounting. The statement also includes changes in retained earnings within its purview so that it is analogous to a statement of net income and retained earnings for a commercial entity. However, recall the earlier caution that enterprise funds, internal service funds, pension trust funds, and nonexpendable trust funds are not primarily profit-seeking and profit-maximizing entities in the same sense as a commercial enterprise.

The final combined financial statement measures sources and uses of financial resources and appears in Exhibit 6 in Appendix G. It is the "Combined Statement of Changes in Financial Position—All Proprietary Fund Types and Similar Trust Funds." As before, the figures in this statement can be matched against figures in individual fund or combining statements of changes in financial position for the proprietary funds and the fiduciary funds subject to the accrual basis of accounting.

In the case of an expendable fund, there is no statement called a statement of changes in financial position at any level, be it at the level of the individual fund, the combining financial statement, or the combined financial statement.

Comparison of Actual and Budget on a Basis Other than GAAP

Another illustrative financial statement included in the illustrative GPFS taken from *1980 GAAFR* is the "Statement of Revenues, Expenditures, and Changes in Fund Balances—Budget (Non-GAAP

Budgetary Basis) and Actual—Special Assessment Fund Type" which is shown in Exhibit 4 of Appendix G. This statement did not appear in *NCGA Statement 1* as one of the basic financial statements described as general purpose financial statements (GPFS). However, *NCGA Statement 1* requires that there be a comparison between actual and the budget on the basis that the budget is prepared even if that accounting basis is not in conformity with GAAP (or what we call MAP) as set out in *NCGA Statement 1.* This means that the actual figures have to be adjusted to the same basis as the budgetary figures so that a meaningful comparison between budget and actual can be carried out. In this illustrative financial statement, we have the budget prepared on a non-GAAP basis. Actual figures in the statement have been adjusted so that they are on the same basis as the budget, so that a meaningful comparison can be made.

Now just why is it that the budget shown in the financial statement of Exhibit 4 of Appendix G is not considered to be, on an accounting basis, consistent with GAAP (or MAP) as set out in *NCGA Statement 1*? In order to get a quick appreciation of the difference between actual on a GAAP basis and on a non-GAAP basis, we should look at special assessment fund actual figures prepared on a basis consistent with GAAP. Such figures can be seen if we look at the combined financial statement shown in Exhibit 2 of Appendix G. In that statement you will find that actual revenues, expenditures, etc., are reported on a basis consistent with GAAP as set out in *NCGA Statement 1.* On the other hand, the actual figures reported in the financial statement in Exhibit 4 are on a non-GAAP basis consistent with the budgetary figures in that statement. A comparison of the two sets of actual figures will reveal the difference between the GAAP and the non-GAAP basis figures.

The basic difference between the two sets of actual figures is that those prepared on a GAAP basis do not include as expenditures $60,000 of debt service that involves the payment of principal on maturing serial bonds. The actual figures prepared on a non-GAAP basis include the $60,000 of debt service, with respect to principal on maturing bonds, as part of actual expenditures. This means that total actual expenditures on a non-GAAP basis come to $377,834 while total actual expenditures on a GAAP basis come to $327,834. The difference is the $60,000 that has been treated in the budget as a budgetary expenditure. The actual figures had to be adjusted for this budgetary expenditure in order to have a meaningful comparison between actual and the budget. It is a requirement of *NCGA Statement 1* that the comparison between actual and the budget be carried out on the same basis as the budget is prepared, even if the budgetary basis is not in conformity with GAAP. *NCGA Statement 1* also requires that actual figures be reported in a financial statement on a basis consistent with GAAP. Both requirements have been met.

The budget for the special assessment fund in the financial statement of Exhibit 4 of Appendix G treats the repayment of debt principal as an expenditure. However, this is not an expenditure from the point of view of municipal accounting principles (MAP) as set out in *NCGA Statement 1* for a special assessment fund. Why not?

When you repay special assessment bonds, at the same time you reduce by equal amounts both the LHS and the RHS of the equation for the special assessment fund. On the LHS, you reduce the asset, "cash." On the RHS you reduce the liability "special assessment bonds payable." There is no effect on the fund balance of the special assessment fund as a result of repaying the principal on special assessment bonds. Expenditures, by the definition of *NCGA Statement 1*, are a use of net financial resources; and in the case of an expendable fund, a use of *net* financial resources must reduce the fund balance of that fund. In the case of the repayment of the principal of the special assessment bonds, the fund balance is unchanged; therefore, expenditures have to be zero. This should explain why the MAP of *NCGA Statement 1* do not treat the repayment of a liability as an expenditure.

THE COMPREHENSIVE ANNUAL FINANCIAL REPORT

The major financial reporting document as set out in *NCGA Statement 1* and elaborated in *1980 GAAFR* is the comprehensive annual financial report. A number of the elements of the CAFR already have been referred to or discussed earlier, in the review of the various financial statements included in the CAFR. The elements of the CAFR are set out in a table of contents for this financial report which appears as Appendix B to this chapter, including each of the illustrative financial statements that we have reviewed. In fact, there is a cross-reference between each of the illustrative financial statements previously discussed and the table of contents.

When we began to review financial statements, the first such statement was for the general fund. It was an individual fund statement. If we look in the table of contents for the CAFR in Appendix B, then just after the general purpose financial statements (GPFS) listed in that table we find the first of the individual fund financial statements. The first such financial statement is the balance sheet for the general fund identified as statement A–1. Now, if we turn to Exhibit 2 in Chapter 37, there we will find the illustrative balance for the general fund taken from the *1980 GAAFR* illustrative CAFR. In the upper right hand corner of that exhibit one finds the identifying cross-reference, A–1, for this statement. The same sort of identifying cross-reference will be found for each of the illustrative statements used from *1980 GAAFR*. In this way, by using the table of contents for the CAFR, one can determine precisely where in the illustrative CAFR each of the illustrative financial statements would be found.

Appendix A contains an illustrative title page for a CAFR. In Appendix C, there is another element of the illustrative CAFR: "An Illustrative Letter of Transmittal from the Chief Executive Officer for a Comprehensive Annual Financial Report." This is followed in Appendix D by "An Illustrative Finance Director's Letter of Transmittal that Functions as an Introductory Section for a Comprehensive Annual Financial Report."

In Appendix E, we have something that one just does not encounter in the financial report of a commercial enterprise. This is the certificate of conformance in financial reporting (COC). What is it, and why is it in the CAFR? There is a brief history and description of the COC program in *1980 GAAFR* (pp. 34–36). The Municipal Finance Officers Association, itself founded in 1906, was instrumental (as noted earlier) in organizing the bodies responsible for generating municipal accounting principles with the formation of the National Committee on Municipal Accounting in 1934. In 1945, the MFOA began an effort to see that MAP would be reflected in a uniform way in the actual financial reporting practices of state and local governmental units. The COC program in financial reporting is a mechanism and an incentive by which the MFOA hopes to establish uniformity in financial reporting. It is a voluntary program. It is not a mechanism by which state or local governments are penalized directly by the MFOA if they do not produce financial reports that qualify for a COC. The COC is not a substitute for an independent audit of the financial statements, but a COC cannot be earned unless the financial statements have been subjected to an independent audit which is in conformance with generally accepted auditing standards (GAAS). GAAS are developed, revised, and maintained by the American Institute of Certified Public Accountants (AICPA). The COC program also has been extended to cover a CAFR of a public employee retirement system.

The discussion on the COC program in *1980 GAAFR* does not deal with the vital topic of the degree of success or nonsuccess of the program. State and local governmental accounting and reporting has been plagued with significant deficiencies over extended periods of time. However, as we have noted earlier, the chapters on municipal accounting principles do not deal with the deficiencies in actual practice.[29]

---

[29]For example, A. J. Simon has published a study that includes references to research on the state of municipal reporting practices. His paper also includes a bibliography of materials pertinent to municipal accounting and reporting set in an economic context. See Abraham J. Simon, "Fiscal Accountability and Principles and Mechanisms of Disclosure for Major Local and State Governments in a Democratic Society," *Collected Papers of the American Accounting Association's Annual Meeting,* August 20–23, 1978, Denver, Colorado (Sarasota, Fla.: American Accounting, Association, 1978), pp. 794–831.

In Appendix F, we have an illustrative audit report from an independent auditor which establishes the fact that the financial statements have been subjected to an independent audit. The auditor starts out by telling us which financial statements have been subjected to an independent audit on which the auditor will render an opinion or, as it has been called, a "certification." Next, we have a statement that the audit was performed in accordance with generally accepted auditing standards. This establishes the quality level of an audit. Next, the auditor provides an opinion as to the degree to which the financial statements have been prepared in accordance with generally accepted accounting principles. The financial statements subject to the auditor's opinion are spelled out. In the illustrative auditor's audit report, the basic financial statements that are the subject of the auditor's opinion are the general purpose financial statements, the combining financial statements, and the individual fund financial statements. Remember that the GPFS are basically combined financial statements. These are the financial statements that are supposed to present the financial position, the results of operations, and the changes in financial position of the governmental unit according to *NCGA Statement 1.*

The combining financial statements and the individual fund financial statements *do not* present the financial position, results of operations, and changes in financial position of the governmental unit itself. The combining and individual fund financial statements refer basically to the financial position, results of operations, and changes in financial position of individual funds or groups of funds. The distinction between GPFS and the individual fund and combining financial statements should be understood, because one must be careful to appreciate which financial statements are subject to the auditor's opinion. In the illustrative auditor's audit report, we are told that the GPFS and also the individual fund and combining financial statements are subject to the auditor's opinion. However, this is not always the case. The auditor may render an opinion only on the GPFS according to *NCGA Statement 1.* That is why *NCGA Statement 1* describes the GPFS as "liftable" financial statements. This means that the GPFS can be issued separately on their own as the basic financial statements of the governmental unit.

By the way, the notes to the financial statements are always considered an integral part of the financial statements. This is the case whether the GPFS are issued as a separate set of financial statements or whether a CAFR is issued by the governmental unit. When the GPFS (or the GPFS plus certain additional financial statements of the CAFR) are subject to independent audit, then the notes to the financial statements being audited are also subject to the same independent audit.

Among the many things that one should keep in mind concerning the financial statements and the independent audit of these statements, one point in particular should be noted. The auditor's opinion that the financial statements are a fair presentation in accordance with GAAP is just that and no more. If one believes that there are significant deficiencies in the accounting principles that independent auditors like to call GAAP, then one must evaluate the auditor's opinion in the light of these believed deficiencies. If one believes that GAAP do not contain significant deficiencies and that they at least achieve acceptable levels of disclosure, then one would evaluate the auditor's opinion somewhat differently. Remember that what independent auditors are fond of calling GAAP, we prefer to refer to simply as municipal accounting principles.

The one part of the CAFR we have not discussed is the part that contains the statistical tables. In *1980 GAAFR* we are told that the statistical tables have been revised somewhat from *1968 GAAFR* and "are part of an NCGA effort to incorporate pertinent disclosures suggested in the MFOA's *Disclosures Guidelines for State and Local Governments* into the CAFR's statistical section. In fact, many of the recommended CAFR statistical section tables are intended to provide information relevant to CAFR users in the government securities market" (p. 32).[30] Earlier, an illustrative statistical table was included in Exhibit 5 of this chapter. Additional illustrative statistical tables are shown in Exhibits 12 and 13. The statistical tables along with the rest of the comprehensive annual financial report provide

Exhibit 12
Illustrative Hypothetical Statistical Table Showing Past Property Tax Levies and Collections

NAME OF GOVERNMENT

PROPERTY TAX LEVIES AND COLLECTIONS

Last Ten Fiscal Years

Fiscal year	Total tax levy	Current tax collections	Percent of levy collected	Delinquent tax collections	Total tax collections	Percent of total tax collections to tax levy	Outstanding delinquent taxes	Percent of delinquent taxes to tax levy
19W3	$ 625,000	610,000	97.6%	15,300	625,300	100.0%	37,583	6.0%
19W4	683,000	666,600	97.6	14,300	680,900	99.7	38,683	5.7
19W5	750,000	730,500	97.4	26,400	756,900	100.9	31,783	4.2
19W6	797,200	779,700	97.8	18,400	798,100	100.1	30,883	3.9
19W7	851,900	830,600	97.5	23,000	853,600	100.2	29,183	3.4
19W8	937,600	921,700	98.3	9,500	931,200	99.3	35,583	3.8
19W9	998,000	983,000	98.5	10,600	993,600	99.6	39,983	4.0
19X0	1,070,000	1,052,900	98.4	16,600	1,069,500	99.9	40,483	3.8
19X1	1,115,600	1,097,800	98.4	14,300	1,112,100	99.7	43,983	3.9
19X2	1,145,000	1,121,000	97.9	12,200	1,133,200	99.0	55,783	4.9

Source: Municipal Finance Officers Association, *Governmental Accounting, Auditing, and Financial Reporting (1980 GAAFR)* (Chicago: MFOA, 1980), Appendix D, p. 209.

[30]The publication referred to in the quote is Municipal Finance Officers Association, *Disclosure Guidelines for State and Local Governments* (Chicago: MFOA, 1979).

Exhibit 13
Illustrative Hypothetical Statistical Table Showing the Ratio of Net General
Bonded Debt to Assessed Value and Net Bonded Debt per Capita

NAME OF GOVERNMENT

RATIO OF NET GENERAL BONDED DEBT
TO ASSESSED VALUE AND NET BONDED DEBT PER CAPITA

Last Ten Fiscal Years

Fiscal year	Popu-lation*	Assessed value (in thousands)	Gross bonded debt(1)	Debt service monies available	Debt payable from enterprise revenues	Net bonded debt	Ratio of net bonded debt to assessed value	Net bonded debt per capita
19W3	18,271	$13,186	$2,490,000	$ 5,391	$1,150,000	$1,334,609	10.12%	$73.05
19W4	19,362	13,882	2,380,000	5,678	1,100,000	1,274,322	9.18	65.82
19W5	20,193	14,706	2,270,000	6,052	1,050,000	1,213,948	8.25	60.12
19W6	21,071	14,818	2,160,000	4,813	1,000,000	1,155,187	7.80	54.82
19W7	22,012	15,603	2,050,000	4,793	950,000	1,095,207	7.02	49.75
19W8	22,985	16,363	1,940,000	5,238	900,000	1,034,762	6.32	45.02
19W9	24,376	16,716	1,830,000	3,716	850,000	976,284	5.84	40.05
19X0	25,562	27,296	1,720,000	4,381	800,000	915,619	3.35	35.82
19X1	27,120	28,172	1,610,000	5,010	750,000	854,990	3.04	31.53
19X2	28,727	28,483	2,400,000	12,572	700,000	1,687,428	5.92	58.74

*Source: Annual school census.

Note:
(1) Includes all long-term general obligation debt.

Source: Municipal Finance Officers Association, *Governmental Accounting, Auditing, and Financial Reporting (1980 GAAFR)* (Chicago: MFOA, 1980), Appendix D, p. 213.

the beginning of a basis for an analysis and evaluation of the economic and fiscal health of a governmental unit.

DIAGRAMATIC OVERVIEW OF FINANCIAL REPORTING PER NCGA STATEMENT 1

NCGA Statement 1 (p. 20) provides a nice diagram so that one can get an overview of the accounting and financial reporting requirements of that statement for a state and local governmental unit. The diagram is shown in Figure 3.

CONCLUSION

We have completed a fairly extensive and intensive review of municipal accounting principles and municipal financial reporting.[31] We

---

[31]The National Council on Governmental Accounting is trying to come to grips with the issue of which activities of a governmental unit to include in the financial statements for that unit. In December 1981, it issued *NCGA Statement 3,* "Defining the Governmental Reporting Entity" (Chicago: Municipal Finance Officers Association, 1981). R. J. Freeman and C. D. Shoulders, in their article, "Defining the Governmental

Footnote 31 *(cont.)*

Reporting Entity," *Journal of Accountancy,* October 1982, pp. 50–63, attempt to evaluate *NCGA Statement 3* and provide an alternative approach. The issue of determining the appropriate reporting entity will remain a difficult problem to resolve. However, both *NCGA Statement 3* and the Freeman and Shoulders analysis provide useful insights.

Also, please note that the National Council on Governmental Accounting (NCGA) continues to produce a stream of pronouncements on various issues. The following will give you an idea of the pronouncements issued by this body at the time that this chapter went to press:

NCGA Statement 1, "Governmental Accounting and Financial Reporting Principles" (Chicago: MFOA, March 1979).

NCGA Statement 2, "Grant, Entitlement, and Shared Revenue Accounting and Reporting by State and Local Governments" (Chicago: MFOA, March 1979.)

NCGA Statement 3, "Defining the Governmental Reporting Entity" (Chicago: new NCGA, December, 1981).

NCGA Statement 4, "Accounting and Financial Reporting Principles for Claims and Judgments and Compensated Absences (Chicago: new NCGA, August 1982).

NCGA Statement 5, "Accounting and Financial Reporting Principles for Lease Agreements of State and Local Governments" (Chicago: new NCGA, December 1982).

NCGA Interpretation 1, "GAAFR and the AICPA Audit" (Chicago: MFOA, April 1976). This interpretation has been superseded by *NCGA Statement 1.*

NCGA Interpretation 2, "Segment Information for Enterprise Funds" (Chicago: new NCGA, June 1980).

NCGA Interpretation 3, "Revenue Recognition—Property Taxes" (Chicago: new NCGA, June 1981).

NCGA Interpretation 4, "Accounting and Financial Reporting for Public Employee Retirement Systems and Pension Trust Funds" (Chicago: new NCGA, December 1981).

NCGA Interpretation 5, "Authoritative Status of Governmental Accounting, Auditing, and Financial Reporting" (Chicago: new NCGA, March 1982).

NCGA Interpretation 6, "Notes to the Financial Statements Disclosure" (Chicago: new NCGA, May 1982).

The NCGA has certain of its work in an incomplete stage as follows:

National Council on Governmental Accounting, *Exposure Draft of a Proposed Statement,* "Financial Reporting for Special Assessments" (May 27, 1982). Comment deadline: October 1, 1982.

National Council on Governmental Accounting, *Discussion Memorandum,* "Budgetary Reporting in State and Local Governments" (September 16, 1982). Comment deadline: January 2, 1983.

National Council on Governmental Accounting, *Exposure Draft of a Proposed Statement,* "Pension Accounting and Financial Reporting, Public Employee Retirement Systems and State and Local Government Employer Entities" (November 1, 1982). Comment deadline: February 1, 1983.

National Council on Governmental Accounting, *Exposure Draft of a Proposed Interpretation,* "Exchanges of Debt Securities" (January 14, 1983). Comment deadline: March 15, 1983.

National Council on Governmental Accounting, *Exposure Draft of a Proposed Interpretation,* "Capitalization of Interest in Governmental Entities" (January 14, 1983). Comment deadline: March 15, 1983.

The NCGA has also issued a theoretical piece:

NCGA Concepts Statement 1, "Objectives of Accounting and Financial Reporting for Governmental Units" (Chicago: new NCGA, March 1982).

Figure 3
Overview of Financial Reporting per *NCGA Statement 1*

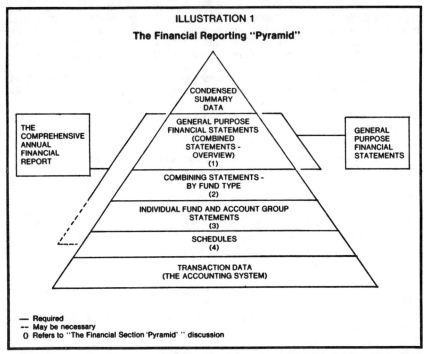

ILLUSTRATION 1

The Financial Reporting "Pyramid"

CONDENSED SUMMARY DATA

GENERAL PURPOSE FINANCIAL STATEMENTS (COMBINED STATEMENTS - OVERVIEW) (1)

COMBINING STATEMENTS - BY FUND TYPE (2)

INDIVIDUAL FUND AND ACCOUNT GROUP STATEMENTS (3)

SCHEDULES (4)

TRANSACTION DATA (THE ACCOUNTING SYSTEM)

THE COMPREHENSIVE ANNUAL FINANCIAL REPORT

GENERAL PURPOSE FINANCIAL STATEMENTS

— Required
-- May be necessary
() Refers to "The Financial Section 'Pyramid' " discussion

Reproduced with permission from National Council on Governmental Accounting, Statement 1, *Governmental Accounting and Financial Reporting Principles* (Chicago: Municipal Finance Officers Association of the United States and Canada, 1979), p. 20. © Copyright 1979 by the Municipal Finance Officers Association of the United States and Canada.

have examined, to some degree, the economic and other foundations for municipal accounting. The financial statements contained in the comprehensive annual financial report of *NCGA Statement 1* for a governmental unit are the basic starting point for any concentrated financial analysis of the financial position and activities of a governmental unit. These statements are the primary sources of financial information that also may have been verified through an independent audit. The statistical tables included in the CAFR provide a modicum of additional information concerning past financial, economic, and demographic trends.

A governmental unit does not operate in an economic, social, demographic, or political vacuum. What is happening locally as well as nationally has a significant impact on the governmental unit. Municipal financial reporting is only one part of the information needed for an in-depth analysis of the economic and financial health of a governmental unit. One would need to have available additional significant indicators of economic, financial, social, demographic, and other trends in order to begin to fill in an overall picture of the environment in which a governmental unit operates. One would have to have a sense of the political dynamics within and external to a particular governmental unit in order to set the various kinds of information into a proper context. However, a good sense of the content and substance of municipal financial reports is a critical link in the financial analysis of governmental units.

APPENDIX A

An Illustrative Title Page for a Comprehensive Annual Financial Report*

NAME OF GOVERNMENT
Comprehensive Annual Financial Report
December 31, 19X2

Prepared by:
Department of Finance

James F. Marling, CPA
Finance Director

Source: Municipal Finance Officers Association, *Governmental Accounting, Auditing, and Financial Reporting (1980 GAAFR)* (Chicago: MFOA, 1980), Appendix D, p. 112.

*The materials included in Appendixes A through H are adapted and reproduced with permission from the Municipal Finance Officers Association of the United States and Canada, *Governmental Accounting, Auditing, and Financial Reporting* (Chicago: Municipal Finance Officers Association of the United States and Canada, 1980). © Copyright 1980 by the Municipal Finance Officers Association of the United States and Canada.

APPENDIX B

An Illustrative Table of Contents for a Comprehensive Annual Financial Report

NAME OF GOVERNMENT
COMPREHENSIVE ANNUAL FINANCIAL REPORT
YEAR ENDED DECEMBER 31, 19X2

TABLE OF CONTENTS

INTRODUCTORY SECTION

Title Page
Table of Contents
Chief Executive Officer's Letter of Transmittal
Certificate of Conformance in Financial Reporting

FINANCIAL SECTION

Exhibit

Auditor's Opinion

Combined Statements - Overview ("Liftable" General Purpose Financial Statements):

Notes to Financial Statements

**Statement/
Schedule**

Financial Statements of Individual Funds:

General Fund:

Special Revenue Funds:

Parks Fund:

State Gasoline Tax Fund:

Motor Vehicle License Fund:

Source: Municipal Finance Officers Association, *Governmental Accounting, Auditing, and Financial Reporting (1980 GAAFR)* (Chicago: MFOA, 1980), Appendix D, pp. 113–115.

Appendix B *(continued)*

Appendix B *(concluded)*

Note: A table of contents should include page number references for all included statements, schedules, tables, etc. Because of the inclusion of this model CAFR within a larger work it was not feasible to separately paginate the contents or to provide page number references in the table of contents. The Introductory Section should also ordinarily include an organization chart and a listing of principal officials of the reporting government.

APPENDIX C

An Illustrative Letter of Transmittal from the Chief Executive Officer for a Comprehensive Annual Financial Report

OFFICIAL LETTERHEAD
OF
GOVERNMENT

March 17, 19X3

Honorable Mayor and
  Members of the City Council
Name of Government

Ladies and Gentlemen:

In accordance with state statutes and local charter provisions, I hereby transmit the annual financial report of the Name of Government as of December 31, 19X2 and for the fiscal year then ended. Responsibility for both the accuracy of the presented data and the completeness and fairness of the presentation, including all disclosures, rests with the City. Management believes that the data, as presented, is accurate in all material aspects; that it is presented in a manner designed to fairly set forth the financial position and results of operations of the City as measured by the financial activity of its various funds; and that all disclosures necessary to enable the reader to gain the maximum understanding of the City's financial affairs have been included.

In developing and evaluating the City's accounting system, consideration is given to the adequacy of internal accounting controls. Internal accounting controls are discussed by the finance director in his accompanying letter of transmittal, and within that framework, I believe that the City's internal accounting controls adequately safeguard assets and provide reasonable assurance of proper recording of financial transactions.

This report has been prepared following the guidelines recommended by the Municipal Finance Officers Association of the United States and Canada. The Municipal Finance Officers Association awards Certificates of Conformance to those governments whose annual financial reports are judged to conform substantially with high standards of public financial reporting including generally accepted accounting principles promulgated by the National Council on Governmental Accounting. The Name of Government was awarded a Certificate of Conformance for its annual financial report for fiscal year 19X1. It is my belief that the accompanying fiscal year 19X2 financial report continues to meet program standards and it will be submitted to the Municipal Finance Officers Association for review.

In accordance with the above-mentioned guidelines the accompanying report consists of three parts:
1) Introductory section, including the finance director's letter of transmittal
2) Financial section, including the financial statements and supplemental data of the government accompanied by our independent auditor's opinion
3) Statistical section, including a number of tables of unaudited data depicting the financial history of the government for the past 10 years, information on overlapping governments, and demographic and other miscellaneous information

Source: Municipal Finance Officers Association, *Governmental Accounting, Auditing, and Financial Reporting (1980 GAAFR)* (Chicago: MFOA, 1980), Appendix D, pp. 116–117.

Appendix C *(concluded)*

State law requires that the financial statements of the Name of Government be audited by a certified public accountant selected by the City Council. This requirement has been compiled with, and our auditor's opinion is included in the financial section of this report.

Although the Name of Government concluded fiscal year 19X2 in a sound financial condition, there are several external areas of concern which may require special attention by the Mayor and Members of the City Council during the present fiscal period.

The state legislature adopted major property tax changes during recent months. These changes include the methods by which real property is assessed and a restructuring of the maximum tax rates which may be levied for certain governmental services. It is my belief that these two changes will have a negative impact of approximately 2 percent on the government's ability to generate real property tax revenues during fiscal year 19X3.

Of concern to the Name of Government, as well as all sectors of the economy, is the continued depressed status of the economy. While to date, the recession has caused only minor reductions in sales tax and other related revenue sources, a prolonged continuation of the depressed state of the economy may cause a need to re-examine the Name of Government's reliance on these types of revenue sources.

Finally, the City Council's decision to limit future expenditure increases to no more than the increase in the consumer price index appears to be giving management the ability to control present and future increases in levels of spending. The members of the City Council should be applauded for this decision and I assure you that as the senior executive of the Name of Government I will continue to do everything in my power to hold current and future increases of expenditures within these guidelines.

The preparation of this annual financial report could not have been accomplished without the dedicated effort of the finance director and his entire staff. Their efforts over the past years toward upgrading the accounting and financial reporting systems of the Name of Government have lead substantially to the improved quality of the information being reported to the City Council, state oversight boards, and the citizens of the Name of Government.

Respectfully submitted,

James S. Remis
City Manager

APPENDIX D

An Illustrative Finance Director's Letter of Transmittal that Functions as an Introductory Section for a Comprehensive Annual Financial Report

OFFICIAL LETTERHEAD
OF
GOVERNMENT

March 10, 19X3

Honorable Mayor, Members of the
City Council, and City Manager
Name of Government

The Comprehensive Annual Financial Report of the Name of Government, for the fiscal year ended December 31, 19X2, is submitted herewith. This report was prepared by the City's Finance Department. Responsibility for both the accuracy of the presented data and the completeness and fairness of the presentation, including all disclosures, rests with the City. We believe the data, as presented, is accurate in all material aspects; that it is presented in a manner designed to fairly set forth the financial position and results of operations of the City as measured by the financial activity of its various funds; and that all disclosures necessary to enable the reader to gain the maximum understanding of the City's financial affairs have been included.

Accounting System and Budgetary Control

In developing and evaluating the City's accounting system, consideration is given to the adequacy of internal accounting controls. Internal accounting controls are designed to provide reasonable, but not absolute, assurance regarding: (1) the safeguarding of assets against loss from unauthorized use or disposition; and (2) the reliability of financial records for preparing financial statements and maintaining accountability for assets. The concept of reasonable assurance recognizes that: (1) the cost of a control should not exceed the benefits likely to be derived; and (2) the evaluation of costs and benefits requires estimates and judgments by management.

All internal control evaluations occur within the above framework. We believe that the City's internal accounting controls adequately safeguard assets and provide reasonable assurance of proper recording of financial transactions.

Budgetary control is maintained at the subfunction level by the encumbrance of estimated purchase amounts prior to the release of purchase orders to vendors. Purchase orders which result in an overrun of subfunction balances are not released until additional appropriations are made available. Open encumbrances are reported as reservations of fund balance at December 31, 19X2.

The Reporting Entity and Its Services

This report includes all of the funds and account groups of the City. It includes all activities considered by the U.S. Bureau of Census to be part of (controlled by or dependent on) the City.

The Metropolitan Airport Authority (MAA), although governed by board members who are directly appointed by the City Commissioners, is considered by Census to be a separate government because: (1) it is an organized entity; (2) it has governmental character; and (3) it is substantially autonomous. Audited financial statements for the Metropolitan Airport Authority are not included in this report. However, such statements are available upon request from the MAA business office at the Metropolitan Airport.

Source: Municipal Finance Officers Association, *Governmental Accounting, Auditing, and Financial Reporting (1980 GAAFR)* (Chicago: MFOA, 1980), Appendix D, pp. 118–22.

Appendix D *(continued)*

The Name of Government Elementary School System is a dependent unit which is considered a part of the Name of Government. Financial data for it are included in the financial statements in this report. The County School District provides secondary education services to students within the jurisdiction of Name of Government. The County system is an independent special district and not part of the Name of Government. Financial data for it are *not* included in the financial statements in this report. However, audited financial statements for the County School District are available upon request from its business office in Ocoya.

The City provides the full range of municipal services contemplated by statute or character. This includes public safety (police and fire), highways and streets, sanitation, health and social services, culture-recreation, education, public improvements, planning and zoning, and general administrative services.

General Governmental Functions

Revenues for general governmental functions totaled $2,542,987 in 19X2, an increase of 9.5 percent over 19X1. General property taxes produced 42.7 percent of general revenues compared to 43.1 percent last year. The amount of revenues from various sources and the increase over last year are shown in the following tabulation:

Revenue Source	Amount	Percent of total	Increase (decrease) from 19X1
Property taxes and penalties	$1,085,462	42.7%	$ 77,768
Licenses and permits	103,000	4.0	6,500
Intergovernmental revenues	1,059,366	41.7	103,366
Charges for services	170,100	6.7	9,700
Fines and forfeits	32,200	1.3	6,900
Other revenues	91,859	3.6	13,989
Total	$2,542,987	100.0%	$218,223

Assessed valuations of $28.5 million represented an increase of 1.2 percent over the preceding year. The nominal increase in assessed valuation is a reflection of the stagnant economic conditions that presently affect Name of Government and the related effect those economic conditions are having on real estate values.

Current tax collections were 95.1 percent of the tax levy, down 0.5 percent from last year. This is the twelfth consecutive year in which current property tax collections have exceeded 95 percent. Delinquent tax collections were slightly less than last year, despite strengthened collection activities. The ratio of total collections (current and delinquent) to the current tax levy was 99.0 percent, a decrease of .7 percent from last year. Allocations of property tax levy by purpose for 19X2 and the preceding two fiscal years are as follows (amounts per $100/assessed value):

Purpose	19X2	19X1	19X0
General Fund	$3.10	$3.11	$3.11
Special Revenue Funds	.64	.56	.50
General obligation debt	.28	.29	.31
Total tax rate	$4.02	$3.96	$3.92

Intergovernmental revenues represented 42 percent of total governmental revenues compared with 41 percent for the preceding year. The growth was primarily the result of a change in the for-

Appendix D *(continued)*

mula for distributing state shared revenues. The additional revenues will continue to be received in future years since the formula change was permanent.

Expenditures for general governmental purposes totaled $2,402,450, an increase of 8.2 percent over 19X1. Increases in levels of expenditures for major functions of the City over the preceding year are shown in the following tabulation:

Function	Amount	Percent of total	Increase (decrease) from 19X1
General government	$ 121,805	5.1	$ (12,395)
Public safety	738,395	30.7	67,095
Highways and streets	502,400	20.9	93,700
Sanitation	56,250	2.3	12,150
Health services	44,500	1.9	7,900
Social services	46,800	1.9	5,400
Culture-recreation	297,350	12.4	10,950
Education	509,150	21.2	(730)
Debt service	85,800	3.6	(1,800)
Total	$2,402,450	100.0%	$182,270

Expenditures for highways and streets increased from 18.4 percent of total general governmental expenditures in the preceding year to 20.9 percent in the current year. This increased level of expenditures is the result of the implementation of a two-year program of maintenance to improve residential streets.

The reduced level of expenditures for education (from 23.0 percent to 21.2 percent) reflects a reduction in purchases of new textbooks and supplies and a reduction in maintenance activities. It will be necessary to increase expenditures for these areas in future years to offset the current year's reduced expenditure level.

Unreserved fund balances and retained earnings in the major operating funds were maintained at adequate levels. The General Fund balance of $144,600 was up $50,300 from last year; the Debt Service Funds balance of $12,572 was up $7,562 from the preceding year, and the $117,020 balance in the Special Revenue Funds was down $16,275.

Debt Administration

The ratio of net bonded debt to assessed valuation and the amount of bonded debt per capita are useful indicators of the City's debt position to municipal management, citizens, and investors. These data for the City at the end of the 19X2 fiscal year were as follows:

	Amount	Ratio of Debt to assessed value (85.8% of present market)	Ratio of Debt to present market value	Debt per capita
Net direct bonded debt	$1,687,428	5.92%	5.08%	$58.74

Outstanding general obligation bonds at December 31, 19X2, totaled $2,400,000, of which $700,000 issued for waterworks improvements are considered to be self-supporting. The remainder of $1,700,000 is considered to be net direct tax supported debt. In addition, $555,000 of special assessment bonds are outstanding. Tables 7 to 14 in the Statistical Section of this report present more detailed information about the debt position of the City.

Appendix D *(continued)*

On March 1, 19X2, $700,000 of general obligation bonds were sold at a favorable effective interest rate of 4 percent; another $200,000 was sold on May 1, 19X2, at an interest rate of 5 percent. The following tabulation presents general obligation bonds issued during the past five fiscal years:

Date of issue	Amount	Average life in years	Effective interest rate	Interest cost per borrowed dollar
March 1, 19X2	$700,000	10.5	2.76	36.7¢
May 1, 19X2	200,000	10.5	3.20	33.2¢

The City's bonds continue to have the same ratings which they have carried for the past several years. These ratings are as follows:

	Moody's Investors Service	Standard & Poor's
General obligation bonds	Aa	AA

Cash Management

Cash temporarily idle during the year was invested in demand deposits, in time deposits ranging from 180 to 365 days to maturity, and in U.S. Treasury bills ranging from 21 to 91 days to maturity as follows: in demand deposits, 62 percent; in time deposits, 29.9 percent; and in U.S. Treasury bills, 8.1 percent. The average yield on maturing investments during the year was 4.8 percent, and the amount of interest received was $36,000. This was $12,300 more than interest on temporary investments in fiscal year 19X1.

Capital Projects Funds

Proceeds of general obligation bond issues are accounted for in Capital Projects Funds until improvement projects are completed. Completed projects and uncompleted construction in progress at year end are capitalized in the General Fixed Assets Account Group. During 19X2, projects costing $944,150 were completed. A detailed summary of project-length Capital Projects Fund revenues and expenditures is included as Schedule D-8 in the Financial Section of this report.

Authorized but unissued bonds at December 31, 19X2, totaled $200,000, but $150,000 of this amount was subsequently sold on February 1, 19X3. After the February sale, unissued bonds totaled $50,000.

The Capital Project Fund balances on hand at December 31, 19X2, were represented primarily by $434,100 in cash, including time deposits, and $640,000 due from the County.

General Fixed Assets

The general fixed assets of the City are those fixed assets used in the performance of general governmental functions and exclude the fixed assets of Enterprise and Internal Service Funds. As of December 31, 19X2, the general fixed assets of the City amounted to $6,913,250. This amount represents the original cost of the assets and is considerably less than their present value. Depreciation of general fixed assets is not recognized in the City's accounting system.

Water and Sewer System

The City's water and sewer utility continued to show moderate gains in operating revenues, number of customers, net income, and debt service coverage. Comparative data for the past two fiscal years are presented in the following tabulation:

Appendix D *(concluded)*

	19X2	19X1
Operating revenues	$672,150	$603,563
Operating income	$107,970	$102,473
Income available for debt service	$337,900	$309,683
Annual debt service	$176,888	$216,408
Coverage (income available for debt service divided by average annual debt service)	1.91	1.45

During the year, $48,000 of regularly maturing revenue bonds were retired in the Water and Sewer Fund. In addition, $50,000 of general obligation bonds, serviced with the earnings of the Water and Sewer Fund activities, were retired.

Independent Audit

The City Charter requires an annual audit of the books of account, financial records, and transactions of all administrative departments of the City by independent certified public accountants selected by the City Council. This requirement has been complied with and the auditor's opinion has been included in this report.

Certificate of Conformance

The Municipal Finance Officers Association of the United States and Canada (MFOA) awarded a Certificate of Conformance in Financial Reporting to the Name of Government for its comprehensive annual financial report for the fiscal year ended December 31, 19X1.

In order to be awarded a Certificate of Conformance, a governmental unit must publish an easily readable and efficiently organized comprehensive annual financial report, whose contents conform to program standards. Such reports must satisfy both generally accepted accounting principles and applicable legal requirements.

A Certificate of Conformance is valid for a period of one year only. We believe our current report continues to conform to Certificate of Conformance Program requirements, and we are submitting it to MFOA to determine its eligibility for another certificate.

Acknowledgements

The preparation of this report on a timely basis could not be accomplished without the efficient and dedicated services of the entire staff of the Finance Department. I should like to express my appreciation to all members of the Department who assisted and contributed to its preparation. I should also like to thank the mayor and city commissioners for their interest and support in planning and conducting the financial operations of the City in a responsible and progressive manner.

Respectfully submitted,

James F. Marling, CPA
Finance Director

APPENDIX E

An Illustrative Certificate of Conformance in Financial Reporting for a Comprehensive Annual Financial Report

Certificate
of
Conformance
in Financial
Reporting

Presented to

NAME OF GOVERNMENT

For its Comprehensive Annual
Financial Report
for the Fiscal Year Ended
December 31, 19X1

A Certificate of Conformance in Financial Reporting is
presented by the Municipal Finance Officers Association
of the United States and Canada to governmental units
and public employee retirement systems whose comprehensive
annual financial reports (CAFR's) are judged to substantially
conform to program standards.

President

Executive Director

Source: Municipal Finance Officers Association, *Governmental Accounting, Auditing, and Financial Reporting (1980 GAAFR)* (Chicago: MFOA, 1980), Appendix D, p. 123.

APPENDIX F

An Illustrative Independent Auditor's Audit Report for a Comprehensive Annual Financial Report

OFFICIAL LETTERHEAD
OF
INDEPENDENT AUDITOR

March 15, 19X3

Honorable Mayor, Members of the
City Council, and City Manager
Name of Government

We have examined the combined financial statements of the Name of Government and its combining and individual fund financial statements as of and for the year ended December 31, 19X2, as listed in the table of contents. Our examination was made in accordance with generally accepted auditing standards and, accordingly, included such tests of the accounting records and such other auditing procedures as we considered necessary in the circumstances.

In our opinion, the combined financial statements referred to above present fairly the financial position of the Name of Government at December 31, 19X2, and the results of its operations and the changes in financial position of its proprietary fund types and similar Trust Funds for the year then ended, in conformity with generally accepted accounting principles applied on a basis consistent with that of the preceding year. Also, in our opinion, the combining and individual fund financial statements referred to above present fairly the financial position of the individual funds of the Name of Government at December 31, 19X2, their results of operations, and the changes in financial position of individual proprietary funds for the year then ended, in conformity with generally accepted accounting principles applied on a basis consistent with that of the preceding year.

Our examination was made for the purpose of forming an opinion on the combined financial statements taken as a whole and on the combining and individual fund financial statements. The accompanying financial information listed as supporting schedules in the table of contents is presented for purposes of additional analysis and is not a required part of the combined financial statements of the Name of Government. The information has been subjected to the auditing procedures applied in the examination of the combined, combining, and individual fund financial statements and, in our opinion, is fairly stated in all material respects in relation to the combined financial statements taken as a whole.

Russum, Feminis, Fucone & Co.

Note: For guidance with respect to the extension of the auditor's opinion to the amounts included in the financial statements as of and for the year ended December 31, 19X1, see *Codification of Statements on Auditing Standards*, American Institute of Certified Public Accountants, New York, par. 505.03 footnote 5.

Source: Municipal Finance Officers Association, *Governmental Accounting, Auditing, and Financial Reporting (1980 GAAFR)* (Chicago: MFOA, 1980), Appendix D, p. 125.

APPENDIX G

An Illustrative Set of General Purpose Financial Statements that Is a Part of a Comprehensive Annual Financial Report

Source: Municipal Finance Officers Association, *Governmental Accounting, Auditing, and Financial Reporting (1980 GAAFR)* (Chicago: MFOA, 1980), Appendix D, pp. 126–32.

Exhibit 1

NAME OF GOVERNMENT

COMBINED BALANCE SHEET—ALL FUND TYPES AND ACCOUNT GROUPS

December 31, 19X2

	Governmental Fund Types					Proprietary Fund Types		Fiduciary Fund Type	Account Groups		Totals (Memorandum Only)	
	General	Special Revenue	Debt Service	Capital Projects	Special Assessment	Enterprise (note 8)	Internal Service	Trust and Agency	General Fixed Assets	General Long-term Debt	19X2	19X1
Assets												
Cash	$255,029	$101,385	$10,889	$434,100	$232,185	$279,296	$29,700	$216,701	$ —	$ —	$1,559,285	$1,232,930
Investments, at cost or amortized cost	65,000	37,200						1,239,260	—	—	1,341,460	1,116,524
Receivables (net, where applicable, of allowances for uncollectibles):												
Taxes, including interest, penalties, and liens (note 2)	61,771	2,500	3,528					580,000			647,799	230,435
Accounts	8,300	3,300		100		24,130					35,830	43,850
Special assessments, including liens					646,035						646,035	462,035
Notes						2,350					2,350	1,250
Loans								35,000			35,000	35,000
Accrued interest	50	25			350			2,666			3,091	4,280
Due from other funds	12,000					2,000	12,000	11,189			37,189	51,220
Due from other governments (note 3)	30,000	75,260		640,000							745,260	116,800
Advance to Internal Service Fund	55,000										55,000	65,000
Inventory, at cost	7,200	5,190				23,030	40,000				75,420	48,670
Prepaid expenses						1,200					1,200	740
Restricted assets: Cash and investments, at cost or amortized cost						306,753					306,753	417,268
Fixed assets (net of accumulated depreciation)—(note 4)						5,769,759	103,100		6,913,250		12,786,109	10,864,206
Amount available in Debt Service Funds										12,572	12,572	5,010
Amount to be provided for retirement of general long-term debt										1,687,428	1,687,428	854,990
Total assets	$494,350	$224,860	$14,417	$1,074,200	$878,570	$6,408,518	$184,800	$2,084,816	$6,913,250	$1,700,000	$19,977,781	$15,550,208

Source: Municipal Finance Officers Association, *Governmental Accounting, Auditing, and Financial Reporting (1980 GAAFR)* (Chicago: MFOA, 1980), Appendix D, pp. 126–27.

Exhibit 1 (concluded)

											Totals (current)	Totals (prior)
Liabilities												
Vouchers and accounts payable	$118,261	$32,454	$—	$29,000	$20,600	$116,471	$15,000	$5,200	$—	$—	$336,986	$179,973
Contracts payable	57,600	18,300	—	69,000	50,000	26,107	—	—	—	—	221,007	503,724
Judgments payable	—	2,000	—	22,600	11,200	—	—	—	—	—	35,800	15,500
Accrued general obligation interest	—	—	—	—	—	14,000	—	—	—	—	14,000	14,100
Other accrued expenses	—	—	—	—	10,700	2,870	—	4,700	—	—	18,270	18,713
Payable from restricted assets:												
Construction contracts	—	—	—	—	—	—	—	—	—	—	—	145,643
Fiscal agent	—	—	—	—	—	139	—	—	—	—	139	—
Matured revenue bonds	—	—	—	—	—	—	—	—	—	—	—	8,000
Matured revenue bond interest	—	—	—	—	—	—	—	—	—	—	—	1,000
Accrued interest	—	—	—	—	—	64,749	—	—	—	—	64,749	66,150
Revenue bonds (note 5)	—	—	—	—	—	48,000	—	—	—	—	48,000	44,000
Deposits	—	—	—	—	—	64,060	—	—	—	—	64,060	55,500
Due to:												
Other taxing units	—	—	—	—	—	—	—	680,800	—	—	680,800	200,000
Other funds	24,189	2,000	—	1,000	—	—	10,000	—	—	—	37,189	51,220
Deferred revenues (note 2)	49,500	1,396	1,845	—	556,200	—	—	—	—	—	608,941	412,951
Advance from General Fund	—	—	—	—	—	—	55,000	—	—	—	55,000	65,000
General obligation bonds payable (note 5)	—	—	—	—	—	700,000	—	—	—	1,700,000	2,400,000	1,610,000
Revenue bonds payable (note 5)	—	—	—	—	—	1,798,000	—	—	—	—	1,798,000	1,846,000
Special assessment bonds payable (note 5)	—	—	—	—	555,000	—	—	—	—	—	555,000	420,000
Total liabilities	249,550	56,150	1,845	121,600	1,203,700	2,834,396	80,000	690,700	—	1,700,000	6,937,941	5,657,474
Fund Equity												
Contributed capital	—	—	—	—	—	1,370,666	95,000	—	—	—	1,465,666	815,000
Investment in general fixed assets	—	—	—	—	—	—	—	—	6,913,250	—	6,913,250	5,174,250
Retained earnings:												
Reserved for revenue bond retirement	—	—	—	—	—	129,155	—	—	—	—	129,155	96,975
Unreserved	—	—	—	—	—	2,074,301	9,800	—	—	—	2,084,101	1,998,119
Fund balance:												
Reserved for encumbrances	38,000	46,500	—	941,500	75,000	—	—	—	—	—	1,101,000	410,050
Reserved for inventory	7,200	5,190	—	—	—	—	—	—	—	—	12,390	10,890
Reserved for advance to Internal Service Fund	55,000	—	—	—	—	—	—	—	—	—	55,000	65,000
Reserved for loans	—	—	—	—	—	—	—	50,050	—	—	50,050	45,100
Reserved for endowments	—	—	—	—	—	—	—	160,865	—	—	160,865	119,035
Reserved for employees' retirement system	—	—	—	—	—	—	—	1,426,201	—	—	1,426,201	1,276,150
Reserved for debt service (note 6)	—	—	12,572	—	(400,130)	—	—	—	—	—	(387,558)	(258,950)
Unreserved:												
Designated for subsequent years' expenditures	50,000	—	—	—	—	—	—	—	—	—	50,000	50,000
Undesignated (note 8)	94,600	117,020	—	11,100	—	—	—	(243,000)	—	—	(20,280)	91,115
Total retained earnings/fund balance	244,800	168,710	12,572	952,600	(325,130)	2,203,456	9,800	1,394,116	—	—	4,660,924	3,903,484
Total fund equity	244,800	168,710	12,572	952,600	(325,130)	3,574,122	104,800	1,394,116	6,913,250	—	13,039,840	9,892,734
Commitments and contingent liabilities (notes 4, 10, 11, 12, and 13)												
Total liabilities and fund equity	$494,350	$224,880	$14,417	$1,074,200	$878,570	$6,408,518	$184,800	$2,084,816	$6,913,250	$1,700,000	$19,977,781	$15,550,208

See accompanying notes to financial statements

Exhibit 2

NAME OF GOVERNMENT

COMBINED STATEMENT OF REVENUES, EXPENDITURES, AND CHANGES IN FUND BALANCES—ALL GOVERNMENTAL FUND TYPES AND EXPENDABLE TRUST FUNDS

Year Ended December 31, 19X2

	Governmental Fund Types					Fiduciary Fund Type	Totals (Memorandum Only)	
	General	Special Revenue	Debt Service	Capital Projects	Special Assessment	Expendable Trust	19X2	19X1
Revenue:								
Taxes and special assessments (note 2)	$ 846,800	$ 189,300	$49,362	$ —	$ 86,000	$ —	$1,171,462	$1,117,694
Licenses and permits	103,000	—	—	—	—	—	103,000	96,500
Intergovernmental (notes 3 and 9)	186,500	831,366	41,500	1,250,000	—	—	2,309,366	1,256,000
Charges for services	91,000	79,100	—	—	—	—	170,100	160,400
Fines and forfeits	33,200	—	—	—	—	—	33,200	26,300
Miscellaneous	18,000	71,359	2,500	3,750	20,664	150	116,423	106,750
Total revenues	1,278,500	1,171,125	93,362	1,253,750	106,664	150	3,903,551	2,763,644
Expenditures:								
General government	121,805	—	—	—	—	—	121,805	134,200
Public safety	258,395	480,000	—	—	—	—	738,395	671,300
Highways and streets	85,400	417,000	—	—	—	—	502,400	408,700
Sanitation	56,250	—	—	—	—	—	56,250	44,100
Health	44,500	—	—	—	—	—	44,500	36,600
Welfare	46,800	—	—	—	—	—	46,800	41,400
Culture and recreation	40,900	256,450	—	—	—	—	297,350	286,400
Education	509,150	—	—	—	—	2,370	511,520	512,000
Capital projects	—	—	—	1,625,500	308,265	—	1,933,765	1,075,035
Debt service:								
Principal retirement	—	—	60,000	—	—	—	60,000	60,000
Interest and fiscal charges	—	—	25,800	—	19,569	—	45,369	35,533
Total expenditures	1,163,200	1,153,450	85,800	1,625,500	327,834	2,370	4,358,154	3,306,268
Excess (deficiency) of revenues over expenditures	115,300	17,675	7,562	(371,750)	(221,170)	(2,220)	(454,603)	(541,624)
Other financing sources (uses):								
Proceeds of general obligation bonds	—	—	—	902,500	—	—	902,500	105,000
Operating transfers in	—	—	—	64,500	10,000	2,530	77,030	89,120
Operating transfers out	(74,500)	—	—	—	—	—	(74,500)	(87,000)
Total other financing sources (uses)	(74,500)	—	—	967,000	10,000	2,530	905,030	107,120
Excess (deficiency) of revenues and other financing sources over expenditures and other uses	40,800	17,675	7,562	595,250	(211,170)	310	450,427	(434,504)
Fund balance at beginning of year	202,500	151,035	5,010	357,350	(113,960)	26,555	628,490	1,062,994
Increase in reserve for inventory	1,500	—	—	—	—	—	1,500	—
Fund balance at end of year	$ 244,800	$ 168,710	$12,572	$ 952,600	$(325,130)	$26,865	$1,080,417	$ 628,490

See accompanying notes to financial statements

Source: Municipal Finance Officers Association, *Governmental Accounting, Auditing, and Financial Reporting (1980 GAAFR)* (Chicago: MFOA, 1980), Appendix D, p. 128.

Exhibit 3

NAME OF GOVERNMENT

COMBINED STATEMENT OF REVENUES, EXPENDITURES, AND CHANGES IN FUND BALANCES—BUDGET (GAAP BASIS) AND ACTUAL—GENERAL, SPECIAL REVENUE, AND CAPITAL PROJECTS FUND TYPES

Year Ended December 31, 19X2

	General Fund			Special Revenue Fund Types			Capital Projects Fund Types		
	Budget	Actual	Variance—favorable (unfavorable)	Budget	Actual	Variance—favorable (unfavorable)	Budget	Actual	Variance—favorable (unfavorable)
Revenues									
Taxes (note 2)	$ 848,000	$ 846,800	$ (1,200)	$ 189,500	$ 189,300	$ (200)	$ —	$ —	$ —
Licenses and permits	125,500	103,000	(22,500)						
Intergovernmental	234,500	186,500	(48,000)	837,600	831,366	(6,234)	1,250,000	1,250,000	
Charges for services	90,000	91,000	1,000	78,000	79,100	1,100			
Fines and forfeits	32,500	33,200	700						
Miscellaneous	19,500	18,000	(1,500)	81,475	71,359	(10,116)	500	3,750	3,250
Total revenues	1,350,000	1,278,500	(71,500)	1,186,575	1,171,125	(15,450)	1,250,500	1,253,750	3,250
Expenditures									
General government	129,000	121,805	7,195						
Public safety	277,300	258,395	18,905						
Highways and streets	84,500	85,400	(900)	494,500	480,000	14,500			
Sanitation	50,000	56,250	(6,250)	436,000	417,000	19,000			
Health	47,750	44,500	3,250						
Welfare	51,000	46,800	4,200						
Culture and recreation	44,500	40,900	3,600	272,000	256,450	15,550			
Education	541,450	509,150	32,300						
Capital projects							1,610,600	1,625,500	(14,900)
Total expenditures	1,225,500	1,163,200	62,300	1,202,500	1,153,450	49,050	1,610,600	1,625,500	(14,900)
Excess (deficiency) of revenues over expenditures	124,500	115,300	(9,200)	(15,925)	17,675	33,600	(360,100)	(371,750)	(11,650)
Other financing sources (uses)									
Proceeds of general obligation bond issues	—	—					902,500	902,500	—
Operating transfers in							65,000	64,500	(500)
Operating transfers out	(74,500)	(74,500)					—	—	
Total other financing sources (uses)	(74,500)	(74,500)	—				967,500	967,000	(500)
Excess (deficiency) of revenues and other sources over expenditures and other uses	50,000	40,800	(9,200)	(15,925)	17,675	33,600	607,400	595,250	(12,150)
Fund balance at beginning of year	202,500	202,500	—	151,035	151,035	—	357,350	357,350	—
Increase in reserve for inventory	—	1,500	1,500						
Fund balance at end of year	$ 252,500	$ 244,800	$ (7,700)	$ 135,110	$ 168,710	$ 33,600	$ 964,750	$ 952,600	$(12,150)

See accompanying notes to financial statements

Source: Municipal Finance Officers Association, *Governmental Accounting, Auditing, and Financial Reporting (1980 GAAFR)* (Chicago: MFOA, 1980), Appendix D, p. 129.

Exhibit 4

NAME OF GOVERNMENT

STATEMENT OF REVENUES, EXPENDITURES, AND CHANGES IN
FUND BALANCES — BUDGET (NON-GAAP BUDGETARY BASIS) AND ACTUAL —
SPECIAL ASSESSMENT FUND TYPE

Year Ended December 31, 19X2

	Budget	Actual	Variance—favorable (unfavorable)
Revenues:			
Special assessments	$ 86,000	$ 86,000	$ —
Miscellaneous	20,000	20,664	664
Total revenues	106,000	106,664	664
Expenditures			
Capital outlay	315,000	308,265	6,735
Debt service	70,400	69,569	831
Total expenditures	385,400	377,834	7,566
Excess (deficiency) of revenues over expenditures	(279,400)	(271,170)	8,230
Other financing sources:			
Operating transfers in	10,000	10,000	—
Proceeds of special assessment bonds	175,000	175,000	—
Total other financing sources	185,000	185,000	—
Excess (deficiency) of revenues and other sources over expenditures	(94,400)	(86,170)	8,230
Fund balance at beginning of year	271,040	271,040	—
Fund balance at end of year	$176,640	$184,870	$8,230

See accompanying notes to financial statements

Source: Municipal Finance Officers Association, *Governmental Accounting, Auditing, and Financial Reporting (1980 GAAFR)* (Chicago: MFOA, 1980), Appendix D, p. 130.

Exhibit 5

NAME OF GOVERNMENT

COMBINED STATEMENT OF REVENUES, EXPENSES AND CHANGES IN RETAINED EARNINGS/FUND BALANCES — ALL PROPRIETARY FUND TYPES AND SIMILAR TRUST FUNDS

Year Ended December 31, 19X2

	Proprietary Fund Types		Fiduciary Fund Types		Totals (Memorandum Only)	
	Enterprise (note 8)	Internal Service	Pension Trust	Nonexpend-able Trust	19X2	19X1
Operating revenues:						
Charges for services	$ 672,150	$88,000	$ —	$ —	$ 760,150	$ 686,563
Interest	—	—	28,460	2,480	30,940	26,118
Contributions	—	—	160,686	—	160,686	144,670
Gifts	—	—	—	45,000	45,000	—
Total operating revenues	672,150	88,000	189,146	47,480	996,776	857,351
Operating expenses:						
Personal services	247,450	32,500	—	—	279,950	250,418
Contractual services	75,330	400	—	—	75,730	68,214
Supplies	20,310	1,900	—	—	22,210	17,329
Materials	50,940	44,000	—	—	94,940	87,644
Heat, light, and power	26,050	1,500	—	—	27,550	22,975
Depreciation	144,100	4,450	—	—	148,550	133,210
Benefit payments	—	—	21,000	—	21,000	12,000
Refunds	—	—	25,745	—	25,745	13,243
Total operating expenses	564,180	84,750	46,745	—	695,675	605,033
Operating income	107,970	3,250	142,401	47,480	301,101	252,318
Nonoperating revenues (expenses):						
Operating grants	55,000	—	—	—	55,000	50,000
Tap fees	22,000	—	—	—	22,000	20,000
Interest	3,830	—	—	—	3,830	3,200
Rent	5,000	—	—	—	5,000	5,000
Interest and fiscal charges	(78,888)	—	—	—	(78,888)	(122,408)
Total nonoperating revenues (expenses)	6,942	—	—	—	6,942	(44,208)
Income before operating transfers	114,912	3,250	142,401	47,480	308,043	208,110
Operating transfers in (out)	—	—	—	(2,530)	(2,530)	(2,120)
Net income	114,912	3,250	142,401	44,950	305,513	205,990
Retained earnings/fund balances at beginning of year	2,088,544	6,550	1,040,800	139,100	3,274,994	3,069,004
Retained earnings/fund balances at end of year	$2,203,456	$ 9,800	$1,183,201	$184,050	$3,580,507	$3,274,994

See accompanying notes to financial statements

Source: Municipal Finance Officers Association, *Governmental Accounting, Auditing, and Financial Reporting (1980 GAAFR)* (Chicago: MFOA, 1980), Appendix D, p. 131.

Exhibit 6

NAME OF GOVERNMENT

**COMBINED STATEMENT OF CHANGES IN FINANCIAL POSITION—
ALL PROPRIETARY FUND TYPES AND SIMILAR TRUST FUNDS**

Year Ended December 31, 19X2

	Proprietary Fund Types		Fiduciary Fund Types		Totals (Memorandum Only)	
	Enterprise (note 8)	Internal Service	Pension Trust	Nonexpendable Trust	19X2	19X1
Sources of working capital:						
Operations						
Net income	$ 114,912	$ 3,250	$142,401	$44,950	$ 305,513	$ 205,990
Add back items not requiring working capital—						
Depreciation	144,100	4,450	--	-	148,550	133,210
Working capital provided by operations	259,012	7,700	142,401	44,950	454,063	339,200
Contributions by subdividers	650,666	--		--	650,666	.
Net decrease in restricted assets	110,515	--	-	. .	110,515	743,386
Investments maturing	—	--	25,000		25,000	20,000
Total sources of working capital	1,020,193	7,700	167,401	44,950	1,240,244	1,102,586
Uses of working capital:						
Acquisition of fixed assets	324,453	7,000	.	.	331,453	846,812
Decrease in long-term general obligation bonds payable	50,000	--	--	-	50,000	50,000
Decrease in long-term revenue bonds payable	48,000	--	—	—	48,000	44,000
Repayment of advance from General Fund	—	10,000	—	—	10,000	10,000
Net decrease in current liabilities payable from restricted assets	143,345	—	—	—	143,345	4,318
Purchase of investments	—	—	145,360	—	145,360	131,000
Total uses of working capital	565,798	17,000	145,360	—	728,158	1,086,130
Net increase (decrease) in working capital	$ 454,395	$ (9,300)	$ 22,041	$44,950	$ 512,086	$ 16,456
Elements of net increase (decrease) in working capital:						
Cash	$ 141,536	$(20,300)	$ 20,121	$ 4,310	$ 145,667	$ 600,105
Investments	—	—	(2,019)	40,500	38,481	—
Receivables	(10,570)	—	—	520	(10,050)	3,217
Due from other funds	(6,000)	(8,000)	2,189	—	(11,811)	(4,923)
Inventory	11,250	14,000	—	—	25,250	(3,414)
Prepaid expenses	460	—	—	—	460	520
Vouchers payable	(72,471)	5,000	1,750	—	(65,721)	(42,427)
Contracts payable	388,250	—	—	—	388,250	(525,400)
Accrued general obligation bond interest	100	—	—	—	100	200
Other accrued expenses	1,840	—	—	(380)	1,460	(11,422)
Net increase (decrease) in working capital	$ 454,395	$ (9,300)	$ 22,041	$44,950	$ 512,086	$ 16,456

See accompanying notes to financial statements

Source: Municipal Finance Officers Association, *Governmental Accounting, Auditing, and Financial Reporting (1980 GAAFR)* (Chicago: MFOA, 1980), Appendix D, p. 132.

APPENDIX H

An Illustrative Set of Notes to Financial Statements where Such Notes Are Considered an Integral Part of the General Purpose Financial Statements of the Comprehensive Annual Financial Report

NAME OF GOVERNMENT
Notes to Financial Statements
December 31, 19X2

(1) Summary of Significant Accounting Policies

The Name of Government was incorporated January 17, 1917, under the provisions of Act 279, P.A. 1909, as amended (Home Rule City Act). The City operates under a Council-Manager form of government and provides the following services as authorized by its charter: public safety (police and fire), highways and streets, sanitation, health and social services, culture-recreation, education, public improvements, planning and zoning, and general administrative services.

The accounting policies of the Name of Government conform to generally accepted accounting principles as applicable to governments. The following is a summary of the more significant policies:

A. Fund Accounting

The accounts of the City are organized on the basis of funds and account groups, each of which is considered a separate accounting entity. The operations of each fund are accounted for with a separate set of self-balancing accounts that comprise its assets, liabilities, fund equity, revenues, and expenditures, or expenses, as appropriate. Government resources are allocated to and accounted for in individual funds based upon the purposes for which they are to be spent and the means by which spending activities are controlled. The various funds are grouped, in the financial statements in this report, into eight generic fund types and three broad fund categories as follows:

GOVERNMENTAL FUNDS

General Fund—The General Fund is the general operating fund of the City. It is used to account for all financial resources except those required to be accounted for in another fund.

Special Revenue Funds—Special Revenue Funds are used to account for the proceeds of specific revenue sources (other than special assessments, expendable trusts, or major capital projects) that are legally restricted to expenditures for specified purposes.

Debt Service Funds—Debt Service Funds are used to account for the accumulation of resources for, and the payment of, general long-term debt principal, interest, and related costs.

Capital Projects Funds—Capital Projects Funds are used to account for financial resources to be used for the acquisition or construction of major capital facilities (other than those financed by proprietary funds, Special Assessment Funds, and Trust Funds).

Special Assessment Funds—Special Assessment Funds are used to account for the financing of public improvements or services deemed to benefit the properties against which special assessments are levied.

PROPRIETARY FUNDS

Enterprise Funds—Enterprise Funds are used to account for operations (a) that are financed and operated in a manner similar to private business enterprises—where the intent of the governing body is that the costs (expenses, including depreciation) of providing goods or services to the general public on a continuing basis be financed or recovered primarily through user charges; or (b) where the governing body has decided that periodic determination of revenues earned, expenses incurred, and/or net income is appropriate for capital maintenance, public policy, management control, accountability, or other purposes.

Internal Service Funds—Internal Service Funds are used to account for the financing of goods or services provided by one department or agency to other departments or agencies of the City, or to other governments, on a cost-reimbursement basis.

Source: Municipal Finance Officers Association, *Governmental Accounting, Auditing, and Financial Reporting (1980 GAAFR)* (Chicago: MFOA, 1980), Appendix D, pp.133–41.

Appendix H *(continued)*

FIDUCIARY FUNDS

Trust and Agency Funds—Trust and Agency Funds are used to account for assets held by the City in a trustee capacity or as an agent for individuals, private organizations, other governments, and/or other funds. These include Expendable Trust, Nonexpendable Trust, Pension Trust, and Agency Funds. Nonexpendable Trust and Pension Trust Funds are accounted for in essentially the same manner as proprietary funds since capital maintenance is critical. Expendable Trust Funds are accounted for in essentially the same manner as governmental funds. Agency Funds are custodial in nature (assets equal liabilities) and do not involve measurement of results of operations.

B. Fixed Assets and Long-Term Liabilities

The accounting and reporting treatment applied to the fixed assets and long-term liabilities associated with a fund are determined by its measurement focus. All governmental funds and Expendable Trust Funds are accounted for on a spending or "financial flow" measurement focus. This means that only current assets and current liabilities are generally included on their balance sheets. Their reported fund balance (net current assets) is considered a measure of "available spendable resources." Governmental fund operating statements present increases (revenues and other financing sources) and decreases (expenditures and other financing uses) in net current assets. Accordingly, they are said to present a summary of sources and uses of "available spendable resources" during a period.

Fixed assets used in governmental fund type operations (general fixed assets) are accounted for in the General Fixed Assets Account Group, rather than in governmental funds. Public domain ("infrastructure") general fixed assets consisting of certain improvements other than buildings, including roads, bridges, curbs and gutters, streets and sidewalks, drainage systems, and lighting systems, *are* capitalized along with other general fixed assets. No depreciation has been provided on general fixed assets.

All fixed assets are valued at historical cost or estimated historical cost if actual historical cost is not available. Donated fixed assets are valued at their estimated fair value on the date donated.

Long-term liabilities expected to be financed from governmental funds are accounted for in the General Long-Term Debt Account Group, not in the governmental funds. The single exception to this general rule is for special assessment bonds, which are accounted for in Special Assessment Funds.

The two account groups are not "funds." They are concerned only with the measurement of financial position. They are not involved with measurement of results of operations.

Noncurrent portions of long-term receivables due to governmental funds *are* reported on their balance sheets, in spite of their spending measurement focus. Special reporting treatments are used to indicate, however, that they should not be considered "available spendable resources," since they do not represent net current assets. Recognition of governmental fund type revenues represented by noncurrent receivables is deferred until they become current receivables. Noncurrent portions of long-term loans receivable are offset by fund balance reserve accounts.

Special reporting treatments are also applied to governmental fund inventories to indicate that they do not represent "available spendable resources," even though they are a component of net current assets. Such amounts are generally offset by fund balance reserve accounts.

Because of their spending measurement focus, expenditure recognition for governmental fund types is limited to exclude amounts represented by noncurrent liabilities. Since they do not affect net current assets, such long-term amounts are not recognized as governmental fund type expenditures or fund liabilities. They are instead reported as liabilities in the General Long-Term Debt Account Group.

All proprietary funds and Nonexpendable Trust and Pension Trust Funds are accounted for on a cost of services or "capital maintenance" measurement focus. This means that all assets and all liabilities (whether current or noncurrent) associated with their activity are included on their balance sheets. Their reported fund equity (net total assets) is segregated into

Appendix H *(continued)*

contributed capital and retained earnings components. Proprietary fund type operating statements present increases (revenues) and decreases (expenses) in net total assets.

Depreciation of all exhaustible fixed assets used by proprietary funds is charged as an expense against their operations. Accumulated depreciation is reported on proprietary fund balance sheets. Depreciation has been provided over the estimated useful lives using the straight line method. The estimated useful lives are as follows:

Buildings	25-50 years
Improvements	10-20 years
Equipment	3-10 years

C. Basis of Accounting

Basis of accounting refers to *when* revenues and expenditures or expenses are recognized in the accounts and reported in the financial statements. Basis of accounting relates to the *timing* of the measurements made, regardless of the measurement focus applied.

All governmental funds and Expendable Trust Funds are accounted for using the modified accrual basis of accounting. Their revenues are recognized when they become measurable and available as net current assets. Taxpayer-assessed income, gross receipts, and sales taxes are considered "measurable" when in the hands of intermediary collecting governments and are recognized as revenue at that time. Anticipated refunds of such taxes are recorded as liabilities and reductions of revenue when they are measurable and their validity seems certain.

Expenditures are generally recognized under the modified accrual basis of accounting when the related fund liability is incurred. Exceptions to this general rule include: (1) accumulated unpaid vacation, sick pay, and other employee amounts which are not accrued; and (2) principal and interest on general long-term debt which is recognized when due.

All proprietary funds and Nonexpendable Trust and Pension Trust Funds are accounted for using the accrual basis of accounting. Their revenues are recognized when they are earned, and their expenses are recognized when they are incurred. Unbilled Water and Sewer Fund utility service receivables are recorded at year end.

D. Budgets and Budgetary Accounting

The City follows these procedures in establishing the budgetary data reflected in the financial statements:

1. Prior to September 1, the City Manager submits to the City Council a proposed operating budget for the fiscal year commencing the following January 1. The operating budget includes proposed expenditures and the means of financing them.

2. Public hearings are conducted at locations throughout the City to obtain taxpayer comments.

3. Prior to November 1, the budget is legally enacted through passage of an ordinance.

4. The City Manager is authorized to transfer budgeted amounts between departments within any fund; however, any revisions that alter the total expenditures of any fund must be approved by the City Council.

5. Formal budgetary integration is employed as a management control device during the year for the General Fund, Special Revenue Funds, Capital Projects Funds, and Special Assessment Funds. Formal budgetary integration is not employed for Debt Service Funds because effective budgetary control is alternatively achieved through general obligation bond indenture provisions.

6. Budgets for the General, Special Revenue, and Capital Projects Funds are adopted on a basis consistent with generally accepted accounting principles (GAAP). Budgets for Special Assessment Funds are adopted on a basis consistent with GAAP except that bond proceeds are treated as other financing sources and bond principal payments are treated as expenditures. Budgetary comparisons presented for Special Assessment Funds in this report are on this non-GAAP budgetary basis.

Appendix H *(continued)*

Budgeted amounts are as originally adopted, or as amended by the City Council on June 27, 19X2. Individual amendments were not material in relation to the original appropriations which were amended.

E. Encumbrances

Encumbrance accounting, under which purchase orders, contracts, and other commitments for the expenditure of monies are recorded in order to reserve that portion of the applicable appropriation, is employed as an extension of formal budgetary integration in the General Fund, Special Revenue Funds, Capital Projects Funds, and Special Assessment Funds. Encumbrances outstanding at year end are reported as reservations of fund balances since they do not constitute expenditures or liabilities.

F. Investments

Investments are stated at cost or amortized cost, which approximates market.

G. Inventory

Inventory is valued at the lower of cost (first-in, first-out) or market. Inventory in the General and Special Revenue Funds consists of expendable supplies held for consumption. The cost is recorded as an expenditure at the time individual inventory items are purchased. Reported inventories are equally offset by a fund balance reserve which indicates that they do not constitute "available spendable resources" even though they are a component of net current assets.

H. Advance to Other Funds

Noncurrent portions of long-term interfund loans receivable (reported in "Advance to" asset accounts) are equally offset by a fund balance reserve account which indicates that they do not constitute "available spendable resources" since they are not a component of net current assets. Current portions of long-term interfund loans receivable (reported in "Due from" asset accounts) *are* considered "available spendable resources."

I. Accumulated Unpaid Vacation, Sick Pay, and Other Employee Benefit Amounts

Accumulated unpaid vacation, sick pay, and other employee benefit amounts are accrued when incurred in proprietary funds (using the accrual basis of accounting). Such amounts are *not* accrued in governmental funds (using the modified accrual basis of accounting). At December 31, 19X2, unrecorded General and Special Revenue Fund liabilities included approximately $32,000 vacation pay, $17,000 sick pay, and $19,000 employee health benefits. These amounts do *not* exceed normal year's accumulations.

J. Comparative Data

Comparative total data for the prior year have been presented in the accompanying financial statements in order to provide an understanding of changes in the City's financial position and operations. However, comparative (i.e., presentation of prior year totals by fund type) data have not been presented in each of the statements since their inclusion would make the statements unduly complex and difficult to read.

K. Total Columns on Combined Statements - Overview

Total columns on the Combined Statements - Overview are captioned Memorandum Only to indicate that they are presented only to facilitate financial analysis. Data in these columns do *not* present financial position, results of operations, or changes in financial position in conformity with generally accepted accounting principles. Neither is such data comparable to a consolidation. Interfund eliminations have not been made in the aggregation of this data.

Appendix H *(continued)*

(2) Property Tax

Property taxes attach as an enforceable lien on property as of January 1. Taxes are levied on March 1 and payable in two installments on June 1 and September 1. The City bills and collects its own property taxes and also taxes for the County School District. Collections of the county taxes and remittance of them to the District are accounted for in the School District Tax Agency Fund. City property tax revenues are recognized when levied to the extent that they result in current receivables.

The City is permitted by the Municipal Finance Law of the state to levy taxes up to $5.00 per $100 of assessed valuation for general governmental services other than the payment of principal and interest on long-term debt and in unlimited amounts for the payment of principal and interest on long-term debt. The combined tax rate to finance general governmental services other than the payment of principal and interest on long-term debt for the year ended December 31, 19X2, was $3.74 per $100, which means that the City has a tax margin of $1.26 per $100 and could raise up to $358,881 additional a year from the present assessed valuation of $28,482,600 before the limit is reached.

(3) Due from Other Governments

Amounts due from other governments include $625,000 due from the County in connection with the construction of the Civic Center, which is expected to cost $2,003,000, with $1,250,000 to be financed through a grant from the County ($625,000 of this amount was paid during 1978). The $625,000 still due from the County is expected to be received when the project is 50 percent complete. Construction is expected to be 50 percent complete by April 1, 19X3, and fully complete by November 1, 19X3.

(4) Changes in General Fixed Assets

A summary of changes in general fixed assets follows:

	Balance Jan. 1, 19X2	Additions	Deletions	Balance Dec. 31, 19X2
Land	$1,225,000	$ 34,500	$ —	$1,259,500
Buildings	2,361,000	614,500	120,000	2,855,500
Improvements other than buildings	535,000	551,750	50,000	1,036,750
Equipment	375,600	91,000	14,100	452,500
Construction in progress	677,650	1,625,500	994,150	1,309,000
Total	$5,174,250	$2,917,250	$1,178,250	$6,913,250

Construction in progress is composed of the following:

	Project authorization	Expended to Dec. 31, 19X2	Committed	Required future financing
Civic Center	$2,000,000	$1,094,000	$ 906,000	None
Mill Street Bridge	250,000	215,000	35,000	None
Improvement District No. 80	200,000	117,100	82,900	None
Total	$2,450,000	$1,426,100	$1,023,900	

A summary of proprietary fund type property, plant, and equipment at December 31, 19X2 follows:

	Enterprise	Internal Service
Land	$ 211,100	$ 20,000
Buildings	447,000	60,000
Improvements other than buildings	3,887,901	15,000
Equipment	1,841,145	25,000
Construction in progress	22,713	—
Total	6,410,559	120,000
Less accumulated depreciation	640,800	16,900
Net	$5,769,759	$103,100

Appendix H *(continued)*

(5) **Changes in Long-Term Debt**

The following is a summary of bond transactions of the City for the year ended December 31, 19X2 (in thousands of dollars):

	General obligation	Revenue	Special assessment	Total
Bonds payable at January 1, 19X2	$1,610	$1,898	$420	$3,928
New bonds issued:				
19X2 Civic Center	700	—	—	700
19X2 Richard Craddock Memorial Recreation Center	200	—	—	200
Improvement District No. 80	—	—	175	175
Bonds retired	(110)	(52)	(40)	(202)
Bonds payable at December 31, 19X2	$2,400	$1,846	$555	$4,801

Bonds payable at December 31, 19X2 are comprised of the following individual issues (in thousands of dollars):

General obligation bonds:

$1,300,000 19W2 Waterworks serial bonds due in annual installments of $50,000 through January 1, 19Y6; interest at 4 percent (this issue is being serviced—principal and interest—by the Water and Sewer Enterprise Fund)	$ 700
$1,400,000 19W2 Street, Bridge, and Drainage Improvements serial bonds due in annual installments of $60,000 to $80,000 through December 1, 19Y2; interest at 3 percent	800
$700,000 19X2 Civic Center serial bonds due in annual installments of $35,000 through December 1, 19Z2; interest at 4 percent	700
$200,000 19X2 Richard Craddock Memorial Recreation Center serial bonds due in annual installments of $10,000 through December 1, 19Z2; interest at 5 percent	200
	$2,400

Revenue bonds:

$1,180,000 Water and Sewer serial bonds due in annual installments of $30,000 to $60,000 through January 1, 19Z2; interest at 3½ percent	$1,090
$820,000 19W8 Water and Sewer serial bonds due in annual installments of $18,000 to $45,000 through January 1, 19Z2; interest at 3½ percent	756
	$1,846

Special assessment bonds:

$350,000 19X1 Improvement District No. 77 serial bonds due in annual installments of $25,000 to $30,000 through July 1, 19Y3; interest at 4 percent	$ 320
$70,000 19X1 Improvement District No. 79 serial bonds due in annual installments of $10,000 through September 1, 19X8; interest at 4 percent	60
$175,000 19X2 Improvement District No. 80 serial bonds due in annual installments of $10,000 through January 1, 19Z0; interest at 4 percent	175
	$ 555

The annual requirements to amortize all debt outstanding as of December 31, 19X2, including interest payments of $1,569,000, are as follows:

Appendix H *(continued)*

Annual Requirements to Amortize Long-Term Debt
December 31, 19X2
(in thousands of dollars)

Year ending December 31	General obligation	Revenue	Special assessment	Total
19X3	$ 265	$ 111	$ 67	$ 443
19X4	258	113	70	441
19X5	252	115	68	435
19X6	246	127	66	439
19X7	240	134	64	438
19X8-Y2	1,105	709	248	2,062
19Y3-Y7	520	654	89	1,263
19Y8-Z2	255	562	32	849
	$3,141	$2,525	$704	$6,370

$12,572 is available in the Debt Service Funds to service the general obligation bonds.

There are a number of limitations and restrictions contained in the various bond indentures. The City is in compliance with all significant limitations and restrictions.

(6) Special Assessment Fund Deficits

The deficits of the Special Assessment Funds (Improvement District Number 77—$273,200 and Improvement District Number 80—$151,980) arise because of the application of generally accepted accounting principles to the financial reporting for such funds. Bond proceeds used to finance construction of special assessment projects are not recognized as an "other financing source." Liabilities for special assessment bonds payable are accounted for in Special Assessment Funds. Special assessments are recognized as revenue only to the extent that individual installments are considered current assets. The deficits of both funds will be reduced and eliminated as deferred special assessment installments become current assets.

(7) Other Required Individual Fund Disclosures

Generally accepted accounting principles require disclosure, as part of the Combined Statements - Overview, of certain information concerning individual funds including:

A. Segment information for certain individual Enterprise Funds. This requirement is effectively met in this report by Exhibits 1, 5, and 6 because the City maintains only one Enterprise Fund.

B. Summary disclosures of debt service requirements to maturity for all types of outstanding debt. This requirement is met by note 5.

C. Summary disclosures of changes in general fixed assets by major asset class. This requirement is met by note 4.

D. Summary disclosures of changes in general long-term debt. This requirement is met by note 5.

E. Excesses of expenditures over appropriations in individual funds. Civic Center Capital Projects Fund expenditures of $1,094,000 exceeded appropriations of $1,075,000. Mill Street Bridge Capital Projects Fund expenditures of $75,000 exceeded appropriations of $74,500. Special Assessment Fund Improvement District 77 expenditures of $204,565 exceeded appropriations of $203,400.

F. Deficit fund balances or retained earnings balances of individual funds. This requirement is met by note 6. No funds, other than Special Assessment Funds, reflected such balances at December 31, 19X2.

G. Individual fund interfund receivable and payable balances. Such balances at December 31, 19X2 were:

Appendix H *(continued)*

Fund	Interfund Receivables	Interfund Payables
General Fund	$12,000	$24,189
Special Revenue Fund:		
Parks Fund		2,000
Capital Projects Fund:		
Mill Street Bridge Fund		1,000
Enterprise Fund:		
Water and Sewer Fund	2,000	
Internal Service Fund:		
Central Garage Fund	12,000	10,000
Pension Trust Fund:		
Employees' Retirement System	10,189	
Expendable Trust Fund:		
Endowment Revenues Fund	1,000	
	$37,189	$37,189

(8) Retirement Commitments

The City sponsors and administers the Employees' Retirement System. It is accounted for as a separate Pension Trust Fund. It covers all City elementary employees except the school teachers, who are eligible for the State Teachers Retirement System, and employees of the Enterprise and Internal Service Funds, who are members of the XYZ Union administered retirement system. The total pension contribution for the year was $89,243, which includes amortization of an unfunded accrued liability of $243,000 over a 17-year period. All administrative costs of the system are borne by the General Fund.

Changes in Fund Balance Reserve for Employees' Retirement System during the year were as follows:

	Total Reserved Fund Balance	Fund Balance Reserved for Employee Contributions	Fund Balance Reserved for Employer Contributions	Fund Balance Reserved for Membership Annuities	Fund Balance Reserved for Undistributed Interest Earnings
Balance, January 1, 19X2	$1,276,150	$461,725	$493,362	$319,496	$1,567
Additions:					
Employee Contributions	64,274	64,274	—	—	—
Employer Contributions	96,412	—	96,412	—	—
Interest Earnings	28,460	10,330	7,730	8,159	2,241
Total Balance and Additions	1,465,296	536,329	597,504	327,655	3,808
Transfers:					
Annuities Awarded	—	(3,547)	(10,639)	14,186	—
Actuarial Adjustments:					
Current Annuities	—	—	1,287	(1,287)	—
Future Annuities	7,650	—	7,650	—	—
Total Revised Balances	1,472,946	532,782	595,802	340,554	3,808
Deductions:					
Expenditures—Annuities	21,000	—	—	21,000	—
Refunds—Deaths	5,495	5,495	—	—	—
Refunds—Resignations	20,250	20,250	—	—	—
Total Deductions	46,745	25,745	—	21,000	—
Balance, December 31, 19X2	$1,426,201	$507,037	$595,802	$319,554	$3,808

The City also contributed $29,447 this year to the State Teachers Retirement System as its share of elementary school teachers' contributions. The City has no further liability to this system. Future deficits would be financed by the state. Data concerning the actuarial status of the system are not available.

The City also contributed $11,313 to the XYZ Retirement System, a union administered plan which covers all City employees paid from the Enterprise and Internal Service Funds. This is a defined contribution (money purchase) plan.

Appendix H *(concluded)*

(9) Intergovernmental Revenues—Debt Service Funds

Under the provisions of state law, the state reimburses the City for a portion of the financing costs of various approved projects. Payments totaling $250,000 have been made through December 31, 19X2 including $41,500 in 19X2 for projects financed by the proceeds of the 19V5 Street, Bridge and Drainage Improvement bonds. These amounts must be used to abate a portion of the tax levied for principal and interest payments due on the approved project bonds. These reimbursements represent approximately 45 percent of the debt service on the 19V5 Street, Bridge and Drainage Improvement bonds and are expected to average approximately $40,000 annually until the bonds mature.

(10) Litigation

The City Council and the City are defendants in litigation seeking damages of $200,000 for violation of civil rights in a zoning decision. The suit alleges that the defendants conspired to down-zone property and refused to accept an application for a building permit by the plaintiff resulting in a violation of his civil rights. Outside counsel for the City is of the opinion that the defendants will prevail.

There are several other pending lawsuits in which the City is involved. The City Attorney estimates that the potential claims against the City not covered by insurance resulting from such litigation would not materially affect the financial statements of the City.

(11) Commitments

Commitments under lease agreements for facilities and equipment provide for minimum annual rental payments as follows:

	Facilities	Equipment	Total
19X3	$ 50,000	$ 25,000	$ 75,000
19X4	50,000	25,000	75,000
19X5	50,000	25,000	75,000
19X6	50,000	25,000	75,000
19X7	50,000	25,000	75,000
Thereafter	135,000	—	135,000
Total	$385,000	$125,000	$510,000

19X2 rent expense was $75,000. Commitments under construction contracts are described in note 4.

(12) Contingent Liabilities

The City participates in a number of federally assisted grant programs, prinicipal of which are the General Revenue Sharing, Community Development Block Grant, Comprehensive Employment Training Act, and Local Public Works programs. These programs are subject to program compliance audits by the grantors or their representatives. The audits of these programs for or including the year ended December 31, 19X2 have not yet been conducted. Accordingly, the City's compliance with applicable grant requirements will be established at some future date. The amount, if any, of expenditures which may be disallowed by the granting agencies cannot be determined at this time although the City expects such amounts, if any, to be immaterial.

(13) Subsequent Event

On February 13, 19X3, the City Council was officially notified that its application for a construction grant from the Environmental Protection Agency (EPA) was approved. Under the grant, the City is to construct a wastewater treatment plant at a total cost of approximately $2,450,000. EPA will finance 75 percent of the total cost, approximately $1,837,500, with the City financing the balance of $612,500 by issuing water and sewer revenue bonds. Construction is expected to commence in late 19X3 with completion currently scheduled for mid-19X5.

Defaults and Related Problems

Case Studies

Case 1: Upgrading New York City's Credit Rating, 1970–1973: A Municipal Analyst's Horror Story*

Judge Theodore Diamond
New York City Civil Court

In August 1977, as part of the "fallout" from New York City's fiscal collapse, the Securities and Exchange Commission (SEC) issued its staff report on New York City securities.[1] The 31-page chapter on credit rating agencies included only a few pages about the upgraded ratings in 1972–73. But how did the ratings go up when financial conditions were getting worse? About the 1970–75 period, SEC stated generally:

> The agencies appear to have failed, in a number of respects, to make either diligent inquiry into data which called for further investigation, or to adjust their ratings of the city's securities based on known data in a manner consistent with standards upon which prior ratings had been based.[2]

• • • • •

> During the period covered by the investigation, as shown below, billions of dollars of New York City's securities were sold or traded predicated upon ratings that were based largely upon unverified data and information furnished by the city to the rating agencies involved. Indeed, the agencies expressly disclaimed any responsibility for the accuracy of the information upon which they acted. Nor did they apparently recognize a responsibility to make diligent inquiry even in the face of adverse facts which came to their attention.[3]

The report emphasized that, while the city supplied data for each sale including a "Notice of Sale" and "Supplementary Report of Essential Facts," it did not have a "Report of Essential Facts" until

---

*Editors' Note: This case study reveals how New York City successfully devised and implemented a political and mass media campaign for pressuring the rating agencies into raising their credit ratings on its debt. The author, who is now a civil court judge in Kings County, New York, was research counsel and director of the research unit of the New York City comptroller's office between 1970 and 1974 and was intimately involved in these events.

[1] U.S. Congress, House of Representatives Committee on Banking, Finance and Urban Affairs, Subcommittee on Economic Stabilization, *Securities and Exchange Commission Staff Report on Transactions in Securities of the City of New York* (95th Congress, 1st Session, August 1977). Hereafter cited as *Staff Report.*
[2] Ibid., "Introduction and Summary," p. 9.
[3] Ibid., Chapter 5, "The Role of the Rating Agencies" p. 1f.

1975. This was irrelevant! The data for such a report was available, and substitutes for "Essential Facts" had been issued in the past.[4] But an interesting question not addressed by the SEC was the extent to which the 1972–73 upgrading was a signal to city officials that they could pressure or bluff the agencies and even the market, and thus enjoy a license for continued irresponsibility in the future.

The *Staff Report* stated that, early in 1972, two New York congressmen held a hearing on credit ratings, and a proposal to impose federal regulation on rating agencies.[5] A December hearing was scheduled by the New York State Senate Select (Goodman) Committee to Investigate the Rating of Tax-Exempt Bonds, and Moody's raised the rating from Baa–1 to A the day before.[6] While Moody's did provide some reasons for its action, the report demonstrated that many fiscal and economic factors were getting worse.[7]

In September 1973, city officials from budget (David Grossman), finance (John Fava), comptroller's office (Sol Lewis) met with Standard & Poor's (S&P), and delivered a written report outlining various improvements in the city's financial, socioeconomic, and accounting areas. After discussion of the report and other documents, and review of the comptroller's Annual Report for 1972–73 in November, S&P determined that an increase in the rating was warranted; and, in December, it was increased from BBB to A.[8] The SEC said that S&P analysts were aware that the data supplied by the city was to some extent a product of fiscal gimmickry (providing six examples), but S&P was "assured" by the city officials that these abuses were being corrected.[9]

WHAT REALLY HAPPENED, AND HOW?

1964–1970

In 1964, City Comptroller Beame issued a report, "New York City Bonds—A Prime Security," arguing for an improved rating from A to AA.[10] In July 1965, Moody's lowered the city's rating from A to Baa. Dun and Bradstreet (D&B) rated bonds in eight categories, with 22 levels of credit risk. It downgraded New York City from "good" to

---

[4]Ibid., p. 10, footnote 2. Such reports had been issued in 1967, 1968, and 1969. The February 1972 Credit Rating Report (see footnote 18), p. 5., was the same as a "Report of Essential Facts."

[5]Ibid., p. 14, footnote 5.

[6]Ibid.

[7]Ibid.

[8]Ibid., p. 15.

[9]Ibid., p. 16f. Also, see footnote 1 on page 17.

[10]The report, dated April 1964, was 18 pages long, had wide margins, little text, and about 1500 words.

"better medium", from risk category 9 to 10. A year later, S&P dropped the rating from A to BBB. In 1968, Moody's subdivided the Baa rating level; and the city got Baa–1, for the best credits in the Baa rating. In 1971, D&B's municipal rating service was merged into Moody's—unfortunately, because D&B reports were more complete.

In 1967 and 1968, City Comptroller Procaccino issued editions of "Essential Facts and Supplementary Information for Investors," about 35 pages long, half filled with financial schedules. In 1969, an election year, the office produced a slick, 50-page report entitled "New York City, An Investment Opportunity; Essential Facts for Investors," which was similar to publications by industrial development agencies.

In the general national prosperity of the late 1960s and the "go-go" years on Wall Street, there appeared to be improvements in the city's financial position. "In the two-year period ending June 30, 1969, the city managed to reduce its net funded debt by $24 million. . . ."[11] In his 1969 book, *The City,* Mayor Lindsay said, "I've seen a bankrupt city become fiscally sound in the space of three years."[12]

Comptroller Beame returned to office in 1970. On January 20, he said, "The city originally lost its A rating because the rating agencies were concerned we were using borrowed money to pay for some day-to-day expenses." Jac Friedgut of Citibank noted (in 1975) that Beame indicated such practices had ceased.[13] In June 1970, the third deputy comptroller advised me, as chief of the comptroller's research unit, to work on the credit rating. Because I had done a 1969 campaign position statement on city finances which identified some major problems, I replied that:

> Any attempt to improve the credit rating should be a long-term effort. . . . If we define an overall program, the banks and credit agencies might be more agreeable to our efforts. More important, if at the end of a year or two we have been able to achieve some of these things, all the more reason why they should go along with us.[14]

1971

In 1971, I indicated that we had to make improvements in the legal requirements and administrative factors which protected bondholders, because we couldn't rely on improvements in the financial and economic well-being of the city, its people, or institutions.

> I believe it unlikely that the general situation will improve in the next decade. No reason for improvement appears on the horizon. The city's

[11]*Staff Report,* Chapter 3, "Role of the City and its Officials," p. 18.
[12]John V. Lindsay, *The City* (New York: W.W. Norton, 1969), p. 17.
[13]*Staff Report,* Chapter 1, "Chronology of Events," p. 162.
[14]Author's memo to Third Deputy Comptroller Julian Buckley, June 23, 1970, p. 1.

master plan projections are quixotic. The results of the 1970 census will be released soon, providing clear and convincing evidence that vast sections of the Bronx and Brooklyn are disaster areas.[15]

However, we developed a strategy after reading all the literature on credit ratings, their purpose, what they measured, the key factors, and the measures used to evaluate each municipality. I was advised by a municipal analyst that factors usually cited as the basis for bond ratings were so extensive that no rating organization could have the time to go into all of them for the thousands of rated bonds.[16] Although rating agencies were competent to adjust a credit up or down based on what was happening in that municipality, their weakness was that they pretended to be able to do more than that—and could not! The strategy called for: (1) a report on the fiscal and economic strength of the city, to be the focus of our efforts; (2) criticizing the validity of the rating system in general; (3) identifying differences between rating agencies about various municipalities; (4) publicizing embarrassing errors by rating agencies; (5) providing situations where rating agencies might express inconsistent statements about what they were doing; (6) calling for government regulation of credit rating agencies.

I still believed that a fiscal improvement program was necessary. I was wrong. No program was ever mentioned, or needed!

Although the comptroller kept asking for the credit rating report in 1971, he did not publicize the issue much. However, he was getting increased pressure from his Technical Advisory Committee on City Debt Management, who indicated that they needed more "help" if they were to "*move* all this city paper."[17]

We resolved that the report would not be a "puff piece" like the "Essential Facts" issued in the 1960s, and we did not repeat silly arguments about how much New York City spent for various services. After all, if New York City spent $3 billion annually on education and the schools were a disaster, that wasn't persuasive! We decided to have lots of text, especially on administrative, social, and economic factors—where we could build up arguments. We were willing to identify problems and discuss them. We made old arguments in new ways, and new arguments. We knew that financial factors had deteriorated badly between January 1970 and June 1971.

Chapter I, a short introduction, described city ratings changes and set forth rating definitions. We did not pretend to be neutral.

> The purpose of this study is to show that New York City's credit rating was unfairly and unnecessarily downgraded. . . . The study will sup-

---

[15]Author's memo to Comptroller Beame, January 25, 1971, p. 1.
[16]Author's discussion with J. Sheafe Satterthwaite, Summer 1971.
[17]Remark to the author by Third Deputy Comptroller Melvin Lechner.

port the city's claim for a higher rating. . . . we believe careful study by the rating agencies of the material in this report justifies an upward adjustment. . . .[18]

Chapter II, "City Debt Structure," was four pages long. It identified the funded debt outstanding on December 31, 1971, and on December 31, 1960. It pointed out that four kinds of funded debt had decreased, two kinds increased; total increase was $1.8 billion. We also identified eight kinds of temporary debt as of December 31, 1971, but without the 1960 comparisons that had appeared in the first draft. The original Chapter II had been entitled, "Factors Considered by Rating Agencies," and was 14 pages long. This did not appear in the final report, but had been useful in developing our strategy.

Chapter III, 32 pages long, was entitled, "Factors Applied to New York City." Originally 26 pages long, it had been largely rewritten by Alice Rubin and included material on: security behind the debt, real estate, construction, changes in attitude, tax collection, socioeconomic factors, headquarters capital, commercial development, port of New York, public assistance, per capita income, recreation capital, etc. About 25% was quotations from reputable organizations.[19] Another 25% was tables which didn't really prove anything but looked good.

Chapter IV, "Comparison of New York City with Other Cities," originally 8 pages, had been immeasurably fortified and expanded by Julie Holtz to 34. This section became a treasure trove of material used in Beame statements during 1972–73. We took the 20 largest cities, added Newark (26th), and compared S&P, Moody's, and D&B ratings. This chapter included sections on repayment, credit reports, description, basic data, and key ratios. It listed favorable quotes about New York City in recent rating reports, and compared them with unfavorable quotes about other cities, arguing that New York City should have been rated as well as other cities with higher ratings. (Incidentally, this does *not* mean that a logical "scoring" system could not be devised and applied—only that the rating agencies didn't have one).

An early draft included a Chapter V, "Effects of the Present Rating," (four pages) that emphasized higher interest costs and eligibility for investment. The one-page Chapter V, "Conclusion," included:

There can be no doubt that the bonds of many of these cities have been

---

[18]New York City Office of the Comptroller, *The Case For Upgrading New York City's Credit Rating,* (February 1972), "Introduction," pp.1–1, 1–3. Hereafter cited as *Credit Rating Report.*

[19]Publications cited were from: Chase Manhattan Bank, Regional Plan Association, New York State Budget Division, First National City Bank, U.S. Census Bureau, Economic Development Council, etc.

rated higher than New York City bonds, even though New York City's economic strengths and its ability to repay its obligations are stronger.

• • • • •

The refusal of the rating agencies to respond favorably to the comptroller's repeated requests for a just upgrading of the city's credit rating has prompted him to call for federal action in this regard. What is needed is the establishment of uniform federal standards in the rating of all municipal obligations in the country, and federal regulation and/or supervision of the rating agencies.[20]

This was followed by an appendix, with 21 financial schedules.

In other words, the report was an attorney's brief—defining the issues in terms most helpful to our client, making our points, undercutting the arguments and credibility of opponents. It was entitled *The Case for Upgrading New York City's Credit Rating.* That implied that an opposing case could be made—for downgrading. True, but no one made *that* case; in fact, it would have been an easier case!

1972

The report was issued on February 17. (The cover page of the report is shown in Exhibit 1.) Letters were sent to Senator Sparkman (Banking, Housing, and Urban Affairs) and Congressman Patman (House Banking and Currency), asking for federal supervision and regulation of credit rating agencies. "I've thought that New York City ought to be at least A," said Beame.[21]

On February 24, he told the Municipal Forum that city bonds were a "top-drawer, blue-chip investment," and "no matter what political, fiscal, or social troubles beset city hall, there is virtually no risk in buying city bonds." Beame said it was riskier to invest in any major corporation in the country.[22]

Beame spoke to the Rockaway Rotary Club on March 1, confident that Congress would supervise rating agencies like the SEC supervised securities, and mentioned the high interest costs resulting from the bad rating.[23]

On March 16, after S&P had reduced the rating of New York State bonds to AA (Moody's had done this in 1964), the state senate appointed a committee to investigate the credit rating of tax-exempt bonds.

---

[20]*Credit Rating Report.* p. V–1.

[21]Comptroller press release 72–36, February 17, 1972; *New York Times,* February 18, 1972, p. 48.

[22]Comptroller press release 72–39, February 24, 1972. Also see release 72–68 of March 27, which repeated these statements.

[23]Comptroller press release 72–42, March 1, 1972

Exhibit 1

THE CASE FOR . . .

UPGRADING NEW YORK CITY'S CREDIT RATING

THE CITY OF NEW YORK
OFFICE OF THE COMPTROLLER

ABRAHAM D. BEAME
COMPTROLLER

FEBRUARY, 1972

On March 27, a few Democratic congressmen from New York City organized a hearing on credit ratings. Carey had to stay in Washington, and Koch sent a staff aide; but congressmen Podell and Murphy were present. Before a friendly group, Beame's rhetoric soared. "Before 1965, my position was that New York City bonds merited a rating of at least AA if not AAA"; and charged that agencies "compared different cities without uniform standards and wind up with ratings which do not accurately reflect relative fiscal strengths." He compared New York City and Newark, with one agency rating Newark higher, one lower, one equal. He called for federal supervision or regulation.[24] Representatives of rating agencies, in testimony, differed on whether lower ratings caused higher interest costs, or whether fiscal problems caused both. Podell suggested that there might be collusion between agencies and underwriters, who would make more money on lower-rated issues. He pointed out that hearings had been held on this subject in the 1960s.[25]

We were also helped because stories about municipal bond sale irregularities were in the news, leading to calls for regulation.

In August, Beame criticized S&P for rating the city's Housing Development Corporation (HDC) better than the city itself, while Moody's rated them one notch *lower*. Beame argued that HDC was a creation of the city; while S&P said there was a State "makeup" provision. A *New York Times* story said, "Privately, however, rating men were dismayed that the two principal services disagreed so much about the quality of the corporation's bonds."[26]

In October, Beame pointed out that, despite poor ratings, New York City bonds had outperformed the market generally in seven out of eight sales over two years.[27] That month, a L. F. Rothschild and Company municipal bond report said of city bonds, "We are of the opinion that the above bonds are entitled to higher ratings than those assigned by the two major investment rating services."[28]

On December 1, Beame called the Moody's Baa–1 rating "an insult to the credit of New York City."[29]

A *New York Times* editorial on December 7, entitled "NYC: Good Risk," seemingly endorsed Beame's position, referring to "the unfairly low credit ratings . . . arbitrarily assigned to this city's offerings."[30]

On December 12, John Nuveen & Company had a large advertisement in the *New York Times* entitled, "There are at least eight good reasons to invest in New York City bonds."[31]

Moody's caved in on December 17, raising the rating from Baa–1 to A. Mayor Lindsay called it a "marvelous Christmas present." Chairman Merola of the City Council's Finance Committee said it

---

[24]Comptroller press release 72–68, March 27, 1972; transcript of congressional hearing before congressmen Bertram Podell and John Murphy, March 27, 1972 (Coast Guard Hearing Room, Old Customs House, New York City).

[25]*New York Post*, April 1, 1972, p. 12; March 28, 1972, p. 67; *New York Times*, March 28, 1972, p. 59.

[26]Comptroller press release 72–145, August 10, 1972; *New York Times*, August 11, 1972, p. 40.

[27]Comptroller press release 72–192, October 18, 1972, a speech at a dinner of the New York City Study Trip for Investors.

[28]Report dated October 23, 1972, p. 1.

[29]Comptroller press release 72–233, December 1, 1972.

[30]*New York Times*, December 7, 1972, p. 36.

[31]*New York Times*, December 12, 1972, p. 73.

was "long overdue."[32] The following day, at a hearing before the State Senate (Goodman) Committee to Investigate the Rating of Tax-Exempt Bonds, Beame declared, "We are entitled to a higher credit rating, and we demand it." Beame asked now for an AA rating, attacked S&P's BBB as "outrageous, unfair, inaccurate, undeserved, and arbitrary; and something must be done about it." He attacked S&P for rating New York State Urban Development Corporation two grades higher than the city. He said that the city's fiscal position had improved since 1971.[33] A former head of S&P's municipal rating activities denied they were arbitrary or capricious, but admitted "ratings are nothing but opinions."[34]

1973

On January 11, Beame complained that S&P had given an improperly high rating to Evergreen Valley bonds, erroneously stating that they were backed by Maine. Evergreen Valley had defaulted.[35]

In March 1973, the city's total debt went over $10 billion. *The Wall Street Journal* defended the rating agencies in an editorial entitled "Roughing the Scorekeeper," and identified some deteriorating factors.[36]

On March 13, a bill to regulate credit rating agencies was introduced in Congress. Beame spoke about it at a speech in Chicago on March 16: "For almost a decade, my argument . . . has been that the rating analysts either don't know what they are doing, or have irrelevant standards; or when their standards *are* relevant, they do not apply them uniformly."[37] A city bond sale for $285 million at just over 5 percent led Beame to announce that the city had outperformed the market. He pressed for an AA rating.[38]

On April 17, Beame criticized an A rating for the United Nations Development Corporation, which had no guarantees and no certain revenue sources.[39]

[32]*New York Times,* December 18, 1972, pp. 1, 69. Moody's Vice President Phillips stated, "New York City has not developed the trend of funding current expenditures we once feared," *Daily News,* December 19, 1972, p. 81.

[33]*New York Post,* December 19, 1972, p. 13; *The Bond Buyer,* December 20, 1972; comptroller press release 72–249, December 19, 1972. For the organization of the Goodman committee, see *New York Times,* March 16, 1972, p. 40.

[34]*The Bond Buyer,* December 20, 1972.

[35]Comptroller's letter to John Pfeiffer of S&P, January 11, 1973; *New York Times,* February 20, 1973, p. 42.

[36]*The Wall Street Journal,* March 12, 1973.

[37]Comptroller press release 73–65, March 16, 1973; press release 73–60, March 13, 1973.

[38]*New York Times,* April 12, 1972, p. 52.

[39]Comptroller press release, 73–93, April 17, 1973, citing a *New York Times* column of April 16 on "Credit Markets," p. 61; *New York Times,* April 18, 1973, p. 43.

Things became ridiculous! The student senate of City University voted to support Beame's campaign for a higher rating. An employee in the graduate school business office got 2,600 signatures on a petition.[40]

On June 1, Moody's gave a city note sale its second highest rating, MIG–2. The city said this "was expected to prepare the climate for a double A rating."[41]

A *New York Times* article on August 19 anticipated regulation of municipal bond sales—to stop fraudulent operations.[42] Wall Street spokesmen were getting nervous at all the talk of regulation. Wallace Sellers of Merrill Lynch, in the *New York Law Journal* of December 10, wrote: "The fact that our issuers are public bodies with little incentive to make misstatements of facts regarding security, and with great incentive to keep issuing costs down, certainly justifies our exemption from the 1933 Act."[43] But he recognized that something had to be done about the bucketshops, and admitted that many less sophisticated people were in the municipal market now in comparison with the past when bonds were bought by institutions or by sophisticated wealthy people with good advisors.

On December 14, S&P raised the city's rating from BBB to A. S&P said, "The financial condition has improved in each of the last two fiscal years, showing an amazing resiliency to withstand budget difficulties."[44] A *New York Times* editorial concluded:

> The city has won its long fight to have its bonds upgraded to A status by both of the country's major credit rating agencies. . . . The improvement . . . climaxes a joint effort by Mayor Lindsay and by Mr. Beame, in his capacity as comptroller, to demonstrate that the fiscal health of New York is strong and getting stronger.[45]

New York City's *Credit Rating Report* may have been the greatest work of fiction in the 20th century. Less than two years after its bond ratings were upgraded, New York City defaulted on its outstanding general obligation notes.

---

[40]Comptroller press release 73–61, March 14, 1973; press release 73–93, April 17, 1973.

[41]*New York Times,* June 2, 1973, p. 41.

[42]*New York Times,* August 19, 1973, Financial Section, p. 1.

[43]*New York Law Journal,* December 10, 1973. p. 35. See comptroller press release 73–60, March 13, 1973, quoting SEC Chairman Casey. For the Beame position, see *The Bond Buyer,* December 10, 1973.

[44]Standard & Poor's statement of December 14, 1973; *New York Times,* December 15, 1973, p. 43.

[45]*New York Times,* December 20, 1973, p. 38.

Case 2: All that Glitters May Not Be an Enforceable and Valid Obligation: The Case of the West Virginia State Building Commission Bonds

James E. Spiotto, J.D.
Managing Partner
Chapman and Cutler

During the latter half of the 19th century, the municipal bond market was faced with various states and local governmental bodies repudiating their obligations on municipal bonds, based upon legal technicalities or outright desire not to pay certain obligations. In response to such problems, the municipal bond market began requiring not only specific legislation or court decisions determining the validity of municipal debt obligations but also opinions by bond counsel as to the validity and enforceability of such debt. As simple as the proposition may appear in the abstract, from time to time municipal-financing parties struggle with the question of whether or not bonds in the hands of bondholders are the valid and binding obligation of the issuing body.

The West Virginia State Building Commission Bonds, Series 1968, in the principal amount of $24.2 million is an example of financing where the question of the validity of the bonds proved fatal to the originally structured debt obligation. While there was support by decisional law from other states, the bonds were invalidated by the supreme court of West Virginia after millions of dollars of bonds were issued and sold. Fortunately, the bonds were later reaffirmed by the state of West Virginia pursuant to a new financing method. However, there was no legal obligation on the part of the state to do so.

FACTS

The principal question raised by the 1968 West Virginia financing was whether the bonds violated constitutional debt restrictions as to the permitted general obligations of the state, since the bonds were issued by the State Building Commission to finance the construction or the acquisition of government buildings and were payable from a fund created by lease payments which, in turn, were paid for by annual state appropriations to various governmental agencies.[1] Indiana, Michigan, Rhode Island, and Oklahoma have in the past upheld sim-

---

[1]Constitutional debt limitations were placed in numerous state constitutions in the latter half of the 19th century, after numerous state repudiations of excessive debt

ilar financing, while New Jersey, Oregon, Georgia, and Wyoming have invalidated statutes which provide for such transactions.

Section 4 of Article X of the constitution of the state of West Virginia provides in relevant part:

> No debt shall be contracted by this state, except to meet casual deficits in the revenue, to redeem a previous liability of the state, to suppress insurrection, repel invasion or defend the state in time of war; but the payment of any liability other than for the ordinary expenses of the state, shall be equally distributed over a period of at least 20 years.

In 1968, the legislature of the state of West Virginia reenacted and amended Article 6 of Chapter 5 of the State Code, thereby creating the State of West Virginia Building Commission and empowering the commission to finance the cost of a project by the issuance of state building revenue bonds, the principal of and interest on such bonds to be payable solely from a special fund. Section 10 of the statute provided that nothing in the article should be construed or interpreted to authorize or permit the incurring of state debt of any kind or nature as contemplated by the provision of the constitution of the state of West Virginia in relation to state debt.

Thereafter, on March 11, 1968, the legislature adopted and approved by resolution the issuance of the bonds, not to exceed the total principal amount of $25 million, for the purpose of acquiring land and constructing new state office buildings and parking facilities. The resolution of the building commission authorizing the bonds specifically provided that no part of the costs of construction were to be paid from any funds, grant, or gifts to be received from the U.S. government or from any other source except the proceeds of the sale of the bonds.

By resolution, the building commission covenanted with the bondholders that the buildings constructed with the proceeds of the bonds would at all times be leased to state agencies under leases sufficient to produce revenues equal to but not less than 130 percent of the average annual principal and interest payment on the bonds and 100 percent of the operating expenses of the system. The resolution of the building commission further provided that no lease or agreement for the use of the system or any of its facilities should pledge the credit or taxing power of the state for the payment of rentals or fees provided for in said leases or agreements.

The bonds themselves specifically provided as follows:

> This bond and the coupons appertaining hereto are payable solely from and executed by a lien upon and pledge of the revenues derived from

---

obligations. The limitations were intended to protect both the states' citizens and bondholders from unnecessary and extravagant debt and bond default. States which repudiated general obligation debt in the 19th century include Florida, Alabama, Louisiana, Mississippi, North Carolina, South Carolina, Georgia, Arkansas, Tennessee, Minnesota, Michigan, and Virginia.

the operation and management of the project and do not constitute an indebtedness of the state of West Virginia of any kind or nature as contemplated by the provisions of the constitution of West Virginia in relation to state debt and the state shall not be obligated to pay this bond or the interest thereon except from the revenues of the system as provided in the constitution. The credit or taxing power of the state shall not be deemed to be pledged to nor shall a state tax ever be levied for the payment of the principal or interest on this bond.

By contracts of lease dated April 1, 1970, the building commission as lessor leased to the state of West Virginia, as lessee for and on behalf of various departments and agencies of the state, office space in the office buildings at a monthly rate of rental which totaled the sum of $2.9 million annually.

Each lease provided that it should continue from "fiscal year to fiscal year" and that it should be considered "renewed for each ensuing fiscal year during the term of the lease, unless it is terminated or modified by agreement of both lessor and lessee." Each lease further provided that "this lease shall be considered canceled, without further obligation on the part of the lessee, if the state legislature or the federal government should subsequently fail to appropriate sufficient funds therefor or should otherwise act to impair the lease or cause it to be canceled."

The entire bond issue of $24.2 million was purchased by an underwriter. The issue was given an A rating by Moody's. The bonds of the series were to mature annually beginning with the year 1972 and ending with the year 1993.

THE LAWSUIT

In 1970, the owners of certain real estate to be acquired through condemnation and included in part of the project sought and obtained a writ of prohibition in the supreme court of West Virginia halting any further action in the eminent domain proceedings. Their basis was that the bonds issued pursuant to the 1968 statute[2] constituted a debt of the state of West Virginia in violation of Section 4 of Article X of the state constitution in view of the fact that rental payments to be used in retiring the bonds would be derived almost exclusively from monies to be appropriated by the legislature to various state agencies and departments.

---

[2]Apparently, State Building Revenue Bonds, Public Safety Series, in the principal amount of $2.5 million and State Building Revenue Bonds, Science and Cultural Center Series, in the principal amount of $1.5 million were also issued and sold pursuant to the statute; but such bonds were not directly questioned by the initial suit. However, such other bonds would be subject to the same constitutional infirmities as the $24.2 million issue.

Although the West Virginia Supreme Court noted that there was a split of authority with respect to the issue of whether such financing created a state debt,[3] the court found that the rental payments were a debt which would necessarily be paid by appropriations in annual installments for over a period of years and by successive legislatures from fiscal year to fiscal year. For this reason, the court determined that the statute pursuant to which the bonds were issued was unconstitutional and created a state debt in violation of the constitution of the state of West Virginia. According to the court, if by its decision the state was embarrassed financially, it was not the fault of the court:

> The parties should have known that this was a questionable procedure and the matter of the validity of these bonds and the question of whether they were general obligations or revenue bonds could have been tested in a proper proceeding in a court of competent jurisdiction before the building commission proceeded to the point where, admittedly, chaos may result because of the decision of the court in this case.[4]

Given the fact that the bonds were sold and the project was basically completed, the court was correct that chaos could have ensued.

SUBSEQUENT HISTORY

The decision of the West Virginia Supreme Court was decided on December 15, 1970, and a rehearing was denied on January 18, 1971. That same year, the state statute was amended to comply with the court's decision. In enacting the amendment, the legislature specifically found that the purpose of the amendment was, inter alia, "to accord statutory recognition to the existing rights, legal and equitable, of the holders of the bonds heretofore issued by the commission, to afford security for the payment of the obligations evidenced thereby, and to provide a special fund for the payment of those obligations."[5]

In the mandamus case which the state quite properly required following the amendments, the West Virginia Supreme Court determined that payment of rent from the state road fund and from a fund to be created and maintained from the sale of alcoholic liquors by the state would not unconstitutionally create state debts in violation of the provisions of the constitution. In the mandamus case, the court also authorized the payment of overdue interest on the Science and

---

[3]The court found that the "special fund doctrine" was inapplicable, as the fund for payment of the bonds was maintained by neither a special excise tax nor a self-liquidating facility.

[4]*State ex rel Hall v. Taylor*, 178 S.E. 2d 48, 59 (W. Va. 1970).

[5]W. Va. Code § 5–6–2 (f) (1971).

Cultural Center Series bonds which had not been paid during the litigation. Therefore, while a default had occurred no dollars of the bondholders were lost.

CONCLUSION

The lesson to be learned from the West Virginia case is basic. In order to ensure that a valid and binding debt is being created, if legal questions are raised which cannot be answered with certainty, it is advisable to have such questions resolved by a court of competent jurisdiction prior to issuing the bonds, rather than run the risk of their invalidity. This is particularly true since such invalidation could jeopardize the issuer's ability to obtain further credit in the marketplace.

Case 3: How Feasible Was the Feasibility Study for the Washington Public Power Supply System Bonds?*

Howard Gleckman
Staff Reporter
The Bond Buyer

Uncritical acceptance of revenue forecasts has come home to roost, perhaps most dramatically, with the Washington Public Power Supply System's (WPPSS) nuclear Projects 4 and 5. An epitaph for investors in the Projects 4 and 5 revenue bonds could well say, "They believed everything they read in the feasibility study and in the official statement."

WPPSS told those investors from the time of its earliest Projects 4 and 5 bond sales that power from the two plants would be necessary to meet the future energy needs of the Pacific Northwest.[1] In July 1976, in a warning regularly cited to the bond market, the federal Bonneville Power Administration (BPA) told the region's utilities that, without the electricity from the two projects, the Northwest

---

*This case study is adapted from *The Weekly Bond Buyer*, Jan. 31, 1983, pg. 3.

[1] Washington Public Power Supply System, Generating Facilities Revenue Bonds, Series 1977A (Nuclear Projects Nos. 4 and 5) Official Statement, March 1, 1977, pp. 15 and 25; also pp. A–9 and A–15 containing letter from R. W. Beck and Associates.

could face an energy shortage by mid-1983.[2] The forecasts were grossly wrong. Power from the two projects, it is now estimated, will not be needed in the region until the end of the century.[3]

Unwanted, plagued by cost overruns and construction delays, the two projects were abandoned in January 1982. By 1983, the supply system was struggling to resolve a financial crisis that threatened default on $2.25 billion in construction bonds sold before WPPSS, its participating utilities, and the bond market finally recognized their mistakes.

The now-terminated projects were planned as the final stage of a two-step effort by WPPSS to build five nuclear plants in Washington State. The power from the two plants was sold to 88 public utilities, which promised to purchase the entire generating capacity of the projects, whatever its cost. Linked with those agreements, called "take or pay" contracts, predictions of the region's need for Projects 4 and 5 power became the underpinning of the plants' feasibility and their bonds' security.

However, the load-growth forecasts cited in the supply system's official statements were not the only projections available by 1977, when WPPSS began its massive borrowing in the tax-exempt market for the two plants. Other estimates, including at least two commissioned by the federal government, projected that conservation generated by rising energy prices would reduce demand far below the forecasts cited by the supply system. Questions about projections relied upon by WPPSS were also raised by the U.S. General Accounting Office (GAO) in a mid-1978 report.[4]

In its March 1, 1977 official statement, WPPSS cited a forecast that projected a 5.5 percent average annual growth rate in energy demand over 15 years. That official statement for the supply system's first major tax-exempt borrowing for construction of the two plants included several charts showing potential energy shortages both for the region and for WPPSS 4 and 5's participating utilities.[5] The

---

[2]Bonneville Power Administration, *Notice of Insufficiency,* July 24, 1976.

[3]This is based upon the consensus of three 1982 load growth forecasts for the region. All three projected a most-likely or mid-range annual growth rate of 1.5–1.7 percent through the end of the century. The forecasts cited are the Washington state legislature's "Independent Review of WPPSS Nuclear Plants 4 and 5" (Hinman Report), March 15, 1982; the draft report of the Northwest Power Planning Council, adopted January 7, 1983; the Bonneville Power Administration's "Forecasts of Electricity Consumption in the Pacific Northwest, 1982." The legislative study suggested the two projects "or a substitute for them" would be needed between 1992 and 1999. The power council draft report suggests that thermal power for the end of the century should come from coal-fired projects rather than WPPSS Projects 4 and 5. The Bonneville forecast suggested the projects might be needed by the early to mid-1990s.

[4]General Accounting Office, "Report to Congress: Region at the Crossroads—The Pacific Northwest Searches for New Sources of Electric Energy," August 10, 1978.

[5]WPPSS, Official Statement, pp. 15, A–9, A–15.

March 1 official statement said, for example, "Early in the 1970s, it became apparent that . . . (WPPSS nuclear Projects 1, 2, and 3) would not provide adequate generating resources to supply the region's growing demand for electrical power beyond the early 1980s".[6] The same forecasts were also used by Bonneville to justify its 1976 warning of a mid-1983 energy shortage unless Projects 4 and 5 were built. How could these forecasts have been so wrong? How could the supply system investment bankers, rating agencies, and investors have ignored what, in hindsight, were key factors of energy price elasticity and economic uncertainty?

Part of the answer may lie in their source. Until 1976, the region had few independent estimates of future power needs. Instead, the primary source of load growth forecasts came from the Pacific Northwest Utilities Conference Committee (PNUCC), a group which represents the utilities themselves. Until 1977, the group's forecasting method was simple. It merely added up the load forecasts of Bonneville and each of the region's 7 investor-owned and 113 public utilities. The sophistication of each of those individual estimates, of course, varied widely. Some utilities provided detailed projections. Others, according to energy officials knowledgeable about the process, merely made "seat of the pants" guesses based on prior historical trends. Although BPA and PNUCC staffs offered technical assistance in preparing the projections, the individual power company forecasts were, in the end, accepted as part of the overall estimate.

That total, called the sum of the utilities projection, in turn became the official regional forecast. It found its way into supply system official statements and Bonneville's own projections. In 1976, it was the basis for BPA's warnings about energy shortages. The forecasts depended on three key assumptions. The first was that the projections should be based, in part, on once-in-a-lifetime "critical water years," when drought sharply reduced hydroelectric power generation. The second was that the region's booming economy of the 1960s and early 1970s would continue without letup for as long as 20 years. The third was that power, then available for less than 1 cent a kilowatt hour, would remain so inexpensive that ratepayers would not reduce consumption in response to higher prices. Although the PNUCC recognized that nuclear- and coal-generated electricity would be more expensive than hydropower—the region's primary source of energy—it took many years before the group expected enough of a cost increase to noticeably affect consumption.

Ironically, much of the increase in electric rates from 1979 to 1983, and the reduced consumption it generated, can be directly attributed

---

[6]Ibid., p. 25.

to WPPSS's own construction program. The least expensive of the WPPSS plants, Project 1, is expected to deliver electricity at about 2.4 cents a kilowatt hour. The most expensive, the now-terminated Project 5, would have provided power at almost 3.5 cents had it been completed at cost estimates made in 1981.[7]

Beginning in 1977, PNUCC did use a computer model to supplement its estimates, but its projections still basically tracked the results of the sum of the utilities method. "The problem with these models is that you need a lot of data, and we just didn't have it," said David Hoff, manager of corporate planning for Puget Sound Power & Light Company and former chairman of PNUCC's forecasting committee.[8]

The PNUCC forecasts, however, contained strong evidence that the group's early estimates may have been overstated about the region's future need for power. After 1974, every annual PNUCC growth estimate declined. Conservation, virtually ignored in early PNUCC estimates, was a factor after 1977. In 1974, for example, PNUCC estimated that utilities in the region would need 17,339 average megawatts of power by 1979–80. In 1977, the group projected 1979–80 energy needs at 15,687 megawatts. The difference was more than the projected output of WPPSS Projects 4 and 5. In 1979–80, utilities in the region actually used 14,866 average megawatts.[9]

The PNUCC forecasts, however, were not the only projections available to WPPSS and BPA, although both agencies chose to discount others. In the spring of 1976, the consulting firm of Skidmore, Owings & Merrill prepared a report at Bonneville's request which concluded that increased conservation in the Northwest would reduce, or even eliminate, the need for all five WPPSS nuclear projects.[10] In October 1976, after a spate of press leaks, BPA made the Skidmore, Owings report public. However, BPA released, at the same time, its own internal analysis that criticized Skidmore, Owings' findings and suggested the projected conservation would never be achieved. Three months later, a second study confirmed many of the Skidmore, Owings conclusions about conservation.

A January 31, 1977 report by the Natural Resources Defense Council (NRDC), a San Francisco-based environmental group, pro-

---

[7]Northwest Power Planning Council, "Development of Resource Targets Issue Paper," November 29, 1982, p. 29.

[8]Northwest Power Planning Council, "Northwest Energy News," April 1982, p. 8.

[9]Washington Energy Research Center, "Independent Review of Washington Public Power Supply System Nuclear Plants 4 and 5. Final Report to the Washington State Legislature," March 15, 1982, p. 77.

[10]Skidmore, Owings & Merrill, "Bonneville Power Administration Electric Energy Conservation Study," July 1976.

jected the region would only need 14,000 average megawatts of power annually by 1995, 2½ times less than estimated by PNUCC.[11] The report, with assumed "vigorous" conservation, was funded by the federal Energy Research & Development Administration, now part of the Department of Energy. According to NRDC's Ralph Cavanagh, the report was "widely distributed and widely publicized" in the region. The study results were reported in both major Seattle daily newspapers on February, 25, 1977.[12] WPPSS's first major Projects 4 and 5 bond sale was a $100 million offering in July 1975 to finance the preliminary engineering. WPPSS did not initiate its heavy borrowing to finance construction until February 23, 1977, after both the Skidmore, Owings and the NRDC studies were completed.

Similar, though less dramatic, conclusions about the region's potential for conservation were reached by the U.S. General Accounting Office, an arm of Congress, in August 1978.[13] The GAO reviewed both the PNUCC estimate of a 4.8 percent energy growth rate through the year 2000 and a second "conventional" 1977 projection by the Northwest Energy Policy Project (NEPP), a group sponsored by the federal government and the states of Washington, Oregon, and Idaho. The accounting arm of Congress said NEPP's midrange forecast of 2.7 percent annual energy growth rate through 2000 was "considered most likely to occur."[14] If that projection was accurate, GAO said, the region showed a strong potential for conservation. GAO recommended a "go slow" attitude towards new thermal projects, including nuclear, and a "thorough assessment" of alternatives.[15]

There were other clues as well. In 1976, the city of Seattle's municipal utility, City Light, decided not to join the construction consortium for Projects 4 and 5, although it was a major participant in WPPSS nuclear Projects 1, 2, and 3. A major factor in its decision was the conclusion of an internal study, called "Energy 1990," which projected that price-induced conservation would dramatically reduce energy demand in the region.[16]

As late as 1979–80, the market and the rating agencies seemed to ignore the growing evidence that the region would not need the power from the two plants in the foreseeable future. Instead, until the market finally closed to Projects 4 and 5 after March 1981, they stressed that the bonds were secured by their take-or-pay contracts even if the

---

[11]Natural Resources Defense Council, "Choosing an Electrical Energy Future for the Pacific Northwest," January 31, 1977.

[12]"An Alternative Energy, Scenario," *Seattle Times,* February 25, 1977, p. A–8; "Regional Energy Plan Keyed to Conservation," *Seattle Post-Intelligencer,* February 25, 1977, p. A–10.

[13]GAO, "Region at the Crossroads."

[14]Ibid., p. iv.

[15]Ibid., p. v.

[16]Seattle City Light, "Energy 1990," 1976.

power was not actually purchased or used. Some investors apparently were convinced that take-or-pay would, in effect, absolve the supply system of its sins. The bonds would be repaid by the utilities which signed take-or-pay agreements, even if the projects' power was not needed or the plants were never completed, argued many on Wall Street.

When originally issued, WPPSS Projects 1, 2, and 3 bonds received Moody's Investors Services' very highest credit rating of Aaa, and the Projects 4 and 5 bonds its A–1 rating. While lower in credit quality, A–1 was designated by Moody's as having the "strongest investment attributes" within the "upper medium grade" of credit worthiness. Standard & Poor's Corporation initially gave WPPSS Projects 1, 2, and 3 bonds its highest rating of AAA, and the Projects 4 and 5 bonds its rating of A$^+$ (which is comparable to Moody's A–1 rating). By June of 1983, Moody's suspended its ratings for the Projects 1, 2, and 3 bonds, and rated the Projects 4 and 5 bonds Caa. Standard & Poor's also had no rating for the Projects 1, 2, and 3 bonds, and rated the Projects 4 and 5 bonds CC, which is defined as the lowest rating above default.

The result of the WPPSS forecasting trap is a $2.25 billion debt for what appears to be a dry hole. A debt which, perhaps predictably, WPPSS's utilities in early 1983 were seeking every legal means to avoid.

Case 4: The Problem Bonds of the Midlands Community Hospital, Sarpy County, Nebraska*

Kent Pierce
Staff Reporter
The Bond Buyer

On January 3, 1983, Midlands Community Hospital in Sarpy County, Nebraska, retired $320,000 in bonds.

The payment was only a small portion of the $19.7 million in bonds outstanding, but it marked the first time the hospital has made a principal payment on schedule since it entered the tax-exempt market 10 years ago.

---

*This case study is derived from an article written by the author published in *The Bond Buyer* ("Nebraska Hospital Is Getting Better after 10 Years of Financial Troubles," January 3, 1983, pp. 1, 55).

The payment was also a sign, the hospital's management said, that a three-year drive to solve the hospital's financial problems was succeeding.

Midlands' troubles began during the planning stages, although they were not apparent until after the hospital's construction.

In the mid-1960s, the board of directors of the Doctors Hospital, an aging 100-bed facility in downtown Omaha plagued by declining patient use and outdated equipment, decided to build a new hospital.

The board selected Papillion, a city situated 12 miles from Doctors Hospital, as the site for the new Midlands Community Hospital. With a population growth rate of 112 percent in the 1960s, Papillion seemed an ideal place to set a new facility. This notion was supported by a feasibility study done by the accounting firm of Arthur Young & Company.

The study estimated patient use according to projected population figures in the area the hospital would serve. It projected occupancy percentages of 59 percent in 1976, the hospital's first year, 71 percent in 1977, and 84 percent by 1978.

Of greater importance to the board, however, was a questionnaire sent by the accounting firm to 562 physicians and 252 dentists in Omaha and Sarpy County which found that 106 physicians and 12 dentists would seek appointment to the staff at Midlands, enough to provide adequate debt coverage.

With these findings in hand, the board decided to proceed with construction.

The study on the surface appeared to be thorough and professional; but as events later proved, the study was terribly flawed.

When the hospital opened in January 1976, there were only three doctors available to admit and treat patients.

Later that same year, a serious revenue shortfall occurred due to an occupancy rate of 30 to 40 patients per day, less than half the rate projected in the feasibility study. It became apparent that revenues and reserves would not be adequate to cover the scheduled debt service payments over the next couple of years. As a result, Midlands was put into receivership by order of the Sarpy County District Court in October 1976. On January 3, 1978, the hospital missed its first principal payment to the bondholders.

"Depending on the medical staff to move 12 miles from Omaha to Sarpy County" was the weak link in the feasibility study's projections, said Morris Miller, former chairman of the board of the Omaha National Bank and now the receiver of the hospital.

"A lot of doctors said they would move, but when the chips were down, they realized that their patient pool was not in Sarpy County but back around their offices in Omaha," he said.

The doctors who had indicated a willingness to practice at Midlands had signed letters of intent. The letters, however, were not legally binding; the physicians could not be forced to work at Midlands.

An additional tactical error was made by the hospital board in its decision to build the hospital before building office space for the doctors. Doctors who were considering a practice at Midlands quickly realized that they would be forced to commute between Papillion and their offices in Omaha. This error did little to attract doctors to Midlands.

Based on faulty assumptions, the hospital's financial foundation quickly crumbled. A review of Midlands' credit rating history illustrates this point.

Moody's originally assigned an investment quality (conditional) Baa rating to both the $19.2 million hospital bond 1973 series and the $2.5 million project completion bond issue of 1976. Offered through the Hospital Authority No. 1 of Sarpy County, Moody's subsequently downgraded the bonds twice. They bottomed out in February 1977 at Caa—which is below investment grade.

Midlands' rating scorecard at Standard & Poor's reflects similar setbacks. After receiving a BBB (provisional) investment grade rating in 1973 and again in 1976, the hospital's credit standing was dropped to D.

The hospital's finances appear to have since improved, but not to the point where its debt is investment grade. The hospital's basic problems are a lack of working capital and the depletion of security accounts, such as the bond reserve fund and the operation and maintenance reserve fund.

Midlands' financial problems have resulted in a negative funds balance. At the end of the 1982 fiscal year (June 30, 1982), the hospital's total funds balance was a negative $3.5 million. Although this figure was down $400,000 from 1980–81 fiscal year figures, it was still a horrible ratio between total assets and total liabilities.

Not surprisingly, investors have shown little interest in the bonds. The bonds traded in February, 1983 at 60 to 70 cents on the dollar but not in great volume. This estimate reflects some gain in price from a low of 38 cents on the dollar, a discount offered during the hospital's most difficult times in the late 1970s.

From this stumbling start, Midlands has slowly progressed toward financial recovery. To conserve funds, more than half of the original staff has been laid off, and the receiver has hired Hospital Corporation of America, a management company that has 145 hospitals in its fold, to run Midlands' day-to-day operations.

Calvin Bremmund, assistant administrator in charge of financing for Midlands, said that the hospital's improved financial condition is due, in part, to the steady growth of "patient days" since the hospital opened in 1976.

Daily bed occupancy rates are indicators of hospital revenues. At Midlands it has risen from a first-year average of about 40 to a 1982 average of 84.

Mr. Bremmund said revenues accumulated from the increased patient days over the last three years have been sufficient to pay back defaulted principal payments dating back to the initial principal payment due in January 1978. With the $320,000 payment on January 3, 1983, Midlands is back on the debt service schedule projected back in 1973.

Another bright note is that the hospital has never missed a semiannual interest payment on either the Series 1973 or the 1976 bonds.

The number of doctors practicing at the Sarpy facility has risen from the dismal figure of three in 1976 to 33 in 1983. Also, the geographic area serviced by the hospital is expected to grow by 30 percent this decade. The hospital today has 208 beds, the same number it opened with.

It would be premature to lift the hospital's receivership for at least another 24 months, declared Mr. Miller who is the receiver of the hospital. He explained that during this period, the hospital management plans to rebuild depleted reserve funds and pay about $1 million in debt remaining from the late 70s. The latter figure can be broken down into bills owed various long-time creditors, such as the utility companies and the general contractor. Mr. Miller hoped that some sort of payback arrangement could be developed involving 10-year bank notes.

When these goals are achieved, he said that a recommendation to lift the receivership will be forthcoming.

In the meantime, Mr. Miller remains optimistic. He predicts that the hospital will succeed because Omaha's metropolitan area is expanding and with it the population of Sarpy County. The more people, the more patients, the better off the hospital.

"Midlands Community Hospital," he said, "was a good idea that took hold before its time."

Case 5: Default of the Beaufort County, South Carolina, Hospital Facilities Gross Revenue and First Mortgage Bonds (Hilton Head Hospital)

George Yacik
Staff Writer
The Bond Buyer

Beaufort County, South Carolina, sold $11.2 million of hospital facilities gross revenue and first mortgage bonds dated June 1, 1974 for the Hilton Head Hospital. The issue consisted of $1.125 million of serial bonds due January 1, 1979 through January 1, 1985, and $10.075 million of 8¼ percent term bonds due January 1, 2005. When these bonds were issued, they had been given medium-grade credit ratings by Moody's of Baa (conditional) and by Standard & Poor's of BBB (provisional). Proceeds from the bond sale were used to construct a 40-bed acute care hospital, a 40-bed skilled nursing facility, and an ambulatory care facility. Construction of the project began March 1, 1974; while completion was originally scheduled for October 1, 1975, the facility began operating a little earlier on August 8, 1975.

Hilton Head Island is a resort area and retirement community off the coast of South Carolina. According to population estimates done by the Sea Pines Company (a local community developer and resort operator), population on Hilton Head more than doubled between 1970 and 1974 to 7,900.[1] The hospital's feasibility study, which was done by Booz, Allen & Hamilton, Inc., took this estimate into account and thus said that such a medical facility would be needed and economically feasible by 1975. It based its projected utilization rate on a projected population on the island of 19,600 by 1980.[2]

However, population growth on Hilton Head began to slow. A special census conducted in April 1975 found that the actual population for 1974 was 6,500, not 7,900 as previously estimated.[3] In addition, the island was hit hard by the national economic recession of 1974–75.

As a result, the hospital's actual patient utilization rate fell far below the estimates in the feasibility study. For example, in March

---

[1] The official statement for the $11,200,000. Beanfort County, South Carolina, Hospital Facilities Gross Revenue and First Mortgage Bonds, Series 1974, dated May 31, 1974, p. A–5.

[2] Ibid, p. A–8.

[3] Standard & Poor's, *Fixed Income Investor*, November 26, 1977, p. 54.

and April 1976 only 50 percent of the acute care beds in the facility were occupied. The failure of the hospital to attract patients occurred not only because of the slow development on Hilton Head but because of the lack of a full-time cardiologist on the hospital's staff, which resulted in a loss of patients to hospitals in nearby Savannah, Georgia.[4] At the same time, staffing levels at Hilton Head Hospital were above those at other comparable hospitals in South Carolina.

In late January 1976, Hilton Head Hospital informed the bonds' trustee, Bankers Trust of South Carolina, that its gross revenues would not cover its operating expenses. For the first 11 months of operation ending June 30, 1976, the hospital incurred an operating loss of $2.19 million.[5] Money in the debt service reserve fund was sufficient to meet coupon payments through July 1, 1977.

The hospital went into technical default when it failed to pay to the trustee on April 1, 1976, one sixth of the bond interest due on July 1, 1976. The reserve fund was fully exhausted in order to meet the July 1, 1977, coupon payment; the coupon payment on January 1, 1978, was not met. The hospital was also in default of a $153,493 note due in February 1977 that was held by the trustee, with interest at 1½ points above the prime rate, and a $52,665 unsecured note held by the Island Investment Corporation.[6]

At that time, the trustee advised that it was in the bondholders' best interest that the hospital remain in operation. The hospital then implemented some staffing and cost-cutting measures, such as moving from a data processing accounting system to a manual system and purchasing drugs and medical supplies from a central supply purchasing bureau. It also began a fund-raising drive. However, at the time of the writing of this case study, the bonds were still in default.

---

[4]Moody's Investors Service, *Municipal Credit Report,* March 22, 1976.

[5]Report of the accountant, McKnight, Frampton, Buskirk and Co., Hilton Head, S.C., September 8, 1977.

[6]Moody's Investors Service, *Municipal Credit Report,* December 18, 1978.

Case 6: The Urban Development Corporation Defaults on Its Notes*

David Herships
Vice President, Public Finance Division
Marine Midland Bank, N.A.

In April 1968, the New York State Urban Development Corporation (UDC) was established by the state legislature to construct subsidized housing in urban renewal areas as well as undertake economic development projects. Less than seven years later, the UDC was on the brink of bankruptcy after defaulting on $100 million in bond anticipation notes on February 25, 1975. With its credit standing ruined, UDC was unable to access the market to refinance the defaulted notes, past-due bank loans, operating expenses, and (most critically) funds to complete construction of half-finished projects. These items totaled almost $700 million. If the projects underway could not be completed, UDC bondholders—$1.1 billion outstanding—would have to look to the state's "moral obligation" pledge for repayment of debt service.[1]

An invasion of the UDC debt service reserve fund and subsequent replenishment by the state had not been contemplated when the moral obligation device had been developed. Moreover, the magnitude of UDC's debt service requirements was difficult for the state to absorb because of its own budgetary difficulties due to the 1975 recession and the rapidly developing New York City financial crisis. The UDC note default was subsequently cured by the state (in May 1975), and a new state agency (the Project Finance Agency) was formed to complete the financing of the unfinished UDC projects.

Nonetheless, although its solvency has since been assured by the state, the UDC crisis shook the world of municipal bond investors. An agency of a major state had defaulted on its obligations, thereby calling into question the credit worthiness of the public authority debt structure of New York as well as other states. In addition, the accountability and the very purpose of public authorities were ques-

---

*The author has drawn information for this case study from the New York State Moreland Act Commission on The Urban Development Corporation and other State Financing Agencies, *Restoring Credit and Confidence* (1978). Mr. Herships was a consultant to the commission. The author's views are his own and do not represent those of Marine Midland Bank, N.A.

[1]Moral obligation bonds are the subject of Chapter 30.

tioned as well. It should be noted that in recent years, the UDC has been able to meet its obligations without dependence on state aid and its financial statements have received an unqualified auditor's opinion.

ORIGINS OF UDC

Faced with deteriorating conditions in the inner cities in the mid-1960s, the governor of New York State, Nelson A. Rockefeller, recommended to the state legislature that it establish a new agency to meet urban housing needs and facilitate economic development as well. The state already had set up the Housing Finance Agency (HFA) in 1960 to finance rental housing at below-market rates after voters had repeatedly rejected a general obligation bond program for the purpose. The HFA bonds were also secured by the so-called moral obligation of the state. The HFA, however, proved to be conservative and would only undertake those housing projects—largely middle-income—which were financially sound. As a result, the riskier, inner-city, low-income housing and urban renewal projects envisioned by the state were not built.

Legislation was enacted creating the UDC in the emotionally charged atmosphere following the assassination of Dr. Martin Luther King, Jr., in April 1968. The role of the UDC, however, while including the financing and construction of low-income subsidized housing, also was unique in that it included unprecedented responsibilities for urban renewal, commercial and industrial development, and the role of developers of so-called new towns.

The UDC was set up to be self-sufficient: that is, project revenues would be applied to payment of principal and interest on the bonds. During the start-up and construction period, however, expenses were to be financed from first-instance state appropriations, and later from capitalized interest. Because of the long delay until project revenues would be available, in order to market the bonds, the state's moral obligation pledge was included in the UDC's financial structure. The moral obligation pledge was the security in part necessary to satisfy the investment community and the rating agencies of the bonds' credit worthiness. As a result, both agencies gave UDC bonds investment grade ratings for the first bond sale in 1971. The ratings may have been partially due to the sound track record established by the HFA since its inception in 1960 as well as to the view that the state, particularly under Governor Rockefeller's leadership, would support its agencies if necessary.

One factor bears special mention. These long, 40-year bonds were not secured by individual project revenues, of which there were many, but were general purpose bonds secured only by the agency's general credit worthiness. In part, this was because of the long lead time of many of the agency's projects and because, during construction, project revenues were not available.

UDC's intent was to finance construction by long-term bond sales as construction progressed. Its first bond sale—for $250 million—occurred in 1971. Both Moody's and Standard & Poor's rated the bonds A—clearly of investment quality in their eyes. UDC subsequently sold $675 million in long-term issues in the market: a $150 million issue in 1972, two issues totaling $300 million in 1973, and two issues for $225 million in 1974. In addition, there was a $200 million private placement of long-term bonds with New York City banks in 1974. This was a substantial amount of debt to be publicly marketed, given the large competing demand for funds by New York City, the HFA, the New York Dormitory Authority, and other New York borrowers, as well as the start-up, speculative nature of the projects.

Nonetheless, even these funds raised from the sale of long-term bonds were insufficient to meet all construction needs, and UDC turned to the short-term market. Short-term bank loans were first made in February 1973. Later, in July 1973, $75 million in one-year bond anticipation notes (BANs) were sold. On February 26, 1974, UDC sold $100 million in BANs rated MIG-2 (of "high quality") by Moody's. These are the notes that were not redeemed at maturity in 1975, defaulting instead.

With bond proceed monies in hand, UDC quickly embarked on a very large-scale construction plan. By 1972, however, financial problems began developing. Simply stated, management had committed for new construction programs that outstripped UDC's ability to raise funds in the market, even though the rating agencies gave the bonds investment-quality ratings. As a result, cash flow problems developed and UDC had to scramble to raise funds. The first external warning sign was when UDC's 1972 financial statements carried disclaimers from their accountants because of the uncertainty of receiving Federal Section 236 housing subsidies, the large amount of deferred projects costs, and concerns whether reserves for mortgage losses were sufficient.

Internal financial controls, weak to begin with, were not adequate to the growing size of UDC's myriad activities. As a result, financial planning and forecasting was inadequate during a critical period of UDC's expansion. New projects were started and construction commitments made based on unrealistic assumptions. Projects were undertaken which later proved to be economically unsound.

UDC's problems grew. By 1973, UDC estimated it needed to borrow $800 million just to complete the $1.2 billion in construction projects then underway. Over half of this amount had to be borrowed by the spring of 1974.

THE 1975 BOND ANTICIPATION NOTE DEFAULT

During 1973 and 1974, several developments occurred that set the stage for the BANs default. First, in 1973 the legislatures of both New York and New Jersey repealed the port authority covenant which limited that body's involvement with mass transit, thereby raising questions in investors' minds whether the state would support its moral obligation debt in time of trouble. Second, while still maintaining its investment-quality rating, in the fall of 1973 Moody's did reduce its rating on the UDC bonds a half a notch from A to Baa1, thereby giving some indication that it was aware of the seriousness of UDC's financial problems. Third, in December 1973 Governor Rockefeller resigned, ending a 15-year tenure and thus removing a driving force from state government. Fourth and last, in the spring of 1974, a major Wall Street underwriter—Morgan Guaranty Trust Company—dropped out of the UDC account as a managing underwriter, because of its concerns over UDC's deteriorating finances.

Due to the above factors as well as tight money market conditions, in May 1974, UDC was unable to market $100 million in short-term notes at reasonable rates, thereby effectively losing a critical source of financing. It was only after long and arduous negotiation with the New York banks that a financing package was assembled in September 1974 that enabled the UDC to raise enough cash to last the balance of the year.

In early 1975, Governor Carey was inaugurated, and his administration began negotiating with the New York banks to resolve the UDC financial crisis. The talks took place amid New York City's deteriorating finances and the uncertain viability of the UDC projects. The UDC's cash needs, estimated at almost $700 million for the next 24 months, proved to be too large an obstacle to be overcome in the few short weeks between the governor's taking office and February 25, 1975, the maturity date of the $100 million in short-term notes. As a result, the UDC was unable to roll over the maturing notes and the default occurred.

Case 7: Default of the Crews Lake Road and Bridge District Bonds

J. Michael Rediker, LL.B.
Partner
Ritchie and Rediker

The Crews Lake Road and Bridge District was organized in December 1974 in Pasco County, Florida, situated approximately 25 miles northwest of downtown Tampa, as a special taxing district containing approximately 1,355 acres of undeveloped land.[1] The district was formed to build and furnish the roads for a land development of approximately 1,208 acres, consisting of approximately 2,111 residential homesite lots of one-third acre each, as well as a development of approximately 147 acres for approximately 100 one-acre homesites.

The district, on July 29, 1977, issued $3.8 million of bearer tax-exempt bonds denominated as general obligation and special assessment bonds, the proceeds of which were to be used primarily to construct a system of roads comprising approximately 27 miles of residential and collector roads, drainage areas, and other appurtenances. The bonds were to be secured by a pledge of annual ad valorem taxes, without limit as to rate or amount, on all taxable real property within the district and by special assessments levied on land within the district, to be made and collected over an approximate 28-year period in an aggregate amount approximately equal to the principal of the bond issue. The Crews Lake bond issue was not secured by any mortgage or lien on the actual property itself lying within the district, which was already subject to a $3 million first mortgage in favor of Chemical Realty, Inc., of New York.

The bonds defaulted on June 1, 1981, and in the spring of 1982 two class actions were brought—one in Florida state court and one in federal district court in Florida—on behalf of the approximately 680 bondholders and against the district, the underwriter, the project developer, the individual commissioners of the district, bond counsel, so-called due diligence (or special) counsel who drafted most of the official statement, counsel for the district, underwriter's counsel, house counsel for the developer corporation, and the trustee bank, among other defendants. In the federal suit, which as of early 1983 was ac-

---

[1]Data for this case study was derived from the second amended complaint in *Kluge et al.* v. *Crews Lake Road and Bridge District et al.,* Case #82–933–T–WC, U.S. District Court, Middle District of Florida.

tively in litigation, bondholders brought claims for violation of Rule 10b–5 under the Securities Exchange Act of 1934, for violation of state securities law, for treble damages under the RICO Act, and for state law claims for breach of trust, conversion of bond proceeds, waste, mismanagement, negligence, and professional malpractice.

Based upon the allegations of the complaint, from the time of conception of the bond issue through closing and sale of the bonds and up to the time of default, a number of substantial problems occurred which were allegedly not disclosed to the bondholders. A significant portion of the alleged wrongs involved the expenditure of bond proceeds for items that were not disclosed in the official statement and were not valid uses of proceeds of the bond issue under the bond resolution, under the laws of Florida, and under the representations as to "use of proceeds" made in the official statement. These expenditures included payments to the project developer (a Florida land development company) to cover its normal operating expenses and overhead; payments to the land developer for the purchase by the district from the land developer of two parcels of land at prices other than arm's length prices; the satisfaction (using bond proceeds) of approximately $500,000 in bank loans of another special taxing district organized by the same developers; the purchase of unneeded equipment and materials from the project developer or entities and other special taxing districts controlled by the project developer; and payment of excessive amounts of legal fees beyond amounts disclosed in the official statement including substantial fees to a law firm which performed legislative lobbying services.

The official statement disclosed (in a balance sheet of the project developer, made part of the appendix to the official statement) that as of a date seven months prior to the bond issuance the project developer had a $158,000 deficit in stockholders' equity. But the bondholders have alleged that the official statement did not disclose the fact that the development company was in arrears, by approximately $248,000, at the time of the bond issuance in the payment of past-due interest on Chemical Realty's $3 million first mortgage on virtually all of the district property. Chemical Realty's mortgage was a lien superior to the bonds, which indeed were not secured by a direct lien upon any of the real estate. The bondholders have also claimed that the official statement did not show that the developer had insufficient cash flow to meet its ongoing operating requirements as well as to pay such past-due interest; they further complained that the real property taxes on the majority of the developer-owned acreage comprising the district were delinquent in one tax year or more at or prior to the time of closing, and that there was a very significant risk that ad valorem tax revenues would be inadequate to pay the principal and interest on the bonds.

The bondholders also complained of the failure to disclose the lack of feasibility of the project. They have pointed out that the district could be developed successfully into one-third acre lots exceeding 2,000 in number *only* with the successful marketing of a separate bond issue for water and sewer facilities, which was never successfully marketed. They have alleged that the resulting per-lot or per-acre purchase cost to potential home buyers, of the land in the district (including in such cost the special assessments and extra ad valorem taxes imposed by the district to support the bond issue together with the cost of installing septic tanks and wells, and with the need for expensive re-engineering of the road system and for ongoing interest costs) made it a virtual certainty that the moderate-income family toward which this development was geared could not afford or would not want to pay such prices, meaning that the project would fail and the bonds would default. In addition, they have alleged the official statement failed to paint a true and accurate picture of exactly how desolate and isolated the land was, including omission of important details as to the lack of any shopping areas, shopping centers, schools, hospitals, municipal services, and other amenities in this rural area.

At least one other similar residential land development project in that area in which this developer had been involved had already gotten into financial troubles or had developed more slowly than projected, and many county officials had opposed this special taxing district project, facts which were not disclosed when the bonds were sold. The developer itself did not have sufficient net worth or cash flow to make the requisite payments of ad valorem taxes and special assessments to support debt service on the bond issue if the lots could not be developed and sold at the rates projected in the official statement; in fact, the developer subsequently defaulted in its tax payments due to support the bonds. The official statement failed to disclose details as to a number of related-party dealings or conflict-of-interest transactions between the district's various commissioners and the developers and between the trustee bank and the developers.

With regard to bond counsel's opinion, including bond counsel's signature on a no-arbitrage certificate, the bondholders have alleged that the bonds constituted arbitrage bonds and that counsel's opinion that the bonds were validly exempt from federal taxation was untrue. They claimed that the district had not been properly organized pursuant to the applicable Florida law and that certain other matters affecting the bond counsel's opinion on validity and enforceability of the bonds had been misstated or omitted from the opinion.

It has turned out that, by the time the bonds defaulted four years after closing, the district had gone into receivership, virtually none of the road system had been constructed, no home sites had been sold, no homes had been built, approximately two thirds of the bond proceeds had already been expended, and the remaining monies in the construction fund were generally regarded by most persons concerned as being inadequate to finance the construction of the facility.

Case 8: The 21-Year Default of the West Virginia Turnpike Commission Revenue Bonds

Sylvan G. Feldstein, Ph.D.
Senior Municipal Specialist
Merrill Lynch, Pierce, Fenner & Smith, Inc.

Charles T. Noona,
Senior Vice President
L. F. Rothschild, Unterberg, Towbin

The original $96 million of the West Virginia Turnpike Commission revenue bonds were sold in early 1952. These are the 3¾ percents dated March 1, 1952, and due December 1, 1989. Because of higher than anticipated construction costs, unanticipated engineering difficulties, higher than estimated real estate costs, and design changes, $37 million in additional bonds had to be sold in 1954. These are the 4⅛ percents dated March 2, 1952, and due December 1, 1989.[1]

While interest on the bonds was capitalized through June 1, 1956, the turnpike opened in October 1954. The turnpike commission agreed to charge tolls adequate to pay all expenses, including debt service. However, revenues were insufficient to pay coupons on a timely basis. The first interest default began with the coupon due June 1, 1958, which was subsequently paid four months later. Also, on March 24, 1959, the West Virginia Supreme Court ruled that bondholders must be paid interest on the defaulted coupons at the same rate as on the bonds. For the next 21 years, the turnpike commission continued to default on all its coupon payments. By June 1, 1969, for example, coupon payments were four years in arrears. The default period ended on December 1, 1979, when the interest coupon was paid when due plus the penalty interest.

---

[1]Data for this case study is from financial statements by Peat, Marwick, Mitchell and Company for June 30, 1981 and 1980, dated August 13, 1981; semiannual report covering the period from January 1, 1981, through June 30, 1981, prepared by the West Virginia Turnpike Commission, dated October 5, 1981; *Moody's Credit Report* of December 3, 1979; and an interview with William H. Rous of John Nuveen & Co., on December 9, 1982.

The turnpike, when originally built, was approximately 88 miles long. It was a two-lane highway extending from Charleston on the north to a junction with U.S. routes 219 and 460 close to the southern border of the state. When the turnpike was planned, it was assumed that connecting highways to the north and south would also be built and that the turnpike would facilitate highway travel between the Midwest and the Southeast.

The turnpike did not attract the amount of long-distance traffic that had been projected. In its early days, the West Virginia Turnpike was anything but a key unit in a network of superhighways. Several miles of the toll road south of Charleston could be avoided by using parallel local roads. Also, connecting interstate highways were not ready. Finally, the traffic engineer overestimated initial commercial vehicle usage. Expected traffic was slow to develop because of the delayed completion of Interstate 77 over the Virginia mountains to the Carolinas.

In the 1970s, the economics of the turnpike began to change in three ways. First, in 1970, the Federal Highway Administration and the West Virginia Department of Highways agreed to provide for, on a respective 90 percent–10 percent financing basis, the upgrading of the turnpike to four-lane federal interstate standards. While the improvements were paid for by the federal and state governments, the tolls were to remain in effect until all the outstanding revenue bonds had been retired. Second, in 1976 Interstate 77 (I77) was opened to traffic from Cleveland, Ohio, to the northern terminus of the turnpike. From the turnpike to the south, I77 was completed through Virginia and North Carolina to South Carolina. Finally, in 1979, Interstate 79 was opened to traffic from Charleston to I90 at Erie, Pennsylvania.

With the completion of the connecting interstate highways and the upgrading of the turnpike, traffic on the turnpike was increased. As an example, in the first six months of 1981, 2,672,846 passenger and commercial vehicles used the turnpike, whereas during the first six months of 1980, 2,322,713 vehicles used the turnpike.

It should also be noted that, while the turnpike is at the time of this writing current in its semiannual coupon payments, the $133 million term maturities are due on December 1, 1989. Although the turnpike commission has since 1982 been retiring some of these bonds through secondary market purchases, it is doubtful that the turnpike will generate sufficient revenues to retire all the term bonds by the scheduled maturity date of December 1, 1989. About half of the bonds are expected to be retired by 1989; the balance will have to be refinanced.

Case 9: The Defaulted Chesapeake Bay Bridge and Tunnel District, Virginia, Series C, 5¾ Percent, Third-Pledge Revenue Bonds

Sylvan G. Feldstein, Ph.D.
Senior Municipal Specialist
Merrill Lynch, Pierce, Fenner & Smith, Inc.

Charles T. Noona
Senior Vice President
L. F. Rothschild, Unterberg, Towbin

In August 1960, $200 million in revenue bonds were sold in order to refund an earlier issue of bonds as well as to build a two-lane, 17.5-mile bridge-tunnel in the lower Chesapeake Bay between the southern tip of the Delmarva Peninsula and Chesapeake Beacon near Norfolk, Virginia. The project was completed and opened to traffic on April 15, 1964.[1]

There are three separate bond securities, each with a final maturity of July 1, 2000. The $70 million Series A bonds have a coupon rate of 4.875 percent and have a first lien on the bridge and tunnel net revenues. The $30 million Series B bonds have a coupon rate of 5.50 percent and have a second lien on the net revenues. The $100 million Series C bonds have a coupon rate of 5.75 percent and a third lien on the net revenues.

Although there is not a formal rate covenant, the traffic engineers are to make recommendations in the schedule of tolls so as "to produce the maximum net revenues possible," and the district will revise its tolls in accordance with the recommendation.[2]

By July 1, 1970, the facility's reserves had been exhausted and the interest on the third-lien, Series C bonds was not paid. The toll road was scheduled to be completed in October 1963. Interest was capitalized in bond proceeds until March 7, 1965. Net revenues were pro-

---

[1]Data for this case study are from the official statement for $200 million Chesapeake Bay Bridge and Tunnel District Revenue Bonds, dated August 1, 1960; annual audit report for fiscal year ended June 30, 1982, for the Chesapeake Bay Bridge and Tunnel District, dated August 3, 1982; annual audit report for fiscal year ended June 30, 1981, for the Chesapeake Bay Bridge and Tunnel District, dated August 14, 1981; and an interview with William Oliver, author of *Moody's Credit Report* of September 19, 1982.

[2]Official statement for $200 million Chesapeake Bay Bridge and Tunnel District Revenue Bonds, p. 26.

jected to be $11,115,000 in 1964 compared with debt service of $10,812,000. Instead, completion occurred on April 15, 1964. Net revenues for the year ending April 30, 1965 were $6,881,626. Annual bond interest was $3,412,500 on the Series A 4⅞, $1,650,000 on the Series B 5½, and $5,750,000 on the Series C 5¾. However, only $1,819,126 was available for the Series C interest.

The coverage for interest on the Series C bonds remained very low through 1974, a period of nine years, when only $1,838,644 was available for that purpose. It was not until 1980, sixteen years after operations began, that Series C interest ($5,750,000) was earned with a slight margin of $1,900,897. Between 1970 and the writing of this case study in January 1983, interest on Series C bonds continues to lag behind. The coupon due January 1, 1979, was paid on June 17, 1982. The total amount of coupon interest in default as of June 30, 1982 was $19,540,966.

Three reasons can be suggested for the default. First, at the time of construction it was hoped that the 17.5-mile, two-lane series of bridges and tunnels would attract a heavy volume of traffic and serve as a major link in the north-south highway system along the Atlantic seaboard. However, competition with the toll-free inland Interstate 95 highway, which includes Maryland's John F. Kennedy Memorial Highway has been keen. As a result, it primarily serves the Delmarva Peninsula community. Automobile traffic tends to be highly seasonal, with the transportation of farm crops during the summer a major factor.

It is interesting to note that at the time of the 1960 bond sale the traffic engineers (Wilbur Smith and Associates of New Haven, Connecticut) had concluded that the project would be successful because of "the desires of motorists to bypass the larger metropolitan areas, and the attractiveness of the flatter topography closer to the Atlantic coastline to commercial vehicles. Both of these advantages are also provided by the Ocean Highway of which the proposed fixed crossing will be a part."[3]

A second reason for the default may be that, due to the numerous collisions by water traffic, the toll facility has had to be closed for long periods of time while repairs were being made to the two-lane structures. Besides increased insurance costs, the closing also resulted in uneven income flows.

A third reason for the default was that the traffic engineers for several years did not believe that a toll increase would be productive.

While toll rates eventually were raised several times and as of April 1, 1982 were at a minimum of $9.00 for passenger cars and light trucks, the district should still continue to be behind in paying

---

[3]Ibid., Appendix I, p. 1–4.

coupon interest on its 5¾ percent Series C bonds. However, for fiscal 1982 (ending June 30, 1982) debt service coverage (including bond amortization) on the first-lien Series A bonds was 3.51 times and on the second-lien Series B bonds it was 5.41 times.

Case 10: The Muir Housing Project Struggles to Come Back from Default*

Kent Pierce
Staff Reporter
The Bond Buyer

On a 10.8 acre lot in Martinez, just outside Oakland, California, there stands the shell of a 100-unit housing project for the low-income elderly that is one month away from completion. The project has been one month away from completion since June 1982. And it will stay one month away from completion for some time to come unless its developer, Muir California Health Recreation and Retirement Facilities, Inc., can pull it out of the financial mess it fell into when it defaulted on a bond interest payment June 1, 1982.

"The whole issue has been a disaster," said Charles L. Gunther, president of Gibralco Inc., the Santa Monica, California, firm which underwrote the $4.2 million bond issue sold to finance the project. "We have been hurt as much or more than anyone else by this affair." Gibralco's reputation has been tarnished, he said, and the company has put considerable time and money into working on the various proposed settlements.

Mr. Gunther's complaint got very little sympathy, however, at a meeting in November, 1982 of more than 100 Muir bondholders in Los Angeles. The meeting was called by the Bank of America, trustee for the bonds sold to finance the project, to discuss alternatives to foreclosure on the project as well as the possibility of foreclosure itself. The bondholders at the meeting—mostly individual investors ranging from doctors and investment counselors to a retired truck driver—represented over $1 million of the $4.2 million bonds sold for the project. It was their first official chance to speak since the bonds went into default, and they took full advantage of it. The meeting ran

---

*This case was adapted by the author from his article which appeared in *The Bond Buyer,* November 22, 1982, pp. 1 and 42.

more than 2½ hours past the scheduled close of 8:30 P.M. as angry investors had their say about the project's past and their concerns about its future.

"We went into the project attracted by the tax exemption and planned to sit back and collect interest as the bonds matured," one bondholder complained. "Now that this is not happening, we do not want to sit back and listen to the verbal gymnastics of attorneys and watch them collect attorneys' fees. We have to get the bondholders involved because it is the bondholders who have their own best interest at heart." Toward that end, the investors ended the meeting by nominating a seven-member bondholder committee to meet with officials of Muir, Bank of America, and the underwriters.

In the circumstances surrounding the Muir default, there are a number of undisputed facts that form the crux of the problems and the focus of all the negotiations.

In May 1981, Muir (a nonprofit health corporation) issued $4.2 million of tax-exempt serial bonds from 1984 to 2009 at yields running from 10 percent to 14 percent. Some of the proceeds were set aside in an interest reserve fund to pay for the first two interest payments in December 1981 and June 1982, and the rest went into buying land, paying bond attorneys, underwriting fees, and construction.

On June 1, 1982, when the project was approximately 80–85 percent complete, the bonds went into technical default because the interest reserve fund came up $60,000 short of the scheduled interest payment. Gibralco and Muir tried to come up with the $60,000, but gave up when it was disclosed that the project was suffering from more serious difficulties. The construction fund was $600,000 short of what it needed to finish the project, and the project's revenue projections were found to be 50 percent too high. With annual revenues originally designed to provide 1.01 to 1.28 times the amount of the bonds due over the first five years of the project, it became readily apparent that the future interest and principal payments could not be made unless the project's finances were restructured.

At that point, Bank of America, acting as trustee, moved to freeze the estimated $590,000 left in the construction fund account and the estimated $220,000 remaining in the interest reserve account. According to Paul Webber, an attorney for the bank, the money has since been reinvested and used to pay for security services, patch holes in the roof, continue insurance coverage, make a project appraisal, and (presumably) pay the bank's attorneys.

Explanations for what caused Muir's various financial problems are fairly simple. At the November meeting of the bondholders, Mr. Webber said that the June 1 interest payment was missed because the project was not generating the funds needed to augment the interest reserve fund.

Why the delay in construction? In an interview last fall, James Snow, secretary-treasurer of Muir, said that construction had been put off and new expenses incurred because of the harsh 1981–82 winter and because of retroactive offsite and onsite requirements placed on construction by the city of Martinez. Bondholders at the November meeting were told that construction costs were running about 20 percent over the original $2.55 million projection.

As for the faulty revenue forecasts, Prefecto Villarreal, director of the Contra Costa Housing Authority (the agency slated to manage the project), explained that the project's success hinged on its appeal to elderly residents with Section 8 rent certificates from the federal Department of Housing and Urban Development. Those certificates are good for rent subsidy money from HUD, the amount of which is based on fair market rental rates which HUD sets for various regions of the country. The feasibility consultant for the project had based his revenue projections on the project being in a region where the 1982 base rental rate was $509; but HUD said that the project was in a region where the rental rate was $347. This mistake, Mr. Villarreal said, meant that the project's forecast of approximately $600,000 in revenues a year was about $200,000 too high.

Various proposals have been made to straighten out the project's financing. A couple of months after the default, Gibralco presented a plan that called for contributions from the bondholders, the county housing authority, and the contractor, Carlo Zocchi. According to Gibralco's calculations, the project could be completed if the housing authority paid for operating the project for five years and for a $121,000 sewer hookup fee, Mr. Zocchi deferred payment of about half of his remaining construction costs for 10 years without interest, and the bondholders agreed to take a 400–basis point reduction on bond repayments. The bondholders eventually would receive full payment on the bonds; and the housing authority would eventually control the project.

It appeared in late summer 1982 that the housing authority might accept the Gibralco proposal. But the political opposition in Martinez and Contra Costa County to the plan convinced the authority to come up with a counterproposal. That plan called for a pooled management fund to pay for the project's operating needs over five years, to which all the major participants could contribute.

Despite some resistance to this plan as well, the county board of supervisors authorized an interest-free loan of $100,000 to the authority to put in the management fund as a substantial gesture of good faith. Additionally, the Martinez council on community development approved a loan from federal community development block grant money to pay for the sewer hookup. With this money in hand, the authority believed it had the bargaining authority to hammer out a settlement.

Bank of America's solution for Muir's problem is to get a grant from HUD to pay for the project's completion—a highly unlikely event—or foreclose on the project. Attorney Webber said the bank feels that the bondholders are innocent bystanders in this affair and should not accept any settlement, including Gibralco's, at their expense. The bondholders' position on all of the preceding proposals remains unclear, though those present at the November gathering expressed an overwhelming desire to take some sort of action.

While the bondholders gave the proposed settlements a relatively sympathetic reception, their mood leaving the Los Angeles hotel was bitter. One investor, who wished not to be named, asked: "Where were all these guys—where was the underwriter, the bond counsel, the Muir people—when all the trouble was taking place? Why weren't the problems—these problems over rental rates, construction costs, and the interest reserve fund—picked up before the bonds were sold to us?"

Said William Jackson, an underwriter at Gibralco: "I think the germ of failure is that a deal can only stand so many things going wrong; and this one just had too many things go wrong."

Case 11: Legal Risks in Controlling Waste Supply: The Akron Experience with the "Put and Pay"

William C. Brashares, J.D.
Partner
Cladouhos & Brashares

One of the standard areas of risk in any municipal revenue bond involving a resource recovery or waste-to-energy project is the risk that the project will not receive a sufficient supply of solid waste to meet its necessary revenue projections.[1] In order to deal with this risk, a variety of approaches have been used. Where the municipal government already handles the collection of a sufficient quantity of solid waste, the only need is for the municipality to commit that supply by contract. More complicated but also workable in some areas are contracts with a number of municipal governments and/or private waste collectors.

In some cases, cities or counties have sought to deal with this risk

---

[1]See Chapter 10 for the credit analysis of resource recovery revenue bonds.

by passing laws requiring private waste collectors to bring waste to the facility. By forcing the waste in this manner and retaining the ability to adjust disposal rates ("tipping fees"), the city can be assured of sufficient revenues to cover operating costs and service its bonds. In areas where the major share of municipal waste is handled by private contractors and where the facility itself may involve significant technological risks which mean uncertainties as to operating costs, this legislative approach, or "flow control," has been particularly attractive.

The city of Akron, Ohio, chose this approach to the supply risk factor in a project financed in late 1976.[2] Acknowledging that it was acting in order to secure financing for its recycle energy system (RES), the city passed an ordinance requiring that all licensed waste collectors bring all waste they collect in Akron to the RES and pay applicable tipping fees. In early 1978, suit was filed in federal district court in Akron by two companies engaged in waste collection in the Akron area and two companies operating sanitary landfills outside of Akron which were receiving waste collected within Akron.[3] The collector-plaintiffs alleged that they would be injured by the flow control ordinance in that it would deprive them of the ability to choose the most economical disposal facility in terms of both cost and location, and also that it would deprive them of whatever opportunity existed for them to extract recyclable materials from waste and sell it. The landfill-plaintiffs claimed that they would be injured in that the business they had previously been receiving from Akron collectors would be cut off by virtue of the Akron ordinance. Some months later another company filed a similar case that was consolidated with the first case. This plaintiff is a company engaged in collecting waste in Akron and separating from that waste all resaleable corrugated cardboard and ferrous and nonferrous materials. This company had been engaged for many years in substantial sales of these recyclables in interstate markets and claimed that the effect of the Akron ordinance would be to force it out of the recycling business altogether since any valuable recyclable materials would have to be delivered to the RES.

THE LEGAL ARGUMENTS

The legal theories upon which these cases were brought were founded on the U.S. Constitution and the federal antitrust laws. The plaintiffs contended that the ordinance would cause a taking of their

---

[2]These are the state of Ohio's Recycle Energy Revenue Bonds, Series 1976 (City of Akron, Ohio, Project).

[3]*Hybud Equipment Corporation et al.* v. *City of Akron et al.* (Nos. 78–1733A and C78–65A) (N.D. Ohio).

property—i.e., the recyclable wastes they collected—without compensation in violation of the Fourteenth Amendment to the U.S. Constitution. They also alleged that the Commerce Clause of the Constitution was violated by this ordinance in that it prevented the continued flow of recyclable materials out of the state of Ohio. The antitrust claim was that, by passing a law that eliminated competition by the plaintiffs in both the disposal market for Akron wastes as well as the recycling markets in which Akron waste was previously sold, both Section 1 of the Sherman Act (which prohibits contracts, combinations, or conspiracies in restraint of trade) and Section 2 of the Sherman Act (which prohibits monopolization) were violated.

The arguments of the defendants, who were the city of Akron, Summit County, and the Ohio Water Development Authority, were that the ordinance did not violate the Fourteenth Amendment's "taking" clause because it was a result of the exercise of the city's police power to deal with a health and safety concern, and that the Commerce Clause was not violated because the effect on commerce was indirect and also justified by the environmental purpose of the RES. As to the antitrust claims, the defendants' principal argument was that they were exempt from the antitrust laws because they are governmental bodies.

The federal district court in Akron, after substantial pretrial discovery and trial of the case, agreed with the defendants on all counts. As to the antitrust issue, the court principally held that Akron was exempt from the antitrust laws because it had been delegated "home rule" powers by the state and, therefore, had the same antitrust immunity that the state itself had under prevailing decisions of the U.S. Supreme Court. The plaintiffs then appealed to the U.S. Court of Appeals for the Sixth Circuit and made essentially the same constitutional and antitrust arguments. The Sixth Circuit again upheld the ordinance on essentially the same reasoning as the district court, but added the suggestion that the antitrust laws might not apply to a city carrying out a traditional governmental function such as waste disposal because it would be inconsistent with the principles of the Tenth Amendment, which reserves to the states powers not expressly granted to the federal government.

THE COLORADO CASE

Plaintiffs then petitioned for *certiorari* in the U.S. Supreme Court, raising the constitutional taking issue and the antitrust exemption issue. Pending before the Supreme Court when the Akron *certiorari* petition was filed was a case from the Tenth Circuit which raised the same antitrust exemption issue, although it related to cable television franchising.[4] The plaintiffs in the Akron case urged the Supreme Court to consider the two cases together since they raised the same antitrust issue. In January 1982, the Supreme Court issued its decision in the Colorado case, rejecting the decision of the Tenth Circuit to the effect that home rule cities have the same antitrust immunity as the state itself. The Court made it clear that, in order for a city or county government to be immune from antitrust liability, it must either be engaging in conduct required by state law or implementing a clear policy of the state favoring monopoly over competition in a particular field. The Court left it unclear whether a local government so acting must have active supervision by a state body in order to permit antitrust immunity.

Following its decision in the Colorado case, the Supreme Court promptly granted *certiorari* in the Akron case, set aside the decision of the Sixth Circuit and remanded the case to the Sixth Circuit to reconsider its decision in light of the Colorado decision. The Sixth Circuit, in turn, has sent the case back to the district court to decide whether any other basis for "state action" antitrust immunity exists and, if not, whether the Akron ordinance violates the antitrust laws.

THE IMPACT ON RESOURCE RECOVERY REVENUE BONDS

What the Akron case means, in the context of flow control laws designed to implement municipal financing in the future, is that attention will have to be given to the nature of the state's role and the way in which laws are structured by the municipalities to avoid substantial risks of legal liability and, thus, enormous financial liability under the federal antitrust laws. One of the major misconceptions about the Colorado and Akron decisions by the Supreme Court is that it outlaws anticompetitive actions by local governments. Those Supreme Court decisions only address the question of whether municipal actions are immune from antitrust challenge. While the Supreme Court has held that they are not immune generally, it has not made clear how the antitrust laws will be applied to municipal conduct that restrains competition. Indeed, the Supreme Court suggested in the Colorado decision that different considerations might apply to anticompetitive municipal conduct than would apply to similar conduct engaged in by private entities. The law probably will not be settled for another 5–10 years as to what kinds of economic or other justifications might be found sufficient by the courts to permit cities to engage in anticompetitive actions. Thus, the problem for resource recov-

---

[4]*Community Communications Company* v. *City of Boulder,* 630 F.2d 704 (10th Cir. 1980), *rev'd,* 102 S. Ct. 835 (1982).

ery project financing in the foreseeable future will be the uncertainty as to how these arrangements will be evaluated.

In order to obtain legal assurance that waste supply measures will not be set aside by antitrust challenge, cities will increasingly turn to contracting mechanisms rather than legislative mechanisms. Furthermore, where a city obtains control of the waste stream by franchise or contract, use of the most competitive bidding or negotiating process and a fairly limited term will be essential to minimize antitrust risk.

Of course, if a state legislature enacts the kind of laws that are necessary to confer antitrust immunity on their cities for flow control ordinances, there is no longer a federal antitrust risk. But this outcome is highly unlikely in most states. First of all, there is broad, almost instinctive political opposition to state laws that push private firms out of a market in which they have long competed. Indeed, state authorities largely support the limitations set by the Supreme Court on municipal anticompetitive actions, as shown by the *amicus curiae* arguments against municipal antitrust exemption by attorneys general of 23 states in the Supreme Court's Colorado case. Second, it is going to be very difficult to draft legislation that anticipates all of the potential areas of anticompetitive conduct that may be necessary to implement a flow control scheme. In other words, the kind of legal straitjacket that may be necessary may not be wearable. What may occur in some states is that a state regulatory body will take all waste collection and disposal operations away from local bodies and control waste flow at the state level in order to implement resource recovery systems developed at the state level as well. This essentially means putting all private waste business under public utility regulation, which historically has not proved popular or economical.

One other lesson from the Akron experience is that municipal flow control measures will face not only a much greater chance of attack but probably a much greater chance of being struck down under the antitrust laws (and possibly the Constitution as well) where recyclable materials are concerned. Ignoring the differences between general municipal waste, which will go to a landfill if it is not burned in a resource recovery plant, and valuable cardboard and metals in the waste stream implicates many traditional businesses. While the waste collector may only be inconvenienced or forced to pay a higher disposal cost, competition in many traditional markets for recycled paper, cardboard, or metals may be severely restrained or eliminated. Courts that might look favorably on laws that only impact on land disposal interests will probably be much less sympathetic to laws that restrain or eliminate recycling firms. It is not particularly popular to argue that the choice of whether to recycle waste paper into new paper or burn it to produce energy should be a legislative rather than an economic one. Of course, combustible recyclable materials such as cardboard often have the highest BTU content and thus are most desired by the resource recovery project. Thus, the value of this part of the waste stream to the project has to be weighed against the increased legal and financing risk of a broad flow control ordinance covering recyclables.

CONCLUSION

In sum, the efforts of municipal governments to control the waste stream by legislation in order to deal with the risk of inadequate waste supply will have to be much more careful and possibly much more limited in light of the Colorado and Akron decisions. Until the courts make clear how these arrangements will be evaluated on their merits, major clouds of uncertainty will continue.

Case 12: The Bellevue Bridge Default

Mark Fury
Staff Writer
The Bond Buyer

The Bellevue Bridge Commission in Bellevue, Nebraska, is paying back coupons 14 years behind schedule.

The commission was established in 1943 to construct, operate, and maintain a bridge across the Missouri River from Bellevue to Council Bluffs, Iowa. Though the bridge carries traffic to and from Iowa, the commission has no jurisdiction outside of Nebraska. In 1950, it issued $2.83 million of revenue bonds to construct the bridge. The bonds were secured solely by toll revenues on the bridge.[1]

The commission began paying interest out of construction funds, having issued enough bond principal to cover three years of interest payments. The bridge was completed on schedule, but five miles of access roads leading to the bridge on the Iowa side were not constructed as the commission had anticipated.[2] As a result, the commission defaulted on its May 1, 1954, interest payment. None of the scheduled semiannual interest payments were made again until June

---

[1]Moody's *Municipal & Government Manual*, 1981, p. 2112.
[2]Ibid.

1, 1972, when the May 1954 coupon was paid. Interest payments have been made sporadically since then;[3] as of November 1982 the Omaha National Bank, the commission's paying agent, paid coupons due May 1, 1968.[4]

The access road problem was rectified when Shields & Company of New York paid $233,000 to pave the five miles of Iowa roads. But the commission's problems were still not over.[5] The commission had estimated that 350 vehicles would cross the bridge each day. In 1957, average daily traffic totaled about 100 vehicles.[6] Then in 1970, Interstate 29 opened five miles north of Bellevue. It provided transportation across the river free of charge.[7]

The 1950 bonds were intended to be 30-year maturities and pay 4 percent coupons. As of early 1983, coupon payments were 14 years behind and no principal had been retired.[8]

[3]Ibid.
[4]Interviews with Officers at the Omaha National Bank.
[5]Moody's, *Manual,* p. 2112.
[6]Ibid.
[7]Interviews with Officers of the Bellevue Bridge Commission.
[8]Interviews with Omaha National Bank Officers.

Case 13: Chicago Defaults on Its Calumet Skyway Revenue Bonds

Sylvan G. Feldstein, Ph.D.
Senior Municipal Specialist
Merrill Lynch, Pierce, Fenner & Smith, Inc.

The original $88 million of the city of Chicago's Calumet Skyway Toll Bridge revenue bonds were sold in December 1954. These are the 3¾ percents dated January 1, 1955, and due January 1, 1995. Because of increased construction costs, $13 million in additional bonds were sold in May 1957. These are the 4⅜ percents dated January 1, 1955, and due January 1, 1995.[1]

The six-lane skyway is about 7.75 miles long connecting the Indi-

[1]Data for this case study is from the official statement for $88 million city of Chicago Calumet Skyway Toll Bridge revenue bonds, dated December 22, 1954; official statement for $13 million city of Chicago Calumet Skyway Toll Bridge revenue bonds, dated April 10, 1957; and *Moody's Credit Report* of November 25, 1980. The author would also like to thank Marilyn Madden of the Merrill Lynch municipal research department for her assistance.

ana Toll Road to the Dan Ryan Expressway (I94) in the center of Chicago. It passes over the Calumet industrial district of river barges, drawbridges, heavy industrial plants, and railroad freight sidings. At the time of the bond sale in the 1950s the traffic engineers, Coverdale & Colpitts of New York City, estimated that the skyway would divert traffic away from other congested routes leading to downtown Chicago. The traffic engineers projected an annual volume of 23 million vehicles using the skyway by 1973. In 1973, traffic volume was only about 9 million vehicles.

In the early 1960s, competing toll-free highways were opened which had the result of diverting traffic away from the skyway. Because of the erratic traffic usage and the projected traffic volume never materializing, Chicago defaulted on its July 1, 1963 coupon payments and all additional payments thereafter. The payments generally have been made three to four years after the due dates, and have included penalties of 5 percent per annum on past-due interest coupons from the date of the defaults to the respective payment dates. For example, the interest coupons due January 1, 1980 were paid on June 9, 1983.

Additionally, it should be noted that, while there is a 1.2 times rate covenant and tolls have been raised over the years, the erratic traffic volume and lack of a maintenance fund have required the payment of necessary maintenance charges out of current gross revenues. By 1980, the accumulated deficit of the skyway was $65,336,000. This included the defaulted interest coupons, the 5 percent penalty per annum on the defaulted coupons, the unpaid sinking fund installments, and $2 million borrowed from the city of Chicago for interest payments.

Case 14: What Really Went Wrong in Cleveland in 1978?

Sylvan G. Feldstein, Ph.D.
Senior Municipal Specialist
Merrill Lynch, Pierce, Fenner & Smith, Inc.

INTRODUCTION

While New York City, Detroit, Boston, and Cleveland all had similar crisis-prone financial problems, only in Cleveland was the municipal government paralyzed and unable to avoid defaulting on December 15, 1978 on a relatively small $15.5 million note loan.[1] New York City's default in December 1975 was on $2.419 billion in notes. Other than Cleveland, no major city in recent memory has presented the public with such macabre scenes as the elected president of the school board being arrested for improper conduct; the local electric utility sending U.S. marshals to attach city assets so as to assure payment of its bills; and part-time city councilmen defiantly boycotting council meetings called by the mayor to deal with urgent city business. While much attention has been paid to the combative personalities of the mayor and city council president as well as the day-to-day verbal posturings of the various political actors at city hall and in the organized labor and business establishments, Cleveland may have defaulted on its notes primarily for one reason. Its mayor lacked the institutional resources to be an effective chief executive who could manage political conflict.

RESTRICTIVE POWERS

In actual practice, because of restrictive Ohio state laws and the city's own 1913 charter, policymaking in Cleveland city government resembled government by mob caucus. At times the mayor was nothing more than a figurehead of power and executive leadership. In fact, the members of the city's school board had terms of office twice as long as that of the mayor. Cleveland's mayor lacked the traditional big-city "carrots and sticks" of unlimited four-year terms of office, ex-

---

[1]Data for this case study is drawn from: selected back issues of the *Cleveland Plain Dealer;* phone interviews with the city's acting budget administrator, Bert Bastock, on January 2 and 8, 1979; phone interviews with the executive director of the Ohio Municipal League on December 29, 1978, and January 3, 1979; preliminary Official Statement (Proof #6) for $25.165 million City of Cleveland Limited Tax Bond Anticipation Note Sale of July 1978, dated June 21, 1978.

tensive appointment and removal powers in the bureaucracies, and strong taxation and budget powers—all of which are used by effective mayors to reward friends and intimidate enemies.

Between 1970 and 1978, Cleveland had operating budget deficits caused by a declining population, stagnant economic resources, and the inability of city hall to bring the budget in line with its limited revenue resources. Unlike nearby Detroit and Pittsburgh—which had even more serious economic and budgetary problems—Cleveland took the easiest political course of action by paying off last year's budget deficit with this year's borrowed monies. As a consequence, Cleveland in 1978 budgeted $28.9 million for paying interest and principal on its bonds, and also was required to retire $40 million in notes. With a general fund budget of $147 million in 1978 and without a new bond sale, voluntary roll-over agreements by the noteholders, or default, Cleveland would have had to use 27 percent of its general fund revenues for the retirement of its notes.

While Cleveland's mayor in 1978, Dennis Kucinich, was elected in a citywide election in November 1977 with 93,172 votes, he had been frustrated in many of his policies by a largely part-time city council in which the average councilman was elected by about 2,500 votes. The council president, when he last had a contest in his ward in 1975, was elected to public office with only 3,665 votes. In strong mayoral cities such as New York, Detroit, Chicago, and Boston, recalcitrance en masse by similar part-time politicians is unheard of. In Cleveland, because of the weakness of the mayor's office, it was an acceptable norm.[2]

TWO–YEAR TERM OF OFFICE

A major weakness of Cleveland's mayor in 1978 was that each term of office was for only two years. This hardly provided the incumbent with sufficient time to establish his own policies and to develop a citywide constituency before he must focus on reelection strategies. The shortness of his term served as an open invitation for political opposition, as his potential rivals could count on the mayor constantly having to divert his energy and resources to reelection concerns while they could hope that they would not have to face punishment by the incumbent if he lost the election. Additionally, unlike other large cities, Cleveland had a unique recall mechanism which allowed his opponents to force him to undergo the pressures of electoral approval even during his two-year term. The mayor survived one such recall vote in August 1978 by a slim margin of a little over 300 votes.

---

[2]It should be noted that, since 1978, the city's charter has been amended to provide a four-year term of office for the mayor as well as for the members of the city council.

LIMITED APPOINTMENT AND REMOVAL POWERS

Another limitation of the mayor's power was that he had no control over many of the city's essential services or over who provided them to Cleveland's residents. The school system was entirely independent of city hall, with its own governing body of seven members who were elected every four years. Mass transit, sewage operations, port development, and welfare were all either county or special district functions. While the city financed the costs of its municipal court system, the mayor had no judicial appointment powers, and court administration was entirely in the hands of an elected clerk. Also, even in the 10 city departments that were nominally under the mayor's control (such as police and fire), he faced well-entrenched bureaucracies supported by 24 public employee unions and a civil service commission that restricted his managerial powers as well.

LIMITED TAXING POWERS

Because of restrictive state laws, the mayor was required to seek electoral approvals for increased property and personal income taxes that were above state-allowed levels. These requirements no doubt greatly weakened the mayor's ability to deal quickly and effectively with budgetary problems as they occurred. The mayor's powers were further weakened by his having to obtain city council approval before a tax resolution could even be placed on the ballot. Vote authorizations were only approved by the city council after much rancorous politicking and bickering with the mayor. As a contrast, in New York City, stringent opposition en masse to the mayor's revenue programs by local legislators would be discouraged by that mayor's ability to punish his enemies through his extensive appointment powers and his control of city programs and services. While as a result of the Jarvis-Gann initiative in California many communities embraced the belief that more curbs on local taxing powers were desirable, Cleveland showed the potential negative results of such restrictions. It is because of these tax restrictions that, at times, government in Cleveland most nearly resembled chaotic policymaking.

LIMITED FEDERAL AND STATE SUPPORT

Still another weakness of Cleveland which further compounded the basic institutional weaknesses of the mayor was that the city, as the result of its declining population, was losing its political influence on the state and national levels as well. The population declined from 914,808 residents in 1950 to an estimated 638,793 in 1975. In 1978, out of a 23-member Ohio congressional delegation, only two members had predominately Cleveland-based constituencies, whereas the congressional delegation from New York City totaled 18 members. Possibly, this difference was an important factor in Washington's refusal to help Cleveland avoid its note default in December 1978; it was stated by a Treasury department spokesman at the time that, unlike New York City's budgetary problems, Cleveland's were "local" in nature.

On the state level, the situation for Cleveland was much the same. Out of 99 state assemblymen and 33 state senators in 1978, only 6 assemblymen and 2 senators were predominately from the city.

CONCLUSION

Other governing bodies contemplating weakening the institutional powers of their own chief executives, such as Cleveland already had done, may well look to this city to see what they can expect. Cleveland's political saga may be a lesson well worth pondering.

Local Bond Securities

Case Studies

Case 15: Tax Allocation Bonds in California

Richard M. Gerwitz
Associate
Merrill Lynch White Weld Capital Markets Group

California is one of a number of states that have provided for some form of tax increment financing. Using it, often to secure tax allocation bonds, redevelopment agencies are able to finance their development and revitalization efforts.

The California Community Redevelopment Law establishes a redevelopment agency in every city and county in the state. Once legislatively activated by the local lawmaking body, an agency can collect tax-increment revenues for specific redevelopment project areas. Each agency also has substantial powers to further its redevelopment efforts. These include: the power of eminent domain; the ability to issue bonds; the ability to acquire, sell, develop, and lease property; and the ability to construct or cause the construction of public buildings. With these powers, redevelopment agencies often acquire property in designated redevelopment project areas, clear and prepare sites for development by installing public improvements, and then lease or sell the site for private development.

Redevelopment agencies receive the necessary revenues for their activities from the property tax growth associated with a successful redevelopment project. Activated agencies submit redevelopment plans for specific redevelopment project areas to the local legislative body for approval. Once approved, the then current assessed value of property within the project area is established as the "frozen base." Annual property tax revenues collected from the application of prevailing local tax rates to the frozen base are distributed, according to existing allocation formulas, to the responsible local agencies (i.e., county, city, and school districts). Any amounts collected from the application of the prevailing tax rate to increases above the frozen base (the tax increment) are distributed to the redevelopment agency. Increment revenues are to be used within the project area from which they are generated. Unless used to secure bonds, this method of property tax distribution continues until the redevelopment plan expires.

Since a redevelopment agency's need for funds generally precedes the receipt of tax-increment revenues, tax allocation bonds (TABs) have become a common revenue-raising device. TABs are secured by a pledge of the future increment revenues realized from the project area for which the bonds are issued. They typically include provision for a reserve fund in an amount equal to maximum annual debt service, and an amount of capitalized interest sufficient to carry the bond issue until increment revenues are available. If TABs are outstanding, tax-increment financing remains in place within the particular project area until all bonds are retired.

The analyst's first concern should be that the redevelopment agency's proceedings have been carried out as required by the Community Redevelopment Law. The opinion of a recognized bond counsel generally provides such assurance. Since the primary security behind a TAB is tax-increment revenue, the analyst will want to closely examine the likelihood of development taking place as expected. The use of independent consultants by the redevelopment agency to certify the agency's projections has become more commonplace in recent TAB financings. The consultant should be recognized within the marketplace and be conversant with local assessment procedures. In addition to a consultant's report, or in those instances where reports are not included, the analyst should be concerned with the status of development used by the agency to make its tax-increment projections. We would tend to avoid those TABs secured by increment projections based on speculative development. Instead, only those developments currently under way or planned for the near-term should be considered. If planned development is included as part of the analysis, the status of construction financing, permits and approvals, and any preleasing should be considered. Also of concern is the historical performance and success of any developer whose project constitutes a major portion of the development. A review of the locality's economy, population, and traditional measures of income and growth as specific to the project site as possible can assist in the analysis of the potential for long-term project success.

The analyst should read the disclosure documents carefully, paying attention to the potential risk factors. Redevelopment agencies have no role regarding the setting of tax rates or the determination of assessed values. Their increment revenues are determined by the application of the locally prevailing property tax rate to assessed valuation as determined by the county assessor. The analyst should therefore be aware of any potential property tax legislation or initiatives which could reduce increment revenues. By cutting both property tax rates and assessed valuations, Proposition 13 caused a temporary crisis in the California TAB market. An analysis of historic property tax rates, assessed values, and tax burden may help to mitigate some fears about future increment reductions.

The agency's financial statements, and financial summaries provided in the disclosure document, should provide information as to how well the agency has operated. Together with material that describes the redevelopment agency, its staff, and other projects in which it is involved, a reasonably good picture should be drawn as to the quality of agency management.

TABs are sometimes issued in a series, and care should be taken to examine each issue's lien position. Calculate the tax-increment coverage of estimated debt service to make sure minimum thresholds of 1.25 times to 1.50 times are met. Coverage should be calculated using tax revenue assumptions tending toward the conservative. Correspondingly, the analyst will want to ascertain that the additional bonds test prevents the issue's security from being diluted. A final point concerns the period during which interest is capitalized: It should be long enough to allow development to take place and generate increment revenues. County assessment procedures regarding the timing of a project's entry on the assessment rolls differ across the state.

Case 16: Certificates of Participation in California

John C. Fitzgerald, Managing Director
Richard M. Gerwitz, Associate
Kenneth D. Ough, Associate
Merrill Lynch White Weld Capital Markets Group

The use of certificates of participation (COPs), a structure which bears similarity to lease-rental bonds, has become more prevalent in recent years as a means to finance equipment and facilities for all types of governmental entities. While not limited to California, COPs have seen their greatest use in the state where Proposition 13 restricted the use of other, more traditional financing structures.

COPs are an extension of the tax-exempt leasing arrangements with private lessors which municipalities have employed over the years for the use and purchase of various equipment. Instead of having the lessor hold the lease for their own account or place it with another financial institution, the agreement is broken up into "certificates of participation", each representing a proportionate interest in the agreement and lease payments. The individual certificates are then offered to the investor through either a competitive or negotiated sale, at which time the lease payment schedule is determined through the assignment of interest rates to the various certificate maturities.

Physically, COPs closely resemble bonds. They are generally offered in $5,000 denominations, have coupons if issued in bearer form, and include the opinion of bond counsel (known as special counsel for a certificate issue) as to their authorization and tax-exempt status. The interest component of the municipality's (lessee's) lease payment is usually paid semiannually, and principal may be retired on a serial or term basis.

While lease-rental bonds are issued by a specially created authority or nonprofit corporation which subsequently leases the improvements to the governmental entity, the lessor for a COP financing is usually a private organization specializing in municipal equipment leasing. Once the lessor enters into the lease agreement and the certificates are delivered, their role is limited. The lessor will typically appoint the lessee as its agent to acquire, or cause the acquisition of the improvements to be leased via an agency agreement, and will assign all rights under the lease agreement, including the right to receive lease payments, to a trustee bank. As assignee of the lessor, it is the trustee bank that breaks the lease up into proportionate interests and offers the certificates, not the governmental entity.

Once issued, lease payments flow from the lessee directly to the trustee for distribution to certificate holders. The trustee also receives all certificate proceeds and maintains the various funds and accounts, including the construction or acquisition fund, and a reserve fund which is generally equal to maximum annual debt service. Should a default occur, the trustee, not the lessor, is the party required to take remedial action. The trustee's role should be detailed in a trust agreement executed by the trustee, the lessor, and the lessee.

Like the leasing arrangements involved in lease-rental bond financings, COPs are attractive to governmental entities, since the lease is not considered a long-term debt and is therefore not subject to debt limits or restrictions. Unlike lease-rental bonds, no interest rate limits apply to COPs and no new authority or nonprofit corporation is necessary. COPs are also not subject to voter approval, although in certain cases involving political subdivisions with their own charter, the lease may be subject to voter referendum. While tax-exempt leases have generally been employed for vehicles and equipment, COPs have been used for a full range of municipal improvements, including administrative buildings, port facilities, sewer and water lines, and computer and telecommunication systems.

The lease underlying the certificates is executory in nature, requiring action on the part of both parties. It is this concept whereby the lease is not considered a long-term debt. However, the lease is therefore subject to annual appropriation by the lessee's legislative body and, in certain states, action to annually renew the agreement. The inability of one legislative body to bind a future legislature as to the appropriation of funds for lease payments is an obvious point of difference between COPs and bonds. Largely as a result of having to annually appropriate funds for lease payments, versus the automatic appropriation of funds for the payment of debt service for a long-term debt, municipal lease obligations are not on the same level of credit worthiness as the entity's general obligation bonds.

When considering COPs, the analyst or investor should be aware of the lessee's need to annually appropriate and the fact that, unlike bonds, leases are not subject to acceleration in the event of default. Instead, the trustee must sue each year to recover the annual lease payment. Because of these factors, those COP issues which are for the acquisition of facilities or equipment critical to the operation of the governmental entity are preferred in terms of investment quality. Given the choice between appropriating funds for essential municipal services and appropriating funds to make lease payments for "nonessential" facilities or equipment, the governing body is likely to choose the former. Since the majority of the facilities leased are special purpose in nature, reletting the facility to another party in the event of nonappropriation may be impossible.

Careful examination of the life of the equipment or facilities financed relative to the term of the lease is also of obvious credit importance. The term of the lease must not exceed the expected life of the improvements. This may involve a certain degree of judgment, particularly in those cases where such equipment as computer or telecommunication systems are being acquired, systems whose usefulness is particularly sensitive to technological obsolescence.

Depending on the source of lease payment, a COP may be secured by either a lease-purchase or installment sale agreement. Lease-purchase must be used if funds are to be appropriated from the lessee's general fund. An installment sale can be employed if payments are to be made from a special fund or fund of an enterprise operation. When an installment sale is used, title to the equipment or facility rests immediately with the lessee. Title rests with the lessor until the end of the agreement when a lease-purchase arrangement is necessary. Since the lessor is not an exempt entity, the facility leased may be subject to property taxes. Recognizing the government purpose of the facilities acquired using this method, however, county assessors will sometimes choose not to assess property taxes. If assessed, property taxes, along with all other incidental charges including facility maintenance, are the responsibility of the lessee. The analyst should therefore be aware of the situation and take the additional costs into account when assessing the lessee's ability to make lease payments.

As with any municipal security, the analyst must depend on the reliability of the opinion of special counsel that all actions necessary to execute the financing have been properly taken and that the entity is properly authorized to enter into such transactions. Where the lease is subject to voter referendum, the period during which such referendum is available should expire before closing and delivery of the certificates. As a lease, rental payments cannot commence until the facility is ready to use. Sufficient capitalized interest must therefore be provided in order to ensure that the acquisition or construction of the project is completed. In order to account for unforeseen delays, the period of capitalized interest should extend several months beyond the scheduled completion date.

Once the analyst feels comfortable with the commitment on the part of the lessee to appropriate funds for lease payments, a more traditional analysis of the entity's ability to pay should be made. First, the source of funds available for lease payments must be identified. If not payable solely from an enterprise fund, in which case a rate covenant is often utilized, the lessee may pledge "all available funds." The analyst must then identify exactly which funds are considered "available funds," taking legal restrictions into account, and then review five years of financials to assess trends, strengths, and weaknesses. As a threshold, one should regard an annual lease payment of 5 percent of available funds as a prudent upper limit. In the case of enterprise fund rate covenants, entities should covenant to institute rates and charges which will produce net revenues available for lease payments 1.25 times greater than that scheduled on an annual basis. We suggest that the analyst examine the trend of rates and charges over the past several years and compare current and future levels relative to nearby jurisdictions. In any case, one should carry out a full analysis of the lessee to assess future ability to pay, including such factors as population, wealth, economic and social trends, assessed property value growth, debt burden, and the political and managerial environment. Other lease obligations should be identified to determine the extent to which the entity has already committed its future revenue stream. Additionally, take note of any potential restrictions on the lessee's revenues from budgetary pressures of other agencies or due to legislative or voter initiatives.

As would be the case for any bond issue, the analyst will want to determine whether or not the security can be diluted by the issuance of parity securities. On the other hand, since lease payments cannot commence until the facility or equipment is ready to use, the analyst should also make sure that either additional securities can be issued for the purpose of completion or that the lessee will and can make sufficient funds available for such purpose. The best situation is where the construction or acquisition cost has been finally determined prior to certificate closing.

Title to the site on which leased facilities are built often rests with the lessee. A policy of title insurance should be evidenced at closing, and the lessor should hold a site lease or have right of access. The site lease or right of access must remain in place until all outstanding certificates are retired or defeased and allow the lessor to sublease the site with the facility in the event of default and reletting. The lessee is also required to maintain adequate insurance as to property damage, personal liability, and business interruption. These policies are particularly important in light of the fact that the facility or equipment must be available for use or occupancy as a prerequisite to receiving lease payments. Lastly, the analyst must also read and understand the flow of funds and identify those situations and under what conditions the certificates can be called for mandatory redemption.

Case 17: Indiana's School Building Corporation Lease Rental Bonds

John W. Illyes, Jr.
Analyst
John Nuveen & Co., Incorporated

The architects of Indiana's Constitution in 1851 designed a debt limitation provision which prevents municipalities from issuing general obligation bonds in excess of 2 percent of assessed valuation. The limitation was certainly reasonable in the context of a mid-19th century agrarian society. Subsequent legislation fixed assessed valuation at one third of actual market value. Together with the constitutional debt limitation, this seriously limited the ability of Indiana school districts to issue general obligation bonds for school construction and caused a severe shortage of schools in the years following World War II.

In 1947, the Indiana General Assembly passed Chapter 273 to overcome both of these financial limitations. The act created School Building Corporations (SBCs), legal entities empowered to issue bonds to construct school facilities and lease them, upon completion, to the sponsoring school districts. Since bonds issued by SBCs are not direct obligations of the school districts, the constitutional debt limitation does not apply.

THE NATURE OF THE CREDIT RISK

There are actually two phases in the life of any physical structure like a school building—construction and operational. The calamities that can befall a school building can occur either during the construction phase or the operational phase. Construction risk has typically been the main concern of prospective investors. This being the case, let us examine some of the ways SBCs can guard against construction risk. Later, we will discuss some of the safeguards designed to cope with operational risks.

Five Ways Construction Risk Is Reduced

1. *Performance bonds* must be provided by contractors covering 100 percent of construction cost. This is the first line of defense against construction risk—the chance that the building may not be finished on time, thus delaying the first lease rental payment.

Nonperformance by the contractor is directly offset by the performance bond. If the building is not completed on schedule, the performance bond enables the SBC to pay another contractor to complete the project.

Occurrences beyond the contractor's control. Performance bonds contain standard provisions relieving the contractor of liability for delays caused by strikes, acts of God, and other events beyond his control. Losses from such noninsurable causes can only be offset by using capitalized interest and investment earnings (see paragraphs 4 and 5 below.)

2. *Builder's risk insurance* must also be provided by contractors covering 100 percent of construction cost. This insurance protects against damage to a building under construction from insurable causes, such as storms and construction mishaps. Excluded, of course, are certain losses, such as those resulting from acts of war, earthquake, or flooding in some areas. These risks are commonly referred to as "force majeure."

3. *Temporary leases* for partial occupancy provide another hedge against construction risk. Given a serious construction delay, the lessee school district may elect to occupy as much of the new building as is tenantable by paying a rental proportionate to the amount of usable space. These temporary rentals may be nominal or substantial. Temporary leases are informal arrangements between the school district and the SBC but are commonly used in Indiana.

4. *Capitalizing interest* beyond the construction period is the fourth offset to construction risk. The risk of delays due to force majeure can be mitigated by capitalizing interest for several months beyond the scheduled completion date. Construction periods for most school building projects range from 12 to 24 months, and an extra 6 months' interest should be built into each financing.

5. *Construction fund earnings* can also offset construction risk and create significant financial latitude in most SBC financings. For

example, a $10 million project to be built over a two-year period, with level draw-downs and interest earning at 13 percent, will produce $1.3 million of investment income. Obviously, most of the $1.3 million will become part of available "sources of funds" in structuring the financing. However, to the extent that the original estimates are conservative, there could be some additional cash throw-off from the construction fund.

Capitalized interest—and construction fund earnings—are the SBCs defense against uninsurable construction risks: force majeure construction delays, force majeure damage to a project during construction, and cost overruns.

Examples of risks related to force majeure were discussed above. The third type of uninsurable construction risk, cost overruns, can be minimized by having firm construction contracts in hand together with 100 percent performance bonds prior to the sale of bonds. Cost overruns attributable to unforeseen change orders can sometimes be reduced by using less expensive building materials where feasible.

Capitalized interest, construction fund earnings, and savings from change orders are the basic tools available during the construction period to offset construction risk. However, they do not afford protection against damage to a completed building from uninsurable causes or rental loss if reconstruction takes over two years. Fortunately, these risks are remote. Strategies to minimize these risks are described below.

Three Ways Operating Risk Can Be Reduced

1. *Fire and extended coverage insurance.* Indiana school districts are required by law to carry policies on completed buildings in amounts equal to 105 percent of replacement cost, as certified by an architect each year.

2. *Rental value insurance* is also required in an amount sufficient to pay principal and interest on the bonds for a period of two years during the time the building is being repaired.

3. *The "double-barreled" back-up that's never been used:* School districts are required by law to levy ad valorem taxes for lease rental payments. A 1967 law not only added state review to local taxing procedure, it also established a new "back-up" source of payment. The State Treasurer is now required to pay lease rentals from state aid due the district, if ever called upon to do so. The law's two key provisions are as follows:

> By statute, the annual rental is payable from unlimited ad valorem taxes levied within the school district. Before the end of each calendar year, the State Board of Tax Commissioners (the

Board) is required to review the district's lease rental levies and appropriations due the next year. If, for any reason, these are insufficient to pay all lease rentals coming due, the Board is required to establish sufficient levies and appropriations.

In the final analysis, if the district's resources are still insufficient, the State shall, upon notification, make the necessary payment from state aid moneys due the district during that calendar year, deducting such payment from the total amount appropriated.

Not only is this second "barrel" for payment in place, it has been successfully tested. The test case involved a $5,660,000 bond issue sold by the Crawford County SBC in 1976. A dispute arose between the building corporation and the district regarding the project—a completed junior-senior high school—with the district claiming improper construction and maintenance. The district refused to pay to the trustee (Corydon State Bank) the lease rental to cover $145,500 of interest due July 1, 1978. After the trustee notified the State Treasurer of the deficiency, the treasurer offered to pay the trustee state aid moneys due the district. Actually, the transfer of state aid moneys was not necessary because the trustee held enough other district funds to pay the coupons.

This 1978 case resulted in an opinion by the State Attorney General which reaffirmed the State Treasurer's responsibility to advance state aid moneys to pay Indiana school district lease rentals. The Attorney General's opinion is expected to be binding on all future State Treasurers without reconfirmation.

EXAMPLES OF PROBLEMS

W. H. (Howard County) SBC, $3,710,000 Bonds, Dated 4/1/ 69. The electrical contractor abandoned this project (an addition to an existing high school) after having erroneously been paid an amount in excess of his contract. Within a relatively short period of time, the same contractor abandoned nine other SBC construction projects. The insurance company that issued the performance bonds for these projects filed for liquidation. However, the available funds—whether capitalized interest, construction fund earnings, or recoveries from third parties—were sufficient in each case to permit recontracting of electrical work and completion of the buildings. Bondholders were paid on time.

Bloomington Schools High School SBC, $10,480,000 Bonds, Dated 6/1/70. Excavation work for Bloomington High School North was being done when extensive limestone was encountered. The contractor stopped construction for three months until an agreement was reached which guaranteed him full payment from recoveries against third parties. The corporation obtained settlements from the architect, engineer, and soil consultant.

Here again settlements from third parties, combined with funds available from the financing, were sufficient to complete construction with no delay in interest payments.

New Castle Community SBC, $733,000 Bonds, Dated 12/5/56. This project—a high school gymnasium—was 75 percent completed when it collapsed. The cause was determined to be either a construction mishap or faulty design. Construction was halted for over a year while the building was redesigned and the contractor and building corporation reached a settlement, allowing completion of the project.

In this case, builder's risk insurance paid the cost of reconstruction but not for the loss of time. The SBC utilized all available sources of funds—capitalized interest, construction fund earnings, insurance proceeds, and settlements from third parties—to finish the building and make timely payments of interest.

CONCLUSION

Since 1949, Indiana's SBCs have had a perfect record of paying debt service. From 1967 on, SBCs have had the added protection of double-barreled security—unlimited ad valorem taxes *plus* the state's pledge to withhold school aid, if necessary, to pay debt service. Since then, the state back-up has been tested once but never used. This commitment—by a fiscally conservative and strong state like Indiana—strengthens SBC security.

Case 18: Oregon's Bancroft Bonds

James C. Joseph
Manager
Municipal Bond Division
State of Oregon

In the state of Oregon, cities, counties, and some special districts may finance certain capital projects through the issuance of "Bancroft" bonds, also known as improvement or assessment bonds. This financing tool has two distinct advantages over the use of general obligation bonds. First, Bancroft bonds are initially secured by an assessment against the benefited property, which frees other taxpayers of the burden of supporting improvements to specific properties. Second, as ultimate security, Bancroft bonds are full faith and credit general obligations of the issuing municipality.

ISSUANCE PROCEDURE

Authorized municipalities in Oregon may issue Bancroft bonds to finance "local improvements." Oregon Revised Statutes (ORS) 223.387 defines a local improvement as:

Street construction or improvement.

Construction or reconstruction of sidewalks.

Street lighting.

Installation of underground wiring or related equipment.

Construction, reconstruction, or repair of any sanitary or storm sewer or water main.

Off-street parking facilities.

Flood control.

Parks, playgrounds, or neighborhood recreation facilities.

For these purposes a municipality may incur indebtedness in the form of Bancroft bonds. For cities, this debt—exclusive of indebtedness for municipal utilities, but inclusive of all other indebtedness—shall not exceed 9 percent of true cash value (ORS 223.295).

Whenever an assessment against a lot or parcel is $25 or more, the owner of that property has the right to file a written application to pay the whole of the assessment in installments. This application shall provide that the assessment will be paid in equal semiannual installments over a period not to exceed 30 years, with interest at such rate as the municipality shall determine.

Notice of a proposed assessment is to be mailed or personally delivered to the owner of each property. The notice shall specify the amount of the assessment proposed and shall state the date by which any objections shall be filed with the municipality. Property owners must be given a minimum of 10 days to respond. The owner of an assessed property may prepay at any time. Funds received from such prepayment shall be placed to the credit of a fund designated the "Bancroft Bond Redemption Fund."

When an assessment is based on an estimate of project cost (and administrative expense) and the actual cost is greater than the estimates, the municipality may make a deficit assessment for the additional cost. If the estimate is greater than the actual cost, provision shall be made for refund of the surplus or excess.

The unpaid balance of an assessment, together with any unpaid balance of previous assessments, may not exceed double the assessed value of the property as shown by the last county tax roll. This limitation does not apply to educational, religious, fraternal, or charitable organizations, or to public corporations subject to such assessments. All unpaid assessments and interest are a lien on each parcel of land or other property, and such liens shall have priority over all other liens and encumbrances.

At any time when an assessment has not been paid for a period of one year, the council or other governing body of the municipality may pass a resolution declaring the total assessment, plus interest, immediately due and payable. It may then take steps to sell the affected lots or tracts. Notice of the delinquency sale must appear, as defined by Oregon statutes, once a week for four successive weeks in a daily or weekly newspaper. Copies of the first of the four published notices shall be sent by registered or certified mail to both the owner and occupant of the property.

Each parcel shall be sold for a sum equal to, but not exceeding, the unpaid lien or assessment thereon plus interest, cost of advertising, and penalty. Sale is made subject to redemption within one year from the date of the certificate of sale. Such redemption may occur by payment of the purchase price, plus 10 percent interest as a penalty and 10 percent per annum interest on the sale certificate.

CONCLUSION

Bancroft bonds are used extensively in Oregon to finance public improvements. In calendar year 1982, Bancroft bonds represented 36.8 percent of all general obligation bonds issued by local governments ($101.98 million of $276.9 million).

Case 19: The New York Metropolitan Transportation
Authority (MTA) Issues Bonds Secured by
Everything that's Not Nailed Down*

Mark Fury
Staff Writer
The Bond Buyer

From the late 1960s through the early 1980s, New York City newspapers periodically spewed out frantic headlines about possible subway fare increases. More often than not, no fare increase came about,
as legislators in Albany strung together yet another package to subsidize it.

The problem of expenses exceeding operating revenues is by no
means new to the New York City subway system. Back in the 1930s,
the then privately owned Interborough Rapid Transit Company, on
the verge of bankruptcy, asked the city for authorization to increase
the five-cent fare. The city's reply was negative. Interborough folded,
and the New York City Transit Authority (NYCTA) emerged as a
city agency to operate the subways with city subsidies to cover revenue shortfalls.

That solution worked well for a while, but the ever-increasing cost
of labor translated into ever-increasing city (and later, state) subsidies. And that, in turn, put mounting pressure on the authority to
keep operating costs down. It got to the point that, in the late 1960s
and early 1970s, the subway system had virtually no capital improvements program. The authority decided to provide only enough maintenance to keep trains running.

By 1980, the system was literally on the verge of collapse. Many
cars rattling through the tunnels in the early 1980s were built in the
1940s. The NYCTA board commissioned a study in 1980 of its capital
needs. By then a sister authority—the Metropolitan Transportation
Authority—had been formed as well. The MTA's state mandate was
to provide for mass transit needs in the 12 New York City and suburban counties that comprise the New York metropolitan area. The
NYCTA and the MTA have identical boards of directors and the same
chairman. Though the NYCTA maintained its status as an autonomous legal entity, it functions as a subsidiary of the MTA.

---

*The material in this article was adapted from a story appearing in *The Weekly
Bond Buyer*, December 13, 1982, page 1, as well as supporting interviews and data
compiled for that article.

The 1980 study included the capital needs of the MTA-at-large, which included the NYCTA, the Manhattan and Bronx Surface Transit Operating Authority (MaBSTOA), the Staten Island Rapid Transit Operating Authority (SIRTOA), the Long Island Rail Road, and the Metro-North Commuter Railroad. At that time, the capital needs through 1990 were put at $14 billion. But by early 1983, the MTA said inflation had put the price tag at $23 billion.

The MTA launched a political campaign to convince the state that the capital was needed. "We have a system that suffered for years from a state of disinvestment and is in a state of gross disrepair," said the MTA's chairman, Richard Ravitch. He added that, "Financing this plan is critical to restoring decent subway service." He warned that if the MTA did not get the capital it needed, the subway system would cease to function.

In the late 1970s, the state legislature had given the MTA a "cash cow" to work with—the Triborough Bridge and Tunnel Authority (TBTA), which operates seven toll bridges and two tunnels, a huge Manhattan parking garage, and a bus shuttle terminal for service to New York airports. Tolls on Triborough river crossings were pushed up to a steep $1.25 per trip by 1982, TBTA collecting nearly $300 million in tolls in that year. TBTA budget surpluses were to be transferred to the MTA.

But $300 million per year, while impressive, are nothing to build a $23 billion capital program on. The MTA decided to outline only those projects which were most urgent and put them into a five-year program running from 1982 through 1987. Those projects, the MTA estimated, would cost $7.2 billion. The MTA board realized that to raise that kind of money in five years, it would have to tap the municipal bond market. The board calculated that TBTA revenues could be pledged to secure about $1.1 billion in long-term bonds; they calculated that other sources would be needed to secure an additional $2.6 billion bonds.

But the mass transit subsidiaries of the MTA have no net revenues. State, city, and federal operating subsidies keep the authority at the center of the red–black seesaw. In 1981, the MTA board came up with three vehicles to fill the $2.6 billion gap: NYCTA gross revenue bonds, MTA gross revenue bonds, and service contract bonds. And they managed to sell the New York state legislature and the rating agencies on the idea of using gross revenues and service contracts as security for bonds. As one MTA official put it, "We'll pledge everything except operating assistance from the federal government." The MTA would pledge that too if it could, but it's against federal law.

NYCTA GROSS REVENUE BONDS

The NYCTA gross revenue bonds, known as transit facilities revenue bonds, are secured by a first lien on gross revenues of the NYCTA, MaBSTOA, and SIRTOA. In addition to farebox receipts, New York City and New York State annual subsidies, revenues from advertising and concessions, and some net revenues from the TBTA can be dedicated to pay bond debt.

The first gross revenue bond issue ever was a $250 million transit facilities revenue bond issue in October 1982. The revenue bond resolution provides that the gross receipts, after being verified each day, will be transferred to an account in the name of the trustee, Manufacturers Hanover Trust Company. The money will be transferred from the trustee's account to the NYCTA account the same day it is received, except on the first of every month, when the trustee will retain one twelfth of the debt service due that year.

The financing is based on the assumption that while the state and city could not necessarily be counted on to bail out the MTA if it failed to pay bondholders, it is assumed that the state and city *can* be relied on to step in if the authority defaults on payments of salaries and bills. The city transit authority generates enough gross revenue to secure the bonds—if the bondholders are paid before workers and creditors. So the revenue bond resolution provides that the bondholders will be paid first.

The New York legislature enacted a bill in 1981 that prohibits the MTA from declaring bankruptcy during the life of the bonds issued for the capital program unless it is in severe financial stress itself. The law does not guarantee that the state will bail the MTA out, but is designed to prevent the MTA from issuing the debt and then absolving itself of the obligations.

A feasibility study on the transit revenue bonds conducted by Charles River Associates of Boston said that, even if the state and city were to refuse to bail out the subway system, demand for subway travel is "inelastic"—that is, it is constant enough for the MTA to raise fares substantially and still have almost the same number of riders.

MTA GROSS REVENUE BONDS

MTA gross revenue bonds, known as commuter facilities revenue bonds, are similar to the transit revenue bonds in that they pledge all gross revenues of the MTA commuter lines—the Long Island Rail Road and the Metro-North Commuter Railroad—except federal operating subsidies. Specifically, state and local subsidies, revenues from advertising and concessions, and some net revenues from the TBTA will secure the bonds, in addition to fares collected.

It should be noted that the price of service has much more effect on the demand for commuter rail service than on transit service demand. If a future increase in operating costs was to be passed on to the riders, alternate means of transportation into the city (such as buses, commuter vans, and private cars) could whittle away at the commuter rail ridership and revenues. However, ridership on the commuter lines did increase 16 percent from 1970 to 1980. At the time of the writing of this case study, none of these bonds have been issued.

SERVICE CONTRACT BONDS

Service contract bonds are secured by special subsidies in the form of service contracts that the MTA gets from New York State. According to the state statute passed in 1981, for the next 35 years the state is obligated to pay up to $52 million annually for the city transit system and $28 million for the commuter lines in the form of service contracts.

BOND RATINGS

Rating agencies varied slightly in their interpretations of the credit worthiness of the two types of securities that have been sold. Standard & Poor's rated the October 1982 transit revenue bond issue BBB-plus; Moody's rated it Baa; and Fitch Investors Service rated it A. The December 1982 issue of service contract bonds, which included $81.25 million in proceeds for transit and $43.75 million in proceeds for commuter facilities, was rated A-minus by Standard & Poor's, A by Moody's, and BBB by Fitch. The December 1982 issue marked the first time bonds were sold that were secured by New York State service contracts.

Case 20: New York City General Obligation Bonds that Have "Double Barrel" Security

Sylvan G. Feldstein, Ph.D.
Senior Municipal Specialist
Merrill Lynch, Pierce, Fenner & Smith, Inc.

INTRODUCTION

Unlike other general obligation bonds of New York City, those issued for elementary and secondary schools have a "double barrel" security feature. Besides being general obligations and thus payable out of general fund revenues and real estate taxes, the bondholder can turn to the state comptroller for direct payment in the event of default by New York City. In this case this security feature is described as well as the specific New York City general obligation bonds that are double-barreled.

HOW THE SECURITY STRUCTURE WORKS

Under Section 99–b of the state finance law, the bondholder can, in a default, file a claim with the state comptroller. This security program is also discussed in Case 23 in terms of how it relates to school districts in New York State.

It is the duty of the state comptroller to immediately investigate the circumstances of the alleged default to determine if it indeed has occurred. If it has, the state comptroller must deduct and withhold from the next succeeding "state aid to education" payment an amount sufficient to pay the bondholders. As of June 30, 1982, outstanding New York City general obligation bonds issued for "school purposes" totaled $655,451,024, and state-aid-to-education payments made in fiscal year 1982 were $800,865,483.[1]

BONDS THAT QUALIFY

Some New York City general obligation bonds issued for school purposes are for higher education, and not for elementary and secondary schools. Since the city does not distinguish on its printed bonds the specific school purpose, the differentiation of the elementary and

---

[1]City of New York comptroller's report for fiscal 1981–82. It should also be noted that the New York City Educational Construction Fund Revenue Bonds, 1972 Series A, also share this security feature. As of October 1, 1982, no more than $46.925 million of the original $51.15 million bond issue remained outstanding.

secondary school purpose bonds from the higher education bonds is
not readily possible visually. It is, however, essential to make such a
distinction. If even a small fraction of the bonds of a particular issue
are for higher education purposes, questions may be raised as to
whether the entire issue qualifies under Section 99–b.

Exhibit 1 lists New York City general obligation school bonds
which are limited to elementary and secondary school construction
purposes. It should be emphasized that, in order for a New York City
general obligation bond to be double-barreled, it must not only have
the correct date of issue, coupon rate, and maturity date, but also it
must state on the face of the bond that it is for "school" purposes. If
it does not, then it does not qualify under Section 99–b.

Exhibit 1
New York City General Obligation Bonds: Elementary
and Secondary Schools Only*

Date of Issue	Coupon	Serials Through
September 15, 1970	7.20%	March 15, 1985
October 15, 1971	7.40	April 15, 1983–87
January 1, 1972	6.90	July 1, 1986
May 1, 1972	6.75	November 1, 1982–86
July 15, 1972	6.50	January 15, 1983–87
January 1, 1973	6.20	July 1, 1983–84
January 1, 1973	5.25	July 1, 1984–87
August 1, 1973	6.90	February 1, 1987–88
August 1, 1973	7.00	February 1, 1984–87
November 1, 1973	7.00	May 1, 1984
November 1, 1973	6.25	May 1, 1984–85
November 1, 1973	5.50	May 1, 1985–88
February 1, 1974	7.00	August 1, 1986
February 1, 1974	5.80	August 1, 1986–87
February 1, 1974	5.50	August 1, 1987–88
March 1, 1974	6.00	September 1, 1983–88
August 1, 1974	8.00	February 1, 1985–89
October 15, 1974	8.00	April 15, 1983–89
February 15, 1975	7.50	August 15, 1989

*The identification of the double-barreled bonds is derived from:
notice of sales for the specific bonds involved; section 99–b of the New
York State Finance Law titled: "Withholding of state aid for school
purposes upon default in payment of obligations of the prospective recipient;" city of New York comptroller's reports for the years: 1947–50
and 1965–75; review of the capital budget working papers for the specific bond issues involved.

DRAWBACKS

Drawbacks of the Section 99–b mechanism in regard to the New
York City general obligation bonds are twofold. First, the Section
99–b mechanism only becomes operational when a bond default has
already occurred. That is, it is a remedy for a default, but does not

prevent one from occurring. Second, state-aid-to-education payments are made only at specified times of the year. Therefore, a default may occur at a time when the state comptroller does not have any appropriated state funds available for the eligible New York City general obligation bondholders. Nonetheless, the mechanism does provide the bondholder with added protection which other New York City general obligation bonds do not have.

Case 21: MAC's Second Resolution Bonds

Sylvan G. Feldstein, Ph.D.
Senior Municipal Specialist
Merrill Lynch, Pierce, Fenner & Smith, Inc.

The Municipal Assistance Corporation (MAC) was created by the state of New York in 1975 to provide financing for the city of New York for capital improvements as well as for funding out the city's budget deficit. As of early 1983, it has issued over $7 billion in municipal bonds under two separate bond resolutions. Under the First General Resolution approximately $1.848 billion has been issued; under the Second General Resolution approximately $5.940 billion has been issued.[1] This case study focuses on the larger of the two bond security structures, MAC's Second Resolution bonds.

THE SECURITY

Pledged revenues are defined as annual appropriations from the state legislature of: (1) general revenue-sharing monies (Per Capita Aid) due the city of New York; (2) sales tax revenues collected by the state from a 4 percent sales tax imposed within the city on most retail sales; and (3) stock transfer tax revenues collected by the state on the transfer of stock and certain other securities.

Annual debt service, operating expenses, and reserve requirements on MAC's First General Resolution bonds have a prior lien on the sales tax and stock transfer tax revenues. After MAC expenses are met, including debt service on the bonds, the remaining monies flow to the city of New York's general fund.

---

[1]These amounts include bonds that could be issued on the exercise of MAC warrants and in connection with MAC's commercial paper program.

THE FLOW OF FUNDS

Sales taxes *plus* stock transfer taxes collected *less* operating expenses of MAC, *less* maximum annual debt service (DS) payable on the outstanding First Resolution bonds *plus* available Per Capita Aid *pays* debt service on the Second Resolution bonds. Below is a table which shows the flow of funds and debt service coverage on the Second Resolution bonds.[2]

Sales taxes.........................	$1,435,000,000
Stock transfer taxes.................	672,000,000
MAC operating expenses............	(11,000,000)
DS on First Resolution Bonds........	(344,000,000)
Net available......................	1,752,000,000
Available Per Capita Aid............	409,000,000
Total available for DS on Second Resolution Bonds	$2,161,000,000
Maximum DS on Second Resolution Bonds..........	$ 803,000,000
DS coverage.......................	2.69 times

Note: For period January 1, 1982–December 31, 1982.

THE ADDITIONAL BONDS TEST

Second Resolution bonds can be issued only if available revenues cover maximum annual debt service on the old and to-be-issued Second Resolution bonds by two times. Additionally, no more than $10 billion in total MAC bonds can be issued. Available revenues used for the additional bonds test are derived from:

1. The *lesser* of either the sales and stock transfer taxes collected over the previous 12 months; or, the amounts estimated to be collected over the next 12 months.
2. The amount of Per Capita Aid paid to MAC during the current year.
3. *Less* maximum annual DS on the First Resolution bonds and MAC operating expenses for the current year.

THE CAPITAL RESERVE AID FUND

A debt service reserve is to be funded at 1.00 times the amount of debt service to be paid in the succeeding calendar year on Second Resolution bonds outstanding and to be issued. This fund is subject to

---

[2]Preliminary official statement for $210,000,000. Municipal Assistance Corporation Series 44 Bonds, dated January 31, 1983.

the legislative makeup provision, the so-called moral obligation. (For additional information about the moral obligation, see Chapter 30.)

CREDIT WORTHINESS STRENGTHS

Below are six aspects of the bond security which provide comfort to the investor.

1. 2.69× Maximum Annual DS Coverage. Available revenues in 1982 would have covered maximum annual DS in 1986 of $802.609 million on outstanding and new Second Resolution bonds as well as bonds subject to issue through the exercise of warrants by an estimated *2.69×*.

It should also be noted that a more conservative formula for determining the maximum annual DS coverage on the Second Resolution bonds is to take the DS on the First Resolution bonds, add it to the maximum DS on the Second Resolution bonds, and then divide that number into the available revenues. Using this formula, the coverage would be *2.17×*.

2. Almost One Year's Maximum Annual DS Reserve. There is a Capital Reserve Aid Fund for the Second General Resolution bonds which, on December 31, 1982, held securities valued at $727.4 million. Maximum annual DS on all the bonds—including bonds that could be issued through the exercise of warrants was estimated to be $803.0 million.

3. Insulation from New York City. Annually, the pledged revenues cannot pass to the city of New York until the DS on the bonds has first been provided for.

It should also be noted that while a legal test of the MAC security structure in a worst-case senario (*i.e.,* a New York City bankruptcy) has not occurred, the authority of the state to appropriate the earmarked monies to MAC has been upheld by the highest state court, and the bond attorneys have opined that the earmarked monies are legally insulated from any possible suits from creditors of New York City or the city itself.

4. The State's "Moral Obligation" Pledge. If the Capital Reserve Aid Fund should have to be used, the state must be notified and may replenish it if the legislature makes an appropriation. While this makeup provision is not mandatory, the state of New York has assisted all other moral obligation bonds where the need occurred.

5. Issuance Test for First Resolution Bonds. There is an issuance test for the First Resolution bonds that limits annual DS to $425 million. (Maximum annual DS in 1983 is $344 million.)

6. Strong Coverage Test Required for New Bond Issues. A two-times coverage test of available revenues for maximum annual DS on the old and to-be-issued Second Resolution bonds is required.

CREDIT WEAKNESSES

Below are four aspects of the bond security which are potential weaknesses to the credit quality.

1. Monies Must be Annually Appropriated. While the state legislature has appropriated Per Capita Aid, the sales tax, and the stock transfer tax to MAC since 1975, under the state constitution, the legislature cannot be legally obligated to do so. Future budgetary problems of the state could adversely influence the amount of Per Capita Aid that is appropriated.

2. Second Lien Bonds. The First General Resolution bonds have a prior lien on the sales and stock transfer tax revenues. However, the Per Capita Aid is not so pledged.

3. Elastic Revenue Base. The sales and stock transfer tax revenues are very elastic and could decline in a prolonged economic recession.

4. Possibly Greater-Increased MAC Issuance. The city is lessening its dependence on MAC and is financing increasingly more on its own. Between FY83 and FY86 the city of New York plans to sell $2.5 billion in general obligation bonds and $795 million in water revenue bonds. If the city, however, should be unable to do this, MAC may be called upon to issue more debt. (It should be noted, however, that pursuant to the act, MAC is limited to $10 billion.)

CONCLUSION

In summary, the credit worthiness of the Second Resolution bonds is strengthened by the high coverage of maximum annual debt service ($2.69\times$); the substantial debt reserve fund ($727.2 million); the insulation of MAC revenues from the city of New York; the state's moral obligation pledge; and the strong two-times coverage test for additional bonds.

The credit worthiness is weakened by the need for the state legislature to annually appropriate the earmarked monies; the prior lien of the First Resolution bonds; the elasticity of the pledged tax revenues; and the uncertainty concerning both the state's and the city's budgetary operations.

Case 22: New York City Housing Authority Bonds that Have Been Converted to the Federal Public Housing Authority Program

Sylvan G. Feldstein, Ph.D.
Senior Municipal Specialist
Merrill Lynch, Pierce, Fenner & Smith, Inc.

INTRODUCTION

Since 1968, certain bonds issued by the New York City Housing Authority that were originally secured only by authority revenues and the guarantee of the city of New York have been converted to a federal program. Because of the strong security features of the federal pledge, such converted bonds are of the highest credit quality. This case study identifies those bonds that are now federally secured and explains how Public Housing Authority bonds are secured.[1]

BACKGROUND

The New York City Housing Authority (NYCHA) was established in 1934 by the city of New York to construct and operate public housing projects for persons of low income. It is the nation's largest and oldest public housing program. Financing for these housing projects has been primarily from three sources. Most projects were financed from proceeds of authority bond sales in which the bonds were secured by a contractual pledge of annual contributions from HUD to be applied first to the payment of principal and interest on the bonds. The annual monies from Washington were paid directly to the paying agent for the bonds, and the bondholders were given specific legal rights to enforce the pledge. These bonds, known as either Public Housing Authority, or New Housing Authority bonds, are of the highest credit quality because of this federal pledge.[2] The second source of

---

[1]Data sources for this case study include: New York City Housing Authority Annual Fiscal Report, dated 12/31/79; calendars of the New York City Board of Estimate, dated 9/18/80, 6/26/80, and 5/29/80; interview with the general manager of the New York City Housing Authority on 9/17/80; interviews with the comptroller of the New York City Housing Authority on 9/17/80 and 9/22/80; and New York City Housing Authority Consolidated Financial Statements, dated 12/31/82.

[2]These bonds are not to be confused with the authority's $27.12 million Section 8 assisted mortgage revenue bonds that were issued in 1978, and which are *not* guaranteed by the U.S. government, though they do receive federal subsidies under certain circumstances.

financing for the authority came from loans made to it by the state of New York. The third source of financing for the housing projects came from the authority's selling its own bonds which were guaranteed only by the city of New York. Each housing project constructed by the authority was financed under either the federal program, the state program, or the city program.

CONVERSION TO THE FEDERAL PROGRAM

Under the federal laws, beginning in the late 1960s certain authority housing projects which had been financed through the sale of authority bonds originally guaranteed only by the city of New York, were incorporated into the federal program. Debt service on authority bonds issued for the housing projects named in Exhibit 1 is now paid by the federal government (HUD) directly to the paying agent for the bonds.

Exhibit 1
**New York City Housing Authority Bonds
that Have Been Converted to the Federal
Program**

Year of Change	*Project Name on Bond*
1968	Colonial Park
	Consolidated City
	(Eastchester City
	Sheepshead Bay, South
	Beach, Woodside)
1972	Elliott
	Dyckman
	Lexington
	Ravenswood
	Riis
	Sedgwick
1979	Arverne
1980	Gun Hill
	Parkside
	Nostrand
	Glenwood
	Todt Hill
	Pelham Parkway
	Berry
	Pomonok

CONCLUSION

In terms of bond security, the above bonds now have the same security features as the ones that had originally been issued as Public Housing Authority, or New Housing Authority bonds.

Case 23: Additional Bondholder Protections for General Obligation Bonds of School Districts in New York State

Sylvan G. Feldstein, Ph.D.
Senior Municipal Specialist
Merrill Lynch, Pierce, Fenner & Smith, Inc.

INTRODUCTION

Because the school districts are located in New York State and are identified with the problems of the state, as well as having unfamiliar names such as the Ausable Valley Central School District and Cheektowaga Union Free School District, their general obligation bonds tend to sell at higher yields than those of school districts located outside the state. There are two unique security features of New York school district general obligation bonds. The first is that any uncollected taxes are reimbursed to the school district by the county, thereby assuring 100 percent school tax collection by the end of the fiscal year. The second is that, if necessary, state aid due the school districts must be used to pay the bondholders.

SCHOOL DISTRICTS IN NEW YORK STATE

School districts in New York State are units of local government created to operate public schools, and authorized to levy real estate taxes and to issue debt including both general obligation bonds and notes. Under the state constitution this debt is payable, if necessary, from the levy of ad valorem taxes on the full value of all taxable property within the boundaries of the respective school districts. For school districts that are in cities with populations under 125,000, there is a debt limit of 5 percent of the issuer's assessed valuation. Within other districts the debt limit is 10 percent as determined by the state legislature. There is no limit on the taxes that can be levied for payment of the debt.

COLLECTION OF TAXES

Tax collectors of the school districts collect the school tax levies, except that in cities of 125,000 or more the city tax collectors also collect the school levies. In towns of less than 125,000 people, the same arrangement can be made by mutual agreement.

WHY THE TAX COLLECTION RATE IS ALWAYS 100 PERCENT

Under New York State law the school districts receive delinquent school tax payments from their respective county treasurers.[1] In this way the school districts receive 100 percent of their annual tax levies, and the counties themselves are responsible for collecting the unpaid taxes. It should also be noted that generally there are two exceptions to this procedure: school districts in Westchester County and school districts located within cities.

IMPORTANCE OF ANNUAL STATE AID PAYMENTS

New York State first began to provide local school districts with annual aid in 1925, when the state began to assist in paying for physical improvements. In 1962 the state began providing school districts with annual aid for operating expenses as well. The state aid monies are derived from a special formula which is based on weighted average daily attendance in the respective school districts compared to the statewide average daily attendance. Some school districts receive up to 85 percent of their revenues from the state of New York; many depend on state aid programs for at least 50 percent. In many if not all school districts, the total amount of annual state aid is substantially more than the annual debt service.

ADDITIONAL BOND SECURITY

If a school district does not pay its debt service, the bondholder (under a New York State law enacted in 1959) can file a statement with the state comptroller, who must deduct and withhold from the next succeeding state aid payment an amount sufficient to pay the bondholder. The security feature is Section 99–b of the State Finance Law.

CASE LAW SUPPORT

Security for bonds of all New York State issuers, including school districts, was further strengthened in November 1976 when the New York State Court of Appeals declared the New York State Emergency Moratorium Act invalid. This was the state law that allowed New York City to postpone redeeming its general obligation notes in November 1975.

---

[1] New York State Real Property Tax Law, Art. 13 (1958, and amended thereafter).

SECTION 99–B DRAWBACKS

There are three aspects of the Section 99–b security structure that the analyst should be aware of:

1. The Section 99–b mechanism only becomes operational when a bond default has already occurred. That is, it is a remedy for a default, but does not prevent one from occurring.
2. State aid to education payments are made only at certain times of the year. Therefore, a default may occur at a time when the state comptroller does not have any appropriated state funds available for the specific school district.
3. Where a school district has defaulted in the payment of interest or principal due upon school bonds, the comptroller is required to withhold and pay from state funds appropriated for the support of common schools the employer's contribution to the New York State Teachers' Retirement System prior to withholding, for payment to the holders of the delinquent bonds, state aid due the defaulting school district.

Case 24: Turning Wastewater into Drinking Water: The Clayton County Water Authority

John W. Coleman, Jr.
Municipal Credit Analyst
The Citizens and Southern National Bank

AUTHORITY STRUCTURE

The Clayton County Water Authority was created under Georgia law in 1955 to construct a water supply and distribution system. The sewer system was started in 1957, expanding the authority's scope. The authority is governed by a seven-member board. Each member is appointed by the Clayton County Board of Commissioners and serves a five-year term. Terms are staggered to eliminate having more than two new members appointed in any one year. The authority establishes rate schedules independent of county or public service commission approval. Daily operations are directed by the manager, who is employed by and reports to the board.

BOND SECURITY

Water revenue bonds issued in 1955 have a first lien on the water system's net revenues; amounts sufficient to retire those bonds are held in the sinking fund. All subsequent bond issues have a lien on system net revenues subject to prior payment of sinking fund requirements for Series 1955 water revenue bonds. The authority has covenanted to maintain, at all times, rates and charges that are sufficient to meet all operating and maintenance expenses, to provide sinking fund payments for current debt service, to accumulate a reserve equal to one year's debt service within 10 years of a new bond issue, and to create and maintain a reserve for water and sewer system extensions and improvements to equal at least $1.5 million dollars. Seventy-five percent of all other monies must be used for system improvements. The other 25 percent could be turned over to the county at the option of the authority.

FLOW OF FUNDS

All operating receipts are deposited into the revenue fund and disbursed: 1) for payment of operating and maintenance expenses, maintaining a $300,000 working capital reserve; 2) for payment of monthly sinking fund requirements, Series 1955 water revenue bonds; 3) for monthly sinking fund requirements for water and sewerage system bonds including a reserve, created by 5/1/87, equal to maximum annual debt service; 4) to the renewal and extension fund monthly residual amounts until a balance of $750,000 is achieved. After all the above requirements have been met, 75 percent of any remaining money will be deposited into the renewal and extension fund, and the remaining 25 percent may be used by the county for any lawful purpose.

ADDITIONAL BONDS

No first lien bonds may be issued. Parity bonds may be issued if: 1) actual net revenues for 12 consecutive months of the preceding 16-month period equal one times the current year's debt service for outstanding first lien and parity bonds; 2) all sinking fund requirements have been met as covenanted; 3) projected net revenues in any future sinking fund year, beginning 12 months after project completion, equal at least 1.5 times maximum annual debt service on outstanding and proposed bonds.

SERVICE AREA

The county is part of the Atlanta SMSA. Spurred by residential development, the population has grown rapidly over the past two decades.

Year	Population	Percent Increase
1960	46,365	102.7
1970	98,043	111.5
1980	150,357	53.4

Located just south of Atlanta, this 149-square-mile county has matured into a suburban community with some degree of industry. Fort Gillem, Ford, General Motors, and Atlanta Hartsfield International Airport provide employment for county and metro area residents.

Overall, Georgia has abundant water resources because of large underground aquifers. However, in northern Georgia counties, underlying rocks have low permeability and can transmit very little water. Thus, water for the region is obtained almost exclusively from surface sources. The Chattahoochee River is the major source of water for metropolitan Atlanta.

Customer base growth has been steady as the combined water and sewer system expanded into unconnected areas. This is particularly true of sewerage customers, as many residents switch over from their own individual systems.

Year	Water Customers	Sewer Customers
1961	3,074	400
1966	9,462	5,198
1971	17,033	10,880
1976	24,817	16,630
1981	28,918	19,907

Currently, water is provided to 80 percent of the population within the service area. Sewer service is provided to 55 percent of the service area population.

THE SYSTEM

Limited water resources dictated the site and structure of combined water and sewer system facilities. Raw water is obtained from Little Cotton Indian Creek and Cotton Indian River located south of Clayton in neighboring Henry County. These two sources supply raw water for the 20 million gallons-per-day (mgd) filter plant on the Little Cotton Indian Creek reservoir. Water is pumped west for storage and distribution. It is repumped for storage and distribution to northern sections of the county. Additionally, Chattahoochee River water

is obtained indirectly from purchase arrangements with the city of
Atlanta. Authority customers are supplied with an average daily flow
of approximately 13.6 mgd of treated water.

USING WASTE WATER FOR DRINKING WATER

Combined effluent is separated and the sludge is dried and pel-
letized. Pellets can be used as a low-grade fertilizer, incinerated into
a fine ash, or mixed with wood chips to fuel furnaces for more pellet
production. Liquid effluent is treated and then distributed onto a
2,650-acre site wetted by 18,000 sprinklers. With phosphates and ni-
trates removed this water, which is now as clean as normal river flow,
flows back into the reservoir. Fast growing pine trees were planted
on the 2,650-acre treatment site, and the trees will be harvested
every 20 years. The timber production also will be used to reduce the
sewer system cost. It was found to be more cost-effective to take land
off the tax rolls for sewerage treatment than to try to build more
costly treatment plants.

FINANCING

Three classes of bonds have financed system facilities. County general obligation bonds were issued in 1955, 1957, and 1964. These
bonds are payable solely from ad valorem taxes. Water revenue bonds
totaling $1.1 million were issued in 1955, representing a first lien on
revenues of the water system. Outstanding first-lien bonds are now
fully funded from amounts held in the sinking fund. Nine issues of
second-lien bonds totaling $23.484 million remain outstanding. These
bonds are technically second-lien obligations until retirement of the
1955 water revenue bonds. However, they do have a first-lien on
sewer system revenues. It should also be noted that 80 percent of the
cost of the sewerage treatment facilities ($43.7 million) was paid by
a federal Environmental Protection Administration grant.

CAPITAL PROGRAM

A $12.5 million bond issue is being planned for extending the wa-
ter supply system. Construction of a new reservoir, a water treatment
plant, and water lines will be financed from bond proceeds and funds
on hand. This will increase water production capacity by approximately 6 mgd, giving the system a total capacity of 26 mgd. Two lines
included in this plan will improve the authority's ability to obtain
water from Atlanta. This capability becomes very important during
warm-weather months if rainfall is below average.

A $12 million bond issue is projected for 1984 to upgrade and expand the sewerage treatment facilities. In 1987, a projected $4–5 million bond issue will fund water and sewer line extension; and of course, service rate increases will be necessary to support coverage requirements for these anticipated debt issues.

Case 25: A "Take or Pay" that Works: The Municipal Electric Authority of Georgia

Jere Dodd, Jr.
Vice President
Robinson Humphrey/American Express Inc.

The Municipal Electric Authority of Georgia (MEAG), which began operations early in 1977, is the wholesale power supplier of 47 municipally owned electric systems in Georgia. In 1980 the systems served areas with a population of 471,437, representing about 8.6 percent of the population of the state. The municipalities have operated their electric systems for many years, with the most recently established system dating from 1929.

MEAG obtains the power it sells primarily from its interests in three coal-fired and two nuclear-fueled generating plants operated by Georgia Power Company. MEAG purchases the balance of its power requirements from Georgia Power and owns an interest in the statewide high-voltage transmission system operated by Georgia Power which it uses to deliver power to its municipal systems. Since its inception, MEAG's wholesale power rates have compared favorably with other wholesale power suppliers in the Southeast.

BACKGROUND

At the beginning of the 1970s the Georgia Power Company, the largest subsidiary of the Southern Company, was the electric supplier for virtually all of the state of Georgia except for Savannah and its environs, which were served by a local utility, and small areas in north Georgia supplied by the Tennessee Valley Authority. Although Georgia Power served most urban areas of the state directly, 50 cities owned their own electric distribution systems which were wholesale customers of Georgia Power. Also, Georgia Power supplied at wholesale 39 federally financed electric membership corporations (formerly known as rural electrification administration cooperatives) which served large areas of the state that were principally rural but also contained rapidly growing suburban areas. Georgia Power's sizable number of wholesale customers made it the largest investor-owned wholesaler of electricity in the United States, exceeded in such sales only by the Tennessee Valley Authority and the Bonneville Power Administration. Thus, a substantial portion of Georgia Power's capital spending was to provide generating capacity for its wholesale customers.

Inflation and soaring interest rates of the 1970s, coupled with sharp increases in fuel costs and large government-mandated expenditures for pollution control, had a heavy financial impact on all electric utilities, which were unable to secure sufficient rate increases quickly enough to offset their rising costs. This shock was felt most strongly by rapidly growing utilities like Georgia Power, which was borrowing heavily to finance its large construction program.

Both Georgia Power and its wholesale customers became concerned about the company's ability to finance its required additions to capacity and about the increased rates that this would entail. After much discussion, Georgia Power agreed to sell interests in certain of its plants and in its high-voltage transmission grid to its wholesale customers so that they could use their own borrowing power to finance a portion of the required capital outlays.

As a result, the electric membership corporations formed what is now the Oglethorpe Power Corporation, a federally financed generation and transmission cooperative; and 47 municipal systems formed the Municipal Electric Authority of Georgia to buy interests in certain Georgia Power facilities. The city of Dalton elected to act alone to buy an appropriate interest; two other small cities decided to remain wholesale customers of Georgia Power Company.

Thus, by the end of the 1970s, the Georgia Power Company was joined in the ownership of some of its generating plants and transmission lines by Oglethorpe Power Corporation, the city of Dalton, and Municipal Electric Authority of Georgia. Georgia Power continued to operate the system as before, acting for itself and its co-owners.

MEAG

Municipal Electric Authority of Georgia, created by the 1975 General Assembly of the state, is an operating electric utility which serves as the wholesale supplier of 47 municipally owned electric distribution systems in Georgia. MEAG supplies these systems (known as its participants) with all of their requirements for electricity except for their allotments of power from federally owned dams, which they purchase from the Southeastern Power Administration. One of these systems has a small amount of generating capacity, but the others purchase all their requirements.

In 1981, MEAG generated about 59 percent of its customers' requirements and bought 26 percent from the Georgia Power Company. The balance of their needs was met by their purchases from the Southeastern Power Administration. MEAG's generating capacity consists of interests in five large units (three coal- and two nuclear-fueled) operated by the Georgia Power Company. MEAG pays its share of the cost of operating these plants and receives its portion of their output. In addition to its operating plants, MEAG has interests in three other generating units (one coal and two nuclear) now being built by Georgia Power.

The authority owns about 1,000 miles of transmission lines which are sufficient to give it a proportionate interest in the statewide high-voltage transmission grid operated by Georgia Power which links the state's generating plants with its distribution systems. MEAG pays its share of the cost of operating this grid and is thereby entitled to deliver electricity from its plants to its customers without payment of additional transmission or "wheeling" charges. This joint transmission system, which is the only such system in the United States, enables MEAG and its participants to realize substantial savings.

From an operational standpoint, MEAG's facilities are an integral part of the Southern Company system. This system—which consists of the Georgia, Alabama, Mississippi, and Gulf power companies—is operated as a corporate power pool much as though it were a single company. Its principal plants are large-scale, coal-fired or nuclear-fueled generating units which are supplemented by smaller hydro and combustion turbine peaking units.

SECURITY FOR BONDS

The authority's bonds are payable from the revenues from its sales of electricity after the payment of expenses of operation and maintenance. The authority has agreed to set its rates at levels which will generate revenues sufficient to pay all expenses and debt service, and a year-end adjustment is made to assure that revenues exactly equal the amounts required.

The authority and its participants have entered power sales contracts that essentially provide that MEAG will be the exclusive supplier of its participants' power requirements except for their allotments from the Southeastern Power Administration. In these contracts, the participants agree to pay rates sufficient to cover all MEAG's costs, including debt service.

These contracts also provide that, if any of MEAG's projects are not completed or are put out of service for any reason, the participants remain liable for their proportionate share of debt service and other expenses related to these projects. The Georgia Supreme Court has ruled that each city's obligation to make payments under these contracts is a general obligation of the city for which it is obligated to levy unlimited ad valorem taxes if necessary.

Normally, however, all payments made by the participants to MEAG will be from the revenues of their electric systems. Should any city default on its obligation, its share would be distributed proportionately among the other participants.[1] A reserve fund, established from a part of the proceeds of the bond issues, which is equal to maximum annual debt service also secures MEAG's bonds.

RATE REGULATION

The act of the 1975 Georgia General Assembly which established MEAG specifically exempted it from any regulation by the Georgia Public Service Commission. The constitutionality of this act has been upheld by the Georgia Supreme Court. The constitution of the state of Georgia exempts municipally owned electric systems from any regulation by the Georgia Public Service Commission. Additionally, neither the authority nor the cities are subject to any federal rate regulation.

REVIEW AND OUTLOOK

When MEAG began operations early in 1977 after the sale of its first bond issue, it launched an ambitious financing program that contemplated the sale of a total of $1.6 billion in bonds between 1977 and 1985 to finance the cost of its interests in the generation and transmission facilities described above. The borrowings required for the four coal-fired generating units (the last of which is expected to go into service in early 1984) and the two operating nuclear units have been very close to original estimates. Thus by early 1984, MEAG will have in service about 71 percent of its planned generating capacity at a cost very close to its original estimates.

However, the remaining 29 percent of its capacity, consisting of interests in two nuclear-fueled units now scheduled for completion in 1987 and 1988, is expected to require $1.2 billion more in borrowing than was originally planned. This large increase was caused not only

---

[1]One of the 47 electric systems that MEAG serves is owned by a county instead of a city. The county's legal responsibility under its contract with MEAG is the same as that of the cities.

by greater construction costs but also by larger financing costs resulting from a four-year postponement of completion and a higher level
of interest rates than originally contemplated.

Case 26: Matching Assets to Liabilities: The Case of the Nebraska Higher Education Loan Program

Michael A. Gort, J.D.
Vice President
Lehman Brothers Kuhn Loeb, Inc.

Diana L. Taylor
Associate
Lehman Brothers Kuhn Loeb, Inc.

The Nebraska Higher Education Loan Program, Inc. (NebHelp), organized in September 1978, is one of the largest student loan programs in the country. NebHelp has issued $376,125,000 of debt since
1978 and has generated significant surplus funds under each of its
indentures. In fall 1982, NebHelp was in a position to initiate the
next step in funding student loan programs, a step permitting a significant increase in the overall average life of outstanding debt and
the release of the surplus monies from each outstanding indenture.

The preferred method of financing a new student loan program has
been through the issuance of long-term bonds with a maturity in excess of 15 years, allowing all loans to be financed through final payout. Between 1980 and 1982, however, the rates in the tax-exempt
market increased dramatically, and the rates necessary to sell long-
term student loan bonds were correspondingly high. The income on a
student loan is dependent upon the 91-day T-bill rate with a guaranteed minimum return of 9.5 percent on most student loans. For purposes of calculating future cash flows and viability of a particular
bond issue, the 9.5 percent minimum return must be sufficient to
cover debt service on the bonds, program administration expenses,
and servicing costs on the loans. In other words, a bond issue with a
true interest cost (TIC) in excess of 9.5 percent is generally not feasible unless funds in addition to the student loans are pledged to pay
debt service. Since long-term bond rates have been significantly
higher than 9.5 percent, since 1980, it has been necessary to utilize
an alternate financing mechanism. Most programs, including Neb-

Help, have settled on three-year bonds backed by a bank credit or liquidity facility. It was intended that, sometime between the time of issuance and maturity, rates would decline sufficiently to allow the 3-year bonds to be taken out with a long-term issue.

During late summer and early fall, 1982, interest rates declined precipitously, allowing long-term issues to be sold within the feasibility constraints imposed by student loan portfolios. At this time, NebHelp had the following debt outstanding:

Issue	Final Maturity	Principal Amount Outstanding
Student Loan Revenue Bonds, 1979 Series A	June 1996	$24,040,000
Student Loan Program Revenue Bonds, 1981 Series A	March 1984	$78,955,000
Student Loan Revenue Bonds, 1982 Series A	June 1985	64,750,000
Variable amount promissory notes	November 1982	21,000,000
Variable amount promissory notes	November 1982	24,000,000
Secured credit note	November 1982	500,000

Prior to the fall rally, NebHelp had intended to refinance only the aggregate $45 million of variable amount promissory notes with a three-year bond issue backed by a bank loan purchase commitment, and to leave all other debt outstanding. As interest rates fell, the potential advantage to be gained by refunding the 1979A and the 1981A bonds in addition to the promissory notes became apparent, and a debt restructuring analysis was initiated to study the effects of various combinations of loan amounts and debt maturities. The 1982A issue was not considered for refunding since it had been issued recently; no loans had been made from its acquisition fund and no surpluses had yet accumulated.

The debt restructuring was designed to match more closely the average life of NebHelp's assets (loan portfolios) and liabilities (outstanding debt). It was found that the most economical way to accomplish this was to refinance $45 million of promissory notes, the 1979A bonds, and the 1981A bonds with two issues—a $51.5 million issue (long-term 1982 Series A) with a final maturity in 1993, and an $87.5 million issue (1982 Series B) due in 1985. The net result was to increase the average life of NebHelp's outstanding debt from 1.695 years to 4.473 years and to free $11 million of surpluses and reserves trapped under each old indenture.

All student loans fall into one of three maturity categories: (1) loans in repayment or grace, all of which have a known payout schedule; (2) loans which have not yet entered repayment and therefore do not have a known repayment schedule, although the date on which they will enter repayment may be estimated based on expected graduation dates; and (3) loans which are scheduled to be acquired from the acquisition fund for which neither expected graduation dates nor repayment terms are known. A bond issue which matches debt service to assets almost exactly can be structured around loans in the first category. The maximum payout period of these loans is 11 years, which includes a 9-month grace period and 120 months in repayment. The 11-year issue was structured around the revenue stream of those loans owned by NebHelp which fell into this first category. All other loans and forward comm......ments owned by NebHelp were used to support the debt service on the short-term issue. Those loans which have entered grace and repayment over the term of the three-year issue will be refinanced with longer-term debt at the end of the three years.

To the extent that loans under the long-term indenture might go into default, the matching of assets and liabilities would be upset. This contingency was prepared for by a right of substitution of loans between the short-term and long-term indentures. Any loans under the long-term indenture which enter deferment can be substituted for loans under the short-term indenture which have entered repayment, keeping the debt service and loan amortization schedules closely matched.

The net effect of refunding the old debt was the significantly increased average life of NebHelp's liabilities and over $11 million of free cash and reserves. Of this $11 million, $7.5 million was used to increase debt service coverage and pay for costs of issuance, leaving $3.5 million free for NebHelp's use.

Case 27: New Jersey's "Qualified Bond Act" Security Program for Local Municipality and School Bonds

Sylvan G. Feldstein, Ph.D.
Senior Municipal Specialist
Merrill Lynch, Pierce, Fenner & Smith, Inc.

INTRODUCTION

In 1976 the governor of New Jersey signed into law two bills (known as "qualified bond" acts) which provide additional security for certain general obligation bonds issued by New Jersey issuers. The chief characteristic of the two laws (one is for municipalities and the other is for school districts) is that selected state aid monies, normally paid directly to the municipality or school district, will be paid directly by the state treasurer to the bond-paying agent.

REVENUE FEATURES

Municipal Qualified Bonds

The selected state aid monies pledged for debt service are the business personal property tax replacement revenues (Public Law 1966, c. 135), and state urban aid funds (Public Law 1971, c. 64). The latter state aid program is available to 24 New Jersey urban municipalities. While these state aid programs could be eliminated or changed, the law provides that any future state aid programs that provide funds in substitution of the above, would be pledged as security for the qualified bonds.

School Qualified Bonds

Under this law, state aid monies pledged for debt service are those available under the Public School Education Act of 1975 (Public Law 1975, c. 212) and four other state aid programs. As with the municipal qualified bonds, the law specifies that, while the specific state aid programs may be eliminated or changed, any future substitute state aid programs would be pledged as security for such qualified bonds.

BOND PAYING PROCEDURES

After the bonds are sold, the issuer certifies to the state treasurer the name and address of the paying agent, the maturity schedule, the interest rate, and debt service payment dates. The state treasurer is then required to withhold from the amount of state aid due the issuer an amount sufficient to pay the debt service on the qualified bonds, and to make this payment directly to the paying agent. The issuer still must include the debt service requirements in its annual budget since the diversion of cash does not represent additional state aid to the issuer, but merely a diversion of cash flow to ensure that the principal and interest on the qualified bonds will be paid promptly.

BOND STRENGTHS

The three strengths of New Jersey qualified bonds are:

1. Debt service payments are made directly by the state treasurer to the paying agents.
2. The State Local Finance Board reviews and authorizes all qualified bond sales under the two laws in order to ensure that state aid more than covers the anticipated debt service.
3. The qualified bonds are also general obligations of the issuing municipalities and school boards.

CONCLUSION

The original purpose of the qualified bond acts was to assist municipalities and school districts (particularly those in urban centers) that had had problems issuing bonds as a result of New York City's fiscal difficulties in 1975. In the opinion of the attorney general of New Jersey, once the qualified bond issue has been approved by the State Local Finance Board and certified to the state treasurer, the earmarked state aid funds cannot be used for any purpose by or on behalf of the issuer other than to pay the required debt service on the qualified bonds.

It should also be noted that future New Jersey legislatures are not necessarily bound by prior legislation, though several of the state aid programs pledged under the qualified bond acts have been in existence for several years.

Case 28: New Jersey's Own Insurance Program for Local School District General Obligation Bonds

Sylvan G. Feldstein, Ph.D.
Senior Municipal Specialist
Merrill Lynch, Pierce, Fenner & Smith, Inc.

INTRODUCTION

Certain general obligation school bonds issued by local governments in New Jersey have a layer of security which is known as a school bond reserve.[1] This reserve, administered by the state treasurer, is to be used to pay debt service on the school bonds if the local governments themselves should ever be unable to do so. This case describes such a reserve, how it works, and which local school bonds are now secured by it. It should be noted that accounting and budget controls for local governments in New Jersey are stringent, and that this reserve adds yet another layer of security to the school bonds.

THE NEW JERSEY SCHOOL BOND RESERVE ACT

This law, passed in July 1980, contractually pledges a portion of the existing New Jersey Fund for the Support of Free Public Schools for paying debt service on certain outstanding, and to be issued, local government general obligation school bonds. Known as the "school bond reserve," this reserve receives revenues from compensation paid to the state for its riparian (i.e., tidewater) lands. These lands, which are now or were formerly covered by the mean high tide, are located around the state and include areas of the Hackensack Meadowlands and some Atlantic City resort properties. The school bond reserve is to contain an amount equal to at least 1½ percent of all outstanding and eligible local government school purpose bonds.

Under the law, if a local government anticipates that it will be

---

[1] Data sources for this case include: state of New Jersey Assembly Bill No. 1706 (introduced May 19, 1980, by Assemblymen Burstein, Karcher, Doyle, Bennent, and by Assemblywoman Garvin); interview with David T. Beale, executive director, New Jersey Department of the Treasury, on August 7, 1980; interviews with Elias Abelson, Esq., Division of Law, state of New Jersey, on August 18, 1980 and June 8, 1983; interview with George Tuttle, Director of Finance, city of Paterson, New Jersey, on August 11, 1980.

unable to make its regular debt service payment, it is obligated to notify the state at least 10 days prior to the payment date. If the local school bonds qualify, the state treasurer shall use monies in the school bond reserve to pay the debt service as it comes due. If monies in the reserve are so used, the state treasurer at least once a year must replenish the reserve with new monies from available riparian rights revenues to bring the reserve back up to its 1½ percent requirement. At December 31, 1982 the book value of the reserve was $15,953,000 which was equal to 1½% of the local government school bonds estimated to be outstanding. At January 31, 1983 the book value of the Fund for the Support of Free Public Schools was $40,065,030.

LOCAL GENERAL OBLIGATION BONDS COVERED BY THE SCHOOL BOND RESERVE

Under the law, the principal and interest on bonds issued since December 4, 1958, by New Jersey counties, municipalities, and school districts and which were for elementary and secondary school purposes, are covered by the reserve. County community college bonds are not affected. Additionally, under the law, each bond so covered and issued subsequent to the effective date of the act (which was July 16, 1980) shall bear the following legend:

> Payment of this obligation is secured under the provisions of the New Jersey School Bond Reserve Act in accordance with which an amount equal to 1½ percent of the aggregate outstanding bonded indebtedness (but not to exceed the moneys available in the fund), of New Jersey counties, municipalities and school districts for school purposes as of September 15 of each year, is held within the state fund for the support of free public schools as a school bond reserve pledged by law to secure payments of principal and interest due on such bonds in the event of the inability of the issuer to make payment.

ALLOWED INVESTMENTS OF THE ASSETS OF THE SCHOOL BOND RESERVE

Under the law the assets of the school bond reserve are composed entirely of direct obligations of the U.S. government or obligations guaranteed by the full faith and credit of the U.S. government. Additionally, at least one third of the securities in the reserve shall mature within one year of their dates of issuance or purchase. On or before each September 15, the state treasurer shall review the investments in the reserve to see that they meet the requirements of the law.

FUTURE AVAILABLE REVENUES FROM
THE STATE'S RIPARIAN RIGHTS

While the school bond reserve now holds $15.9 million, it has a claim to all future revenues derived from the state's riparian rights. It should be noted that, while the state estimates potential revenues as being as high as $100 million, there had been attempts through state referenda and court cases to restrict the state's riparian rights and the amounts that the state can collect on the sale of its rights as well.

STRENGTHS AND WEAKNESSES OF
THE SECURITY STRUCTURE

While the school bond reserve (as an insurance reserve and from actuarial insurance aspects) provides additional protection to the eligible general obligation bonds, there are certain aspects of this security structure that should be noted. First, the school bond reserve is only reviewed annually (September 15 of each year) to determine if its holdings equal at least 1½ percent of the outstanding local school bonds. Second, responsibility for notification of a potential default rests with the issuer. Third, the monies generated by the riparian rights are relatively small when compared to the total debt service payable on the eligible bonds.

The Federal Municipal Bankruptcy Law

APPENDIX

James A. Moyer
LeBoeuf, Lamb, Leiby & Macrae

I. DESCRIPTION OF CHAPTER 9 OF THE BANKRUPTCY ACT

In 1978, the United States Congress adopted Chapter 9 of the Bankruptcy Reform Act of 1978 (sometimes referred to as Chapter 9 of the Bankruptcy Act),[1] which modified and changed Chapter IX of the Bankruptcy Act[2] (also called the Former Act) and its amendments to provide a more flexible, legal, and procedural mechanism for public entities, such as states, municipalities, political instrumentalities and agencies, to seek the protection of the United States bankruptcy courts. This chapter *(a)* describes Chapter 9 as it now exists and *(b)* describes alternative actions for states or municipalities which are unable or do not desire to pay debt service or other creditors' claims. The material here is a dichotomy. Part is a tedious recapture of the essence of statutory and case law, and part is the reporting of some mundane facts and events which produce stress, nightmares, headaches, and general uneasiness among holders of debt obligations.

---

[1]Bankruptcy Act, Pub. L. 95–598, Nov. 6, 1978, 92 Stat. 2621, as amended.
[2]Chapter IX of the Bankruptcy Act of 1937.

The threat and effect of a default cannot be overlooked or ignored by an issuer or purchaser of municipal short- or long-term obligations. *Default* is the term used when a debtor *does not* promptly pay on presentation at maturity the principal of or interest on a bond or note. Just so we do not get too immersed in the procedural vagaries of the Bankruptcy Act or municipal analysis, please examine the following for its emotional content:

> When we find in state legislation a departure from true honor—when selfish ambition, and the passion of avarice have a controlling influence on the minds of men in public station then may we bid farewell to all hope of protecting the rights and the interests of those who are subject to the will and the power of men thus depraved . . . With such men, the oath of office 'faithfully and impartially' to execute the high trust committed to their care is trampled under foot.[3]

This is not a quotation from a Midwest institutional noteholder in 1975 about New York City's moratorium on paying debt service. Rather, it is a statement about the hardship wrought by the state of Rhode Island in repudiating and compromising debt incurred during the Revolutionary War. The claims against Rhode Island took many years to resolve, and a number of creditors received some moneys, but many suffered the hurt of delay and partial loss of principal and forgone interest.

The most recent adjustment to the mechanism for the settlement or composing of claims against municipalities became effective on April 8, 1976, in the form of amendments to and revisions of the Former Act. The 1976 revision was incorporated into the Bankruptcy Act effective in 1978 in almost the identical form. The intent of Chapter 9 is to provide a sensible procedure for a municipality having financial difficulty to work with its creditors to adjust or settle indebtedness. The intent of Chapter 9 is to enable the municipal entity to seek respite from debt payment while developing and having confirmed a plan for debt adjustments. Chapter 9 is similar in purpose to Chapter 11 of the Bankruptcy Act, which has the ultimate effect of enabling a corporation to reorganize its affairs, with one significant difference. Municipal entities exercise sovereign powers which cannot be impaired by the federal government nor therefore by the bankruptcy courts. Generally, no court order or decree may interfere with the political or governmental powers of the debtor municipal entity, its property or revenue, or any income-producing property. The most significant distinctions between private and municipal bankrupts are

---

[3]John W. Richmond, *Rhode Island Repudiation: Or the History of the Revolutionary Debt of Rhode Island*, 2d ed. (Providence, R.I.: Sayles, Miller & Simons, 1855).

that the alternative of liquidation is not available for a municipal entity and involuntary filings or adjudications of bankruptcy are not available against municipal entities.

II. REVIEW AND ANALYSIS OF CHAPTER 9

Municipal debt adjustment under Chapter 9 is different from the effect of the Bankruptcy Act on an individual or private corporation. Severe limitations are placed upon the powers of the bankruptcy court in a municipal debt adjustment proceeding as a consequence of the 10th Amendment to the United States Constitution and the decisions of the Supreme Court on the United States upholding municipal bankruptcy legislation.[4] The bankruptcy court is not really involved in the operation of the municipal entity during the time that it is undergoing financial reorganization. The bankruptcy court has no power to control expenditures for municipal services or any of the activities of the municipal entity.[5] A 1940 court decision states the intent and scope of Chapter 9:

> The Bankruptcy Act limits the power of the court to the composition of indebtedness and to the carrying on of the usual business transactions, which includes the making of necessary expenditures in connection therewith, jurisdiction over the governmental affairs of the municipality, or of its property, is limited to such purposes. The court is merely authorized to determine insolvency, or inability to meet debts as they mature, and whether the plan is proposed in accordance with the provisions of the statute, and whether it has been accepted by the number of creditors provided, and whether the petitioner is in a position to carry out the terms of the plan, and whether it is equitable, for the best interest of the creditors, and nondiscriminatory.[6]

The functions of the bankruptcy court focus on determining whether the voluntary petition of the municipal entity is properly filed, approving the petition, assisting in the formulation of a plan of debt adjustment, and confirming and implementing the plan. The municipal entity seeking the protection of the bankruptcy court may gain substantial benefit from the powers of the bankruptcy court. When the most powerful of these provisions, automatic stays of contracts, exist, the municipal entity is permitted to adjust nondebt contractual relationships like executory contracts and unexpired leases, and the municipal entity is also given the authority to borrow moneys

---

[4]Collier Vol. 4, Sec. 900.02.
[5]11 U.S.C., Sec. 904.
[6]Matter of Willacy County Water Control & Improvement District No. 1, 36 F. Supp. 36,39 (S.D. Tex. 1940).

to continue operations by offering a court-approved high priority to assure a prospective creditor of the likelihood of repayment.[7]

The first test for a municipal entity under Chapter 9 is to become eligible for relief. As we mentioned before, municipal entities cannot be compelled to seek involuntary relief under the Bankruptcy Act. Because of the protection afforded by the bankruptcy court, controversies may arise over whether or not a municipal entity is eligible for relief. A holder of a bond or note may oppose the seeking of court protection by a municipal entity because the ability to mandamus or enforce the payment of the obligations may be stayed, limited severely, restricted, or nullified by the bankruptcy court. Also, courts generally do not seek to foster proceedings before them and often limit access to only those petitioners clearly meeting the jurisdictional standards. Only an entity that is a municipality is eligible for relief under Chapter 9. "Municipality" is defined to mean "political subdivision or public agency or instrumentality of a State."[8]

The four eligibility requirements a municipality must satisfy are as follows:

First, the municipality must be "generally authorized to be a debtor under [Chapter 9] by State Law, or by a governmental officer or organization empowered by State Law to authorize such entity to be a debtor under such [Chapter 9]."[9]

Second, the municipality must be "insolvent or unable to meet such entity's debts as such debts mature.[10] "Insolvent," as defined in the Bankruptcy Act, means a "financial condition such that the sum of such entity's debts is greater than all of such entity's property, at a fair valuation.[11] The concept of insolvency does not have practical application to a municipal entity because there is no mechanism for liquidation under Chapter 9. The reality of the situation facing a municipal entity seeking relief under Chapter 9 is that there is an inability to raise sufficient revenues through taxes or otherwise to pay obligations as they mature. The desire or need to seek the protection of the bankruptcy court becomes most evident when the imposition of taxes over and above those already imposed has the counterproductive effect of causing more tax defaults and tax foreclosures. This negative effect results from the inability of the private property or private activities within the municipality to support the taxes imposed.

Third, the municipal entity must "desire to effect a plan to adjust such debts.[12] A municipal entity may not use Chapter 9 to evade cred-

---

[7]11 U.S.C. Sec. 365, 901(a), 11 U.S.C. Sec. 364.

[8]11 U.S.C., Sec. 101 (29).

[9]11 U.S.C., Sec. 109 (c) (2).

[10]11 U.S.C., Sec. 109 (c) (3).

[11]11 U.S.C., Sec. 101 (20).

[12]11 U.S.C., Sec. 109 (c) (4).

itors or effect a delay. The petition must be designed to result in a plan of adjustment of debts by which creditors' claims will be satisfied or discharged.[13] This requirement has not been widely interpreted by courts but could be utilized by creditors protesting the acceptance of a petition by a bankruptcy court or used by a bankruptcy court itself in an effort to reject consideration of a petition.

Fourth, it is required that the municipal entity:

> (A) has obtained the agreement of creditors holding at least a majority in amount of the claims of each class that such entity intends to impair under a plan in a case under such chapter [Chapter 9]; (B) has negotiated in good faith with creditors and has failed to obtain the agreement of creditors holding at least a majority in amount of the claims of each class that such entity intends to impair under a plan in a case under such chapter [Chapter 9]; (C) is unable to negotiate with creditors because such negotiation is impracticable; or (D) reasonably believes that a creditor may attempt to obtain a preference.[14]

The third element is the most useful one and was inserted in the 1976 amendatory law.[15] The intent is to enable major municipalities to seek the protection of Chapter 9 where negotiation with creditors is extremely difficult and where many of the creditors who hold bearer debt obligations cannot be identified or even contacted. The fourth element is sometimes of critical importance in providing the debtor municipal entity with an opportunity to seek a stay against aggressive creditor action while attempting to negotiate a plan of adjustment.

A municipal entity that satisfies the previously described criteria may seek the protection of a bankruptcy court by filing a voluntary petition. Only the municipal entity itself may file the petition. In the case of an unincorporated tax or special assessment district that does not have its own officials, the petition may be filed by the governing authority or the board or body having authority to levy taxes or assessments to meet the obligations of the district.[16] The bankruptcy court may entertain objections to the petition and, after notice and a hearing, dismiss the petition if the debtor did not file the petition in good faith or if the petition does not meet the requirements of Chapter 9. If the petition is not dismissed, the municipal entity shall be entitled to an order of relief and to the protection of the bankruptcy court.

The ability of a municipal entity to seek relief under Chapter 9 is

---

[13]Collier, Vol. 4, Sec. 900.03.
[14]11 U.S.C., Sec. 109 (c) (5).
[15]Collier, Vol. 4, Sec. 900.03.
[16]11 U.S.C., Sec. 921.

tempered by two key sections in Chapter 9. Section 903 of the Bankruptcy Act states:

> This chapter [9] does not limit or impair the power of a State to control, by legislation or otherwise, a municipality of or in such State in the exercise of the political or governmental powers of such municipality, including expenditures for such exercise, but—
> (1) a State law prescribing a method of composition of indebtedness of such municipality may not bind any creditor that does not consent to such composition; and (2) a judgment entered under such law may not bind a creditor that does not consent to such composition.[17]

Section 904 of the Bankruptcy Act provides:

> Notwithstanding any power of the court, unless the debtor consents or the plan so provides, the court may not, by any stay, order, or decree, in the case or otherwise, interfere with—
> (1) any of the political or governmental powers of the debtor;
> (2) any of the property or revenues of the debtor; or
> (3) the debtor's use or enjoyment of any income-producing property.[18]

These two sections provide a glimpse at the relationships between the states and the federal government under the Constitution. The effect of these two sections is to limit the ability of the bankruptcy court to interfere with a state's control over its municipal entities and in turn to control the conduct of the affairs of a municipal entity. Of course, the municipal entity must consent to the exercise of power by the bankruptcy court, but such consent cannot extend beyond the scope of Chapter 9. In order to avoid conflicts under the Constitution of the United States resulting in a test of the limits of Chapter 9, Section 904 acts as a safeguard. Remember that a bankruptcy court may exercise its inherent power and may issue seemingly draconian orders which hinder or disrupt commercial entities. However, Section 904 serves to restrict activities of the bankruptcy court in the exercise of its authority.

The view of the Supreme Court of the United States concerning the limits of Chapter 9 can be covered quickly. In *Faitoute Iron & Steel Co.* v. *City of Asbury Park,* the Supreme Court stated:

> The principal asset of a municipality is its taxing power and that, unlike an asset of a private corporation, cannot be available for distribution. An unsecured municipal security is therefore merely a draft on the good faith of a municipality in exercising its taxing power. The notion that a city has unlimited taxing power is, of course, an illusion. A city cannot be taken over and operated for the benefit of its creditors, nor can its creditors take over the taxing power. Indeed, as far as the

---

[17]11 U.S.C., Sec. 903.
[18]11 U.S. C., Sec. 904.

Federal Constitution is concerned, the taxing power of a municipality is not even within its own control—it is wholly subordinate to the unrestrained power of the State over political subdivisions of its own creation.[19]

This perceptive interpretation of the law was written by Justice Frankfurter in 1941. A further court statement on the limitation of bankruptcy courts is:

> A municipal corporation . . . is a representative not only of the State, but is a portion of its governmental power . . . The State may withdraw these local powers of government at pleasure, and may, through its legislative or other appointed channels, govern the local territory as it governs the state at large. It may enlarge or contract its powers or destroy its existence.[20]

The essence of the relationship between Chapter 9 and the taxing power reserved to the states is that Chapter 9 may only serve to protect the rights of municipal creditors and enable the enforcement of obligations incurred by municipal entities as long as neither the power to levy taxes is usurped nor the existence of the municipal entity impaired. The question of whether Chapter 9 constitutes impermissible interference with a state's control over its municipalities is unanswered at this time. However, if creditors in a Chapter 9 proceeding are too vigorous in pressing their demands upon the municipal entity, the following view of Justice Frankfurter may prevail:

> . . . if taxes can only be protected by the authority of the State and the State can withdraw that authority, the authority to levy a tax is imported into an obligation to pay an unsecured municipal claim, and there is also imported the power of the State to modify the means for exercising the taxing power effectively in order to discharge such obligations, in view of conditions not contemplated when the claims arose. Impairment of an obligation means refusal to pay an honest debt; it does not mean containing wages and means for paying it.[21]

Perhaps, the limits of Chapter 9 will be litigated in the future, but to date, the bankruptcy court has demonstrated sufficient self-restraint to protect its own power and ability to function.

The administrative provisions of Chapter 9 are fairly clear, but the interaction with other provisions of the Bankruptcy Act have developed tremendous controversies and analytical matrices which affect the marketability of tax-exempt obligations. Once a petition is filed, the chief judge of the United States court of appeals for the circuit embracing the municipal entity in which the case is commenced des-

---

[19]*Faitoute Iron & Steel Co.* v. *City of Asbury Park*, 316 U.S. 502, 509 (1941).
[20]*United States* v. *Railroad Company*, 17 Wall 322, 324; *Hunter* v. *Pittsburgh*, 207 U.S. 161.
[21]*Faitoute Co.* v. *Asbury Park*, 316 U.S. 502, 511 (1942).

ignates the bankruptcy judge to hear the petition and to supervise the conduct of the case.[22] The petition may be objected to and a hearing held. If the petition is not dismissed, the bankruptcy court shall order relief.[23] Appeals may be taken from an order of the bankruptcy court, but the filing of an appeal cannot restrict, stay, or delay the bankruptcy court in proceeding under Chapter 9.

Section 922 of the Bankruptcy Act effectively provides that all actions or claims against a municipal entity and the holders of municipal assets or assets which can become subject to possession by the municipal entity are stayed.[24] This section alone has and will continue to provide substantial opportunity for lawyers, municipal analysts, and bankers to worry about municipal indebtedness. The stay is of action against an officer or inhabitant of the debtor or against taxes or assessments owed to the debtor. It prohibits a creditor from bringing an action against an inhabitant of the debtor owing taxes to the debtor where the creditor seeks to collect the debt by collection of taxes that are owed to the municipality. The creditors are stayed from any attempt to enforce a lien on taxes owed to the municipality or to collect taxes directly from an inhabitant. Relief from the stay provisions occurs upon dismissal or closing of the case, upon discharge of the debtor, or upon request for relief from the stay.

The next three provisions in Chapter 9 cover notice, the list of creditors, and the effect of the list of claims.[25] Under Chapter 9 there are three distinct instances requiring notice: (1) commencement of a case under Chapter 9, (2) an order of relief, and (3) dismissal of a Chapter 9 case. The notice must be published not less than once a week for three successive weeks in at least one newspaper of general circulation published within the district in which the case is commenced, and in such other newspaper having a general circulation among bond dealers and bondholders as the bankruptcy court designates.[26] The Rules of Bankruptcy Procedure are specific in their description of the procedures and actual form for notice. The notice requirements are intended to comply with the requirements of due process provisions under the Constitution.[27] The debtor municipal entity must also file a list of creditors with the bankruptcy court to comply with the due process clause in the Constitution and to enable the proper notice to be given to creditors.[28] Generally, the list of cred-

---

[22]11 U.S.C. Sec. 921 (b).
[23]11 U.S.C. Sec. 92 (c).
[24]11 U.S.C. Sec. 922.
[25]11 U.S.C. Sec. 923, 924 and 925.
[26]11 U.S.C. Sec. 923.
[27]Fifth Amendment to the United States Constitution.
[28]11 U.S.C. Sec. 924.

itors is filed with the petition, but the bankruptcy court may require that it be updated or completed if it is evident that the list is incomplete as to actual creditors or the information required. The applicable Rule of Bankruptcy Procedure requires the debtor municipal entity to list creditors of each class, show the amounts and character of their claims, whether secured or unsecured, the nature of any security, and, so far as is known, the name and address or place of business of each creditor and whether the claim is disputed, contingent, or unliquidated in amount.[29] A list of the names and addresses of the holders of record title, legal or equitable, to real property subject to assessment or taxation must be provided too.

Section 925 of Chapter 9 establishes that the filing of the list of creditors and claims, other than those which are listed as disputed, contingent, or unliquidated, constitutes prima facie evidence of the validity and amount of claims.[30] The practical effect is that a creditor does not have to get notice of the bankruptcy petition, search the list to determine if a claim was filed on its behalf, and then prove the existence and value of the claim. Holders of bearer bonds are saved the inconvenience and expense of having to file claims to participate in the proceeding, since their claims would be deemed to be filed and allowed. A proof of claim will be required to be filed by the creditor, however, if the claim appears on the list of creditors as disputed, contingent, or unliquidated.[31] Under the Bankruptcy Act, "disputed" means that liability on the claim is not agreed upon by the debtor and the creditor, "unliquidated" means that the dollar amount of the claim is either not agreed upon or is unknown, and "contingent" means that not all of the factors that are essential to the creation of liability have yet occurred.[32]

Section 926 of the Bankruptcy Act is perhaps the most powerful provision or least equal to Section 922 in power.[33] It is also the most discussed, analyzed, and agonized over provision in Chapter 9. Before discussing some of the concepts that have emerged as almost a subculture in municipal, legal, and analytical practice, it is appropriate to review what Section 926 contains. The Section states:

> If the debtor refuses to pursue a cause of action under Section 544, 545, 547, 548, 549 (a), or 550 of this title, then on request of a creditor, the court may appoint a trustee to pursue such course of action.[34]

---

[29]Public Law 95–548; Sec. 405 (d), Rules of Bankruptcy Procedure, Chapter IX Rule 9–7.

[30]11 U.S.C. Sec. 925.

[31]Id.

[32]Collier, Vol. 4, Sec. 925.02.

[33]11 U.S.C. Sec. 926.

[34]Id.

Should the debtor municipal entity fail to bring a cause of action against one of its creditors during the course of a Chapter 9 proceeding, a creditor may petition the bankruptcy court by motion to have a trustee appointed to exercise the avoiding powers. The avoiding powers are: Section 544, which is the strong arm power and enables the trustee to exercise the rights and powers of the debtor to avoid, rescind or cancel any transfer of property of the debtor municipal entity or any obligation incurred by the debtor municipal entity that is voidable; Section 545, which is the avoiding of the fixing of a statutory lien on property of the debtor municipal entity to the extent that such lien, among other things, becomes effective only when the debtor municipal entity commences a Chapter 9 proceeding or is not perfected or enforceable against the property of the debtor municipal entity at the time of the filing of the Chapter 9 petition or is a claim for rent; Section 547, which is the preference provision and contains the perhaps most discussed provision in Chapter 9; Section 548, which enables the trustee or a creditor to avoid any transfer of an interest of the debtor municipal entity in property, or any obligations incurred by such debtor, that was made or incurred on or within one year before the date of the filing of the Chapter 9 petition, if the transfer or obligation was fraudulent, was for less than fair market value, was a sham, or was less than a good faith transaction or was made while the debtor municipal entity was insolvent; Section 549, which provides that transactions executed by the debtor municipal entity after the commencement of a Chapter 9 proceeding may be avoided by the court or the trustee; and Section 550, which empowers the trustee to recover for the benefit of the estate the property transferred or its value from almost any transferee with the exception of a transferee that takes the property for value, in good faith, and without knowledge of the voidability of the transfer being avoided. These provisions are powerful and are generally only limited by equity and applicable law that permits the perfection of a security interest in the property which the trustee wishes to seize. Generally, a creditor, in order to defeat the avoiding power, must perfect his interest in accordance with applicable law and the Uniform Commercial Code, and the perfection must relate back to a time prior to the commencement of the bankruptcy proceedings in order to overcome the trustee's or debtor municipal entity's power of avoidance.

The next section, Section 927, gives the appearance of being nothing more than a procedural provision.[35] It covers mandatory and permissive dismissal by the bankruptcy court after notice and hearing and has not yet been voluminously interpreted through litigation.

---

[35] 11 U.S.C. Sec. 927.

Section 927 provides that the bankruptcy court may dismiss a Chapter 9 case for cause, including:

(1) want of prosecution;
(2) unreasonable delay by the debtor [municipal entity] that is prejudicial to creditors;
(3) failure [by the municipal entity] to propose a plan within the time fixed by the [bankruptcy court];
(4) if the plan is not accepted within any time fixed by the [bankruptcy court];
(5) denial of confirmation of a plan under [Chapter 9];
(6) if the [bankruptcy court] has retained jurisdiction after confirmation of a plan
   (a) material default by the debtor [municipal entity] with respect to a term of such plan; or
   (b) termination of such plan by means of the occurrence of a condition specified in such plan.[36]

Also the bankruptcy court shall dismiss a Chapter 9 case if confirmation is refused.[37] This mandatory dismissal provision is similar to one of the grounds for permissive dismissal and perhaps is redundant. The significance of this section is that the bankruptcy judge has wide discretion and substantial powers. A recalcitrant municipal entity could find itself without the protection of the bankruptcy court. A discharge would probably be detrimental to the creditors because they could only pursue their rights under state statutes without any assistance from the bankruptcy court.

The final sections in Chapter 9 concern the plan for debt adjustment, the supervision of the bankruptcy court in having the plan implemented, and the confirmation of the plan. The debtor municipal entity has the obligation of proposing the plan for the adjustment of the debtor's debts.[38] The debt adjustment plan can be filed when the bankruptcy petition is filed or at a later time fixed by the bankruptcy court. Because of the 10th Amendment to the U.S. Constitution, the bankruptcy court and the creditors cannot propose a plan of adjustment because that would be an interference with the established powers of the debtor municipal entity to control future taxes and expenditures. Chapter 9 does not contain a detailed procedural structure to assist a debtor municipal entity in formulating a plan for debt adjustment. The debtor municipal entity has the right to modify the plan for the adjustment of debts before the court confirms the plan. In addition, the debt adjustment plan may be modified after confirmation by the bankruptcy court even though the Bankruptcy Act does not

---

[36]11 U.S.C. Sec. 927 (a).
[37]11 U.S.C. Sec. 927 (b).
[38]11 U.S.C. Sec. 941.

make specific provisions for this.[39] Obviously, over time the debt adjustment plan may need modification, and the bankruptcy court should not be refused an opportunity to continue to keep a workable plan in place. Furthermore, a debt adjustment plan for a municipal entity is generally a longer-term commitment than a corporate reorganization for the parties involved. The Borough of Fort Lee, New Jersey, took almost 40 years to work through its plan, and the city of Wanchula, Florida, took 14 years.

The debt adjustment plan shall be confirmed by the Bankruptcy Court if the following are satisfied.

(1) the plan complies with the provisions of this title [Bankruptcy Act] made applicable by sections 103 (e) and 901 of this title;

(2) the plan complies with the provisions of this chapter [Chapter 9]

(3) all amounts to be paid by the debtor or by any person for services or expenses in the case or incident to the plan have been fully disclosed and are reasonable;

(4) the debtor is not prohibited by law from taking any action necessary to be taken to carry out the plan;

(5) the plan provides that each holder of a claim of the kind specified in section 507 (a) (i) [the priority provision] of this title will receive, on account of such claim, property of a value, as of the effective date of the plan, equal to the allowed amount of such claim, except to the extent that the holder of a particular claim of such have waivered such payment on such claim; and

(6) the plan is in the best interest of creditors and is feasible.[40]

This Section makes Chapter 11 of the Bankruptcy Act applicable to Chapter 9 proceedings. Chapter 11, which controls corporate reorganizations, is generally more specific in enumerating the requirements to be met by the debtor in possession in order to have a plan approved. The carryover provisions provide that (1) the debtor municipal entity propose the plan in good faith,[41] (2) the plan must be accepted by each class of creditors that is impaired under the plan,[42] (3) excluding insiders like elected officials, at least one class of creditors that is impaired under the plan has consented to the plan,[43] and (4) the debtor municipal entity may avail itself of the "cram-down" provisions.[44]

The cram-down provisions enable the debtor municipal entity to seek confirmation of the debt adjustment plan by classes of creditors

[39]*American United Life Ins. Co.* v. *Maines City,* 117 F.2nd. 574 (Fifth Cir., 1941); *Wells Farge Bank and Union Trust Co.,* v. *Imperial Irrigation District,* 136 F.2d 53 g (Ninth Cir., 1943).

[40]11 U.S.C. Sec. 943.

[41]11 U.S.C. Sec. 1129 (a) (3).

[42]11 U.S.C. Sec. 1129 (a) (8).

[43]11 U.S.C. Sec. 1129 (a) (10).

[44]11 U.S.C. Sec. 1129 (b).

that are impaired by the plan and have not accepted the plan. Conscious refusal to accept the plan, like a refusal of municipal labor unions or the inability to give notice and an opportunity to be heard to the holders of bearer bonds, may dictate the use of the cram-down provisions. The standard applied is to test whether the plan does not discriminate unfairly and is fair and equitable with respect to each class of claims that is impaired under and has not accepted the plan.[45] In a nutshell, if the plan protects the legal rights of a dissenting claim in a manner consistent with the treatment of other claims whose legal rights are intertwined with those of the dissenting claims, then the plan does not discriminate unfairly with respect to the dissenting class.[46] In a Chapter 9 plan, the fair and equitable standard becomes an equitable doctrine because the assets of the municipal entity cannot be valued in determining the relative benefits to be passed to the several classes of creditors.

For the purpose of confirming a debt adjustment plan under Chapter 9, the federal courts have included a feasibility standard. This means that there is a reasonable prospect that the debtor municipal entity will be able to generate adequate tax revenues and control expenses to have sums sufficient to make the payments required under the plan. The gist of a debt adjustment proceeding under Chapter 9 can be distilled into the following:

> Where future tax revenues are the only source to which creditors can look for payment of their claims, considered estimates of those revenues constitute the only available basis for appraising the respective interests of different classes of creditors. In order that a court may determine the fairness of the total amount of cash or securities offered to creditors by the plan, the court must have before it data which will permit a reasonable, and hence an informed, estimate of the probable future revenues available for the satisfaction of creditors.[47]

In addition, before the bankruptcy court confirms the plan with the effects of a cram-down, it must be evident that the debtor municipal entity is exercising its taxing power to the fullest extent possible for the benefit of its creditors.[48] Much attention has been directed to the cram-down provisions, but the reality is that the area of municipal debt adjustment has not had much litigation yet under the new Bankruptcy Act by classes of creditors alleging that some special favor or inducement was accorded to another class.

The next several paragraphs in Section 943 provide that all of the costs and expenses associated with a Chapter 9 proceeding be identi-

---

[45]11 U.S.C. Sec. 1129 (b) (2).
[46]Kenneth Klee, "All You Ever Wanted to Know About Cram Down under the New Bankruptcy Code," *American Bankruptcy Law Journal*, 53 (1979), p. 133, 142.
[47]Collier, Vol. 4., Sec. 943.03.
[48]*Fano* v. *Newport Heights Irrigation District*, 144 F.2d 563 (Ninth Cir., 1940).

---

fied and that provisions be made in the plan for the payment of those having a priority. Generally, the bankruptcy court can continue to monitor the payment of funds and the reimbursement of expenses in connection with a Chapter 9 case to ensure that the expenses are reasonable and that there is full disclosure of whose rights and interests are affected directly by the debt adjustment plan and directly or indirectly by compensation arrangements. In the past, the debtor municipal entity and the creditors may have suffered some harm where attorneys, banks, fiscal advisors, and municipal agents profited from the restoration of the municipal credit or at least an improvement in the creditworthiness of the defaulted obligations when the debt adjustment plan was confirmed. Administrative expenses are entitled to a priority, and the bankruptcy court must make provisions for payment when confirming the debt adjustment plan. Obviously, "administrative expenses" include allowable attorneys' and accountants' fees, court costs, costs of giving notice or of preparing materials for distribution to creditors. But what about operating expenses of the debtor municipal entity during the pendency of the Chapter 9 proceedings? Under Chapter 11, the bankruptcy court is charged with the responsibility of "preserving the estate."[49] There is no estate in a Chapter 9 proceeding. Perhaps in time there will be direction about whether wages, salaries, benefits, services, supplies, and debt service during the pendency of a Chapter 9 proceeding are allowable administrative expenses.

The final requirement for confirmation of a plan in a Chapter 9 case is that the plan "is in the best interest of creditors and is feasible."[50] If the classes of creditors do not consent to the debt adjustment plan, the fair and equitable requirement may be applied by the bankruptcy court, but if all classes cannot, then the tests of best interests and feasibility are met because the creditors are placed in a better position under the plan than they would be without a plan. The test also gives the bankruptcy court an opportunity to protect the creditors by withholding confirmation until the plan devotes sufficient available resources to creditors. In effect, the best interest test provides a floor for payments under the debt adjustment plan, and the feasibility test provides ceiling.[51]

Once the debt adjustment plan is confirmed by the bankruptcy court, the plan is binding on all creditors, and the debtor and the debtor municipal entity can be discharged. The debtor municipal entity is given complete relief by the plan and the order of confirmation, and the debtor's affairs are totally adjusted by the plan and the order, notwithstanding any failure of creditors to participate in the debt ad-

---

[49]11 U.S.C. Sec. 503 (b) (1) (A).
[50]11 U.S.C. Sec. 943 (b) (6).
[51]Collier, Vol. 4 Sec. 943.03.

justment case or in the plan confirmation proceeding. All creditors are bound by the plan even though they did not accept the plan or even participate, and the bankruptcy court may issue injunctions to make effective the order confirming the plan. The discharge from Chapter 9 occurs when the following have been completed:

(1) confirmation of the debtor's plan;
(2) deposit by the debtor of considerations to be distributed under the plan with the disbursing agent appointed by the court;
(3) a determination by the court that securities deposited with the disbursing agent "will constitute, after distribution, a valid legal obligation of the debtor" and "that any provision made to pay or secure payment of such obligation is valid."[52]

In undertaking the discharge, the bankruptcy court must appoint a disbursing agent to receive, hold, and distribute the moneys and other property to be paid to the creditors. The bankruptcy court may appoint the debtor municipal entity or an institution like a trust company to serve as the disbursing agent. The final requirement is that if refunding obligations or some types of new debt are to be issued by the debtor municipal entity, the bankruptcy court shall add the extra assurance that the obligations are valid. Once the discharge is effective, the debtor municipal entity has the protection of a court approved release of all debts incurred up to the time of the filing of the petition under Chapter 9.

The bankruptcy court may retain jurisdiction over the case for such period of time as is necessary for the successful execution of the plan and shall close the case when administration of the case has been completed.[53] Where the creditors are paid under the plan and have no reason to seek assurance of performance by the debtor municipal entity, the bankruptcy court ceases all involvement quickly. Practically, because there is no estate to liquidate, creditors receive new indebtedness of the debtor municipal entity. Typically, refunding obligations have a longer maturity in order to reduce annual debt service and to cause a reduced burden on tax revenues. Under these circumstances, the supervision of the bankruptcy court may continue for many years to assure that the plan will be performed. Of course, the bankruptcy court has the authority to reopen the case and modify the plan after confirmation. Perhaps the actual or conjectural threat of continuing jurisdiction is one facet of bankruptcy which is aptly unappealing to municipal entities and their creditors.

The extent of Chapter 9 petitions is not a significant absolute number. From 1970 to 1979, there were 11 petitions filed under Chapter 9, while the average number of annual bankruptcy cases filed was

---

[52]Collier, Vol. 4 Sec. 944.03.
[53]11 U.S.C. Sec. 945.

208,619.[54] In reviewing the period from 1938 to 1972, 362 cases were filed with the debtor municipal entities admitting an aggregate indebtedness of \$217,230,541;[55] \$140,614,796 of this aggregate sum was paid or to be paid under confirmed plans, and \$76,615,745 were losses.[56] Perhaps the presence of Chapter 9 has been a significant deterrent. Its complexity and the existence of the perceived unlimited powers of the bankruptcy court may have discouraged potential cases from arising or may have pushed municipal borrowers and creditors to be more discerning in their borrowing arrangements.

Finally, it should be noted that this review of Chapter 9 does not truly reflect the impact of the Bankruptcy Act on municipal entities. With the exponential growth of revenue-supported tax-exempt indebtedness, project financing, and industrial development bonds, other provisions in the Bankruptcy Act affect municipal entities. Also, increased tension created by the pressure to maximize investment return has impaired municipal entities' abilities to withstand harm when private financial institutions become subject to debt adjustment, reorganization, or bankruptcy proceedings or are utilized to enhance credit worthiness of municipal borrowers.

---

[54]1981 Annual Report of the Administrative Office of the United States Courts, p. 18.

[55]George H. Hempel, "An Evaluation of Municipal 'Bankruptcy' Laws and Procedures," *Journal of Finance* X (1973), p. 1339, 1342.

[56]Ibid., p. 1342.

Glossary

Compiled by
Sylvan G. Feldstein
Merrill Lynch, Pierce, Fenner & Smith, Inc.

Additional Bonds Test. A legal requirement that additional bonds that will have a claim to revenues already pledged to outstanding revenue bonds can only be issued if certain financial or other requirements are met first.

Ad Valorem Tax. A state or local government tax based on the value of real property.

Advanced Refunded Bonds. Bonds for which monies have been already placed in escrow to be used for paying debt service.

Assessed Valuation. The worth in dollars placed on real estate and/or other property for the purpose of taxation.

Authority or Agency. A state or local unit of government created to perform a single activity or a limited group of functions.

Authorizing Ordinance. A law which when enacted allows the unit of government to sell a specific bond issue or finance a specific project.

Average life. The average length of time an issue of serial bonds and/or term bonds with mandatory sinking funds and/or estimated prepayments are expected to be outstanding.

Balloon Maturity. An inordinately large amount of bond principal maturing in any single year.

Bond or Note. A security whereby an issuer agrees, by written contract, to pay a fixed principal sum on a specified date (maturity date) and at a specified rate of interest.

Bond Counsel. A lawyer who writes an opinion on the security, tax-exempt status, and issuance authority of a bond or note.

Bonded Debt. That portion of an issuer's debt structure represented by outstanding bonds.

Chinese Coverage. A rate covenant that specifies that rates charged are to provide cover only to the extent necessary to pay for debt service operations, and *required improvements* with excess monies being credited against the succeeding year's revenue requirements. The term "chinese coverage" is also used to describe the liberal approach to the calculation of coverage for a second lien revenue bond. This is usually done by subtracting the debt service on the first lien bonds from the available revenues and then calculating the coverage figure. A more conservative approach is to combine the debt service of both liens and then derive the coverage figure.

Covenant. A legally binding commitment by the issuer to the bondholder.

Coverage. This is the margin of safety for payment of debt service on a revenue bond which reflects the number of times the actual and/or estimated project earnings or income for a 12-month period of time exceed debt service that is payable.

Debt Limit. The maximum statutory or constitutional amount of debt that the general obligation bond issuer can either issue or have outstanding at any time.

Debt Ratio. The ratio of the issuer's general obligation debt to a measure of value, such as real property valuations and personal income.

Debt Service. Required payments for principal and interest.

Debt Service Reserve Fund. An account established as a back-up security for an issuer's bonds.

Default. Failure to pay in a timely manner principal and/or interest when due, or the occurrence of an event as stipulated in the Indenture of Trust resulting in an abbrogation of that agreement.

Delinquent Taxes. Property taxes which have been levied but remain unpaid on and after the due date.

Direct Debt. In general obligation bond analysis, the amount of debt which a particular local unit of government has incurred in its own name or assumed through annexation.

Double-Barreled Bond. A bond with two distinct pledged sources of revenue such as earmarked monies from a specific enterprise or grant-in-aid program as well as the general obligation taxing powers of the issuer.

Feasibility Study. A financial study provided by the issuer of a revenue bond that estimates service needs, construction schedules, future project revenues and expenses.

Fiscal Year. A 12-month time horizon by which state and local governments annually budget their respective revenues and expenditures.

Flow of Funds. The annual legal sequence by which enterprise revenues are paid out for operating and maintenance costs, debt service, sinking fund payments, etc.

Full-Faith-and-Credit. A phrase used primarily in conjunction with state general obligation bonds to convey the pledge of utilizing all taxing powers and resources, if necessary, to pay the bondholders.

Funded Debt. Total debt which is issued and outstanding. Does not include other debt such as short-term loans and notes.

General Obligation Bond. A bond secured by a pledge of the issuer's taxing powers (limited or unlimited). More commonly the general obligation bonds of local governments are paid from ad valorem property taxes and other general revenues.

General Property Tax. A tax levied on real estate and personal property.

Gross Debt. The sum total of a state or local government's debt obligations.

Gross Revenues. Generally, all annual receipts of a revenue bond issuer prior to the payment of all expenses.

Industrial Development Bonds. Bonds used to finance facilities for private enterprises, water and air pollution control, ports, airports, resource recovery plants, and housing, among others.

Interim Borrowing. (1) Short-term loans to be repaid from general revenues or tax collections during the current fiscal year; (2) short-term loans in anticipation of bond issuance or grant receipts.

Issuer. A state or local unit of government which borrows money through the sale of bonds and/or notes.

Joint and Several. A form of contract in which each of the signers is obligated for the full contract amount if other signers should default.

Lien. A claim on revenues made for a specific issue of bonds.

Maximum Annual Debt Service. The maximum amount of principal and interest due by a revenue bond issuer on its outstanding bonds in any future fiscal year.

Negative Pledge Covenant. This term is usually used in conjunction with a hospital revenue bond in which the bondholders do not have a mortgage interest in the facility. Instead, the issuer covenants that the revenue generating facilities will not otherwise be pledged or mort gaged.

Net Bonded Debt. Gross general obligation debt less self-supporting general obligation debt.

Net Revenue Available for Debt Service. Usually, gross operating revenues of an enterprise less operating and maintenance expenses but exclusive of depreciation and bond principal and interest. "Net revenue" as thus defined is used to determine "coverage" on revenue bond issues.

Official Statement. A document (prospectus) circulated for an issuing body prior to a bond sale with salient facts regarding the proposed financing.

Overlapping Debt. The proportionate share of the general obligation bonds of local governments located wholly or in part within the limits of the reporting unit of government which must be borne by property owners within the unit.

Parity Bonds. Revenue bonds which have an equal lien or claim on the revenues of the issuer.

Pay-As-You-Go. A phrase that means that capital projects are being permanently financed from current operating revenues or taxes rather than by borrowing.

Put Bond. A bond which can be redeemed on a date or dates prior to the stated maturity date by the bondholder. Also known as an "option tender" bond.

Qualified Legal Opinion. Conditional affirmation of the legal basis for the bond or note issue.

Rate Covenant. A legal commitment by a revenue bond issuer to maintain rates at levels to generate a specified debt service coverage.

Ratings. Various alphabetical and numerical designations used by institutional investors, Wall Street underwriters, and commercial rating companies to give relative indications of bond and note credit worthiness.

Refunding Bond. The issuance of a new bond for the purpose of retiring an already outstanding bond issue.

Repo. A financial transaction in which one party "purchases" securities (primarily U.S. government bonds) for cash and simultaneously the other agrees to "buy" them back at some future time according to specified terms. Municipal bond and note issuers have used repos to manage cash on a short-term basis.

Revenue Bond. A municipal bond whose debt service is payable solely from the revenues derived from operating the facilities acquired or constructed with the proceeds of the bonds.

Security. The legally available revenues and assets from which are derived the monies to pay the bondholders.

Self-Supporting Bonds. Bonds payable from the earnings of a municipal utility enterprise.

Special Assessment Bond. A bond secured by a compulsory levy made by a local unit of government on certain properties to defray the cost of local improvements and/or services.

Tax Base. The total resources of the community that is legally available for taxation.

Technical Default. Failure by the issuer to meet a requirement of the bond covenant other than for debt service.

Underlying Debt. The general obligation bonds of smaller units of local government within a given issuer's jurisdiction.

Zero-Coupon Bond. A municipal bond in which no current interest is paid, but instead at bond maturity the investor receives compounded interest at a specified rate.

Name Index

Note: Lightface page numbers are in Volume I; boldface page numbers are in Volume II.

Note: Lightface page numbers are in Volume I; boldface page numbers are in Volume II.

Note: Lightface page numbers are in Volume I; boldface page numbers are in Volume II.

Note: Lightface page numbers are in Volume I; boldface page numbers are in Volume II.

Subject Index

A

Account group, 473
  in budget, **499–500**
  in combined balance sheet, **598**
  general fixed assets and, **558**
Accounting; *see also* Amortization;
    Corporate accounting; Depreciation;
    Municipal accounting; *and*
    Municipal financial reporting
  cash-basis of, **450, 455 n**
  colleges and universities and, **276**
  financial, **442–47**
  general obligation bond credit analysis
    and, **128–29**
  managerial, **442–43**
  uniform standards of, **638**
Accounting Principles Board (APB),
    445 n, 451 n
Accrual accounting; *see* Municipal
    accounting
Accrued interest, 26
Active immunization, 534
Active portfolio management, 576; *see
    also* Commercial banks
Actual accounts, budgets and, **498–99**
Additional-bonds test
  municipal electric systems and, **266–67**
  revenue bonds and, 116
Additional parity indebtedness, hospital
    revenue bond and, **166–67**

Adjusted basis, of a capital asset, 37, 38
Adjusted gross income, 41
Administrative Procedure Act (APA),
    652
Administrative rules, of Municipal
    Securities Rulemaking Board, 663–
    64
Advanced refunding bonds
  escrow accounts of, 700–702
  refunding issues and, 224–25, 226, 227
Aftertax bond performance; *see* Taxed
    portfolio
Aftertax capital gain; *see* Capital gains
Aftertax conventional yield-to-maturity,
    494–96
Aftertax coupon return, taxable bond
    and, 487–88
Aftertax interest-on-interest, taxable
    bond and, 488–90
Aftertax realized compound yields, 493–
    94
Aftertax yield; *see* Yield
Agencies, governmental, **11**
Agency funds, **484–85, 488, 505, 534,
    631**
  balance sheet of, **535**
Agreement among underwriters, 247
Aid for Families of Dependent Children
    (AFDC), **41–42**
Airline Deregulation Act of 1978, **224–25**

Note: Lightface page numbers are in Volume I; boldface page numbers are in Volume II.

Note: Lightface page numbers are in Volume I; boldface page numbers are in Volume II.

Note: Lightface page numbers are in Volume I; boldface page numbers are in Volume II.

Note: Lightface page numbers are in Volume I; boldface page numbers are in Volume II.

Note: Lightface page numbers are in Volume I; boldface page numbers are in Volume II.

Discount rate—*Cont.*
  maturity and, 516–21
  net yield, 303, 324
  not an original discount, 40–41
  original issue discount, 38–40, 261 n–
    62 n
  penalty yields on a, 261–63
  price volatility and, 309
  sale or exchange of a, 38–41
  yield on, 345–47
Discount rate
  Bond Buyer Index and, 287–90
  maturity yield spreads and, 292–96
  quality spreads and, 291, 292, 293
  selling at a discount, 10
  yield forecasted with, 285, 287–90
Discounted value; *see* Present value
Discounting, 65, 68
Discriminant analysis; *see* Multiple
    discriminant analysis
Disposition, of general fixed assets, **563–
    64**
Diversification swap, 604–5
Divided account, syndicate account as,
    176
Doctrine of sovereign immunity, general
    obligation bonds default and, **90**
Dollar bonds, 24
  brokers trading, 183, 188
Dollar-weighted return (DWR), 617–20
Double-barreled bonds, 18, 114, 121, 233,
    123
Double deductible, effective tax rate,
    and, 59
Double-up option, 442, 451, 452, 455
Dow Jones Capital Market Wire,
    municipal bond funds and, 600
Durable goods sector, credit risk analysis
    interest due to decline of, **5**
Duration, 534, 535–38; *see also*
    Immunization
  bond equivalence and, 560
  elasticity and, 280
  price volatility and, 298, 299–303
  of a security, 91–93
  set yield factor expressed in terms of
    adjusted, 323–24

E

Early redemption option; *see* Put bonds
East New York Savings Bank v. *Hahn*,
    94
Economic development authorities
    (EDAs), **202, 203**; *see also* Small-
    issue industrial development
    revenue bonds

Economic good, **418**
  market good as; *see* Corporate
    accounting
  nonmarketable good as; *see* Municipal
    accounting
Economic models, market efficiency
    measured by, 459–61
Economic Recovery Tax Act of 1981
  federal tax rate and, 54
  state and local taxes and, 47
Education, as impure public good, 425–
    29, 430
Effective annual interest, 68
Effective par rate, 484–86, 508
  tax-exempt, 498–500
  in taxed portfolios, 496–97
Effective tax rates; *see* State and local
    tax treatment
Efficiency of market; *see* Market
    efficiency
Eisenhower College, closing of, **282–83**
Elasticity, 280
Elderly; *see* Life care revenue bonds
Electric revenue bonds; *see* Public power
    revenue bonds
Elementary school education, as impure
    public good, **425–29, 430**
11-Bond Index, 342
Employee benefits
  as general long-term debt, **570**
  modified accrual basis of accounting
    and, **491**
Employers, general obligation bond
    credit analysis with review of, **133**
Enabling legislation, underwriters
    counsel and, 238–39
Enacted rates, 51, 52–53
Encumbrances
  balance sheet and, **520–21**
  in budget, **497–99**
  reserved for, **520–21**
Energy-related taxes, **48–49**
Engineering report, public power
    revenue bonds and, **271**
Enterprise fund, **481–82, 488, 505,
    542–43, 630**
  balance sheets of, **545, 547, 549–53**
  individual fund balance sheets for,
    597
Enterprise revenue bonds, **543 n**
Equity capitalization, seaport revenue
    bond credit analysis and, **144**
Equivalent taxable yield, 45–46
Erie R. Co. v. *Public Util. Comm'rs*,
    107 n
Ernst & Ernst v. *Hochfelder*, 634, 636,
    638

Escrow accounts
low-yielding state and local
government series (SLGS), and,
700
refunded bonds and, 22
Escrow funds
funded bonds and, **338**
mixed, **338**
pure, **338**
refunded bonds and, **339**
Estimate revenues, in budget, **499**
Evergreen financing, tax-exempt
commercial paper and, **407**
Exclusion principle
private ownership and, **438–40**
public areas for pedestrian use and,
423, 425, 426, 458–62
Expectations hypothesis, term structure
of interest rates and, 280, 281
Expected yield, probability models for
contingent takedown options and,
445–49
Expendable fund, **485–86, 488, 513–14**
financial statements for, **584–87**
fund accounting and, **513**
modified accrual basis of accounting
for, **486**
statement of revenues, expenditures,
and changes in fund balances for,
582–87, 610–12
Expendable trust funds, **483, 488, 505,
533–34**
balance sheets of, **535**
Expendables, 427
Expenditures
in budget, **497, 498**
for an expendable fund, **580–87, 610–
12**
as financial outflows, **586**
modified accrual basis and, **454–57,
486, 489–96**
Expenditures associated with assets,
modified accrual basis of accounting
and, **494–96**
Expenses, financial statements using,
588–90
Externalities, education and, **427–28**
Extraordinary mandatory bond
redemption, single-family mortgae
bond and, **238–40, 241, 242**

F

Face rate; *see* Coupon rate
Face value; *see* Par value
Fair practice rules, Municipal Securities
Rulemaking Board and, 669–70

Faith and Credit Clause, of the New
York constitution, **94–95**
Faitoute Iron & Steel Co. v. *City of
Asbury Park,* **94, 95, 96, 740–41**
Family Assistance Plan, 41
*Farmers and Mechanics Savings Bank of
Minneapolis* v. *State of Minnesota,*
50
Feasibility study
life care communities and, **372–73**
for mortgage money, **242–43, 248;** *see
also* Credit risk analysis *and*
Hospital revenue bonds
Federal aid; *see* State and local
governments
Federal Deposit Insurance Corporation
(FDIC), **288**
enforcement authority and, 649
Federal funds rate
Bond Buyer Index (BBI) and, 285–87
yield forecasted with, 284, 285–87
Federal Guaranteed Student Loan
program (GSL), 20, 135, 136
Federal Housing Authority (FHA)
insurance
construction loan notes and, **390–91,
396–97, 398–99**
multifamily housing revenue bonds
and, **289–90**
multifamily mortgage hospital
revenue bonds and, **348–51**
single-family mortgage revenue
bonds and, **234, 235, 236, 245**
super sinkers and, 396–99
Federal income tax treatment
energy-related severance, **48–49**
equivalent taxable yield and, **45–46**
interest deductibility and
acquired bonds and, 33–36
for financial institutions, 36
marginal tax rates and, 45
regulatory and legislative aspects of,
697–99
on sale or exchange of bond, 36–37
capital gain or loss for corporations,
43–44
capital gain or loss for individuals,
41–43
purchased at a discount, 38–41
purchased at premium, 37–38
statutory exemption of interest, 30–32
arbitrage bonds and, 33
industrial development bonds and,
32
Federal Insured Student Loan program
(FISL), 20, 135–36, 179, 180; *see also*
Student loan revenue bonds

Note: Lightface page numbers are in Volume I; boldface page numbers are in Volume II.

Note: Lightface page numbers are in Volume I; boldface page numbers are in Volume II.

Note: Lightface page numbers are in Volume I; boldface page numbers are in Volume II.

Note: Lightface page numbers are in Volume I; boldface page numbers are in Volume II.

Note: Lightface page numbers are in Volume I; boldface page numbers are in Volume II.

Municipal bond funds, 7, 584–602
  amortized cost and, 587
  capital appreciation potential, 592, 595
  credit ratings and, 592, 598–99
  credit risk and, 600–601
  general, 592, 596
  government and, 601
  high-yield, 592, 594
  intermediate term, 587, 592, 593
  maturity risk and, 600
  with no maturity restriction and with
    high credit ratings, 587, 590–91
  open-end, 586–92
  penny rounding and, 587
  portfolio analysis of, 592, 595, 596–99
  selection, 595, 600–602
  short-term, 586–87, 588–89, 592
  Unit Investment Trusts, 585–86
Municipal Bond Insurance Association
  (MBIA), 150, 406–7, 408, 409, 410,
  411, **411**
Municipal bond trustee; *see* Trustee
Municipal electric systems; *see* Public
  power revenue bonds
Municipal Finance Officers Association
  (MFOA), 417, 637–38, **466**
  disclosure guidelines and, 633–34
  official statement and, 246
Municipal financial reporting; *see also*
  Balance sheets; Comprehensive
  annual financial report; Disclosure;
  and Financial statement
  modified accrual basis and, **491–96**
  National Council on Governmental
    Accounting and, **606 n–7 n**
  objectives of for taxpayers and
    investors, **436–38**
  overview of, **606, 608**
  as public good, **434–36**
Municipal multipliers, 383
Municipal securities brokers, 187–89,
  203, 641–42
  compliance examinations for, 656–57
  Municipal Securities Rulemaking
    Board and, 661, 665–66, 668
  regulation, 686–88, 689, 690
Municipal securities dealers, 640–42
  compliance examinations for, 656–57
  decline in number of, 465
  diverse intrastate and bond price, 202
  Municipal Securities Rulemaking
    Board and, 661, 665–66, 668
  regulation, 686–88, 689, 690
Municipal Securities Full Disclosure Act
  of 1977, 663 n, 692

Municipal Securities Rulemaking Board
  (MSRB), 247, 623, 626, 627, 643,
  660–79, 687–88
  administrative rules, 663–64
  call provisions and, 14–15
  compliance with rules of, 656–58
  definitional rules, 665
  disclosure requirements and values of,
    235
  enforcement of rules of, 654–60
  equal regulation goals, 670
  fair practice rules and, 669–70
  general rules, 665
  goals, 670–73
  industry involvement with, 673–74
  interpretive notices and advisory
    opinions of, 658–60
  official statement filed by, 9
  operational aspects rules, 667–68, 670–
    71
  professional qualifications rules, 665–
    67, 671–72
  rulemaking authority, 651–54, 660–63
  rulemaking goals conflict and, 670–72
  rules of, 663–70
  Securities and Exchange Commission
    and, 650–51, 675–78
  specificity of rules of, 672–73
  syndicate practices and, 668–69
  underwriters counsel and, 249–50
Municipal utility district revenue bonds,
  21
Municipalities; *see* Local government

N

National Association of Securities
  Dealers, Inc. (NASD), 649
National Committe on Governmental
  Accounting, **466**
National Committee on Municipal
  Accounting (NCMA), **466**
National Council on Governmental
  Accounting (NCGA), **468, 606 n–7 n**
  Statement 1, **468, 469, 470–72, 504–
    8;** *see also* Financial statements;
    Municipal accounting; *and*
    Municipal financial reporting
National Health Planning and Resource
  Development Act of 1974 (PL 93-
  641), **375**
National Housing Act, Federal Housing
  Administration insurance and, **289**
NCGA; *see* National Council on
  Governmental Accounting

Note: Lightface page numbers are in Volume I; boldface page numbers are in Volume II.

Note: Lightface page numbers are in Volume I; boldface page numbers are in Volume II.

Note: Lightface page numbers are in Volume I; boldface page numbers are in Volume II.

Note: Lightface page numbers are in Volume I; boldface page numbers are in Volume II.

Note: Lightface page numbers are in Volume I; boldface page numbers are in Volume II.

Note: Lightface page numbers are in Volume I; boldface page numbers are in Volume II.

Note: Lightface page numbers are in Volume I; boldface page numbers are in Volume II.

Note: Lightface page numbers are in Volume I; boldface page numbers are in Volume II.

Note: Lightface page numbers are in Volume I; boldface page numbers are in Volume II.

Note: Lightface page numbers are in Volume I; boldface page numbers are in Volume II.

Note: Lightface page numbers are in Volume I; boldface page numbers are in Volume II.

Note: Lightface page numbers are in Volume I; boldface page numbers are in Volume II.